For Ellen,

12.25.90

Collage
Critical Views

Studies in the Fine Arts: Criticism, No. 31

Donald B. Kuspit, Series Editor

Professor of Art History
State University of New York at Stony Brook

Other Titles in This Series

No. 22	*Postminimalism into Maximalism: American Art, 1966–1986*	Robert Pincus-Witten
No. 24	*Artwords 2: Discourse on the Early 80s*	Jeanne Siegel, ed.
No. 27	*Feminist Art Criticism: An Anthology*	Arlene Raven, Joanna Frueh, and Cassandra L. Langer, eds.
No. 29	*Pop Art: The Critical Dialogue*	Carol Anne Mahsun, ed.
No. 30	*Georgia O'Keeffe: The Critical Response, 1916–1929*	Barbara Buhler Lynes
No. 32	*Art in the Public Interest: Critical Writings*	Arlene Raven, ed.

Collage
Critical Views

Edited by
Katherine Hoffman

With a Foreword by Kim Levin

U·M·I Research Press
Ann Arbor / London

Produced and distributed by
UMI Research Press
an imprint of
University Microfilms Inc.
Ann Arbor, Michigan 48106

Library of Congress Cataloging in Publication Data

Collage : critical views / edited by Katherine Hoffman.
p. cm. — (Studies in the fine arts. Criticism ; no. 31)
Bibliography: p.
Includes index.
ISBN 0-8357-1933-2 (alk. paper)
1. Collage 2. Art, Modern—20th century. I. Hoffman. Katherine, 1947- . II. Series.
N6494.C6C65 1989 709'.04—dc19 88-37072
British Library CIP data is available.

For Sean, Kristen, Geoffrey, and Ashley

The real voyage of discovery . . .
consists not in seeking new landscapes, but in having new eyes,
in seeing the universe with the eyes of another, of a hundred others,
in seeing the hundred universes that each of them sees.
Marcel Proust, *La Prisonnière*

Contents

Figures

Foreword

Collage is the all-purpose twentieth-century device. Over the years it has become a repository for the most diverse concerns of artists and critics. As these essays reveal, the concept of collage absorbs ideas the same way the technique fuses stray images, objects, and materials, assimilating whatever the course of modern art, life, and history has happened to bestow upon it. Along with assemblage (its three-dimensional equivalent) and montage (its counterpart in photography, film, and video), collage has been a carrier of the crucial issues of the modern era.

Used by one revolutionary style after the next, collage has supported Freudian, Marxist, narrative, semiotic, feminist, and deconstructivist readings, as well as formalist ones. Collage can convey disjunctions of form, conjunctions of content, or disruptions of context. It can express absurdity or velocity, relativity or flatness, fusion or anarchy. It can allude to mechanical reproduction or erotic encounter, can be an agent against causality or an economic critique. It can point to predecessors in women's craftwork or tribal fetishes, and to affinities with Third World politicized folk art.

This technique—which takes bits and pieces out of context to patch them into new contexts—keeps changing, adapting to various styles and concerns. And it's perfectly apt that interpretations of collage have varied according to the intellectual inquiries of the time. From our vantage point near the end of the century we can now begin to see that collage has all along carried postmodern genes. Pieced together with byproducts from the modern world, collage—the most literally materialistic of mediums—has always contained information that pointed beyond modernism. The germs of appropriation and simulation can be found in the earliest recycled scraps in Cubist collages. The seeds of media manipulation are latent in juxtapositions governed by Surrealist desire. Built into the nature of the technique is an argument against purity, newness, and unlimited progress—those optimistic ideals of modernism. The flip-side of our century's horn of produced and consumed plenty is profligate waste. The omnipresent technique of modern fragmentation exudes postmodern impurities. These essays track new ways to see and think about collage.

Kim Levin

Preface

Writing in 1948, in reference to a retrospective exhibition of collages held at the Museum of Modern Art, James Thrall Soby described collage as a "key manifestation of our epoch's visual sensibility. . . . And there can be no real question as to the importance of collage in twentieth century art."[1] For that same exhibition, Margaret Miller, director of the exhibit, wrote in a press release, "Collage cannot be defined adequately as merely a technique of cutting and pasting, for its significance lies not in its technical eccentricity but in its relevance to two basic questions which have been raised by twentieth century art: the nature of reality and the nature of painting itself."[2] As a significant twentieth-century art form, collage, with its multiple layers and signposts, has allowed for the possibility or suggestion of countless new forms and realities.

Collage and its extended principles and forms have inspired artists and writers of this century to explore new territories and ways of seeing that have been revolutionary. The intent of this volume is to gather together some of the critical voices that in recent years have explored the state and impact of collage in the twentieth century. The earliest piece is Clement Greenberg's 1959 essay, "Collage," which pointed to collage as an important turning point in modern art. Many of the pieces are new, written for this volume. The essays, diverse in discipline, content, and methodology, are examples of the great diversity of critical thought that has been inspired by the medium of collage. The writings of artists, critics, and scholars are included. The essays themselves form a type of collage of different viewpoints concerning the role of collage and its related areas, such as papier collés, assemblage, montage, etc., in the twentieth century. Through a multifaceted approach, as illustrated in the diversity of the essays, it is intended that the multiple dimensions of collage and its principles be better seen and understood in the context of our complex, contemporary world.

A collection of this type can by no means include all that has been written in the last thirty years on collage and extensions of collage. Those essays that appear here are examples of the different types of critical voices that have emerged and are emerging. The first chapter of the book, "Collage in the Twentieth Century: An Overview," is included to set the philosophical, theoretical, and art historical stage for the essays that follow. Quotations from the artists are included to stand as complements and/or counterpoints to the critical essays. The bibliography is limited to selected sources beginning in 1958, with Clement Greenberg's "The Pasted Paper Revolution."

It is hoped that this volume will inspire further artistic and critical inquiry into a medium that has had such a profound impact on the history of twentieth-century art. For as William Seitz has written,

> [I]t must be recognized with approval and pleasure that, in addition to enriching and adulterating the themes and forms of painting and sculpture, makers of assembled art have wrought a truly magical transformation: from banality and ugliness, dispersion and waste, tawdriness and commercialism, they have created challenging, meaningful, and often beautiful objects ordered by principles inseparable from this century.[3]

Notes

1. James Thrall Soby, "The Importance of Collage," *Saturday Review of Literature* 6 November 1948, p. 36.
2. Margaret Miller, cited in William Seitz, *The Art of Assemblage* (New York: Museum of Modern Art, 1961), p. 6.
3. William Seitz, *The Art of Assemblage,* p. 92.

Acknowledgments

The seeds for this project were sown during my participation as a fellow in the Institute for the Study of Avant-Gardes at Harvard University during the summer of 1987, which was directed by Susan Suleiman and Alice Jardine and funded by the National Endowment for the Humanities. Through group discussions and independent reading, I was inspired further to explore questions surrounding the subject of collage.

Instead of an exhaustive list of thank-yous, I would like to acknowledge the assistance of the various personnel at the libraries that I used, in particular the Fogg Art Museum library and the Bradford College library. Most importantly, I would like to thank the contributors to this volume for their cooperation and support for the project. Finally, I would like to thank my husband, Sean Gresh, for his support and his exemplary creative energies, and my children, Kristen, Geoffrey, and Ashley, whose creative spirits and art works, many of which have been collages, are of unending inspiration.

1

Collage in the Twentieth Century: An Overview

Katherine Hoffman

Grasping for Realities— The Philosophical and Theoretical Background

Collage may be seen as a quintessential twentieth-century art form with multiple layers and signposts pointing to a variety of forms and realities, and to the possibility or suggestion of countless new realities. As Clement Greenberg wrote, "Collage was . . . a major turning point in the whole evolution of modernist art in this century."[1] Or as Gregory Ulmer has written, "By most accounts collage is the single most revolutionary formal innovation in artistic representation in our century."[2] Once considered a folk art, collage in the twentieth century has emerged as both a medium and an idea, and has led to some of the most significant developments in art and criticism in our time.

In the emergence of collage as a major fine arts form, it is important to consider it in the context of changing concepts of time, space, and reality that have evolved as the twentieth century has progressed. With the advent of a new century, artists, scientists, and philosophers began to shatter nineteenth-century monism and concepts of a monolithic Absolute. Writing in 1933, Herbert Read pointed to the character of these changes:

> But I do think we can already discern a difference in kind in the contemporary revolution: it is not so much a revolution, which implies a turning over, even a turning back, but rather a break-up, a devolution, some would say a dissolution. Its character is catastrophic. . . . We are now concerned not with a logical development of the art of painting in Europe, not even with a development for which there is any historically parallel, but with an abrupt break with all tradition. . . . The aim of five centuries of European effort is openly abandoned.[3]

Dualism and pluralism began to replace nineteenth-century monism. Philosophers such as Henri Bergson began to attack old monoliths such as Truth and introduce new concepts of time and perception. For Bergson time was "no longer the principle of dissolution and destruction, no longer the element in which ideas, and ideals lose their value . . . [W]e are not merely the sum total of the individual moments of our life, but the result of the everchanging aspects which they acquire through each new moment.[4] For Bergson, "before" and "after" were not important. Rather time was continuous duration and there were no definite fixed objects in time. Further, Bergson felt that one could view the world in two ways—intellectually and intuitively. Intuition allowed for the direct perception of the inner core of an object and enabled one to transcend the everyday facts of external appearance.

Freud and the new psychologists began to shatter rationalism and probe into both the unconscious and conscious mind. Freud's early books, *The Interpretation of Dreams* (1900), *The Psychopathology of Everyday Life* (1904), *Three Essays on the Theory of Sexuality* (1905), and *Totem and Taboo* (1913), opened the doors to the world of dreams, nightmares and revelations, and brought forth a wealth of material for artists and writers. The first psychoanalytical congress was held in 1908.

While Freud challenged accepted views of psychology, Max Weber and Emile Durkheim laid the foundations for modern sociology. Thorstein Veblen wrote the *Theory of the Leisure Class* (1899) and coined the phrase "conspicuous consumption." Sorel's well-known *Reflections on Violence,* with its conception of the function of myth, appeared in 1908.

Discoveries in the world of science also touched the arts. The disintegration of the atom, Einstein's theory of relativity, and quantum physics began to shake people's faith in the reality of a given, concrete, visible world. There was no longer one true vision of reality but the possibility of the perception of multiple realities. Theories in quantum physics and the New Physics affected the relationship of the viewer and the work of art.

> The New Physics tells us that an observer cannot observe without altering what he sees. Observed and observer are interrelated in a real and fundamental sense . . . [T]here is a growing body of evidence that the distinction between "in here" and the "out there" is illusion. . . . Access to the physical world is through experience. the common denominator of all experience is the "I" that does the experiencing. In short, what we experience is not external reality, but our interaction with it.[5]

It is with this background that Modernism, and collage as a fine art form, were born in the early part of the century. Artists and writers of the early twentieth century were sensitive to trends and conflicts in the larger society, and sought new forms and languages.

> What they had to say was listened to and understood by only a minority at the time; only later when the War had swept away the old order of European society and finally destroyed the values in a way which everyone could see, was it recognized that the imagination of the painters and poets, the scientists and the thinkers, of the 1900s had reached out to see in advance the world (which they were helping to create), that improbable, disturbing, fragmented world in which we still live.[6]

For some, this breaking away from an established order implied a sense of chaos, and the vocabulary of chaos—disintegration, fragmentation, dislocation. But as James McFarlane points out, Modernism may also be seen as bringing a new kind of integration to the forefront:

> But the defining thing in the Modernist mode is not so much that things fall apart but that they fall *together* (recalling appropriately the derivation of "symbol" from *symballein,* to throw together). In Modernism, the centre is seen exerting not a centrifugal but a centripetal force; and the consequence is not disintegration but (as it were) superintegration.[7]

The concepts of disintegration, fragmentation, and integration are perhaps particularly important for the medium of collage.

In the passage from a modern to a postmodern era, there have continued to be challenges to and changes in perceptions of reality. We are now in an age of pluralism and interchangeability, and stand as "others among others."[8] But pluralism has become almost like an institution, rather than a celebration of individual works and theories.

One of the areas of concern for postmodernist versus modernist thought has been the concept of representation. As Frederic Jameson writes, "Modernism's formulation of the problem of representation [was] borrowed from a religious terminology which defines representation as 'figuration,' a dialectic of the letter and the spirit, a 'picture language' (*Vorstellung*) that embodies, expresses and transmits otherwise inexpressible truths."[9] Postmodernism is characterized by its "resolution to use representation against itself to destroy the binding or absolute status of any representation."[10]

> In the visual arts, the post-modernist critique of representation proceeds by a similar attempt to undermine the referential status of visual imagery and with it, its claim to represent reality as it really is, whether this be the surface appearance of things (realism) or some ideal order lying behind or beyond appearance (abstraction). Postmodern artists demonstrate that "reality," whether concrete or abstract, is a fiction, produced and sustained only by its cultural representation.[11]

Jean Baudrillard, in his *For a Critique of the Political Economy of the Sign* (1981), deals with reality as an effect of signification. He goes further with his concept of the precession of the "simulacra." At the beginning of his essay, "The Precession of Simulacra," he quotes from Ecclesiastes, "The simulacrum is never that which conceals the truth which conceals that there is none. / The simulacrum is true."[12] Baudrillard notes the effect of mass media and the television in determining the nature of reality.

> Simulation is no longer that of a territory, a referential being, or a substance. It is the generation by models of a real without origin or reality: a hyperreal. The territory no longer precedes the map, nor survives it. Henceforth, it is the map that precedes the territory—PRECESSION OF SIMULCRA—it is the map that engenders the territory . . . [O]f the same order as the impossibility of rediscovering an absolute level of the real is the impossibility of staging an illusion. Illusion is no longer possible, because the real is no longer possible.[13]

Baudrillard's position is complemented by what one might call a poststructuralist position that

> adds: not only is the bourgeois individual subject a thing of the past, it is also a myth; it *never* really existed in the first place; there have never been autonomous subjects of that type. Rather this construct is merely a philosophical and cultural mystification which sought to persuade people that they "had" individual subjects and possessed this unique personal identity.[14]

In his essay, "Post-Modernism and Consumer Society," Frederic Jameson describes the schizophrenic experience (derived largely from the work of French psychoanalyst Jacques Lacan) as a basic feature of postmodernism. He sees schizophrenic experience as "an experience of isolated, disconnected, discontinuous material signifiers which fail to link up into a coherent sequence."[15] Thus the individual and individual subject in the postmodern era, according to some theorists, have lost their identities, and are afloat in space and time, grappling with concepts of, and relationships to, a variety of realities. In confronting the world and grappling with changing concepts of reality/realities, artists and critics have found the medium of collage with its multilayers of significance to be a particularly viable and flexible medium, as the century has progressed.

For many, collage has often been associated with the concept of the avant-garde.[16] The term avant-garde, of military origins, is often used as meaning that which is in opposition to an established cultural order; it means, as *Webster's New Collegiate Dictionary* suggests, "in any art, the most daring of the experimentalists and innovators of original and startlingly unconventional designs, ideas and techniques during a particular period." The emergence of the avant-garde in this century is usually associated with the rise of modernism, as a liberating and sometimes utopian moment/movement. The avant-garde "sought to transcend representation in favor of the signifier, its liberation from the 'tyranny of the signified.' "[17] Picasso's *Still-Life with Chair Caning* (1912), often viewed as the first Cubist collage, where Picasso glued a piece of oilcloth with a woven caning pattern to the surface, thereby indicating the presence of a chair without traditional methods, may be seen as an avant-garde piece.

Within the realm of the avant-garde there often appears to be a tension between individual and "collective" thought. For instance, how much did Picasso and Braque give up their individuality in a "collective of two" in working toward innovations in collage? Today some feel the avant-garde is dead, yet some of the motives of the avant-garde, a need and desire for a critical art and an art of change, a shared sense of purpose, are still with us. And for a number of artists and critics the medium of collage, in its diversity of materials and format and its potential for multiple and layered meanings, is one that can answer the call of the avant-garde.

The Medium of Collage and Its Evolution in the Twentieth Century

Thus far, in setting the philosophical and theoretical stage for the growth of collage and criticism thereof, the term collage has been used without differentiating among the variety of collage forms. Before proceeding further it seems important to briefly make such distinctions. The French word *collage,* from the verb, *coller,* means "pasting, sticking, or gluing" onto a surface, for example, the application of wallpaper. (In slang, the word collage means an illicit love affair, which may have delighted Picasso and Braque. The past participle *collé* refers to something fake or pretend in slang.) *Papier collé* is a somewhat narrower form of collage referring only to the use of paper, and often referring to the paper collages of the Cubists. Picasso is usually credited with the beginnings of the use of collage by modern artists, while Braque is usually credited with the innovation of *papier collé* or pasted paper in *modern* art (Herta Wescher found a Japanese *papier collé* of the tenth century used as a background for calligraphy).[18]

The term assemblage, associated with collage, refers in French and English to "the fitting together of parts and pieces," and has been applied to both two- and three-dimensional forms. Dubuffet used the term in 1953 for a series of *assemblages d'empreintes* resulting from a group of small collages of butterfly wings. Dubuffet felt that the term collage should be reserved for the collages made in the period 1910–20 by Picasso, Braque, the Dadaists, etc. In 1954 Dubuffet extended his work to three dimensions. Today the concept may include all forms of composite art and processes of juxtaposition.

Décollage, the opposite of collage, refers to "ungluing," or taking off or destroying or dissolving an image, as in the work of Austin Cooper or Wolf Vostell. *Découpage* or "cutting" refers to a method of decorating painted furniture and wood surfaces with cutouts of flowers, fruits, etc., and to a cleanly cut collage of new paper, such as the Matisse cut-outs.

Photomontage, the assembling of photographs by pasting or other means, although seen in the middle of the nineteenth century, refers particularly to the use of photographs in collages by Dadaists and other artists, beginning early in this century. The word was derived from the German verb *montieren,* similar to the English verb "to assemble." The term montage and variations on it have also been used in relationship to film, particularly by Sergei Eisenstein, in *The Film Sense* (1942). There he refers to metric, rhythmic, tonal, overtonal, and intellectual montage.

With this brief clarification of terms, one may proceed with a description of the evolution and proliferation of collage and collage principles from the beginning experiments of Picasso and Braque to the present, as background for the critical essays that follow. Discussion here will focus on innovations in form and content for various time and stylistic periods, rather than on extensive description of all that has been done.

The first experiments in collage as a legitimate art form may be seen in the work of Picasso, Braque, and other Cubists such as Juan Gris. Cubist painting began to portray simultaneity in time and space. Collage introduced an interaction between the pictorial surface and the "real environment," and freed the artist from the technicalities of brushwork. Maurice Raynal's article on collage in the *Section D'Or* of 1912, probably the first written discussion of collage, although not really favorable to the use of collage elements, implied that the appearance of collage "was due to the artists' distaste for photographic illusionism in painting, and they felt it preferable to substitute for an exact copy of an object (for example the label on a bottle), a portion of the object itself."[19]

Although there has been some dispute concerning who did the "first" collage recognized as a fine art form, Picasso or Braque, it is the spirit of the endeavor that seems more important. Indeed, Picasso and Braque worked in close collaboration from 1908 to 1912. Kahnweiler writes,

> It is obvious that it was a joint discovery if one calls it a discovery. These two painters were then working so closely together that it is not certain that the one who did the first "papier collé" had really had the idea first. They might have talked about it before. . . . It is generally admitted that the first one was "Compotier" done by Braque in summer 1912 at Sorgues.[20]

Picasso was most likely influenced by the assembled and synthetic qualities of African objects that used materials such as beads, shells, and fabric. Pierre Daix has compared Picasso's use of collage to the concept of *bricolage,* or the putting together of odds and ends: "The act of pasting and constructing . . . was in the first instance, a return to 'bricolage.' . . . This new 'craft' gave birth to new freedom . . . to a certain crudity of execution which again made Picasso into his own primitive."[21]

The Cubists' use of materials such as grained papers, newspaper clippings, and wallpaper allowed for a complex interplay between illusion and reality, and for the transformation of one reality into another. Unlike paintings, the collages could point to the paradox between "the true and the false." Were wallpaper patterns that formed part of a guitar, or newspaper that formed the sound hole of a guitar part of a guitar, part of another context or object from which the wallpaper or newspaper was taken, or signposts pointing to other meanings and questions? Did the guitar halves in some works refer to the female torso? The play and interplay of meanings becomes complicated. What was presented, re-presented, and represented, and conversely, what was *not* presented or represented behind the pasted pieces is complex.

In the use of newspaper, bottle labels, etc., one also sees both the confrontation and integration of "high" and "low" cultures. Thomas Crow writes, "The principle of collage construction itself collapses the distinction between high and low by transforming the totalizing creative practice of traditional painting into a fragmented consumption of already existing manufactured images."[22]

Picasso and Braque both wrote about their experiments in collage and the significance of the medium for them. Their statements and those of other artists that follow here may be seen as complements and counterpoints to critics' viewpoints. Picasso:

> The purpose of the papier collé was to give the idea that different textures can enter into a composition to become the reality in the paintings that competes with the reality in nature. We tried to get rid of "trompe l'oeil" to find a "trompe l'esprit". . . . And this strangeness was what we wanted to make people think about because we were quite aware that our world was becoming very strange and not exactly reassuring.[23]

Braque:

> It is not enough to make the painted object visible, it must also be made tangible.
>
> A painter trying to make a circle would only make a ring. Possibly the look of it may satisfy him but he will have doubts. The compass will restore his certainty. The papier collés in my drawings have also given me a kind of certainty.
>
> The papier collés, the imitation wood—and other elements of the same nature—which I have used in certain drawings, also make their effect through the simplicity of the facts, and it is this that has led people to confuse them with trompe l'oeil, of which they are precisely the opposite. They too are simple facts, but created by the mind and such that they are one of the justifications of a new figuration in space.[24]

Once collage was utilized by the Cubists, other artists and movements began to realize the potentials of the medium. The Futurists found in collage and construction ways to proclaim their ideals of a machine age—speed, dynamism, lines of force, simultaneity, motion, etc. There was an emphasis on process and intuition as cited in Bergson's writings. To express such concepts visual imagery was often derived from the machine.

F. T. Marinetti, poet and editor, developed a form of concrete poetry, called "words of freedom" that was similar to collage. The artists who signed the "First Manifesto of Futurist Painting," Boccioni, Balla, Severini, Carrà, and Russolo, all experimented with cutting and pasting in their works. In a letter to Raffaele Carrieri, Severini recalled the significance of Picasso's and Braque's work and the significance of collage materials for him in attempting "to comprehend the sense of a more profound and secret inner reality."

> As regards the so-called papier collés I can tell you with precision that they were born in 1912 in the zone of Montmartre. As I remember it, Apollinaire suggested the idea to me after having spoken of it to Picasso, who immediately painted a small still-life onto which he applied a small piece of waxed paper (the type that was used for the tablecloths in the bistros of Paris). I tried to glue some pailletes and multicolored sequins onto forms of ballerinas in movement. I next saw a collage of Braque, perhaps the first, made of what seemed to be wood and large sheets of white paper on which he had sketched to a large extent with a black crayon. During my trip to Italy in August of 1912 I naturally spoke about the technique to Boccioni and he, in turn, to Carrà. During 1913 the first futurist experiments in this field saw the light of day. The reasons for which Apollinaire gave us these suggestions, as I remember them from conversations of a later date, were: in the first place the need, that time, to comprehend the sense of a more profound and secret inner reality which would have been born from the contrast of materials employed directly as things placed in juxtaposition to lyrical elements.[25]

In 1912 Umberto Boccioni called for new and up-to-date materials for sculptors, to escape the traditional bronze and marble statues. In his *Technical Manifesto of Futurist Sculpture,* he wrote,

> A sculptural composition must not be made throughout from a single work, in order to heighten its power of expression. To mention only a few: glass, wood, cardboard, cement, horsehair, leather, cloth, mirror, light, etc. . . . [W]ith the aid of transparent bottles, glass disks, sheets of metal, illumination from within and without, we can bring to expression the planes, movements, tones, and half tones of a new reality.[26]

Further, Boccioni advocated

> a Futurist sculpture, whose basis will be architectural, not only as a construction of masses, but in such a way that the sculptural block itself will contain the architectural elements of the sculptural environment in which the object exists. . . . [T]he cogs of

> a machine might as easily appear out of the armpits of a mechanic, or the lines of a table could cut a reader's head in two, or a book with its fanned-out pages could intersect the reader's stomach.[27]

Boccioni's *Fusion of a Head and a Window,* an assemblage which included a real wooden window and fastener, was done in 1911 or 1912. Proceeding from the Cubists' in-depth examination of textures, objects, and spatial juxtapositions, the Futurists were also openly concerned with social and aesthetic theories and propaganda, and with how the materials they used could serve their goals. The fragment of newsprint in Boccioni's *Cavalry Charge* (1915) helps identify the battle which is the subject of the painting with collaged element. Carrà's well-known free word collage of pasted papers and newsprint, on cloth mounted on wood, *Patriotic Celebration* (1914), is a swirling spiral where the typography is at once a type of propaganda message and a mass of interpenetrating fragments, sounds, and colors.

At the same time the Cubists and Futurists were experimenting with collage and assemblage, so, too, were Russian artists and poets. According to Herta Wescher, collage was apparently born in Russia in about 1912 with publications of young poets such as David Burliuk, Alexei Kruchenykh, and Vladimir Mayakovsky.[28] Artists such as Rosanova, Goncharova, Malevich, and Popova collaborated with the poets in illustrating the text pages and often used brightly colored collaged papers on the book jackets. Malevich did a number of collages in the early teens that he called "alogical" associations, using abstract forms, words, and representational objects. He wrote, "The alogical collusion of two forms . . . illustrates the moment of struggle between logic, the natural law, bourgeois sense and prejudice."[29] An example of this alogical style, *Private of the First Division* (1914) (fig. 1.1), marks a transition from his Cubist work to his nonrepresentational painting. The contrast of the collaged and figurative areas with the blank square and lower open end of the piece is striking. With the collaged words such as "Thursday," "President Vasnyetsov," "snuff box," and the mounting of a thermometer, the viewer finds himself floating disconcertingly among various realities.

Along with Kasimir Malevich, Vladimir Tatlin also experimented with new materials in his constructions and what he called "painting reliefs," which included materials such as metal and wire mesh. In 1915 he began to make "counter-reliefs" from wire stretched across the corners of rooms, that looked almost like airplanes. To some, such as the writer Fritz Karpen, such work was outrageous, while to others such as Konstantin Umansky, the work was laudable. In his book, *Neue Kunst in Russland, 1914–19,* Umansky wrote of Tatlin's work: "A triumph of the intellectual and the material, the negation of the right of the spirit to isolated autonomy, a

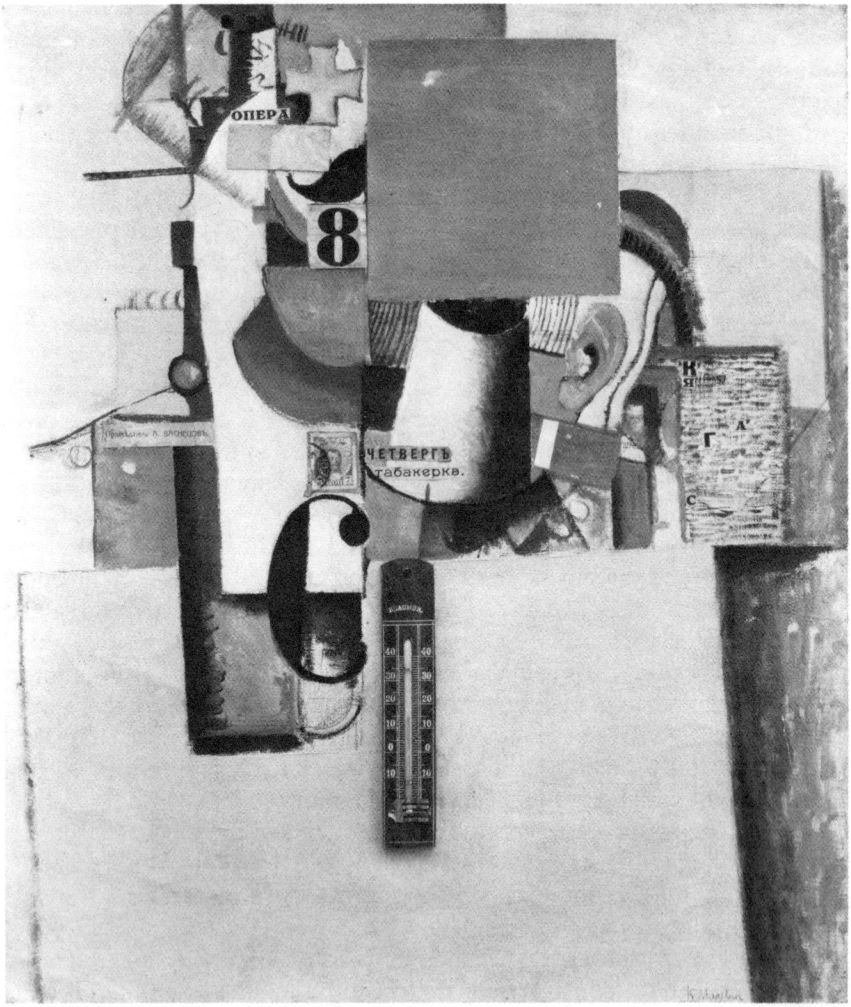

Figure 1.1. Kasimir Malevich, *Private of the First Division,* 1914
Oil on canvas, with collage of postage stamp, thermometer, etc., $21\frac{1}{8}'' \times 17\frac{5}{8}''$.
(Collection, The Museum of Modern Art, New York)

quintessence of contemporary reality, of sovereign technique, of victorious materialism—it is thus we must define the counter reliefs which have relegated within quotation marks all such sacrosanct words as Art, Painting, Picture."[30]

With the advent of the Russian Revolution artists also became involved with posters, wall newspapers, and street decorations. This "agit-prop" art, determined by Rosta, the Russian Telegraph Agency, often was in the form of large wall montages, with revolutionary slogans and words. For the first time art was accessible to all levels of Russian society, not just the wealthy and privileged classes. Perhaps most effective were the agit-prop trains sent to educate people in the countryside about Soviet doctrine. The trains themselves were like giant collages, vividly painted and plastered with pamphlets and posters.

Photomontage became a "preferred constructivist medium," gathering momentum with the publication of *Lef* (Journal of the Left Front of the Arts, 1923–25).[31] The fourth issue of *Lef* included an unsigned statement entitled "Photomontage," stressing the importance of the photograph as document:

> By photomontage we mean the use of the photograph as an illustrative means. A combination of photos replaces a composition of graphic images. The sense of this substitution is that the photo is not a sketch of a visual fact, but an exact fixation of it. This exactness and documentariness give the photo a power of influence over the observer which a graphic image can never obtain. . . . Up to now a qualified photo, i.e. an artistic one, has always tried to imitate painting and drawing, which is why its production has been weak, and has not revealed the possibilities there are in photography. Photographers supposed that the more like a picture the photo was, the more artistic and better it would be. In reality, however, the result has turned out quite the reverse: the more artistic it is, the worse it is. Photography has its own possibilities for montage and has nothing in common with the composition of pictures. These [possibilities] should be made clear.[32]

Developments in Russian cinema paralleled the developments in photomontage. Figures such as Vertov and Eisenstein played important roles in the world of cinema. Dziga Vertov organized the group Kino-Eye in Moscow in 1922. His Kino-Pravda (Cinema Truth) films were mounted out of contemporary photographic documents organized in dynamic and rhythmic sequences. Vertov's well-known *Man with a Movie Camera* is an example of brilliant editing and montage effects. A contrapuntal structure depicting a working day, the film shows a variety of working processes from factory and post office to the actual making of the film. For Vertov the cinematic techniques could reveal truth that was not readily visible to the eye.

Sergei Eisenstein is well known for his work in various levels of montage. In his films he often favored the collision of contradictory shots to provoke the audience. He wrote, in *Film Form,*

> Is the method of overtonal montage unrelated to our previous experience, artificially grafted onto cinematography, or is it simply a quantitative accumulation of one attribute that makes a dialectic leap and begins to function as a new qualitative attribute?
>
> In other words is overtonal montage a dialectical stage of development within the development of the whole montage system of methods, standing in a successive relation to other forms of montage?
>
> These are the formal categories of montage that we know:
>
> 1. Metric Montage . . . 2. Rhythmic Montage . . . 3. Tonal Montage . . . 4. Overtonal Montage . . . 5. Intellectual Montage. . . .[33]

Collage used for political and commercial concerns continued in the Bauhaus but with a different spirit than that of the Russians. Bauhaus students were taught to examine the nature and use of different materials, and the optical and tactile qualities of materials such as wood, glass, tree bark, furs, woven fabrics, etc. Collages and montages of various materials were made, showing contrasts of varied materials. During the last period of the Bauhaus, students in Joost Schmidt's applied graphics class received instruction in the techniques of photomontage.

Beyond its use in teaching, collage at the Bauhaus was also used for posters and announcements for special events. Collages were made as birthday cards for Gropius and others. The photomontages that Moholy-Nagy began to make in 1924 provided a strange optical tension between two and three dimensions, because of the sculptural qualities of the figurative details. He called these pieces ''photo-sculptures,'' and described them in his book, *Malerei, Fotografie, Film* (1925), as ''assembled out of various photographs . . . an experimental method of simultaneous representation. They compressed . . . interpenetration of visual and verbal wit in an uncanny union of the imaginary with the real, but at the same time, they could narrate, stand solidly on their own in a way more real than life itself.''[34] Moholy-Nagy and other Bauhaus artists also did commercial art commissions, often using typographical and photomontage techniques.

The glory of the freeing elements of collage is perhaps no better seen than in the work of the Dada and Surrealist artists. Formed in 1916 in Zurich, the young Dada group pushed forth its nihilistic spirit in a variety of ''anti-art'' formats—nonsense poems, songs, collage, etc. The German actor and playwright Hugo Ball, who operated the Cabaret Voltaire in Zurich, who is usually considered the founder of the Dada movement, was joined by figures such as Tristan Tzara, Marcel Janco, Richard Huelsenbeck, and Jean Arp. Tzara wrote of the revolutionary aspect of the *papier collé*. "Papier collé, in all its different aspects, marks in the evolution of painting the most poetic moment, the most revolutionary, the touching flight toward the most viable hypotheses, a greater intimacy with daily truths, the insurmountable affirmation of the temporary, and of temporal themes, the supremacy of the idea."[35] He described the writing of a poem by making a collage.

> To make a dadaist poem
> Take a newspaper.
> Take a pair scissors.
> Choose an article as long as you are planning to make your poem.
> Cut out the article.
> Then cut out each of the words that make up this article and
>   put them in a bag.
> Shake it gently.
> Then take out the scraps one after the other in the order in
>   which they left the bag.
> Copy conscientiously.
> The poem will be like you. . . .[36]

Jean Arp created some of his reliefs and collages strictly by chance, thereby breaking with traditions such as intentionality, purpose, composition, and the concept of the artist as an individual, unique originator. Beyond the work done during the height of the Dada movement, in the 1930s Arp did a series of collages and reliefs, based on a principle he called constellation, that had to do with nature's continuous cycles, dissolution and regeneration:

> The forms I created in the years 1927–1948 which I called cosmic forms
> were vast forms
> which could englobe a multitude of forms . . . I constellated these forms
> "according to the laws of chance"
> . . . These cosmic forms seemed to be mute
> because their language is out of reach of human waves of perception.[37]

Arp related some of the collages of this time not only to decay in nature but also to the decay of art, and to his mother's death. The torn papers in these works often were fragments of destroyed drawings and prints. The pieces are in some ways an attempt to accept the inevitability of decay and death, and an attempt to express in new formats regenerative powers: "I had accepted the transcience, the dribbling away, the brevity, the impermanence, the fading, the withering, the spookishness of our existence. Not only had I accepted it, I had even welcomed transience into my work as it was coming into being."[38] Arp often referred back to the Dada movement as his source. "Dada is the basis of all art. . . . Dada is direct like nature and tries to assign each thing to its essential place. . . . Life is the goal of art, art can misunderstand its means and merely reflect life instead of creating, such means are then illusionist, descriptive, academic.''[39]

Dadaism spread rapidly through Europe at the end of World War I. In Hanover, under the leadership of Kurt Schwitters, the Dada spirit continued. With Schwitters, collage seemed to come into full bloom as an artistic medium able to stand beside painting. From his collection of a vast variety of stickers, stamps, postmarks, buttons, nails, silver foil, art papers, matches, etc., Schwitters brought a number of new materials to the realm of collage. He wrote,

> Every means is right when it serves its end. . . . What the material signified before its use in the work of art is a matter of indifference so long as it is properly evaluated and given artistic meaning int he work of art. And so I began to construct pictures out of materials I happened to have at hand, such as streetcar tickets, cloakroom checks, bits of wood, wire twine, bent wheels, tissue paper, tin cans, chips of glass, etc. These things are inserted into the picture either as they are or else modified in accordance with what the picture requires. They lose their individual character, their own special essence (Eigengift) [*sic*], by being dematerialized (entmaterialisiert) they become material for the picture.[40]

Schwitters gave to his work the name MERZ, from a piece bearing the name MERZ, cut out of a KOMMERZ UND PRIVATBANK advertisement. He wrote of his MERZ concept, ''My work, indeed, did not answer to the old classifications such as: Expressionism, Cubism, Futurism, and all the others. Therefore I called all my pictures . . . MERZ pictures, the name of the most characteristic one . . . I myself am now called MERZ.''[41] Schwitters's Hanover apartment became a Merzbau, a cavern of old lumber, strangely molded plaster, and other materials that might be called an early ''environment.'' Schwitters sold his collages at a standard price of twenty marks, and actually made his living from painting academic portraits. He made a sharp ''distinction between his academic 'art *for* commerce' and that other 'art *from* commerce,' the commercial castoffs that he retrieved, poeticized, and rededicated to an art cleansed of the mundane, a lucid art pure and completely purposeless in any practical sense.''[42]

Berlin Dada was equally iconoclastic and more boldly political. Collages, cartoons, photomontages, and writings by figures such as Baader, Citroën, George Grosz, Raoul Hausmann, Herzfelde, Hannah Höch, and Huelsenbeck attacked the European political establishment. In a manifesto titled *Synthetisches Cino der Malerei* Hausmann wrote,

> The doll a child throws away, a brightly colored scrap of cloth, are more essential expressions than those of all the jackasses who wish to transplant themselves for all eternity in oil paints into an endless number of front parlors. . . . In Dada, you will find your true state: wonderful constellations in real materials, wine, glass, cardboard, cloth, organically matching your own consummate, inherent unsoundness, your own shoddiness.[43]

Collage and photomontage were important as polemical and political tools. In an interview Hannah Höch commented on their use of montage:

> Actually, we borrowed the idea from a trick of the official photographer of the Prussian army regiments. . . . But the aesthetic purpose, if any, of this very primitive kind of photomontage was to idealize reality, whereas the Dada photomonteur set out to give something entirely unreal all the appearances of something real that had actually been photographed. . . . Our whole purpose was to integrate objects from the world of machines and industry in the world of art.[44]

The spirit of Dada also infiltrated New York with the assistance of Francis Picabia, who came to New York in 1913 to see the impact of the Armory Show. He injected a proto-Dada spirit into Alfred Stieglitz's *Camera Work* and *291*, the journal of Stieglitz's gallery 291. Arthur Dove, part of the inner Stieglitz circle, was one of the few Americans in the early part of the twentieth century to use collage materials. Different than the Cubist or Dada collages, Dove's collages tended to be thematic or associational, sometimes nostalgic in evoking memories of the past, as in his *Grandmother* of 1925 (fig. 1.2). Dove was drawn to the rhythms of the water and earth as well, and like a number of other artists of his time, aspired toward a "visual music" through his work.

> To feel the power of the ground or sea, and to play or paint it with that in mind, letting spirit hold what you do together rather than continuous objective form, gaining in tangibility and actuality as the plane leaves the ground, to fly in a medium more rare and working with the imagination that has been built up from reality rather than building back to it.[45]

> There is no such thing as abstraction.
> It is extraction, gravitation toward a certain direction, and minding your own business.
> If the extract be clear enough its value will exist.
>
> It is nearer to music, not the music of the ears, just the music of the eyes.
> It should necessitate no effort to understand. Just to look, and if looking gives vision, enjoyment should occur as the eyes look.[46]

Dada as a group activity died by about 1921, as the spontaneous character of the movement dissolved, as arguments and public demonstra-

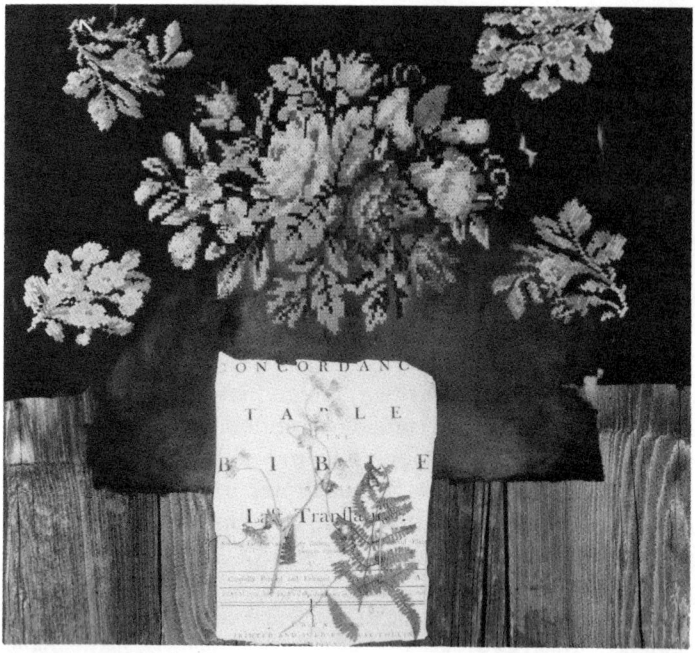

Figure 1.2. Arthur G. Dove, *Grandmother,* 1925
Collage of shingles, needlepoint, page from the Concordance, pressed flowers, and ferns, 20″ × 21¼″.
(Collection, The Museum of Modern Art, New York. Gift of Philip L. Goodwin [by exchange])

tions began to prevail. A number of Dada artists became Surrealists and rallied around André Breton when he issued his Surrealist Manifesto in 1924. Breton listed men such as Lautréamont, Freud, Trotsky, and Hippolyte Taine as ideological precursors to the movement. Breton worked with Max Ernst about 1922 on experiments in automatism in both drawing and writing. With Max Ernst collage became more than a medium. It became a philosophy, as Ernst formulated his "collage idea." He was fascinated with the collage method as it allowed him to use irony, wit, and narrative. Unlike Schwitters, Ernst found a wealth of material in books and catalogues, including scientific engravings and Victorian book illustrations. The line engravings allowed him to conceal the joining together of separate images to form a new image. He did a number of collage-scenarioed books such as *La Femme 100 têtes, Une Semaine de bonté,* and *Rêve d'une petite fille qui voulut entrer au Carmel.* Ernst's imagination brought forth whole new worlds to the viewer as he experimented with a variety of techniques such as frottage, décollage, fumage and décalcomanie. In Ernst's work memories, dreams, materials, events, etc. collide, and are transformed. He wrote of his collage work,

> I am tempted to see in collage the exploitation of the chance meeting of two remote realities on an unfamiliar plane . . . cultivating the effects of a systematic bewilderment, according to the view of André Breton . . . coupling two apparently uncoupleable realities on a plane apparently unsuitable to them. . . .
>
> Under the title *Natural History* I brought together the first results obtained by the procedure of frottage (rubbing) from *The Sea and the Rain to Eve, the Only One We Have Left.*
>
> I emphasize the fact that, through a series of suggestions and transformation arising spontaneously—in the way things do in hypnagogic visions—the drawings thus obtained increasingly lose the character of the original material (wood, for example) and assume the aspect of images of an unhoped for precision, of a kind likely to disclose the initial cause of the obsession or to produce some semblance of that cause.[47]

The impact of Ernst's collage idea can be further seen when one searches for realities on a continuum between the polarities that Ernst might subtly juxtapose or suggest, such as the constructive and the destructive, the rational and the irrational, the beautiful and the ugly, the sane and the insane, etc.

Other Surrealists concerned with juxtaposing disparate and oppositional elements also used collage and collage elements. Dali's 1929 painting with collage, *Accommodations of Desire,* shows a variety of sexual and psychologically oriented images combined in a dreamlike landscape. Dali's "paranoiac-critical activity" described in his book *La Femme visible* (1930), where he proposed a state of mind disoriented from the outside world, pushed further the search for new realities that occupied the Surrealists and others.

> The way in which it has been possible to obtain a double image is clearly paranoiac. By the double image is meant such a representation of an object that is also, without the slightest physical or anatomical change, the representation of another entirely different object, the second representation being equally devoid of any deformity or abnormality betraying arrangement.[48]

World War II disrupted the Surrealist movement, but its spirit survived. Surrealist techniques and ideas influenced a number of American artists. Joseph Cornell's complex boxes of disparate objects and elements, juxtaposed in enigmatic constructs, followed his contact with the Surrealists, particularly Max Ernst. Peggy Guggenheim's international collage exhibit, at her newly founded Art of this Century Gallery in New York in 1943, brought forth three young American artists—Robert Motherwell, William Baziotes, and Jackson Pollock—who all applied Surrealist automatic methods to collage for the exhibit. Of the three, only Motherwell continued to work in collage as a major form of expression. As part of the heroic abstract expressionist generation, Motherwell found collage to be a liberating form through which he could explore spontaneous and gestural elements. Although painting and collage have been parallel activities for Motherwell, he sees them as distinct. He sees his collage work as "autobiographical," and his paintings as "large simplifications." He has written of collage,

> The sensation of physically operating on the world is very strong in the medium of the papier collé or collage, in which various kinds of paper are pasted to the canvas. One cuts and chooses and shifts and pastes, and sometimes tears off and begins again. In any case, shaping, arranging such a relational structure obliterates the need, and often the awareness of representation. Without reference to likeness, it possesses feeling because all the decisions in regard to it are ultimately made on the grounds of feeling.[49]

> Collages are a modern substitute for still-life. . . . My painting deals in large simplifications for the most part. Collage in contrast is a way to work with autobiographical material—which one wants sometimes. . . . I do feel more joyful with collage, less austere. A form of play. Which painting, in general, is not, for me, at least.[50]

Motherwell's collages, such as *The Red and Black #53* (1987) (fig. 1.3), continue to carry the lyrical and transcendent sensibilities that characterize much of his work.

Lee Krasner, married to Jackson Pollock, also contributed to the development of collage in the world of Abstract Expressionism. Although she was primarily a painter, collage was one of her favorite media. In an interview with John Bernard Myers she spoke of her use of collage:

> I long ago asked myself what collages can do. The Cubists made collages to emphasize the ambiguity of flat surfaces, to indicate volume, even depth, in order to abolish con-

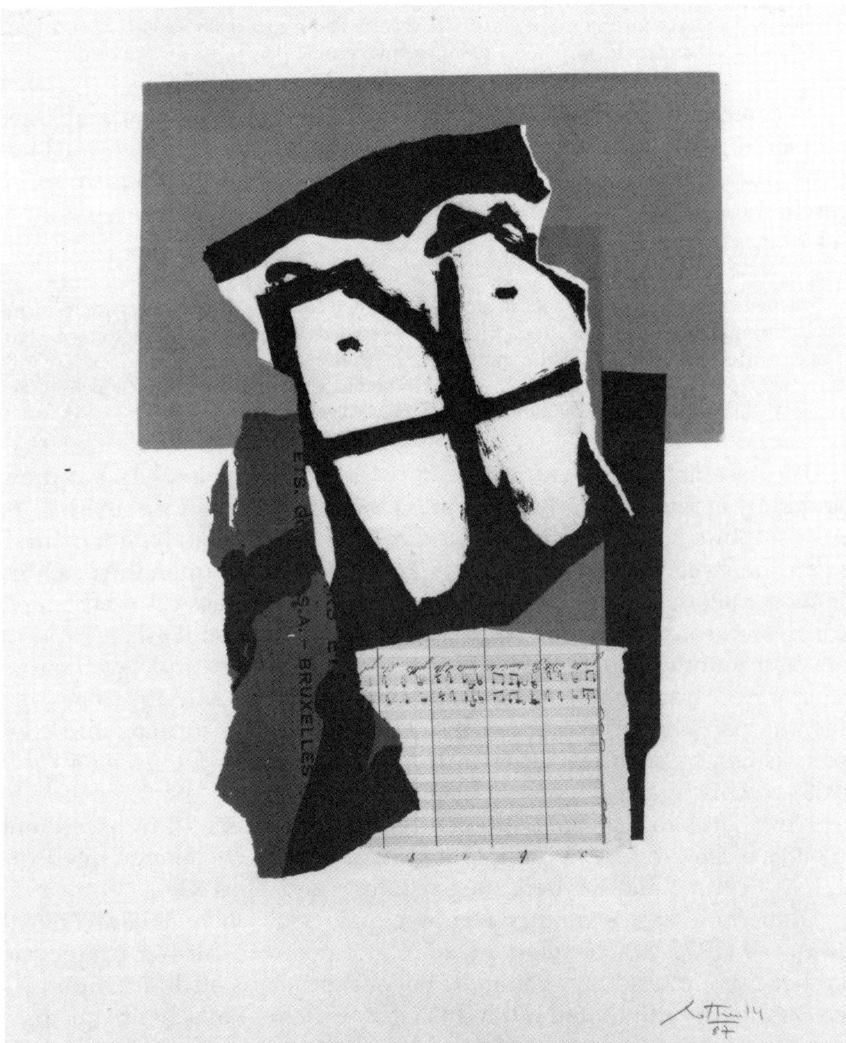

Figure 1.3. Robert Motherwell, *The Red and Black #53,* 1987
Collage on Whatman paper, 32″ × 25″.
(Collection of the artist. Photo by Ken Cohen; courtesy of M. Knoedler and Co., Inc.)

ventional perspective. The Surrealists used collage for purposes of surprise and irrationality, sometimes to fool the eye. Other serious artists, Kurt Schwitters for instance, composed abstract structures with refuse, *Merz;* and still others created lyric sensory images, as Anne Ryan did so enchantingly. My collages have to do with time and change, and are for me the appropriate means to express such experiences. I have other things in my head when I paint, or make new prints, or do a mosaic.[51]

In contrast to Motherwell and Krasner, Jean Dubuffet's assemblages and paintings elicited the name art brute for the brutally primitive qualities of the work. He continuously explored materials and techniques, as he searched for a primeval Earth Image that extended beyond man, animal and plants. For him,

the name collage is a critic's term, a pre-established category for stereotyped art forms and trite and conventional ideas. My assemblages are a whole cycle of pictures pasted, cemented or sewn, and of little statues—made from butterfly wings, fragments of torn newspaper . . . you can see that, even if the name collage pleased me (which it does not) still it could not embrace all these works, all these materials.[52]

The assemblage concept as we know it today was explored and expanded by artists such as Richard Stankiewicz and John Chamberlain as junk sculpture became acceptable and collage existed in a dynamic three-dimensional space. Stankiewicz and Chamberlain drew upon the machine for their materials. Gone were the days of heroic, classical marble and bronze statues that were, to some, elitist. Instead, Chamberlain's use of smashed automobiles and Stankiewicz's wheel, dog, and lever parts, transformed traditional notions of both sculpture and the machine. Machine parts became alive and transformed in new formats and contexts, as can be seen in pieces such as Stankiewicz's *Europa on a Cycle* (1953) or Chamberlain's *Essex* (1960).

New paths for collage were made as the abstract and transcendent qualities of the Abstract Expressionists' works were challenged by artists such as Robert Rauschenberg, Jasper Johns, and Yves Klein. From 1953 on, Rauschenberg, with his combine paintings such as *Bed* (1955), *Monogram* (1955–59), or *Pilgrim* (1960), attempted to further bridge the gap between art and life, going far beyond previous such attempts. As Leo Steinberg has pointed out in his *Other Criteria,* Rauschenberg "proposed the flatbed of work-surface plane as the foundation of an artistic language that would deal with a different order of experience."[53] Although some of these pieces hung on the wall, they referred back to horizontals upon which one sat, worked, slept, etc. Steinberg wrote further of Rauschenberg's innovations,

> What he invented above all was, I think, . . . a pictorial surface that let the world in again. Not the world of the renaissance man who looked for his weather clues out of the window; but the world of men who turn knobs to hear a taped message, ''precipitation probability ten percent tonight,'' electronically transmitted from some windowless booth. Rauschenberg's picture plane is for the consciousness immersed in the brain of the city.[54]

Rauschenberg also incorporated techniques of reproduction such as silkscreen, transfer drawings, etc. into his work. For some, such as Douglas Crimp, Rauschenberg's work is very much a part of a postmodern aesthetic:

> The fiction of the creating subject gives way to the frank confiscation, quotation, excerptation, accumulation and repetition of already images. Notions of originality, authenticity and presence, essential to the ordered discourse of the museum, are undermined. Rauschenberg steals the *Rokeby Venus* and screens her onto the surface of *Crocus,* which also contains pictures of mosquitoes and a truck, as well as a reduplicated Cupid with a mirror. She appears again, twice, in *Transom,* now in the company of a helicopter and repeated images of water towers on Manhattan rooftops.[55]

And Rauschenberg himself has written of his work:

> In the third Artist Show at the Stable Gallery, my collage, SHORT CIRCUIT, 1955, was motivated by the protest that there had not been any new artists invited to exhibit. Therefore, I invited four artists: Jasper Johns, Stan Vanderbeek, Sue Weil and Ray Johnson to give me works to be built into my collage. Only two paintings were ready in time to be installed into the major piece. The collage also contains the autograph of Judy Garland, and one of the first programs of a John Cage concert. Because Jasper Johns' flag for the collage was stolen, Elaine Sturtevant is painting an original flag in the manner of Jasper Johns' to replace it. This collage is a documentation of a particular event at a particular time and is still being affected. It is a double document.[56]

> Painting related to both art and life. Neither can be made. (I try to act in that gap between the two.) I am trying to check my habits of seeing, to counter them for the sake of greater freshness. I am trying to be unfamiliar with what I'm doing.[57]

Jasper Johns began to challenge our illusions of what everyday objects and events were—a flag, a broom, a target, a number, etc. beginning in 1955 with his target constructions. The French artist Yves Klein pushed too to work in the gap between art and life, as he progressed from his monochrome overall paintings in the late 1950s to sponge reliefs and assemblage sculptures to ''event-paintings'' such as his imprints of female bodies with paint on paper mounted on canvas.

In the sixties, the world of Pop Art provided a stimulus for collage, as focus was placed on the everyday object and television, electric signs, advertisements, comic strips, etc., were elevated to the realm of fine art. In London the 1956 Whitechapel Gallery exhibition called "This Is Tomorrow" featured a Pop Art collage, *Just What Is It That Makes Today's Homes So Different, So Appealing,* by Richard Hamilton. The piece showed two "pin-up" figures, male and female, in a mechanized environment of mass culture. A vacuum cleaner, tape recorder, and television were accompanied by a music hall program, sentimental comic strip, can of ham, etc. The Whitechapel show brought together painters, sculptors, and architects, evoking an environmental "collage" event. Also included in the exhibit was an environmental piece, consisting of a blow-up of Robbie the Robot, who was sixteen feet high with flashing eyes and teeth. In the catalogue for the exhibit Hamilton wrote,

> We reject the notion that tomorrow can be expressed through the formal presentation of rigid formal concepts. Tomorrow can only extend the range of the present body of visual experience. What is needed is not a definition of meaningful imagery but the development of our perceptive potentialities to accept and utilize the continual enrichment of visual material.[58]

In some American Pop collage pieces, the raw and bare qualities of Pop objects and materials appeared, as in *7 Up* (1961), a painted plaster wall projection by Claes Oldenburg; *Cinema* (1963) by George Segal; and the combines of readymade objects such as household tools and lawnmovers on painted surfaces by Jim Dine. Pop Art was only one of the elements that bombarded and transformed life in the sixties.

Media of all types—print, electronic, etc.—brought continuous and discontinuous events in unrelated times and places to the individual. The transferral and amassing of information was like a collage of disparate times and places in the "global village." There was a sense of the possibility of connectedness but at the same time there existed a sense of alienation, of individuals afloat in a world turned upside down.

As the sixties progressed there appeared to be a greater desire for the integration and interaction of art and life, as in the work of Allan Kaprow. His early collages evolved into Happenings or what he called a "collage of action." A striking aspect of artists who organized Happenings and Events was their frequent political and social involvement. The viewer was pushed to have not only an aesthetic response, but also to immerse him/herself completely in the event at hand. Building on the Happening, artists such as Jean Tinguely and Wolf Vostell dealt with elements of destruction in their work. Tinguely's self-destroying piece of 1960, *Homage to New York,* which was designed to make music and create paintings, and which included a bathtub and piano, struck strongly at notions of permanence and stability, introducing a subtle sarcasm into the Museum of Modern Art courtyard on that cold March day when the piece self-destructed. Wolf Vostell fractured and destroyed imagery in his erasure décollages. He has explained,

> Proceeding from self-dissolving, self-destroying and self-exhausting factors in experience . . . I coined the idea of décollage. For me, this was the beginning of a change of taste and the inclusion of the environment in the form of experiences in my work.
>
> Duchamp discovered Readymades and the Futurists claimed noise as art. A primary characteristic of my work and that of my colleagues is that the Happening includes whatever noise, movement, object colour, or psychology enters into the total work of art. Because of this, I assert that life and people are art.[59]

Vostell was also responsible for the first U.S. environmental installation using a television set, in the Smolin Gallery in 1963. The polarities of death and destruction/birth and creation are embraced simultaneously in works such as those by Vostell and Tinguely.

The immediacy of the Happening was extended to Performance art. Gilbert and George transformed themselves into living and assembled sculpture, and brought a sense of humor to performance art. In one of their best-known pieces, *The Singing Sculpture* (1971), they covered themselves with metallic paint, wore "proper" English suits, stood on a table and appeared as marionettes mouthing words to a prewar song that is the title of the piece. In more recent work they have presented themselves through documentation of large-scale photomontages and photograms.

A performance artist once associated with the Fluxus movement in Germany is Nam June Paik, who moved from electronic music composition to work in video. He proclaimed in the mid-sixties that "as collage technique replaced oil paint, the cathode ray tube will replace the canvas,"[60] and "My experimental TV is not always interesting, but not always uninteresting like nature which is beautiful / not because it changes beautifully / but simply because it changes."[61] In 1965 Paik had his first gallery exhibit in the U.S. at the Galeria Bonino. In 1967 his *Electronic Blues*, involving viewer participation, was installed at the Howard Wise Gallery. Paik achieved notice for a number of pieces he created for the classical cellist Charlotte Moorman. One, *Bra for Living Sculpture* (1969), showed the cellist wearing a bra made of two miniature television sets. Mechanical and human attributes were juxtaposed and exchanged as the viewers' perceptions of realities were altered. What was perhaps once considered intimate and private, the bra, suddenly became exposed and public. Other important video/performance events in the late sixties included the following:

1966 Nine Evenings: Theater and Engineering organized by Billy Klüver, with collaboration of forty engineers and ten artists with video projections in a number of pieces.

1967 WGBH-TV in Boston, "What's Happening, Mr. Silver?" with host David Silver, and experimental collage/information series in which several dozen inputs were mixed live and at random.

1969 "T.V. as a Creative Medium," the first American exhibit devoted entirely to video.

The medium of video with its potential for multiple layers of time (what might be called a collage of and in time for some pieces) and images, and its potential for widespread distribution, has in many ways gone far beyond the canvas, and extended principles of collage. Some video pieces have involved the spectator in both the perception of and the realization of the piece. Unlike film, which must be processed before it can be screened, video imagery can be recorded and played immediately. The spectator may no longer be a passive receiver but engaged in giving meaning to the work.

In the sixties the arrangement and assemblage of various elements also appeared in Minimalist and Earth art. Carl Andre's assembled land and floor pieces were collections of what he called "particles" existing in a specific space and time. Sometimes Andre placed such elements in random urban settings. Beginning in 1968, Robert Smithson dealt with the placement and displacement of earth materials and the interaction of the "real" site and the "nonsite," as the Cubists might have done with found materials and the picture surface. In 1968 Smithson relocated shards of sandstone from New Jersey to a New York gallery and piled them in a mirror-lined corner, creating a "nonsite" from a particular organic site. Later, moving out of the gallery space to specific earthpieces, Smithson continued to be interested in metaphors of flux and change. "One's mind and the earth are in a constant set of erosion . . . [I]deas decompose into stones of unknowing."[62]

A different approach to assemblage was seen in the work of Louise Nevelson, whose work, although forceful and strong, evoked a sense of a very private and intimate world. The struggle of stereotypic male/female qualities appears inherent in the work as she described it. Concerning enclosing her sculpture in boxes, she wrote in 1956:

> I wanted to be more secretive about the work and I began working in the enclosures. . . . There's something more private about it for me and gives me a better sense of security. I feel that my works are definitely feminine. . . . A man simply couldn't use the means of, say, fingerwork to produce my small pieces. They are like needlework. . . . My work is delicate; it may look strong, but it is delicate. . . . My whole is in it, and

> my whole life is feminine. . . . Women through all ages could have had physical strength and mental creativity and still have been feminine. The fact that these things have been suppressed is the fault of society.[63]

Nevelson's use of found objects, fragments, and wholes, often in a grid format, appeared in some instances to be a re-exploration of a Cubist-like space.

The decade of the 1970s brought an era of eclecticism. Artists as diverse as Laurie Anderson, Joseph Beuys, and Vito Acconci extended the legacy of the Event and the Happening. An artist such as Romare Bearden came to greater recognition following his Museum of Modern Art retrospective in 1971. An art of life, drawing upon experiences of the rural South, urban New York, Bearden's collages in their kaleidoscopic qualities and evocation of jazz forms speak to the viewer with compassion. Bearden's *Odysseus* series was perhaps symbolic of his search to reclaim his past and articulate its significance for a contemporary world (fig. 1.4).

> I paint out of the tradition of the blues, of call and recall. You start a theme and call and recall. When I begin a work now, I first put down several rectangles of color, some of which, as in a Rembrandt drawing, are of the same proportion as the canvas. I next might paste a photograph (or piece of paper), perhaps of a head, in the general layout of the composition. When that is accomplished, I attempt ever more definite statements, superimposing other materials over those I started with. I try to move up and across the surface . . . avoiding deep diagonal thrusts and the kind of arabesque shapes favored by the great Baroque painters. Slanting directions I regard as tilted rectangles, and I try to find some compensating balance for these relative to the horizontal and vertical axes of the canvas. . . . I like the language to be as classical as possible, but I don't want complete reductionism. What I like about Cubism is the emphasis on the essentials of painting. And what I don't like about Cubism is . . . that a lot of it overcrowds the space.[64]

Miriam Schapiro searched for a collective past and present, based on women's experiences. With Judy Chicago she directed the Womanhouse project in Los Angeles in 1971 and with Sherry Brody she collaborated on the *Dollhouse* in 1972. Judy Chicago's *Dinner Party* was a collective and a collaborative monument to the work of women. Schapiro's discovery of feminism led her to femmage, using a synthesis of collage, geometric forms, and decorative fabrics that combined modernist forms with objects and materials of feminine history and experience.

On yet another path, Frank Stella in the 1970s moved increasingly toward three-dimensional assembled painted reliefs, which along with other works of the period began to destroy the traditional boundaries between the individual art forms of painting and sculpture. Stella's *Painted*

Figure 1.4. Romare Bearden, *Odysseus Leaves Nausicaa*, 1977
Collage, 32″ × 44″.
(Courtesy of the Cordier-Ekstrom Gallery, New York. Photo by eeva-inkeri)

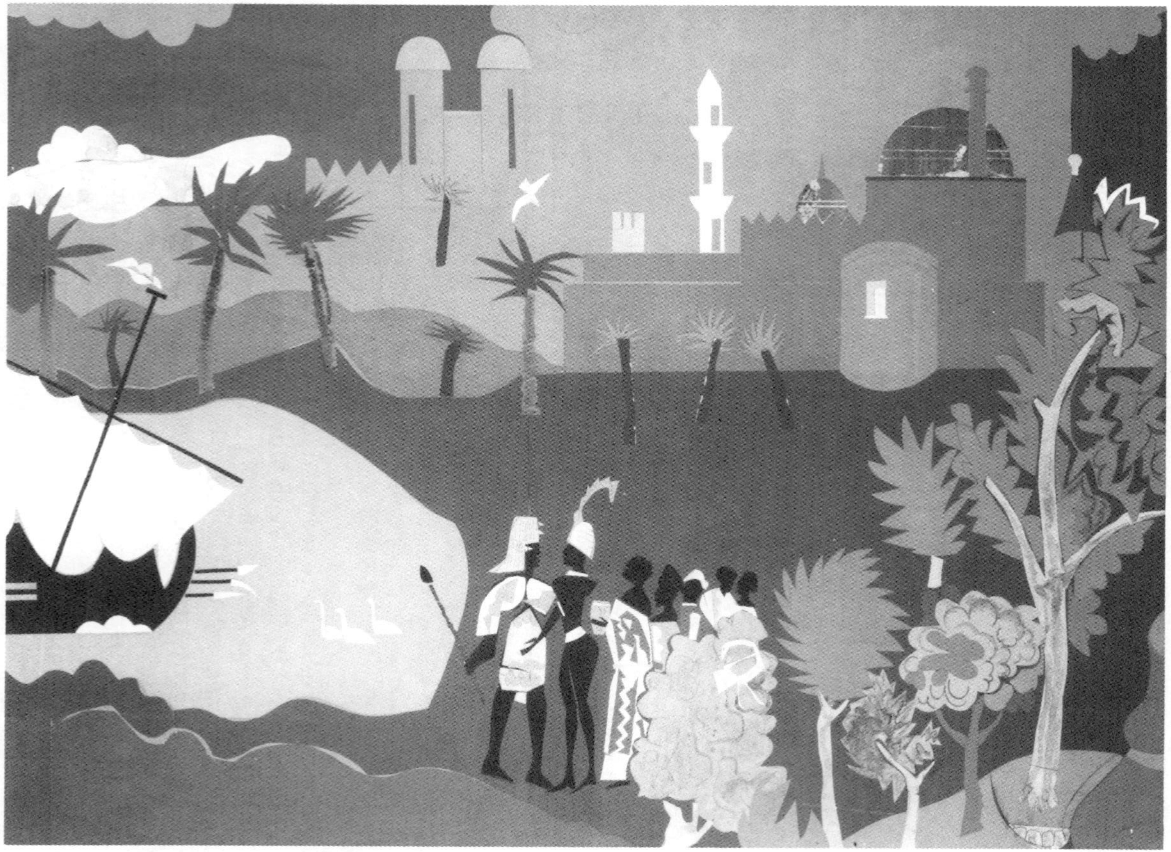

Bird series and *Shards* series, for instance, are filled with a dynamism of color, shape, space, and energy that causes the viewer to catch his breath. A Baroque spirit seems to have invaded modern forms. Once again collage techniques and principles had helped open the door to new territories of content and technique.

It is perhaps appropriate to note here that in the mid- and late-sixties polymer acrylics were developed which, when applied to paper and collage materials, provided a permanency and hardness unobtainable previously. A range of polymers, from a thin emulsion that dries hard and clear to the thick polymer pastes usable for embedding heavy objects, enabled artists to more easily overcome technical problems of collage. In addition, the development of polymer paint colors brought a fast-drying, brilliantly colored palette that was more adaptable to collage than oil paints.

As the seventies turned into the eighties, many artists searched for new heroes beyond the world of Modernism. There began a search for new heroic forms and content, and new aggressive explorations of allegory and myth. Neo-Expressionsim was born, and with it, energized surfaces filled with what might be called collage elements—such as broken crockery, straw, photographic processes, etc. Appropriation, pastiche, deconstruction are critical terms of Post-Modernism and of this decade. The appropriation of images from their original contexts and the mixing of such in new contexts has brought new ways of viewing iconography. Some Post-Modernists have come to accept a nonlinear view of time where fragments of the past become the present. As Andrew Solomon has pointed out, ours is both a historicist and aestheticist era, one in which sheer attractiveness seems to reign both in art and in the mundane," which "has considerable bearing on the apparent fact that ours is above all a synthetic era, one in which the greatest art is 'merz' art—a matter of wittingly random collages."[65] Collage methods in our time are used not only technically and physically, but also metaphorically and conceptually, in the arrangement and rearrangement of ideas and images in a variety of contexts. And deconstructionism, in pointing out the culturally dictated character of myths and narrative, has upset a myriad of traditions.

In these times we see Anselm Kiefer's apocalyptic and mythic paintings where the application of straw and sand, of overprocessed photographs, lacquer, and even fire enhance the expressive power of his work. We see Julian Schnabel's epically scaled, richly textured and aggressive paintings that involve such materials as broken crockery, plates, roots, and wood. In some instances, Schnabel revives archetypal myths and themes and shocks us with his bold and dramatic surfaces. David Salle's appropriation and assembling of disconnected images quickly shows the viewer where he/she may stand at this point in the century—often overloaded with media, mythical imagery, and information systems, and sometimes schizophrenic, torn between realities. Salle borrows from Minimalism's stained fields, continues Jasper Johns's juxtaposition of contrasting images, and borrows from art history, comic books, popular illustrations, etc. He often uses a variety of materials such as the oil, acrylic, table/fabric on canvas in his 1985 *Miner.*

Robert Longo is no less dramatic in his large assemblages that may contain sculpture (wood carving, stone, intaglio, or bronze casting), painting (acrylic, spray paint, and gold leaf), drawing, silkscreen, and photography. His work—such as *All You Zombies (Truth before God)* (1986) (fig. 1.5) or *Ornamental Love*—often contains taut contradictions in imagery and format, creating a rising tension based on ambiguity. Longo says of the role of the artist, "Artists are like guardians of culture. I'm totally obsessed with the idea of human value. I feel that I'm contributing to my culture, posing certain questions about living and the pressures of living today."[66]

Jean Tinguely deals with the motif of death in his *Cenodoxus Isenheim Altarpiece* (1981), where he reinterprets and transforms *Cenodoxus,* a Baroque play, and Matthias Grünewald's *Isenheim Altarpiece* (ca. 1510–15). Tinguely's altarpiece is a motorized openwork relief in triptych format, asking the viewer to face death in a more direct and more savage manner than the sixteenth-century piece could ever do. The mechanized assemblage of parts, including a skull, a large blue, wooden wheel, bouquets of feathers, and red and yellow rusty metal bars, enforces a confrontation of sacred and profane, of high and low culture. The collage and assemblage elements, on formal and conceptual levels, allow Tinguely to raise questions through the piece that traditional materials and methods would not have made possible.

Appropriation has been seen in a variety of guises in this decade. The intimate polaroid photographic collages, such as *Watchers* by John O'Reilly (fig. 1.6), gently incorporate a variety of imagery that is at various times parodic and approving. The ambiguities of past and present, new and old, fragment and whole, subtly call out to the viewer. O'Reilly has written of his work,

> I have worked in paper collage since 1961. The polaroid collages emerged from this background 4 years ago to meet artistic needs for a new kind of clarity.
>
> The polaroid process carries with it the suggestion of personal intimacy—photography, in general, appears to me more connected to a public, professional statement.
>
> The collages often suggest the art studio as an intimate stage. I am in the work as it is being made as one would be as an actor in an intimate situation—I am less the private person to myself in the completed collages.

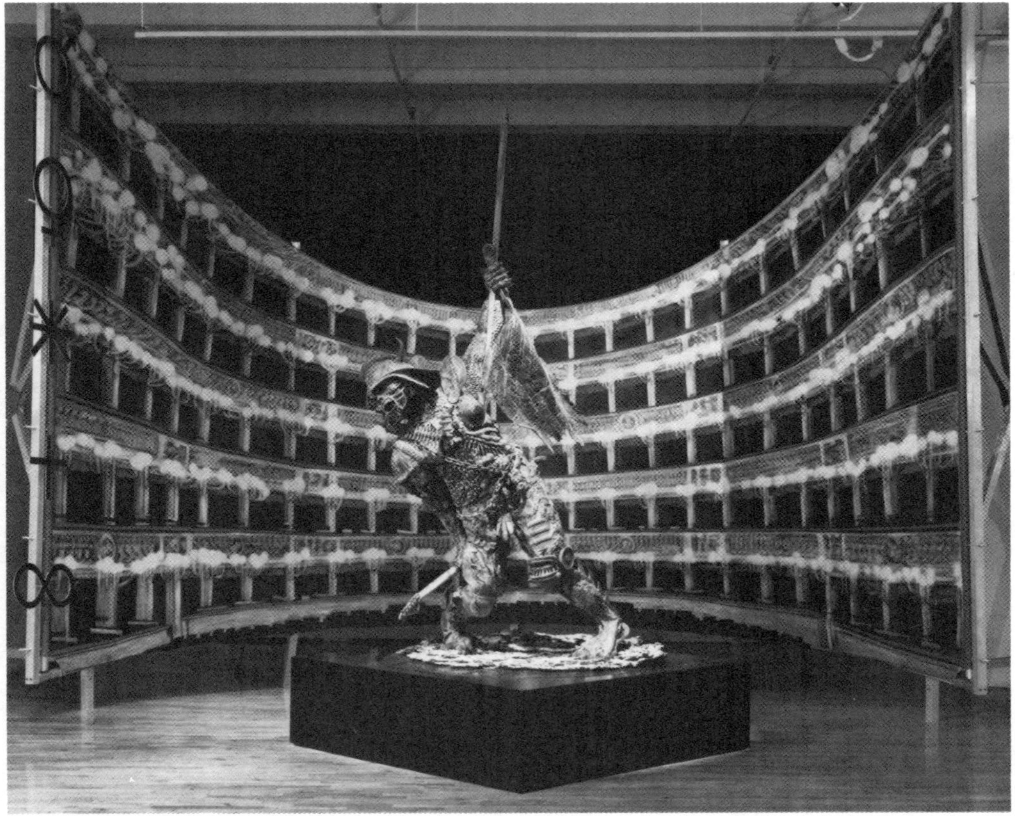

Figure 1.5. Robert Longo, *All You Zombies (Truth before God)*, 1986
Cast bronze, mechanized steel pedestal, aluminum; acrylic, charcoal, and graphite on canvas, 167½″ × 195″ × 177½″.
(Courtesy Metro Pictures, New York. Photo by Bill Jacobson Studio)

Figure 1.6. John O'Reilly, *Watchers*, 1987
Polaroid collage, 2¾″ × 6½″.
(Courtesy Howard Yezerski Gallery)

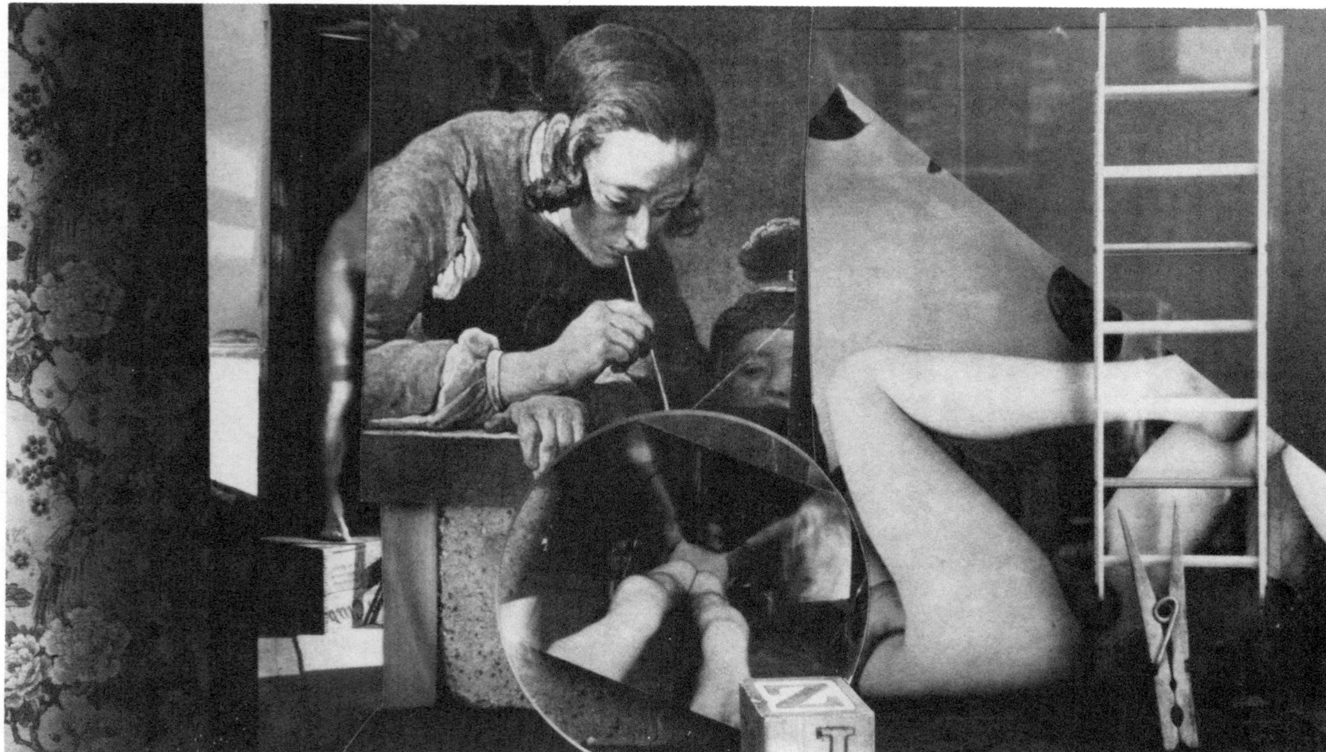

> I seek a timeless, boundless space in which the actual and art are identical. The photographic medium helps me present this imaginative truth under the guise of a reality point of view.
>
> Nudity is, in part, an attempt to deny historical time to myself.
>
> The collages should appear seamless to those who want that effect; seamed to those with a more collaged eye. I intend them to have photographic clarity while remaining ambiguous regarding whether they are photographs.
>
> The works are small in size while suggesting larger scale in content and space. Diminutive size suggests both a preciousness in terms of quality and opposed to this is feeling, a scale sense of the snapshot.[67]

On a somewhat larger scale, the photographs of the Starn Twins, often in a collagelike format, with torn-edged pieces, point frequently to contemporary searches for heroes, and set up new visions of traditional heroic imagery, as in *Christ (Stretched).*

Krzysztov Wodiczko uses photographic "montage" effects in his large-scale projections of objects and body parts onto public buildings and monuments, thereby creating a sense of disruption and dissonance at the site. Often commenting on society, Wodiczko has created over forty outdoor spectacles in the U.S., Europe, and Canada in the last seven years. These include the projection of chains and padlocks on the New Museum of Contemporary Art in New York (1985) and a swastika projected on South Africa House, Trafalgar Square (1985). Heroic and antiheroic attributes become complexly intertwined.

Looking inward rather than outward, Barbara Kruger, in her use of montage techniques—juxtaposition, superimposition, intertwining of text and image, etc.—seeks to explore and expose stereotypes and clichés concerning the self, as one sees in her 1983 untitled piece with the words, "You are not Yourself" [see fig. 15.14]. She is concerned with gestures and signs, rather than action.

> In Kruger's work, the strategic value Lacan attributes to pose is doubled and redoubled . . . . She stages for the viewer the techniques whereby the stereotype produces subjection, interpellates him/her as subject . . . [I]n Kruger's double inversion, the viewer is led ultimately to reject the work's address, this double postulation, this contradictory construction. There is risk, of course, that this will take the form of yet another gesture—a gesture of refusal. It can, however, be an active renunciation. Against the immobility of the pose, Kruger proposes the mobilization of the spectator.[68]

Activist in a different sense than Wodiczko, Kruger, or work with obvious political and social content is the collaborative work of Tim Rollins and K. O. S. (Kids of Survival). Rollins, an artist and teacher, and a group of South Bronx teenagers from broken and poor homes, working together, have created a group of powerful drawings and collage-paintings. The works are not only a collaboration of members of a group but also a collaboration between the artists and the world around them, as is suggested in the very act of collage. Books are literally and figuratively the basis for much of the work. The group reads a book such as Kafka's *Amerika* and responds visually and verbally. A book is often taken apart and the pages glued onto Belgian linen, which is used as a ground for some of the painting. Some of the text may be left open to the viewer. The final visual works are inspired by the connections between the actual reading of the book, the teenagers' own lives, and additional imagery such as that of Picasso. Important are not only the products, which are now owned by major museums and collectors, but also the process. The collective problem solving that must go on and the life-giving force that has lifted the Kids beyond the web of an impoverished future are significant aspects of the work. The work is perhaps more "activist" than actual "political" images as one considers Rollins's long-term goal to raise enough money to found an accredited high school in the Bronx that uses art as the basis of an entire curriculum. The work of Rollins and K. O. S. also shows an unusual interplay between text and visual elements. A piece such as *Amerika X* (fig. 1.7) gives the viewer a new context in which to consider the nature of language, literature, and the tension between visual and verbal statements.

In a consideration of the extension of collage principles in a postmodern era, it seems important to briefly mention their impact in architecture. As Colin Rowe and Fred Koetter indicate in their *Collage City,*

> It is suggested that a collage approach, an approach in which objects are conscripted or seduced from out of their context, is—at the present day—the only way of dealing with the ultimate problems of, either or both, utopia and tradition; and the provenance of the architectural objects introduced into the social collage need not be of great consequence. . . . Societies and persons assemble themselves according to their own interpretations of absolute reference and traditional value; and up to a point, collage accommodates both hybrid display and the requirements of self-determination.[69]

One may cite architects such as Charles Moore or Frank Gehry as examples. Moore's Piazza d'Italia, with its historicist and fantasy elements, combines archeology, modernism, commerce, and theater. Frank Gehry's buildings are often literal collages of diverse materials such as corrugated metal or chain link. The sixty-five-foot-high, recently constructed Gehry structure for an exhibit at the Washington Building Museum (1988) is like a cubist tower of sheet metal, with powerful geometric shapes and raw finishes.

Thus collage principles, and extensions and variations of collage, have opened the door to an endless stream of artistic and critical innovations and expressions. Collage may indeed be seen as a quintessential twentieth-century art form. It is in the context of the developments in

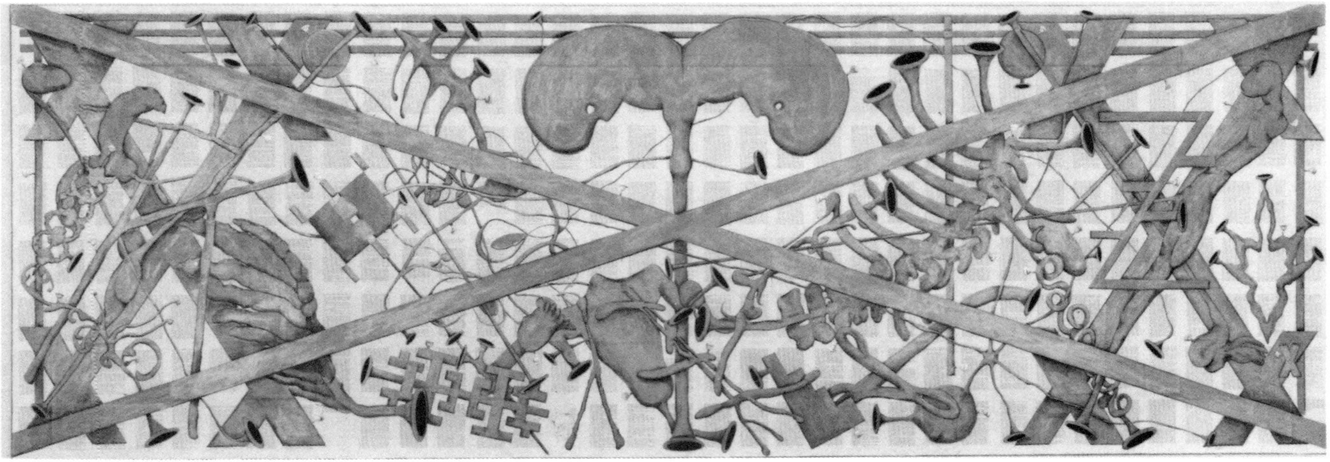

Figure 1.7. Tim Rollins and K. O. S., *Amerika X,* 1986–88
Watercolor, charcoal and bistre on bookpages on linen, 60″ × 175″.
(Courtesy Jay Gorney Modern Art, New York)

collage, from the first Cubist experiments to the present, that the following critical essays have been written. They, in a sense, are a collage of viewpoints concerning the state and impact of collage in the twentieth century.

Notes

1. Clement Greenberg, "Collage," in *Art and Culture* (Boston: Beacon Press, 1961), p. 70; reprinted in this volume (pp. 67–77), p. 67.
2. Gregory Ulmer, "The Object of Post-Criticism," in Hal Foster, ed., *The Anti-Aesthetic: Essays on Postmodern Culture* (Port Townsend, Wash.: Bay Press, 1983), p. 84; reprinted in this volume (pp. 383–412), p. 384.
3. Herbert Read, quoted in Malcolm Bradbury and James McFarlane, eds. *Modernism* (Middlesex: Penguin Books, 1976), p. 20.
4. Henry F. May, *The End of American Innocence* (New York: Alfred Knopf, 1959), pp. 238–39.
5. Gary Zukav, *The Dancing WuLi Masters: An Overview of the New Physics* (New York: William Morrow and Co., 1979), p. 92.
6. Allan Bullock, "The Double Image," in Bradbury and McFarland, *Modernism*, p. 70.
7. James McFarlane, "The Mind of Modernism," in Bradbury and McFarland, p. 92.
8. Hal Foster, "The Problem of Pluralism," *Art in America* (January 1982): 14.
9. Frederic Jameson, "In the Destructive Element Immerse," *October* 17 (Summer 1981).
10. Ibid.
11. Craig Owens, "Representation, Appropriation and Power," *Art in America* (May 1982): 21. For a discussion of representation and collage see also Rosalind Krauss, "Representing Picasso," *Art in America* 68 (December 1980): 90–96.
12. Ecclesiastes, quoted in Jean Baudrillard, "The Precession of Simulacra," in Brian Wallis, ed., *Art after Modernism: Rethinking Representation* (New York: The New Museum of Contemprary Art, in association with David Godine Publishers, Boston, 1984), p. 253.
13. Ibid., pp. 253, 266.
14. Fredric Jameson, "Post-Modernism and Consumer Society," in Hal Foster, ed., *The Anti-Aesthetic: Essays on Postmodern Culture* (Port Townsend, Wash.: Bay Press, 1983), p. 115.
15. Ibid., p. 119.
16. Some of the material in the following paragraphs is derived from discussion notes taken at the National Endowment for the Humanities Institute for the Study of Avant-Gardes, Harvard University, Summer 1987.
17. Craig Owens, "The Discourse of Others: Feminists and Post Modernism," in Foster, *The Anti-Aesthetic*, p. 59.
18. Herta Wescher, *Art Aujourd'hui* 5 (February 1954): 3.
19. John Golding, *Cubism: A History and an Analysis, 1907–14* (London: Faber and Faber, 1959), p. 104.

20. Daniel-Henry Kahnweiler, letter to Harriet Janis, 4 Feb. 1961, Harriet Janis and Rudi Blesh, *Collage—Personalities, Concepts, Techniques* (Philadelphia and New York: Chilton Co., 1962), p. 15. For further discussion of Kahnweiler's ideas and of Picasso's 1912 *Guitare* of sheet metal and wire as "at once the origin of 'synthetic' Cubism and of a new era in the history of Western sculpture," see Yve-Alain Bois, "Kahnweiler's Lesson," *Representations* (Spring 1987): 33–68.

21. Pierre Daix, *Picasso, The Cubist Years 1907–16, A Catalogue Raisonné of the Paintings and Related Works* (Boston: New York Graphic Society, 1979), p. 103.

22. Thomas Crow, "Modernism and Mass Culture," in Benjamin H. D. Buchloh, Serge Guilbant and David Sokin, eds., *Modernism and Modernity, The Vancouver Conference Papers* (Halifax: The Press of the Nova Scotia College of Art and Design, 1981), p. 246.

23. Quoted in Françoise Gilot and Carlton Lake, *Life with Picasso* (New York: McGraw-Hill, 1964), p. 70.

24. Georges Braque, the line "It is not enough to make the painted object visible, it must also be made tangible," is quoted in *Encyclopedia of World Art,* vol. 9, p. 598. The remaining lines are from "Thoughts on Painting," 1917, quoted in Edward Fry, *Cubism* (New York: McGraw-Hill), pp. 147–48.

25. Gino Severini, letter to Raffaele Carrieri, cited by Carrieri in his *Futurism* (Milan: Edizione del Milione: distributed by Harry Abrams, 1969), p. 117.

26. Umberto Boccioni, *Technical Manifesto of Futurist Sculpture,* cited in Marjorie Perloff, "The Invention of Collage," in Jeanine Parisier Plottel, ed., *Collage* (New York: New York Literary Forum, 1983), p. 20.

27. Quoted in Herta Wescher, *Collage* (New York: Harry Abrams, 1968), p. 52.

28. Herta Wescher, *Collage,* p. 85.

29. Kasimir Malevich, cited in Herta Wescher, *Collage,* p. 94.

30. Konstantin Umansky, cited in Wescher, *Collage,* p. 101.

31. Dawn Ades, *Photomontage* (London: Thames and Hudson, 1976), p. 72.

32. Quoted in Dawn Ades, *Photomontage,* p. 72.

33. Sergei Eisenstein, *Film Form* (New York: Harcourt Brace, 1949), p. 72.

34. Quoted in Wescher, *Collage,* p. 266.

35. Tristan Tzara, "Le Papier collé ou le Proverbe en peinture," *Cahiers d' Art* 6 (1931): 62.

36. Quoted in Blesh and Janis, *Collage,* p. 56.

37. Jean Arp, cited in "Constellations and Cosmos," in Jane Hancock, *Arp 1886–1966* (Minneapolis, Minn.: The Minneapolis Institute of Arts, 1987), p. 122.

38. Ibid., p. 123.

39. Ibid., p. 122.

40. Translation in Werner Schmalenbach, *Kurt Schwitters* (New York: Abrams, 1967), p. 94.

41. Quoted in Blesh and Janis, *Collage,* p. 63.

42. Ibid., p. 64.

43. From Raoul Hausmann, ''Synthetisches Cino der Malerei,'' *Courrier Dada,* p. 40; in Wescher, *Collage,* p. 136.

44. Hannah Höch, ''Dada Photo Montage,'' in Herschel Chipp, ed., *Theories of Modern Art,* (Berkeley: University of California Press, 1968), p. 396.

45. Arthur Dove, cited in Dickran Tashjian, *Skyscraper Primitives, Dada and the American Avant-Garde* (Middletown, Conn.: Wesleyan University Press, 1975), p. 198.

46. Arthur Dove, cited in Dorothy Rylander Johnson, *Arthur Dove: The Years of Collage* (College Park, Md.: University of Maryland Art Gallery, 1967), p. 20.

47. Max Ernst, ''Beyond Painting,'' *Cahiers d'Art* (1936), cited in Gaëtan Picon, *Surrealists and Surrealism 1919–1939* (New York: Rizzoli Publications, 1977), pp. 56, 94.

48. Salvador Dali, cited in Blesh and Janis, *Collage,* p. 83.

49. Robert Motherwell, cited in ''Paint, Paste and Plane,'' by David Rosand, in Jeanine Plottel, *Collage,* p. 132.

50. Robert Motherwell, in *An Exhibition of the Work of Robert Motherwell* (Northampton, Mass.: Smith College Museum of Art), p. 8.

51. Lee Krasner, cited in John B. Myers, ''Naming Pictures,'' *Artforum* (November 1984): 73.

52. Jean Dubuffet, letter to Harriet Janis, *Vence,* 16 Dec. 1969; in Blesh and Janis, *Collage,* p. 224.

53. Leo Steinberg, *Other Criteria* (New York: Oxford University Press, 1972), p. 85.

54. Ibid., p. 90.

55. Douglas Crimp, ''On the Museum's Ruins,'' in Foster, The *Anti-Aesthetic,* p. 53.

56. Robert Rauschenberg, cited in Elayne H. Varian, *Art in Process: The Visual Development of a Collage* (New York: Finch Museum of Art, 1967).

57. Robert Rauschenberg, cited in William Seitz, *The Art of Assemblage* (New York: Museum of Modern Art, 1961), p. 116.

58. Richard Hamilton, cited in Eddie Wolfram, *History of Collage* (New York: Macmillan Publishing Co., 1975), p. 159.

59. Wolf Vostell, cited in Wolfram, *History of Collage,* p. 178.

60. Nam June Paik, cited in Corinne Robins, *The Pluralist Era: American Art, 1968–1981* (New York: Harper and Row, 1984), p. 225.

61. Ibid., p. 224.

62. Robert Smithson, cited in H. H. Arnason, *History of Modern Art,* 3rd ed. (Englewood Cliffs: Prentice-Hall, 1986), p. 576.

63. Louise Nevelson, cited in Wendy Slatkin, *Women Artists in History, from Antiquity to the 20th Century* (Englewood Cliffs: Prentice-Hall, 1985), pp. 152–53.

64. Romare Bearden, cited in Avis Berman, ''Romare Bearden,'' *ARTnews* (December 1980): 60, 63.

65. Andrew Solomon, ''Something Borrowed Something Bloom,'' *Artforum* (May 1988): 122.

66. Robert Longo, cited in Howard N. Fox, *Avant-Garde in the Eighties* (Los Angeles: Los Angeles County Museum of Art, 1987), p. 22.

67. John O'Reilly, letter to Katherine Hoffman, June 1988.

68. Craig Owens, "The Medusa Effect, or The Specular Ruse," *Art in America* (January 1984): 97–105.

69. Colin Rowe and Fred Koetter, *Collage City* (Cambridge, Mass.: MIT Press, 1978), pp. 144–45.

2

Collage: The Organizing Principle of Art in the Age of the Relativity of Art

Donald B. Kuspit

*By the early twentieth century, concepts of "absolute" values and ideas had been replaced by ideas of relativism and relativity in many circles of artistic and intellectual thought. Donald Kuspit, in examining expanded concepts of relativity in the work of figures such as Jerome Kagan, Alfred North Whitehead, and Karl Mannheim, and the relationship of their work to collage, illustrates how collage may be seen as "*the *exemplification of the use and dominance of relativity in modern art." As Kuspit writes, "Collage is a demonstration of this process of the many becoming the one, with the one never fully resolved because of the many that continue to impinge upon it. Every entity is potentially relevant to every entity's existence. This is the relativistic message of collage: the keeping in play of the possibility of the entry of the many into one, the fusion of the many into the one."*

The first part of the task is to define relativity for the purposes of this discussion; the second part is to bring it to bear on collage, conventionally described (if I may fall back on the dictionary) as "an agglomeration of fragments such as matchboxes, bus tickets, playing cards, pasted together and transposed, often with relating lines or color dabs, into an artistic composition of incongruous effect." The dictionary definition concludes with the statement: "It is a type of abstraction."[1] Note the emphasis on the following: agglomeration, fragments, transposition to an abstract plane, and incongruous effect. Collage composition does not

---

This article originally appeared in *Relativism in the Arts,* edited by Betty Craig (Athens: The University of Georgia Press, 1983).

cohere, and there is nothing inherent to it. It is the beginning—one might say, the model—for what has come to be called "junk art," being in a sense no more than an accumulation of the detritus of daily life in a composition that can only loosely be called a "synthesis." It implies an easy shift from the material of life to the material of art—the self-evidence of the relationship between the two. Decisions are involved in its creation—from the choice of material to the "composing" of the incongruous effect—but these seem secondary to the expectation of easy crossover between life and art, the easy "translatability" of the one into the other, with only minor artistic adjustments, represented in the dictionary definition by "relating lines or color dabs." However, these relational factors are crucial, for they complete the crossover. On them, as the formal confirmation of transposition, depends the success of the collage—its viability as a "structure" of relationships between fragments of material, and as a demonstration of the reversible relationship (the continuum) between life and art. The gathering together which collage is about becomes abstract and assumes the mantle of art only when token signs of art are added to the mix; i.e., only when it is aestheticized by being "treated" (shall we say "purified"?) with the residue from a convention of art, traces that once signaled a full-fledged act of artistic creation. The artistic fragments refine the life fragments, giving them appeal to a more contemplative level of consciousness than is customary in everyday life, making them safely formal and aesthetically significant. "Laundered," the life fragments have—to use the critical term supposedly indicative of heightened aesthetic awareness—a "crispness" they did not have in life. This crispness is the sign of their autonomy, their new presence, ineffable as well as spontaneously eternal. The life fragments have been raised from a transient to an eternal present as painlessly as possible. The whole process is so patently a mockery of conventional conceptions of art-making—so summary a practice of the theory of art as imitation of nature—that it becomes hard to take collage seriously as art. It brings the whole idea of art into question, or else makes it seem a risky yet superficial venture.

At first glance, then, the collage approach to art—however much it is assumed to give familiar aesthetic results (whether it does or does not quickly becomes a matter of debate)—does not imply the most rigorous sense of art. This is where the idea of relativity becomes relevant; it accounts for that apparent lack of rigor and becomes a means of tracing its implications and finally of justifying it. The collage is only relatively, rather than absolutely, art. The word "only" signals the seeming sense of inadequacy of the collage in comparison to "real" art—the fall from aesthetic grace and decline in general status of art when it becomes all too obviously relative to life, and above all relative in itself, structurally indecisive or uncertain. It is thus no longer clearly autonomous or self-reliant, and when its relative condition is recognized as incurable, it is no longer self-evidently art. The collage seems adrift in a limbo that is neither life nor art, at least by the strictest standards. It seems to have lost its center of gravity, the clarity of its intention as art. It seems to be an agglomeration of literal fragments of life and art—the letter of both, without the spirit of either.

To speak of the relativity of art seems to reduce it to absurdity, to correlate with the methodological absurdity of transposing the important idea of relativity from the realm in which it originated to a realm in which it does not belong and in which it loses importance. To generalize the principle of relativity from physics to art—to exploit it beyond the boundaries of its customary usage—is inevitably to reduce art to pure physicality, for in its scientific usage relativity is descriptive of the workings of physical reality. To use it nonscientifically is to use it prescriptively, and so to misuse and falsify it. Relativity can only falsify what Baudelaire called "artificial existence," the art which is one of the things in what Hannah Arendt calls the " 'artificial' world of things" created by work. If, as Arendt says, "the human condition of work is worldliness,"[2] and the world of the work of art is not the same as the material reality that physics investigates, then to reduce art to its physicality—literalness, as it is called by Modernism—is to deny its worldliness, and thereby to deny its identity as art. It is also to become estranged from the work that went into the making of art, as well as to disparage that work by characterizing it, presumptuously and prematurely, as merely physical.

But the idea of the relativity of art is not a reductionist strategy. On the contrary, it signals an expanded sense of the possibilities and effectiveness of art—an expanded sense of the meaning of creativity and of art's worldly role. This becomes clear when we recognize that relativity (and collage) presents itself as a solution to an epistemological rather than a physical problem: the problem of *conceiving* art, not simply the problem of receiving or perceiving what is already regarded as art. The latter unavoidably reflects the former, but is logically secondary to it. The philosophical generalization of relativity by Alfred North Whitehead makes its epistemological character self-evident, as does the self-conscious employment of the idea of relativity in psychological and sociological thinking, perhaps most obviously in the works of Jerome Kagan and Karl Mannheim. Here I will use their expanded conception of relativity—increasingly pertinent and analytically precise as it passes from metaphysical to psycho-social and historical meaning—as a scalpel to dissect collage, conceived as the case in point of the relativization of art, i.e., as *the* exemplification of the use and dominance of relativity in Modern art. The modern tendency to relativize both the structure and meaning of art self-consciously accelerates with collage. Relativity becomes the determinant of art's immanent structure and worldly consequence—the inescapably central factor in (to use Whitehead's language) the primordial and consequential nature of the work of art. From Cubist collage on, art can never be understood as anything but relative in its nature, and experience of it can never be anything but relative. In Kant's language, from the modern period on, it is a "transcendental illusion" to assume that art can be "complete" or absolute—that it can exist entirely in itself, on its own terms, rather than relative to those which can never be mistaken for art, which resist becoming those of art, and which are ostensibly indifferent to art, i.e., the terms in which life is given.

Whitehead defines the "principle of relativity" as follows: "That the potentiality for being an element in a real concrescence of many entities into one actuality, is the one general metaphysical character attaching to all entities, actual and nonactual; and that every item in its universe is involved in each concrescence. In other words, it belongs to the nature of a 'being' that it is a potential for every 'becoming.' "[3] In the course of spelling out the implications of "the principle of universal relativity," Whitehead remarks that it "directly traverses Aristotle's dictum, '[A substance] is not present in a subject.' On the contrary, according to this principle an actual entity *is* present in other actual entities. In fact, if we allow for degrees of relevance, and for negligible relevance, we must say that every actual entity is present in every other actual entity."[4]

The ontological emphasis is Whitehead's; it amounts to an insistence on the actuality or presence of each entity in every other entity. That actuality is hardly demonstrable, at least on the level of everyday perception. Rather, it influences our expectations. We look for the variety of other entities in any one entity, rather than regarding that one entity as self-same—self-identified. It is identifiable in terms of its synthesis of other entities, each of which remains a possible part of itself. Collage is a demonstration of this process of the many becoming the one, with the one never fully resolved because of the many that continue to impinge upon it. Every entity is potentially relevant to every other entity's existence, is potentially a fragment in every other entity's existence. This is the relativistic message of collage: the keeping in play of the possibility of the entry of the many into the one, the fusion of the many into the one. Concrescence is, in effect, never finished, however much there may be the illusion of completeness. This is the poetry of becoming—the poetry of relativity—and it is what collage is about: the tentativeness of every unity of being because of the persistence of becoming, even when absolute entity-ness seems achieved.

The incongruous effect of the collage is based directly on its incompleteness, on the sense of perpetual becoming that animates it. It is always coming into being; it has never "been," as one can say of the more familiar, "absolute" type of art. It is always insistent yet porous, never resistant and substantive. Its parts always seem to be competing for a place in some unfinished scene, as if to finally give it the necessary accent that makes it complete. Yet nothing in the collage is necessary; each part is forever contending with every other, pushing every other part out of place, until the very idea of a place in an order becomes meaningless. Even the idea of displacement does not focus what is occurring in the collage. What counts is that it remains incompletely constituted, for all the fragments that constitute it. There is always something more that can be added to or taken away from its constitution, as if by some restless will. The collage seems unwilled, and yet it is willful. The collage is a metaphor of universal becoming, becoming that is arbitrary if self-conscious, as much a matter of blind momentum as directed process. For Whitehead, becoming is finally directed by the "desire" of each entity to be itself by becoming more than itself, in a "decisive" way. Indeed, decision is the final step of concrescence for Whitehead. Decision is described in a subjective way as involving positive and negative prehensions, i.e., ap-prehensions of entities that seem relevant and irrelevant to one's becoming. The subject forming itself is not aimlessly adrift on a turbulent sea of becoming, but steers itself through this sea by *deciding* what might or might not be relevant to its being at any given moment of its becoming. Entities prehended positively become parts of the subject's actuality, "ingress"—to use another Whiteheadean term—into its existence, become constitutive of its concreteness.

Collage sums up, as it were, this process of assimilation: the tentativeness of being in the face of its own becoming, the uncertainty or ambiguity of the workings of becoming. Collage, for the first time in art, makes uncertainty a method of creation, apparent indeterminacy a procedure. Entities rejected for inclusion remain associated with the subject that chooses another kind of actuality, as the defining contour or fringe of that actuality. Collage—and we are talking about Cubist collage, as the first truly relativistic and self-conscious use of collage—is very much about these dark fringes, these absences, as well as about the positive presence of positively ap-prehended fragments. The informal fringe and the formal assertion of substance exist side by side in the collage, subtly mingling to generate its energy. This is a material togetherness, not simply a togetherness of signs, as formalist analysis—lately revived in semiotic terms—would have it.[5] That is, it has to do only secondarily with issues of representation and abstraction; primarily, it is about the establishment of a particular kind of artistic, subjective concreteness. The integration of substance and fringe may not give the kind of unity of being that is customarily regarded as grounding the work of art's necessity. It does, however, constitute a concretely becoming artistic subject which has its unity as much in the potentiality of its becoming as in the actuality of its presence.

This point is made clear when one recalls that, in his original definition of relativity, Whitehead remarked that "non-actual" as well as actual entities could be elements in a real concrescence. The "relating lines or color dabs" of the collage—the vestigial use of primary artistic constituents—are such nonactual (abstract) entities, signs of what Whitehead calls "eternal objects." Color is particularly remarked as such an object, as well as geometric form—always implicit in the use, even the most amorphous automatist use, of line. In collage we find abstract elements as material fragments—elements of a code of abstraction that no longer perform the abstractive function but exist as entities in their own right. These fragments of art have equal status with fragments of life in the collage; they are as concrete, for the purposes of becoming, as life. They have no privileged position in the process of artistic becoming, just as the fragments of life (the traditional model of art) do not constitute a privileged source or root of art. There is no clear-cut, single ground of art in the collage: art is no longer either representational (an imitation of nature issuing in an illusion of life) or abstract (a formal construction issuing in a style). It is a creative, subjective choice of elements emblematic of becoming in general. The being of nature and the being of form lose their primacy in the subjective decisions of art, which can move freely between them to achieve its becoming. They unite in a dialectic of ap-prehension which is under subjective control. They are both subsumed in the actuality of the concrete work of art—"worked over" until they become art. The becoming of art is located not in life or style, but in the relativity of relations between them in a particular situation of concrescence. The collage replaces privilege with equivalence, definitions of artistic being with deconstructions of artistic becoming, unity with energy. The field of the work of art reveals itself more as determined by subjective work than as determined by a preconception of art as a certain kind of object, whether life-referencing or self-reflexive.

Let us get more particular, as a way of bringing the subjective character of the relativistic work of art to the fore—as a way of showing how the decisions that constitute the concrescence of a particular work of art are relative. Jerome Kagan, writing about "the need for more relativistic definitions of selected theoretical constructs" in psychology, asserts:

> "Relativistic" refers to a definition in which context and the state of the individual are part of the defining statement. Relativism does not preclude the development of operational definitions, but makes that task more difficult. Nineteenth-century physics viewed mass as an absolute value; twentieth-century physics made the definition of mass relative to the speed of light. Similarly, some of psychology's popular constructs have to be defined in relation to the state and belief structure of the organism, rather than in terms of an invariant set of external events. Closely related to this need is the suggestion that some of the energy devoted to a search for absolute stimulus characteristics of reinforcement be redirected to a search for the determinants of attention in the individual.[6]

What are the determinants of the artist's attention? Clearly, this question is more to the point of discovering the fundamentally relative situation of the work of art in its modern condition than are questions of subject matter and style—and than are inquiries as to what a truly modern subject matter and a truly modern style would be. There is no absolute definition of modern; "modern" in fact means this absence of or active indifference to absoluteness. No subject matter or style is, once and for all, modern. Only the artist's living attention is modern; only in exercising his powers of ap-prehension is he up to date. By its seeming indifference to the fragments that constitute it—conveyed by the seemingly random way in which those fragments are gathered together—the collage forces us to turn from the fragments to the attention that selected them, the individuality they acquire by being brought together by a particular kind of attention. They themselves, simply by being fragments, exist in attenuated form as stimuli—but never with any absoluteness, only relative to an individual's attention. Why they might be stimulating depends on that attention and individuality. As Kagan says, "If a stimulus is to be regarded as an event to which a subject responds or is likely to respond then it is impossible to describe a stimulus without describing simultaneously the expectancy, and preparation of the organism for that stimulus. Effective stimuli must be distinct from the person's original adaptation level. Contrast and distinctiveness, which are relative, are part and parcel of the definition of a stimulus."[7]

For Kagan, this correlates with Whitehead's subjective process of positive and negative prehension, on the basis of a previously actualized ap-prehension (categorization) of actuality: "Man reacts less to the objective quality of external stimuli than he does to categorizations of those stimuli." The categorization or belief structure which is the already existing core of the entity in process of becoming controls, to a great extent, future actualization or concrescence of the entity. Its subjectivity is already bound by its beliefs, its categorization of its own actuality and that of the entities that constitute its world. Such categorical belief gives it formal closure and seeming unity—a sense of stable identity, however limited. In collage, implicit belief or preexisting categories of orientation—unconscious conditions of choice not necessarily known even to the artist—determines entry into the field of operations, the field of artistic becoming. The fragments that find their way into the field are only superficially found by chance. Chance is a disguise for the uncertain yet highly personal significance they are felt to have. They are fascinating because they are the objects of a belief that only half knows itself, and so experiences the world in a chance way. The fragments are experienced as profoundly meaningful, but the meaning cannot be spelled out completely and never seems to truly surface—which is what leaves the artist free to arrange the fragments as he wishes, in a whimsical or a willful way. This gives the collage an aura of creative freedom which is crucial to its sense of liveliness and to the artist's sense of self-determination. Freedom and chance, the determinate fragments and the indeterminate sense of their relation, become con-fused, making the fragments even more stimulating than expected.

All of this seems obvious, but there is a tension, the possibility of self-contradiction in the situation that is less obvious but at its center. The significance the artist finds in the fragments involves as much the deconstruction as the objectification of a belief—dissolving as well as acting upon an existing, if implicit, categorization of the world. This destructive dialectic is typical of the difficulty surrounding any attempt to "recover" a subjective sense of significance from an objective world, particularly when the objects of that world are regarded as absolute and the subject is understood to exist relative to them. Under such conditions, the subject always imagines that its consciousness of itself is a false consciousness. Its consciousness of objects is a true consciousness, and however much it may work against that consciousness by dealing with "deteriorated" objects—worn fragments of objects, suggestive of the relative way objects exist as objects—those objects remain intractable enough to obscure or mute the sense of self that arises from resistance to them. The objects, however fragmentary, dominate the subject's sense of itself; and yet the subject's power of belief in the objects has been shaken. Its categorization of the world seems close to collapse, if only because of its unwillingness to trust itself in the face of the objects of the world. They can be defied, if not dismissed, by being spontaneously rather than categorically regarded—by being regarded relativistically, rather than absolutely. This, at the least, frees the self from its own self-centeredness, the sense of a center that it acquires by reason of its belief structure. The belief structure is up for grabs in the relativistic situation of the collage—and the self is inwardly freed from objects, if not externally free of them.

Objectivity is no longer a categorical imperative, but can be creatively conceived. A sense of spontaneity emerges which freshens the sense of individuality. This sense of spontaneity arises, in part, from the resistance of the self to its own unconscious categorization of the world, which becomes conscious in the course of being acted upon. And that very act sets the self against itself, which is one of the sources of its revived sense of individuality.

The collage is the scene of this struggle between an objective and subjective sense of worldliness. The subjective tries to defeat its own sense of what is typically objective by seeing all objectivity in relative terms, which at the same time restores its sense of its own primordial becoming. A sense of subjective, "artistic" becoming emerges in the collage, forever obscure or uncertain in its attribution of meaning—its categorization of or beliefs about the world—because it sees any definitive meaning as detrimental to its sense of becoming, as inhibiting of its sense of its own creative, powerful individuality. Yet that individuality refuses to presuppose itself, and it only reluctantly presupposes objects. It conceives of itself entirely in terms of complete openness—what Smithson called an "open limit"—to becoming. It assumes that it is possible to exist on a completely open horizon of ap-prehension, in which no prehension is preordained as positive or negative. It desires to achieve a state in which choice is unnecessary, in which momentum comes not even from one's resistance to one's own choices, but from entirely selfless becoming, from loss in the creative flux of cosmic becoming. This is the impossible ideal: the loss of both subjectivity and objectivity in the ceaseless flow of entities, the loss of even the most elementary sense of the world in a primordial sense of becoming, in which all choices of being are so relative as to be irrelevant, in which all commitments seem superficial in terms of the total flow of things and feelings. In collage, one is ideally totalized by this indeterminate yet insistent flow.

In practice, the collage displays a situation of irreducible tension between a subjectivity eager to identify itself yet incapable of completely doing so, and an objectivity in the process of breaking down—objects in the process of losing their hold on subjects. If, as Kagan says, "contrast" is "an important key to understanding the incentives for human behavior,"[8] then a major incentive for modern artistic behavior is recognition of the contrast between dynamic becoming, overcoming all beliefs about being, and the undertow of a residual sense of being in this becoming. It is about the dynamics of belief—what Nietzsche called the desire for self-overcoming, so as to become freshly concrete. It is about the primal contrast that emerges when relativity invades the scene of being.

The collage, then, epitomizes the state of contrast between categorization of actuality and expectation of becoming—between categorization which determines expectation, and expectation which rebels against categorization by finding fresh stimulation in the world. The collage demonstrates rebellion against determining beliefs in the very act of articulating them through the choice of fragments. More obviously, the collage is a sum of contrasts which never totalize into a single kind of stimulation. Such lack of totalization, of complete objectification of stimuli in a single object, is crucial to the success of the collage. The sense of a restlessly shifting range of stimuli is the essence of the collage—a restlessness reflecting the individuality of the artist's becoming, as embodied in the willfulness of his attention. The unsettled state of the collage is itself emblematic of the will to individual becoming which emerges from the display of fragments. The collage is a relative state of artistic affairs, where relativity indicates the restlessness of individuality in the process of becoming. As such, the collage becomes emblematic of the task of art at least since Baudelaire: the redemption of individuality in mass society, with its standardizations or categorizations—its banalization or deindividualizing of belief. Collage makes poetry with the prosaic fragments of dailiness. The poetry is a matter not just of recognizing the legitimacy of choosing one's own context of life from the universal dailiness and thereby in some sense escaping it, but of not getting locked into or trapped by this context. It is to be regarded as no more than a means of operating in the dismal dailiness, to be changed or discarded as soon as it, too, becomes a possessive, standard routine. Art teaches one to stay ahead of or to transcend dailiness by manipulating it, juggling its variables in endlessly interesting combinations. This implies a certain purposelessness, but also the playful purposefulness of continuing to become individual, even if the becoming is only pretending in a world that is "un-becoming" because it is banal—a world that has ceased to be anything but itself. The essential playfulness of the collage is a direct acknowledgment of the relativity of individuality in the world, as well as a way of expanding that world to include it, and of expanding individuality to include the world. One can view this ironically, but to do so implies a serious dedication to irony as the only way of individualizing in a world of standard categories.

Ironical contrast seems almost a mannerism in Cubist collage from the start, but it is so relentlessly pursued that it becomes visionary. Relativity shows itself succinctly in irony, which, however limited and transient—however quickly it becomes a cliché—becomes emblematic of the dialectic between individual and world, the emergence of each in the other. The limited becoming of the individual in the world—perhaps limited to his being relatively artistic, ironically artistic—in the last analysis turns out to be essential to the becoming of the world, whose own concrescence is inseparable from its individuation. Collage, relativistic art, implies such inseparability as an ultimate. It exists against all the forces that would absolutize one kind of being at the expense of the becoming of all other beings, thereby destroying the individuality of all kinds of being. This simple defiance, which is at the heart of relativism in Modern art and in the collage, becomes possible only when one explodes the object of art into theoretically innumerable fragments that never make more than an ironical whole. Those fragments establish an ironical individuality and locate that individuality in an ironical attention to detail that never adds up to a whole. With collage, art becomes a marginal, ironical way of coming into being without fully realizing one's being, i.e., one which is unassimilable by any other being, one which is free of subjective becoming.

Karl Mannheim offers a further qualification of relativism with his idea of "existential relativity." This idea "is far from implying a relativism under which everybody and nobody is right; what it implies is rather a *relationism* which says that certain (qualitative) truths cannot even be grasped, or formulated, except in the framework of an existential correlation between subject and object."[9] In the course of characterizing "the existential relativity of knowledge," Mannheim remarks that "the situation facing our thinking today appears as follows: various groups are engaged in existential experiments with particular order patterns, none of which has sufficient general validity to encompass *in toto* the whole of present-day reality."[10] From art's point of view this is not the worst state of affairs; it makes for an easier "existential correlation between subject and object," a dialectic which does not have to trouble with validity because it is an experiment in ordering reality, rather than a way of decisively determining it. Such an existential experiment is a way of acknowledging its relativity.

The collage is an "existential experiment with particular order patterns" grounded by the self-conscious belief in the impossibility of ever finding one with general validity. In fact, the desire is *not* to find one, for that would be to interfere with or even to stop the experiment by making it serious. It would be to end the individuality of the experiment—to destroy it as an experiment in individuality. It would be to end its usefulness as the resistance of an individual against the implicitly assumed (if incompletely articulated) general validity of the social order.

Relativistic art denies the as-if absoluteness or assumed validity of the daily world of modern society—the daily order of a society that pretends to be traditionless. Relativistic art thus keeps it true to itself, asks it to trust the restless sense of becoming that comes with being self-consciously modern rather than the aspiration to universality by which it seeks to become generally valid. At the same time, relativistic art—collage—is the labor by which the modern world gives birth to a tradition of sorts, i.e., a determinate focusing of itself in a "transcendent" order. The structure that passes for tradition is tenuously evident through collage sedimentation of dailiness; it is as though collage was a delta at the end of a river of becoming, in whose very fertile soil one might grow new ideas of order. In another metaphor, collage is the fleeting archaeological residue of a society still in process of hectic becoming, a random—flirtatious—display of signs which that world self-consciously examines to read its destiny, as if they were sibylline. (Destiny is always rooted in tradition, even in the case of the "tradition of the new" that collage displays.) But there is an essential ambiguity in the collage, for its refractive revelation of the inner life of modern dailiness, leading to a sense, however makeshift, of a structured dailiness implying a tenable if insecure tradition, is countered by its own dogged experimentalism or speculative stance, whose uncertainty directly correlates with the turbulence of modern becoming. This ambiguity—an inescapable structural fault, as it were—shows that collage is in perpetual deconstructive motion. In collage we watch the dailiness which is the veneer on—reification of—a supposedly generally valid social order deconstruct into a self-contradictory, experimentally realized—and so impossible to understand as generally valid or "traditional"—order. It is feverishly relational, existential; in no way can it be regarded as based on a preexisting paradigmatic order. It is constitutionally unstable, with further experimentation its only fallback position. This deconstructive experimentalism is quintessentially modern; it implies modern social belief in the relativity of all worlds, with their relativity to one another existentially prior to the separate tradition of each, for each is only fully known through its relation to the other. (This belief is masked and simplified by the concept of pluralism, which presupposes "spiritually" equivalent worlds, none superior nor more ordered and sustainable—"traditional"—than another.)

This circular relativism completes itself in Mannheim's conception of "perspectivistic" knowledge as the only way of avoiding historicist or nihilistic relativism, in which every point of view is regarded as equally valid. It is not that—in the collage, as everywhere in the modern world—every point of view is equally valid because none is generally valid. Rather, it is that a point of view or perspective must be self-consciously established, to the extent that it not only knows its own nature but can also deconstruct itself. Perspectives are not simply given; they are not stumbled upon and accepted as long-lost relatives. Instead, they must be worked up or, if already given, worked into, made one's own—experienced as emerging from one's own becoming.

There is already an implicit perspective in the seemingly random fragments of the collage. It is not simply the subjective attitude that results from a certain kind of individualizing attention, but an objective perspective implicit in the kind of things that are likely to end up as fragments and to be brought into the collage. The perspective is implicit in the fragments themselves, and individual attention seeks it out, tries to conform to it as well as to manipulate it for ironical (incongruous) effect.

This perspective in the things themselves implies that collage exists not only subjectively but also as a return to what Mannheim calls "the pre-theoretical vis-à-vis." (Mannheim uses the word *Gegenüber*—here translated as "vis-à-vis"—to avoid the word *Gegenstand* or object).[11] This seems to contradict what was implicit earlier, and what seemed at the very core of the relativistic character of the collage: namely, the idea of the impossibility of an unmediated relationship with reality. This relationship would be one of direct intuition rather than of dialectical or existential correlation, and it would seem to deny the very premise of "relationism." Yet, as noted at the beginning, the material fragments that constitute the collage exist in a certain raw state, and they keep sinking back into a pretheoretical state by reason of the dubious success of their synthesis into a conventionally unified art object. By not fully objectifying as art—by not absolutely *being* art—they present themselves as objects that seem to resist not only art but also any mediation, and thus they present themselves pretheoretically. This means that the worldly perspective inherent in them can be discovered—that, in not reaching the level of absolute art, they have fallen back into the general world. In failing to achieve an artificial existence, they appear opposite it as clues to the nature of being-in-the-world. They lose their status as physical stimuli and become sedimented meanings of worldliness, artifacts found in a particular excavation at a particular site of the world. The collage becomes simply a way of panning for the golden meanings of the world, an archaeological investigation into a present (if hidden) truth.

More precisely, the collage undermines our ideas about things by refusing to establish them in a systematic relationship, reducing them to the elements of artistic experience. As Mannheim says, systematization is "the first ordering of the 'elements of experience.' "[12] By not subsuming them in this primary order, collage sets them over against us so that they appear unmediated or pretheoretical, with an inherent perspective of their own. The collage becomes a medium in which real things can be discovered in their objective meaningfulness, as well as one in which artistic things can be invented for the purpose of achieving meaningfulness, i.e., ironical individuality. The duplicity or doubleness of the collage is a direct demonstration of its relativistic character. Self-contradictory, it seems more self-determining or self-created than if it were completely worldly or completely artistic in the conventional, absolutistic sense.

The collage is, then, self-relativizing. When we think of Mannheim's conception of "the self-relativization of thought and knowledge," we realize that he is describing their collage—artistic—character in modern times.[13] The instrument of self-relativization, for Mannheim, is the epoche, "a type of suspension of the validity of a judgment"—in the case of art, the judgment of taste.[14] Taste cannot be brought to bear on the collage, where the consensus of taste no longer determines artistic value. Taste, an eighteenth-century idea that reached a climax of use with this century's conception of Modernism, was a short-lived means of establishing an aristocratic mainstream of art within a situation of its increasing democratization, i.e., its increasing openness to life. This openness is partly Romantic in origin—recall Goethe's idea that Romanticism means that no subject matter is alien to art. But, perhaps more crucially, it has to do with the sense of the expanded means of art, with art's eagerness to share in the explosion of technique characteristic of the Industrial Revolution. Taste involves keeping a restraint on technique, insisting that only the traditional media are sure sources of art. Collage destroys the very idea of a medium, of any one "pure" mode of art. With collage, art is nowhere and everywhere; it becomes a freewheeling way of dealing with random material, emblematic of fragmented experience. Modern experience seems fragmented because one never knows what will impinge upon it, what will turn up in it. It is radically open—radically democratic—because it distrusts categorizations of experience as much as it uses them. It discards its belief structure in the very moment of acting on it, initiating a new concrescence—discovering fresh possibilities of experience—in the very moment of acting on the ground of the old one. Subjective being is constantly being overturned by objective becoming, with its unexpected entities presenting themselves for ingression in one's existence. The entities represented by the fragments of the collage, however much they may be familiar and everyday, come to be part of oneself in a new way because one's attitude toward them "artistically" changes.

Mannheim describes self-relativization as "a new form of relativization introduced by the 'unmasking' turn of mind," which is inseparable from "the emergence of a new system of reference."[15] Collage is an unmasking of art and life as they grope toward new systems of self-reference. The fragmentary character of both is revealed, and from the fragments a new revelation emerges—not mechanically, but by way of what Whitehead calls the "creative flux" of the fragments. The establishment of this condition of creative flux—for Whitehead the category of categories, the ultimate category, the final generalization of the principle of relativity—is what collage is about, so that, in the "atomistic competition" between fragments (to use Mannheim's description of competition in democracy), a new sense of systematic possibilities for both life and art might emerge. The unmasking of old systems is necessary to establish the sense of creative flux and the possibility of new systems, new actualizations of meaningful form. This unmasking, as Mannheim says, "does not aim at simply rejecting certain ideas so much as at disintegrating them. . . . To unmask an idea, thus, is not to refute it theoretically, but to destroy its effectiveness."[16]

Collage destroys the effectiveness of the idea that the imitation of nature is the basis of art—the idea that art's highest achievement is not simply to create an illusion of life, but to function as a kind of representation of it. Life can be directly referenced—directly incorporated into art—but not symbolically referenced. Or at least such symbolic referencing or representation of life is no longer the primary task of art, but simply one element in it. Collage also destroys the idea that life is a stable whole, indivisible—or rather, that the division of life will destroy it. Life still exists in fragments which afford new opportunities for experiencing it, new opportunities for finding meanings in it. Art and life become unexpected in the collage, which gives us the opportunity for a creative relationship with both of them. Neither is destroyed by having traditional ideas about it undermined. The disintegration of such traditional ideas which collage represents—for both life and art—does not disintegrate either. On the contrary, in collage what is most essential in both is revealed: their reality as creative fluxes. They have the same root: the relativistic, creative flux of democratic becoming.

What creative flux means in the practice of collage is described by Mannheim: "We understand, looking at things from our perspective, the possibility and necessity of the other perspectives; and no matter what our perspective is, we all experience the controlling 'stubbornness' of the data (*Gegebenheiten*)."[17] The data of life and art—the fragments—indisputably exist, but there is no necessary logic by which they can be ordered. Their "inner necessity" is found in the intention of our own perspective, our own subjective pursuit of meaningfulness—our own willingness to suspend our customary judgments, our categorical understanding of reality, the reality of life and art. The implication of collage, which appears arbitrary and so disturbing, is that it is extraordinarily difficult to suspend the given meanings, the expected forms, the obligatory order, the traditions (whether personal or social) by which we live, and to establish a creatively open horizon. It is a simple enough message, even socially proclaimed—the message of individual openness. But it is rarely acted upon, and it is generally regarded as a foolish, romantic rebellion against inescapable limits. But the stubbornness, the givenness of the data of life and art are not the same as the supposedly logical limits set upon them and used to control them. All such control aims to dominate them in the name of a specific perspective, which becomes a cause—to enlist them in the service of a self-styled heroic, universal cause. Returning to the roots of art and life—to creative flux—in the collage, we realize that no perspective is universal or absolute. From the matrix of fragments of both life and art, subjective perspective must be allowed to freely arise, as a dialectical response—a dialectical emergence.

This makes the collage the climactic realization of the romantic principle in art. Mannheim summarizes this principle by quoting Novalis:

> The world must be romanticized. That is the way to its original meaning. Romanticizing means nothing but raising to a higher level of quality. Through that operation the lower self is identified with a higher self, since our soul consists of a series of qualitatively different levels. This operation is still completely unknown. In giving a noble meaning to the vulgar, a mysterious appearance to the commonplace, the dignity of the unknown to the known, the semblance of infinity to the finite, I romanticize it.[18]

With collage, relativity becomes *the* way of romanticizing the world, counteracting what Breton calls "miserabilism," "the depreciation of reality in place of its exaltation."[19] By fragmenting the stubborn datum of reality until it becomes a raw stimulus—a fragmentation which encourages relationism and perspectivism to reconstitute reality into an exalted or mysterious semblance of a whole—the collage raises "our soul," as well as the world, "to a higher level of quality." Both come to seem infinitely extensive while bound to an irreducible stubborn fragment of reality.

For Mannheim, there is something fake as well as necessary about this forced march to the depths, this depreciation of the surface to evoke enigma where there may be none. As he says, "the romantic preoccupation with these 'depths' was not a true one. The predominance of the subjective approach introduced an arbitrary element into its interpretations and prevented the thinker from really getting inside his subject."[20] The elusiveness of the collage, its deliberate cultivation of relativity of appearance to undermine the absoluteness of reality—to get behind that façade of absoluteness in order to recover the reality of its becoming, its dialectical metamorphosis in its concretizing of its world—is at once an attempt "to sound the 'depths' of the soul" and "an ideological dressing-up of things as they are."[21] Collage accomplishes both. It evokes the sense of an independent depth of consciousness, of consciousness directed toward itself, clarifying its own perspective; and it evokes the sense of consciousness dressing up "things as they are" with the "profundity" of its own perspective, with the subjectivity of its own interpretation of reality. The seemingly unqualified subjectivity of the perspective counts for more than its regulatory power over reality. In response to Braque's dictum, ''I love the rule that rectifies the emotion,'' Juan Gris said, ''I love the emotion that rectifies the rule.''[22] And as one art historian observes, ''nowhere did he [Gris] so completely give himself over to his feelings as in his collages, on which he conferred a highly personal magic, interlocking reality and unreality like meshed gears.''[23]

The untraditional collage is preferable to the traditional painting because of its greater romantic possibilities, the greater freedom of expression possible in it, and the greater ease with which traditional ideas of what a work of art should be—the realization of a ''definitive'' style and an imitation of nature—can be dismissed. Relativism is the ideal instrument for romanticization of reality—the flotsam and jetsam of everyday life set adrift in the collage—because it denies certitude of style and nature, of ideals and models for art that might lead to its perfection. Instead of trying to perfect art and to indicate that art is a perfection of life, the collage, in an attempt to ''keep alive a certain germ of experience . . . always splits up and relativizes what we believe to be 'rational' and 'objective,''' revealing a hidden ''world of 'pure experience.' ''[24] The myth of pure experience—immersion in creative flux—sustains collage, not only dismissing traditional ideas of the purpose of art, but also dismissing Modernist ideas that the ''art'' in art has to do with its making. The collage seems casually, even flimsily made, deliberately flawed as a constructed object. It has a ramshackle, helter-skelter look, as though the artist were unsuccessfully trying to clean up an accident. But it is precisely by being poorly made, as it were, that it ''breaks into the 'here and now,''' ''the first form of utopian consciousness.''[25] By being inadequate as an object it acquires ''an ecstatic center''[26] beyond its constituents. No longer strictly ''congruent with existence''—and so no longer contained by even the thinnest illusion of a circumference, except by reason of its technical termination—the collage seems to center experience in the intensity of its immediacy, heightening our sense of the stubbornness with which it is given and the stubbornness with which we at once assimilate and resist it by means of our relative perspectives on it.

In sum, the collage is an awkward amalgam of three unresolved elements: (1) purely worldly elements, especially such fragments of dailiness as newspapers; (2) purely artistic elements such as line, color, and shape—the typical constituents of form; and (3) mixed or impure elements, or residual images of an imitated nature, ranging from the famous imitation wood grain and chair caning to traces of such domestic objects as clay pipes and such studio props as guitars. Gris's use of the mirror seems to summarize such elements, for it unequivocally demonstrates the illusory character of imitation by making the ''imitation'' of reality unmistakable. The elements are already ''relative'' by reason of their displacement from the life-world into the "art world," and by reason of their fragmentary state. Taken together, seen relative to one another, their relativity seems irresistible and fundamental. For all the stubbornness with which they are given, they can never again be regarded as *absolutely* given. They are an experiment in time and space—which shows that the old idea of Modern art as an experiment concerned with articulating the fourth dimension has, for all its charming naiveté, a certain truth to it. It is an imprecise but still perceptive way of acknowledging the relativity of concrescence, and of acknowledging Modern art as the major exemplification of such relativity.

Notes

1. *Webster's New Collegiate Dictionary,* 2nd ed.
2. Hannah Arendt, *The Human Condition* (Garden City, N.Y.: Doubleday Anchor Books, 1959), p. 9.
3. Alfred North Whitehead, *Process and Reality* (New York: Humanities Press, 1955), p. 33.
4. Ibid., p. 79.
5. See Rosalind Krauss, "Re-presenting Picasso," *Art in America* 68 (December 1980): 90–96.
6. Jerome Kagan, "On the Need for Relativism," in *The Ecology of Human Intelligence,* ed. Liam Hudson (Baltimore: Penguin Books, 1970), pp. 134–35.
7. Ibid., p. 135.
8. Ibid., p. 136.
9. Kurt H. Wolff, ed., *From Karl Mannheim* (New York: Oxford University Press, 1971), p. 226.
10. Ibid., p. 247.
11. Ibid., p. xxii.
12. Ibid., p. xxiii.
13. Ibid., p. xxxi.
14. Ibid., p. xxv.
15. Ibid., p. xxxiii.
16. Ibid.
17. Ibid., p. xxxv.
18. Ibid., p. xliv.
19. André Breton, "Away with Miserabilism!" in *Surrealism and Painting* (New York: Harper and Row, 1972), p. 348.
20. Wolff, ed., *From Mannheim,* p. xlv.
21. Ibid.

22. Herta Wescher, *Collage* (New York: Harry N. Abrams, 1979), p. 29.

23. Ibid.

24. Wolff, ed., *From Mannheim,* p. xlvii.

25. Ibid., p. lxiv.

26. Ibid., p. lxiii.

3

Collage: Philosophy of Put-Togethers

Harold Rosenberg

Near the beginning of his essay, Harold Rosenberg quotes Tristan Tzara's description of collage "as the most poetic, the most revolutionary moment in the evolution of painting." Rosenberg goes on to point to various problems with some interpretations and descriptions of collage, such as the Museum of Modern Art's 1961 Assemblage exhibit, and Herta Wescher's 1971 book, Collage. *He stresses the need to consider collage not only as part of art history, but also as a dramatic, revolutionary upheaval in that history. Collage should be seen as "a kind of adversary" within the realm of modern art. For Rosenberg, there is an important element of mockery inherent in collage, and he sees collage as corresponding to contemporary "illusion-producing processes" such as advertisements, films, political campaigns, news stories, etc. For him, "Collage is the primary formula of the aesthetics of mystification developed in our time. It is the visual vocabulary of what Walter Benjamin called 'the age of mechanical reproduction'; it reflects the absurdity of representing things and images in a universe of forces and energies."*

Collage is a way of making art, but it is not a specific art form, nor is it a style. Cutting and pasting have been practiced in the kindergarten, by housewives making their own home decorations, by Matisse at the culmination of his powers. In itself, collage has no aesthetic or intellectual character: it has been employed for centuries to compose craft objects, such as arrangements of artificial fruits and flowers and colored papers, or to arouse surprise by sewing real buttons on a painted garment or inserting an actual clock in the tower of a landscape. In our cen-

This article originally appeared as a chapter in *Art on the Edge,* by Harold Rosenberg (New York: Macmillan Publishing Company, 1975).

tury, however, collage has become more than a technique or genre for folk artists and amateurs. It has entered into painting and sculpture as an intrinsic part of their history. The incorporation of scraps of paper, cloth, printed matter, coins into compositions of painted forms was hailed by the Dadaist Tristan Tzara as "the most poetic, the most revolutionary moment in the evolution of painting." Considering the many different things that are now done with collage, this revolution is not easy to define. An elegant composition of colored papers by Esteban Vicente seems to have little in common with a box of forks and spoons by Arman. Both were included in the "Assemblage" exhibition at the Museum of Modern Art a dozen years ago, but that show was organized on the how-to-do-it concept of collage, and it was chaos, intellectually and aesthetically.

Presumably, the components added to the canvas or sculpture contribute qualities to a collage that paint or plaster cannot achieve. But the significance of these additions varies importantly in works belonging to different categories—for instance, in the paintings of Adja Yunkers with their rigorous strategy of superimposed bands, as compared to the torn, rugged automobile parts of John Chamberlain's sculptures. For Yunkers, strips of painted paper provide a restrained variation of the surface that could not quite be matched by built-up strands of pigment; that is to say, he uses collage to obtain a formal low-relief figure on a flat ground. In contrast, Chamberlain's chunks of crushed, rusted, enamelled metal convey a sensation of physically menacing edges and fears associated with wrecked cars; when his work gained attention, artists took to noticing junk piles. Critics who consider Chamberlain's assemblages to be merely a translation into three dimensions of the forms of de Kooning and Kline (which are especially apparent as influences in Chamberlain's *paintings*) dismiss the aura of highway, crack-up, and obsolescence clinging to Chamberlain's material. So, too, do those who, defending his originality, praise his progress from his junk works to the ones executed in new metals, foam rubber, and plastics. Chamberlain's recourse to the wreckers' lot was his primary creative act; his work in other mediums has to win interest on new grounds (which in my opinion it has failed to do). A similar instance of diminution of quality with a change of materials occurred when the Italian Alberto Burri renounced the stained and patched burlap sacks with which, in the 1950s, he had his début in the United States. In collage, the introduction of an emotionally expressive physical component can enable a work to surmount its formal background as well as the inventive limitations of the artist.

For Tzara, the revolution of collage consisted in its incorporating "a piece of everyday reality which enters into relationship with every other reality that the spirit has created." This idea of collage as a mixture of realities belonging to different orders identifies modern assembled art with a metaphysical principle beyond mere technique. Collage opens art to the common stuff of daily life, to Rimbaud's "poetic junk" of the city streets, in order to fix in time and place the abstractions of form. The collage revolution brings to an end the age-old separation between the realm of art and the realm of things. With collage, art no longer copies nature or seeks equivalents to it; an expression of the advanced industrial age, it appropriates the external world on the basis that it is already partly changed into art. Painting and sculpture encompass tangible entities that have origins and functions of their own. The newspaper cuttings in *Man with a Hat,* at the Museum of Modern Art (fig. 3.1), not only supply compositional and color elements but refer to tuberculosis and dental care, and, according to a note in a catalogue by William Rubin, were snipped from the December 3, 1912, issue of *Le Journal.*

The unity of collage lies in the metaphysics of mixing formal and material realities through introducing the concreteness of the paste-in. As art, collage lacks an independent history. Herta Wescher's *Collage** is actually a history of art movements since Cubism, retold in terms of pasting and assembling. A monumental accumulation of data, it is receptive to works in every mode of modern art in which a shuffling of materials or images has been employed—from a photomontage of a pair of hands with wide-open eyes in their palms to an abstract composition of rope, leaves, and rags. Wescher calls the roll of Cubists, Futurists, Dadaists, and so on, gives brief biographical accounts of their careers in collage, and quotes their views on the advantages of using nonart substances. Albers "urged the students [at the Bauhaus] to make use of rubbish for the simple reason that he found it too expensive to provide fresh materials for their class exercises," and artists working in different places, periods, and styles also stressed the economical aspect of collage in legitimizing substitutes for art supplies, especially during crises of war and depression. In contrast, for Johannes Itten, like Albers a Bauhaus master, the attraction of waste lay in its tactile variety: his students were instructed "to keep our eyes open, while out walking, for rubbish heaps, refuse dumps, garbage buckets, and scrap deposits as sources of material by means of which to make images (sculptures) which would bring out unequivocally the essential and the antagonistic properties of individual materials."

Several artists cited by Wescher reiterate the thought expressed by Tzara regarding the bringing of everyday reality into painting and

---

*Herta Wescher, *Collage* (New York: Harry N. Abrams, Inc., 1971).

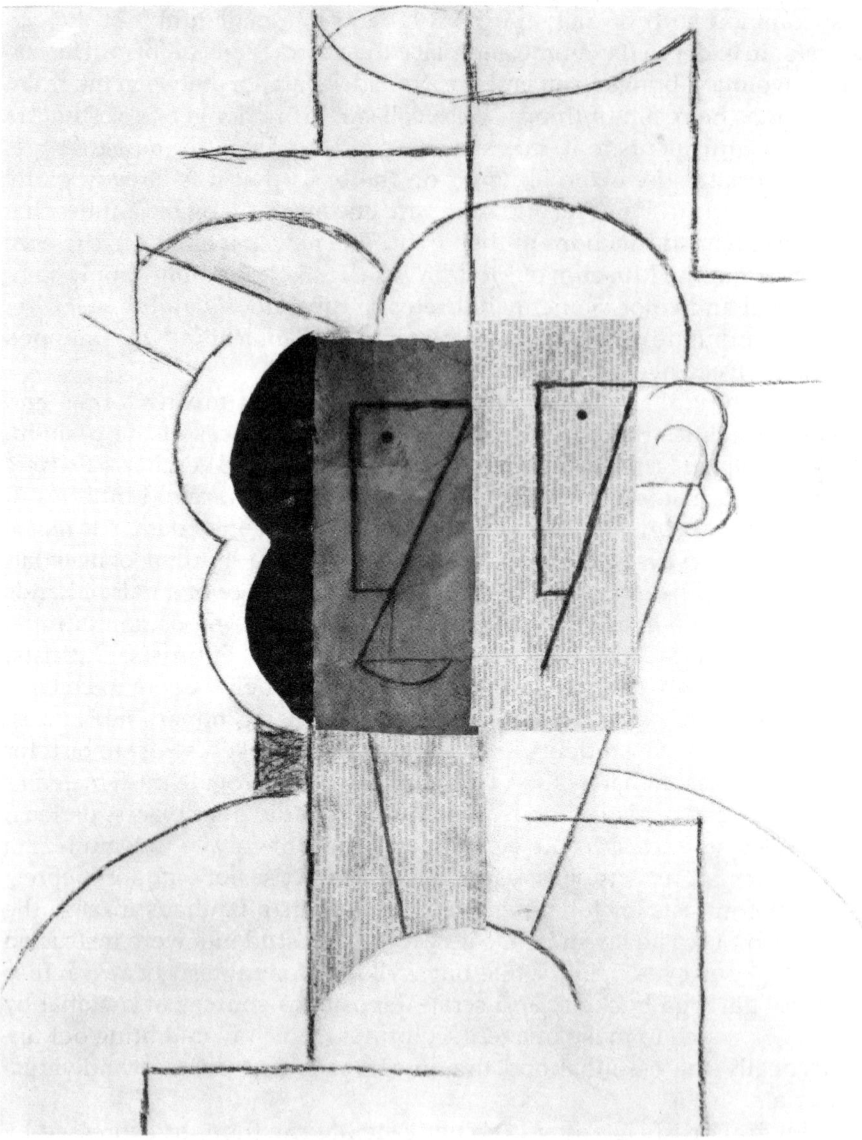

Figure 3.1. Pablo Picasso, *Man with a Hat,* December 1912
Cut and pasted papers, brush and ink, charcoal,
24½″ × 18⅝″.
(Collection, The Museum of Modern Art, New York. Purchase)

sculpture, but there is no discussion of what this radical adulteration means, and the problem is submerged in the encyclopedic survey. *Collage* mentions large numbers of craftsmen, including architects, photographers, and members of art-related professions, who have made collages after the models of leading Dadaists and Constructivists. But a précis of, say, the career of Ladislav Sutnar in Prague or the contribution of H. H. Stuckenschmidt to the Berlin Dada Fair is not a satisfactory substitute for analysis of why collage became so pervasive in twentieth-century creation. The net effect of Wescher's volume is to present collage as a technique for producing avant-garde paintings and sculptures by other means. Photographs of collages are often indistinguishable from photographs of paintings and reliefs, since the inserted elements tend to blend with the painted forms: even when newspaper clippings supply a clue, there is the possibility that the artist has reproduced them on the canvas. In any case, the visual effect of the paper-covered area is similar to that of a painted one. The dangers of relying on reproductions in presenting developments in art are serious enough in painting and sculpture, but they are immensely heightened in dealing with collage. Wescher has grouped her illustrations from Cubist through Abstract Expressionist, and this facilitates the presentation of collage as a technical variation within the history of modern styles.

Collage is part of art history, but it also represents a decisive upheaval in that history; Tzara, among others, was justified in using the word "revolutionary." Collage changed the relation between painting and the world outside painting. The combining of formal qualities with crude fact in Cubist collage contained the seeds of antiart that have flourished in the half century that followed; to arrive at found objects, readymades, conceptual art, information art, antiform heaps, or earth art it is necessary only to discard Picasso's compositional objectives in *Man with a Hat* and to elaborate upon his pasted-in news items and aging paper (process art). From collage it is logical to move outside the picture to the aesthetic appropriation of bottle racks and ticker tape; in *Guitar* Picasso cancels the picture frame as an enclosure by painting it on the canvas.

Collage is the form assumed by the ambiguities that have matured in our time concerning both art and the realities it has purported to represent. Collage manifests itself in modern art modes as a kind of adversary within the mode itself. No sooner is a new manner established in painting or sculpture than it is duplicated in alien materials that seem to make painting and sculpture superfluous: one of the earliest assaults on Action painting was the "combine paintings" of Rauschenberg, begun in 1953 and described by Wescher as follows: "Into paintings with the techniques of American Action painting he inserts wildly disparate objects which he integrates by dashing paint over them. Whatever he can lay hands on is serviceable: pieces of cloth, underclothing, frames and wood panels of earlier days, objects useful and useless. Empty fields of color are filled with letters and words. News photos of current events are slapped down side by side with irrelevant drawings.'' There is an inherent element of mockery in collage: the put-together is like a painting, but without the effort of painting or the need to know how to paint. Its materials, besides being inexpensive, have the air of having been picked up by chance, so the collage seems to say to the spectator, ''See how easy it is to make a work of art.'' In Picasso's *Guitar* the sheet of paper representing the guitar is fastened to the canvas with pins, though it seems to be held down by a nail, which is actually a paper cutout with painted trompe-l'oeil shadows. Parody upon parody upon parody—but the use of pins has the effect of a method even more casual than pasting, and Picasso's easy-does-it attitude dramatizes itself unmistakably in *Baboon and Young* with its head of toy automobiles and its tail of a length of spring. The undermining of refinement in art through masterworks of old nailed boards and chicken wire, broken bottles, and soiled wrappings is in keeping with the spirit of derision that collage brings into painting and sculpture.

The mingling of object and image in collage, of given fact and conscious artifice, corresponds to the illusion-producing processes of contemporary civilization. In advertisements, news stories, films, and political campaigns, lumps of unassailable data are implanted in preconceived formats in order to make the entire fabrication credible. Documents waved at hearings by Joseph McCarthy to substantiate his fictive accusations were a version of collage, as is the corpse of Lenin, inserted by Stalin into the Moscow mausoleum to authenticate his own contrived ideology. Twentieth-century fictions are rarely made up of the whole cloth, perhaps because the public has been trained to have faith in ''information.'' Collage is the primary formula of the aesthetics of mystification developed in our time. It is the visual vocabulary of what Walter Benjamin called ''the age of mechanical reproduction''; it reflects the absurdity of representing things and images in a universe of forces and energies.

In the vision of collage, the identity of an object is suspended between its practical reality and the conceptual whole in which it is set. A banknote incorporated in a collage has surrendered its simple character as money and undergone aesthetic transformation. A friend of mine was shocked when this principle was violated by burglars who plucked a twenty-dollar bill from a collage hanging on his wall. Collage invites the spectator to respond with a multiple consciousness in which forms, objects, and images are interchangeable. The robbers rejected this invitation by identifying the banknote as exclusively money—a giveaway to the police,

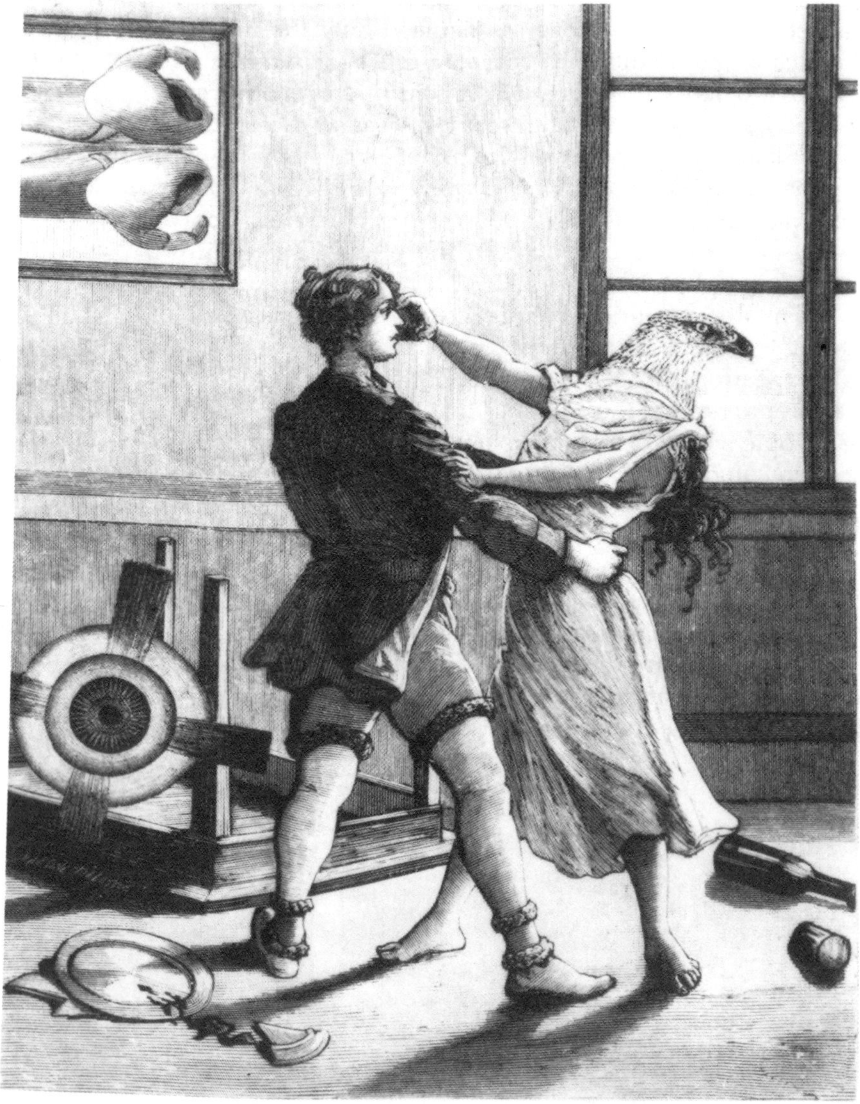

Figure 3.2. Max Ernst, Plate from *Une Semaine de bonté* or *Les Sept éléments capitaux*, 1934
Reproduction of collage of cut-up wood engravings from popular magazines of the late nineteenth century, 11⅛″ × 9″.
(Collection, The Museum of Modern Art, New York. The Louis E. Stern Collection)

thought my friend, that they belonged to the lower cultural orders. Like realistic painters, the thieves recognized only the monomorphic realm of appearances solidified by common sense—a realm in which money is a category of its own and is not to be confused with other green rectangles. To cope with sensibilities of this sort, my friend reflected, the artist ought to have used a painted copy of a banknote instead of a genuine one; when the thieves tore it off the canvas, they would have discovered that the back was blank. In his view, people who break into apartments have a special need for the education in the problematic nature of visual experience supplied by collage.

As in other twentieth-century creations, there is a vein of farce in collage: its exposure of the duplicity of art is comparable to the tradition in the theatre, from Pirandello to Genet, of an actor's stepping out of character to remind the audience that "this is a play" and that actors are real people whose profession is pretending to be someone else. Through its interchanging of things and images of them, collage has provided the artist with the means of dissolving reality into endless visual absurdities. The use of these means is most obvious in the collages of Dadaists and Surrealists, such as Ernst (fig. 3.2), Picabia, and Magritte, but the instruments of farce provided by collage were already fully operative in Picasso's 1913 *Guitar,* in which the navel of a female figure is represented by a tiny circle of newsprint. The current "return to nature" in painting constitutes an abandonment of the comical questioning of appearances that has been the major interest of art since Cubism.

4

Collage

Clement Greenberg

Clement Greenberg's 1959 essay calls collage "a major turning point in the evolution of Cubism and therefore a major turning point in the whole evolution of modernist art in this century." Greenberg's emphasis is on the formal qualities and innovations of Cubism and Cubist collage. He discusses aspects of flatness, shading, shape, etc., in Picasso's, Braque's, and Gris's collage works. Indeed, flatness begins to almost become a metaphor for larger values and meanings. As Greenberg writes, "Because of the size of the areas it covers, the pasted paper established undepicted flatness bodily, *as more than an indication or sign. Literal flatness now tends to assert itself as the main event of the picture, and the device boomerangs: the illusion of depth is rendered even more precarious than before."*

Collage was a major turning point in the evolution of Cubism, and therefore a major turning point in the whole evolution of modernist art in this century. Who invented collage—Braque or Picasso—and when is still not settled. Both artists left most of the work they did between 1907 and 1914 undated as well as unsigned; and each claims, or implies the claim, that his was the first collage of all. That Picasso dates his, in retrospect, almost a year earlier than Braque's compounds the difficulty. Nor does the internal or stylistic evidence help enough, given that the interpretation of Cubism is still on a rudimentary level.

The question of priority is much less important, however, than that of the motives which first induced either artist to paste or glue a piece of extraneous material to the surface of a picture. About this, neither Braque nor Picasso has made himself at all clear. The writers who have

---

This article originally appeared as a chapter in *Art and Culture,* by Clement Greenberg (Boston: Beacon Press, 1961).

tried to explain their intentions for them speak, with an unanimity that is suspect in itself, of the need for renewed contact with "reality" in face of the growing abstractness of Analytical Cubism. But the term "reality," always ambiguous when used in connection with art, has never been used more ambiguously than here. A piece of imitation-woodgrain wallpaper is not more "real" under any definition, or closer to nature, than a painted simulation of it; nor is wallpaper, oilcloth, newspaper or wood more "real," or closer to nature, than paint on canvas. And even if these materials were more "real," the question would still be begged, for "reality" would still explain next to nothing about the actual *appearance* of the Cubist collage.

There is no question but that Braque and Picasso were concerned, in their Cubism, with holding on to painting as an art of representation and illusion. But at first they were more crucially concerned, in and through their Cubism, with obtaining *sculptural* results by strictly nonsculptural means; that is, with finding for every aspect of three-dimensional vision an explicitly two-dimensional equivalent, regardless of how much verisimilitude might suffer in the process. Painting had to spell out, rather than pretend to deny, the physical fact that it was flat, even though at the same time it had to overcome this proclaimed flatness as an aesthetic fact and continue to report nature.

Neither Braque nor Picasso set himself this program in advance. It emerged, rather, as something implicit and inevitable in the course of their joint effort to fill out that vision of a "purer" pictorial art which they had glimpsed in Cézanne, from whom they also took their means. These means, as well as the vision, imposed their logic; and the direction of that logic became completely clear in 1911, the fourth year of Picasso's and Braque's Cubism, along with certain contradictions latent in the Cézannian vision itself.

By that time, flatness had not only invaded but was threatening to swamp the Cubist picture. The little facet-planes into which Braque and Picasso were dissecting everything visible now all lay parallel to the picture plane. They were no longer controlled, either in drawing or in placing, by linear or even scalar perspective. Each facet tended to be shaded, moreover, as an independent unit, with no legato passages, no unbroken tracts of value gradation on its open side, to join it to adjacent facet-planes. At the same time, shading had itself been atomized into flecks of light and dark that could no longer be concentrated upon the edges of shapes with enough modeling force to turn these convincingly into depth. Light and dark in general had begun to act more immediately as cadences of design than as plastic description or definition. The main problem at this juncture became to keep the "inside" of the picture—its content—from fusing with the "outside"—its literal surface. *Depicted* flatness—that is, the facet-planes—had to be kept separate enough from *literal* flatness to permit a minimal illusion of three-dimensional space to survive between the two.

Braque had already been made uncomfortable by the contraction of illusioned space in his pictures of 1910. The expedient he had then hit upon was to insert a conventional, trompe-l'oeil suggestion of deep space *on top* of Cubist flatness, between the depicted planes and the spectator's eye. The very un-Cubist graphic tack-with-a-cast-shadow, shown transfixing the top of a 1910 painting, *Still Life with Violin and Pitcher,* suggests deep space in a token way, and destroys the surface in a token way. The Cubist forms are converted into the illusion of a picture within a picture. In the *Man with a Guitar* of early 1911 (in the Museum of Modern Art), the line-drawn tassel and stud in the upper left margin is a similar token. The effect as distinct from the signification, is in both cases very discreet and inconspicuous. Plastically, spatially, neither the tack nor the tassel and stud *acts* upon the picture; each suggests illusion without making it really present.

Early in 1911, Braque was already casting around for ways of reinforcing, or rather supplementing, this suggestion, but still without introducing anything that would become more than a token. It was then apparently, that he discovered that *trompe-l'oeil* could be used to undeceive as well as to deceive the eye. It could be used, that is, to declare as well as to deny the actual surface. If the actuality of the surface—its real, physical flatness—could be indicated explicitly enough in certain places, it would be distinguished and separated from everything else the surface contained. Once the literal nature of the *support* was advertised, whatever upon it was not intended literally would be set off and enhanced in its nonliteralness. Or to put it in still another way: depicted flatness would inhabit at least the semblance of a semblance of three-dimensional space as long as the brute, undepicted flatness of the literal surface was pointed to as being still flatter.

The first and, until the advent of pasted paper, the most important device that Braque discovered for indicating and separating the surface was imitation printing, which automatically evokes a literal flatness. Block letters are seen in one of his 1910 paintings, *The Match Holder;* but being done rather sketchily, and slanting into depth along with the depicted surface that bears them, they merely allude to, rather than state, the literal surface. Only in the next year are block capitals, along with lowercase letters and numerals, introduced in exact simulation of printing and stenciling, in absolute frontality and outside the representational context of the picture. Wherever this printing appears, it stops the eye at the literal plane, just as the artist's signature would. By force of contrast alone—for wherever the literal surface is not explicitly stated, it seems implicitly denied—everything else is thrust back into at least a memory of deep or plastic space. It is the old device of the *repoussoir,* but taken a step further: instead of being used to push an illusioned middleground farther away from an illusioned foreground, the imitation printing spells out the real paint surface and thereby pries it away from the illusion of depth.

The eye-undeceiving *trompe-l'oeil* of simulated typography supplements, rather than replaces, the conventional eye-deceiving kind. Another literally and graphically rendered tassel and stud imbeds flattened forms in token depth in Braque's *Portuguese* (1911), but this time the brute reality of the surface, as asserted by stenciled letters and numerals, closes over both the token illusion of depth and the Cubist configurations like the lid on a box. Sealed between two parallel flatnesses—the depicted Cubist flatness and the literal flatness of the paint surface—the illusion is made a little more present but, at the same time, even more ambiguous. As one looks, the stenciled letters and numerals change places in depth with the tassel and stud, and the physical surface itself becomes part of the illusion for an instant: it seems pulled back into depth along with the stenciling, so that once again the picture plane seems to be annihilated—but only for the fraction of another instant. The abiding effect is of a constant shuttling between surface and depth, in which the depicted flatness is "infected" by the undepicted. Rather than being deceived, the eye is puzzled; instead of seeing objects in space, it sees nothing more than—a picture.

Through 1911 and 1912, as the Cubist facet-plane's tendency to adhere to the literal surface became harder and harder to deny, the task of keeping the surface at arm's length fell all the more to eye-undeceiving contrivances. To reinforce, and sometimes to replace, the simulated typography, Braque and Picasso began to mix sand and other foreign substances with their paint; the granular texture thus created likewise called attention to the reality of the surface and was effective over much larger areas. In certain other pictures, however, Braque began to paint areas in exact simulation of wood graining or marbleizing. These areas, by virtue of their abrupt density of pattern, stated the literal surface with such new and superior force that the resulting contrast drove the simulated printing into a depth from which it could be rescued—and set to shuttling again—only by conventional perspective; that is, by being placed in such relation to the forms depicted within the illusion that these forms left no room for the typography except near the surface.

The accumulation of such devices, however, soon had the effect of telescoping, even while separating, surface and depth. The process of flattening seemed inexorable, and it became necessary to emphasize the surface still further in order to prevent it from fusing with the illusion. It was for this reason, and no other that I can see, that in September 1912, Braque took the radical and revolutionary step of pasting actual pieces of imitation woodgrain wallpaper to a drawing on paper, instead of trying to simulate its texture in paint. Picasso says that he himself had already made his first collage toward the end of 1911, when he glued a piece of imitation caning oilcloth to a painting on canvas. It is true that his first collage looks more analytical than Braque's, which would confirm the date he assigns it. But it is also true that Braque was the consistent pioneer in the use of simulated textures as well as of typography; and moreover, he had already begun to broaden and simplify the facet-planes of Analytical Cubism as far back as the end of 1910.

When we examine what each master says was his first collage we see that much the same thing happens in each. (It makes no real difference that Braque's collage is on paper and eked out in charcoal, while Picasso's is on canvas and eked out in oil.) By its greater corporeal presence and its greater extraneousness, the affixed paper or cloth serves for a seeming moment to push everything else into a more vivid *idea* of depth than the simulated printing or simulated textures had ever done. But here again, the surface-declaring device both overshoots and falls short of its aim. For the illusion of depth created by the contrast between the affixed material and everything else gives way immediately to an illusion of forms in bas-relief, which gives way in turn, and with equal immediacy, to an illusion that seems to contain both—or neither.

Because of the size of the areas it covers, the pasted paper establishes undepicted flatness *bodily,* as more than an indication or sign. Literal flatness now tends to assert itself as the main event of the picture, and the device boomerangs: the illusion of depth is rendered even more precarious than before. Instead of isolating the literal flatness by specifying and circumscribing it, the pasted paper or cloth releases and spreads it, and the artist seems to have nothing left but this undepicted flatness with which to finish as well as start his picture. The actual surface becomes both ground and background, and it turns out—suddenly and paradoxically—that the only place left for a three-dimensional illusion is in *front* of, *upon,* the surface. In their very first collages, Braque and Picasso draw or paint *over* and *on* the affixed paper or cloth, so that certain of the principal features of their subjects *as depicted* seem to thrust out into real, bas-relief space—or to be about to do so—while the rest of the subject remains imbedded in, or flat upon, the surface. And the surface is driven back, in its very surfaceness, only by this contrast.

In the upper center of Braque's first collage, *Fruit Dish* (in Douglas Cooper's collection), a bunch of grapes is rendered with such conventionally vivid sculptural effect as to lift it practically off the picture plane. The trompe-l'oeil illusion here is no longer enclosed between parallel flatnesses, but seems to thrust through the surface of the drawing paper and establish depth *on top* of it. Yet the violent immediacy of the wallpaper strips pasted to the paper, and the only lesser immediacy of block capitals that simulate window lettering, manage somehow to push the grape cluster back into place on the picture plane so that it does not "jump." At the same time, the wallpaper strips themselves seem to be pushed into depth by the lines and patches of shading charcoaled upon them, and by their placing in relation to the block capitals; and these capitals seem in turn to be pushed back by *their* placing, and by contrast with the corporeality of the woodgraining. Thus every part and plane of the picture keeps changing place in relative depth with every other part and plane; and it is as if the only stable relation left among the different parts of the picture is the ambivalent and ambiguous one that each has with the surface. And the same thing, more or less, can be said of the contents of Picasso's first collage.

In later collages of both masters, a variety of extraneous materials are used, sometimes in the same work, and almost always in conjunction with every other eye-deceiving and eye-undeceiving device they can think of. The area adjacent to one edge of a piece of affixed material—or simply of a painted-in form—will be shaded to pry that edge away from the surface, while something will be drawn, painted or even pasted over another part of the same shape to drive it back into depth. Planes defined as parallel to the surface also cut through it into real space, and a depth is suggested optically which is greater than that established pictorially. All this expands the oscillation between surface and depth so as to encompass fictive space in front of the surface as well as behind it. Flatness may now monopolize everything, but it is a flatness become so ambiguous and expanded as to turn into illusion itself—at least an optical if not, properly speaking, a pictorial illusion. Depicted, Cubist flatness is now almost completely assimilated to the literal, undepicted kind, but at the same time it reacts upon and largely transforms the undepicted kind—and it does so, moreover, without depriving the latter of its literalness; rather, it underpins and reinforces that literalness, re-creates it.

Out of this re-created literalness, the Cubist subject reemerged. For it had turned out, by a further paradox of Cubism, that the means to an illusion of depth and plasticity had now become widely divergent from the means of representation or imaging. In the Analytical phase of their

Cubism, Braque and Picasso had not only had to minimize three-dimensionality simply in order to preserve it; they had also had to *generalize* it—to the point, finally, where the illusion of depth and relief became abstracted from specific three-dimensional entities and was rendered largely as the illusion of depth and relief *as such:* as a disembodied attribute and expropriated property detached from everything not itself. In order to be saved, plasticity had had to be isolated; and as the aspect of the subject was transposed into those clusters of more or less interchangeable and contour-obliterating facet-planes by which plasticity was isolated under the Cubist method, the subject itself became largely unrecognizable. Cubism, in its 1911–12 phase (which the French, with justice, call "hermetic") was on the verge of abstract art.

It was then that Picasso and Braque were confronted with a unique dilemma: they had to choose *between* illusion and representation. If they opted for illusion, it could only be illusion per se—an illusion of depth, and of relief, so general and abstracted as to exclude the representation of individual objects. If, on the other hand, they opted for representation, it had to be representation per se—representation as image pure and simple, without connotations (at least, without more than schematic ones) of the three-dimensional space in which the objects represented originally existed. It was the collage that made the terms of this dilemma clear: the representational could be restored and preserved only on the flat and literal surface now that illusion and representation had become, for the first time, mutually exclusive alternatives.

In the end, Picasso and Braque plumped for the representational, and it would seem they did so deliberately. (This provides whatever real justification there is for the talk about "reality.") But the inner, formal logic of Cubism, as it worked itself out through the collage, had just as much to do with shaping their decision. When the smaller facet-planes of Analytical Cubism were placed upon or juxtaposed with the large, dense shapes formed by the affixed materials of the collage, they had to coalesce—become "synthesized"—into larger planar shapes themselves simply in order to maintain the integrity of the picture plane. Left in their previous atomlike smallness, they would have cut away too abruptly into depth; and the broad, opaque shapes of pasted paper would have been isolated in such a way as to make them jump out of plane. Large planes juxtaposed with other large planes tend to assert themselves as *independent* shapes, and to the extent that they are flat, they also assert themselves as silhouettes; and independent silhouettes are apt to coincide with the recognizable contours of the subject from which a picture starts (if it does start from a subject). It was because of this chain reaction as much as for any other reason—that is, because of the growing independence of the planar unit in collage as a *shape*—that the identity of depicted objects, or at least parts of them, reemerged in Braque's and Picasso's papiers collés and continued to remain more conspicuous there—but only as flattened silhouettes—than in any of their paintings done wholly in oil before the end of 1913.

Analytical Cubism came to an end in the collage, but not conclusively; nor did Synthetic Cubism fully begin there. Only when the collage had been exhaustively translated into oil, and transformed by this translation, did Cubism become an affair of positive color and flat, interlocking silhouettes whose legibility and placement created allusions to, if not the illusion of, unmistakable three-dimensional identities.

Synthetic Cubism began with Picasso alone, late in 1913 or early in 1914; this was the piont at which he finally took the lead in Cubist innovation away from Braque, never again to relinquish it. But even before that, Picasso had glimpsed and entered, for a moment, a certain revolutionary path in which no one had preceded him. It was as though, in that instant, he had felt the flatness of collage as too constricting and had suddenly tried to escape all the way back—or forward—to literal three-dimensionality. This he did by using utterly literal means to carry the forward push of the collage (and of Cubism in general) *literally* into the literal space in front of the picture plane.

Some time in 1912, Picasso cut out and folded a piece of paper in the shape of a guitar; to this he glued and fitted other pieces of paper and four taut strings, thus creating a sequence of flat surfaces in real and sculptural space to which there clung only the vestige of a picture plane. The affixed elements of collage were extruded, as it were, and cut off from the literal pictorial surface to form a bas-relief. By this act he founded a new tradition and genre of sculpture, the one that came to be called "construction." Though construction-sculpture was freed long ago from strict bas-relief frontality, it has continued to be marked by its pictorial origins, so that the sculptor-constructor Gonzalez, Picasso's friend, could refer to it as the new art of "drawing in space"—that is, of manipulating two-dimensional forms in three-dimensional space. (Not only did Picasso found this "new" art with his paper guitar of 1912, but he went on, some years afterwards, to make some of the strongest as well as most germinative contributions to it.)

Neither Picasso nor Braque ever really returned to collage after 1914. The others who have taken it up have exploited it largely for its shock value, which collage had only incidentally—or even only accidentally—in the hands of its originators. There have been a few exceptions: Gris notably, but also Arp, Schwitters, Miró, E. L. T. Mesens, Dubuffet and, in this country, Robert Motherwell and Anne Ryan. In this context, Gris's example remains the most interesting and most instructive.

Braque and Picasso had obtained a new, self-transcending kind of decoration by reconstructing the picture surface with what had once been the means of its denial. Starting from illusion, they had arrived at a transfigured, almost abstract kind of literalness. With Gris it was the opposite. As he himself explained, he started out with abstract flat shapes, to which he then fitted recognizable images and emblems of three-dimensionality. And whereas Braque's and Picasso's subjects were dissected in three dimensions in the course of being transposed into two, Gris's first Cubist subjects tended—even before they were fitted into the picture, and as if preformed by its surface—to be analyzed in two-dimensional and purely decorative rhythms. It was only later that he became more aware of the fact that Cubism was not a question of decorative overlay and that the resonance of its surfaces derived from an abiding concern with plasticity and illusion which informed the very renunciation of plasticity and illusion.

In his collages almost more than anywhere else, we see Gris trying to solve the problems proposed by this fuller awareness. But his collages also show the extent to which his awareness remained incomplete. Because he continued to take the picture plane as given and therefore not needing to be re-created, Gris became perhaps too solicitous about the illusion. He used pasted paper and trompe-l'oeil textures and lettering to assert flatness, but he almost always completely sealed the flatness inside an illusion of conventional depth by allowing images rendered with relatively sculptural vividness to occupy, unambiguously, too much of both the nearest and farthest planes.

Because he shaded and modeled more abundantly and tended to use more explicit color under his shading, Gris's collages seldom declare their surfaces as forthrightly as Picasso's and Braque's collages do. Their total *presence* is thus less immediate and has something about it of the removedness, the closed-off presence, of the traditional picture. And yet, because their decorative elements function to a greater extent solely as decoration, Gris's collages also seem more conventionally decorative. Instead of the seamless fusion of the decorative with the plastic that we get in Picasso and Braque, there is an alternation, a collocation, a mere juxtaposition of the two; and whenever this relation goes beyond juxtaposition, it leads more often to confusion than to fusion. Gris's collages have their merits, but only a few of them deserve the unqualified praise they have received.

But many of Gris's oils of 1915–18 do deserve their praise. In all justice, it should be pointed out that his paintings of those years demonstrate, perhaps more clearly than anything by Braque or Picasso, something which is of the highest importance to Cubism and to the collage's effect upon it: namely, the liquidation of sculptural shading.

In Braque's and Picasso's very first papiers collés, shading stops being pointillist and suddenly becomes broad and incisive again, like the shapes it modifies. This change in shading also accounts for the bas-relief effects, or the velleities to bas-relief, of the first collages. But large patches of shading on a densely or emphatically patterned ground, such as woodgrain or newsprint, tend to take off on their own when their relation to the model in nature is not self-evident, just the way large planes do under the same circumstances. They abandon their sculptural function and become independent shapes constituted by blackness or grayness alone. Not only did this fact contribute further to the ambiguity of the collage's surface; it also served further to reduce shading to a mere component of surface design and color scheme. When shading becomes that, all other colors become more purely *color.* It was in this way that positive color reemerged in the collage—recapitulating, curiously enough, the way "pure" color had emerged in the first place for Manet and the Impressionists.

In Analytical Cubism, shading as shading had been divorced from specific shapes while retaining in principle the capacity to inflect generalized surfaces into depth. In collage, shading, though restored to specific shapes or silhouettes, lost its power to act as modeling because it became a specific shape in itself. This is how and why shading, as a means to illusion, disappeared from the collages of Braque and Picasso, and from their Cubism, never really to reappear. But it was left to Gris, in his pictures of 1915–18, to elucidate this process and its consequences for all to see—and, in doing so, to produce, finally, triumphant art. Gris's Cubism in this period—which is almost as much Analytical as it is Synthetic—separated, fixed and immobilized, in oil on wood or canvas, some of the overlapping stages of the transformation that Cubism had already undergone in Braque's and Picasso's glued and pasted pictures. The cleanly and simply contoured solid black shapes on which Gris relied so much in these paintings represent fossilized shadows and fossilized patches of shading. All the value gradations are summed up in a single, ultimate value of flat, opaque black—a black that becomes a color as sonorous and pure as any spectrum color and that confers upon the silhouettes it fills an even greater weight than is possessed by the lighter-hued forms which these silhouettes are supposed to shade.

In this phase alone does Gris's art, in my opinion, sustain the main tenor of Cubism. Here, at last, his practice is so completely informed by a definite and steady vision that the details of execution take care of themselves. And here, at last, the decorative is transcended and transfigured, as it had already been in Picasso's, Braque's and Léger's art, in a monumental unity. This monumentality has little to do with size. (Early and late, and whether in Picasso's hands or Braque's, Cubism has never lent itself with entire success to an outsize format. Even Léger's rather splendid big pictures of the late 1910s and early 1920s do not quite match the perfection of his smaller-scale Cubism of 1910–14.) The monumentality of Cubism in the hands of its masters is more a question of a vision and attitude—an attitude toward the immediate physical means of pictorial art—thanks to which easel paintings and even ''sketches'' acquire the self-evident self-sufficiency of architecture. This is as true of the Cubist collage as of anything else in Cubism, and perhaps it is even truer of the collage than of anything else in Cubism.

5

The Realism and Poetry of Assemblage

William C. Seitz

Taken from the 1961 Museum of Modern Art catalogue, The Art of Assemblage, *William Seitz's text emphasizes the poetic qualities of assemblage. For him, assemblage is a "method with disconcertingly centrifugal potentialities. It is metaphysical and poetic as well as physical and realistic." The catalogue to the 1961 exhibit was described on the jacket as "the first book to recognize collages, 'readymades,' 'found objects,' ' surrealist objects,' 'combine paintings,' and the other varieties of assemblage as diverse manifestations of a common tradition which (though fascinating parallels and prototypes can be found for it in primitive and popular art) is unique to the twentieth century."*

The memory throws up high and dry
A crowd of twisted things;
A twisted branch upon the beach
Eaten smooth, and polished
As if the world gave up
The secret of its skeleton,
Stiff and white.
A broken spring in a factory yard,
Rust that clings to the form that the strength has left
Hard and curled and ready to snap.
T. S. Eliot, "Rhapsody on a Windy Night"

The catalogue of the exhibition [*The Art of Assemblage,* Museum of Modern Art, 1961] lists the materials incorporated in each work. It suggests the

---

limitless diversity that relates assembled art to the world. The finished works, moreover, are usually closer to everyday life than either abstract or representational art. Such objects as Victor Brauner's *Wolf-Table,* Edward Kienholz's *Jane Doe,* or George Herms's *The Poet,* however arresting, strange, or poetic may be their effect, resemble furniture more than they do sculpture; they fit more naturally in a living room than they do in a museum. A similar shortening of psychological distance results from the treatment of materials: one's hand is drawn toward the frayed holes in Burri's sacks as unconsciously as toward a tear in a pair of trousers.

Intrinsic to the medium of assemblage is an entirely new relationship between work and spectator: a reconquest, but by different means, of the realism that abstract art replaced. In 1915 (for an exhibition at the Tanner Gallery in Zurich) Jean Arp spoke out ''against illusion, fame, artifice, copy or plagiarism,'' and ''for reality, the precision of the indefinable, rigorous precision.'' The participating artists, he said later, ''were disgusted with oil painting and were searching for new materials.''[1] It was perhaps Picasso's unwillingness to take this step to complete abstractness that led him, in 1923, to assert that an artist must know how to ''convince others of the truthfulness of his lies.''[2]

Even Gris, who composed ''flat architecture'' in entirely nonrepresentational forms, chose to overlay his abstraction with realism: to ''adjust the white so that it becomes a paper and the black so that it becomes a shadow.''[3] When he interpolated illustrations, pieces of mirror, or typographical clippings, replacing a deductive image by a fragment of the environment, the metaphysic of juxtaposition was barely posed: the reality problem raised by assemblage is a new and different one that has little to do with illusionism or *trompe-l'oeil* devices. When the scene behind the gold frame came forward and began to crack up or fade out (as it did in Mondrian's art of 1910–15), abstract pictorial elements became more ''real'' than what they represented, and the gap between painting and sculpture narrowed until, in the abstract *tableaux-objets* that followed, the distinction was almost obliterated. Abstract painting and sculpture substituted a second reality, self-contained and objective, for the surrogate reality of illusionism. Not only did it narrow the gap between flat and three-dimensional media, but also that between art and everyday life. A final step, from art to the presentation of objects assembled in ordinary daily acts and without aesthetic intention, is taken in Daniel Spoerri's ''snare pictures.'' Often dramatic and perceptually compelling, they are ''situations prepared by chance,'' selected, glued together, and presented vertically rather than horizontally.[4] ''Spoerri doesn't pretend to create works of art,'' Alain Jouffroy writes, ''nor does he proclaim that his works exalt non-art or anti-art.''[5] In precisely the same spirit, Mimmo Rotella, Raymond Hains, and the other salvagers of lacerated posters rip down portions of the environment and present them as pictures. The critic Pierre Restany has dubbed this group "the new realists." "What they offer us," he writes, "is an entire aspect of the real, captured in its objective integrity, without transcription of any sort. Never, at any moment is it a question of re-creation, but on the contrary of an expressive transmutation."[6] "However one chooses to categorize them, the assemblages exhibited by these men should be compared to those in which the arrangement is the result of "art" rather than accident and choice. The challenge that Duchamp presented to our minds when he exhibited a bottle rack and a urinal—a challenge compounded in Spoerri's project for a combined grocery store and art gallery where each avocado pear, yam, and bottle of olives would be labeled ATTENTION: WORK OF ART—should not be sidestepped.

Just such extreme actualism—i.e., the inclusion of a Coca-Cola bottle rather than the representation of one—is intrinsic to assemblage; but it points to only one layer of meaning, and only certain works exemplify it sharply or purely. In thought-provoking ways assemblage is poetic rather than realistic, for each constituent element can be transformed. Physical materials and their auras are transmuted into a new amalgam that both transcends and includes its parts. When, as in a primitive cult object, a shell becomes a human eye because of its context, the accepted hierarchy of categories (as the surrealists delighted in pointing out) is disrupted. When the meanings of highly charged units impinge on a poetic as well as on a physical or visual level, significant expression becomes possible.

The assembler, therefore, can be both a metaphysician and (because his units are loosely related rather than expository) a poet who mingles attraction and repulsion, natural and human identification, ironic or naïve responses. Because overtones and associations as well as physical materials are placed in juxtaposition, it could almost be said that a constellation of meanings can exist independently of the colors, textures, and forms which are its carriers. In fact, three levels of operation can be specified: that of tangible materials; that of vision, at which colors and other formal qualities alter each other and blend like tastes or scents; and finally that of "literary" meanings. "Many diverse images, borrowed from very different orders of things," Bergson wrote in his *Introduction to Metaphysics,* "may, by the convergence of their action, direct the consciousness to the precise point where there is a certain intuition to be seized. By choosing images as dissimilar as possible, we shall prevent any one of them from usurping the place of the intuition it is intended to call up."[7]

Certain works of assemblage, with an attraction like that of green-encrusted bronzes or the unnamable artifacts of a people far away or long dead, seem to emit a magical halo: an aura too ephemeral to be ascribed to sensory stimuli, but so existent as to seem measurable. Unfortunately it is on this level (that of wizardry as well as art) that the value of a work can easily be missed or misinterpreted. It is one of the limitations of civilized human beings to be more readily convinced by syllogistic discourse than by words or forms poetically related: it is easy to disbelieve what is written in a plastic language.

Figuratively, the practice of assemblage raises materials from the level of formal relations to that of associational poetry, just as numbers and words, on the contrary, tend to be formalized. Transmutation tends also to move in the opposite direction in Abstract Expressionist painting, in which the subject is absorbed into the medium. But when textures and tones totally created by the artist take on a tactile or visual effect of actuality—as do the graffiti, "texturologies," and "topographies" of Dubuffet, the "rhinoceros hide" surfaces of Jan Lebenstein, the carved wood surfaces of Lucio Muñoz, or the relief paintings of Tàpies—the two tendencies, which might be called "radiative" and "absorptive," meet. In the assemblages of Wagemaker, Bouras, Tumarkin, and others, assertive plastic substances provide a field into which *objets trouvés* are pressed.

Assemblage is a method with disconcertingly centrifugal potentialities. It is metaphysical and poetic as well as physical and realistic. When paper is soiled or lacerated, when cloth is worn, stained, or torn, when wood is split, weathered, or patterned with peeling coats of paint, when metal is bent or rusted, they gain connotations which unmarked materials lack. More specific associations are denoted when an object can be identified as the sleeve of a shirt, a dinner fork, the leg of a rococo chair, a doll's eye or hand, an automobile bumper, or a social security card. In both situations meaning and material merge. Identities drawn from diverse contexts and levels of value are confronted not only physically, within the limits of the work they form, but metaphysically and associationally, within (and modified by) the unique sensibility of the spectator. Even taken in isolation, the possible meanings of objects and fragments are infinitely rich, whereas (except in special cases like that of John Flannagan, whose images conform to the natural contours of stones and boulders) professional art materials such as paint, plastic, stone, bronze, etc., are formless and, in the Platonic sense, are pure essences of redness, hardness, or ductility. Found materials are works already in progress: prepared for the artist by the outside world, previously formed, textured, colored, and even sometimes entirely prefabricated into accidental "works of art."

John Chamberlain's decision to work with sections of scrap automobile bodies and other painted metal solved the problem of polychromy in sculpture at one stroke. The use of non-art materials has put an unprecedented range of new formal qualities at the artist's disposal;

but unless he carefully obliterates marks of the origin and history of each element, these qualities inevitably transcend abstractness of form, texture, and color. It goes without saying that modes of fabrication and varieties of craftmanship also relate to content. Tearing, cutting, burning, pasting, stapling, nailing, sewing, welding, and the use of heavy plastic substances can do much more than separate or join. Expressive neatness or sloppiness of craftsmanship ranges from the oversolidity of H. C. Westermann's *About a Black Magic Maker* to the loose works of experimenters like Kaprow or Whitman whose fluttering creations of newspaper and rags, doctrinaire in their fragility, are barely jointed to each other at all. The raw construction of Jean Tinguely's demented machines provides a large part of their expressive power, and Edward Kienholz (a cabinetmaker by trade) ironically hides the thoroughness of his craftsmanship behind an appearance of sloppy workmanship. At the other pole of this spectrum one is moved by the feminine delicacy with which the fragile and transparent materials of Anne Ryan are overlaid, and the ephemeral precision of Joseph Cornell's boxes.

The function of materials in assemblage cannot be explained in terms appropriate for orthodox media. In *papiers collés* such as *Bottle of Suze,* Picasso used printed matter simply to get a gray tone, as so many other collagists have done since; where the type is larger, it provides an oscillating pattern. But Apollinaire sanctioned the use of numbers and letters as pictorial elements because, although "new in art, they are already soaked in humanity."[8] Whether it can be read or not, a fragment of newsprint has a wholly different meaning from the page of an old book, a crumbling and yellowed manuscript, a political poster, or a legal document. Its message may be central to the work's theme, as is the news clipping included in Boccioni's *Cavalry Charge,* or, as in Schwitters's word fragment MERZ, it can carry the challenge of a manifesto.

The expansion of this idea beyond typography to include the entire range of materials and objects postulates endless possibilities. If they are to be even partially assessed, it is necessary to consider the multiplicity of meanings and implications that lie between garish newness and total disintegration, artifact and natural form, machine and hand fabrication, or between socially esteemed and tabooed objects.

The fabric of meaning woven by materials can cover the distant in time and space, awakening a romantic response to ruins, architectural and sculptural fragments, and the evocative richness of old walls or ritual vessels. As element is set beside element, the many qualities and auras of isolated fragments are compounded, fused, or contradicted so that—by their own confronted volitions as it were—physical matter becomes poetry. Directed, intentionally or unconsciously, by an artist's intellectual position, emotional predisposition, or any other conditioning attitude or coloration, a vast repertoire of expression—exultant, bitter, ironic, erotic, or lyrical—can be achieved by means different in kind from that of painting and sculpture, but akin to those of literature.

An artist, as Marcel Duchamp has emphasized, is never more than partially cognizant of what his work communicates.[9] Whatever his intention may be, he cannot sidestep the symbolic meaning of objects, nor can his audience. Collagists from Gris to Man Ray, Cornell, Cohen, and Baj have employed mirrors. Who can ignore the fascination of this strange object that dissolves its own surface but brings into being a counterpart of the real world? How can its presence in a work of art not carry something of the potency that it had for the primitive mind? Of the myth of Narcissus? Of the childhood delight in Alice's liberation from everyday life? Of the incantation that begins: "Mirror, mirror, on the wall"? Of one's discovery of infinity in "barbershop" reflections? Of the daily mystery of confronting one's self in reverse?

The history of assemblage, from Picasso and Man Ray on, is punctured with the sharp points of nails. Used expressively, how can they fail to elicit at least a tremor of the meaning they have in a thousand crucifixions painted between the sixth and twentieth centuries? Forks, knives, dishes, and other eating utensils, playing cards, ropes, flags, clocks, shoes, wheels—these objects contain immeasurable layers of significance. Dolls and mannequins, common in surrealist objects, used by George Cohen during the fifties, and recently by Kienholz, Conner, and many others, elicit a range of references which can be erotic, ludicrous, or horrible; separate parts of the body, as in Cohen's *Anybody's Self-Portrait* or Arman's *Little Hands,* can stir unrealized emotions frightening to contemplate. John Latham works almost exclusively with old books: revered or feared, for centuries treasured or burned, how can one imagine their full potential as expressive form and symbol? These examples are few, but they serve as a passing allusion to the enormous variety of subject matter accessible to an assembler: an unending reverberation of object meanings that, because of their associations, reach back to the origins of human consciousness and to the depth of human personality.

Attitudes and Issues

Assemblage is a new medium. It is to be expected, therefore, that it should be the carrier of developing viewpoints for which orthodox techniques are less appropriate. It has indeed provided an effective outlet for artists of a generation weaned on Abstract Expressionism but unwilling to mannerize Pollock, de Kooning, or other masters whom they admire. Because of their concern for subject matter, painting and sculpture are not their only influences. Many cultivate attitudes that could be labeled "angry," "beat," or "sick"; they inherit a malaise shared by authors such as Kafka, Sartre, Beckett, and Ionesco. Certain of their attitudes are comparable to those of the Dada period; but why (especially considering the overtone of tired academicism which it can imply) is the prefix "neo" more applicable in 1961 than it was in 1921? Social and emotional life is scarcely more secure at present than it was during the youth of Jarry, Vaché, Schwitters, or Duchamp.

The current wave of assemblage owes at least as much to Abstract Expressionism (with its Dada and Surrealist components) as it does to Dada directly, but it is nevertheless quite differently oriented: it marks a change from a subjective, fluidly abstract art toward a revised association with environment. The method of juxtaposition is an appropriate vehicle for feelings of disenchantment with the slick international idiom that loosely articulated abstraction has tended to become, and the social values that this situation reflects. The technique of collage has always been a threat to the approved media of oil painting, carving, and casting. Inherent in Kurt Schwitters's MERZ collages, objects, environments, and activities (which, in various ways, all incorporated the spectator and the life around him into the fabric and structure of the work) was an impatience with the line that separated art from life. The medium of which Schwitters must be recognized as *le grand maître,* still expanding after more than forty years, cannot be dismissed as the affectation of a group of incompetents. It is an established mode of communication employing words, symbols, and signs as freely as it does pigments, materials, and objects. Wordlessly associative, it has added to abstract art the vernacular realism that both Ingres and Mondrian sought to exclude by the process of abstraction.

Assemblage has become, temporarily at least, the language for impatient, hypercritical, and anarchistic young artists. With it, or admixtures of it with painting and sculpture, they have given form to content drawn from popular culture: more recent equivalents, as the English critic Reyner Banham argues, of Boccioni's love of "all anti-art manifestations of our epoch—café-chantant, gramophone, cinema, electric advertising, mechanistic architecture, skyscrapers . . . nightlife . . . speed, automobiles, aeroplanes and so forth."[10]

For the first time since the period of the Futurists, the automobile, for example, has been effectively dealt with by the plastic arts, but with an emotional tone that is not at all the same. By now, the automobile has become a mass killer, the upholstered love boat of the adolescent, and the status symbol of the socially disenfranchised. In our period the impact of these "insolent chariots" is at least as great as previously was that of the horse—whose role as a living symbol could be said to have ended with the agonized scream of the disemboweled victim in Picasso's *Guernica.* In his magnificent bronze of 1951, *Baboon and Young,* Picasso used a miniature automobile body to simulate the head of an ape.

It is no longer delight with mechanization that is represented. John Chamberlain salvages smashed, bent, and rusted car bodies, but only, he says, for their color and form. Jason Seley uses nothing but bumpers, and as a counterforce to the elegance of his compositions, he emphasizes their previous function. César takes a *méchant* pleasure in seeing deviscerated auto body shells compressed into dense blocks of steel collage. James Dine, in a ''happening'' named *Car Crash,* and in a series of gouaches and collages, has dealt with the automobile as a symbol of love and death. Richard Hamilton, an English artist who admires Marcel Duchamp, juxtaposes the forms of female models with those of Chryslers and electric kitchen equipment. William Copley, an American Surrealist painter working in France, draws attention to the comic gaudiness and erotic symbolism of the automobile. Larry Rivers paints the front ends of Buicks. In addition to plumbing and other scrap metal, Richard Stankiewicz uses cylinder blocks and tire chains to make satiric personages or carefully structured abstract assemblages.

The themes beginning to pass through the doors of art museums are (once again, as in the days of Courbet) those described by Gide as ''the squalor of reality.''[11] Or, in a more current—and perhaps therefore a more apt—phrase, Allan Kaprow speaks of ''the nameless sludge and whirl of urban events.''[12] All is not grumbling, ''jazz,'' and ''kicks,'' however: it is not hard to discern behind these vernacular subjects a striving, embittered by disenchantment, but mystical and moral as well as irascible and sexual. It is in part an outcome of insecurity that is more than economic, and of the aesthetic individualism that, following the failure of liberal politics during the thirties and forties, provided, a motive force for Abstract Expressionism.

The vernacular repertoire includes beat Zen and hotrods, mescalin experiences and faded flowers, photographic bumps and grinds, the *poubelle* (i.e., trash can), jukeboxes, and hydrogen explosions. Such subjects are often approached in a mystical, aesthetic, or ''arty'' way, but just as often they are fearfully dark, evoking horror or nausea: the anguish of the scrap heap; the images of charred bodies that keep Hiroshima and Nagasaki before our eyes; the confrontation of democratic platitudes with the Negro's disenfranchisement; the travesty of the Chessman trial. Indeed, in the United States, a network of artists could be identified who, quite independently and with no political affiliation, incorporate or represent in their work flags, shields, eagles, and other symbols of democracy, national power, and authority, with mild amusement or irony, with unconcealed resentment and scatological bitterness, or simply as totally banal images.

Adjunctive to the identification with popular culture, but more whimsical, is a group of objects whose elements can be manipulated, removed, added to, or reassembled by the spectator: these elements include balls that drop, playing cards that can be moved from hook to hook, boxes and openings from which mementos can be removed and replaced by others, tablets on which notes may be written, or toy pianos that can be played. The spectator is invited to be a participant in a childlike sort of game.

Another group of works, related to the international trend toward mobile constructions in the tradition of Duchamp, Moholy-Nagy, Gabo, and Calder combines assemblage with mechanical movement.

''Resist the anxious fear to fix the instantaneous, to kill that which is living,'' warns Jean Tinguely, whose most recent work, influenced by Rauschenberg and Stankiewicz, fuses the tradition of kinetic art with that of assemblage.[13] On a dank evening in March 1960, Tinguely's ''self-constructing and self-destroying work of art,'' *Homage to New York* (white and stately five minutes before its maiden performance, and compounded of a mélange of materials ranging from bicycle wheels and dishpans to an upright piano), vibrated and gyrated, painted pictures, played music, and magnificently but inefficiently sawed, shook, and burned itself to rubble and extinction in the sculpture garden of the Museum of Modern Art. A year or so earlier the British junk man and eccentric Gustave Metzger was making ''expendable art'' with acid brushed onto stretched nylon: ''as the acid is applied, it dissolves in patches, the edges curl and a pattern is formed.''[14] He has also proposed sculpture that will disintegrate more slowly, ''by undergoing a continual destructive process such as the action of acid or some other errosive [*sic*]. This type of work could also be destroyed by the action of natural elements—rain and humid atmosphere under normal circumstances will almost certainly corrode completely a thin piece of iron or mild steel within a decade at the outside.''[15]

Common to many of the controversial ideas, attitudes, and activities cited in the preceding paragraphs is a dissatisfaction, ranging from impatience to nihilism, with the limitations traditionally imposed by the idea of art, the sequestered atmosphere and geometric enframement of the museum, and—though the spotlight of success and fashion is constantly shifting toward allegedly avant-garde innovations—the whirl of dealers, collectors, and soaring prices. Yet, by a process of reciprocal thesis and antithesis oscillating with the speed of alternating current, a negative position needs only to be stated to be immediately countered by a return to art for its own sake within the same camp: one must surely agree with Basil Taylor that ''the spirit of art–antiart is of the greatest significance in the history of our time.''[16]

Allan Kaprow, in a manuscript of 1960, ''Paintings, Environments, and Happenings,'' advocates ''a quite clear-headed decision to abandon craftsmanship and permanence,'' and ''the use of obviously perishable media such as newspaper, string, adhesive tape, growing grass or real food,'' so ''no one can mistake the fact that the work will pass into dust or garbage quickly.''[17] The medium of refuse, according to Kaprow (but over the objections of certain of his associates), can ''force once again the eternal problems of what may be (or become) art and what may not. The intellectuals' typical disdain for popular culture, for the objects and debris of mass production, is as always a clear instance of aesthetic discrimination: *this* is fit for art; *that* is not. Such high-mindedness is not at all different from the seventeenth century's belief in the greater value of 'noble' themes over genre ones.''[18]

Although the connection is far too dispersive to make precise, the productions known as ''happenings,'' presented by Kaprow, James Dine, and other New York artists at the Reuben Gallery and elsewhere, had their origin in painting and collage. Kaprow explains their expansion for ''agglomerates'' to three-dimensional assemblages large enough for a spectator to enter, to become an element of, and even to alter if he chooses. Finally, surrounding and including not only their authors but their audience as well, ''happenings'' involve movements, costumes, sounds, lights, and scents as well as forms and colors. The producers of ''happenings'' have no common program, but their most evident general aim seems to be the spatialization or immobilization of time, sequence, and movement. The performances avoid climax or denouement in order to imprint a series of sharp images on the minds of the audience. Separated actions, related only by their impact on each other, take place simultaneously, leading to an effect described by a reviewer of Claes Oldenburg's *Fotodeath* as the ''extended exposure of a picture.''[19]

Recognizing the connection of New York ''happenings'' with painting, sculpture, and assemblage, and the unquestionable success of a few performances, one must nevertheless assert that, to date, many have resembled amateur theatricals. It is interesting to note, indeed, that many works of the avant-garde film and the professional theater have an analogous antinarrational tendency which could be described, in its avoidance of a definite conclusion, by the advice André Gide gives himself in his ''Journal'' of *The Counterfeiters:* ''This novel will end sharply, not through exhaustion of the subject, which must give the impression of inexhaustibility, but on the contrary through its expansion and by a sort of blurring of its outline. It must not be neatly rounded off, but rather disperse, disintegrate.''[20]

In quite the same way, the theme of assemblage is dispersed by the consideration of ''happenings'' and similar activities going on in New York and other centers throughout the world—especially when they take place in museum gardens, railroad stations, rifle ranges, Venetian gondolas, or autobuses. Certain of these events differ from the routine occurrences "outside" only in the special kind of attention which they demand.

The importance of assemblage to modern art is surely beyond question. It is nevertheless always hard to avoid judging, either positively or negatively, by extrinsic criteria: by what one supposes will be the outcome of the principles a work exemplifies, or simply by a prejudice for or against the tendency or group that it seems to represent. The challenge presented to the plastic arts by the new wave of assemblage should nevertheless not be evaded, but surely pseudo innovation should never be embraced because it seems to be *le dernier cri.* Yet the need of certain artists to defy and obliterate accepted categories, to fabricate aggressive objects, to present subjects tabooed by accepted standards, to undermine the striving for permanency by using soiled, valueless, and fragile materials, and even to present ordinary objects for examination unaltered—these manifestations are signs of vitality. They once more demonstrate the necessity for artists to flee the current circle of approval while seeking recognition on another level, to return again from abstraction to nature, to work with the materials of life rather than art.

Those who decry such developments as dishonest or deplorable, as evidence of commercialism, capitulation to jaded fashion, moral decay, or worse—and such views are held by many who are neither stubborn conservatives nor who reject venturesome art—should surely be heard. On the opposite side—though who can honestly declare himself to be entirely in one camp or the other?—lies an unqualified faith in the purity of the regenerative human activity of art no matter where it may lead. Somewhere between these opposed prejudices lies the realization, supported by history, that Western art is, has always been, and should continue in a state of ferment and constant redefinition. And it must be recognized with approval and pleasure that, in addition to enriching and adulterating the themes and forms of painting and sculpture, makers of assembled art have wrought a truly magical transformation: from banality and ugliness, dispersion and waste, tawdriness and commercialism, they have created challenging, meaningful, and often beautiful objects ordered by principles inseparable from this century.

Notes

1. Marcel Jean, *The History of Surrealist Painting* (New York: Grove Press, 1960), p. 66.
2. Alfred H. Barr, Jr., *Picasso: Fifty Years of His Art* (New York: The Museum of Modern Art, 1946), p. 270.

3. Daniel-Henry Kahnweiler, *Juan Gris: His Life and Work* (New York: Valentin, 1947), p. 138.
4. From a catalogue of a Spoerri exhibition, Milan, Galleria Schwarz, 1961.
5. Ibid.
6. In an unpublished MS, Paris, 1961.
7. Quoted by Shattuck, *The Banquet Years,* p. 264.
8. Guillaume Apollinaire, *The Cubist Painters,* 2nd ed. (New York: Wittenborn, Schultz, 1949), p. 21.
9. Marcel Duchamp, ''The Creative Act,'' in Robert Lebel, *Marcel Duchamp* (New York: Grove Press, 1959), pp. 77–78.
10. Reyner Banham, in *Arts Magazine* 35, no. 3 (December 1960): 37.
11. André Gide, *The Counterfeiters: with Journal of ''The Counterfeiters''* (New York: Knopf, 1959), p. 396.
12. Allan Kaprow, *Paintings, Environments, and Happenings* (Old Bridge, N.J., 1960).
13. Quoted by Basil Taylor in ''Art—Anti-Art,'' *The Listener* (London), 12 November 1959, p. 281.
14. See Jasia Reichhardt, ''Expendable Art,'' *Architectural Design* (London) 30, no. 10 (October 1960): 421. Jean Tinguely's *Homage to New York* is also discussed.
15. Ibid.
16. Basil Taylor, ''Art—Anti-Art,'' p. 819.
17. Kaprow, *Paintings, Environments, and Happenings,* p. 12a.
18. Ibid., p. 12.
19. Jill Johnson, in *Art News* 60, no. 2 (April 1961): 57.
20. Gide, *The Counterfeiters,* p. 415.

6

Picasso and the Typography of Cubism

Robert Rosenblum

Robert Rosenblum's pivotal essay moves away from formalist interpretation of Cubist collages to the subject matter of printed words and papers as he skillfully points to levels of meaning in the Cubist collages beyond the formal language. Rosenblum's careful delineation of possible puns, plays on words, fusions of words and visual imagery, the use of wit and irony, etc. enriches conceptually and intellectually the formal language of Cubism. Further, Rosenblum points to the great impact of this "typography": "In this light the Cubist sensibility to the kaleidoscopic assault of words and advertising images to be found in the most commonplace urban situations represents the first full-scale absorption into high art of the typographical environment of our century. So important was this insight that the consequences—from the social aggressiveness of words in Futurism and Dada to the aesthetic ironies of commercial imagery in Pop Art—are still to be assessed."

By now it is a commonplace of art history to say that the innovations of Cubism altered the structure of Western painting to a degree unparalleled since the Renaissance. Indeed, so drastic were Cubism's shattering and reconstruction of traditional representations of light and shadow, mass and void, flatness and depth that discussions of Cubist art have rightly concentrated upon the nature of these overwhelming changes. But for most commentators, the formal revolutions wrought by Cubism are so arresting that many secondary aspects of Cubist art tend to be neglected, particularly those which, at least at first glance, seem to be

---

This article originally appeared in *Picasso in Retrospect,* edited by Sir Roland Penrose and John Golding (New York: Harper and Row, 1980).

peripheral or even irrelevant to the multiple new visual problems posed. Above all, the subject matter of the great masters of Cubism—Picasso, Braque, and Gris—has been of minimal interest, for the themes they preferred—single figures, still lifes, and less often, landscapes—were so traditional that, in themselves, they hardly detracted attention from the most antitraditional Cubist language into which they were translated. And with this broad assumption in mind—that the subject matter of Cubism plays an intellectually and emotionally neutral role in the restless formal explorations of Cubist art—even the most unconventional aspect of Cubist subject matter, that is, the abundant intrusion of words and printed papers culled from everyday life, has often been construed as a device primarily oriented toward the solution of the successive formal problems raised by the rapid changes of Cubist structure in the years between 1910 and 1914. How many times have we read that the introduction of hand-painted and stencilled words by Braque and Picasso in 1910–11 was a means of asserting the flatness of the picture plane; or that the pasting of bits of newspaper onto canvas or paper, beginning in 1912, was motivated by the need for enriching the lean textural vocabulary of Cubism![1] Such explanations are by no means incorrect, but their exclusivity has blinded most spectators to the possibility of additional interpretations that would enrich, rather than deny, the formal ones. Indeed, this indifference to the actual reading matter in Cubist art has often been so deeply ingrained that, on more than one occasion, the date printed on a newspaper used in a Picasso *papier collé* has been overtly contradicted by the date assigned to the work by historians and cataloguers.[2] The question, simply, is this: could it really have been that Picasso and his fellow Cubists chose the words, the newspaper clippings, the calling cards, the cigarette-paper packets, the advertisements, the bottle labels, even the kind of typeface (roman, italic, Gothic) with total indifference to their potential verbal meaning or associative value?

Consider, to begin with, the recurrent references to newspapers in Picasso's Cubist paintings, drawings,and collages. Although at times, Picasso painted, stencilled, pasted, or drew the names of such French newspapers as *L'Indépendant, Excelsior,*[3] *Le Moniteur,*[4] *L'Intransigeant,*[5] *Le Quotidien du Midi,*[6] *Le Figaro,*[7] as well as the Spanish newspaper, *El Diluvio*[8] and the new Italian Futurist periodical, *Lacerba,*[9] it was, above all, *Le Journal* which recurred in these works as well as in those of Braque and Gris.[10] Characteristically for the aesthetic of Cubism at its most inventive, even this ephemeral commonplace, that daily newspaper read by Picasso and other Parisians, is thoroughly transformed. Like the objects that surround them—whether figures, stringed instruments, bottles, wine glasses—the letters on the masthead, LE JOURNAL, are subjected to constant metamorphosis, changing from lucid, discrete wholes to ambiguous, interdependent fragments. Indeed, it is almost a rule that in no Cubist work of Picasso does the entire newspaper name, LE JOURNAL, appear; [11] and even when it is most legible, as in a *papier collé* of winter 1912–13, where it hovers together with a siphon, wine glass, and violin upon a drawn tabletop, the article, LE, is omitted. Far more commonly, it is shattered into yet smaller parts. Thus, in the case of a painted still life of 1914, the same two-syllable newspaper title is broken into three syllabic parts, JO/UR/NAL, the verbal equivalent of the planar dissection of Cubist objects, and this release from conventional verbal completeness permits, in turn, a whole series of permutations and combinations that, to be understood, must often be *read* as well as *seen*. Students of Cubism have frequently used the metaphor of a pun to characterize the visual ambiguities so intrinsic to Cubist art, but in fact, such puns exist on a more literal, verbal level as well. Like his fellow Cubists, Picasso was a member of that literary generation which included the greatest punster in the history of Western literature, James Joyce. And in more personal terms, too, Picasso was an intimate of such Parisian poets as Apollinaire, who, in the *Calligrammes* of 1914,[12] confounded words and images with a newfound typographical freedom; and of Max Jacob, who was often obsessed with the possibility of endless transmutations of common words.[13] And among his fellow artists, such Dadaists as Duchamp and Picabia would delight in elaborate puns that, at simpler moments, parallel variations on LE JOURNAL. Thus, Duchamp once provided a parody dictionary entry for another Dadaist, Man Ray, whom he defined as: n.m. synon. de Joie*jouer*jouir.[14]

It is exactly this kind of multiple verbal-visual reading of similar sounds and letters (*joie*=joy; *jouer*=to play; *jouir*=to enjoy or, in sexual slang, to come) that we can trace in Picasso's metamorphoses of LE JOURNAL. Freed from an absolute form and meaning by the Cubist aesthetic of the relative and the ambiguous, this prosaic word can take on new guises in new contexts. Thus, a simple transformation can be achieved merely by bisection. In *Still Life with a Bottle of Vieux Marc,* dated spring 1913 (but usually misdated spring 1912),[15] LE JOURNAL becomes LE JOUR (the day). But with bisections at different points in the word, other, more evocative puns are also made possible. Thus, JOURNAL can become just JOU, a word fragment that, in French, conjures up the root of the verb *jouer,* to play, a concept that is not only generally appropriate to Picasso's first collage,[16] with its capricious interplay of multiple realities, where the true and the false, the handmade and the machine-made are constantly shuffled, but is even more specifically appropriate to *The Card Player* of 1913–14, whose playing cards—part revealed, part concealed—are echoed in the almost clandestine disclosure of the first letters, JOU, of the newspaper included on the table top.

In other cases, the fusion of word and image is more complex, in the manner of an Apollinaire *calligramme* whose disposition of letters creates an image of the subject described. Thus, in the *Still Life with Skull* of 1913, which repeats the macabre *memento mori* still-life theme that Picasso had already introduced in 1907,[17] the grey, papery, masklike skull merges with the equally grey and papery newspaper in an evocative way. The vowels OU of JOURNAL are obscured by the lower part of the skull, whose nasal cavity suggests a carat which points upward to the eye cavities, whose rounded hollows fulfill, as it were, the visual and verbal expectation of the concealed vowels. The same kind of fusion of an image and the word JOURNAL occurs, without such grim associations of time and death, in a later still life, *The Saucepan* of 1919 by Juan Gris, whose verbal and visual punning so often rivals that of his compatriot Picasso. In this example, the J and U of the newspaper title are obliterated by the presence of a wine glass, whose sloping sides isolate the letter O. As a result, this vowel funcitons ambiguously as both a single letter, excerpted from JOURNAL, and as a description of the round rim of the glass, transformed by Gris's flattening and geometricizing stylizations into an oval.

Elsewhere, still other possibilities are extracted from the simple verbal premise of LE JOURNAL. In Picasso's *Student with a Newspaper* of 1913–14, one finds the intrusion of a slightly off-color pun, here perfectly suited to the schoolboy grin of the scarecrow figure, who wears a broad-brimmed *faluche,* the French student's cap: the JO is dropped, leaving URNAL, a combination of letters easily associated with URINAL.[18] The same joke recurs in an earlier still life context [see fig. 8.1], where the newspaper title, URNAL, is followed by another fragment, UN COUP DE THE, which, heading an article about the Balkan Wars that appeared on 4 December 1912, originally read UN COUP DE THEATRE. Moreover, with the multiplicity characteristic of the Cubist aesthetic, the phrase UN COUP DE THE may evoke not only tea, but also the title of Mallarmé's famous poem, "Un Coup de dés n'abolira jamais le hasard," whose typographical freedom was a major inspiration to the poets in Picasso's circle,[19] and whose titular subject, a die, was a common object in Picasso's still lifes.[20]

The sullying of the ostensibly pure and cerebral character of Cubism with risqué verbal puns can be demonstrated in other works by Picasso. In depicting a still life and a man with guitar, both of 1913 (fig. 6.1), Picasso continues his and Braque's frequent intrusion of lettering inspired by posters, in this case announcements of a GRAND CONCERT.[21] Again, through simple Cubist bisection, Picasso evokes, instead of GRAND CONCERT, GRAND CON,[22] a commonplace French insult that is further compounded, in 1917, in the lettering (as well as the position of hand and bow) of a sandwich man costume for the ballet *Parade,* which adds à la Jarry's *Ubu Roi,* MERD, to the suggestion of GRAND CON.

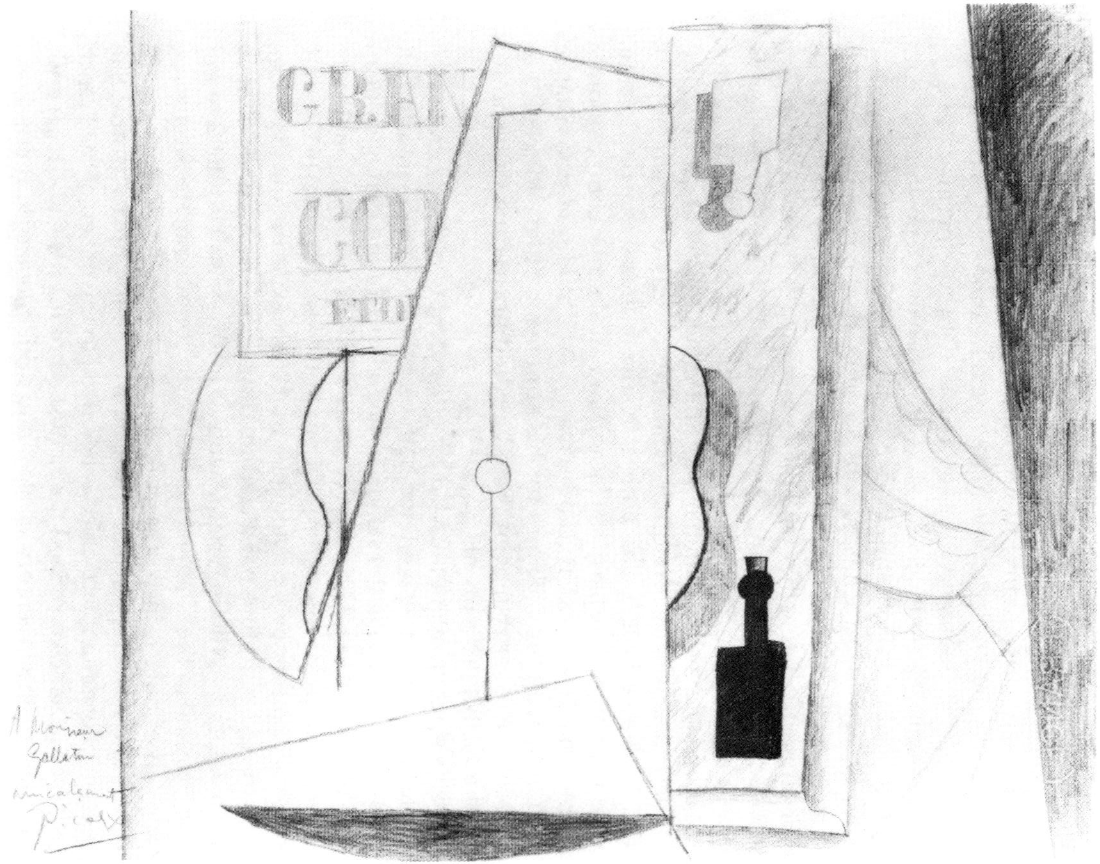

Figure 6.1. Pablo Picasso, *Guitar and Bottle,* 1913
Pencil on paper, 12″ × 15¾″.
(Philadelphia Museum of Art. A. E. Gallatin Collection)

Far more clandestine and witty is the lascivious joke concealed in a masterly collage of 1912–13 [see fig. 8.4], which substitutes for the commonplace of the newspaper title, LE JOURNAL, a collection of pastings that advertise two famous Parisian department stores, LA SAMARITAINE and AU BON MARCHÉ. Above, we see a commercial drawing of a properly dressed lady, cut off at the waist; below, the label of the *lingerie* and *broderie* department at the Bon Marché; and below that, in much smaller letters that point directly up to the word "lingerie" and that, in turn, partly fill a pictorial "hole" in the jigsaw puzzle compactness of this collage, we read the fragmented words TROU ICI (hole here).

The stimulus of brand names, labels, advertisements, posters was constant in the Cubist milieu and, in two cases, Picasso even managed to combine the very word Cubism with a commerical commonplace, the trade name, KUB, of a bouillon cube that is still sold in France today. Here the letters KUB, together with the number 10 (the price in centimes), are imposed upon the schematic drawing of a cube, which then, as now, appears in the advertisement. In fact, the unexpected topicality of this familiar French advertising emblem for the milieu of avant-garde painting was seized as well by Mondrian, who, engrossed by Cubism in Paris between 1912 and 1914, made both a relatively literal drawing of this advertisement on a Montparnasse facade and an abstract composition in which the same letters, KUB, can be read.[23] And it is said, too, that in 1911, upon arriving in Collioure for his summer holiday, Matisse was chagrined to discover that even there he could not escape Cubism, for he found a KUB poster on his house.[24]

Picasso's singling out of the KUB advertisement was clearly motivated by the joke on Cubism that it offered both verbally and, in the transparent cube drawing, visually. In the same way, his choice of the popular slogan (and title of a brochure),[25] NOTRE AVENIR EST DANS L'AIR (our future is in the air), for inclusion in three Cubist still lifes of spring 1912[26] may allude to his and Braque's private joke that their experiments in collage and constructed sculpture paralleled the innovative techniques of such pioneer aviators as Wilbur Wright, whose death on 30 May 1912 might even have provided the stimulus for Picasso to commemorate this topical phrase by inscribing it in works of art.[27]

Most often, however, Picasso's selection of commonplace words, like his selection of commonplace objects, belonged to the milieu of the French café (whose ambiance provided the richest stimulus for Cubist art) and, in particular, to the inventory of alcoholic drinks available there. Even in a pair of such casual Cubist drawings as those made during the summer of 1912, Picasso chose to record, with the eye of a *flâneur* on holiday, 1) a café corner with chair and tabletop laid out with newspaper headlines

(*La Vie au Gran . . .*), bottle, glass, and in the background, lettering with the price (50 centimes) of Munich beer; and 2) a street facing the old port of Marseille, where the nearly illegible scaffolding of Cubist hieroglyphs, punctuated by an anchor, is suddenly given a prosaic point of visual entry by the lettering, APERITIF, on a café awning, by the fragment of a street sign, LA CANE (BIERE?), and by the no less literal rendering of figures at a café table and of the carriages below.

From such cafés Picasso selected the names and labels of apéritifs like Pernod, Anis del Mono, and Suze; brandies like Hennessy, Vieux Marc, and Françoise; and ales like Bass, all of which turn up with the frequency of the daily newspaper and are subjected to similar metamorphoses. Picasso especially enjoyed a kind of Cubist prestidigitation of these identifying labels, that is, a constant oscillation of their levels of fact and fiction. At times, as in the case of a bottle of Suze, he actually pasted a real label onto a Cubist bottle; elsewhere, at the opposite extreme, he would label a bottle of Bass with his own, irregular hand lettering in typographical contrast to the printed lettering on a calling card and the label of a package of tobacco. But at other times, with even richer Cubist wit, he would further compound these levels of fact and fiction by identifying a Cubist bottle neither by hand nor by the actual label, but rather by pasting a newspaper advertisement for the alcohol in question. Such is the case in a still life of 1914, where the lettering RHUM simultaneously identifies the contents of the Cubist bottle and suggests the presence of the newspaper itself on the still life table (fig. 6.2), or yet more ambiguously, in an earlier *papier collé* of December 1912,[28] where, if we trouble to read the trapezoidal column of advertisements Picasso selected from the newspaper, we discover not one, but two possibilities—MARC 'A LA CLOCHE' and VIN DESILES—for identifying the exact contents of the drawn bottle to which the clipping has been affixed. And with still greater duplicity, Picasso could also turn a bottle of BASS into a playing card simply by isolating the AS (French for ACE) of BASS on a flat plane and locating it next to a floating symbol of a playing card club. The result is an ace of clubs split into verbal and symbolic fragments that, like the evocative JOU of the JOURNAL which hovers on this table top, keep changing identities.

Such Cubist conundrums are quite as common in the labelling of the bottles of Picasso's compatriot, Juan Gris. On his café tabletops, even humble bottles of Beaujolais can suddenly be transformed into verbal jokes. Often, the word BEAUJOLAIS is fragmented to a simple BEAU, which, in addition to taking on adjectival status that might define the quality of the wine, could even confuse the wine drinker into thinking that he had a bottle of Beaune; and in one case this word fragment joins

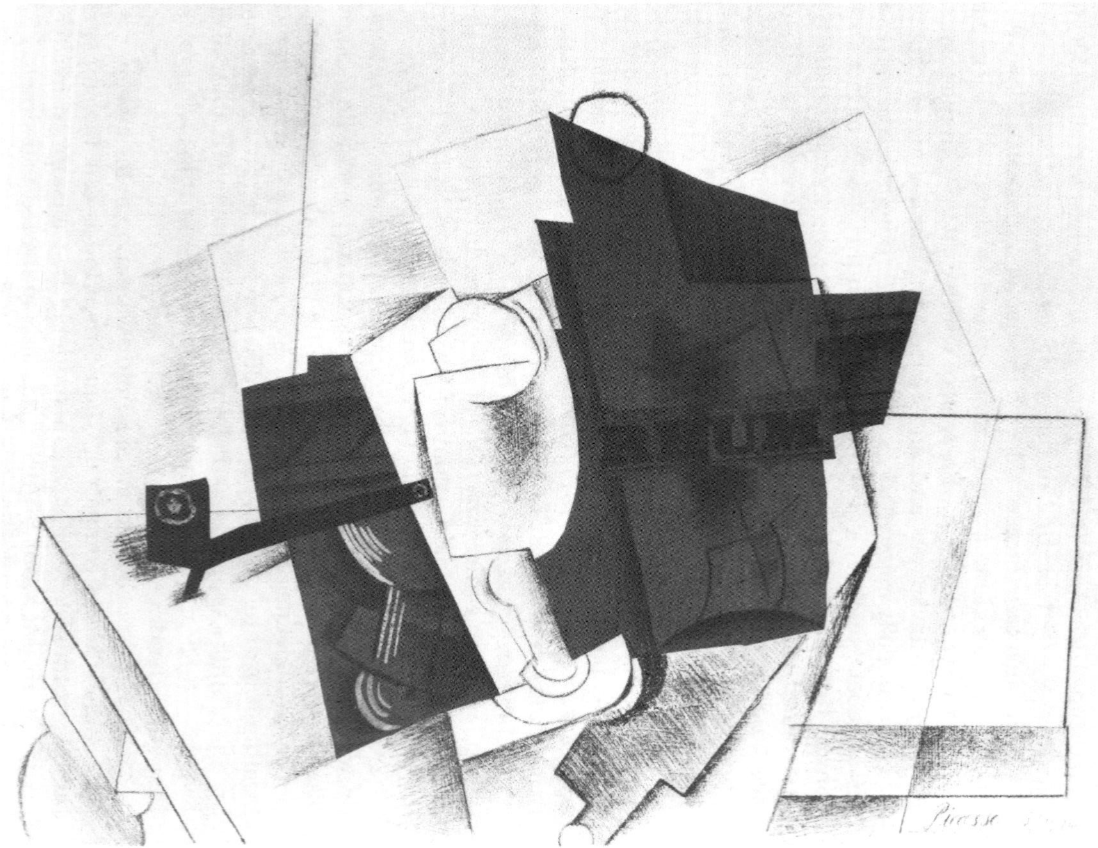

Figure 6.2. Pablo Picasso, *Pipe, Glass, Bottle of Rum*, March 1914
Pasted paper, pencil, gouache on cardboard, 15¾″ × 20¾″.
(Collection, The Museum of Modern Art, New York. Gift of Mr. and Mrs. Daniel Saidenberg)

verbal forces with the equally fragmented newspaper title, LE JOURNAL, so that the two elide in a new phrase that begins, BEAU JOUR (beautiful day). In another example, Gris offers the most comic metamorphosis of all. Here, in identifying a bottle of red wine, he permits only the letters EAU to show on the label (originally B*eau*jolais, B*eau*ne, or Bord*eau*x), and thereby performs his own Cubist version of the Miracle at Cana. And in yet another case, the name of the popular apéritif, DUBONNET, is observed on a matchholder and faceted into separate syllables—BON and NET[29]—which again provide a permutation of verbal meanings that creates the exact linguistic counterpart of the Cubist visual legerdemain that questions the identity of objects through fragmentation and elision (fig. 6.3).

Like newspapers and the brand names of alcohol, references to music are as common in the Cubist dictionary of words as in the Cubist repertory of still life objects. Although Braque, in particular, alluded often to classical music, with sprinklings of words like SONATE, ETUDE, DUO, ARIA, RONDO, or even the names BACH, MOZART, KUBELICK, it was popular music that dominated most Cubist art. For Picasso especially, popular songs provided further possibilities for the piquant intrusion of the commonplace within the arcane visual environment of Cubist art. These may range from unspecificed waltzes[30] to a mazurka like *Trilles et Baisers,* [31] from more sentimental songs like *Sonnet* (after Pierre Ronsard)[32] to the famous habanera, *La Paloma.*[33] But the most frequent musical reference is undoubtedly MA JOLIE, words excerpted from the refrain—"O Manon, ma jolie, mon coeur te dit bonjour!"—of a popular song, *Dernière chanson,* written by Fragson in 1911.[34] Shortly after, in the winter of 1911–12, the phrase MA JOLIE appears in Picasso's work, at first in the magisterial figure painting now commonly known by this title, although originally catalogued by Zervos as *Femme à guitare.*[35] The inclusion of the phrase MA JOLIE in this complex, nearly indecipherable Cubist context can be interpreted in many ways.[36] For one thing, it functions here as a pseudo-title, mocking with its impersonal lettering and its position at the bottom of a nearly illegible painting the identifying title one might find on a picture in a museum. For another, it must have provided in 1911–12, the time of the song's debut and success, a jolting reminder of a popular tune, known to all, in the midst of an avant-garde pictorial style, understood by few. Indeed, this abrupt confrontation between a new experimental art of overt difficulty and an easily comprehensible fragment culled from popular art is paralleled at exactly the same time, 1911, by Stravinsky, who, in the first scene of *Petrouchka,* suddenly introduced into a daring new musical fabric of polyharmony and polyrhythm (the musical counterpart of Cubist visual multiplicity) a simple and lilting popular melody—"Elle avait un' jambe en bois"—which he had often

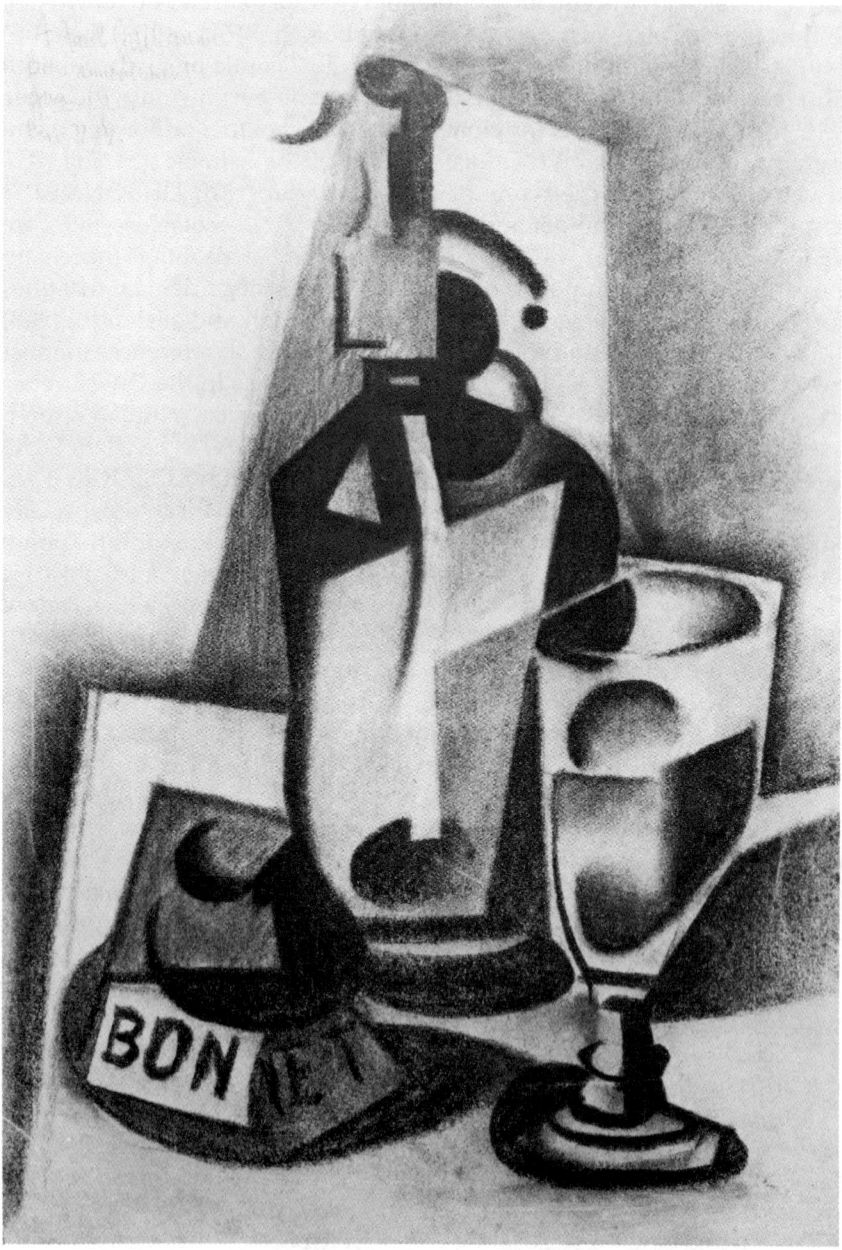

Figure 6.3 Juan Gris, *The Siphon*, 1917
Conté crayon on paper, 18¾″ × 12½″.
(Philadelphia Museum of Art. A. E. Gallatin Collection)

heard played on a hurdy-gurdy outside his window in Beaulieu.[37] But Picasso's use of the phrase MA JOLIE could have, with typical Cubist ambiguity, yet another meaning, this time private and sentimental rather than public and aesthetic. For Picasso's new girlfriend of the Cubist years, Marcelle Humbert, was called "Eva" by the artist, who, on 12 June 1912, wrote to his dealer Kahnweiler that he loved her and would write her name on his pictures.[38]

That name, EVA, like a still life object or the words of a newspaper clipping, was subjected to Cubist metamorphoses which combined it with the refrain MA JOLIE. In one case, JOLIE, in its role as half of the song phrase, is inscribed above EVA, offering an adjectival embellishment to a lover's tribute to his loved one. Elsewhere, Picasso inscribes more explicitly J'AIME EVA [see fig. 8.6].[39] But more often—at least twelve times[40]—he simply writes or stencils MA JOLIE, which in this context becomes, as it were, a clandestine reference to Eva in the guise of a public reference to a popular song.

Again, Picasso's exploration of song titles for secret allusions or puns was paralleled by Gris. In one particularly witty example, a café still life of 1913, Gris inscribes on his tabletop a fragmentary sheet of music which reads AUPRES DE MA BLONDE, the name of the well-known French folksong, and locates this title next to a fluted beer glass, of a kind so common in his still lifes. A joke may well have been intended, for French café slang refers to a glass of light beer as *une blonde,* a reference that would here unite, in a verbal and visual joke, the love song and the beer glass. In a similar example, Gris establishes yet another connection between word and image. Here, in a still life of 1914[41] which includes a package of coffee, a bottle, two cups, and a newspaper, the clipping at the left reports on the French invasion of the Moroccan city of Tazza and diagrams these military maneuvers on a map. Again, the juxtaposition of the printed word TAZZA and the drawn shadow of a Cubist cup at its right would hardly seem accidental; for especially to Gris, a Spaniard in France, the word TAZZA would offer a kind of Romance language pun on both French *tasse* and Spanish *taza.* Even in lesser Cubist masters like the American Max Weber, this kind of punning can be found (perhaps expectedly in his case, in view of his efforts to create in *Cubist Poems* of 1913[42] the verbal equivalent of his pictorial Cubist aesthetic). In his representation of a scale, painted in 1915, the stencilled word AVOIRDUPOIS hovers precariously in letter fragments that echo the movement of the balancing mechanism, and is then translated into a visual joke by the contents of the scale: a mound of peas (*pois*).

It was the words and images of the newspaper clippings, however, that tended to produce the wittiest and most clandestine jokes in Cubist art. Consider a Picasso *papier collé* of 1913, in which a trapezoidal newspaper clipping, pasted upside down, enlivens an unusually ascetic drawing of a still life. One might well ask why Picasso had chosen to paste this clipping upside down, and the answer, to begin with, might be that this position contributes to the Cubist sense of weightessness, of gravity-defiant objects. But if one also takes the trouble to read the small print, one sees that the upper portion is an advertisement for an electric light bulb, which is illustrated, and that the text boasts that this bulb is "la seule qui éclaire dans toutes les directions" (the only one which gives light on all sides) and "la seule qui se place *indifféremment* dans toutes les positions" (the only one which can be placed in any position at all)—which is exactly what Picasso has done. Indeed, the location of the commercial illustration of the bulb in the center of a skeletal linear network transforms this bottle-shaped volume into a lamp base (with arced shade), yet another example of Cubist sleight-of-hand.

The same attention might be paid to an earlier *papier collé* of winter 1912–13, where a clipping from LE JOURNAL joins visual, verbal, and conceptual forces with the dissected wine glass that is drawn upon it. To begin with, the square frame of the diagram provides another geometric variation among the trapezoid of the siphon at the left, the spiral of the violin at the right, and the circle and parallelogram of the wine glass's lip and bowl. But even more, the diagram within the newspaper frame is delightfully appropriate, for it illustrates, as the caption explains, "Comment on pose une ligne à 1000 mètres de fond" (how to lay a line at a depth of 1000 meters). Here, in a cross-section of the sea, almost Cubist in its schematic transparency, a fishing boat is seen dropping a line that visually connects with the drawn circle of the wine glass's lip and that almost seems to attempt to anchor, with its plumb-line verticality, the swaying, teetering rhythms of the Cubist objects set afloat around it.[43] In gravitational contrast to Picasso's deep-sea fishing, Gris, on one occasion, used a newspaper diagram to make his still life airborne (fig. 6.4). Here, the illustration, formally analogous to the checkerboard squares to the right, shows us the lower part of a dirigible, whose swollen arc seems to hover under the base of a wine glass that, with an almost Futurist path of movement, floats up to the left-hand corner, as if propelled skyward by this fragment of an airship.[44]

Gris, in fact, was especially canny about choosing newspaper clippings that pertained to the aesthetic of Cubism, whether in terms of gravity,[45] the interplay of fact and fiction, the technique of collage itself, or the question of signatures. In one case, *The Table* of 1914, the headlines of the lead article announce LE VRAI ET LE FAUX . . . , an appropriate comment on a still life that constantly confuses, in a manner worthy of

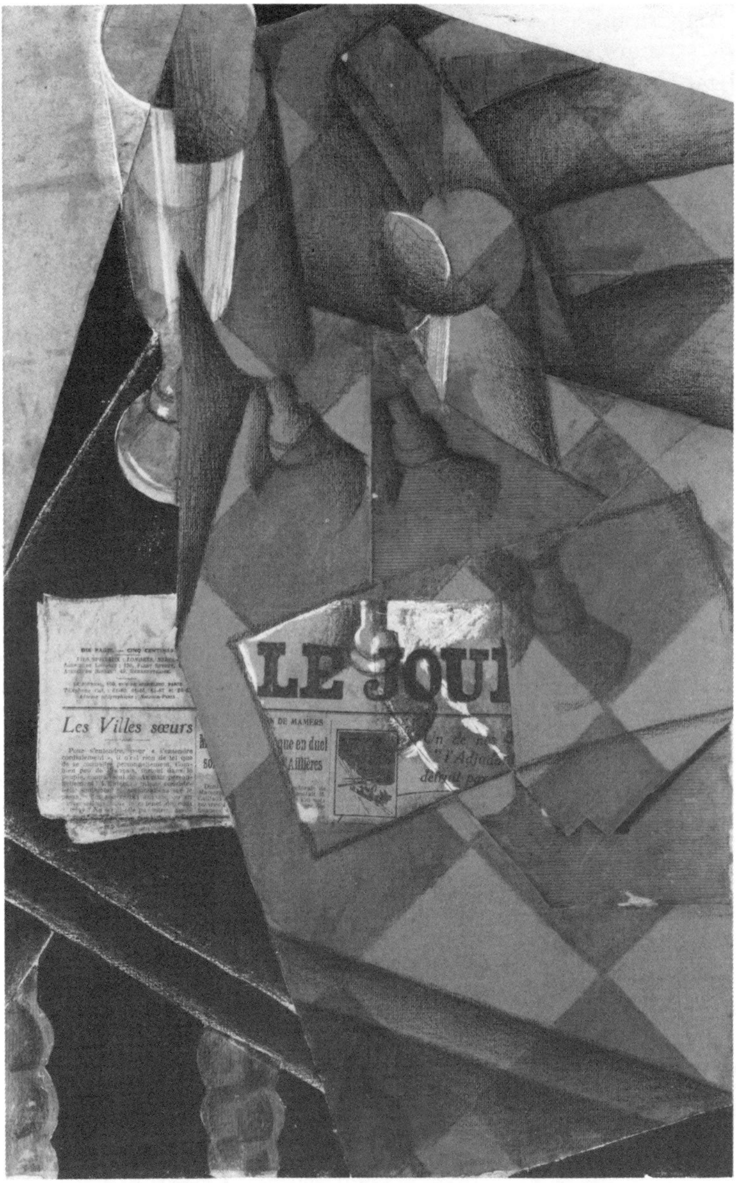

Figure 6.4. Juan Gris, *Glasses and Newspaper,* May 1914
Gouache, conté crayon, and chalk on paper mounted on canvas, 24″ × 15″.
(Smith College Museum of Art, Northampton, Massachusetts. Gift of Joseph Brummer, 1921)

Pirandello, the true and the false components in an array of illusionistic devices that range from the *trompe-l'oeil* key to actual pastings from books and newspapers.[46] Moreover, at the extreme right, another newspaper clipping offers a joke on the Cubist aesthetic: the upper half of a photograph of a man's head, whose face disappears beneath an opaque plane, is topped by the word fragment DISPAR . . . , which might be *disparu* or *disparition* (disappeared or disappearance), a reference, as it were, to the missing person who vanishes in accord with the Cubist principle of the fragmentary and the elusive.

In another collage of 1914, *The Teacups,* Gris alludes to the very technique of pasting papers. Here, a pair of before-and-after photographs of the statue of a lion on its plinth in the Place de la Concorde demonstrates, as the caption explains, "Une des conséquences de la loi restreignant l'affichage électoral" (one of the consequences of the law restricting the posting of electoral notices). The text of the article,[47] not included in Gris's clipping, actually went on to explain how the photograph at the left showed the statue in January 1889, during the electoral campaign between Jacques and General Boulanger, whereas that on the right showed the same statue just yesterday (i.e., 25 April 1914). The lesson was that the picturesqueness of these pasted posters may have been lost, but that beauty and cleanliness had certainly won. It is almost as if Gris jestingly suggested that henceforth the technique of Cubist collage was to be a subversive activity, not only made illegal by the new law, but aesthetically condemned as ugly and untidy.[48] And in yet another collage of 1914, Gris offers perhaps his wittiest newspaper clipping of all. A faceless gentleman is concealed behind a newspaper, LE MATIN, and a glass of beer, evoking perhaps the sinister mystery associated with that famous fictional detective Fantômas, so popular in Paris at the time, thanks to Marcel Allain and Pierre Souvestre's book (1911) and the cinema serial made from it by Louis Feuillade.[49] The article that faces us bears out this allusion to criminology. Entitled "Bertillonnage: On ne truquera plus les oeuvres d'art," it refers to the famous French criminologist, Alphonse Bertillon, who had devised a new system that would prevent forgeries. The small print, only partially included by Gris, goes on to propose that artists fingerprint their own works, so that authentic works could be distinguished from forgeries by criminological methods, an idea approved, so the newspaper reported, by such painters and sculptors as Harpignies, Bonnat, and Rodin. The article went on further to include a diagram of fingerprints, a fact which may well have stimulated Gris's idea of permitting the naturalistically drawn fingers of the invisible man to make their imprint, as it were, on the front of the newspaper as a kind of mock signature.[50]

The very idea of true and false works of art and true and false signatures could hardly have been more timely to the Cubist milieu.[51] Indeed, in the same year, 1914, Gris was sharp-eyed enough to find his own name in LE JOURNAL as part of a headline, and used it comically as a mock signature that might have unsettled Bertillon's criminological methods (fig. 6.5).[52] But it was Picasso, above all, who experimented with the typographical jokes and disguises potential to a signature in a Cubist work of art. It should be remembered, to begin with, that in the period 1908–13, Picasso, like Braque, almost never signed his Cubist pictures on the front side, presumably to underline their anonymity. When such a signature does, in fact, appear on the front of a Cubist picture it generally has been added by Picasso at a much later date in order to authenticate it.[53] But given this voluntary proscription of traditional signatures, Picasso began to find Cubist fictions that could reintroduce his signatory identity in as unexpectedly witty and stealthy ways as his surreptitious references to Eva in the guise of the song phrase "Ma jolie." In a tiny, oval still life, probably dating from spring 1912,[54] Picasso painted a letter with a handwritten inscription, "Monsieur Picasso, 11 Bd. de Clichy, Paris," which functions, with typical Cubist double entendre, as both an imitation of a real letter addressed to the artist and the artist's own handwritten signature.[55] Perhaps, too, it was the same impulse to break the facade of pictorial anonymity in 1911–12 that may help to explain Picasso's occasional choice, at this time of his and Braque's greatest stylistic convergence, of specifically Spanish motifs: Spanish words, references to the bull fight, and in one case, even the bright red and yellow Spanish flag, which forms a background to the bullring phrase SOL Y SOMBRA.[56]

By 1914, however, Picasso once more began to sign his pictures in an explicit way, except that now, in many cases, his signature was the subject of the same kind of metamorphoses which characterized his Cubist treatment of other objects and typographical elements. In one such work, his signature reappears in the unexpected role of a mock printed label, affixed to a frame as mock as the rope frame on the first collage. This, in turn, encloses a matting of speckled paper, upon which is illusionistically affixed a small still life drawing which casts a mock shadow. Like Pirandello's *Six Characters in Search of an Author,* this collage keeps juggling layers of artistic illusion, which here reach their most ambiguous point in the *trompe-l'oeil* nameplate. Together with the decorative paper border, which parodies the baroque carved frame of a traditional masterpiece, the nameplate ennobles, as if in a museum display, the modest little Cubist still life of pipe and music score (again "Ma jolie"). And as a further complication, the printing on the nameplate, though nominally

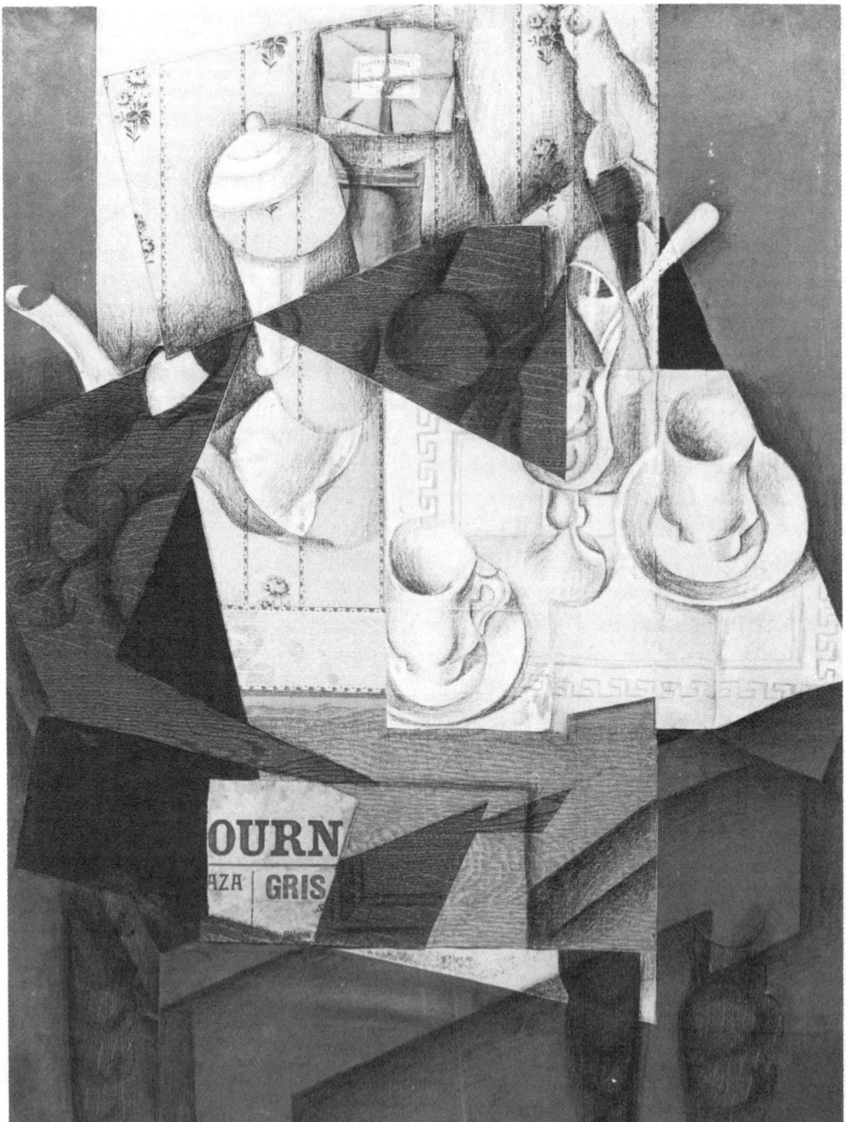

Figure 6.5. Juan Gris, *Breakfast*, 1914
Pasted paper, crayon, and oil on canvas,
31⅞″ × 23½″.
(Collection, The Museum of Modern Art, New York. Acquired through the Lillie P. Bliss Bequest)

impersonal in its block letters, is nevertheless sufficiently irregular to suggest that it, unlike the decorative frame, is handmade, not machinemade, so that all facts and fictions are cast into doubt. And later, in 1918, Picasso added still another level of complication by signing the *trompe-l'oeil* name plate on a little still life not with impersonal block letters, but rather with his usual personal signature, a hand-painted flourish underlined and followed by the date, 18.[57] Such ideas, in fact, even preceded Cubism; for already before 1900, Picasso had made many casual drawings that included *trompe-l'oeil* frames and labels, as in the case of a portrait drawing of his friend Hermen Anglada, presented within a pseudo-frame whose prominent inscriptions identify both the sitter and the artist.

The aggrandizement of a Cubist still life to the pretensions of framed and labelled museum pieces must have seemed at the time a particularly ironic joke, for Picasso could hardly have suspected then that one day his modest studio experiments would, indeed, be publicly displayed and esteemed in the company of earlier masterpieces of Western painting. The joke, in fact, was shared by other Cubists. For example, Braque, in his *Music* of 1914, enclosed a still life in an irregular, biomorphic frame, outside of which he added a *trompe-l'oeil* nameplate that also functions, like Picasso's, as both an official museum label and (since it is handmade) a mock signature and equally confounds the proper boundaries of the work of art.[58] Gris, too, was later to explore the joke in 1917, when he enclosed a Cubist still life with an elaborate *trompe-l'oeil* frame, at the top of whose arced grey boundaries are inscribed, as if by machine, the artist's name and the date of the work: JUAN GRIS 12–17. Again, the frame and the label are, so to speak, both inside and outside the picture, and the signature itself is both true (having been made by the artist's own hand) and false (having been imitated from an impersonal inscription made by a machine).

An even more complex example of mistaken identities in Cubist signatures may be found in a work of 1914 by the Mexican master Diego Rivera, who was then part of the Cubist milieu in Paris. Included in a Cubist still life of a glass and carafe is a real telegram received by the artist, with his name and address (16 rue du Départ) handwritten by an anonymous postal clerk, presumably with the *trompe-l'oeil* fountain pen (then a new invention) that hovers beside it. In contrast to this "signature" of the artist, hastily scrawled in ink by someone else, is another signature, this time drawn by the artist himself on the table's rounded edge, as if carved in wood in impersonal block letters. The Cubist delight in confounding identities reaches a baffling climax here, for the overtly impersonal, printed signature is, in fact, the true one, made by the artist's own hand, whereas the overtly personal, handmade one is, in fact, the false one, made by a stranger.

The idea of a signature that could mimic styles of writing other than the artist's own appealed particularly to Picasso. Even before 1900, first as a child and then as a prodigious young artist in Madrid and Barcelona, Picasso made endlessly imaginative and abundant doodles in which he experimented with all manner of monogram and signature, ranging from lettering styles that echoed the inventive new shapes of Art Nouveau typography to those that mimicked the traditional elegance of cursive script.[59] In the Cubist years, this precocious diversity was revived and expanded, not only by signatures in the form of a nameplate, but also by signatures in the form of a calling card. In one example, a still life of ca. 1914,[60] a papery plane with a dog-eared upper right-hand corner has the artist's name stencilled upon it, continuing in the realm of signatures Picasso's earlier use of stencilled letters to suggest the more impersonal realm of posters and newspapers.[61] Here, the artist's traditional hand-written flourish is transposed to stencilled lettering that seems to be stamped upon a calling card, which is then dropped upon the table with the other still life objects. That the card is dog-eared suggests, according to traditional rules of etiquette, that the owner of the card has paid a personal visit, but found no one at home.[62]

The same kind of wit (used as well by the Futurist Carlo Carrà after a visit to Paris in 1914)[63] could be applied to the calling cards of Picasso's friends. Already in spring 1912, Picasso translated the fact of a friend's visit into a pictorial fiction. According to Gertrude Stein,[64] she and Alice B. Toklas visited Picasso in his new studio on the Rue Ravignan; but finding him not at home, she left her calling card there, only to discover a few days later that Picasso was working on a painting which included the card on the lower right-hand corner of a table.[65] This hand-painted illusion of a calling card, inscribed by Picasso MIS [*sic*] GERTRUDE STEIN, was to be transformed, two years later, into a real calling card in a still life of 1914. This time, the story is even more complicated, at least according to Miss Toklas,[66] who recounted that she and Gertrude Stein, again finding Picasso not at home, left a dog-eared calling card to signify their visit. Picasso then stripped off the real folded corner, and, replacing it with a *trompe-l'oeil* fold, included it in a still life of a die and a package of cigarettes. To compound the irony, so prophetic of the switched identities that later would characterize Miss Stein's Cubist idea of writing her own autobiography in the guise of Miss Toklas's autobiography, Picasso then left the still life for Miss Stein and Miss Toklas at 27 rue de Fleurus as a kind of Cubist calling card in which the identity of the original owners had been completely absorbed, as it were, by the identity of Picasso and his art.[67]

In another example of 1914, Picasso used the actual calling card of André Level (a dealer and the author of a book on Picasso published in

1928). Here, in a manner rivalling Diego Rivera's confusion of signatory identities, the card provides the typographical stimulus for Picasso's own signature (in the lower right-hand corner), which imitates the elegant italic type used for the printing of Level's name. Indeed, this joke of handwriting, in which the artist's handmade signature mimics the elegance of a name printed on a calling card, occurs often in Picasso's work of 1914[68] (as well as in the work of Braque[69] and the Futurist Gino Severini;[70] and once, quite explicitly, Picasso signs his name in a cursive script upon an illusionistic piece of paper that suggests an analogy in typeface and shape to a real calling card.[71]

The chameleon guises of Picasso's signatures in these works enormously enriched the Cubist idea of the artist as a kind of actor-magician, who could suddenly appear in surprising roles within the shifting realities of his own pictorial stage. Moreover, these various kinds of handwriting and typefaces correspond to the characteristic Cubist insistence that no one way of representing a thing was absolute. Indeed, just as Picasso explored a wide variety of illusionistic and symbolic means to represent Cubist figures, landscapes, and still life objects, so, too, did he compile, as it were a typographical dictionary that similarly provided the multiple means of representing words in art. If in actual writing techniques he could range from the hand-painted to the hand-drawn, from the stencilled to the machine-printed, in choice of writing style he could be equally diverse. Thus, the words in his Cubist years not only appear in the guise of roman and italic type, in their many variations, but at times extend to less familiar typefaces and even alphabets.

In one case, this pleasure in exploring diverse ways of representing words led him to include a phrase written with the Russian alphabet. Kahnweiler recalls that several of Picasso's pictures which had been on loan at an exhibition in Moscow organized by the "Jack of Diamonds" Group were returned carefully wrapped in Russian posters.[72] Picasso was sufficiently fascinated with these Russian words to incorporate them into a Cubist picture of music-making: a woman strumming a stringed instrument. Characteristically, Picasso was interested not only in the formal patterns of the Russian letters, but in their meaning; in fact, according to Gertrude Stein, Picasso, about this time, had troubled to learn the Russian alphabet from his Russian friends, the painter Serge Férat (called G. Apostrophe) and his sister the Baronne d'Oettingen (called Roche Grey).[73] For, the words he has copied from the poster—БОЛ . . . КОНЦЕРТ—are taken from the phrase transliterated as BOLSHOI CONCERT, i.e., the announcement of a "big concert," which is perfectly appropriate to the musical subject at hand as well as being a phrase used in French (*grand concert*) in other Cubist works.[74]

But even within the customary range of Western script, Picasso was endlessly curious about typographical variety. In a painting of 1911, the Cubist hieroglyphs that include a flower in a vase, a fan, and a wine glass are brusquely juxtaposed with a daily newspaper, whose bisected name, *L'Indépendant,* is surprising not only in its sudden legibility within a nearly illegible pictorial vocabulary, but in its use of as old-fashioned and picturesque a typeface as Gothic within this avant-garde pictorial context. Moreover, Picasso's eye was constantly alert to the lesser variations of typeface invented in modern advertising.[75] Thus, when he included a packet of cigarette papers in his Cubist still lifes and identified the brand as JOB, he was careful to imitate in the lettering the lozenge-shaped "O" that still characterizes the product (fig. 6.6).[76] Indeed, Picasso's scrutiny of such typographical variants must have been stimulated in good part by the innovations of commercial art and, in particular, the posters of La Belle Epoque, which provided him and his fellow Cubists in Paris with a ubiquitous visual environment.[77] Thus, in a typical *fin-de-siècle* poster design for JOB by Jane Atché, not only does one find at the lower right-hand corner the distinguishing letter forms that label the product and that recur in Picasso's still life, but any number of other variations on typographical styles, right down to the Picasso-like contrast of the artist's signatory flourish with the roman letters above. Moreover, such posters often explored a wide variety of visual tricks that prophesy Cubist techniques—the *trompe-l'oeil* shadows cast by the letters JOB below, or the spatial intertwining of the chiffonlike smoke with the perfectly flat letters JOB above.

In this context, it should be remembered that already in the late nineteenth century—witness Toulouse-Lautrec, Denis, Bonnard, Vuillard—ambitious painters had been involved in poster design and had become increasingly aware of the role of words and lettering in their art, and that the Cubist generation was an heir to this tradition. Like Gris, who made book illustrations and newspaper drawings both as a youth in Madrid and in his pre-Cubist years in Paris,[78] not to mention such other artists as Villon, Duchamp, and Marcoussis, who also were to belong to the Cubist milieu,[79] Picasso, in his early years, was often obliged to leave the art-for-art's-sake ambiance of the studio for the practical realities of commercial illustration[80] and, in fact, remained throughout his life one of the masters of modern poster design.[81] Thus, looked at from the point of view of Cubism, even so modest and youthful a design as the menu card Picasso designed about 1898 for the Barcelona café Els Quatre Gats[82] offers prophecies of the more intricate juggling of words and images that abound in the Cubist years. Here, the more traditional illustrative techniques that describe the casual stance of the waiter, bottle in one hand, platter in the other, are contrasted with the flattening letters of the name

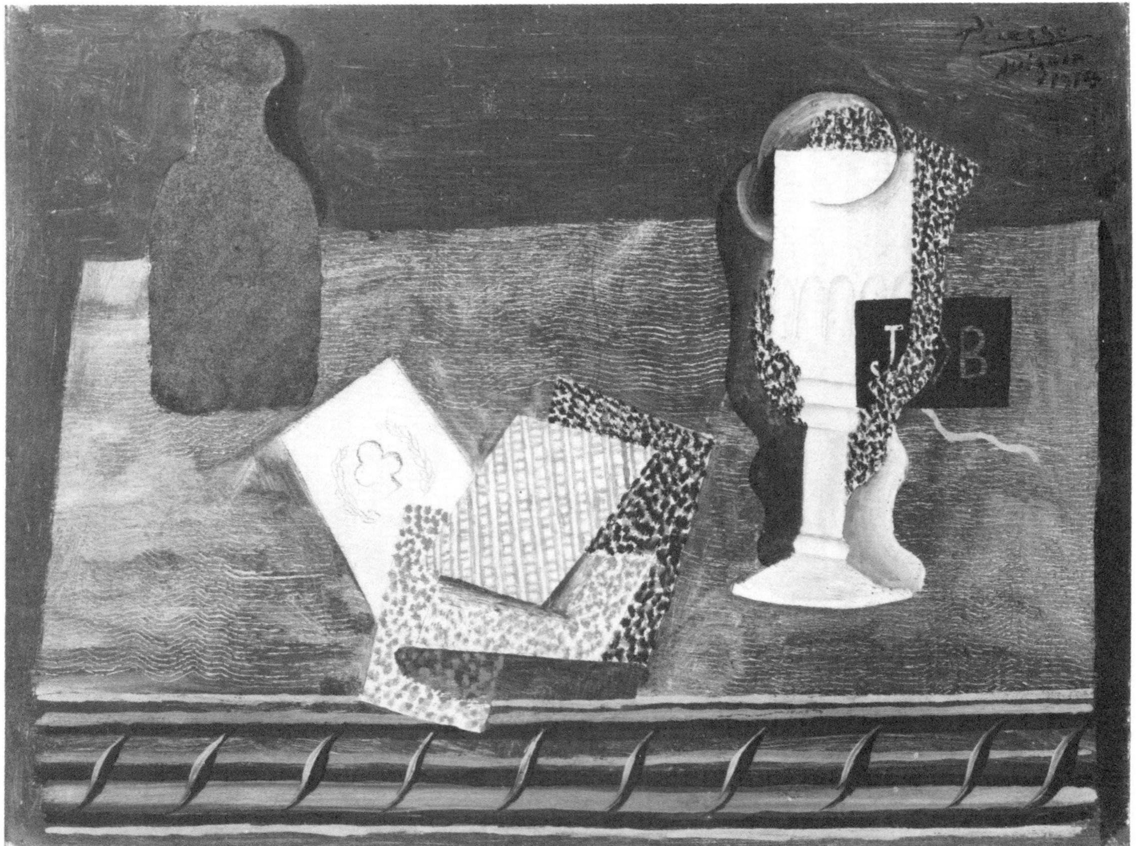

Figure 6.6. Pablo Picasso, *Still Life: Bottle, Playing Cards, and Wine Glass on a Table,* Summer 1914
Oil on panel, 12⅜″ × 16⅞″.
(Philadelphia Museum of Art. A. E. Gallatin Collection)

of the café—4 GATS—and the weightless announcement of the PLAT DEL DIA (plat du jour), whose identification presumably would have been inscribed in the empty frame below. Indeed, just such a potpourri of letters, whether printed or handwritten, and varying degrees of illustrative description, from the naturalistic to the schematic, recurs constantly in the Cubist years, and even, at times, in the context of what might be called Cubist menu cards. Thus, the Barcelona menu card is brought up to date in several Cubist still lifes where Picasso displays the typographical repertory to be found at any restaurant table. In two such works, Picasso reproduces the Art Nouveau lettering of the word RESTAURANT itself, floating in the background as if seen on a window, and then, in the foreground, presents the diner with a flurry of words, numbers, and scripts that range from the block letters of a bottle of *moutarde de Dijon* or the word MENU itself to the handwritten word fragments *boeu(f), veau, trip(es), 40 (centimes)* that describe the *carte du jour.* Amid this profusion of letters, Picasso then juxtaposes the more palpable facts of the table: a more illusionistic rendering of a knife and fork against, in one case, a roast chicken, in the other, a ham.[83] Or, on the contrary, are these Cubist still life objects less real than the letters and numbers, which can suddenly seem so literal a record of prosaic visual truths?

Surprisingly, then, such Cubist still lifes can be thought of not only as inhabiting the private, cerebral world of an artist's ivory tower, but also as exploring the most ordinary printed, handwritten, stencilled, pasted typographical facts experienced by any twentieth-century urban man. Thus, the familiar assertion that Picasso is always a realist may not even demand, for the Cubist years, so abstract or metaphysical an interpretation of realism as is often attempted. For not only do the words that proliferate in Cubist art enrich intellectually the ambiguous formal language of Cubism with equally ambiguous verbal double entendres, but they also establish, with startling vividness, Cubism's connections with the new imagery of the modern world. Like Apollinaire in his epic poem *Zone* (1913), Picasso embraced the realism of the printed word that abounded in the city. When Apollinaire sings the praises of "prospectuses, catalogues, posters," of "newspapers and cheap detective stories," of "inscriptions on walls, street signs, name plates, notices,"[84] he might almost be cataloguing the very repertory of printed matter that stimulated Picasso and his fellow Cubists. In this light, the Cubist sensibility to the kaleidoscopic assault of words and advertising images to be found in the most commonplace urban situations represents the first full-scale absorption into high art of the typographical environment of our century. So important was this insight that the consequences—from the social aggressiveness of words in Futurism and Dada to the aesthetic ironies of commercial imagery in Pop Art—are still to be assessed.[85]

Notes

This article is a considerably revised and amplified version of a lecture, "The Typography of Cubism," first given at a meeting of the College Art Association of America in Los Angeles, 28 January 1965, and subsequently repeated in many universities and museums in the United States and England. The idea that the choice of words in Cubist art could involve intentional puns and jokes seems to have been largely a product of the growingly nonformalist interpretation of Cubism common to the 1960s. In my own *Cubism and Twentieth-Century Art* (New York, 1960), I made several such suggestions (e.g., pp. 64, 72, 96, 121). Other examples were offered in Harriet Janis and Rudi Blesh, *Collage: Personalities, Concepts, Techniques,* (Philadelphia, 1962) pp. 18ff., although most of these—from the reference to upside-down nickelodeon slides in Picasso's first *papier collé* (1908; Christian Zervos, *Pablo Picasso: Oeuvres,* 33 vols. [Paris: Cahiers d'Art, 1932-] 2: 66), where the words AU LOUVRE are inverted, to the pun on "du Louvre" in the Spanish word fragment DILUV (Zervos, 2: 348)—may strike one as somewhat farfetched. Subsequent studies of Cubism have tended to be increasingly open to these possibilities. See, e.g., Edward Fry, *Cubism* (New York, 1966), pp. 29, 31; Nicholas Wadley, *Cubism* (London, 1970), pp. 80–82; as well as the catalogue entries by George Downing and Daniel Robbins on Gris and Picasso in *The Herbert and Nanette Rothschild Collection* (Providence, Rhode Island School of Design, 1966). Recently, I have been able to consult an unpublished Master of Arts thesis at Columbia University, which deals with a major theme of my own essay: J. Charlat Murray, *Picasso's Use of Newspaper Clippings in His Early Collages,* 1967. Inevitably, many of the examples and interpretations coincide with those in my lecture and in the present essay, although the range of allusions in Miss Murray's readings of Cubist words tends to be more speculative than mine. I have tried to acknowledge, in notes, the new material in her thesis that I have found relevant to my own arguments. After my own article was completed in 1971, I was able to share its specific contents and general ideas with William Rubin during the preparation of his admirable catalogue, *Picasso in the Collection of the Museum of Modern Art* (New York, 1972). In his analyses of the use of words in specific works by Picasso, he has been kind enough to acknowledge his debts to this article and astute enough to make many fresh observations of his own.

1. The most lucid analysis of Cubist words and collage elements from a purely formal viewpoint is Clement Greenberg, "The Pasted-Paper Revolution," *Art News* 67 (1958): 46–49.

2. For a conspicuous example, see Zervos, *Picasso,* 2: 348, where the Barcelona newspaper, *El Diluvio,* is clearly dated 31 March 1913, but the catalogue caption dates the work "printemps 1912." I have discussed this and other dating problems related to the newspaper clippings in Rosenblum, "Picasso and the Coronation of Alexander III: A Note on the Dating of Some *Papiers Collés, Burlington Magazine* 113 (October 1971): 604–6.

3. Zervos, 2: 406.

4. Zervos, 2: 765.

5. Zervos, 2: 729; 3: 118, 142, 293.

6. Zervos, 2: 339.

7. Zervos, 2: 335. This issue of *Le Figaro* is, exceptionally, an old one, dated 28 May 1883. For more on Picasso's use of this old newspaper, see Rosenblum, "Picasso and the Coronation."

8. Zervos, 2: 348.

9. Zervos, 2: 461. Another collage that uses *Lacerba* is not included in Zervos. It is, however, illustrated in H. Wescher, *Die Collage* (Cologne, 1968), pl. 16.

10. Braque and Gris, incidentally, considerably enlarged Picasso's repertory of newspapers by including *Le Courrier, Le Petit Eclaireur, L'Echo d'Alger, Le Réveil, Le Matin, Gil Blas,* etc.

11. The only exception I have found to this rule is Zervos, 6: 1239, a small watercolor there dated 1914 or 1915.

12. The *calligrammes* and other poem-images by Apollinaire are now most conveniently anthologized in Michel Décaudin, ed., *Oeuvres complètes de Guillaume Apollinaire* (Paris, 1966), vol. 3.

13. See, for example, Jacob's puns on the phrase "les ménages déménagent," discussed in Jean Rousselot, *Max Jacob au sérieux* ([Rodez], 1958), pp. 170ff. More on this is included in Gerald Kamber, *Max Jacob and the Poetics of Cubism* (Baltimore, 1971).

14. See the catalogue, *An Exhibition . . . of the Works of Man Ray* (London: Institute of Contemporary Arts, 1959), unpaginated.

15. For the question of the date of this work, see Rosenblum, "Picasso and the Coronation," p. 604.

16. On the dating of this first collage, see ibid., note 9. It should be added that, although this work is considered to inaugurate the collage period of Cubism, Picasso had earlier, in 1908, used a piece of pasted paper on a drawing (Zervos, 2: 66).

17. The skull was an important motif in the first conception of the *Demoiselles d'Avignon,* where a figure holding a skull was seen entering a brothel (Zervos, 2: 19), but it was then eliminated. It recurs however in two still lifes of 1907 (Zervos, 2: 49, 50).

18. The point is already made in Rosenblum, *Cubism and Twentieth-Century Art,* p. 96; repeated in N. Wadley, *Cubism,* p. 80.

19. Mallarmé's poem was first published in *Cosmopolis* (May 1897): 417–28; and then republished separately (Paris, 1914) at the peak of the Cubist artistic and literary movement.

20. A die is found, for example, in Zervos, 2: 469, 490, 501, 512, 525, 789, 830, 832–38, 840, 847, 852.

21. The tradition of using poster announcements in Cubist art would seem to begin with Braque's *The Portuguese* of spring 1911, with its stenciled letters (GRAND)D BAL, and Picasso's *Still Life on a Piano* (Zervos, 2: 728), which also uses a stencilled poster fragment CORT(OT), presumably announcing a concert by that pianist. For the problem of the date of the Picasso, see below, note 61.

22. See also Rosenblum, "Picasso at the Philadelphia Museum of Art," *Bulletin, Philadelphia Museum of Art* (January–March, 1967): 183.

23. Mondrian's use of this advertisement and its precedent in Picasso's work are discussed in Robert P. Welsh, *Piet Mondrian, 1872–1944* (The Art Gallery of Toronto, 1966), pp. 144, 146. Douglas Cooper (*The Cubist Epoch* [London 1970], p. 106) has also suggested that the spelling KUB may have influenced the Parisian tendency to refer to "le Cubisme" as "Der Kubismus," i.e., something foreign and German.

24. See Pierre Cabanne, *L'Epopée du Cubisme* (Paris 1963), pp. 147–48.

25. As pointed out in John Richardson, ed., *Picasso: An American Tribute* (New York: The Public Education Association, 1962) ''Cubism,'' no. 7.

26. The other two are Zervos, 2: 312, 734. Zervos dates the latter of these winter 1911–12, but its similarity to the other two and, above all, to the rope-framed first collage (Zervos, 2: 294) suggests that they must all date from the same time, spring 1912.

27. The connection between the aeronautics slogan and Picasso's comments on his and Braque's interest in the making of aeroplanes as analogous to the making of Cubist constructions (as well as Picasso's reference to Braque as ''mon cher Vilbure'') was first made by Roland Penrose (*Picasso: His Life and Work* [London, 1958], p. 161). It is repeated in Cooper, *The Cubist Epoch*, p. 59.
    It should be added that the aeronautics motif was aggrandized in the Cubist mileu by La Fresnaye's *Conquest of the Air* (1913) and Delaunay's *Homage to Blériot* (1914), and that, in at least one case, a watercolor still life of 1915, with an aeroplane viewed through a window, Picasso was to refer more literally to aviation. (Illustrated in J. Richardson, Cubism, no. 24.)

28. The newspaper clipping comes from *Le Journal*, 3 December 1912, p. 5.

29. In other paintings by Gris, both of 1912, two other facets and syllable combinations of a DUBONNET matchholder are seen: (a) DU (illustrated in D.-H. Kahnweiler, *Juan Gris: His Life and Work* (rev. ed.), [New York, 1969], p. 23) and (b) DUBON (illustrated in James Thrall Soby, *Juan Gris* [New York, 1958], p. 17). It should be added that a modern advertisement for DUBONNET uses a comparable series of puns (DU, DU BON, DUBONNET) and may have existed, in a similar form, earlier in the century. If so, it would offer yet another case of the confluence of commercial imagery and Cubist art.
    Marcoussis, too, included verbal fragments of the alcohol brand names found on matchholders, as in *Le Pyrogène ''Quinquina''* (1912) and *Le Pyrogène ''Byrrh''* (1914), illustrated in Jean Lafranchis, *Marcoussis, sa vie, son oeuvre* (Paris, 1961), p. 22, pl. 30.

30. Zervos, 2: 366, 372.

31. Zervos, 2: 413.

32. Zervos, 2: 772.

33. Zervos, 2: 786.

34. I believe the first writer to pinpoint this reference was Maurice Jardot, in his exemplary catalogue, *Picasso* (Paris; Musée des Arts Décoratifs, 1955), no. 26.

35. Zervos, 2: 244. It is there dated ''printemps 1911,'' although its style has suggested to later chroniclers of Cubism a somewhat later date, i.e., winter 1911–12.

36. See also Rosenblum, *Cubism and Twentieth-Century Art*, pp. 64ff.

37. Contrary to what Stravinsky thought, the song was copyright by its composer, Emile Spencer, to whom royalties on performances of *Petrouchka* then had to be paid. For further details, see Eric Walter White, *Stravinsky: The Composer and His Works* (Berkeley and Los Angeles, 1966), p. 162, note 10.

38. '' . . . et je l'aime beaucoup et je l'écrirai sur mes tableaux.'' (Quoted by M. Jardot, *Picasso*, no. 30, and often repeated by subsequent writers.) For further comments on ''Eva'' see R. Penrose, *Picasso, His Life and Work*, pp. 169–70. Gertrude Stein also discloses

the identity of "Ma jolie" in reference to the inscription in a still life of spring 1912 (Zervos, 2: 321), (*The Autobiography of Alice B. Toklas* [New York, 1933], p. 136).

39. Zervos, 2: 352, 364.

40. The frequency of this phrase is even greater than the nine examples cited by Jardot (*Picasso,* no. 26). It is found in Zervos, 2: 244, 306, 321, 341, 351, 445, 446, 503, 505, 525, 526, 527.

41. The collage was often dated 1913, although research in a periodical room would have disclosed that the newspaper clipping from *Le Matin* is dated 12 May 1914.

42. Published in London by Elkin Matthews.

43. That this particular clipping might be relevant to the imagery of the work was first suggested briefly by Lawrence Alloway ("Against Picasso," *Art International* 4, no. 8 [25 October 1960], p. 46, note).

44. The newspaper clipping comes from an account in *Le Journal,* 3 May 1914, of the explosion of the dirigible "L'Adjutant-Reau" near Verdun.

45. A related example here would be his use of the upper half of a clipping about a "train volant," whose aerial wires are just visible and contribute to the Cubist sense of a new airborne realm in tune with the twentieth century. On this collage, see the exhibition catalogue, *The Herbert and Nannette Rothschild Collection,* no. 60 and unpaginated notes on Gris.

46. See also Rosenblum, *Cubism and Twentieth-Century Art,* p. 121.

47. The clipping is taken from *Le Matin,* 26 April 1914. The text reads: "Un des lions de la Place de la Condorde en janvier 1889, à l'époque de la lutte électorale entre Jacques et le Général Boulanger. Le même (à droite) photographié hier. Le pittoresque y a perdu, mais l'esthétique et la propreté y ont certainement gagné."

48. The irony of this clipping in a collage context has also been commented on briefly by E. Fry, p. 31; and Nicholas Wadley, *Cubism,* p. 81.

49. The masked emblem of Fantômas is even included in a Gris still life of 1915 (illustrated in Kahnweiler, *Juan Gris,* p. 261). Kahnweiler, in fact, comments on Gris's fascination with this fictional detective (ibid., p. 49). For further references to the importance of Fantômas in the Cubist mileu, see J. Charlat Murray, *Picasso's Use of Newspaper Clippings,* p. 54.

50. The full article, of which Gris provides only a provocative fragment, can be read in *Le Matin,* 3 February 1914. Bertillon, incidentally, died only ten days later (13 February), a fact which might have made the inclusion of this article in Gris's papier collé all the more topical.

51. A brief reference to the general relevance of this headline, "On ne truquera plus . . . ," to Cubism is also made by Wadley.

52. I believe this joke was first pointed out in print by Thomas Hess ("Paste Mixed with Paint," *ARTnews* 47 [October 1948]: 25, caption).

53. For a succinct and informative discussion of the problem of Picasso's signatures during the Cubist period, see Maurice Jardot's "Note sur les signatures de Picasso et les titres de ses tableaux" in the indispensable catalogue, *Picasso* (Paris: Musée des Arts Décoratifs, 1955), in the unpaginated section "Documents." The question of signatures in Cubist art was raised earlier by Kahnweiler, pp. 124–25.

54. Zervos dates it winter 1911–12, but in view of its similarity to such other oval still lifes as Picasso's first collage (Zervos, 2: 294), also misdated by Zervos winter 1911–12, and now generally dated no earlier than May 1912 (see above, note 16), it is probably to be advanced in time. The address on the painting, however—11 Bd. de Clichy—provides a *terminus ante quen,* since Picasso left that address on his return from Sorgues in October 1912.

55. An idea similar to this painting of a letter may be found earlier in a drawing of 1911 which inscribes a palette with: PICASSO, ARTISTE PEINTRE, 11 BD. DE CLICHY, PARIS (Zervos, 6: 1134). See also the painted letter in Marcoussis's *Nature morte à l'échiquier* (1912), illustrated in J. Lafranchis, *Marcoussis,* p. 23.

56. The other Spanish word fragments include: (PUBLI)CIDAD, DON, and BARCE (LONA). For other Spanish allusions in Picasso's Cubist works, see Zervos, 2: 319 (with the inscription ENTR(EE) AUX AREN(ES)); 362 (the so-called *Aficionado,* with its reference to the bullfight periodical, *Le Torero,* and to Nîmes, a city whose arena is still used for bullfights); and 348 (with the clipping from the Barcelona newspaper, *El Diluvio*). For more on Picasso and Spain during the Cubist years, see the sections on Céret in Josep Palau i Fabre, *Picasso en Cataluña* (Barcelona, 1966), pp. 160ff.

Gris, too, may have wished to suggest obliquely his Spanish identity, not only by the inclusion in his still lifes of such alcohols as Jerez de la Frontera and Anis del Mono, but by such overtly Spanish subjects as the *Torero* of 1913, illustrated in Kahnweiler, p. 47.

57. For other related works, with mock frame and nameplate, see Zervos, 2: 478, 500, 552. Picasso also signed, in his natural handwriting, the illusionistic borders around many still lifes of 1917–19 (e.g., Zervos, 3: 102, 121, 140, 367; 6: 1411, 1432).

58. See also Rosenblum, *Cubism,* p. 98, where a parallel in Duchamp's work is indicated. It should be added that Braque used a *trompe-l'oeil* nameplate in other works, the earliest of which seems to be the *Still Life, Sorgues,* dated, without explanation, 1912/14 in the exhibition catalogue, *The Herbert and Nannette Rothschild Collection,* no. 18. Perhaps the mock frame, with the nameplate, postdates by two years the picture within it. For a later example by Braque, see *Still Life with Fruit Dish and Guitar* (1917), illustrated in John Richardson, *Georges Braque,* Penguin Modern Painters. (1959), pl. 14.

59. The Museo Picasso, Barcelona, contains dozens of examples of these calligraphic variations on the theme of the artist's own signature, beginning with the elegant inscriptions on the pages of his schoolboy's Latin grammar books of 1891–92 and continuing with countless typographical inventions and imitations that even include replicas of his artist-father's signature.

60. The date of 1914 is Zervos's, although the many overlapping transparencies and chiaroscuro effects suggest that the date may be more convincingly located in 1913.

61. Presumably, the first example of the use of stencilled letters in Picasso's work is Zervos, 2: 728, with the inscription CORT (for the pianist Cortot?). Zervos dates this winter 1910–11, but Jardot contends, to my eye correctly, that on stylistic grounds, it must be no earlier than spring 1911 (*Picasso,* no. 23). Such a dating raises the question already posed by Rosalind Krauss in her review of the exhibition, "The Cubist Epoch" (*Artforum* 9 [February 1971]: 35), of whether Braque's use of stencilled letters in *The Portuguese* precedes (as is generally claimed) or follows Picasso's.

Picasso's use of a stencilled signature was also taken up by Diego Rivera, who stencilled his initials on paintings in 1914, and by Jacques Villon, who, as late as 1924 (*The Jockey*), stencilled his entire name on a painting. The inclusion of stencilled letters in paintings was most recently revived with the greatest invention by Jasper Johns.

62. The refinements of the situation are explained in such a standard French etiquette book as La Baronne Staffe, *Règles du Savoir-Vivre dans la Société Moderne,* 15th ed. (Paris, 1890), p. 224: "La corne signifie qu'on est venu en personne et, dans ce cas elle équivaut à une visite, qui doit être rendue comme si elle avait été reçue."

63. In the *Sintesi circolare di oggetti,* reproduced and discussed in Marianne W. Martin, *Futurist Art and Theory, 1909–1915* (Oxford, 1968), fig. 192 and pp. 192–93. (For a more legible reproduction, in color, see H. Wescher, *Die Collage,* p. 67.) The inscription on the calling card reads: C. D. Carra, Pittore Futurista, Milano. Prof. Martin suggests that the tilting of the card and wine glass against the siphon allude to a bout of drunkenness. In any case, the intersection of the plane of the siphon and the upper right-hand corner of the calling card creates the effect of a dog-eared card.

64. The incident is recounted in G. Stein, *The Autobiography of Alice B. Toklas* (New York, 1933), p. 136, a reference kindly called to my attention by Miss Margaret Potter.

65. For further comments on this painting and its title, see *Four Americans in Paris; the Collection of Gertrude Stein and Her Family* (New York: The Museum of Modern Art, 1970), p. 171. This painting, incidentally, is misidentified in Jaime Sabartès, *Picasso; documents iconographiques,* (Geneva, 1954), fig. 194 and pp. 329–30, as the work Picasso executed on a wall of the villa *Les Clochettes* at Sorgues and then had transferred to canvas. This wall decoration, which a M. Couturier remembered as containing a mandolin, a musical score inscribed "Ma Jolie," and a bottle of Pernod, is to be identified rather with Zervos, 2: 351.

66. The story is told in Edward Burns, ed., *Gertrude Stein on Picasso* (New York, 1970), in the unpaginated catalogue.

67. For another complex example in Picasso's work of this kind of double identity, see Zervos, 2: 493, a curious quartet of still lifes (1914), of which the two on the left are by Picasso and the two on the right by Derain. But in the still life with playing cards in the lower left-hand corner, Picasso has painted a stamped letter addressed by hand to André Derain. This suggestion of Derain's signature is all the more paradoxical since it occurs in the painting executed by Picasso rather than in the adjacent painting, executed by Derain.

68. See Zervos, 2: 454, 457, 787. There are other signatures of this year that stand more ambiguously between the cursive script and Picasso's usual signature (e.g., Zervos, 2: 469, 530), as if the natural and the artificial were being combined.

69. As in the italic signature on *The Musician* (1917–18), illustrated in J. Richardson, *Georges Braque,* pl. 13.

70. In Severini's *Portrait of Paul Fort,* the calling card of the poet, Fort, is pasted onto the canvas, and its italic type is imitated by Severini in the inscription in the lower right-hand corner. The work is illustrated in the catalogue, *Collagen* (Zurich: Kunstgewerbe Museum, 1968), p. 79, where it is misdated 1913, despite the date of December 1914 printed on one of the collage elements, the periodical *Poèmes de France.*

71. On this drawing, see also R. Rosenblum, "Picasso at the Philadelphia Museum," p. 183.

72. The story is recorded in an interview of Kahnweiler by Hélène Parmelin in *Picasso; oeuvres des Musées de Leningrad et de Moscou et de quelques collections parisiennes* (Paris, 1955), p. 20. I am grateful to Miss Margaret Potter for this and the following reference.

73. See Gertrude Stein, *The Autobiography of Alice B. Toklas* (New York, 1933), p. 195. The context suggests that this took place in the winter of 1914–15, although the picture in question is dated 1913–14 by Zervos. Since Férat had known Picasso in Paris since 1910, the Russian lesson may well have taken place somewhat earlier than implied by Stein's narrative.

74. The other letters and numbers (which offer a contrast in terms of the use of numbers and the Latin alphabet) are less easily read. The FRA refers perhaps to a price (francs), the 9½ to the time (i.e., 9½ heures).

75. This is fully as true of Gris, who, in a still life of 1915, even imitated the complex typographical variety on the labels of both a bottle of Bass and a package of Quaker Oats (illustrated in J. Soby, *Juan Gris,* p. 51), thereby providing a kind of Cubist prophecy of Andy Warhol's paintings of Campbell's soup cans.

76. A package of Job cigarette papers also turns up in a still life of 1916, not included in Zervos, but illustrated in J. Richardson, "Cubism," no. 27.
   It has been suggested by J. Charlat Murray (p. 26) that the references to JOB in Picasso's still lifes are also puns on Max Jacob's name.

77. For a useful survey of these French posters, see the exhibition catalogue, *Cent ans d'affiches: "La Belle Epoque"* (Paris: Bibliothèque des Arts Décoratifs, 1964).

78. See Soby, pp. 11–12. Gris's illustrations for José Santos Chocano's *Alma América—Poemas Indo-Españoles* (Madrid, 1906) and the Parisian humorous journal *L'Assiette au beurre* (to which he contributed from 1908 to 1910) offer a surprisingly large repertory of proto-Cubist ideas, ranging from flattening, geometric stylizations of figure drawing and eccentric perspective schemes to complex interplays of words and images.

79. Some of the newspaper illustrations of the young Cubists are discussed in Jean Adhémar, "Les journaux amusants et les premiers peintres cubistes," *L'Oeil* No. 4 (15 April 1955): 40–42.

80. See, for example, his illustrations for the Madrid periodical, *Arte Joven* (31 March 1901), most conveniently reproduced in Anthony Blunt and Phoebe Pool, *Picasso, the Formative Years: A Study of His Sources* (London, 1962), fig. 57. Here, as elsewhere, words and images are interwoven, including even the repetition of the title, *Arte Joven,* on the paper the woman is reading.

81. See Joseph K. Foster, *The Posters of Picasso* (New York, 1964).

82. This menu card was published for the first time in Blunt and Pool, and discussed in the caption for figs. 1–9.

83. The former still life with a chicken (Zervos, 2: 347) is dated by Zervos 1912, a date repeated in D. Duncan, p. 206. Nevertheless, the easy legibility of this still life, as well as its stylistic and thematic closeness to 534 (dated by Zervos 1914), suggest that it, too, should be dated 1914 rather than 1912.
   For an earlier, less legible example of such a restaurant still life, see Zervos, 2: 308 (1911–12), where a "pigeon aux petits pois" is presented against the inscription CAFE. For a later, more legible one, see Zervos, 2: 430 (1913), where a *papier collé* roast chicken (duck? goose?) is set against a drawn menu, wine glass, bottle, and knife.

84. This enumeration of urban printed matter comes from the following lines in Apollinaire's *Zone*:

> *Tu lis les prospectus les catalogues les affiches qui chantent tout haut*
> *Voilà la poésie ce matin et pout la prose il y a les journaux*
> *Il y a les livraisons à 25 centimes pleines d'aventures policières . . .*
> *Les inscriptions des enseignes et des murailles*
> *Les plaques les avis à la façon des perroquets criaillent . . .*

85. The realization that many formal and iconographic aspects of Cubism may be in good part inspired by commercial imagery seems to have been very slow in coming to historians and critics of the movement, but the advent of Pop Art in the early 1960s may have opened the possibility of such interpretations. For some preliminary comments in this direction, see N. Wadley, pp. 69ff.

7

Picasso's Collages and the Threat of War, 1912–1913

Patricia Leighten

Building on the work of Robert Rosenblum, Patricia Leighten explores the newsprint texts in Picasso's Cubist collages of 1912–13. She carefully delineates the anarchist and Symbolist milieu that "helped form Picasso's view of himself as an artist in society, his ideas about spontaneity and the inspiration of the artist, and about the virtues of 'unsophisticated' primitive art." For Leighten the newsprint in these Picasso collages, rather than being formal passages of color and texture, are, instead, a way to integrate anarchist issues into his art. Unlike a number of other critics writing on Picasso, Leighten alludes to Picasso as a political figure, struggling (in his words) "as a true revolutionary."

> *From 1905 on, one diplomatic crisis followed on another in rapid succession. The shock of Tangiers—as Péguy put it—within the space of . . . two hours introduced a new epoch in his own life, as it did in the history of his country and of the world. For the next decade the youth of Europe lived and breathed in an atmosphere of impending war.*
>
> H. Stuart Hughes, *Consciousness and Society: The Reorientation of European Social Thought, 1890–1930*

Anarchist ideas played a crucial role in Picasso's use of newsprint in his Cubist collages of 1912–13, not only influencing his choice and placement of news items but also inspiring the original act of introducing into his art, in the most literal way, the issues and events of the current Balkan

---

This article originally appeared in *The Art Bulletin* 67, no. 4 (December 1985). Reprinted by permission of the College Art Association of America, and by permission of the author.

wars. Picasso's early encounter with anarchism in the artistic circles of Barcelona and Paris had a profound impact on his development as an artist, and is an intrinsic part of the social and aesthetic background necessary to an understanding of his work prior to World War I. Picasso was not a doctrinaire anarchist with a program "hidden" in his work, but rather one of scores of artists of the 1890s and early 1900s inspired by the utopian visions of the larger libertarian movement, as it meshed with the international Symbolist movement in art and literature. Anarcho-Symbolist ideas helped form Picasso's view of himself as an artist in society, his ideas about spontaneity and the inspiration of the artist, and about the virtues of "unsophisticated" primitive art. The anarchists' social critique and romantic revolutionism also exerted a discernible influence on Picasso's early work—especially evident in the Blue Period—but was most articulately manifested in his early collages, both in style and, more surprisingly, in content.

Picasso's collages have traditionally been seen as his most highly abstract works. This has been due partly to our formalist bias, partly to Picasso's own desire to obfuscate his creative processes and his impatience with earnest inquiries concerning his "meaning." However, a close look at many of the newspaper clippings incorporated into the collages shows them to be not arbitrary bits of printed matter, nor mere signs designating themselves, but reports and accounts, meticulously cut and pasted to preserve legibility, of the events that heralded the approach of World War I and the anarchist and socialist response to them. Such reports represent more than half of the newsprint clippings in Picasso's collages of 1912–14, the years in which the body of his collages were made. (Another quarter introduces macabre accounts of suicide, murder, and vandalism, which accumulate to depict, with the blackest humor, a world gone mad; the remainder largely alludes to the art and café world, including such items as theater listings and advertisements for tonic wines.) These political reports had special resonance for an artist deeply tied to the anarcho-symbolist, antimilitarist traditions of Barcelona and who was daily immersed in the raging arguments over the pan-European war universally acknowledged to be threatening. Further, the pieces of newsprint are often wittily and tellingly tied to the Cubist images of the cafés, where such arguments and discussions about the threat of war took place; the iconography of the early collages insistently sets us among the tables, bottles, liqueurs, and, indeed, newspapers of an artistic and political bohemia.

This aspect of Picasso's collages suggests significant revisions for our critical view of the Cubist period. Scholars have long been preoccupied with the brilliance of Picasso's and Braque's formal innovations, and it was only in the last decade that Robert Rosenblum discussed at length the role of wordplay in the masthead and headline fragments in the papiers-collés. Other recent studies have revealed ideas, themes, witticisms, and personal revelations in Picasso's proto-Cubist works, most concentrating on *Les Demoiselles d'Avignon*.[1] Some scholars have argued that the very presence of "content" in *Les Demoiselles* proves its distinction from the so-called content-neutral Cubist period proper; it can be argued as easily, however, that the overlapping meanings in this seminal painting hint at richly layered content that can be sought fruitfully in Picasso's subsequent work. Picasso's political background and response to contemporary events are by no means the only perspectives from which to view his art; but they are significant yet neglected aspects of the early modernist movement in general, and of Picasso's work of the *avant-guerre* in particular. This study demonstrates the importance of political ideas and passions for Picasso's Cubist period, however idiosyncratic and inconsistent was his own version of anarchism. If Peter Kropotkin's anarchist aesthetics called upon artists to create a revolutionary art, Picasso's radical Cubist style made of this aesthetic imperative a liberating assault on tradition, on the past, and hence, as contemporary critics of Cubism did not fail to notice, on society. These anarchist motives are most manifest, not only in style but in content as well, in the collages of autumn 1912, which came to fruition during the First Balkan War when Picasso and his bohemian milieu were deeply agitated by world events and preoccupied with issues of pacifism, militarism, and war. Furthermore, Picasso's absorption with these new issues of form and content virtually supplanted the activity of painting until the beginning of 1913. Of all two-dimensional works executed in the autumn and winter of 1912, thirty-nine were collages while only twelve were paintings, including oil, watercolor, and gouache. Although Picasso's "politics" doubtless changed considerably over the period from the 1890s to 1912, his early schooling as an "anarchist artist" played a renewed, in fact, a more powerful and mature role in his art under the impress of the threat of a general societal upheaval. But it is impossible to appreciate this aspect of the collages without first recognizing the impact made on Picasso by his first immersion in the highly politicized and militantly "modernist" atmosphere of Barcelona, and the somewhat different influence that anarchist attitudes and ideas in France exerted on his work after his move to Paris in 1904.

Anarchism and Picasso's Barcelona Period

It has been said many times that the youthful Picasso spent his time with anarchist sympathizers at Els Quatre Gats, the café-meeting place or *tertulia* of the avant-garde in Barcelona, and second home to Picasso at this time.[2] The overlap of the artistic with the political in Barcelona in the 1890s was far more extensive than has yet been recognized. To the avant-garde of that city, identification with the anarchist cause meant a great deal more than sympathy for the downtrodden masses or for the outrageous acts of individual violence that later came to characterize anarchism in the popular imagination. The rise of the anarchist movement in the nineteenth century was in direct response to the development of a rich body of theory rivaling Marxism.[3] Such writers as Pierre-Joseph Proudhon, Mikhail Bakunin, and Peter Kropotkin were widely read throughout Europe, and their theories particularly appealed to avant-garde writers and artists in the second half of the century. Courbet, Wagner, Mallarmé, Pissarro, Signac, Jarry, and Apollinaire, to name only some of the better known figures, numbered themselves among those who equated artistic with political liberation in anarchist terms. *Symbolisme* especially came to be associated with the anarchist movement and its creed of extreme individualism as a stand against bourgeois society.[4]

Proudhon and later anarchists rejected the social system in which they lived, and offered an ideal vision of an anarchist future. They were antiauthoritarian, anti-industrialist, antimilitarist, antipatriotic, antiparliamentarian, antiproperty, and antireligion; they were pacifist and internationalist; they embraced individual independence and liberty, the social necessity and moral virtue of work, and imagined a future society of small groups enjoying ''natural'' relations of interdependence and ''mutual aid.'' Although regional pride and ethnic differences were approved, nationalism and patriotism were despised as manipulative fictions that exploited laborers and inevitably led to wars waged for the profit of those in power. Proudhon, living as he did during the rise of the conscript army, saw war as the most tragic injustice of the social system.[5] Antimilitarism became one of the most important themes in the later nineteenth-century libertarian movement, and is of special significance for Picasso's work immediately prior to the First World War.

The Russians Bakunin, an active revolutionary and organizer, and Kropotkin, the great thinker of the movement in the late nineteenth century, built on Proudhon's ideas, so that by the 1880s and 1890s we can speak of a body of anarchist thought.[6] Bakunin added the violence of an activist, and for a time—which he later regretted—he embraced Sergei Nechaev's ''propaganda of the deed,'' which rationalized and glorified individual acts of terrorism.[7]

Kropotkin felt that the real solution to society's ills lay with the peasantry, in part because they still had those primitive roots of mutualism which he saw as the natural form of society: men and women, if uncorrupted by coercive government, will naturally and freely aid their fellows in pursuit of the general well-being of all. Kropotkin developed an aesthetic theory out of the profound conviction that ''primitive'' societies—and "primitive" arts—express themselves in more "natural," more spontaneous, and therefore truer, ways. Aesthetic theory and the role of the artist were central issues for the anarchists in a way that distinguishes them from the Marxists.[8] Kropotkin believed artists were critical to the success of anarchism, and exhorted them to hasten the revolution by behaving as if it had already taken place. Though Kropotkin himself seems to have envisioned an "ideal" art along the lines of ancient Greece, his theories inspired two generations of revolutionary art. For the modern artist to cultivate strategies of primitivism and spontaneity in both art and life was to rebel against the static forms of bourgeois morality and bourgeois art. Kropotkin's primitivism, and emphasis on the role of art in changing social consciousness, constituted much of the appeal of anarchism to the artistic and literary generation of the 1880s and 1890s, along with the romanticism of *la propagande par le fait*. All of these convictions were acted out in Picasso's art in the period from 1897 to 1914.[9]

Anarchism was particularly strong in Spain, not only in the cosmopolitan centers but in the countryside, where its themes accorded with those of a strong and politicized folk culture.[10] Barcelona was anarchism's best and last stronghold in Europe, playing a critical part in the Spanish Civil War of 1936–39. As the capital of the ancient province of Catalonia, Barcelona was traditionally oriented more towards Europe than Madrid, and became the major industrial center of Spain, which further linked it to the north. At the turn of the century, the rich industrialists of Barcelona became fervent Catalan nationalists, and the Catalan language, customs, and artistic traditions were energetically revived.[11] Mingling with this *catalanismo* was a working-class movement that was more purely anarchist. The two movements shared many attitudes, foremost among them a settled hatred of the Madrid government. Barcelona was the most politically agitated city in Spain, and the witness of increasing violence around the turn of the century.[12]

The artistic and literary movement was an intrinsic part of this politically charged atmosphere in Barcelona in the 1890s. As several recent studies and an exhibition have shown, Els Quatre Gats played a significant role in focusing the modernist movement and providing a center for the avant-garde artists and radical writers of several generations from 1897 to 1903.[13] In such a city, at such a time, it would have been next to impossible, had one so desired, to remain impervious to poverty, labor unrest, and government oppression. The artists and writers of Barcelona, and especially Picasso and his circle, did not wish to ignore the social realities; on the contrary, they paid particular attention to them, and inevitably this experience colored their view of the world and the art they made.

A large and politically avid audience supported an enormous volume of anarchist publications during the years Picasso lived in Barcelona (1895–1904). There were anarchist daily newspapers, preeminently *La Vanguardia,* no fewer than eleven anarchist periodicals publishing weekly or monthly, and art journals with openly anarchist sympathies such as *Joventut, Cu-Cut!,* and *Catalonia.* All of these periodicals published discussions and translations of European and American anarchist and writers whom they saw as allied to the movement, including Proudhon, Bakunin, Kropotkin, Tolstoy, Nietzsche, Wagner, and Mallarmé. And the list of Spanish literary anarchist and radical writers is large: based in Madrid, Pío Baroja, Azorín (J. Martínez Ruiz), and Miguel de Unamuno; and based in Barcelona, Alfredo Opisso, Pompeu Gener, Joan Maragall, Jaume Brossa, Alexandre Cortada, and others. Picasso knew most of the Spanish figures, and Opisso, Brossa, and Gener were particular friends.[14]

Many of the political and literary figures familiar from the anarchist press appeared in the numerous art journals published in Barcelona during the same period; most of these journals explicitly or implicitly supported *catalanismo,* and many further espoused *anarquismo,* despite the periodic danger of fines and imprisonment.[15] *Joventut,* for example, had a separatist editorial policy and extensively published the anarchist criticism of Picasso's longtime friends Brossa and Gener, who introduced the writings of Nietzsche to Barcelona.[16] Many articles appeared in *Joventut* attacking the idea of "art for art's sake" as a "perilous 'Dilettantism'" lacking social consciousness.[17] Picasso's first published drawings appeared in *Joventut,* including his *symboliste* illustration for Joan Oliva Bridgman's poem *El Clam de las verges* (12 July 1900), "the cry of the virgins" for equality and sexual liberation.[18] Journals such as *Els Quatre Gats, Pèl & ploma,* and *Catalunya artística* were more cautious, and announced their radicalism and support of *catalanismo* largely through publishing socially critical drawings by Catalan artists.

Even the older *modernistas* Santiago Rusiñol and Ramón Casas—whose Catalanist politics were actually rather conservative—were assimilated to the anarchist camp. For example, in his review of "La Exposición General de Bellas Artes—Pt. III," in *La Illustración iberica* of 2 June 1894, Alfredo Opisso declared that Rusiñol, Casas, and Zuloaga—a Valencian peasant painter—represented "without doubt, the Bakunin, the Nietzsche, the Kropotkin of the Spanish section."[19] Opisso, father of Picasso's friend Ricardo Opisso, far from being alone in making his Catalanist and leftist views part of his art criticism, is typical of this politically charged artistic milieu. Miguel Utrillo, Angel Guimerá, Narcis Oller, Jaume Vrossa, Pompeu Gener, Masso y Torrents, and Joan Maragall, who represent the entire range of *catalanismo,* all wrote highly politicized art and literary criticism for Barcelona's periodicals and moved in Picasso's circle.

Luis Graner, among the older generation, rejected the Spanish tradition of moralizing genre. His paintings concentrated not on peasants, but on the most deprived classes of the poor. Works such as *Tavern Interior*[20] and his depictions of beggars and ragpickers influenced the whole of the younger generation of socially concerned artists—including Picasso—who looked beyond a sentimental glorification of the peasants to an unsentimental depiction of their new urban reality.[21] Many of these younger artists met at La Llotja, the art academy in Barcelona. Isidro Nonell, Ricardo Canals, Ricardo Opisso, Ramón Pichot, and Joaquin Mir left the academy to paint "real life" in the outskirts and poor districts of Barcelona. Known as the Colla S. Martí (S. Martí group) after one of these slums, they were the group of painters with whom Picasso early became associated. All of the members of the Colla S. Martí concerned themselves with social themes, none more explosively than Nonell in his antiwar and antigovernment series of 1898, *España después de la guerra* (Spain after the War). In the 1890s, Canals concentrated on working-class entertainments and gypsies. Mir sketched scenes of life in the poor districts, as in his *Bosquejos barceloneses* of 1899. Opisso made numerous sketches of peasants at work, but also recorded the pathetic plight of "urban peasants" in various works, such as *Soup Line* of 1899.[22] The large majority of the images of these artists through the turn of the century directly concerned social themes, and constituted a collective outcry against the social system responsible for the heartbreaking conditions they recorded.

Picasso emerged from this milieu as the anarchist artist-hero who adopted these themes and carried them into the twentieth century. In his earliest work of the late 1890s and early 1900s, he painted savagely satirical works of bourgeois comfort and decadence, while at the same time drawing many records of the impoverishment and anger of the lower classes. In the Blue Period, from 1901 to 1904, he openly sympathized with the wretched, urban poor: their hunger, their broken family ties, and their alienation from the earth, which, in contrasting works of his, gives peace and harmony to the lives of rural peasants.

Much recent literature has shown to what a large extent Picasso was a part of the *modernista* movement in Barcelona, and to what a large degree he was early influenced by its painters.[23] But the specifically political character of the art of the *modernistas* and, more particularly, of Picasso's work in this period has not been properly studied. As early as April 1896, Picasso saw the art of Rusiñol, Casas, Graner, Nonell, and Mir in the same exhibition in which he showed *The First Communion* of 1895–96.[24] From this time the subjects of his work coincide with that of the Colla S. Martí in recording the street life of Barcelona's poor suburbs, its destitute mothers with children, its beggars and laborers. Among those painters, Nonell was the most important since he particularly befriended the younger Picasso, letting him use his studio in Barcelona in 1899 and again in Paris in 1900. He and Picasso also had studios in the same building on the Calle de Comercio in the winter and spring of 1904, and therefore were certainly aware of each other's work on a continuing basis. Pool has convincingly demonstrated the crucial confluence of subject and style in their work of this period.[25].

Well before the Blue Period, Picasso made sketches of beggars. In a number of related drawings (variously dated 1897–98 and 1898–99 by Cirlot, though it seems probable that they were done at the same time), a violinist, a woman with a baby, and a little girl with her hand out all beg on a street corner. In the one illustrated here (fig. 7.1), a working man in his Catalan smock, cap, and narrow trousers gives a donation to the child; above, Picasso has written ''Caridad'' (''charity'').

When Picasso went to Paris, he found a similar environment and recorded it in his art. *Scène de rue (Rue Lepic),* Paris, 1900,[26] which today might appear to be an impressionistic view of modern city life, was read more accurately by Picasso's contemporaries. When it was included in Picasso's show at Berthe Weill's gallery in 1904, Maurice Le Sieutre wrote in the preface to the catalogue, ''One senses the painter is interested in the tone which modern misery strikes in the suburbs of Paris. Here on the ramparts are vulgar couples; at the crossroads of crowded streets there are idlers, workers, women, all unfortunates, abject and weary, rough, indistinct, worn down, tossed by life like pebbles by the sea.''[27]

In the years 1902 to 1904, Picasso concentrated increasingly on representing the experience of poverty and alienation, and its effect on small family groups. Numerous works depict a woman with an infant, seemingly abandoned by society altogether, wandering next to the sea. Although they now have neutrally descriptive, auction-house titles such as *Woman and Child on the Shore,* or more obviously formalist titles such as *Mother and Child in Profile,* these works were originally exhibited at Berthe Weill's in late 1902 with titles like *La Misère: Mère et enfant,* [28] which more clearly point to their social content. A madman—Picasso called him *El loco* —who lived in Barcelona was painted and drawn by Picasso several times in 1903 and 1904.[29] Such an outcast had no place anywhere in his urban society and compares tellingly with the subject of Picasso's *El tonto* (the idiot), Barcelona, 1903,[30] a village idiot who was cared for within the traditional rural social structure and was neither ragged nor hungry. Picasso not only depicted this pathetic outcast but pointed up the exaggerated imbalance of wealth in Spanish society in a work ironically titled *Caridad,* Barcelona, 1903 (fig. 7.2), which shows a grotesquely fat bourgeois giving a coin to *El loco* as he sits grimly in the street with his emaciated little dog.

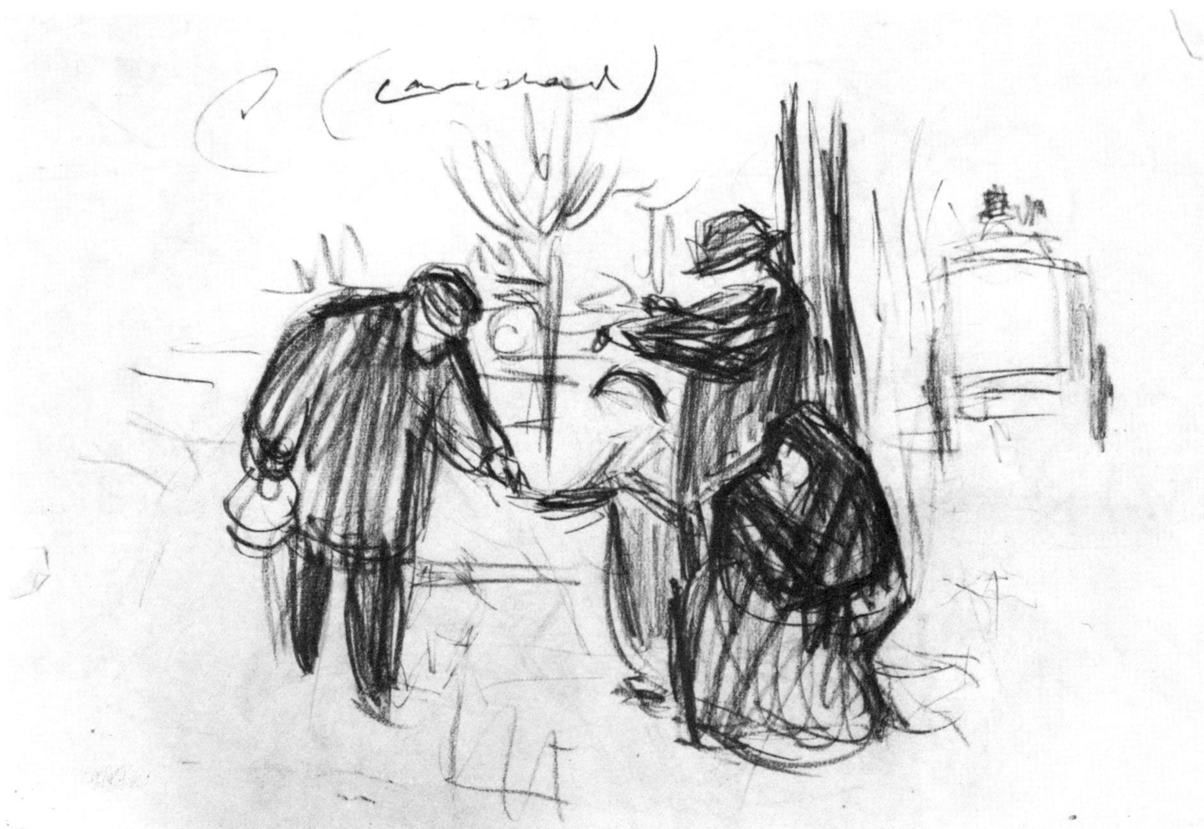

Figure 7.1. Pablo Picasso, *Caridad*, 1897–99
Conté crayon on paper, 23.2 cm × 33.8 cm.
(Museu Picasso, Barcelona. Photo: Museu Picasso)

Figure 7.2: Pablo Picasso, *Caridad*, 1903
India ink and colored crayons on paper, 26 cm × 36 cm.
(Collection Marcel Mabille, Brussels. Photo: M. Mabille)

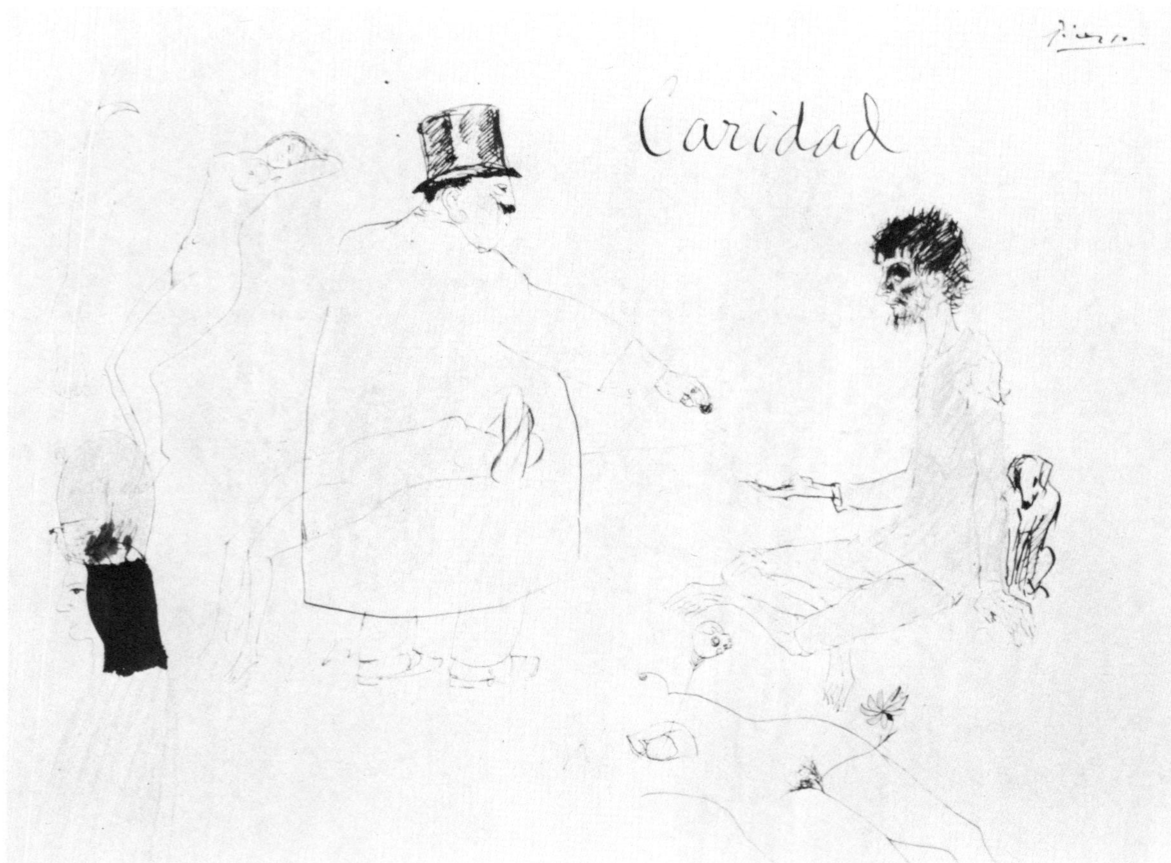

Another group of drawings that are related stylistically and thematically in these early years concerns a kind of street violence acted out almost daily in Barcelona following the unprecedented growth of the anarchist movement and increasing attempts to suppress it. Moreover, Madrid had its own share of troubles when Picasso lived there in 1897–98. At least twelve drawings in the Museo Picasso in Barcelona, all from 1897–99, depict violent street fights and confrontations. Assailants, victims, and horrified onlookers are actors in knifings, assassinations, and mob scenes in both cities.

One group of three drawings shows a street assassination or murder. In the first two, a man holds out his arm to keep back those running up to view the victim, huddled over by two men.[31] The third drawing, *After the Fight,* 1898 (fig. 7.3), depicts a different moment in a similar scene. This time, two victims lie in the street, one clutching his stomach, while a group of men turns and hurries away. Whether the assassins are among them, or they are merely a crowd who cannot afford to get involved, remains unclear.

Another drawing in this group, *Street Fight* of Madrid, 1897–98,[32] shows an angry mob led by a man holding a knife, stopped by an imposing figure protecting the inert body of a man behind him. All of the figures appear to be workers; given the political climate in Spain in the late 1890s, this certainly records some form of workers' protest. The final sketch dealing with this subject is *Study for a Poster for "El Liberal,"* 1900 (fig. 7.4), an anarchist newspaper published by Picasso's friend Carles Junyer-Vidal; it depicts a demonstration of poor men and women yelling angrily from beneath the inflammatory masthead. These drawings testify to Picasso's awareness of the political violence of the time, evidencing his direct observation of the cities' upheavals. The themes of all these works discourage the idea that Picasso's Blue Period expresses merely sentimental or autobiographical preoccupations, rather than, as Sabartés articulately phrased it, a "testimony of conscience," with all the conscious intention that implies.[33]

Final evidence of Picasso's politicized consciousness in that early period is provided by the avant-garde journal *Arte joven,* which he published with Francisco Asis de Soler in Madrid in 1901, for it constitutes an important record of his sympathies and prejudices. Leading figures of the literary and artistic avant-garde of Madrid and Barcelona lent work to the new journal, especially those sympathetic to and associated with the anarchist movement: poems by Miguel de Unamuno and Alberto Lozano, stories by Pío Baroja and Rusiñol, articles by and about Pompeo Gener—who introduced Nietzsche to Spain—and J. Martínez Ruiz (Azorín), drawings by Nonell and Baroja, translations from Catalan and

Figure 7.3. Pablo Picasso, *After the Fight,* 1898
Conté crayon on paper, 13 cm × 21 cm.
(Museu Picasso, Barcelona. Photo: Museu Picasso)

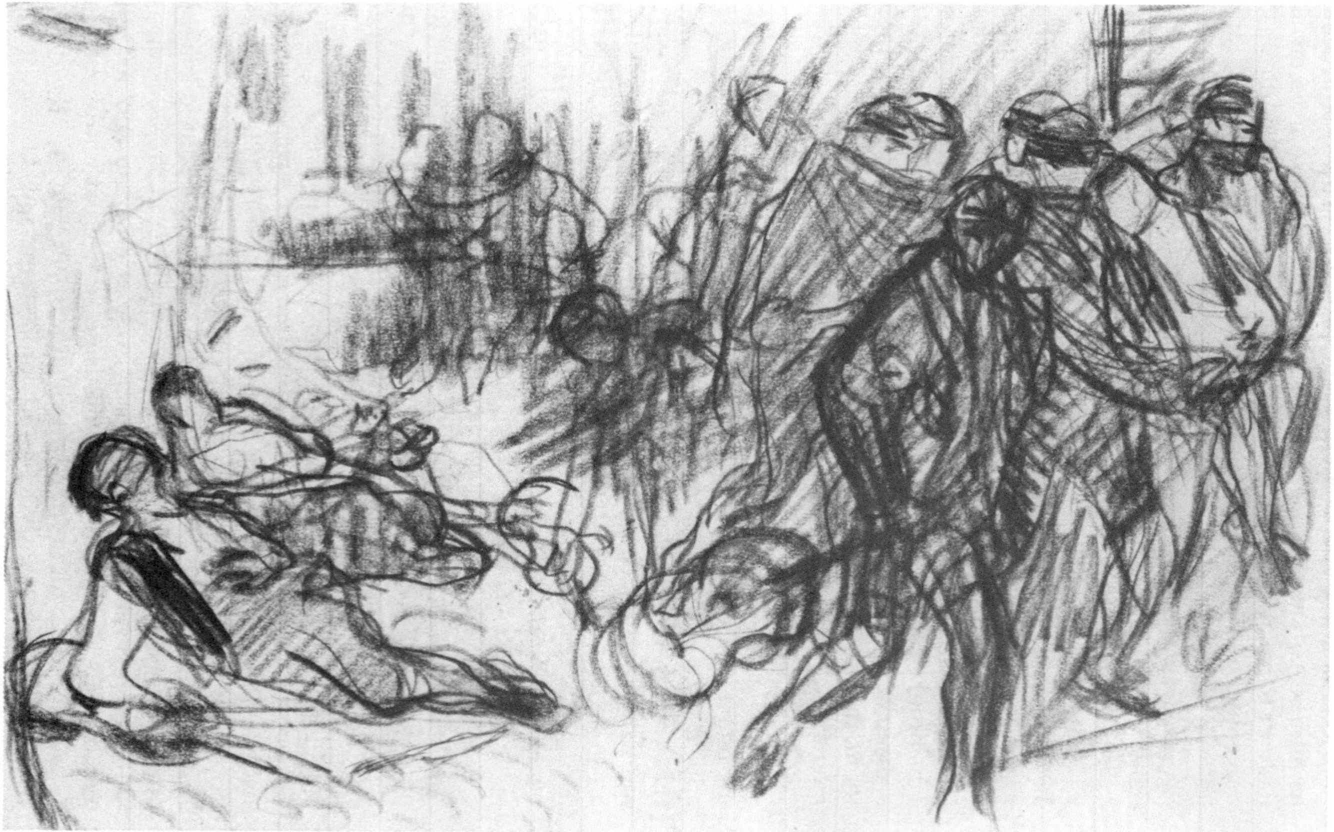

Figure 7.4. Pablo Picasso, *Study for a Poster for "El Liberal,"* 1900
Conté crayon on paper, 33.7 cm × 36.3 cm.
(Museu Picasso, Barcelona. Photo: Museu Picasso)

a "Letter from Barcelona, to the intellectuals of Madrid" by Ramón Reventós, which attempted to establish political and artistic links between the two cities. The advertisements supporting the magazine were few but, for our purposes, very telling: for the café Els Quatre Gats; *Arte joven* and *Madrid* (a journal projected by Picasso and Asis de Soler but never realized); and a list of translations published by Rodriguez Serra, including Kropotkin's *Memoirs of a Revolutionist* and *The Conquest of Bread;* Ruskin's *Of Queen's Gardens,* a powerful tract criticizing the economic and industrial system; and Nietzsche's *The Origins of Tragedy* and *The Twilight of the Gods.* This constituted a menu of the most frequently reprinted and discussed books of the Spanish avant-garde.[34]

General themes of the Spanish Symbolist movement—primitivism, faith in natural instinct, exaltation of childhood—accompanied concretely political ones, making *Arte joven* even more anarchist than its Catalan models. Picasso's and Soler's introductory statement in the *número preliminar,* following a cover drawing of poor peasants, announced their idealistic aims in highly politicized language:

> It is not our intent to destroy anything: our mission is more elevated. We come to construct. The old, the decrepit, the worm-eaten will sooner or later fall down by itself, the powerful breath of civilization is enough and will take care of pulling down that which obstructs us. . . .
>
> We come to the struggle with much enthusiasm, with much energy, with a tenacity that will never be able to spare the old.
>
> Come, then, to the struggle, ours that will triumph if we fight with faith. Come and you will not forget that *to struggle is to succeed.*[35]

In the same issue, Lozano's poem, "Drops of Ink," began "I am a mystic in Art who appears an atheist, because I arrogantly deny all authority, and scoff at theories, ancient and modern."[36]

Such anarchist rhetoric was also put to less metaphorical uses. For example, in the third issue Picasso and Asis de Soler published a passionate article by Martínez Ruiz declaring war on what they considered the farce of Spain's electoral system:

> The State is evil; the State is authority and authority is the tax that impoverishes the peasant, the hardship that kills in the factory, the one-fifth duty that decimates the villages and leaves the countryside exhausted, the inadequate wages, the humiliating alms, the law, in short, that controls everything and tyrannizes over everything. . . . We do not wish to impose laws nor that laws impose on us; we do not wish to be governors nor that anyone govern us. Monarchists or republicans, reactionaries or progressives, all are at bottom authoritarians. Let us be inert to the invitation to politics. Democracy is an iniquitous lie. To vote is to fortify the age-old injustice of the State.[37]

After this purely Proudhonian analysis—the socialists were unpopular in Spain because they consented to work within the system—Martínez Ruiz presented the alternative offered by the artists, who generally felt themselves to be the leading cadres of the revolution: "We will hasten this end: We will work for this dawn of peace and right. Art is free and spontaneous. Let us make life artistic. Propellers and generators of life, artists would not want laws or borders. As for our free bohemia, our aspiration is that it become the bohemia of all humankind."

Picasso, according to an article of 1901 promoting the new Madrid journal in *Pèl & ploma,* was the real force behind the venture.[38] As Pool suggests, it is telling that the only periodical over which Picasso had control should express social and political commitment so flamboyantly.[39] Most significantly, the ideas expressed in this journal affirm that many of Picasso's early drawings and paintings were informed by the peculiarly Spanish marriage of art and politics. Picasso went so far as to sign, along with his friends Carlos Casagemas, Francisco Asis de Soler, Josep Cardona, and eighty others, a "Manifesto of the Spanish Colony resident in Paris," which appeared on the front page of *La Publicidad,* a Barcelona daily, on 29 December 1900, and demanded both the release of the political prisoners—mostly anarchists—who were still being held in Montjuich following the antimilitarist agitations of 1898, and amnesty for the exiles who had fled to France to avoid military service.[40] Picasso did not again engage in this kind of political activism until the Spanish Civil War of 1936–39, and it demonstrates the nature of his early commitment to the anarchist movement, which he was to modify over the subsequent years. Politically, he was one with his milieu in the avant-garde circles of Madrid and Barcelona; artistically, he took their outrageous theories more to heart, and pursued an increasing boldness and antiacademicism in his style that finally went beyond that of his Spanish peers. But he not only maintained a strong adherence to the anarchist aesthetic as he pushed his art in Paris to increasingly revolutionary stages over the next ten years, he also continued to deal, both metaphorically and concretely, with political issues that were central to the concerns of the anarchist artists with whom he had matured in Spain.

Anarchism and Picasso's Cubist Period

Paris, the intellectual home of anarchism, mothered strong anarchist and socialist movements.[41] Both groups influenced the course of events in late nineteenth-century France, but it was anarchism that, almost exclusively, won the adherence of the literary and artistic avant-garde.[42] With ideas formed among Barcelona's radicals, Picasso moved to Paris in 1904 and almost immediately found his way into an artistic circle with a history of anarchist thinking and activity that paralleled his Barcelona experience. The anarchist view of the role and importance of the artist provided a serious rationale for styles of art (and behavior) that to the uninstructed seemed to be outrageousness for its own sake. Exasperated critics were not wrong to call such self-conscious bohemianism "anarchist," as they frequently did.[43] From this moment until the war, Picasso's work passed rapidly from narrative, socially critical painting through an experimental primitivism almost unimaginably violent—*Les Demoiselles d'Avignon* is Picasso's *la propagande par le fait*—to the most daring collaborative artistic revolution of the early twentieth century: Cubism and the collages.

Picasso made his way into the French Symbolist/anarchist circle with remarkable rapidity. Taking over a studio in the Bateau-Lavoir in April of 1904, he soon met Guillaume Apollinaire and André Salmon.[44] By the autumn, Picasso and Max Jacob were accompanying them to the various soirées of the older Symbolists, including the gatherings sponsored by the journals *La Plume* and *Vers et prose.* There Picasso met the group of artists and writers who embraced anarchism: Alfred Jarry, Paul Fort, Félix Fénéon, Laurent Tailhade, Gustave Kahn, Emile Verhaeren, Stuart Merrill, Paul Signac, Paul Sérusier, Charles Morice, and a host of lesser figures including the anarchist Mécislas Golberg, who was writing *La Morale des lignes.*[45]

Apollinaire and Salmon, like Picasso, also had anarchist histories. At school in Nice in the mid-1890s, Apollinaire had produced an anarcho-Symbolist newspaper, *Le Vengeur,* with poems and articles by himself ("Guillaume Macabre") and his friend Toussaint-Luca.[46] In Paris between 1903 and World War I, he edited and contributed to anarchist and left-wing periodicals and avant-garde reviews, becoming the regular art critic for *L'Intransigeant* and *Le Mercure de France* in 1910 and 1911, respectively.[47]

In his criticism, Apollinaire defended every manifestation of modernism, sounding all the visionary themes of anarchist aestheticians. Thus, the new art was not merely different from that of the past—Cubism was extolled as "the most audacious school that ever existed"—but this art played a "social role" in heralding a new beauty and a new era of wholly changed attitudes towards humanity.[48] Apollinaire presented Picasso in *Les Peintres cubistes* in 1913 as the exemplar of the new artist: "A new man, the world is his new representation. He enumerates the elements, the details, with a brutality which is also able to be gracious. New-born, he orders the universe in accordance with his personal requirements, and so as to facilitate his relations with his fellows. The enumeration has epic grandeur, and, when ordered, will burst into a drama."[49] Apollinaire's "new" men re-order the universe; what they write and paint will only be fully intelligible to the future because art will be freed from its shackles. Such utopian themes and images are the stuff of the anarchist dreams that Apollinaire, Picasso, and a whole generation grew up on. Apollinaire acknowledged in much of his criticism this aesthetic shared with Picasso; throughout the prewar period they not only influenced but incited each other to greater artistic audacity and outrageousness.

Salmon confirmed his early and continuing anarchism many times. He was responsible for organizing the wild soirées of *Vers et prose* at the Closerie des Lilas. Much later he wrote a history of the libertarian movement, *La Terreur noire,* in which he addressed the issue of how he and his generation were, though antimilitarists, led into fighting in the war, an issue to which we will return.[50]

In my dissertation I demonstrated the ways in which anarchist ideas manifested themselves in Picasso's work from his overtly political Barcelonese drawings through his subsequent periods, when the influence of anarchist ideas was felt more obliquely. Here it will suffice only to mention the stages leading to their extraordinary, articulate manifestation in the collages. During the Rose Period of 1904–05 Picasso identified the artist with *saltimbanques,* or wandering acrobats and entertainers, whom he saw as rejected and misunderstood by a culture undeserving of their innocence or their art—a theme frequent in the work of the *modernistas* Rusiñol and Opisso.[51] That Picasso identified precisely with the *saltimbanques'* survival and persistence on society's edges does not make them mere symbols of the artist's struggle, nor mitigate the political component of their plight as actual representatives of their kind.

Starting in 1906, Picasso pursued various kinds of "primitivism"—based on Iberian, African, Caledonian art—as alternative cultural forms. The Iberian works frequently offered an arcadian vision, as in *The Harvesters* of spring 1907 (fig. 7.5), which was cast in the forms of an indigenous, "spontaneous," Spanish primitivism. The African works, on the contrary, challenged the norms of Western art in violently overturning inherited conventions for the treatment of human form. The conflation of "African" forms with a traditional subject—the female nude—was shocking, indeed explosive, in *Les Demoiselles d'Avignon;* but the combination became even more appalling when used to attack the Church and its art, as in *Mother and Child* of 1907 (fig. 7.6), with its formulaic madonna and child composition, halo, and blue robe.[52]

Picasso's subsequent Cubism fulfilled the anarchist aesthetic dictum, echoing Baudelaire's statement that art must express its own time. The Cubist style developed in rather loose and unscientific affiliation with various ideas that seemed to the artists to be especially "modern" and characteristic of the new century, for example, Bergson's philosophy, Princet's mathematics, and William James's perception psychology, whose relevance for Cubism have been investigated by scholars in the last several decades.[53] The newest, most radical and audacious direction for Picasso was formal abstraction, which Braque and he pursued until the war. The features of their adventurous new style were apparent to critics from the very beginning: the increasing difficulty of identifying the hermetic image, with its fragmentation of form, ambiguous treatment of space, suppression of color, and the oblique and conceptual relationship to the material world. Yet, Picasso's drive to be artistically radical, which helped to push the development of Cubism at its swift pace (from the Cézannesque distortions of 1909 to the nearly abstract collages of 1912 in only four years), was impelled not by the *Kunstwollen* of the style alone, but also by his dedication to the idea of the revolutionary in art. This was Picasso's "political act."

Indeed, during its public life from 1908 until after the war, the Cubist movement never escaped charges that it was purposely attacking the social facade in violating artistic traditions. Critics representing the range of political opinion from the left to the extreme right repeatedly discussed Cubism in highly politicized language, whether for purposes of praise or censure, which suggests not only the existence of an audience that perceived the revolutionary nature of the style in political terms, but also a calculated—indeed unavoidable—awareness of their politicized audience on the part of the artists.[54] Cubism came most visibly onto the public political stage in the Chamber of Deputies on 3 December 1912 in the debate on whether to censor the style as an abominable, "antinational," and "foreign" influence on French art, or at the least to refuse to allow it to be exhibited in the national palaces—a move that, had it succeeded, would have kept Cubist paintings out of the annual Salon d'Automne at the Grand Palais.[55] This heated debate manifests those political tensions, to which the art world also responded, which were engendered by the growing nationalism and war hysteria of the prewar period.

The critics' and Deputies' politicizing responses to the Cubist style and its attack on tradition would not have taken Picasso by surprise. When, in 1944, immediately following the liberation of Paris, Picasso joined the French Communist Party, he made political statements that have generally been understood as metaphorical (or delusional), but which I believe he intended literally. His utterances are usually oblique and ironic; yet, in the emotional climate following the liberation, he declared with rare candor and thoroughness his lifelong commitment to artistic revolutionism. In his first explanatory statement, an interview with Pol Gaillard in October 1944, Picasso said,

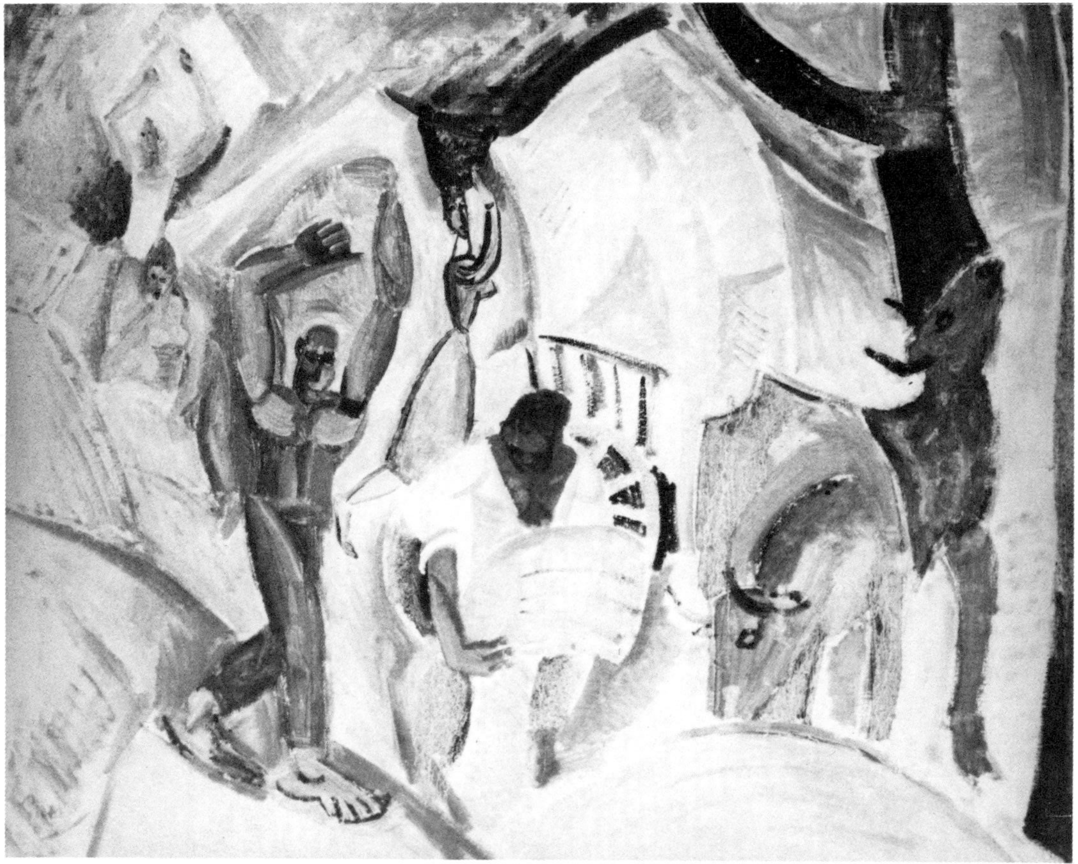

Figure 7.5. Pablo Picasso, *The Harvesters,* Spring 1907
Oil on canvas, 65 cm × 81.3 cm.
(Thyssen-Bornemisza Collection, Lugano. Photo: Thyssen-Bornemisza Collection)

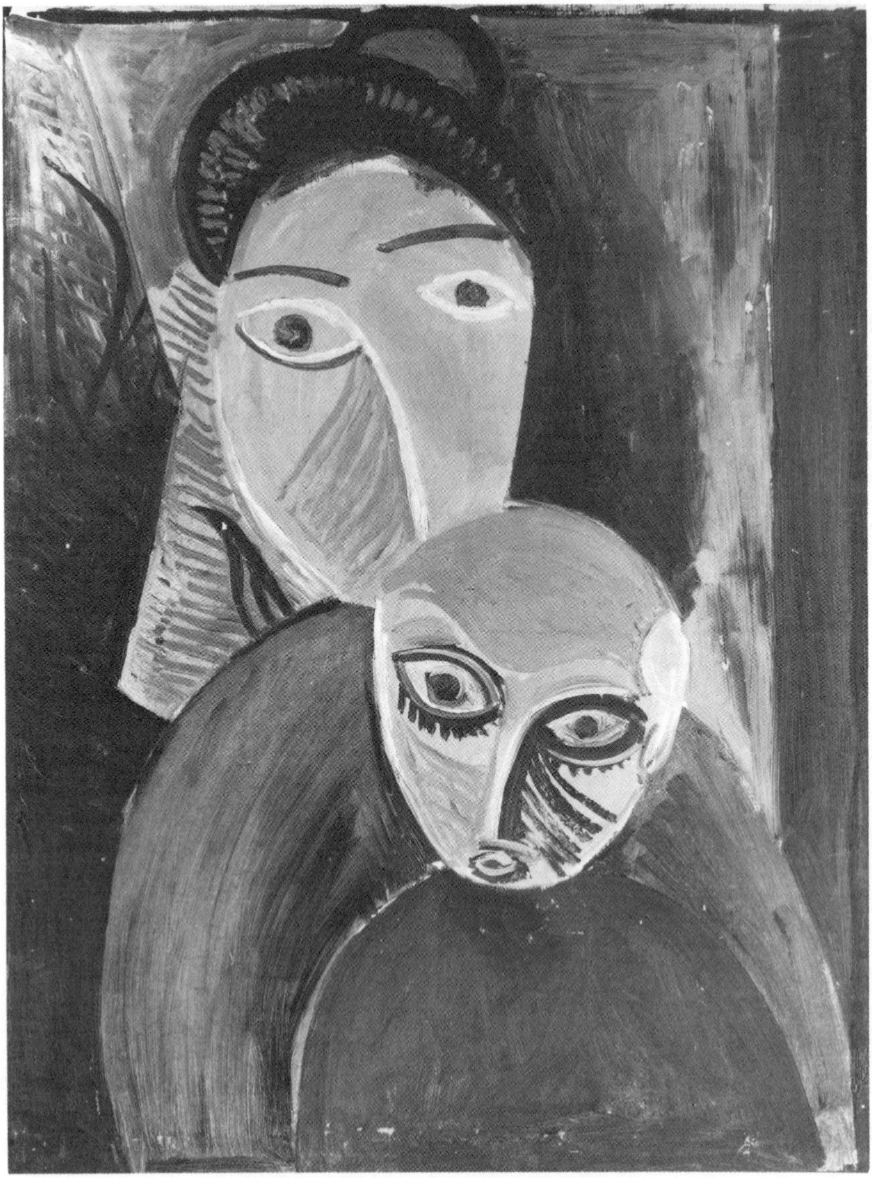

Figure 7.6. Pablo Picasso, *Mother and Child,* 1907
Oil on canvas, 81 cm × 60 cm.
(Musée Picasso, Paris. Photo: Musées Nationaux)

> My joining the Communist Party is the logical outcome of my whole life, my whole work. Because, I'm proud to say, I have never considered painting as an art of simple pleasure, of diversion; I have wanted, through drawing and through color, since those were my weapons, to penetrate always more deeply into knowledge of the world and of men, in order that this knowledge liberate us all more each day; I have tried to say, in my own way, that which I held to be the most true, the most just, the best, and that was naturally always the most beautiful, as the greatest artists well know.
>
> Yes, I am conscious of having always struggled by means of my painting, as a true revolutionary. But I have understood now that even that does not suffice; these years of terrible oppression have demonstrated to me that I must fight with not only my art, but my whole self.[56]

The next spring, following much heated debate in the press, some of which expressly accused him of insincerity and of having stated that art and politics had nothing in common, Picasso composed an official written statement to counter the offensive suggestion that, as an artist, he was apolitical:

> What do you think an artist is? An imbecile who has only his eyes if he's a painter, or ears if he's a musician, or a lyre at every level of his heart if he's a poet, or even, if he's a boxer, just his muscles? On the contrary, he's at the same time a political being, constantly alive to heartrending, fiery or happy events, to which he responds in every way. How would it be possible to feel no interest in other people and by virtue of an ivory indifference to detach yourself from the life which they so copiously bring you? No, painting is not done to decorate apartments. It is an instrument of war for attack and defense against the enemy.[57]

As Picasso most succinctly summed up in a less passionate and more characteristically aphoristic way, "It is not necessary to paint a man with a gun. An apple can be just as revolutionary."[58] The art by means of which he struggled "as a true revolutionary," from his early years in Barcelona to the war, led him to overturn virtually all the artistic conventions, pictorial and procedural, remaining at the turn of the century; and this art developed during a period of intense political agitation and instability in which Picasso's circle had a particular interest.[59]

In France in the years leading up to the war, frequent clashes between strikers and the state forced attention to the plight of the workers.[60] One result of the repression of the labor movement and the persecution of its leaders was the growth and increasing militancy of the anarchist movement and the Confédération Générale du Travail, the syndicalist arm of the anarchist movement, which recorded 300,000 members in 1906, 400,000 in 1908, and 600,000 in 1912. At the same time, the more moderate socialists were gaining voters and seats in Parliament. The left-wing movements in France over a wide spectrum of opinion gained tremendously during the *avant-guerre* in numbers and in political power.[61]

Anarchists, as has been seen, embraced the working-class revolution and advocated the use of violence strikes to achieve their ends. More important, however, was their utopian vision of a future society, in fighting for which they were fiercely opposed to nationalism and war. In 1905 the "First Moroccan Crisis"—alluded to in the epigraph to this essay—awakened France to the possibility of war with Germany.[62] The French Foreign Minister Delcassé had made a secret deal with England and Spain, agreeing on colonial spheres of influence and setting up a French protectorate in Morocco. Wilhelm II, who cherished thoughts of a German colonial empire, was furious at having been left out of the consultations. Claiming the jeopardy of Germany's economic interests, he sailed into Tangiers, landing with sword symbolically drawn to announce his readiness to go to war over the issue. Negotiations went on for a year and war seemed imminent until the Settlement of Algeciras in 1906. But even this accord was temporary, and for the next seven years Morocco was the pretext for continual tests of strength and calls of bluff between Germany and France, as both prepared for war.

The other major crisis of the years immediately prior to World War I was the First Balkan War, which was of special importance for Picasso's work. When Poincaré became France's premier and foreign minister in 1912, he rapidly began to gear up for war with Germany, which he thought would be "short but glorious." One of his first moves was uncritically to support Russian designs on the Balkans. Czar Nicholas II formed the secret "Balkan League" with Serbia and Bulgaria in March 1912, assuring war with Turkey and Austria-Hungary, and hence Germany, whose interests they threatened. When Poincaré himself visited Russia, pledging full support for Russia's plans for war and a rapid buildup of Franch military strength, the stage was set for World War I. On 15 October 1912, Montenegro, Serbia, Bulgaria, and Greece declared war on Turkey. After expelling the Turks, in November Serbia laid claim to a large part of Albania in the Austro-Hungarian Empire and Austria mobilized. But because Russia's military preparations were incomplete, the czar failed to come in with Serbia; treaty discussions began in London and dragged on until May 1913. The Second Balkan War amounted to a few weeks' skirmish and ended in a final treaty in August 1913. While much blind optimism prevailed, many accurately saw the Balkan wars as a dangerous preview of a general European war. When a year later World War I did break out, the immediate event that sparked it was the assassination of Archduke Francis Ferdinand of Austria-Hungary by a Serbian nationalist.[63]

"The end of militarism is the mission of the nineteenth century," Proudhon had written in 1861.[64] After the Moroccan Crisis of 1905, the burning issue for both anarchists and socialists was whether the workers would or should fight in the war that already seemed inevitable. Most on the left hoped that when called upon to shed their blood for capitalist "warmongers," workers internationally would recognize their class brotherhood, refuse to fight, and rise up to prevent war altogether. This was the course advocated by France's leading socialist, Jean Jaurès, right up to the moment of his assassination three days before France mobilized its armies. He sensibly dreaded the outbreak of war; but others, thinking that war would trigger revolution, clamored for it. In France alone in 1910, a million socialist votes encouraged the hope that the workers were ready.[65]

Numerous anarchist and socialist congresses met during the *avant-guerre* to formulate positions against militarism and the coming war. A congress in Amsterdam in 1904 founded the Association Internationale Antimilitariste. They published an "affiche aux conscrits" that read,

> When they command you to fire your guns on your brothers in misery . . . workers, soldiers of tomorrow, you will not hesitate, you will not obey. You will fire, but not on your comrades. You will fire on the gold-braided old troopers who dare to give you such orders. . . . When they send you to the border to defend the coffers of the capitalists against other workers, abused as you are yourselves, you will not march. All war is criminal. At the mobilization order, you will answer with an immediate strike and with insurrection.[66]

Although the AIA was soon crushed by the government, its recommendations were embraced with increasing frequency. The anarchosyndicalist Confédération Générale du Travail (CGT) repeatedly published a *Manuel du soldat* advising desertion or the spreading of revolutionary propaganda in the barracks; at the CGT congress in Marseilles in 1908, the delegates agreed to proclaim a general strike at any declaration of war. Desertion and absenteeism in the French army grew at an alarming rate in response to this powerful and widely disseminated critique of the military establishment: 5991 in 1902; 14,067 in 1907; 12,000–13,000 in 1912.[67]

Socialists likewise met to consider tactics for preventing war. From 1907 on, Jaurès became famous for his stand against imperialism and the machinery of war, traveling all over France to plead and argue for peace to hundreds of thousands who came to listen. As the war approached, more and more support seemed to gather behind his arguments; for example, a speech he gave in a working-class district of Paris on 25 May 1913, organized in only two days, drew a crowd of 150,000. The anarchists and socialists organized demonstrations so huge and enthusiastically critical of the government that Premier Barthou threatened to crack down further on the labor movement.[68] In the end, the government ignored the message from the left with impunity and the French nation in a patriotic fever marched off to a war ultimately more destructive than any had imagined, whether "warmongers" or workers.

It would have been nearly impossible in Paris in those years to have remained oblivious to the scope of this left-wing antiwar movement, which drew attention to the plight of workers as well as to the machinations of armaments manufacturers and government ministers. D.-H. Kahnweiler, Picasso's dealer and friend after 1907, remembers those politicized years before the war:

> As for my political ideas, I was a leftist. For example, I took part in a demonstration on the grave of Zola, who had just died. . . . I was still, you remember, a very young man, so the only way I could show my interest was to participate in demonstrations and meetings, which I did. I heard Jaurès, Pressensé, all the great socialists of the day. I took part in demonstrations. The Dreyfus case was fairly recent, and the political atmosphere was still very unsettled. The right wing was very restless, and the left wing was full of enthusiasm.[69]

Picasso, far from remaining impervious to such events, was galvanized by them. Maturing in radically anarchist and pacifist Barcelona, he was equipped to understand the machinations and jockeying for war that such events represented. According to the anarchists, war is on one level madness and on another level exploitation of the workers as cannon fodder in the interests of armaments manufacturers and profiteers. While the fever of patriotism in France grew around him and the press became more and more hysterical, Picasso explored these issues through "quoting" with the newsprint he selected and through juxtaposition of such quotations with the still life images in his collages of 1912–13. Such associations range from black humor to black horror, and embody threats to the civilization represented by the work itself. The subtle interaction of these elements makes Picasso's antiwar posture apparent and reveals it to be consistent with the anarchist views expressed in his earlier work. That Picasso steadily stood against the war is confirmed by his refusal to be caught up in the final panicked rush to "defend civilization" that overtook all his French friends, including the antimilitarist Salmon. Even Apollinaire, who, like Picasso, was from a neutral country, changed his citizenship in order to fight on the French side. It took considerable courage in the face of Kropotkin's much-publicized support of the Allied cause, and doubtless loss of esteem in the eyes of a patriot like Braque, to maintain a pacifist stance at such a heady moment.[70]

A reading of the newspaper clippings in many of Picasso's collages reveals them to be reports and accounts of events with special political meaning, constituting a journalistic diary of the period. Most were carefully cut out to preserve legibility, and sometimes whole columns of print remained intact. Where Picasso cut into the text of an article, he often clearly retained its sense. Furthermore, the clippings did not innocently reflect front page news; it can be observed that Picasso selected from all parts of the newspaper, including the financial pages. (In his collages, Braque demonstrated little interest in such *actualités,* though he was cutting scraps out of the same newspapers from which he and Picasso were making supposedly random selections.)[71]

It seems possible that the very development of the use of newsprint in Picasso's collages—a full year before Braque's—could have been directly motivated by a desire to work these anarchist issues into his art. No more concrete way could be imagined of pulling Cubism back from the brink of total abstraction, a denouement steadfastly avoided by both Picasso and Braque. And no more democratic way could be found for the project of subverting the high art of oil painting than that of introducing such easily readable articles, on such universally engaging subjects. Following the recent redating by Daix and Rosselet of Picasso's Cubist works, we now know that the first time Picasso ever used a scrap of newsprint in a collage was in *Guitar, Sheet-Music and Wine Glass* of autumn 1912 (fig. 7.7), either his first or second experiment with *papier collé.* Concerning the current Balkan war, this first headline, from *Le Journal* of 10 November 1912, dispatched from Constantinople, reads "La Bataille s'est Engagé" ("The Battle Is Joined"), referring literally to the war and perhaps metaphorically to Picasso's own struggle with the issues it raised, as well as to the formal challenge represented by the unprecedented and outrageous use of the collage in art.[72] The fear that the Balkan war would lead to a pan-European war and the frantic (if insincere) peacemaking efforts by the other European powers were recorded in the newspapers in the following months, and in Picasso's subsequent collages. These anxieties, introduced into the tranquility of the still life, seem to threaten the fragile pleasure of a civilized peace: wine and music in a wallpapered room.

The second time that Picasso used newsprint in a collage, *Violin* of autumn 1912 (fig. 7.8), the article he chose describes the occupation of St.-Jean-de-Medua by the Montenegran army and discusses the desire of the Turks to continue the fighting.

Bottle of Suze of autumn 1912 (fig. 7.9), the third work in which Picasso used newsprint, contains a report, dated "16 Novembre," of the Serbian advance toward Monastir in Macedonia, including accounts of the wounded, descriptions of battle movements, and speculations on how long besieged Adrianople could hold out against famine. Picasso often deepens our sense of the tragedy of war by including, alongside accounts of strategy and battle movements, gruesome descriptions of war's victims. This collage includes the following account (fig. 7.9a) of a cholera

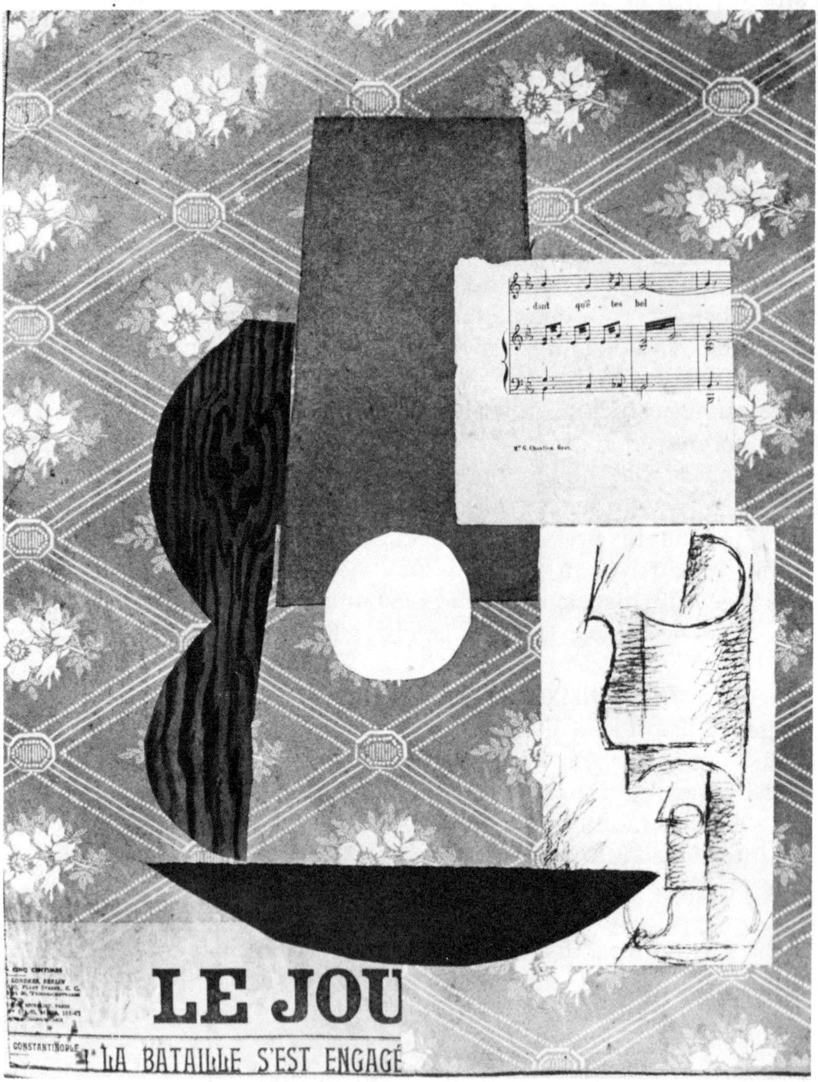

Figure 7.7. Pablo Picasso, *Guitar, Sheet Music and Wineglass,* November 1912
Pasted papers, gouache and charcoal on paper, 48 cm × 36.5 cm.
(Marion Koogler McNay Art Institute, San Antonio. Photo: McNay Art Institute)

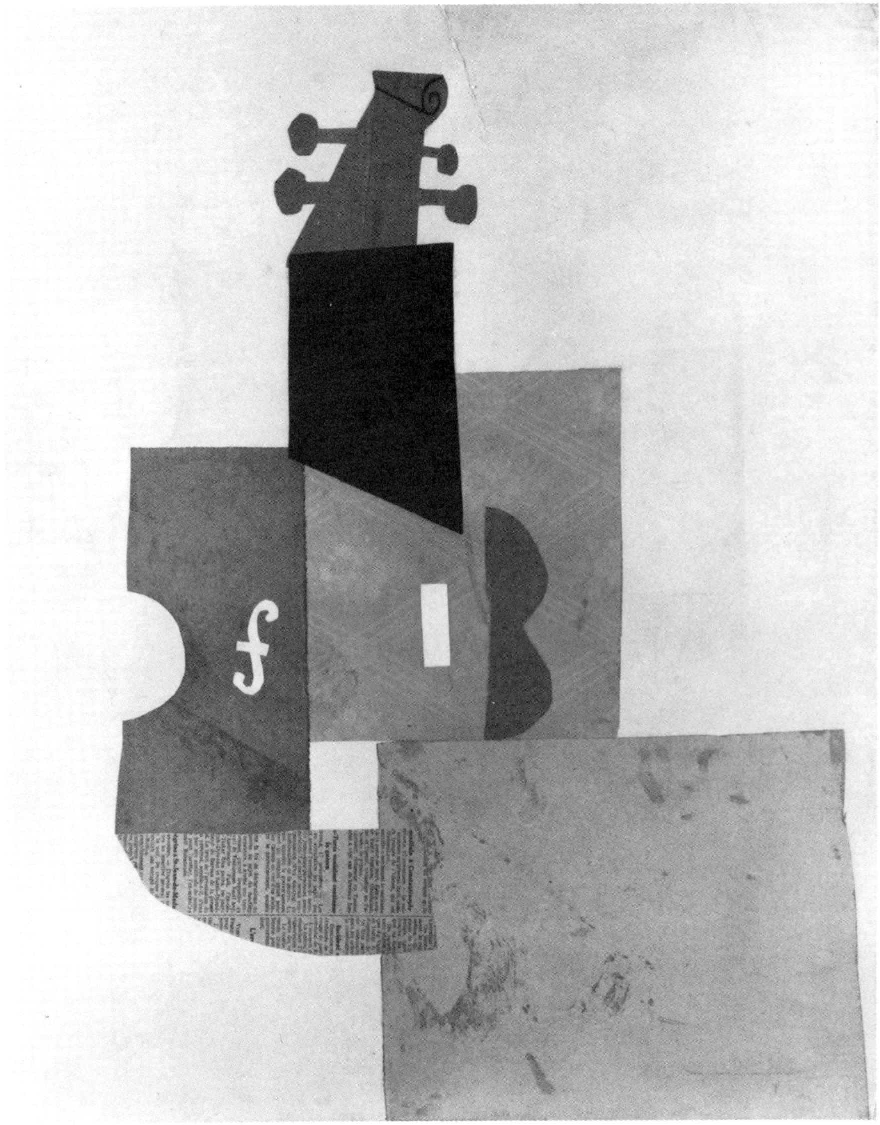

Figure 7.8. Pablo Picasso, *Violin,* November 1912
Pasted papers on paper, 65 cm × 50 cm.
(Musée Picasso, Paris. Photo: Musées Nationaux)

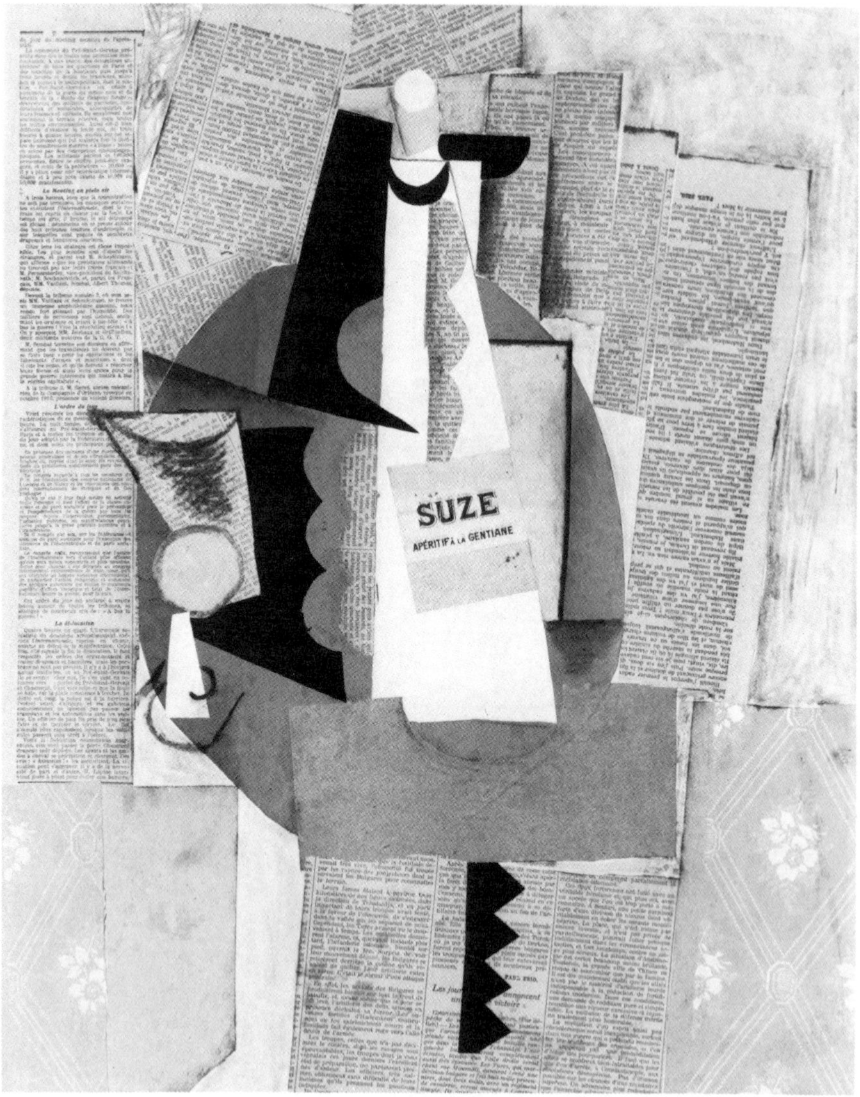

Figure 7.9. Pablo Picasso, *Bottle of Suze,* November 1912
Pasted papers, gouache and charcoal on paper,
64.5 cm × 50 cm.
(Washington University, St. Louis. Photo: Washington University Gallery of Art)

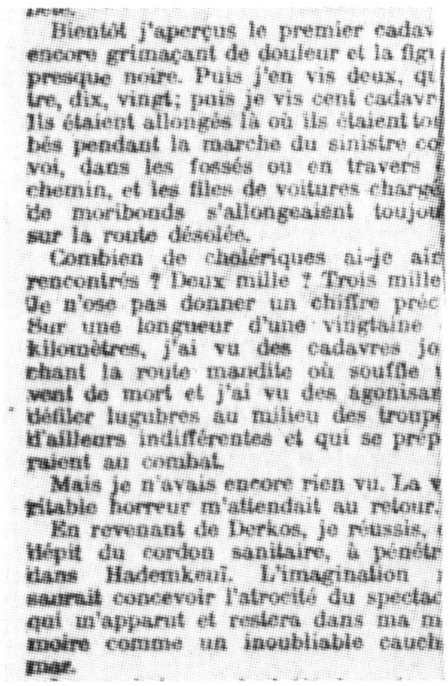

Bientôt j'aperçus le premier cadav
encore grimaçant de douleur et la fig
presque noire. Puis j'en vis deux, q
tre, dix, vingt; puis je vis cent cadavr
Ils étaient allongés là où ils étaient to
bés pendant la marche du sinistre co
voi, dans les fossés ou en travers
chemin, et les files de voitures charg
de moribonds s'allongeaient toujo
sur la route désolée.

Combien de cholériques ai-je ai
rencontrés ? Deux mille ? Trois mille
Je n'ose pas donner un chiffre préc
Sur une longueur d'une vingtaine
kilomètres, j'ai vu des cadavres jo
chant la route maudite où souffle
vent de mort et j'ai vu des agonisa
défiler lugubres au milieu des troup
d'ailleurs indifférentes et qui se prép
raient au combat.

Mais je n'avais encore rien vu. La v
ritable horreur m'attendait au retour.

En revenant de Derkos, je réussis,
dépit du cordon sanitaire, à pénétr
dans Hademkeui. L'imagination
saurait concevoir l'atrocité du specta
qui m'apparut et restera dans ma m
moire comme un inoubliable cauch
mar.

Figure 7.9a. Detail of Figure 7.9

epidemic among the Turkish soldiers, which can be read as pacifist statement since the Turks, "the enemy," are seen sympathetically:

> Before long I saw the first corpse still grimacing with suffering and whose face was nearly black. Then I saw two, four, ten, twenty; then I saw a hundred corpses. They were stretched out there where they had fallen during the march of the left convoy, in the ditches or across the road, and the files of cars loaded with the almost dead everywhere stretched themselves out on the devastated route.
>
> How many cholerics did I come upon like that? Two thousand? Three thousand? I don't dare give a precise figure. Over a distance of about twenty kilometers, I saw cadavers strewing the cursed route where a wind of death blows and I saw the dying march, ominous in the middle of troops indifferent and preparing themselves for combat.
>
> But I had seen nothing yet.[73]

These vivid descriptions of the horror and agony of war placed upside-down in the still life—an image of the world turned on its head—are forced into a dialogue with a report on the other side of the collage of a mass socialist/anarchist/pacifist meeting, 40,000 to 50,000 strong, with lengthy quotations from the speakers that, in effect, voice the leftist position. This article—right-side-up in the composition—reports that "the most listened-to speakers were at first the foreigners, and among them M. Scheidemann [a leading German socialist], who affirmed 'that the German proletarians will not fire on their French brothers.'" "M. Sembat ended his speech affirming that the workers ought not to seek death 'for the capitalists and the manufacturers of arms and munitions.'" And a third speaker articulated the threat inherent in all we have seen here by his opening words: "In the presence of the menace of a general [Euro]pean war. . . ."[74]

After these first three works, a cluster of collages, difficult to place in an exact sequence but all dating to late November–early December 1912, recorded the progress of the fighting, the preliminary negotiations for peace, and closely related subjects.[75] *Man with a Violin* (fig. 7.10), for example, includes in the upper left a report on an action by the miners of the Nord and the Pas-de-Calais, and in the center left an article in which the Minister of the Navy defends himself in Parliament against accusations that, if war was declared, the fleet would be undersupplied in powder, munitions, and fuel. In an adjacent column, a reporter in Bulgaria speculates on whether the Balkan war will escalate and whether "if a third power intervenes, Germany will throw itself into the balance." His column continues in the lower left, describing the preliminaries for peace negotiations at Tchataldja. At the bottom of the picture a partial cutting, apparently reporting a discussion in the Chamber, concerns itself with the "antimilitarist campaign" and "the extreme left."[76] Thus, these articles mingle the subject of the Balkan war with worker discontent and

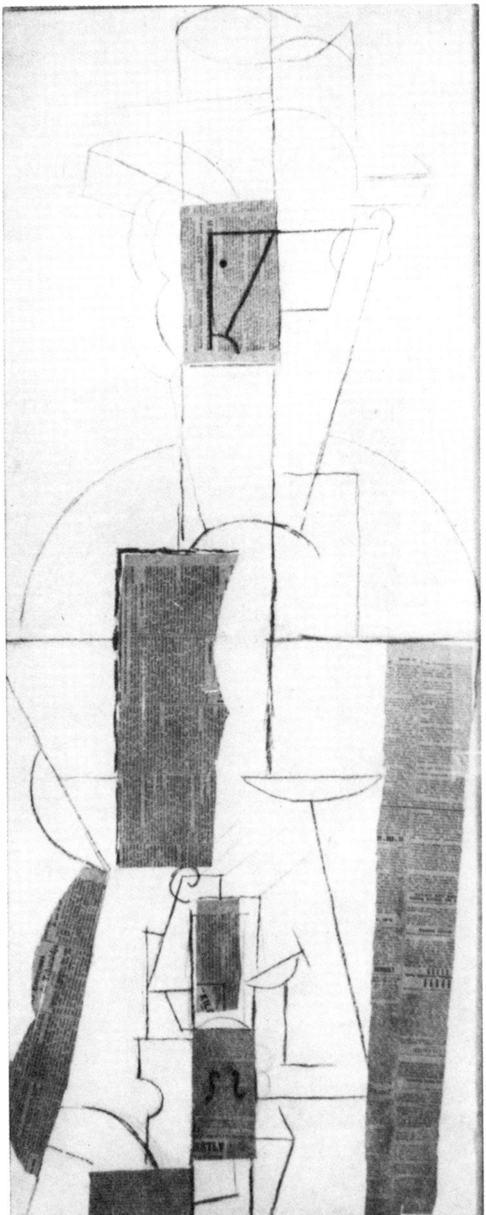

Figure 7.10. Pablo Picasso, *Man with a Violin,* Autumn-Winter 1912 Pasted papers and charcoal on paper, 123.5 cm × 46 cm. *(Private collection, New York. Photo: The Museum of Modern Art, New York)*

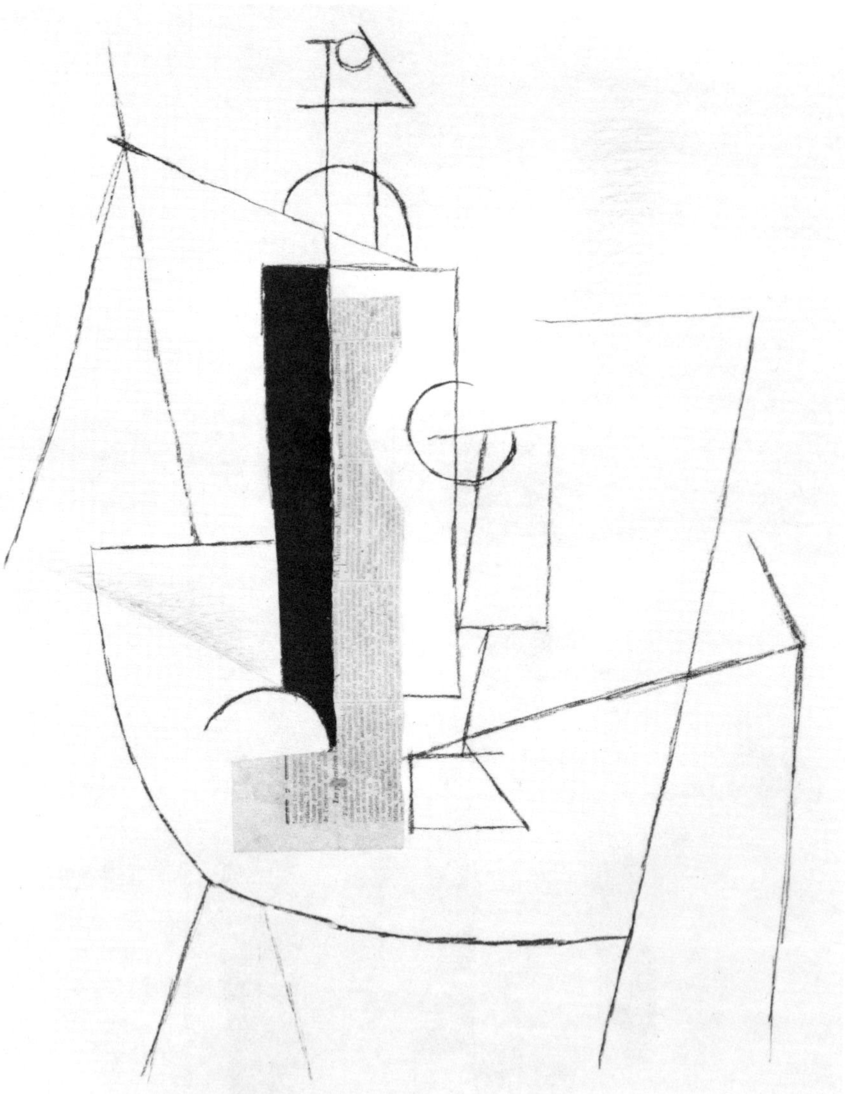

Figure 7.11. Pablo Picasso, *Bar Table with Bottle and Wineglass,* Autumn–Winter 1912
Pasted paper, ink and charcoal on paper,
62.5 cm × 47.3 cm.
(Metropolitan Museum of Art, New York. The Alfred Stieglitz Collection. Photo: Metropolitan Museum)

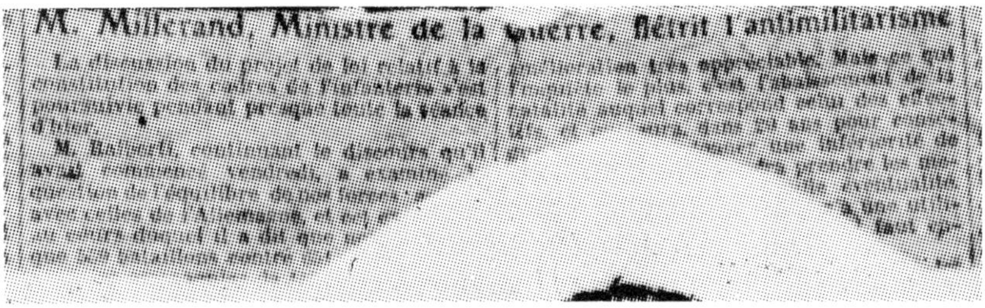

Figure 7.11a. Detail of Figure 7.11

the pacifist/anarchist movement and allude to the threat of a larger war in which France would be involved.

In *Bar Table with Bottle and Wineglass* of autumn-winter 1912 (figs. 7.11 and 7.11a), we read that M. Millerand, once a leading socialist but now minister of war, has "blasted" the antimilitarists for resisting the passage of a law expediting the French military build-up. In the series to which this work belongs stylistically, including *Bottle and Wineglass* and *Table with Bottle and Guitar,* both of autumn-winter 1912 and both containing dispatches concerning the unstable armistice signed on 3 December 1912,[77] the newsprint is circumscribed by the outline of the bottle, suggesting its role as the bottle's liquid and, by extension, the stuff on which French culture is temporarily drunk.

During 1912 and 1913 Picasso made approximately eighty collages of which fifty-two contain newspaper text; of these, at least half deal with the Balkan wars and the economic and political state of Europe, most produced in the autumn and winter of 1912.[78] (Picasso continued to make collages in 1914 but lost interest in dealing with the world events recorded in the newsprint; newsprint appears in only four of the approximately forty-six collages made that year.) The diaristic quality of the series would be incomplete without the actual announcement of peace in the First Balkan War; this appears, cut from *Le Journal* of 4 December 1912, in *Bottle and Wineglass.*[79]

It is worth noting that the iconography of the collages from autumn to winter 1912 is more strictly that of the Paris café than the later collages of 1913 and 1914, in which a larger percentage of the newspaper items Picasso incorporated suggest other, less serious, themes. The background of *Bottle on a Table* of autumn-winter 1912 (fig. 7.12) consists of a single sheet from the 3 December *Le Journal* turned upside-down—the financial page—which almost entirely discusses the impact on European economies of the shaky armistice that followed the First Balkan War. Stock markets plunge as repesentatives of the great powers meet in London to settle boundaries and reparations and attempt to balance the interests contending in the Balkan peninsula; while some profit from war, others suffer disastrously. Thus, this collage affirms the direct link between war and the economic health of nations. That the isolated bottle seems to rest on a table formed by the newspaper itself suggests that the economic structure making café life possible rests on the uncertain and despotic whimsy of uncontrollable world events, a suggestion tragically borne out two years later in 1914 when the world was indeed turned upside-down. Picasso, through his early immersion in the anarchist view of the world and of war, would have been well equipped to foresee this.

How do we make sense of these cuttings from *Le Journal* in the context of works traditionally considered Picasso's most highly abstract? Picasso, who had embraced a political view that despised the diplomatic maneuvering of these years and rejected patriotic jingoism, would have been drawn into discussions with his French friends about their expected roles in the coming war. Many of them, like Picasso, had grown up in the intellectual atmosphere of anarcho-Symbolism and certainly voiced their pacifism at this time: Signac, Salmon, Vlaminck.[80] Others, like Braque, expected to answer the call of *la patrie.* In the end, virtually the entire avant-garde marched off to war, including the virulent antimilitarists. Kropotkin amazed everyone by publicizing his fears of a German "threat to civilization," and encouraging participation in the war.[81] As noted above, even Apollinaire changed his citizenship from Polish to French so that he could fight with his French brothers to "defend civilization."[82] Picasso, though from a neutral country, still would have had to justify his noncombatant position, given the passionate rhetoric aroused by the threat of a general European war. With such ominous events and promises of hostility as the clippings in these collages evidence, the discussions and arguments must have grown intense in cafés all over Paris. With their settings of bottles, glasses, café tables, and newspapers, these works not only depict the physical setting of the artistic bohemia, where political arguments were part of the daily fare, but suggest the contents of such arguments by selectively importing the news itself into that heady atmosphere.

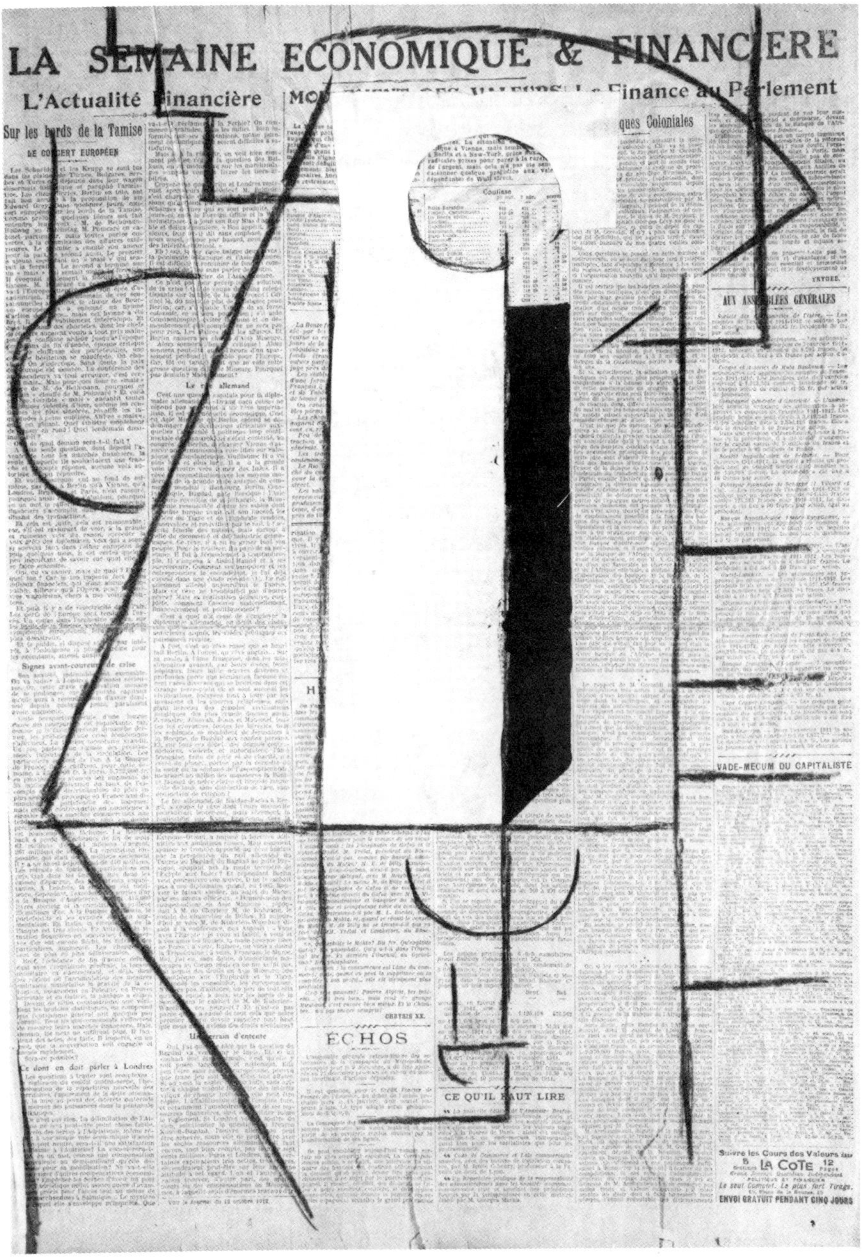

Figure 7.12. Pablo Picasso, *Bottle on a Table,* Autumn 1912
Pasted papers and charcoal on paper,
62 cm × 44 cm.
(Musée Picasso, Paris. Photo: Musées Nationaux)

Picasso, as has been seen, juxtaposed readable columns of newsprint whose authors insistently reiterated subjects of specific concern to left-wing radicals: war, war profiteers, machinating politicians, ministerial abuses of power, strikes and strike-breaking, anarchist and pacifist anti-war demonstrations. The news items accumulate to project an image of French politics as venal, power-mongering, and posing a crazy threat to all those values of humanity and civilization which Picasso's work had always, in various ways, embraced. The articles can be seen as addressed to an audience of *Le Journal* readers, that is, those who constituted his immediate society and whom he expected to read, as well as to contemplate, his collages; this would explain why he incorporated so few Spanish newspapers in the collages as a group and none in late 1912.[83] *Le Journal,* a mass circulation Republican daily that encouraged in its reporters a somewhat disrespectable emphasis on the prurient and the gory, was the ideal vehicle for importing into the café settings of the collages the widely publicized war news—and those macabre "human interest" stories of murder, suicide, and vandalism which make up another quarter of the newsprint items used in 1912–14. Picasso never employed anarchist or radical newspapers, which would have replaced description with polemic. His use of the traditional still life as an arena for his Spanish radicalism ironically acknowledges his anomalous position in French culture, in which, in so many ways, he refused to participate. An anarchist would have said, "refused to legitimate." (For example, he publicly exhibited in France only two or three works during the entire life of the Cubist movement.)[84] The incorporation of the columns of newsprint for their associational values remains as radical an introduction of the real world into an otherwise illusionistic context as the incorporation of those letters, signs, and headline fragments to whose meanings we are already alert. But at the same time they extend the revolutionary nature of such intrusions by representing through their selection literally revolutionary viewpoints. And, perhaps more significantly, such news items firmly orient the outrage to traditions of image and craft in the political philosophy that justified it. They, more than any other of the collage elements, suggest Apollinaire's meaning in his explication of the appearance of "actual objects" in the collages: "new in art," he wrote in *Les Peintres cubistes,* "they are already soaked with humanity."[85]

It may seem curious that there is no contemporary art criticism that articulates this reading of Picasso's collages—apart from the general critical view of Cubism as the saboteur of the past—but it is less surprising when we recollect that Picasso never exhibited them. Perhaps best equipped to understand the depth of what Picasso was doing in the collages I have discussed here, Apollinaire only rarely referred to specific works in his art criticism, and, even then, never discussed them at length. He preferred high-blown generalizations, which almost exclusively characterized this genre of his writing, though he frequently cast such generalizations in politicized language that was more than merely metaphorical.[86] Further, the monthly journal that Apollinaire co-directed with Jean Cerusse from 1912 to 1914, *Les Soirées de Paris,* followed the events of the Balkan wars almost as closely as did Picasso's collages.

The most telling response to the political aspect of Picasso's collages comes from neither journalists nor art critics but from the work of Juan Gris. Gris, after a period of making a living by selling socially critical and political cartoons to such journals as *L'Assiette au beurre,* developed a unique and brilliant Cubist style, following the artistic maneuvers of his Spanish compatriot at several removes (in style and time) but with attentive absorption.[87] Gris's use of newsprint in his collage differs from that of the other Cubists; for example, he cut out and combined letters to create false headlines, leaving room for none of the doubts regarding conscious intention that Picasso's and Braque's collages can still inspire. Picasso's groundbreaking use of newpsrint in his collages of the Balkan war period, before Gris was making papiers-collés of any kind, did not pass Gris unnoticed; but not until 1914, in the first year of his concentrated exploration of the medium of collage, did political and military events inspire Gris to make similar use of newspaper headlines and texts to manifest his political consciousness. For example, *The Package of Coffee* of 1914 contains a battle map of Ulm; *Still-Life, Glasses and Newspaper* of 1914 shows the folded front page of the May 3rd edition of *Le Journal,* exhibiting an illustration and article about a dirigible explosion at Verdun; and *The Checked Tablecloth* of 1915 contains an illusionistic copy of *Le Journal* with only one legible headline: COMMUNIQUES OFFICIELS, suggesting a life taken over by and obsessed with the war, as Gris's was at the time. Other works of this period contain articles about the conduct of the war itself and contain newspapers representing a variety of political attitudes towards its events, including *Excelsior, Le Matin, Le Figaro* and *Le Journal.*[88] It is notable that it was Gris, a Spaniard, who most honored Picasso's incorporation of news events and political issues in his art; but more significantly, Gris's work of 1914 and 1915 affirms the ease with which a contemporary perceived and imitated the incorporation of political subjects in Picasso's collages.

In such works as *Playing Cards, Wineglass and Bottle of Rum (''Vive la France''),* Avignon, summer-autumn 1914, with its crossed flags taken from the mobilization posters, Picasso seemed to enjoy poking fun at his friends' patriotism at a time when many thought, like Poincaré, that the war would be ''short but glorious.''[89] Expressing his pacifist convictions,

Picasso did not enlist. But whatever his arguments may have been in 1914, they could not suffice after the much publicized (and exaggerated) atrocities of the German march through Belgium.[90] Apollinaire, in an essay written from the front in March 1915 listing the whereabouts of the scattered French avant-garde, informed the interested public that Picasso was too ill to fight:

> Derain is in a motorcycle unit in the North, Georges Braque was recently in Le Havre as a second lieutenant, Fernand Léger is at the front with the supply corps, Albert Gleizes has been at the front since the outbreak of war, and Dufy is in Le Havre, waiting. . . . R. de la Fresnaye is doubtless still in Lisieux. Groult suffered an arm wound. The sculptor Duchamp-Villon is a medical aide in Saint-Germain; the painter and engraver Laboureur is at the Château of Nantes, serving as an interpreter for the British Army. . . . There was a rumor that Robert D[elaunay] is in San Sebastián, but I cannot bring myself to admit the truth of this unlikely assertion. . . . Picasso, whose health is too weak to allow him to do anything other than his invaluable work as an artist, ''has outdone Ingres in his admirable drawing without even trying,'' according to a letter I received.[91]

Picasso almost certainly never intended to fight.[92] His claims of ill health are now known to be hypochondriacal if not chimerical, and are belied by photographs of the strapping young man that date from that period.[93] Of particular interest, though, is the shift in justification for Picasso's noncombatant position. For many anarchists at the time, the brutal events forced a reevaluation in the face of the German ''threat to civilization'' so feared by Kropotkin. Picasso, we know, felt extremely lonely in Paris with the dying Eva; understandably, he was obsessed with death, and embarrassed in front of soldiers who were wounded or on leave.[94] In a drawing of 1915 (fig. 7.13), he depicted himself standing in a deserted Paris; the only other visible creatures are a little dog, and, in the distance, an overweight man with a cane, who was obviously unfit for active duty. Yet Picasso maintained his unpopular moral position throughout the war and, indeed, throughout his life: the few explicitly political works in his career—such as *Guernica* of 1937, *The Charnel House* of 1945, or the *War* and *Peace* murals of 1952—are all pacifist images, against war in general, according to Picasso, and they confirm the pacifism expressed earlier in his life and work.[95]

To sensitize ourselves to the social and political background of the collages, and to consider the ways in which Picasso was able to manipulate relevant themes, is not to suppose that he was methodically and secretively encoding each collage with anarchist directives, nor even that a single, unchanging anarchist outlook characterizes his work of the *avant-guerre.* For Picasso to exhibit unwavering consistencies in his work through this

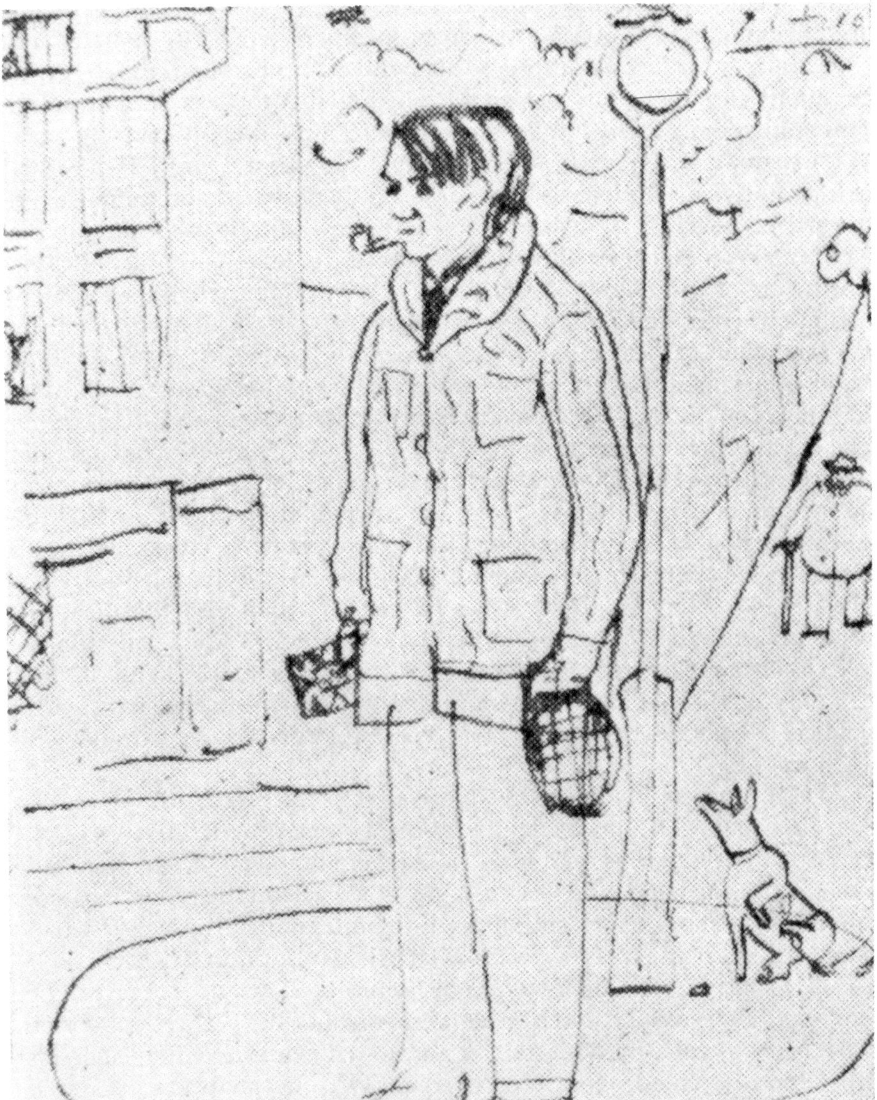

Figure 7.13. Pablo Picasso, *Self-Portrait,* 1915
Pen and ink on paper, 15 cm × 11.5 cm.
(Present location unknown. Photo after 1975 sale catalogue for London Arts Group of Detroit)

period, in politics as in anything else, would be highly uncharacteristic. And the complex impulses behind the development of the Cubist style are attributable to a myriad of concerns. But it would be equally uncharacteristic for Picasso utterly to suspend, in his Cubism, those preoccupations and thematic threads which tie together the rest of his oeuvre. This study points to the impact that anarchist ideas had on his early work in Barcelona and Paris, and suggests that he was not cooly indifferent to the cataclysmic upheavals of his day. He shared ideas and themes with the artists, poets, and political theorists with whom he associated in his early career. It has been difficult to imagine the degree to which Picasso was aware of and deeply connected to current political events precisely because he embraced a body of social theory now largely ignored. Political interpretations of Picasso's work of this period have been offered—by Max Raphael, Clement Greenberg, Meyer Schapiro, John Berger, and, most recently, T. J. Clark—but in every case, Picasso has been forced into a Marxist interpretation of art and society.[96] The desire to work out a model of historical determinism, and the dislike and/or ignorance of anarchism on the part of many Marxist critics, has prevented them from seeing the conscious political component of Picasso's relations to culture. Though their aims and, in fact, achievements have varied widely, most have applied Marxist theories to Picasso's role as an artist with the firm and sometimes arrogant assumption that he was no more conscious and intellectual a political creature than the anti-intellectual artist he pretended to be. Except for Sabartés's view of the Blue Period and the later overtly political works, Picasso's art has been interpreted as unrelievedly apolitical.

Yet if much of his work—from the street sketches of 1897–99 to the collages—has been viewed as mere formal experiment, it is true that Picasso himself later prompted us to see them that way. Apart from *Arte joven* on the one hand, and *Guernica* and later work on the other, Picasso's ambivalence about expressing himself unambiguously, in either artistic or verbal statements, has generally masked his political convictions. Secretive and private, his revolutionism informed his art. He refused to explain to those who could not see. Asked about his aesthetic theory in 1904, he eloquently fired his gun—a gift from the quintessential anarchist artist Jarry.[97] Asked about Negro art in 1920, he snapped, "Connais pas!"[98] Yet Picasso's adherence to these anarchist attitudes and ideas in his early life, and his expression of them, however obliquely and allusively, in even his most radically abstract works, substantiates the affirmation he voiced in later years that he had always struggled, by means of his painting, "as a true revolutionary."

Appendix

Journal officiel de la Chambre des Députés, 3 Dec. 1912, 2918–29:

M. Jules-Louis Breton: Depuis quelques années, sous prétext de rénover l'art, de moderniser ses procédés, de créer des formes nouvelles, des formules inédites, certains exploiteurs de la crédulité publique se sont livrés aux plus folles surenchères d'extravagances et d'excentricités.

Je ne songe nullement à leur en contester le triste droit, mais je ne puis admettre que notre administration des beaux-arts se prête à ces plaisanteries de très mauvais goût et livre gracieusement nos palais nationaux pour des manifestations qui risquent de compromettre notre merveilleux patrimoine artistique.

(Très bien! très bien! sur divers bancs.)

Et cela d'autant plus que ce sont pour la plupart des étrangers qui viennent ainsi chez nous, dans nos palais nationaux, jeter consciemment ou inconsciemment le discrédit sur l'art français. . . .

Il est en effet, messieurs, absolument inadmissible que nos palais nationaux puissent servir à des manifestations d'un caractère aussi nettement antiartistique et antinational.

(Applaudissements.)

M. Marcel Sembat [an acquaintance and supporter of Picasso, Matisse, and modernism in general]: C'est aux peintres cubistes qu'il l'a dû. . . .

Qui donc contestera, même dans les milieux où l'on est le plus vite alarmé sur la [*sic*] tendances révolutionnaires, la valeur des [juges] et la sûreté de leur goût? . . .

Mon cher ami, quand un tableau vous semble mauvais, vous avez un incontestable droit: c'est de ne pas le regarder, d'aller en voir d'autres; mais on n'appelle pas les gendarmes!

Notes

I would like to thank Jack J. Spector and Joan M. Marter of Rutgers University for their many fruitful suggestions and unfailing encouragement. Thanks also go to my colleague William I. Homer, and to Cleo McNelly Kearns and George Kearns, for discussing with me the many implications of this subject. I would also like to express my appreciation to the University of Delaware for a General University Research Grant, which supported a research trip to France and Spain in the summer of 1983, and to the Delaware Humanities Forum for a Research Fellowship in 1984–85, which provided support for the completion of the manuscript.

1. Significant recent studies include R. Rosenblum, "Picasso and the Typography of Cubism," in Roland Penrose and John Golding, eds., *Picasso in Retrospect* (New York:

Harper and Row, 1980); reprinted in this volume, pp. 91–120; and "The *Demoiselles d'Avignon* Revisited," *ARTnews* 72 (April 1973): 45–48; L. Steinberg, "The Philosophical Brothel," *ARTnews* 71 (September 1972): 20–29 and (October 1972): 38–47; W. Rubin, "Cézannisme and the Beginnings of Cubism," in W. Rubin, ed., *Cézanne—The Late Work* (New York, 1977), pp. 151-202, and "From Narrative to 'Iconic' in Picasso: The Buried Allegory in *Bread and Fruitdish on a Table* and the Role of *Les Demoiselles d'Avignon*," *Art Bulletin* 65 (1983): 615–49; M. Gedo, "Art as Exorcism: Picasso's 'Demoiselles d'Avignon,'" *Arts Magazine* 55 (October 1980): 70–82; R. Johnson, "The Demoiselles d'Avignon' and Dionysian Destruction," *Arts Magazine* 55 (October 1980): 94-101, and "Picasso's 'Demoiselles d'Avignon' and the Theater of the Absurd," *Arts Magazine* 55 (October 1980): 102–13; and L. Nochlin, "Picasso's Color: Schemes and Gambits," *Art in America* 68 (December 1980): 105–23 and 177–83.

2. For example, Penrose, pp. 46ff; P. Cabanne, *Pablo Picasso: His Life and Times* (New York, 1977), p. 30; W. Boeck, *Picasso* (New York, n.d.), p. 113; and Blunt/Pool, passim.

3. The best work in English on the anarchists is Joll. See also Woodcock Maitron; and E. Hobsbawm, *Primitive Rebels: Studies in Archaic Forms of Social Movement in the 19th and 20th Centuries* (New York, 1959), esp. chap. 5, "Millenarianism II: The Andalusian Anarchists."

4. The major study of this subject is Herbert. Her book thoroughly establishes the crucial significance of social theory for many artists and writers of the period, most particularly the Symbolist and Neoimpressionist avant-garde of the 1880s and 1890s, though more study could be done on the distinctions between anarchism and socialism; see also Egbert.

5. Joll, pp. 69ff.

6. Kropotkin's most influential works were *The Conquest of Bread* (Paris, 1892) (London, 1977) and *Mutual Aid: A Factor in Evolution* (London, 1902), originally published as articles in French periodicals in the 1890s and frequently reprinted in Spain.

7. See Joll, pp. 95ff., and, for a more extensive discussion, E. Carr, *Michael Bakunin* (London, 1937).

8. See A. Reszler, *L'Esthétique anarchiste* (Paris, 1973), pp. 44ff. Kropotkin discussed his ideas on art at greatest length in *The Conquest of Bread,* which was widely and popularly read in Spain:

   > When a Greek sculptor chiseled his marble he endeavored to express the spirit and heart of the city. All its passions, all its traditions of glory, were to live again in the work. But today the *united* city has ceased to exist; there is no more communion of ideas. The town is a chance agglomeration of people who do not know one another, who have no common interest. . . . What fatherland can the international banker and the ragpicker have in common? Only when cities, territories, nations, or groups of nations, will have renewed their harmonious life, will art be able to draw its inspiration from *ideals held in common* (trans. in H. Read, ed., *Kropotkin: Selections from His Writings* [London, 1942], p. 145).

9. See Leighten, passim.

10. Proudhon was especially influential in Spain, where excerpts of his writings were translated and published in the scores of anarchist and avant-garde periodicals (see Joll, 78; Alvarez Junco, passim; M. Bookchin, *The Spanish Anarchists: The Heroic Years 1868–1936* [New York, 1977]; and Brenan, chapter on anarchism, passim).

11. See Cervera's important study, and A. Cirici Pellicer, *El arte modernista catalán* (Barcelona, 1951).

12. See Brenan, pp. 217–18; H. Thomas, *The Spanish Civil War* (New York, 1961), p. 14; J. Read, *The Catalans* (London, 1978), p. 173; and E. Peers, *Catalonia infelix* (New York, 1938) (Westport, Conn., 1970), pp. 137–39.

13. See Blunt/Pool, Cervera, and McCully. Of these writers, McCully avoids any mention of political awareness on the part of these artists, going so far as to deny the primacy of subject matter in the work of Nonell, who, with his reiterated depictions of the homeless beggars, gypsies, and shamelessly abandoned soldiers who constituted the social scandals of the day, was certainly the most overtly politically conscious artist of all the *modernistas*: "Nonell's interests, however, lay less in social commentary than in the straightforward sketching and observation of life around him, and in experimentation with techniques" (McCully 22). Cervera points to many of the political influences and social conditions that formed a large part of the artistic environment in Barcelona. Pool, more than anyone, draws connections between specific works and contemporary political writing in Barcelona.

14. Alvarez Junco, pp. 630–33, has compiled a complete bibliography of all anarchist journals published in Spain in the period; of all translations of anarchists and radical writers outside Spain in the political and litarary press (this does not include art journals), pp. 634–55; and a good bibliography, though not exhaustive, of translations of artists and literary figures, and of articles on art and revolution, pp. 77–85 and 89–92.

15. *La Renaixensa* (1871–1905); *La Illustracío catalana* (1880–1903); *L'Avenç* (1881–84; 1889–93); *La Ilustración iberica* (1883–98); *Catalonia* (successor to *L'Avenci* (1898–1900); *Luz* (1898); *Hispanis* (1899–1903); *Els Quatre Gats* (1899); *Pèl & ploma* (successor to *Els Quatre Gats;* 1899–1903); *Joventut* (1900–06); *Catalunya artística* (1900–05); *La Ilustracío Llevantina* (1900–01); *La Semana catalanista* (1900); *Forma* (successor to *Pèl & ploma*/ 1904–07). See Cervera, chapter 7, "Periodicals," passim.

16. Cervera, p. 163.

17. See Domingo Marti y Julia, "L'Art a Catalunya," *Joventut* (6 December 1900): 673, quoted in Cervera, p. 182.

18. Illustrated in Blunt/Pool, fig. 39.

19. Quoted in Cervera, p. 199 (author's trans.).

20. Illustrated in ibid., fig. 38 (undated).

21. Ibid., pp. 61–62.

22. See ibid., pp. 62–64; E. Jardí, *Nonell* (Barcelona, n.d.), pp. 58–62 and 102–10; and McCully, p. 50. For illustrations see Cervera, figs. 41 and 42; Jardí, figs. 25–29 and 39–42; McCully, figs. 22 and 23; and Blunt/Pool, fig. 63.

23. The three major works on this subject are Blunt/Pool, McCully, and Cervera.

24. Cirlot, p. 27.

25. Blunt/Pool, pp. 11–12, and figs. 60–77 with text.

26. See Daix/Boudaille, A. 5.

27. Ibid., p. 238.

28. Ibid., p. 206.
29. Ibid., x.5, x.6, viii.1.
30. Ibid., D.ix.17.
31. Cirlot, figs. 73 and 578.
32. Ibid., fig. 129.
33. Blunt/Pool. p. 19.
34. See Alvarez Junco, pp. 634–55.
35. P. Picasso and F. Asis de Soler, "Arte joven," *Arte joven* (15 March 1901): 1 (author's trans.).
36. A. Lozano, "Gotas de tinta," in *Arte joven* (15 March 1901): 3 (author's trans.).
37. J. Martínez Ruiz, "La Vida," *Arte joven* (15 April 1901): 2–3 (author's trans.).
38. *Pèl & ploma* (15 March 1901): 7.
39. Blunt/Pool, p. 11.
40. See "La Amnestía se impone" and "Manifiesto de la colonia española residencia in París," *La Publicidad* (29 December 1900): 1. Though Picasso was not really one of the exiles (his uncle paid his military exemption fee until 1908; P. O'Brien, *Pablo Ruiz Picasso* [New York, 1976], p. 56), it is noteworthy that he counts himself among them in order to add his voice to the protest. He was, in fact, back in Spain by the time the manifesto appeared.
41. See Maitron; Goldberg; Joll; Woodcock; B. Tuchman, *The Proud Tower: A Portrait of the World Before the War, 1890–1914* (New York, 1966); J. and M. Lough, *An Introduction to Nineteenth Century France* (London, 1978); and Herbert.
42. See Herbert, passim; A Lehmann, *The Symbolist Aesthetic in France: 1885–1895* (Oxford, 1950, pp. 18ff.; Egbert, pp. 45ff.; and R. Poggioli, *The Theory of the Avant-Garde* (Cambridge, Mass., 1968), pp. 97ff.
43. The art critics in the left, centrist, and, especially, right-wing press often discussed modern art in terms of radical politics. Their assumption that every work of art functions in relation to the desire to preserve or change the status quo reveals the high degree to which French culture at the turn of the century was politicized, for Picasso's audience as much as for Picasso himself. For specific equations of Cubism with anarchism, revolutionism, amorality, and willful distruction of the past, see, for example, Coriolès, "A propos de l'internationalisme en art," *Le Gaulois* (3 January 1910): 2, Sâr Péladan; "Le Salon d'Automne," *Le Revue hebdomadaire* 20 (1911): 405–16; André Pe'raté, "Le Salon d' Automne," *Le Correspondant* (25 October 1911): 308–16; J. d'Aoust, "La Peinture cubiste, futuriste . . . et au-delà," *Livres et art* 1 (March 1912): 153–56; and Camille Mauclair, "La Peinture 'nouvelle' et les marchands," *La Revue* 98 (1912): 429–42. For a contemporary discussion of this politicized attitude, see Fernand Roches, "Le Salon d'Automne de 1912," *L'Art décoratif* 14 (20 November 1912): 281–328.
44. W. Rubin, ed., *Pablo Picasso: A Retrospective* (New York, 1980), p. 56.
45. J. Golding, *Cubism: A History and an Analysis 1907–1914* (London, 1959), pp. 23–24; Penrose, pp. 143–44; Herbert, pp. 102ff. See M. Golberg, *La Morale des lignes* (Paris, 1908); and P. Aubery, "Mécislas Golberg et l'art moderne," *Gazette des beaux-arts* 66 (1965): 339–44.

46. M. Adéma, *Apollinaire,* trans. D. Folliot (New York, 1955), p. 15; R. Shattuck, *The Banquet Years: The Origins of the Avant-Garde in France, 1885 to World War I* (New York, rev. ed., 1968), p. 257.

47. Apollinaire and Salmon started an avant-garde review, *Le Festin d'Esope, Revue des belles lettres,* which ran in nine issues from November 1903 to August 1904. Arne Hammer, an editor of the pacifist *L'Européen,* was associated with the new review and Jarry contributed poetry and advice. Samples of the contents of *Le Festin d'Esope* include stories and poems by Apollinaire; poems by Salmon and Jarry; an article by the Polish anarchist Mécislas Golberg on passive resistance; "Chronique," a column probably by Apollinaire discussing a radical socialist group; political commentary by Apollinaire's friend "Thrank-Spirobeg" (Faik bég Konitza,) an Albanian revolutionary; and a translation from Czech, "Lettre d'un condamné à son défenseur," by Otakar Theer. Political concerns in the short life of *Le Festin* equaled, indeed paralleled, the literary ones, as they would again in Apollinaire's journal of 1912–14, *Les Soirées de Paris.* For an account of Apollinaire's bizarre friendship with Faik bég Konitza, see F. Steegmuller, *Apollinaire: Poet among the Painters* (New York, 1963), pp. 91–94 and 102–03.

48. G. Apollinaire, 'The New Painting: Art Notes," *Les Soirées de Paris,* April–May 1912, in L. Breunig, ed., *Apollinaire on Art: Essays and Reviews, 1902–1918,* trans. S. Suleiman (New York, 1972), pp. 223–25.

49. Apollinaire, *The Cubist Painters: Aesthetic Meditations, 1913,* trans. L. Abel (New York, 1949), p. 23.

50. Salmon, p. 11.

51. McCully, p. 130. See Rusiñol's *L'Allegria que passa* (1898), fig. 43.

52. For studies of primitivism and modern art, see R. Goldwater, *Primitivism and Modern Art* (New York, 1938; rev. ed., 1967); J. Laude, *La Peinture française (1905–1914) et l'art nègre* (Paris, 1968); and the recent catalogue from the Museum of Modern At, W. Rubin, ed., *'Primitivism' in 20th Century Art* (New York, 1984), esp. J. Paudrat, 'The Arrival of Tribal Objects in the West from Africa," pp. 125–75; and Rubin, "Picasso," pp. 241–343.

53. See, for example, C. Gray, *Cubist Aesthetic Theories* (Baltimore, 1953); L. Henderson, "A New Facet of Cubism: 'The Fourth Dimension' and 'Non-Euclidean Geometry' Reinterpreted," *Art Quarterly* 34 (1971): 410–33; and M. Teuber, "Formvorstellung und Kubismus oder Pablo Picasso und William James," in S. Gohr, ed. *Kubismus* (Cologne, 1982), pp. 9–57.

54. See above note 46.

55. See *Journal officiel de la Chambre des Députés,* 3 December 1912, pp. 2918–29: see Appendix.

56. Picasso, "Pourquoi j'ai adhéré au parti communiste," interview with Pol Gaillard, *L'Humanité,* Paris, 29–30 October 1944 (author's trans.).

57. See A. Barr, *Picasso: Fifty Years of His Art* (New York, 1946), pp. 245ff.; trans. pp. 247–48.

58. "Shafts from Apollo's Bow, 9. A Blast from the North," *Apollo* 46 (October 1947): 90.

59. See Leighten, chap. 3, for a discussion of the political concerns in Apollinaire's journalism and the anarchist activism of such friends and acquaintances of Picasso's as Kees Van Dongen, Maurice Vlaminck, et al.

60. In response to strikes by miners of the Nord and the Pas-de-Calais in 1906, by dockers of Nantes, vineyard workers of the Midi, and the electricians of Paris in 1907, and by construction workers in 1908, the government dispatched military troops who fired on the assembled strikers, killing twenty and wounding six hundred sixty-seven in these three years. The fact that the Radical government of Clemenceau lent its police power to the employers encouraged disillusion and class hatred. Even the old socialist Briand, in the name of national defense and patriotism, used government power to break an important transport strike in 1910. See Tuchman (as in n. 41), pp. 515–16 and 532; and Goldberg, pp. 353–68. See also E. Dolléans, *Histoire du mouvement ouvrier,* 3 vols. (Paris, 1936–53), II, *1871–1936.*

61. Goldberg, p. 368; Joll, pp. 202ff.

62. Goldberg, pp. 342ff.

63. Ibid., pp. 429ff.; and E. Helmreich, *The Diplomacy of the Balkan Wars, 1912–1913* (Cambridge, Mass., 1938; repr. 1969).

64. Proudhon, letter to Romain Rolland, 3 June 1861; quoted in Joll, p. 69.

65. Goldberg, pp. 380ff.

66. Quoted in Maitron, p. 349 (author's trans.).

67. Goldberg, p. 351; Maitron, p. 350.

68. Goldberg, pp. 382–83 and 442.

69. D. Kahnweiler, *My Galleries and Painters* (Paris, 1961; New York, 1971), interview with F. Crémieux, p. 23.

70. André Salmon, in *La Terreur noire,* pp. 500ff., discussed the atmosphere in the days of the mobilization: Jaurès was dead and "Kropotkin était d'accord avec les poilus." Passions ran high at that time. Vlaminck, who was fiercely pacifist and did his war service by working in a factory, was horrified by the enthusiasm for the war of his longtime friend and artistic collaborator André Derain, and he claimed it completely ended their friendship; see A. Derain, *Lettres à Vlaminck,* intro. and commentary M. Vlaminck (Paris, 1955), pp. 213–20.

71. See I. Monod-Fontaine and E. Carmean, Jr. *Braque: The Papiers Collés* (Washington, D.C., 1982), for a complete catalogue of Braque's collages.

72. Daix/Rosselet, p. 287, "The newspaper, bottom left, dates from 10 November 1912, and is the oldest one that I have been able to discover."

73. Author's translation.

> Bientôt j'aperçus le premier cadav[re] encore grimaçant de douleur et la fig[ure] presque noire. Puis j'en vis deux, qu[a]tre, dix, vingt; puis je vis cent cadavr[es.] Ils étaient allongés là où ils étaient tombés pendant la marche du sinstre co[n]voi, dans les fossés ou en travers [le] chemin, et les files de voitures chargé[es] de moribonds s'allongeaient toujou[rs] sur la route désolée.
>
> Combien de cholériques ai-je ain[si] rencontrés? Deux mille? Trois mille[?] Je n'ose pas donner un chiffre préc[is.] Sur une longueur d'une vingtaine [de] kilomètres, j'ai vu des cadavres jo[n]chant la route maudite où souffle u[n] vent de mort et j'ai vu des agonisan[ts] défiler lugubres au milieu des troupe[s] d'ailleurs indifférentes et qui se prép[a]raient au combat.
>
> Mais je n'avais encore rien vu.

74. Author's translation. "Les plus écoutés sont d'abord les étrangers, et parmi eux M. Scheidemann, qui affirme 'que les prolétaires allemands ne tireront pas sur leur frères français' . . ."; "M. Sembat termine son discours en affirmant que les travailleurs ne doivent pas se faire tuer 'pour les capitalistes et les fabricants d'armes et munitions' . . ."; "En présence des menaces d'une guerre [euro]péene généralisée. . . ."

75. *Violin* (Daix/Rosselet, No. 524); *Wineglass, Violin and Newspaper* (Daix/Rosselet, No. 527); *Head of a Man* (Daix/Rosselet, No. 532); *Man with a Violin* (Daix/Rosselet, No. 535) (fig. 7.10); *Head of a Man* (Daix/Rosselet, No. 538); *Table with Bottle, Wineglass and Newspaper* (Daix/Rosselet, No. 538); *Table with Bottle, Wineglass and Newspaper* (Daix/Rosselet, No. 542); *Bottle and Wineglass* (Daix/Rosselet, No. 544); *Bottle and Wineglass* (Daix/Rosselet, No. 549); *Table with Bottle and Guitar (Daix/Rosselet, No. 550); Bottle on a Table* (Daix/Rosselet, no. 551) (fig. 7.12); *Table with Bottle and Wineglass* (Daix/Rosselet, No. 554).

76. Author's translation. "Toutefois, si une tierce puissance intervenait, l'Allemagne jetterait son épée dans la balance"; "campagne antimilitariste" and "l'extrême gauche."

77. *Bottle and Wineglass* (Daix/Rosselet, No. 549) and *Table with Bottle and Guitar* (Daix/Rosselet, No. 550). See also Daix/Rosselet Nos. 543, 544, 546, 547, 552, and 553.

78. I have been unable to obtain photographs with legible details of eleven of the fifty-two collages, several of which are destroyed or lost. It is likely that some of them would raise the percentage of political clippings further.

79. Daix/Rosselet, No. 549.

80. Paul Signac, a longtime anarchist supporter and close friend of the leading French anarchist intellectual Jean Grave, expressed his extreme disillusion at Grave's support for the French cause when the war actually came (repr. in R. Herbert and E. Herbert, "Artists and Anarchism: Unpublished Letters of Pissarro, Signac and Others—II," *Burlington Magazine* 102 [1960]: 520):

    > . . . laissez-moi vous confier, mon cher ami, qu'un de mes grands chagrins en ces horribles temps, a été causé par votre évolution au début de la guerre. Nourri de vos principes, de ceux de Reclus, de ceux de Kropotkine,—car c'est vous qui m'avez formé—je n'ai pu comprendre que vous admettiez la guerre, et que vous ne protestiez pas contre le déchaînement de cette horreur, que vous puissiez faire une différence entre la bonne et la mauvaise guerre—Vous m'avez enseigné que la guerre est mauvaise, toujours, atroce.

    See also M. Vlaminck, *Dangerous Corner,* trans. M. Ross (New York, 1961).

81. André Salmon in *La Terreur noire,* p. 500, discussed the impact of Kropotkin's outspoken call to defend the Allied cause against the Germans, a shocking reversal of his lifelong position against any and all wars.

82. Steegmuller (as in n. 47), pp. 28ff.

83. Letters written to Gertrude Stein as early as 1909 show that Picasso's French was perfectly adequate to understand the subtleties of the articles pasted into these works; in comparison with letters written to Max Jacob in 1902, his French had considerably improved after his move to Paris.

84. See Daix/Rosselet, p. 259, and Rubin (as in n. 44), p. 122. It is true that this is not the typical strategy for avant-garde artists supporting the anarchist cause: Pissarro and Signac, for example, gave money and donated prints and paintings to help support

Jean Grave's *Les Temps nouveaux* (Herbert, p. 188). Not only did Picasso not follow suit, he also made a point of refusing to sell drawings to left-wing satirical magazines, such as *L'Assiette au beurre,* which featured artists and friends that he certainly admired, including Théophile Steinlen and Van Dongen, and remained a source of income and publicity for Picasso's generation, including Juan Gris, Jacques Villon, Louis Marcoussis, and Franz Kupka (see Penrose, pp. 104–05 and S. Appelbaum, *French Satirical Drawings from 'L'Assiette au beurre'* [New York, 1978]). Without knowing his thoughts on this subject, however, one can only note that he never fully participated in the French art world on its own terms. And while he readily sold works to interested buyers—he was dependent, as were most contemporary artists, on the bourgeois art market—he had twice earlier abandoned saleable styles in order to pursue his Blue Period work, and later his ''African'' style and proto-Cubism. Arguably, collages are less saleable than the traditional and more permanent oils on canvas.

85. Apollinaire (as in n. 49), p. 21.

86. J. Tharaud, ''La Guerre des Balkans,'' *Les Soirées de Paris* 10 (November 1912): 289–92; ''Nos collaborateurs dans les Balkans,'' ibid., 320; and A. Tudesq, ''La Guerre des Balkans,'' *Les Soirées de Paris* 11 (December 1912); 338–41. See Leighten, pp. 133–48, for a discussion of Apollinaire's criticism.

87. Soby, *Juan Gris* (New York, 1958), pp. 11–12, and M. Rosenthal, *Juan Gris* (New York and Berkeley, Calif., 1983), pp. 11–12; see also Appelbaum (as in n. 84), pp. 74–77.

88. See Soby (as in n. 87), figs. 45, 46, and 60; see also figs. 39 and 58, and Rosenthal (as in n. 87), figs. 55, 57, 59, and 73.

89: Daix/Rosselet, No. 782; see also Daix/Rosselet, 337, and Goldberg, 429.

90. See B. Liddell Hart's lucid account of the war, *A History of the World War 1914–1918* (London, 1934); see also K. Silver, ''*Esprit de Corps:* The Great War and French Art, 1914–1925,'' passim, Ph.D. diss., Yale University, 1981, for an analysis of the quick move toward patriotism among avant-garde artists at the beginning of the war.

91. Apollinaire, ''Living Art and the War,'' *Le Petit messager des arts et des industries d'art,* 1 March 1915, trans. in Breunig (as in no. 48), *Apollinaire on Art,* pp. 439–40.

92. Although Cabanne (as in n. 2), p. 172, reports that Picasso considered joining the Foreign Legion—a telling if authentic later fiction—the artist doubtless agreed with the pacifism of his Barcelona friends, of whom Brenan writes, p. 173: ''When in 1914 the syndicates began to reorganize and to prepare again for action the European war broke out and caused a split in the Anarchist ranks, some (especially the younger generation) being neutral and pacifist and others favouring the Allies.''

93. See documentary photographs in Daix/Rosselet, p. 359.

94. Cabanne (as in n. 2), p. 172.

95. The complex issue of whether Picasso was promoting a Communist Party line in his work after 1944 or making generally pacifist statements is still much debated. Whether he was successfully manipulated by the French Communist Party or not, Picasso viewed himself, in such works as *Massacre in Korea* of 1951 and the *War* and *Peace* murals of 1952, as once more taking a life-long position—one strongly flavored with anarchist aesthetics—on pacifism:

> To call up the face of war I have never thought of any particular trait, only that of monstrosity. Still less of the helmet or uniform of the American or any other army.

I have nothing against the Americans. I am on the side of men, of all men. Because of that I could not imagine the face of war separated from that of peace. Even peace came to my mind only with the attributes of the absolute needs of humanity and the full liberty of everyone on earth. Art must put forward an alternative (quoted in D. Ashton, *Picasso on Art: A Selection of Views* [New York, 1977], p. 158).

96. See M. Schapiro, ''Nature of Abstract Art,'' *Marxist Quarterly* 1 (1937): 77–98, reprinted in M. Schapiro, *Modern Art, 19th and 20th Centuries: Selected Papers* (New York, 1978), p. 185–211; C. Greenberg. ''Avant-Garde and Kitsch'' (1939), and ''On the Role of Nature in Modernist Painting'' (1949), both reprinted in *Art and Culture: Critical Essays* (Boston, 1961), pp. 3–21 and 171–74; J. Berger, *The Success and Failure of Picasso* (London, 1965); M. Raphael, *Proudhon, Marx, Picasso: Trois études sur la sociologie de l'art* (Paris, 1933), trans. in G. Schiff, *Picasso in Perspective* (Englewood Cliffs, N.J., 1976), pp. 106–16; and T. Clark, ''Clement Greenberg's Theory of Art,'' *Critical Inquiry* 9 (1982): 139–56; see also A. Hauser, *The Social History of Art*, vol. 4 (New York, 1951), pp. 230–34. The following quotation from Raphael, p. 106, illustrates the exclusively formal reading of Cubist works common to all these writers and the profoundly misleading lengths to which it can go:

> During the first phase [to 1906] the content and spiritual conception of the subject predominate; during the [Cubist phase] it is the form-creating elements—the modeling, problems of composition and form, of method and execution. . . . His almost unvarying theme during the sentimental phase was drawn from the fringes of nature and society: blind men, paralytics, dwarves, morons; poor people, beggars; Harlequins and Pierrots; prostitutes; tightrope dancers, acrobats, fortune tellers, strolling players; clowns and jugglers. One must not see here anything resembling social criticism, any sort of accusation against the bourgeois order. Very much like Rilke, Picasso looks upon poverty as a heroic thing and raises it to the power of myth. . . . Far from regarding it as a social phenomenon which it is up to those afflicted to abolish, he makes of it a Franciscan virtue heralding the approach of God.

In *The Moment of Cubism and Other Essays* (New York, 1969), p. 27, Berger, who admires the revolutionary step taken by the inventors of Cubism, nevertheless does not credit them with the purposefulness of their act, insisting with unfounded confidence and rather tortured logic that: ''I must emphasize again that the Cubists were not aware of all that we are now reading into their art. Picasso and Braque and Léger kept silent because they knew that they might be doing more than they knew.''

97. M. Jacob, *Cronique des temps héroiques* (Paris), pp. 48–49; A. Salmon, *L'Air de la Butte* (Paris, 1945), p. 35; Penrose, p. 118.

98. *Action* 3 (April 1920): 26.

Bibliography

Alvarez Junco, J. *La ideologia politica del anarquismo español (1868–1910)*. Madrid, 1976.
Blunt, A., and P. Pool. *Picasso, the Formative Years: A Study of His Sources*. London, 1962.
Brenan, G. *The Spanish Labyrinth*. Cambridge, 1943.
Cervera, J. *Modernismo: The Catalan Renaissance of the Arts*. New York, 1976.
Cirlot, J. *Birth of a Genius*. New York, 1972.
Daix, P., and J. Rosselet. *Picasso, the Cubist Years 1907–1916: A Catalogue Raisonné of the Paintings and Related Works*. Boston, 1979.
______. *Picasso: The Blue and Rose Periods: A Catalogue Raisonné, 1900–1906*. New York, 1967.

Egbert, D. *Social Radicalism and the Arts: Eastern Europe—A Cultural History from the French Revolution to 1968.* New York, 1970.
Goldberg, H. *The Life of Jean Jaurés.* Madison, Wis. and London, 1968.
Herbert, E. *The Artist and Social Reform: France and Belgium, 1885–1900.* New Haven, Conn., 1961.
Joll, J. *The Anarchists.* New York, 1966.
Leighten, P. "Picasso: Anarchism and Art, 1897–1914," Ph.D. diss., Rutgers University, 1983.
Maitron, J. *Histoire du mouvement anarchiste en France (1880–1914).* Paris, 1951.
McCully, M. *Els Quatre Gats: Art in Barcelona around 1900.* Princeton, N.J., 1978.
Penrose, R. *Picasso: His Life and Work,* rev. ed. New York, 1973.
Salmon, A. *La Terreur noire.* Paris, 1959.
Woodcock, G. *Anarchism: A History of Libertarian Ideas and Movements.* New York, 1962.

8

Mallarmé, Picasso, and the Newspaper as Commodity

Christine Poggi

Moving from Rosenblum's and Leighten's readings of Picasso's newspaper clippings in his collages, Christine Poggi explores the role of the newspaper in Picasso's collage by probing and emphasizing "the connoted meaning of newspaper itself in an artistic milieu, still largely dominated by Symbolist values." Poggi discusses the role of the newspaper in transforming language into a commodity. She suggests that Picasso's introduction of the newspaper into the realm of painting was a critique of its fine art status on a number of levels. As she points out, "the artist's use of newspaper and other mass-produced materials pointed toward the obsolescence of contemporary cultural hierarchies and theories of representation, in an age in which cultural artifacts had become commodities."

In 1832, the unabridged edition of Victor Hugo's *Notre-Dame de Paris* appeared, containing the previously omitted chapter entitled "Ceci tuera cela."[1] Hugo had coined this now-famous dictum, roughly translated as "this will kill that," to refer to the gradual decline and death of the great public art of architecture in the wake of Gutenberg's invention of the printing press. For Hugo, it was inevitable that the book should sound the death knell of the medieval cathedral, despite the fragility of the printed page in comparison to carved stone. The greater power of the book lay in its efficiency of means: cheap, and quickly produced, an edition was soon scattered like a flock of birds in the wind. Hugo described the effects of thought expressed through the two forms of writing, that of the press and that of architecture, in the following terms:

This article originally appeared in *The Yale Journal of Criticism* 1, no. 1 (Fall 1987). Reprinted by permission of the author.

> In the form of the press, thought is more imperishable than ever; it is volatile, unseizable, indestructible. It mingles with the air. In the time of architecture, thought made itself into a mountain and powerfully mastered a century and a place. Now it has turned itself into a flock of birds, scatters in the four winds, and occupies at once all positions in the air and in space.[2]

Hugo believed the invention of the press to be the greatest event in history and described it as "the mother of revolutions.[3] Written in November 1830, "Ceci tuera cela" undoubtedly reflected Hugo's understanding of the vital role played by the press in bringing about the July Revolution of 1830.[4] For Hugo, the rise of the press inevitably entailed a total transformation in modes of expression, promoted the democratization of culture, and finally, of political power.

A mere four years after publishing "Ceci tuera cela," Hugo might have concluded his chapter with the triumph, not of the book, but of the newspaper, an even more formidable agent in the democratization of culture. Prior to the 1830s, newspapers had attracted a limited readership due to the expensive subscription system, a slow distribution process outside of urban areas, and the lack of even minimal literacy among the majority of the French. In 1836, however, Emile de Girardin founded *La Presse,* the first successful low-cost daily newspaper in France.[5] The success of Girardin's innovation lay in his strategy of doubling circulation by cutting subscription costs in half.[6] This was achieved by supplementing subscription income with advertising and by attracting new readers through the invention of a new literary form, the *roman-feuilleton,* or serial novel. The daily installments of these novels, printed on the bottom quarter, or *rez-de-chaussée* (literally, the ground floor), of the front page, were an immediate success, encouraging many who had never before felt the need of a newspaper to subscribe. Once it was discovered that novels sold newspapers, the rest of the press hastened to imitate Girardin's formula.[7] A new form of commercial novel writing soon emerged, in which the exigencies of serialization displaced older narrative structures.[8] Authors were careful to fit their installments to the allotted space, to end episodes on a note of suspense, and to fill their stories with intrigue, dramatic coincidence, violence, and pathos. A number of favored themes characterized the new form: the horror and fascination of the underworld; crime and social deviance, especially prostitution; the downfall and salvation of the poor and innocent. These novels engaged the popular imagination in a way that traditional literature, and especially poetry, found extremely difficult to compete with. Alexandre Dumas's novel *Le Capitaine Paul* gained *Le Siècle* five thousand new subscribers in less than three weeks.[9] Eugène Sue's *Les Mystères de Paris,* published by *Le Journal des Débats* between 1842 and 1843, became the most widely read novel of the nineteenth century in France, far surpassing the novels of Balzac and Stendhal.[10]

During the course of the Second Empire, despite stringent government censorship, the publishing industry witnessed further expansion. Transported by railroads, newspapers now reached even remote rural areas, making urban culture more accessible and advancing the process of cultural homogenization. With the appearance of *Le Petit Journal* in 1863, the first paper to be printed on a rolling press and to be sold for a mere five centimes, it became possible for anyone to own a copy of a newspaper.[11] The popularity of this national tabloid and its many imitators, available in train stations and cafés throughout France, soon rendered the itinerant book peddler's trade obsolete.[12] The circulation of local papers also rose dramatically, tripling after the Prussian War, and continuing to rise into the first decade of the twentieth century.[13] By the 1880s there were seventy daily newspapers in Paris alone, attesting to the emergence of a new mass audience for printed matter.[14] The phenomenal growth of the newspapers was accompanied by the growth of literacy among all classes, although the cities still outpaced the countryside. These developments had many profound effects, among them a blurring of the formerly precise boundaries between the literate and the illiterate, and between the role of the journalist and that of the novelist, poet, or critic.

Prior to these transformations, it had been possible to distinguish between the gentility and the lower classes in France at least in part on the basis of cultural refinement, especially the ability to read. With the advent of nearly universal literacy by the end of the nineteenth century, however, mere reading could no longer provide a stable ground for class differences or cultural hierarchies. A new hierarchical opposition, however, gradually displaced the older one, now marking the differences between those who read newspapers and those who read books, especially poetry. This opposition became a determining one for the Symbolist generation of writers and poets, who conceived their writing as a form of protest against the penetration of the values and logic of the marketplace into the very structure and reception of literature.

Stéphane Mallarmé, who had experienced the growing marginalization of the poet in contemporary society and the erosion of a genuine public sphere for noncommercial writing, defined his own poetry as the "other" of the writing in the newspapers. "Poetry," he wrote in "The Evolution of Literature," "is everywhere in language where there is rhythm, everywhere except on posters and the back page of newspapers."[15] The vehemence of Mallarmé's denunciation of the newspaper and the poster, a theme that appears throughout his critical essays, issued from his aversion to their commercial use of language. If he singled out the back page of the newspaper for special derision, it was because this was the page that contained the greatest number of advertisements and *petites annonces.* For Mallarmé, then, the newspaper and the poster exemplified the prevailing tendency to transform language into a commodity, thereby rendering its qualitative value as symbol into mere exchange value. In "Crises of Poetry," Mallarmé characterized all contemporary writing, with the exception of (pure) literature, as a form of journalism. He further described this "crude" or "elementary" use of language as a popular but superfluous equivalent for the silent exchange of money:

> One of the undeniable desires of my time is to separate, in view of their different purposes, the dual state of the word, crude or immediate here, there essential.
>
> To narrate, to teach, even to describe, this is what is current, even though for each one, it would suffice perhaps to exchange human thought by taking or placing in the hand of others, silently, a coin; the elementary use of discourse caters to that universal *reporting,* in which, literature excepted,[16] all the genres of contemporary writing participate.[17]

Moreover, journalistic writing had for some time encroached on the territory of literature proper. Due to the popularity of the serial novel true fiction (*fiction proprement dite*) or imaginative narrative (*le récit, imaginatif*) could be found frolicking in the "well-frequented" pages of the dailies.[18] Mallarmé noted that the feuilleton, traditonally on the *rez-de-chaussée* of the newspaper, now "supported the mass of the entire format," even displacing the news, while "no one made allusion to verse."[19]

It was in vivid contrast to the debased forms of journalistic writing, then, that Mallarmé conceived the purity and ideality of his unrealized project for a great "spiritual book." This contrast was most explicitly evoked by the metaphors Mallarmé used to describe the difference in the physical appearance of newspaper and book, and the consequences this difference must have for the experience of reading. In his essay of 1895 "The Book: A Spiritual Instrument" Mallarmé wrote,

> I now propose to examine, technically, how this rag [the newspaper] differs from the book, which is supreme. The newspaper provides an opening; literature[20] flows into it at will.
>
> Now—
>
> The foldings of a book have, with respect to the page printed large, an almost religious significance, which is less striking, however, than their thickness when they are piled together, offering a minuscule tomb, certainly, for the soul.[21]

Vis-à-vis the book, the newspaper is thin: its open pages, a mere parody of the pages of the book, contain no depth or hidden meanings. The religious significance of depth and foldings, however, also implies a sexual metaphor, and Mallarmé compares the book to a virgin, whose folded leaves hide mysterious depths. The reader who cuts the pages is like the book's first lover, and reading, transfigured, becomes an act of consummation.

> The virginal folding back of the book, once more, willing/lends for a sacrifice from which the red edges of ancient tomes once bled; the introduction of a weapon, or paper knife, to establish the taking of possession. How much more personal later, will be our consciousness without this barbaric simulacrum: when it joins the book, taken here, there, varied melodically, guessed like an enigma—almost recreating it. The folds will perpetuate a mark, intact, inviting one to open or close the page, according to the master. So blind and negligible a process, the crime that is consummated, in the destruction of a frail inviolability.[22]

Thus, although marking the site of possession, for Mallarmé the cut folds of the book remain forever intact, pure, virginal.[23] By comparison, the newspaper is already defiled. To read a newspaper is to encounter the flat, open pages of the commodity, which, like the prostitute, disports itself with all comers. Nothing remains hidden, unknown, privileged: "The newspaper, its full sheet on display, acquires in the printing process an improper result, of plain, sloppy marking: no doubt, the striking and vulgar advantage of it, in everyone's view, lies in [*gise dans*=*gisant*=a recumbent effigy on a tomb] its mass production and circulation."[24]

For Mallarmé, the language of the newspaper also revealed its commercial servitude in the arbitrariness of the column format. He writes of the annoying and dangerous influence the newspaper has upon the book, citing in particular "the monotonousness of its always unbearable columns, which are merely strung down the page by hundreds."[25] The Futurist poet F. T. Marinetti, who sought in so many ways to reject his Symbolist heritage, would later praise this feature of the newspaper. He found the unrelatedness of the juxtaposed articles exhilarating and described them as if they formed a readymade collage.

Mallarmé, of course, admitted ironically that the format of the book, too, was useless but dreamed of a new poetry that would overcome the arbitrariness of the vertical column as well as that of standard typography. This new poetry would also guarantee a truthful relation of sound to meaning. The poet deplored the perverse effects of chance (*le hasard*) that had put the sounds of the word *nuit*, so bright, and of the word *jour*, so sombre, in opposition to their meaning.[26] As Mallarmé conceived it, the task of the new poetry was to prevail over *le hasard* by giving primacy to the aural and optical, rather than representative, function of words. Language, by its material presence on the page, would obliterate the exterior world and conjure in its place a rarefied realm of pure, formal relationships. This was the project he envisioned as the ideal book, an architecturally structured and fully premeditated work in which every aspect of language would contribute to the jewellike radiance of the overall effect.

The poem in which Mallarmé most conspicuously attempted to achieve something of his ideal was "Un Coup de dés jamais n'abolira le hasard" ("A Throw of the Dice Will Never Abolish Chance"), first published in 1897. He conceived this poem as approximating the horizontal flow of a musical score, in direct contrast to the tyranny of the newspaper's vertical columns. Words appear scattered across the page, like the image of a constellation evoked in the conclusion of the poem,[27] but their place and typographical character have been carefully considered for expressive effect. Every effort has been made to return individual letters to their primordial splendor, to arrest the movement of the eye and the flow of narrative, to let the silence of the white spaces speak. Here unity lies in the simultaneous mise en scène of the double page, rather than in the perfected single line. At the same time, the flowing words suggest the mobility of music, with its hesitations, embellishments, and continuations. Mallarmé, writing once again of his "spiritual book," suggests the meaning these innovations had for him:

> The book, which is a total expansion of the letter, must draw from it, directly, a mobility and spacious, through correspondences, must institute a play, unknown, which confirms the fiction.
>
> There is nothing fortuitous there, where chance seems to capture the idea, the formal disposition is the equal [*l'egal* = equal to the task, legal, legitimate]. Do not judge, therefore, these words—industrial or having to do with materiality.[28]

In another passage from this essay, Mallarmé further emphasizes the difference of his new poetic system from that of the commercialized forms of the newspaper:

> I, in turn, misunderstand the true meaning of this book and the marvel implied by its structure, if I cannot, knowingly, imagine a given motif in view of a special place and height on the page, according to the fall of light on it or on the work. No more of those successive, incessant, back and forth motions of our eyes, a line finishes, to the next, to recommence: such a practice does not do justice to our delight, having immortally broken, for an hour, with everything, in realizing our fantasies. Otherwise or without this execution, as of music on the keyboard, actively measured by the pages of a score, who would not rather shut their eyes and dream?[29]

Ideas such as these of Mallarmé were prevalent among Symbolist poets, artists, and critics, many of whom shared his aspiration to create an autonomous art free of all reality.[30] Not surprisingly, they frequently associated an excessive concern with the imitation of reality with journalism, casting upon that symbol of modern life all the despised connotations of materialism. The Symbolist critic and painter Maurice Denis, for example, in an essay of 1896, described the current followers of the impressionists in these derogatory terms: "Work after nature was the last safeguard of the craft of the painter. In these last years one has succeeded in bypassing it completely. One does nothing more than note sensations, art is nothing more than the newspaper of life. It is journalism in painting. . . . It is the eye that devours the head."[31]

Given the prevalence of such attitudes at the turn of the century, it seems likely that Picasso's frequent choice of newspaper as a collage material reflected a self-conscious, ironic negation of Symbolist values. We know that Picasso was familiar with Mallarmé's poetry,[32] and in fact, the newspaper headline in one of his earliest collages from late 1912 (fig. 8.1) is cropped to produce "Un Coup de Thé" from "Un Coup de Théatre," so that a pun on Mallarmé's famous poem emerges from the very newspaper format the poet detested. Mallarmé had found the strident boldness of newspaper headlines particularly offensive, and in "Un Coup de dés" had dispersed the title on successive pages to integrate it with the overall form of the poem.[33] Picasso, on the other hand, takes special delight in newspaper titles, often choosing to engage in a play of all the possible puns contained in the word *journal,* which is also the generic name of all newspapers. One of the better-known examples of this wordplay is *Guitar and Wineglass,* another early collage from the fall of 1912 [see fig. 7.7], in which "Le Jou" (suggesting the game, or the play) appears just above the title of an article, "La Bataille s'est Engagé" (the battle has begun), which has been interpreted as making allusions both to the Balkan wars and to the beginning of the challenge of collage itself as a new pictorial form. Another collage, from the winter of 1912 (fig. 8.2), bears the fragment "URNAL," which has been variously interpreted as a reference to the critic Maurice Raynal, one of the first critics to champion a collage work (although he later denounced this practice), and as a mocking reference to *urinal.* Attention has been drawn to these puns and jokes as well as to the numerous clippings about the Balkan wars by art historians such as Robert Rosenblum[34] and, more recently, Patricia Leighten,[35] who have demonstrated that Picasso's newspaper clippings are meant to be read for the black humor and political associations they reveal. And indeed, for the most part, the clippings respect the verticality of the columns and are placed upright within the pictorial field so that they can be read with relative ease. What has not been sufficiently emphasized, however, is the connoted meaning of *newspaper* itself in an artistic milieu still largely dominated by Symbolist values.[36]

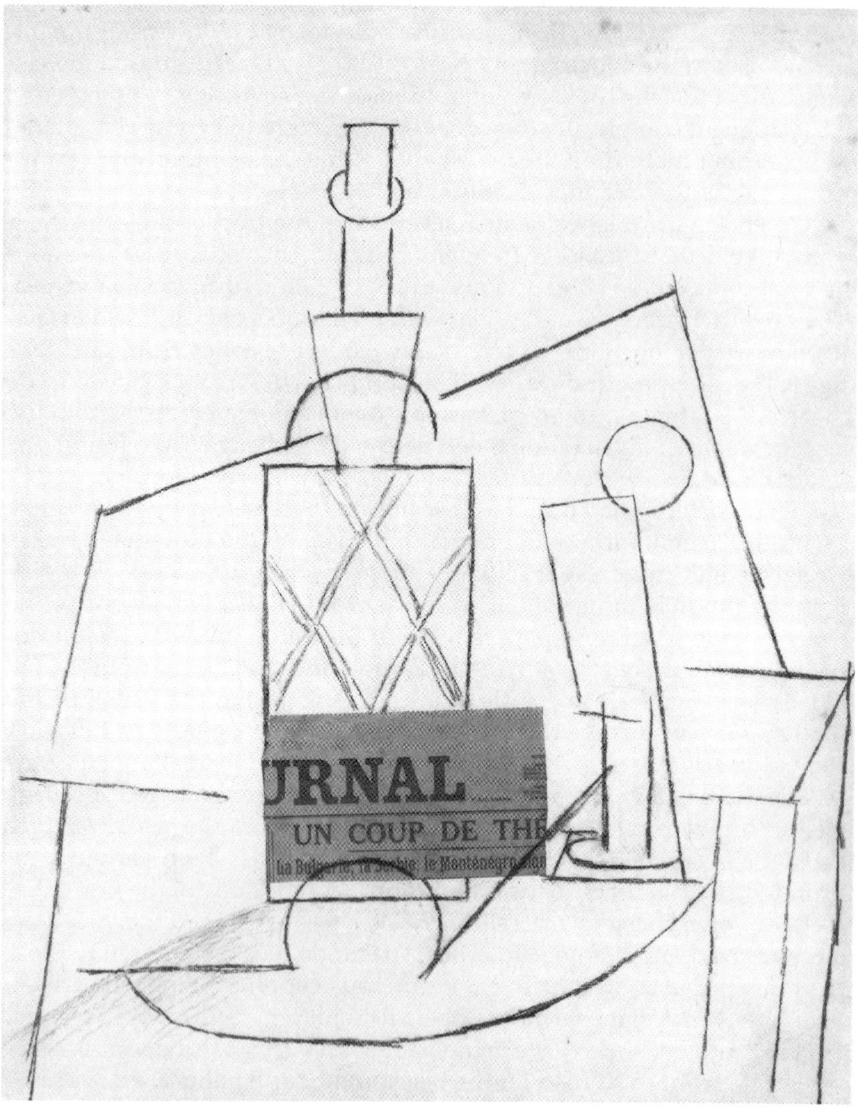

Figure 8.1. Pablo Picasso, *Bottle, Glass and Newspaper on a Table,* 1912
Pasted paper and charcoal on paper.
(Cliché Musée National d'Art Moderne, Paris. Photo: Ch. Bahier-Ph. Migeat. Copyright ARS N.Y./SPADEM, 1988)

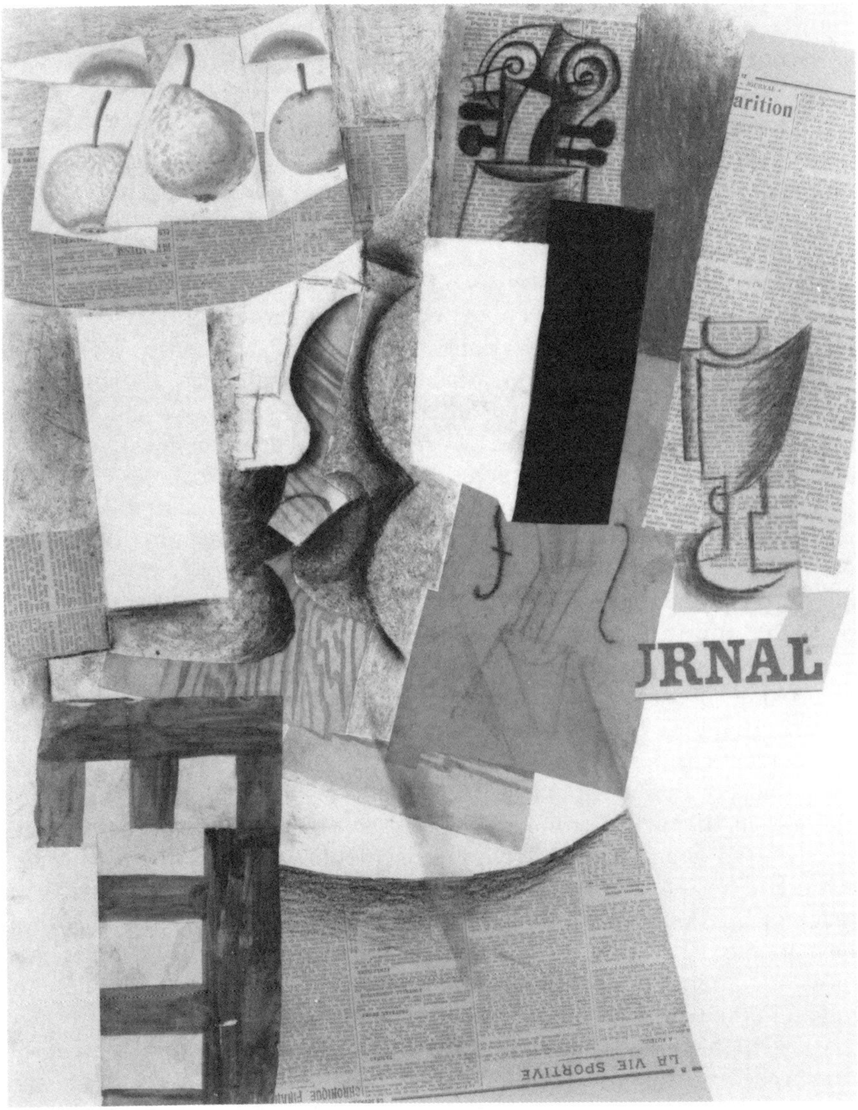

Figure 8.2. Pablo Picasso, *The Violin (Violin and Fruit)*, 1913
Colored papers and charcoal on paper,
25½″ × 19½″.
(Philadelphia Museum of Art. A. E. Gallatin Collection. Copyright ARS N.Y./SPADEM, 1988)

Certainly Picasso, as an early-twentieth-century artist, faced many of the same material conditions that had prompted the ivory tower, purist attitudes of the Symbolists. His early and consistent refusal to exhibit his works in any of the Parisian salons or to contribute illustrations to satirical magazines, even when most destitute, indicates the strength of his desire to remain free of the pressures of public taste and of the marketplace. Nevertheless, the eruption of newspaper fragments within the previously homogeneous and pure domain of painting must be interpreted as a critique of Symbolist ideals and, indeed, of Symbolist theories of representation.

In Picasso's collages, everything once banished or suppressed from the autonomous, pure realm of art now reappears within the text of the newspapers: contemporary political and social events, serialized romances, scientific discoveries, advertisements of all kinds, the want ads. The collage *Bottle and Glass on a Table*[37] of late 1912 prominently displays a newspaper clipping of liqueur advertisements, used to signify both the label and contents of the depicted bottle. In another collage from this period, a full newspaper sheet serves as the ground for a still life of a bottle on a table [see fig. 7.12], in which the title "La Semaine Economique et Financière" (The Economic and Financial Week) can scarcely be missed despite its inverted position. Serialized romances also turn up, in *Violin*[38] and in *Head of a Man with a Hat* (fig. 8.3), both of late 1912.

One of the most interesting uses of newspaper, and particularly of advertising, occurs in a small collage of early 1913, *Still Life: "Au Bon Marché"* (fig. 8.4). Here, Picasso creates a collage with materials from the commercial world, including newspaper clippings and cheap wallpaper. The subject of this work of art, in turn, alludes to its material origins by taking as its theme the promiscuity of the commodity. Through the placement of two department store advertisements, one from *La Samaritaine* at top and another from the *Bon Marché* at center, Picasso constructs an image of the bourgeois female which ironically conforms to that of the mass media. She appears in this collage in her exemplary dual role as both consumer of goods and as object of desire, that is, as intimately involved in the world of commodities. As Robert Rosenblum has observed, the placement of the fragments suggests a rather clandestine joke: at the top we see the torso of a woman, then an advertisement for lingerie, and just below, inserted into a gap in the wallpaper background and jutting into the lingerie advertisement, are the words "un trou ici" (a hole here).[39] Picasso's pun may also be a private joke, referring to Apollinaire's first pornographic novel, written in 1901, *Mirely, ou le petit trou pas cher.*[40] On a more overt level, the humorous erotic allusions of this collage play on a popular late-nineteenth- and early-twentieth-century theme, the dubious

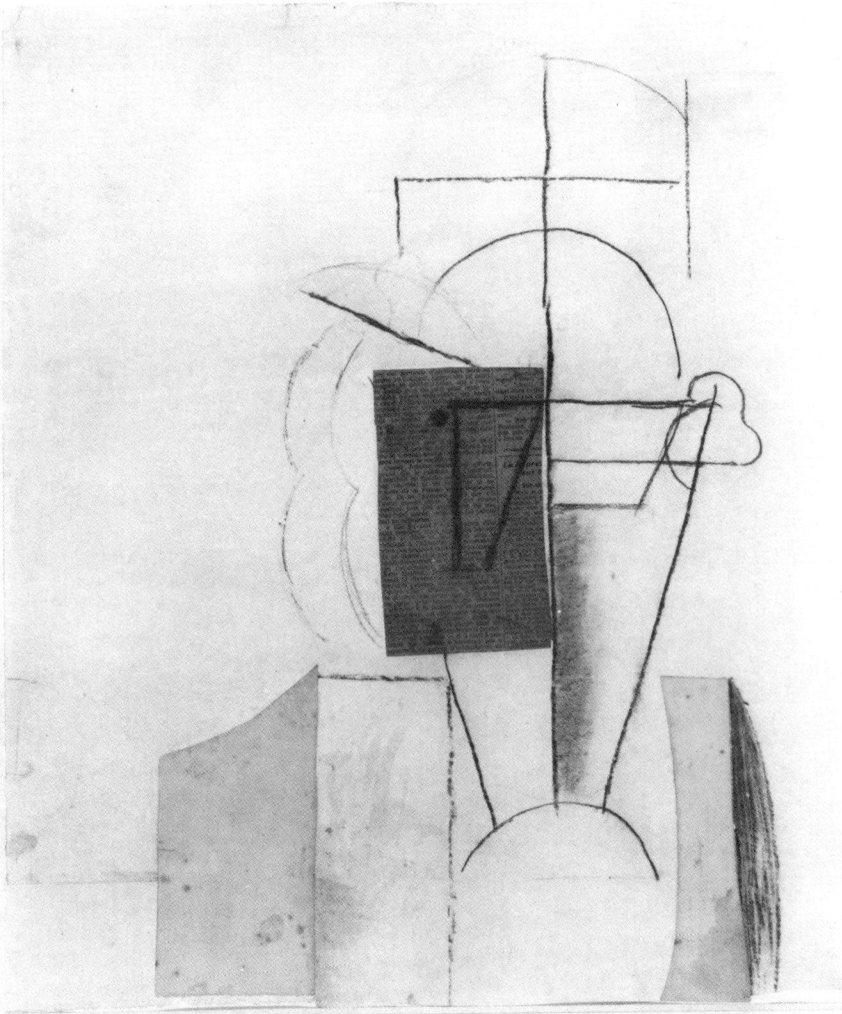

Figure 8.3. Pablo Picasso, *Head of a Man with a Hat,* 1912
Charcoal, graphite, laid paper and newsprint on white laid paper, 57.3 cm × 47.9 cm.
(Fogg Art Museum, Harvard University. Anonymous gift in memory of Frederick B. Deknatel. Copyright ARS N.Y./SPADEM, 1988)

Figure 8.4. Pablo Picasso, *Still Life: ''Au Bon Marché,''* 1913
Collage.
(Private collection. Copyright ARS N.Y./SPADEM, 1988)

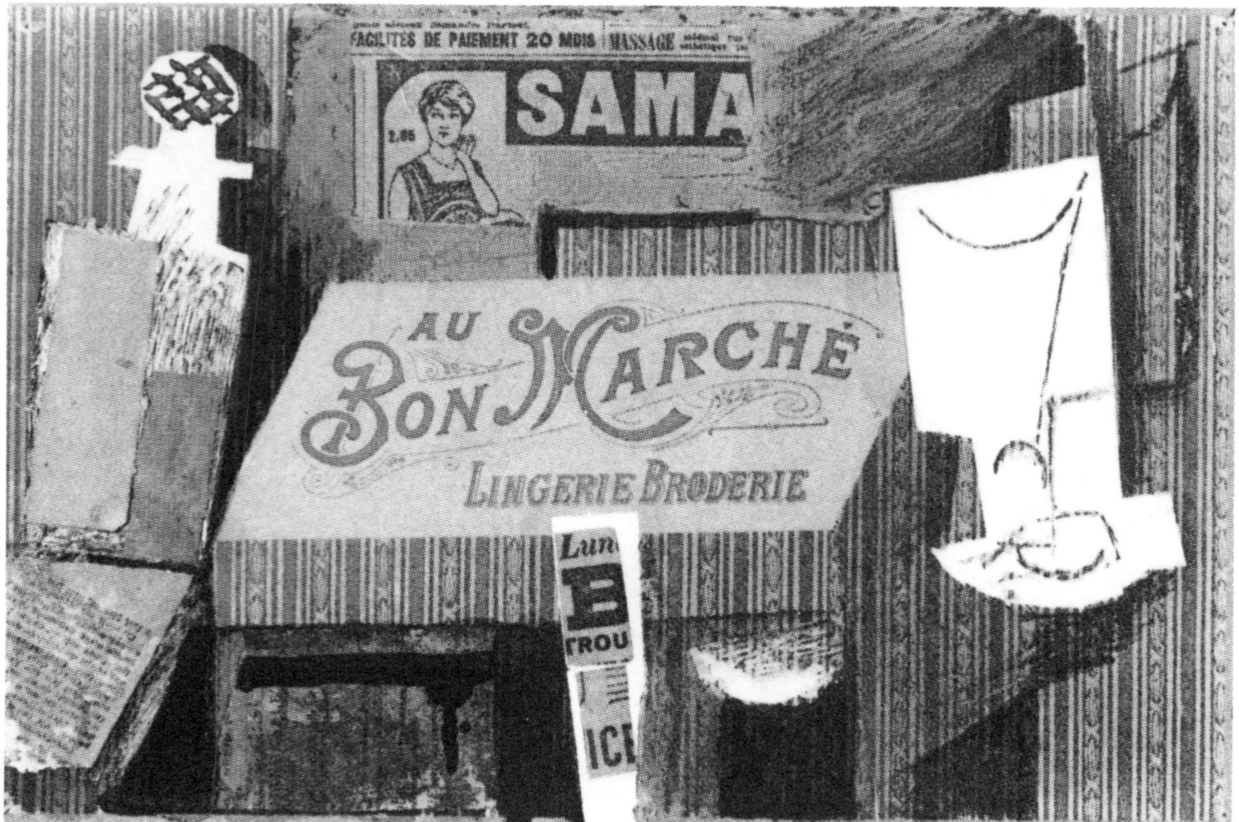

morality of the department store salesgirl. Contemporary writers complained that such girls, naive and no longer in the safety of their homes, might succumb to the temptations now surrounding them, while at the same time they hinted that these salesgirls were a new source of danger, out to seduce the men they encountered. More important, some writers protested that such women could not be easily distinguished from the *bonne bourgeoise,* and this threatened to lead to undesirable social and moral confusion. To counter such claims, department store owners established elaborate precautionary systems, sometimes, as in the case of the early *Bon Marché,* including the isolation of the female from the male workers.[41] Despite such efforts, the sexuality of the salesgirl remained a source of obsessive fascination and low humor.

Part of the irony of this collage, however, is that while alluding to such themes, the *trou* cropped from the newspaper also refers to the pictorial gaps or "holes" created by perspectival illusion in the flat surface of the picture plane. Such pictorial holes were themselves of ill repute during the late nineteenth and early twentieth centuries, implying deception about the nature of the medium. One of the rallying cries of the Symbolists (including artists and critics such as Paul Gauguin, Emil Bernard, Albert Aurier, and Maurice Denis) had been the necessity of a return to the pre-Renaissance aesthetics of *décoration,* especially mural decoration. Rejecting the perceived decadence of illusionistic easel painting, Symbolist artists sought to reflect the structure of the pictorial support in the work itself, by avoiding deep perspectival holes that made walls appear to vanish. In Picasso's collage, the newspaper text asserts the presence of a *trou,* without, however, creating the illusion of one. The hole remains an effect of writing pasted to a visibly flat, wall-like ground. For in a sense, it *is* a wall that is depicted here, although one must still ask—what sort of wall? The striped, golden wallpaper ground and the allusion to a woman in lingerie suggest that this is an intimate interior, perhaps a boudoir. Yet the wine glass at right and the bottle at left convert the scene to a café setting, while the overall effect of the collaged advertisements evokes a poster-covered urban wall. Thus advertising, one of the subsidiary industries that developed in response to early capitalist mass marketing techniques, presides over the collapse of the boundaries between the private and public realms, assimilating the interior to the street. Walter Benjamin captured the essence of this phenomenon in his essay on Baudelaire when he wrote,

> If the arcade is the classical form of the *intérieur,* which is how the *flâneur* sees the street, the department store is the form of the *intérieur*'s decay. The bazaar is the last hangout of the *flâneur.* If in the beginning the street had become an *intérieur* for him, now this *intérieur* turned into a street, and he roamed through the labyrinth of merchandise as he had once roamed through the labyrinth of the city.[42]

As more and more areas of private experience seemed to become subject to the laws of the market, not surprisingly nineteenth-century theories of originality as self-expression were gradually undermined. One of the earliest signs of a new conception of the creative process, and particularly of originality, appears in Picasso's first series of collages executed during the autumn of 1912. In place of the unique, expressive marking of the artist's hand, still of primary significance in Symbolist and Fauvist works, we find for the most part fragments of previously established codes of representation: newspaper clippings, bits of wallpaper, musical scores. In *Guitar and Wineglass* even the drawn glass appears as a readymade element. It reads like a familiar quotation from Picasso's previous Cubist reconstructions of simple objects. In these collages, originality derives from the imaginative manipulation of conventional signs, rather than from a spontaneous encounter between self and nature. This attitude toward representation suggests, in part, a return to the classical theory of invention, which relied on the recombination of previously known compositional elements or schemata. But whereas an academic artist was taught to base his art on the conventions of the finest art of the past, Picasso appropriated elements from the contemporary world of popular culture and mass communication. Here again, the preponderance of newspaper in Picasso's collages is significant. Newspaper, perhaps more than any other cultural artifact, embodies the principle of reproducibility in utter negation of the unique or privileged object, for any copy of a newspaper is as good as any other. Moreover, with a life span of only a day or perhaps a week, it quickly assumes the status of refuse, thereby exemplifying the principle of obsolescence inscribed in the very nature of the commodity. Thus, Picasso's introduction of newspaper within the realm of painting suggests a critique of its fine art status on several fronts. It challenges the uniqueness and durability of the work of art, traditionally defined in opposition to the products of mass culture. It redefines the creative act as a manipulation of iterable, arbitrary signs, like those of writing. It also implicitly points to the conventionality of seemingly original, spontaneous signs for the revelation of the self, such as sketchlike brushstrokes or heightened color. By 1912, it was no longer possible for Picasso to use such techniques without irony. When he stencilled "Ma Jolie," the easily recognized fragment of a popular song,[43] to his canvases (fig. 8.5) or wrote "J'aime Eva" (a reference to his current mistress) in overtly childlike handwriting on a heart-shaped piece of gingerbread and glued it to his canvas (fig. 8.6), it was to underscore the paradox involved in the attempt to express a personal emotion with a public language. Picasso's collages imply that this highly clichéd language is the only language available. It was the impossibility of inventing a purely expressive, uncontaminated

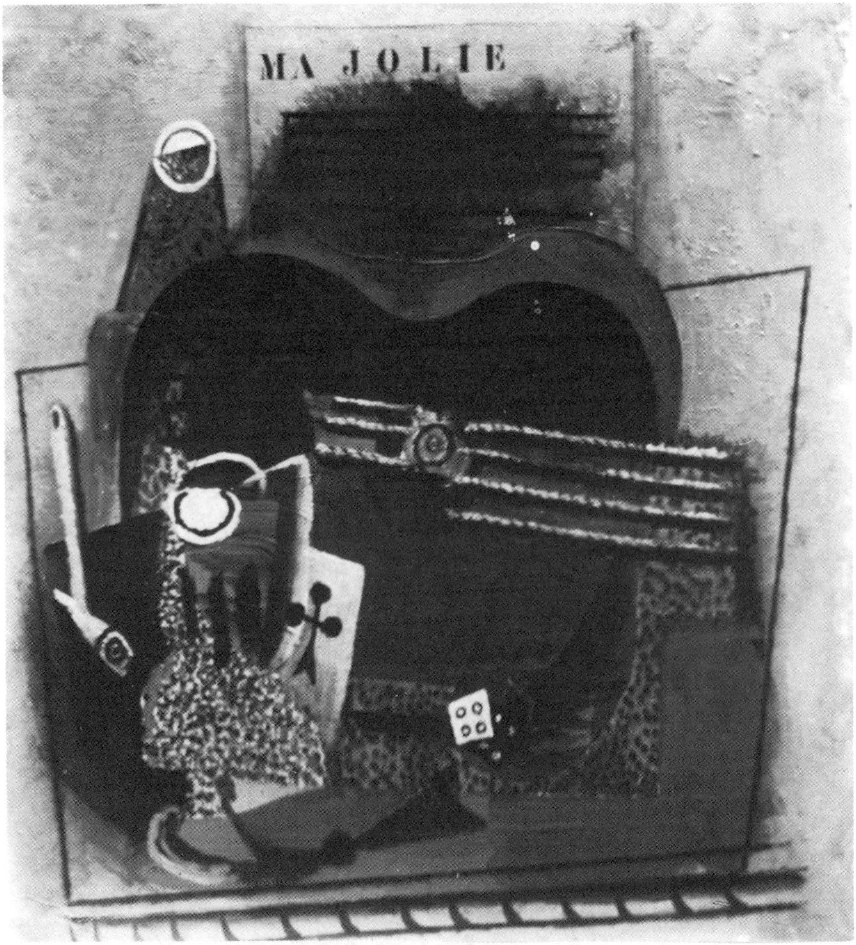

Figure 8.5. Pablo Picasso, *Pipe, Glass, Playing Card, Guitar, Die ("Ma Jolie")*, 1914
Oil on canvas, 45 cm × 40.5 cm.
(Galerie Louise Leiris, Paris. Copyright ARS N.Y./SPADEM, 1988)

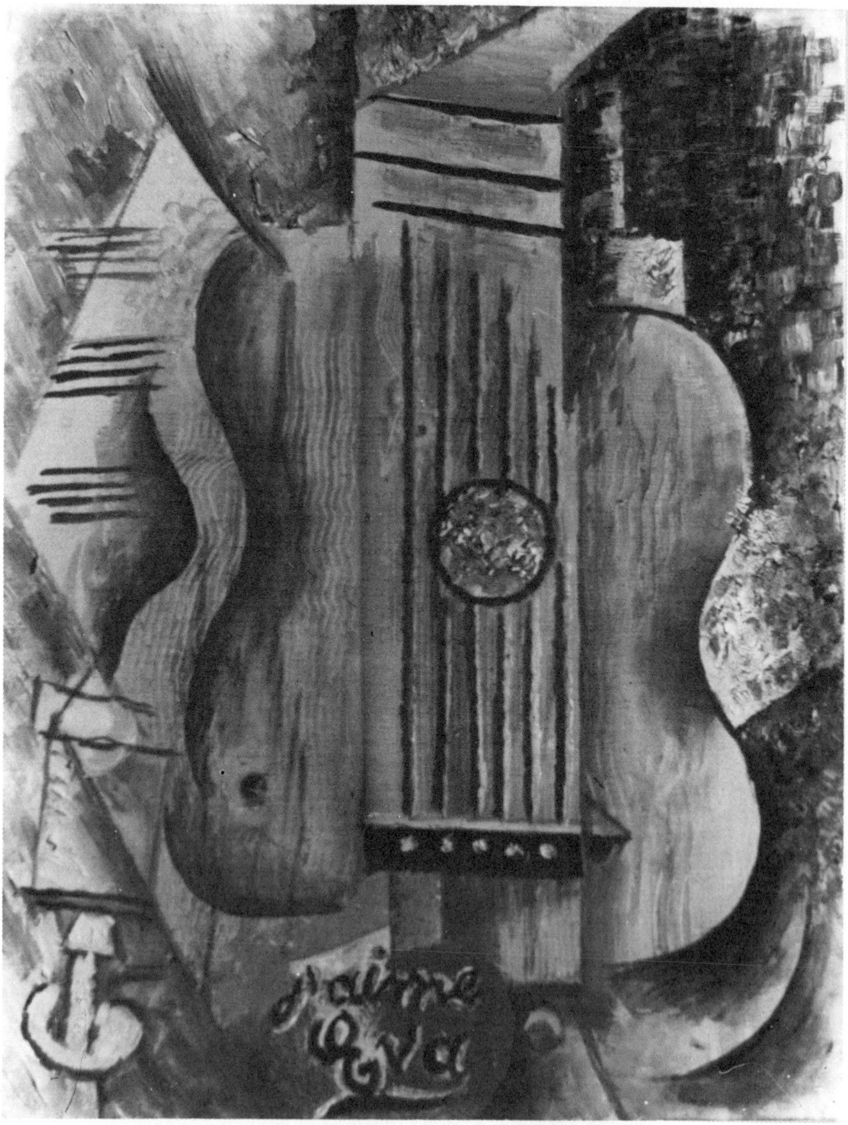

Figure 8.6. Pablo Picasso, *Guitar: "J'aime Eva,"* Summer 1912
Oil on canvas, 41 cm × 33 cm.
(Galerie Louise Leiris, Paris. Copyright ARS N.Y./SPADEM, 1988)

personal language (that would still be a language) that Picasso revealed in these works.

Here the aesthetics of Mallarmé and Picasso converge once again. For although Mallarmé believed that a true work of art was unique, or should be,[44] his conception of the poem as pure, independent object precluded causal references to the self, or what he called "the audible breathing" of the poet. In "Crisis of Poetry" Mallarmé spoke of the impersonality of his poetic ideal:

> The pure work implies the elocutionary disappearance of the poet, who cedes the initiative to words, brought into collision by their mobilized inequality. They illuminate themselves through reciprocal reflections like a virtual swath of fire sweeping over precious stones, replacing the audible breathing in ancient lyric poetry or the personal and passionate control of the phrase.[45]

For Picasso, however, the effacement of the self did not gesture toward the pure, expressive radiance of words. Rather, the artist's use of newspaper and other mass-produced materials pointed toward the obsolescence of contemporary cultural hierarchies and theories of representation, in an age in which cultural artifacts had become commodities.

Notes

1. A version of this essay was delivered on 14 February 1987, at the annual meeting of the College Art Association held in Boston, Mass. I would like to thank the Georges Lurcy Foundation and the Whitney Humanities Center at Yale University for providing me with a fellowship during the year 1985–86, allowing me to carry out the research and writing of this paper. I am also grateful to Aline Elliot for her assistance with the Mallarmé translations.

2. Victor Hugo, *Notre-Dame de Paris* (Paris: Librairie Générale Française, 1972), p. 234:

   > Sous la forme imprimerie, la pensée est plus impérissable que jamais; elle est volatile, insaisissable, indestructible. Elle se mèle à l'air. Du temps de l'architecture, elle se faisait montagne et s'emparait puissamment d'un siècle et d'un lieu. Maintenant elle se fait troupe d'oiseaux, s'éparpille aux quatre vents, et occupe à la fois tous les points de l'air et de l'espace.

3. Ibid.

4. The early years of Louis Philippe's reign witnessed the greatest period of freedom of the press thus far experienced in France. This freedom gave rise to a host of oppositional journals, repesenting both legitimist and republican attacks on the person and policies of Louis Philippe as well as on the very principle of constitutional monarchy. The government responded with the severe Laws of September, voted in in 1835, which put an end to this brief period of exceptional political liberty; they did not, however, impede the growth of the press in part because of the cuts in subscription rates. For a history of the press under the July Monarchy see Henri Avenel, *Histoire de la presse française depuis 1789 jusqu'à nos jours* (Paris: Flammarion, 1900), pp. 303–83.

5. Hugo, along with many other of the most renowned writers of the period, became a contributor, writing on social questions. With the advent of the Second Republic and nearly complete freedom of the press, Hugo founded his own newspaper, *L'Evénement*, its first issue appearing on 1 August 1848. Later, in exile in Belgium, he wrote a scathing denunciation of the censorship laws promulgated by the Second Empire in his book *Napoléon le petit.* See Avenel, *Histoire de la presse française,* pp. 451–52.

6. Emile de Girardin first experimented with cutting subscription costs in early 1835, when he founded *Le Journal des connaissances utiles.* This journal's successor, *La Presse,* appeared on 1 July 1836, at a cost of forty francs per year rather than the standard eighty francs. Girardin reasoned that it would be easier to acquire ten thousand subscribers at the lower rate than one thousand at the higher rate. His success was even greater than he had anticipated; after three months, *La Presse* counted twenty thousand subscribers. Ibid., p. 368.

7. Notably, the conservative *Journal des Débats* was the only paper not to reduce its price of eighty francs without suffering diminished influence or prosperity. Ibid., p. 369.

8. For a fascinating discussion of the new serial form and the narrative structures it engendered, see Peter Brooks, "The Mark of the Beast," in *Reading for the Plot: Design and Intention in Narrative* (New York: Vintage Books, 1985), pp. 143–70.

9. This newspaper, founded the same day as *La Presse,* and with nearly identical principles, eventually became even more successful than its competitor, attaining a circulation of thirty-eight thousand within a few years.

10. Balzac, who had incurred great debts during his brief attempt to establish his own printing press, was only too well aware of the choices faced by a young, aspiring writer of his day: an unscrupulous but financially successful career as a journalist, or a long, arduous attempt to be a writer of literature, with little hope of recompense. This theme is the subject of the second part of his three-part novel *Lost Illusions,* in which journalists are characterized as men of little principle who have turned the press into an instrument for achieving social advancement and political power. Balzac himself, however, had contributed to many newspapers during the twenties and thirties and had even played a role in founding and directing some of them.

11. *Le Petit Journal,* founded by Moïse Millaud, revolutionized the French press by achieving, almost immediately, the unheard of circulation of one hundred thousand copies per day. By 1900 the figure had surpassed one million. This wide distribution was made possible by use of the rolling press, invented by Hippolyte Marinoni, who eventually became director of the paper. The *presses rotatives* could print forty thousand papers per hour. Other papers were forced to follow suit and eventually five centimes became the standard cost of a daily paper. See Avenel, *Histoire de la presse française,* pp. 491, 853–65.

12. Eugen Weber, *Peasants into Frenchmen: The Modernization of Rural France, 1870–1914* (Stanford: Stanford University Press, 1976), p. 466.

13. Ibid., p. 468.

14. Norman Stone, *Europe Transformed, 1878–1919* (Cambridge, Mass.: Harvard University Press, 1984), p. 14.

15. "Le vers est partout dans la langue où il y a rythme, partout, excepté dans les affiches et à la quatrième page des journaux." "Sur l'évolution littéraire." *Oeuvres complètes* (Pléïade edition), Henri Mondor and G. Jean-Aubrey, eds. (Paris: Editions Gallimard, 1945), p. 867.

16. From the context of this statement, it is clear that Mallarmé intends to contrast literature with journalism. At times in his critical essays, however, the term *literature* assumes a negative value in relation to the pure art of poetry.

17. "Crise de vers," ibid., p. 368:

> Un désire indéniable à mon temps est de séparer comme en vue d'attributions différentes le double état de la parole, brut ou immédiat ici, là essentiel.
>
> Narrer, enseigner, même décrire, cela va et encore qu'à chacun suffirait peut-être pour échanger la pensée humaine, de prendre ou de mettre dans la main d'autrui en silence une pièce de monnaie, l'emploi élémentaire du discours dessert l'universel *reportage* dont, la littérature exceptée, participe tout entre les genres d'écrits contemporains.

18. "Plutôt la Presse, chez nous seuls, a voulu une place aux écrits—son traditionnel feuilleton en rez-de-chaussée longtemps soutint la masse du format entier. . . . Mieux, la fiction proprement dite ou le récit, imaginatif, s'ébat au travers de 'quotidiens' achalandés, triomphant à des lieux principaux, jusqu'au sommet; en déloge l'article de fond, ou d'actualité, apparu secondaire." "Etalages," ibid., p. 376.

19. "Personne ne fit d'allusion aux vers," ibid., p. 373.

20. Here Mallarmé is speaking of debased forms of literature, such as the *roman feuilleton.* This negatively valued literature is opposed to poetry in the ideal form of the book. See note 16 above.

21. "Sur l'évolution littéraire," ibid., p. 869:

> Je . . . techniquement, propose, de noter comment ce lambeau diffère du livre, lui suprême. Un journal reste le point de départ; la littérature s'y décharge à souhait.
>
> Or—
>
> Le pliage est, vis-à-vis de la feuille imprimée grande, un indice, quasi religieux: qui ne frappe pas autant que son tassement, en épaisseur, offrant le minuscule tombeau, certes, de l'âme." Ibid., p. 379. Mallarmé had also compared literature to a tomb in a passage in "The Evolution of Literature": "For me, the situation of the poet in this society that does not permit him to live, is the situation of a man who isolates himself in order to sculpt his own tomb" [Pour moi le cas d'un poëte, en cette société qui ne lui permet pas de vivre, c'est le cas d'un homme qui s'isole pour sculpter son propre tombeau].

22. "Le Livre, instrument spirituel," ibid., p. 381:

> Le reploiement vierge du livre, encore, prète à un sacrifice dont saigna la tranche rouge des anciens tomes; l'introduction d'une arme, ou coupe-papier, pour établir la prise de possession. Combien personnelle plus avant, la conscience, sans ce simulacre barbare: quand elle se fera participation, au livre pris d'ici, de là, varié en airs, deviné comme une énigme—presque refait par soi. Les plis perpétueront une marque, intacte, conviant à ouvrir, fermer la feuille, selon le maitre. Si aveugle et peu un procédé, l'attentat qui se consomme, dans la destruction d'une frêle inviolabilité.

23. Jacques Derrida has discussed the paradoxical meanings of the fold in Mallarmé's writing in "The Double Session," in *Dissemination,* trans. Barbara Johnson (Chicago: University of Chicago Press, 1981), pp. 173–286. As Derrida puts it, "But in the same blow, so to speak, the fold ruptures the virginity it marks as virginity. . . . But after the fact, it still remains what it was, a virgin, beforehand, faced with the brandished knife" (p. 259).

24. "Journal, la feuille étalée, pleine, emprunte à l'impression un résultat indu, de simple maculature: nul doute que l'éclatant et vulgaire avantage soit, au vu de tous, la multiplication de l'exemplaire et, gise dans le tirage." "Le Livre," *Oeuvres*, p. 380. The use of an invented word, *gise*, should be noted. Mallarmé had already suggested that a *tome* (book) was like a *tombeau* (tomb) for the writer of literature. Here, however, through the conjunctions of the sounds *gise dans* [*gisant*], he implies that the improper use of hte press results in a stillborn (horizontal) writing, incapable of flight from the earth. Death and flight are metaphors that circulate throughout Mallarmé's opposition of poetry and journalism, and sometimes they serve to suggest a hidden relationship between these two apparently contradictory forms of writing.

25. " . . . une monotonie—toujours l'insupportable colonne qu'on s'y contente de distribuer, en dimensions de page, cent et cent fois." Ibid., p. 381.

26. "Crise de vers," ibid., p. 364:

> . . . mon sens regrette que le discours défaille à exprimer les objets par des touches y répondant en coloris ou en allure, lesquelles existent dans l'instrument de la voix, parmi les langages et quelquefois chez un. A côté d'*ombre*, opaque, *ténèbres* se fonce peu; quelle déception, devant la perversité conférant *à jour* comme à *nuit*, contradictoirement, des timbres obscur ici, là clair. Le souhait d'un terme de splendeur brillant, ou qui'il s'éteigne, inverse; quant à des alternatives lumineuses simples—*Seulement*, sachons *n'existerait pas le vers*: lui, philosophiquement rémunère le défaut des langues, complément supérieur.

27. The final part of Mallarmé's poem reads: " . . . UNE CONSTELLATION / froide d'oubli et de désuétude / pas tant / qu'elle n'énumère / sur quelque surface vacante et supérieure / le heurt successif / sidéralement / d'un compte total en formation / veillant / doutant / roulant / brillant et méditant / avant de s'arrêter / à quelque point dernier qui le sacre / Toute Pensée émet un Coup de Dés." Ibid., p. 477.

28. "Le livre, expansion totale de la lettre, doit d'elle tirer, directement, une mobilité et spacieux, par correspondances, instituer un jeu, on ne sait, qui confirme la fiction.
Rien de fortuit, là, où semble un hasard capter l'idée l'appareil est l'égal: ne juger, en conséquence, ces propos—industriels ou ayant trait à une matérialité." "Le Livre," ibid., p. 380.

29. Ibid.:

> A mon tour, je méconnais le volume et une merveille qu'intime sa structure, si je ne puis, sciemment, imaginer tel motif en vue d'un endroit spécial, page et la hauteur, à l'orientation de jour la sienne ou quant à l'oeuvre. Plus le va-et-vient successif incessant du regard, une ligne finie, à la suivante, pour recommencer: pareille pratique ne représente le délice, ayant immortellement, rompu, une heure, avec tout, de traduire sa chimère. Autrement ou sauf exécution, comme de morceaux sur un clavier, active mesurée par les feuillets—que ne ferme-t-on les yeux à rêver?

30. Charles Morice, for example, writing in 1889, shared Mallarmé's views on the distinction between journalism and literature: "I don't think I have to specify in what ways literature and journalism, although they employ the same alphabet, constitute two arts absolutely foreign to each other" [Je ne pense pas avoir à spécifier en quoi la Littérature et le Journalisme, bien qu'ils emploient le méme alphabet, constituent deux Arts absolument étrangers l'un à l'autre]. *La littérature de tout à l'heure* (Paris: Perrin et Cie, 1889), p. 292, n.I. Morice explained his aversion to journalism in the following terms: "The very idea of *selling* a poetic object is repugnant to one's honor: an archaic

and epic point of view. . . . But this very action is contrary to logic since it is *la rue du Sentier,* in the last analysis, that is the arbiter of art as well as of commerce, since in other terms, art has become a trade'' [L'idée seule de *vendre* la chose poétique répugne à l'honneur: point de vue archaique et légendaire. . . . Mais le fait même répugne à la logique depuis que c'est *la rue du Sentier,* en dernière analyse, qui est l'arbitre de l'art aussi bien que du commerce, depuis, en d'autres termes, que l'art est devenu un commerce] (ibid., p. 291).

31. ''Le travail d'après nature était la dernière sauvegarde du métier de peintre. On est arrivé ces dernières années à s'en passer complètement. On ne fait plus que noter des sensations, l'art n'est plus que le journal de la vie. C'est le journalisme dans la peinture. . . . C'est l'oeil qui mange la tête.'' Maurice Denis, ''Les Arts à Rome ou la Méthode Classique,'' *La Spectateur catholique,* nos. 22, 24 (1896), reprinted in *Théories 1890–1910* (Paris: L. Rouart et J. Watelin Editeurs, 1920), pp. 52–53.

32. Maurice Raynal reported seeing books by Verlaine, Rimbaud, and Mallarmé in Picasso's studio in the rue Ravignan (prior, that is, to 1909), in *Picasso* (Paris: G. Crès & Cie, 1922), pp. 52–53.

33. In ''The Mystery in Letters,'' Mallarmé advises those who would read to confront the whiteness of the page ''forgetful even of the title which would speak too loudly [oublieuse méme du titre qui parlerait trop haut].'' ''Le Mystère dans les lettres,'' *Oeuvres,* p. 383.

34. Robert Rosenblum, ''Picasso and the Typography of Cubism,'' in Roland Penrose and John Golding, eds., *Picasso in Retrospect* (New York: Harper and Row, 1980); reprinted in the present volume, pp. 91–120. Subsequent page references to this article are to pages in the present volume's reprint.

35. Patricia Leighten, ''Picasso's Collages and the Threat of War, 1912–13,'' in *The Art Bulletin* 67, no. 4 (December 1985); reprinted in the present volume, pp. 121–70.

36. ''Picasso's Musical and Mallarmean Constructions,'' *Arts Magazine* 51 (March 1977): 127. Ron Johnson mentions Mallarmé's aversion to the newspaper in connection with his analysis of Picasso's collages and constructions but does not emphasize its commercial associations. He is more interested in demonstrating the similarities between Picasso's constructions and Mallarmé's aesthetics than the differences. Thus his analysis turns on concepts of chance, suggestion, and creativity as a destructive process. Of the newspaper he says,

> Picasso in fact became a poet of puns and word fragments, turning to printed words, whereas Mallarmé used visual processes to add another dimension to his poetry. Mallarmé thought of the book as a spiritual instrument in contrast to the newspaper, which he compared to the sea. It was the newspaper and its mechanical sense of lettering that Picasso subverted to his own semiotic purposes. He not only used the newspaper for its form (flatness) and value (stark dark light contrasts) with many reversible effects, but began using the letters to create an abreviated [*sic*] telegraphic poetry. . . . Perhaps there is a more immediate relationship to Apollinaire's *Calligrammes* and to Alfred Jarry's puns in this fragmentation process, sense of surprise, and humor than to Mallarmé, but it is the latter who began the process.

37. See Pierre Daix and Joan Rosselet, *Le Cubisme de Picasso* (Neuchatel, Switzerland: Editions Ides et Calendes, 1979), no. 547.

38. See ibid., no. 525.

39. Rosenblum, ''Picasso and the Typography of Cubism,'' pp. 94–95.

40. Apollinaire continued to supplement his meagre income as poet and critic by writing and editing pornography, and Picasso was certainly aware of this activity. Apollinaire's first published work, interestingly, albeit under another man's name, was the bulk of the serial novel *Que faire?*, which appeared in *Le Matin* in 1900. Apollinaire was never paid by the hack journalist, Esnard, who signed the installments written by various authors. For an account of Apollinaire's publications, see Roger Shattuck, ''The Impresario of the Avant-Garde,'' in *The Banquet Years: The Origins of the Avant-Garde in France, 1885 to World War I* (New York: Random House, Vintage Books, 1968), pp. 253–97.

41. For a history of the *Bon Marché,* the first large department store in France, see Michael B. Miller, *The Bon Marché: Bourgeois Culture and the Department Store, 1869–1920* (Princeton: Princeton University Press, 1981).

42. Walter Benjamin, *Charles Baudelaire: A Lyric Poet in the Era of High Capitalism* (London: Verso Editions, 1983), p. 54.

43. The lyrical fragment ''Ma Jolie'' was excerpted from the refrain of Fragson's ''Dernière chanson,'' written in 1911 and popular during 1911 and 1912. The refrain was as follows: ''O Manon, ma jolie, mon coeur te dit bonjour!'' See Rosenblum, ''Picasso and the Typography of Cubism,'' p. 99. Rosenblum credits Maurice Jardot with this reference.

44. '' . . . car l'oeuvre, seule ou préférablement . . . .'' ''Le Livre,'' *Oeuvres,* p. 381.

45. ''L'oeuvre pure implique la disparition élocutoire du poëte, qui cède l'initiative aux mots, par le heurt de leur inégalité mobilisés; ils s'allument de reflets réciproques comme une virtuelle traîné de feux sur des pierreries, remplaçant la respiration perceptible en l'ancien souffle lyrique ou la direction personnelle enthousiaste de la phrase.'' ''Crise de Vers,'' ibid., p. 366.

9

Decoding Collage: Signs and Surfaces

Wendy Holmes

Through a reading of various critical commentaries on Cubist collage, Wendy Holmes sheds further light on the complexities of collage, particularly when viewed from a semiotic perspective. As she writes, "A look at the critical commentary on Cubist collage, should therefore, afford a rare opportunity to observe art historians coming to terms with signs within the content of their ordinary involvements with works of art and outside of the polemics of theoretical and methodological 'crisis' in which 'semiotics' figures as a loaded term." Holmes considers, in particular, the "semiotic insights and problems" in the critical writings of Rosalind Krauss, Clement Greenberg, Robert Rosenblum and Pierre Daix. She also raises a number of provocative questions such as "What is the nature of a 'sample'?" or "Is collage a system or part of another system?"

> *Cubism is no different from any other school of painting. The same principles and the same elements are common to all. The fact that for a long time Cubism has not been understood and that even today there are people who cannot see anything in it, means nothing. I do not read English, an English book is a blank to me. That does not mean the English language does not exist and why should I blame anybody else but myself if I cannot understand what I know nothing about?*
>
> Pablo Picasso, 1923

As juxtapositions of fragments of language and fragmented images *trompe-l'oeil* illusions, real things, and things that are illusions, the great early Cubist collages of Braque and Picasso are generally recognized as configurations of extreme semiotic density. In such compositions as Picasso's *Still Life with Chair Caning* and *Compote Dish with Fruit, Violin, and Glass* of 1912, questions about visual signification are so baldly posed as to *force* their commentators to attend to their semiotic character. A look at the critical commentary on Cubist collage, should, therefore, afford a rare opportunity to observe art historians coming to terms with signs within the context of their ordinary involvements with works of art and outside of the topical polemics of the theoretical and methodological "crisis" in which "semiotics" figures as a loaded term. If the findings of art historians represent the understanding of "competent readers" of the "code" of Cubism, semiotic paraphrase and analysis should be able to explain their differences in relation to their diverse presuppositions and interests in signs.

Considering the importance of what Clement Greenberg called "the pasted paper revolution" as "a major turning point in the evolution of Cubism, and therefore a major turning point in the whole evolution of modernist art in this century,[1] collage has received little independent study. Readings of collage are inextricably bound to readings of Cubism in general and, as Kenworth W. Moffat's succinct summary suggests, these fall into three major categories.

> Almost from the beginning there has been, at least implicitly, a division of opinion as to whether Cubism is essentially an art of realism or abstraction. With characteristic disregard for consistency Apollinaire managed to maintain both things at the same time. And perhaps his was the best appraisal: Cubism was a realist art but was moving toward abstraction ("le peinture pure"). Metzinger and Gleize's, Kahnweiler's as well as almost all subsequent studies of the movement stress the representational character of Cubism while abstract artists from Mondrian to Hans Hofmann emphasize its purely formal significance and imply (indeed sometimes state) that they have drawn the logical conclusions from Cubism—conclusions which the original Cubists themselves had failed to draw. Conversely, writers of the "realist" persuasion generally see non-objective art as a "misunderstanding" of "true" or "pure" Cubism (usually this means only the Cubism of Picasso, Braque, Gris). They point to the way that Picasso and Braque always shied away from the completely non-figurative and how they often seemed anxious to "reaffirm" their connection with the real world."[2]

The various accounts which are roughly characterized above as Cubism-as-realism, Cubism-as-abstraction, and Cubism-as-transition also apply to collage, which, in many ways, stands to earlier and later phases of Cubism as Cubism stands to antecedent and subsequent art. The collages of Braque and Picasso are crucially situated, by most accounts, in the transition or even *as the transition* from analytic to synthetic Cubism, marking the shift between the style's more representational and presentational moments. Alternatively, the introduction of extraneous things and fragments to the traditional homogeneity of drawn or painted surfaces may be regarded as either a new literalism which affirms art's immediate presentational values or a novel reaffirmation of visual art's representational traditions. Of course, most critical commentary includes discussion of all three aspects, so it is only in relation to what is designated as its most significant feature that the terms "realism," "abstraction," and "transition" distinguish among variant interpretations of Cubist collage.

Rosalind Krauss's overlapping articles, "Re-presenting Picasso"[3] and "In the Name of Picasso,"[4] are, in a way, deconstructive of both the "realist" and "abstractionist" views represented, for her purposes, by Robert Rosenblum and Clement Greenberg. In its structuralist aspect, the text of Pierre Daix's *catalogue raisonné* of Picasso's works of 1907 to 1916, which covers the period of prolific collage production, lays the ground for Krauss's own structuralist discussion which seeks to correct and expand Daix's position, but departs radically from his assumptions to offer a novel reassessment of collage's semiotic foundations. Krauss reads Daix and Rosenblum and others through Ferdinand de Saussure, and she reads Saussure through Roland Barthes and Jacques Derrida. She is not concerned with "doing justice" to any of the theorists that she represents and misrepresents for her own purposes. By focusing my discussion on the same small group of art historians as representative of widely held views and presenting a rough semiotic overlay of their positions, as well as Krauss's critiques, I hope to illustrate the range of semiotic questions and art historical answers which cluster around Cubist collage.

Signs and Things

Acknowledging that "there is no question but that Braque and Picasso were concerned in their Cubism with holding on to painting as an art of representation and illusion,"[5] Clement Greenberg is militantly antirealism and proabstraction, which is also to be proliteralism and proconcreteness. In response to the notion that the introduction of extraneous real things onto the purity of the painted or drawn surface reaffirms realism or strengthens the bond between art and reality, he asserts that such substances as wallpaper and cloth and newspaper are certainly no more real than paint on canvas and that the only grain of truth in the Realism theory is that the Cubist artists chose to preserve the representational function of their art. In his influential articulation of the transition theory, Greenberg characterizes collage as a means to the end of enhanced flatness *in painting* rather than a truly independent medium of lasting interest to the artists: "Neither Picasso nor Braque ever really returned to collage after 1914."[6] Collage turns Cubism and ultimately modernist painting, away from "illusion" and toward an overt acknowledgement of the literal flatness of the painted surface.

As signs of surface, collage elements replace or reinforce lettering, whose absolute frontality also draws attention to the flatness of its support, the textural effects that Braque and Picasso achieved by mixing sand with paint and painted simulations of woodgrain and marble textures, all of which function similarly to stress the literal two-dimensionality of the picture plane and thereby strengthen the residual illusions of depth and volume elsewhere in the Cubist picture. But the pasted paper is different from these other devices: It "establishes undepicted flatness *bodily,* as more than an indication or sign."[7] In Braque's and Picasso's first collages (*Still Life with Chair Caning* and *Fruit Dish*) the bits of simulated oilcloth and wood that are affixed to the surfaces are such superior exemplars of flatness that "the only place left for a three-dimensional illusion is in *front* of, *upon,* the surface."[8]

The Cubists' ultimate rejection of *illusion,* in Greenberg's narrative, does not entail a rejection of *representation;* the two are distinct from each other insofar as illusions simulate three-dimensional spaces and volumes, qualities which can never be actually manifest on or in the painted surface, while representations may be exorcized of all volumetric and spatial properties, becoming planar shapes whose two-dimensionality is continuous with the literal flatness of a paper or canvas surface. Visual representation is independent of illusion, defined by Greenberg as nonconformity or noncompliance with the literal qualities of a particular medium. As far as Braque and Picasso are concerned, only when the lessons of collage were translated into paint "did Cubism become an affair of positive color and flat, interlocking silhouettes whose legibility and placement created allusions to, if not the illusion of, unmistakable three-dimensional identities."[9]

The account of collage that Robert Rosenblum provides in *Cubism and Twentieth-Century Art,* like his account of Cubism as a whole, includes transitional, abstractionist, and realist aspects, but these are subordinate to his view of the *continuity* of Braque's and Picasso's "Cubist dialectic between art and reality"[10] or illusion and reality or illusion and symbol. The terms of Rosenblum's dialectic shift, but it is clear that his main interest is in the coexistence and interpenetration of *different varieties of signs* in Cubist creations and that these differences are established, to his mind, by the nature of their distinctive modes of connection to the extrasemiotic realm. Before collage, the "unliteral vocabulary" of Cubist signs is already established: "Confronted with these various alphabetical, numerical, and musical symbols, one realizes that the arcs and planes that surround them are also to be read as symbols, and that they are no more to be considered the visual counterparts of reality than a word is to be considered identical with the things to which it refers."[11] Rosenblum assumes that it is uncontroversial and self-evident that images and words normally stand in different relations to "reality," that Braque and Picasso sometimes employ languagelike visual symbols that are distinct from illusions, and that collage introduces "material references" into an already mixed Cubist collection of signs.

Although Daix consistently uses the Saussurian terms "signifier" and "signified," the fact that he never defines "sign" or refers to Saussure prompts Krauss to provide a brief primer to Saussure as support for her own semiotic perspective. She stresses the conceptual generality of the "signified" and its difference from the "referent," that real-world entity which has no place in the purely linguistic purview of Saussure. A sign, consisting of a material signifier and a conceptual signified, is a "substitute, stand-in, proxy for an absent referent," and, therefore, a "grounding of the terms of representation on absence—the making of absence the very condition of the representability of the sign."[12] Krauss's emphasis on absence as the "structural condition" for the operation of signs and sign systems seems to lead her to deny full semiotic status to "illusionistic depiction"—visual representation in the traditional sense:

> Whereas illusionistic depiction attempts to simulate the *presence* of objects, words effect no such simulation. Instead, they are part of a system of *re*presentation, with the prefix "re-" distancing the word-as-sign both temporally and substantively from its referent. The sign is a surrogate, substitute or proxy acting in the absence of the actual object. Collage, as Daix shows, is a thoroughgoing submission to the action of the sign; it reformulates the visual as language. Through the logic of collage the guitar, the compote, the wineglass, are banished from the image to be reconjured only through the play of signs—representation as a self-conscious system of substitutions.[13]

Krauss adopts Saussure's definition of the linguistic sign as the definition of sign-in-general and stresses its grounding in *absence* rather than in *convention*—which is more generally understood as the common feature of languages and nonlinguistic systems of signs. This odd emphasis, which I do not find in Saussure, is laid out prior to discussion of the differential nature of signs, which is everywhere in Saussure. Whereas Greenberg defines "illusions" in relation to specific media, Krauss regards them as the making-present-of-objects, close enough to objects to call their semiotic status into question. If "illusionistic depiction" is only quasirepresentational, surely Rosenblum's "material references" are too much present to have any semiotic status whatsoever according to Krauss's initial description of "sign."

What is not provided in the Saussurian discussion, which applies only to the arbitrary signs of language, is some account of *modes of signification* such as Peirce's icon, index, and symbol or Nelson Goodman's denotation, exemplification, and expression, which foreground the differences among signs. Briefly, Peirce's well-known triad classifies signs according to whether they take their signifying powers from social convention (symbol), resemblance (icon), or causality (index); since a dyadic relation is not in itself semiotic or mediating, icons and indices also have conventional aspects which determine the conditions of their usage as signs. According to Peirce's most general definition:

> An *Icon* is a sign which refers to the Object that it denotes merely by virtue of characters of its own, and which it possesses, just the same, whether any such Object actually exists or not. It is true that unless there really is such an Object, the Icon does not act as a sign; but this has nothing to do with its character as a sign. Anything whatsoever, be it quality, existent individual, or law, is an Icon of anything in so far as it is like that thing and used as a sign of it.[14]

There are enough ambiguities in this short statement to keep Peirce scholars arguing for years. However, for my purposes it establishes the double basis of iconic representation in the intrinsic qualities of signifiers and in the interpretive recognition or "use" of likeness. Icons as a class do indeed have greater "presence" than symbols in the sense that a picture is said to be worth a thousand words since they lack the capacity to refer with the bald generality of "man," "table," or "musical instrument." To refer, icons must characterize, exhibit, or describe. According to how they describe, Peirce classifies icons as: *images,* which share some perceptible quality or qualities with their referents; *diagrams,* which manifest similar structural relations; and *metaphors,* which function by means of parallelism or analogy.[15] Although anything may function as a symbolic substitute for anything else by virtue of agreement between the users of signs, icons are a special class of substitutes which "can only have a similar Object" (referent, in other terms), which "more strictly speaking, can only be an idea."[16]

"Illusions" are iconic images which Braque and Picasso modify, augment, analyze, and displace by iconic diagrams, linguistic symbols, visual symbols, and other varieties of signs. With the dispersal or fragmentation of iconic continuity, which implies that the relations among images are also iconic—relative to relations among visible things, Daix points to the importance of what he calls "clue objects"—iconic details or fragments—in referring to objects and establishing space.[17] The slice of lemon, the key or knob of a drawer, the nail, the pipe, are not only more tightly rendered than what surrounds them, but they imply the existence of supporting planes, drawers, or tables, or walls, so that spatial and situational contexts coalesce around them, created by the viewer out of ambiguous spaces or shapes. Some such small-scale details, like the curving shapes of the sound holes of the violin or the round hole in the middle of a guitar, become so familiar through the Cubists' repetition that they become independent symbols of musical instruments, recognizable in the absence of other clues even when they are positive shapes. Daix, Rosenblum, and Krauss in summarizing Daix refer to the Cubist separation and dispersal of iconic aspects or qualities or texture, color, and shape which were formerly concentrated in discrete objects and are now laid out next to each other as the independent variables of the images they displace.

There are tantalizing glimpses of Braque and Picasso's *systematic* dismantling of iconicity in Daix's reports, but, because he possesses the most rudimentary of semiotic distinctions—"signifier/signified," "pictorial/optical," "clue-object," "ideogram"—his descriptions are not systematic. He calls forms or qualities of form "signifiers" and the subjects or objects of diagrammatic reference "signifieds," and amasses details pertaining to the successive Cubist modifications of signs and space. Without plumbing the depth of Peirce's semiotic theory, his fundamental distinctions between icon, index, and symbol would clarify and enhance Daix's analysis of Cubist signs. In some respects, the substitution of "iconic image" for "illusion" may be a trivial one, for Greenberg, Rosenblum, and Daix *assume* that illusions signify in something like the way that Peirce describes, but in others the Cubist displacement of iconic functions into symbolic and indexical signs is amenable to closer semiotic description than the vocabulary of ordinary critical language can provide.

But what of brute things? Rosenblum calls the pieces of oilcloth or paper or rope that are used as collage materials "material references" and Greenberg suggests that such untransformed material, literally or bodily occupying the surface of collage, are other than signs. Nelson Goodman, who devotes a great deal of attention to samples and swatches and examples, supports Rosenblum's view. Describing exemplification as "an important and widely used mode of symbolication in and out of the arts," which he defines as "possession plus reference," Goodman asserts that any thing may function as an example of something that it is or some property that it has.[18] Or, to be more precise, things exemplify predicates which are accurately applied. Goodman puts the same constraints of *possession* and *use* on examples that Peirce puts on icons—and he regards "expression" as metaphoric exemplification. Therefore, in spite of the radical iconoclasm of Goodman's understanding of visual representation, his definition of exemplification coincides with Peirce's ideas on iconicity in important respects so that examples or samples may be regarded as a fundamental category, perhaps the most fundamental category, of iconic signs.[19]

The most far-reaching development of Goodman's theory of exemplification is in its recuperation of meaning of the most "pure," "literal," or "abstract" of artistic signs.

> The properties that count in a purist painting are those that the picture makes manifest, selects, focuses upon, exhibits, heightens in our consciousness—those that it shows forth—in short, those properties that it does not merely possess but *exemplifies*, stands as a sample of. . . . A work of art, however free of representation and expression, is still a symbol even though what it symbolizes be not things or people or feelings but certain patterns of shape, color, texture that it shows forth.[20]

There is nothing for Greenberg to disagree with in Goodman's claims, which elucidate what Greenberg assumes—that forms have meaning in relation to systems of forms; ''presence'' has a mediated aspect which does not detract from immediacy; and the modernist shift that collage plays a part in effecting is described anew as the change from representational to exemplifying signs.

In contrast to painted colors and shapes, however, collage elements are samples of alien stuffs or things. There could be no better illustration of Goodman's claim that *which* of its various properties or predications a sample exhibits is dependent upon the semiotic system it falls within.[21] In a book of samples, a piece of wallpaper or oilcloth does not normally exemplify ''wallpaper'' or ''oilcloth'' or ''wallpaper/oilcloth sample'' (or size or shape) but only its specific pattern and coloration. As a part of an artistic configuration, a piece of wallpaper or oilcloth does become a sample of a sample and exhibits its ''wallpaperness'' in an entirely different way; a property that was semiotically inert is activated in the new context of painted or drawn shapes. Alternatively, ''material references'' could be construed as indices of the real things of which they were once part, indices of their mechanical production, as Rosenblum observes, or indices of the formative acts of cutting and pasting which brings them to their present place. Goodman's analytic interest in the logical disentanglement of the modal and polysemic complexities of artistic signs is mirrored on the plane of interpretation by Rosenblum's focus on the interactions of signs and modes of signification as *the over-arching theme* of Cubist art which is brilliantly particularized in individual collages.

Rosenblum is struck, for example, by the use of readymade illusion in *Still Life with Chair Caning,* Picasso's first collage.

> This pasting or, to use the now familiar French term, *collage,* is perhaps even more probing in its commentary on the relations between art and reality than any of such earlier Cubist devices as *trompe l'oeil* or painted symbols, since the result now involves an even more complex paradox between ''true'' and ''false.'' The oilcloth is demonstrably more ''real'' than the illusory Cubist still-life objects, for it is not a fiction created by the artist but an actual machine-made fragment from the external world. Yet, in its own terms, it is as false as the painted objects around it, for it purports to be chair caning but is only oilcloth. To enrich this irony, the most unreal Cubist objects seem to have a quality of true depth, especially the *trompe l'oeil* pipe stem, which is rendered even more vivid by juxtaposition with the flatness of the *trompe-l'oeil* chair caning below.[21]

Rosenblum uses *trompe-l'oeil* to distinguish relatively distinct images like the pipe stem from more stylized representations, as well as to describe flat areas of simulated textures, like wallpaper or woodgraining or caning, which might indeed fool the eye, momentarily or in photographic reproductions of works.[22] The oilcloth caning is a readymade icon of ''caning,'' and sample of oilcloth which becomes chair caning by means supplemental specifying signs. As a substitute for the artist's rendering of cane patterning, the oilcloth may cause the viewer to reflect upon their difference, as Rosenblum does above, but if the caning were real, some of its significations and effects would be the same. The word ''caning,'' a piece of patterned oilcloth, a fragment of actual chair caning, and an artist's *trompe-l'oeil* rendering may be symbols or icons or examples of the same (idea of a) thing, but the varying connotations of ''skill,'' ''tradition,'' or ''mechanical reproduction'' which are created by the artist's choice of one or another means of denotation create the allusive density which Rosenblum describes.

In the brief interpretive description quoted above, Rosenblum clearly takes account of the varieties of signs that Goodman describes in logical terms. Their perspectives of the art historian/critic and the semiotician/logician are different. Rosenblum is interested in the meanings of works and Goodman is interested in how works mean what they do. But, in the context of Krauss's meditations on representation and naming, how does Rosenblum come to represent the inadequacy of art historical interpretation and a flat ''positivist'' or ''realist'' comprehension of signs? Krauss discusses ''Picasso and the Typography of Cubism,''[23] and not Rosenblum's more general treatments of Cubism and collage in *Cubism and Twentieth-Century Art,* from which I have quoted. In both there are aspects of the Realism theory; collage elements and linguistic signs are viewed as guides to intelligibility, the former as ''material references to nonartistic realities,''[24] and the latter as the mundane signage of urban life, which, however ambiguous, ''establish, with startling vividness, Cubism's connections with the new imagery of the modern world.''[25]

Krauss asks of Rosenblum's account of a ''Cubist conundrum'' in which the letters EAU on a bottle label are taken as a reference to Beaujolais, Beaune, or Bordeaux:[26]

> But are the labels EAU and JOU a set of transparent signifiers, the nick-names of a group of objects (the newspaper, the winebottle) whose real names (Journal, Beaujolais) form the basis for this labor of the Cubist pun? Is the structure of Cubist collage itself supportive of the semantic positivism that will allow it to be assimilated into the art history of the proper name? Or are the word fragments that gather on the surfaces of Picasso's collages instead a function of a rather more exacting notion of reference, representation, and signification?[27]

Krauss has so far developed her sketch of "the art history of proper names" in relation to "the autobiographical Picasso" and explanations of works that rely on references to Olga or Dora Maar or Jacqueline, and also in a short general discussion of naming and referring, in which it is suggested that classical theories of mimesis which limit meaning to reference, donation, extension, and lack dimensions of intention or connotation persist or enjoy a revival in art history at the present time. There is much that should hit home to art historians in the first part of this discussion, especially as it concerns the relentless mining of the contexts of artistic production for new "facts" of questionable aesthetic relevance. However, Cubist collages and paintings bear names on their surfaces, proper names like BACH, MOZART, KUBELICK, MISS STEIN, MISS TOKLAS, and ANDRE LEVEL, as well as LE JOURNAL, L'INDEPENDENT, LE FIGARO, and PERNOD, SUZE, and VIEUX MARC, and the signatures of BRAQUE, PICASSO, and GRIS, which are transformations of normal signings, as Rosenblum explains, so that his discussion of the names and nouns and wordplay that are pervasive in Cubist works is of an entirely different order than the gratuitous introduction of nominal particulars that shifts the focus of attention from texts to contexts and signs to things. Rosenblum looks at what the Cubists do with names in relation to what they do with images, and the interactions and enfusions of their "double register" of signs. It is hard to read "semantic positivism" into the ambiguity, paradox, and instability that he finds.

Krauss's thumbnail critique of Daix involves the same charge of "semantic positivism" that she makes about Rosenblum's discussion of Cubist typography: Daix pays too much attention to "bottle," "table," and "violin," the signifieds of still life paraphernalia, making it "easy to convert the issue of the collage-sign into as question of semantics, that is, the sign's transparent connection to a given referent."[28] And, "because the power and interest of collage go well beyond the capacity of element *a* to refer to object *x*, Daix's search for the ideogrammatic or pictographic mark does not exhaust the implication of collage as a signifying system."[29] Krauss suggests that Daix and Rosenblum, as practitioners of realist reconstruction and seekers of certitude, piece together Cubism's shattered images, given common sense and proper reference to linguistic fragments, and restore to the seamed and polyseamed surfaces of collage the semblances of comforting illusions that were.

Krauss implies that Daix and Rosenblum, especially Rosenblum as the designated realist, overlook both the formal structures of collage and the "differential" nature of signs. Greenberg, on the other hand, understands that collage marks the choice between illusion and representation, but he doesn't express this understanding in the language of signs.

What is left for Krauss to do, then, is 1) to clarify the differential aspect of signs and give Greenberg's insights semiotic form; as it turns out, this will also enable her to 2) challenge Greenberg's modernist privileging of presence and reveal that absence, not presence, is the ''master term'' of Cubist collage, 3) discover that collage elements embody formal oppositions, and 4) characterize Cubist collage as metalanguage.

Relations and Functions of Signs

The two sets of ''differential'' relations which are fundamental to all sign systems are described in terms of the ''twofold character of language'' below:

> The addressee perceives that the given utterance (message) is a COMBINATION of constituent parts (sentences, words, phonemes, etc.) SELECTED from the repository of all possible constituent parts (the code). The constituents of a context are in a state of CONTIGUITY, while in a substitution set signs are linked by various degrees of SIMILARITY which fluctuate between the equivalence of synonyms and the common core of antonyms. . . . A given significative unit may be replaced by other, more explicit signs of the same code, whereby its general meaning is revealed, while its contextual meaning is determined by its connection with other signs within the same sequence.[30]

This dual relationship of signs to other signs in the manifest configurations in which they are embedded (*in presentia,* in Saussure's terms) and to the sign system as a whole (*in absentia,* or mnemonically), is foundational for semiotic studies of a great many levels and types. E. H. Gombrich, for example, constructs his powerful theory of artistic expression on the differential nature of signs, explaining how responses to *artist's choices* of colors and shapes differ from ''physiognomic perception'' of colors and shapes outside of the ''structured matrix'' of an organized medium and a particular stylistic code.[31] Both Gombrich and Goodman understand the ''meanings'' of abstract art as connotations of feelings and values which develop on the basis of the differential functions of signs—and they also understand the dynamic and shifting dimensions of artistic expression as emergent from disjunctions between productive and interpretive codes.[32] Jakobson, on the other hand, gives semiotic articulation to the premise that what counts aesthetically is present to perception in the contiguous configurations of the artistic ''message'' or text, which collapses the normal distance between message and code.[33] Jakobson's differentiation of the *aesthetic function* of signs as fulfilling an interpretive interest in the message as formulated, in contrast to the referential, emotive, and metalingual functions which all lead away from the particulars of specific configurations toward their paraphrasable content, what signs may reveal about their producers, and the operation of codes has direct relevance to Krauss's complaints about "the art history of proper names" and art historical equations of meaning with reference, which are largely unjustified, I think, as far as Rosenblum and Daix are concerned.

In his study of Cubist typography, Rosenblum explores the different significations that similar elements—such as pieces of newspaper or variations of the word JOURNAL—take on in different compositional contexts; and in his discussion of *Still Life with Chair Caning* he clearly responds to the connotations of Picasso's choice of materials and the polysemic functions that elements may take on (oilcloth=caning/plane/nonpainting). Daix, on the other hand, understands his own *method* as semiotic precisely in respect to the differential aspect of signs. Daix replaces "myth" by "work" in Lévi-Strauss's statement: "Light is shed on every work or version of a work by what it transforms, distorts, opposes, denies or affirms."[34] He proposes to emulate the radically comparative procedures of Lévi-Strauss in the text of his *catalogue raisonné* which attempts to elucidate the *functions* of collage elements and other devices in Picasso's Cubist idiom by comparing their relationships and uses across the corpus of works produced by Picasso between 1907 and 1916.

The point that Krauss wants to make, in relation to the differential operation of signs, is that collage elements are polysemic, but not only that, they are polysemic in peculiar ways. In Picasso's *Compote Dish with Fruit, Violin and Glass* (Daix no. 530), for example, "the single patch of wood-grained paper ambiguously allocated to table and/or musical instrument composes the sign for open, as opposed to closed form. Yet the piece of wood-graining terminates in a contour that produced the closed silhouette of a neighboring form."[35] This leads to the conclusion that:

> In the great, complex Cubist collages, each element is fully diacritical, instantiating both line and color, closure and openness, plane and recession. Each signifier thus yields a matched pair of formal signifieds. Thus if the elements of Cubist collage do establish sets of predicates, these are not limited to the properties of objects. They extend to the differential calculus at the very heart of the formal code of painting. What is systematized in collage is not so much the forms of a set of studio paraphernalia, but the very system of form."[36]

What does this mean? It is entirely uncontroversial that collage elements take on a variety of semiotic functions, over and above signifying "studio paraphernalia," and ambiguous connotations of opacity and transparency, positive and negative, closure and openness, and so forth. Here is how Greenberg describes the same ambiguity:

> In the later collages of both masters, a variety of extraneous materials are used, sometimes in the same work, and almost always in conjunction with every other eye-deceiving and eye-undeceiving device they can think of. The area adjacent to one edge of a piece of affixed material—or simply of a painted form—will be shaded to pry that edge away from the surface, while something will be drawn, painted, or even pasted over another part of the same shape to drive it back into depth. Planes defined as parallel to the surface also cut through it into real space, and a depth is suggested optically which is greater than that established pictorially.[37]

But how do we get from the discontinuity or ambiguity that everyone recognizes to "the matched pair of formal signifieds" and "the very heart of *the* formal code of painting?" Such matched signifieds as opacity and transparency or closure and openness are, in systems of images in which they are employed, antonymical—they cannot have the same signifier. To neutralize antonyms, as the Cubists do, is to create extreme ambiguity, to violate the system of the image code. But the matched pairs of *formal signifieds* that are listed above are not antonyms—they are the terms of Wölfflin's principles of art history, structuralized and returned as bipolar oppositions through a series of analogies and assumptions that I will not attempt to describe.[38]

Whereas Greenberg stresses the absorption of the illusion of depth by the fact of flatness, how the presence of the flat collage shapes "releases and spreads" flatness, Krauss fixes upon what collage makes absent, conceals, removes from view:

> For it is the affixing of the collage piece, one plane set down on another, that is the center of collage as a signifying system. . . .
>
> The collage element as a discrete plane is a bounded figure; but as such it is a figure of a bounded field—a figure of the very bounded field which it enters the ensemble only to obscure. The field is thus constituted inside itself as a figure of its own absence, an *index of a material presence* [italics added] now rendered literally invisible. The collage element performs the occultation of one field in order to introject the figure of a new field, but to introject it *as* figure—*a surface that is the image of eradicated surface.* It is this eradication of the original surface and the reconstitution of it through the figure of its own absence that is the master term of the entire condition of collage as a system of signifiers.
>
> The various resources for the visual illusion of spatial presence becomes the ostentatious subject of the collage-signs. But in "writing" this presence, they guarantee its absence. Collage thus effects the representation of representation. This goes well beyond the analytic Cubist dismemberment of illusion into its constituent elements. Because collage no longer retains these elements; it signifies or represents them.[39]

This extremely subtle argument, in which "absence" figures so heavily, rests entirely on the earlier claim that absence is the "structural grounding" for signs in a sense that goes well beyond the structuralist understanding of "significant absence," the negative mark, or the zero degree opposition through which absences are enabled to signify because presences, which also signify, are systemically possible. The collage element can signify only because it makes the original surface of the canvas absent. *It is a sign because it causes absence.* It is as she states an *"index"* of a material presence that it conceals. At the heart of "Re-presenting" and "In the Name," as they apply to collage, is another note on the index, which is conjoined through "absence" to the preceding structuralist discussion of signs, and a recuperation of the *icon,* which was discounted earlier on as too much present to fulfill the Saussurian conditions for signs. The collage element is an index of the surface that it makes absent and, at the same time, an iconic "facsimile" of the surface whose flatness and boundedness it replicates. Because any flat, painted shape could carry the iconic function of the collage element—as both the figure of a ground and a ground for other figures—it is the conjunction of icon and index or else indexicality by itself that is crucial to Krauss's tenuously balanced argument. The collage manner of covering and concealment by means of the addition or superimposition of materials *that are planes* is conceived as completely different from the addition or superimposition of substances which are not planes—like paint mixed with sand or just paint. Krauss's argument verges on tautology—the master term of collage is collage.

But does the index function spatially or temporally? Does it refer to what it covers up or to the act of covering? Such surface disturbances as fingerprints, footprints, tracks, and imprints of all varieties are not generally regarded as referring to the substances or surfaces that bear them—the expanse of wet sand, say, or the wall of a cave—which undergo physical alteration by either sinking down or receiving new material. Is it the concealed surface or the additive act that is signified by the indexical sign? As an elemental semiotic potential, anything made can indicate its manner of making, just as anything can serve as an example of what it is. To read as an example or to read as an index may be more or less aesthetically relevant, depending on the code of production and the code of interpretation which is in effect. But in semiotic descriptions other than Krauss's very strained and idiosyncratic adaptation of Saussure, "absence" is not necessary to activate the play of signs and *re*-presentation is not absent from Cubism before collage.

Art Historians and Semiotics

The semiotic concerns and levels of operation of the four commentators converge and diverge in various ways. There is less difference between Daix's "announced" semiotic perspective and Greenberg's and Rosenblum's unannounced semiotic perspectives than Krauss's summary of Daix's findings would lead one to believe. He concentrates on the signs that replace images in representing still-life subjects and on Cubist space. He is the only one of the four that conceives of his *method* as semiotic, loosely related to the myth readings of Levi-Strauss, for whom to know what a sign means is to discover another sign that can stand in its place. Daix's list of surface-stressing substitutes is essentially the familiar one discussed at length by Greenberg and duly noted by everyone since—the frontally aligned lettering, the sand mixed with paint, the trompe-l'oeil textures, the pasted planes. Daix does not add to Greenberg's account of how these devices impinge on other elements of Cubist pictures, agreeing with Greenberg, letting his account stand. The point that, above all else, *collage elements are formal substitutes for effects of painting* is supported by profuse comparisons of collages with "companion" drawings and paintings, some of which share the same linear "armature" and are clearly conceived as sets or series.[40]

The existence of so many companions of collage raises questions about Krauss's splitting off the system "collage" from the system "Cubism." Only Krauss isolates collage, though Greenberg's essay is similarly focused on collage. Is collage a system or part of another system? If collage is what opens the Cubist surface to representation, how does Cubist painting mean? For semiotic studies which make general claims about how systems work it is of the utmost importance that the corpus of messages or texts isolated for study truly reflect a "language state" that is operative for the users of language at a certain synchronic moment or limited slice of time. If the selected corpus is too narrow or too broad, then the relations among signs are misrepresented—their differential structures are deformed—and if collage elements can substitute for effects of painting that sometimes carry the same general compositional functions then Cubist collage cannot be discussed in isolation from Cubist painting. Daix's disregard of the difference in substances in which the Cubist signs are manifest is structurally proper—the traffic code, for instance, employs many substances as well as the preexisting signs of ordinary language and stylized images but it is still *one code*—though in other ways Daix's structuralist veneer is extremely thin. What is structuralist about his method is thoroughly enmeshed in "the art history of proper names," biographical narrative, the confidences of Picasso, and the wisdom of earlier critics—including Greenberg and Rosenblum. In its very eclecticism, Daix's method is far more art historical than structuralist but, at the same time, it demonstrates the structuralist proclivities of art history as a discipline that is fundamentally analytic rather than hermeneutic, one that routinely categorizes, contrasts, and compares.[41]

There is no reason that signs should not be studied diachronically or historically,[42] unless the purposes of semiotic investigation are on a par with those of structural linguistics which seeks to provide an ''explicit representation, by a system of rules and norms, of the implicit knowledge of those who successfully operate within the system.''[43] The temporal slice considered by Daix (and Greenberg) is narrow enough to count as synchronic, but in Daix's account it is packed with important incidents which unfold sequentially, month by month and season by season, in excruciating diachronic detail. To the extent that both Daix and Greenberg focus on *changes* in how things were represented and *changes* in Cubist space, they can never describe the ''language'' of Cubism as an operative code, a complete system of signs adequate for whatever Braque and Picasso ''have to say'' at any given time and adequate for interpreters to ''get the message'' of individual works of art. Krauss, on the other hand, ducks the problem of synchrony and diachrony—and also the necessity of dealing with Cubism as an independent code whose rules and norms are yet to be discovered—by the tactic of naming Wölfflin ''the father of art historical structuralism'' and his empirically derived points of contrast between Renaissance and Baroque style as the rudiments of a great atemporal system, the ''code in relation to which style can be either manifested or perceived.''[44]

The *bricolage* of semiotic and art historical bits from which Krauss's reading of collage is constructed takes its plausibility mainly from points of overlap with what art historians generally believe about Cubism. Cubism is ambiguous; why not the site of embodied formal oppositions? Cubism is ''about'' representation in some fundamental way; why not metalanguage? Many readers will not understand the new and special way that Krauss wishes metalanguage and representation to be understood, but they will understand that it is some kind of methodological tour de force to arrive at absence as the key to the most ostensibly full and augmented of Cubist inventions, which is surely the main purpose of her elaborate circumlocution of collage and Cubist signs.[45] But one point that she makes most vividly is of fundamental importance to the semiotics of Cubism and collage: As she says, *objects are absent* in cubist art—the plane of imagistic denotation is absent—and it is not reconstituted by the fullness of iconic aspects or elements or the density of metonymic fragments which take its place.

Krauss moves from the plane of denotation to that of metalanguage, but a passing observation of Jakobson's on ''the manifestly metonymical orientation of Cubism, where the object is transformed into a set of synecdoches,''[46] which he does not develop into any full-fledged discussion of Cubist art, together with his discussion of the *systematic breakdown* of language in different forms of aphasia, introduces a different semiotic perspective and a parallel to the breakdown of the language of images in Cubist art.

Jakobson explains anomia—the loss of names and the loss of descriptive precision—as an impaired internalized code and an inability to discriminate among signs and things on the basis of similarity and dissimilarity, while a generalized grammar or pattern of linkages remains.[47] The ability to comprehend and make sense that survives in anomia is entirely context-dependent, reliant on cues provided by the external circumstances of utterance and on the framework of connectives that allows one word to follow from another in the contiguous chain. Jakobson's comments on the similarity disorder are richly suggestive of Cubist disruptions of images and the compensatory sense-making devices which take their place—the survival of the organizational scaffolding and the mundane frame of reference, the displacement of intact images into spatial contiguities, the interdependences of shapes and their purely positional coherence, metonymic condensations and expansions of every conceivable type, and the intermittent incidences of linguistic or imagistic fluency on collaged patches coming from outside the system and retaining their distinctness from other Cubist signs. But even if Cubism does not, under closer scrutiny, hold up as a sort of anomia of images, the parallelisms and divergencies of Krauss's theory of collage and Jakobson's discussion of aphasia are worth closer examination. According to Jakobson, however, metalanguage involves exactly those discriminations of similarity and that understanding of language as system which the sufferers of anomia have lost.[48]

Whereas Greenberg, Daix, and Krauss are, in different ways, concerned with collage in relation to systems of forms, Rosenblum focuses more on the contiguous relations of signs in individual collages. In "Picasso and the Typography of Cubism," newspaper is not read as "plane" or "luminosity" or "surface" but read actually as newspaper. The subject of Rosenblum's study of Cubist typography—language, words, letter forms—is signs. His approach is not historical but loosely organized around such recurring motifs as names of newspapers, brand names of alcoholic beverages, music, newspaper clippings, allusions to Cubism, proper names, and signatures. He charts the transformations and derivations of *Le Journal* through a broad selection of collages and paintings. His study is not semiotic, however, in point of view, in the sense of orienting investigation or organizing findings according to some general theory of signs or some encompassing framework of semiotic distinctions. Since differential relations exist on every level of a system—a point that becomes obscured in Krauss's discussion—the dimensions of denotation and connotation which interest Rosenblum could be systematized according to the structuralist bipolar scheme, or they could be overlaid by discussion of their iconic, indexical, and symbolic dimensions or projected into the field of Goodman's logical constructs. Either of the latter alternatives might clarify or sharpen the sorts of distinctions and interactions of different semantic modalities that interest Rosenblum, but since neither Goodman's nor Peirce's semiotics yields a readily applicable mode of analysis, they could only provide a supplemental discourse and some elemental points of distinction to operate in counterpoint to Rosenblum's discussion of Cubist signs. Still, nonstructuralist semiotics seems vastly more *appropriate* for application to collage and, perhaps, to most visual signs. The problem with structuralism outside of its linguistic setting, as many theorists have noted, is that although it posits specific procedures for categorization and analysis of a corpus, it is often fuzzy at either end, in specifying just what questions it proposes to answer or what the results of analysis mean.

Rosenblum shows how the device of collage permits the cooption or quotation of materials that are not only samples but are samples of signs, most often the signs of ordinary language or ordinary schematic drawing which take on ironic connotations in the Cubist milieu. The mundane still life, which is generally the enframing subject of Cubist collage, is thereby expanded to take in all the news that is fit to print or picture, and the "transparent" visual and verbal codes of everyday transactions are retained for Cubist use. This is a function of collage that cannot be duplicated by "effects of painting," and, as Rosenblum demonstrates, it was one that was appreciated and exploited by the artists—in some of their works. But uniqueness is not essence. Arguments about the central or essential function of collage simply duplicate in miniature the realist, abstractionist, and transitionalist arguments about Cubism. There is no essence of Cubist collage or "key" or "master term" or semiotic depth at which its secret is revealed—which is not to say that existing descriptions are individually satisfactory or collectively adequate or that deeper or closer semiotic studies could not function as elucidating tools. What the collective studies of art historians do reveal is collage as a supremely multiple and mutable device capable of operating on several semiotic strata simultaneously, sometimes assuming a primary semantic position and sometimes sinking back into form.

Notes

1. Clement Greenberg, "Collage," in *Art and Culture* (Boston: Beacon Press, 1961), p. 70; reprinted in present volume (pp. 67–77), p. 67. Subsequent page references to this article are to pages in the present volume's reprint.
2. Review of Douglas Cooper's *The Cubist Epoch, Art Bulletin* 56, no. 2, (June 1974): 305.

3. Rosalind Krauss, "Re-presenting Picasso," *Art in America* 68, no. 10 (December 1980): 91–96.
4. Rosalind Krauss, "In the Name of Picasso," in *The Originality of the Avant-Garde and Other Modernist Myths* (Cambridge/London: The MIT Press, 1985), pp. 23–40.
5. Greenberg, p. 68.
6. Ibid., p. 74.
7. Ibid., p. 71.
8. Ibid.
9. Ibid., p. 74.
10. Robert Rosenblum, *Cubism and Twentieth-Century Art* (New York: Harry N. Abrams, Inc., 1960), p. 70.
11. Ibid., p. 66.
12. Krauss, "In the Name of Picasso," p. 33.
13. Krauss, "Re-presenting Picasso," p. 94.
14. Charles Sanders Peirce, "Logic as Semiotic: The Theory of Signs," *Philosophical Writings of Peirce,* Justus Buchler, ed. (New York: Dover Publications, Inc., 1955), p. 102.
15. Peirce, p. 105.
16. Peirce continues: "For it must produce an Interpretant idea; and an external object excites an idea by a reaction upon the brain."
17. *Picasso: The Cubist Years 1907–1916* (Boston: New York Graphic Society/Little, Brown, and Company), pp. 83–84.
18. *Languages of Art* (Indianapolis/New York: The Bobbs-Merrill Company, Inc., 1968), pp. 52–53.
19. Nelson Goodman, *Ways of Worldmaking* (Indianapolis/Cambridge: Hackett Publishing Company), p. 65.
20. Goodman, *Languages of Art,* p. 53.
21. Rosenblum, *Cubism and Twentieth-Century Art,* p. 68.
22. Peter Burger, for example, refers to Picasso's oilcloth as a piece of woven basket somewhere in his *Theory of the Avant-Garde,* which is mentioned in Benjamin Buchloh's *Art in America* review (November 1984) as evidence of Burger's distance from works of visual art.
23. In Roland Penrose and John Golding, eds., *Picasso: 1881/1973* (London: Paul Elek Ltd., 1980), pp. 48–75; reprinted in the present volumes, pp. 91–120. Subsequent page references to this article are to pages in the present volume's reprint.
24. Rosenblum, *Cubism and Twentieth-Century Art,* p. 70.
25. Rosenblum, "Picasso and the Typography of Cubism," p. 112.
26. Ibid., p. 99.
27. Krauss, "In the Name of Picasso," p. 32.

28. Ibid.

29. Krauss, ''Re-Presenting Picasso,'' p. 94.

30. Roman Jakobson and Morris Halle, *Fundamentals of Language* (The Hague: Mouton, 1975), p. 75.

31. In *Art and Illusion,* especially ''The Beholder Share'' (New York: Bollingen Foundation, 1965), pp. 181–287, and ''Expression and Communication,'' *Meditations on a Hobby Horse* (New York, Phaidon Press, 1971), pp. 59–61.

32. Goodman, *Languages of Art, 45–56* Gombrich, especially in ''Visual Metaphors of Value in Art,'' *Meditations on a Hobby Horse,* pp. 12–44.

33. ''Linguistics and Poetics,'' in Thomas A. Sebeok, ed., *Style in Language* (Cambridge, Mass.: MIT Press, 1960), p. 358.

34. Daix, p. 9.

35. Krauss, ''In the Name of Picasso,'' p. 35.

36. Ibid., p. 37.

37. Greenberg, p. 72.

38. Wölfflin is discussed specifically in ''Re-presenting Picasso'' but not in ''In the Name of Picasso.''

39. Krauss, ''In the Name of Picasso,'' p. 37.

40. Daix, p. 114.

41. For discussion of the analytic focus of art historical studies compared to prestructuralized literary studies: Svetlana and Paul Alpers, ''Ut Pictura Noesis? Criticism in Literary Studies and Art History,'' *New Literary History* 3 (Spring 1972): 437–58.

42. For discussion of Prague School Structuralism's conception of systematic change see: F. W. Galen, *Historic Structures: The Prague School Project, 1928–1946* (Austin: University of Texas Press, 1984).

43. Jonathan Culler, *Structuralist Poetics* (Ithaca: Cornell University Press, 1975), p. 9.

44. Krauss, ''Re-presenting Picasso,'' p. 93.

45. Krauss's discussion includes strategically placed ''ifs'' and the section of ''In the Name of Picasso'' in which her ideas on collage are developed is headed by Robert Rauschenberg's legendary portrait or its quotation: ''This is a portrait of Iris Clert if I say so.'' Perhaps we are meant to take everything that follows conditionally.

46. Jakobson and Halle, p. 92.

47. Ibid., pp. 77–84.

48. Ibid., p. 82.

10

Space Craft: Collage Discourse

Harry Polkinhorn

Harry Polkinhorn points to the importance of approaching collage as "a particular process practiced by artists in a given historical period." He examines a number of different critical discourses on collage, as he considers the problems of critics "idealizing the 'category' of collage among a variety of others . . . to advance their own arguments concerning modernism and postmodernism." For Polkinhorn the materials and process of collage may ultimately serve "not in understanding the world, now an impossibility, but in interacting with it so as to change it."

Words

Most recent discussions of collage in art have approached it as a *technique* of revolutionary importance in early modernism; in the standard critical moves to chart the foundations of modernism, Picasso (and sometimes Braque) is credited with the invention of this supposed technique, which then spread to the other arts, eventually eroding the boundaries between them. As I hope to demonstrate, misunderstanding an art-making process by not grounding it sufficiently in the historical specifics of its use by artists easily leads to inflated claims for its significance. Thus, Perloff states that the invention of collage

> reflects a profound change in verbal art as well, calling into question the traditional boundaries between "prose" and "verse," between the genres—lyric, novel, drama—as well as between the media. It is also in this period that we witness the coming into prominence of such hybrid genres as the manifesto, the performance, the artist's book, the visual poem, the documentary novel—offshoots of collage art that have become increasingly important in our own time.[1]

It was not only collage, of course, that examined the divisions between genres, a function of most Western European art since at least the

Renaissance. In any event, as Wolfram has amply shown, by the early twentieth century collage as an art practice had had a very long history both in Western and Eastern cultures.[2] To attribute its invention, then, to artists in the early twentieth century (even its purported appropriation by artists for the interrogation of representation in visual art) must itself be examined as a coded move to set apart practices, intentions, and achievements of a group of artists as significantly different from what preceded them in the drive to create modernism categorically.

However, Wolfram's implicit corrective to the misapplications of art historical and literary critical periodizations, while certainly welcome, must be complemented by a fuller political contextualization of the process than has been offered to date. That is, the descriptive-anecdotal accounts of which collage's history is made up, together with formal analyses and "close readings" such as Greenberg's,[3] require a synthesis at the next stage of development of commentary on collage if indeed this practice is to be approached as a distinctive feature of the art-making of our time. Only in this way will we be able to gain some understanding of how the discourse upon the art with which we are concerned in fact operates.

One can see an analogous strategy in Marchán Fiz's analysis in *Del arte objetual al arte de concepto.* Once "the object" (especially the art object) was separated from its historical/sociological context, all kinds of possibilities opened up. Among these is that of the Duchampian gesture. States Fiz, "The gesture achieved the status of a category of an artistic *provocation* against the concept and the object of bourgeois art. And this gesture of provocation is considered as art."[4] By the same token, embedded in collage as a historically conditioned category of discourse we have the gesture of rejection of the process of apprenticeship and all that it is based on—hierarchy, order, the political economy of liberalism. The gesture itself is now worthy of the label "art," its end product having been set free to drift in the relatively free space of contemporary culture. What I am suggesting here, in addition to a critical analysis of collage discourse itself, is the theoretical advisability of viewing collage as an art-making process, and the political implications of this gesture in our time.

Because collage was practiced by artists whose work came to be classified as "avant-garde," originally a military term, the rhetoric of direct political action (assault, revolution) came to be associated with this process. According to this model, representational art was that produced for the ruling class, specifically the bourgeoisie, whereas avant-garde art sought the overthrow of the sociohistorical status quo. With regard to the explicitly political debates which have accompanied discussions not only of collage but of all experimental art processes in the early twentieth century, Pastorello's comments on montage apply equally to collage: "*Montage is not a subversive category in itself* . . . the category of montage is then *anti-naturalist* and *anti-'realist'* (or if one prefers anti-materialist mechanical)."[5] This of course is not to imply that allegedly *new* processes were not seen as bound up with the programs of revolution; quite the contrary.

The point here is that the debates must be as fully contextualized as possible. Pastorello thus continues, "The debate over montage spills right over into the problem of montage as technique. This debate, drawn to a close in the USSR in 1932 by a decree, and prolonged during the thirties among the exiled Germans, is not a debate between advocates of *form* and *content* but a battle between two lines, between two conceptions of revolution. . . . "[6] Unless we approach collage as a particular process practiced by artists in a given historical period, claims as to its ultimate significance for modernism lose all force. For example, note a diametrically opposite reading to the above, which has been suggested by Hofmann: "Curiously enough, in breaking away from the Renaissance dogma of a work of art as an original and coherent whole produced by one man, this process is close to the didactic art of the Middle Ages, which was not concerned to reproduce reality but to illustrate exemplary situations by prototypes and 'exempla' familiar to everyone."[7] Although the prototypes have become aesthetically untreated materiality itself (newspaper, wallpaper, caning, cigarette packages, ticket stubs, etc.), which bears out the observation that collage at least temporarily explodes high culture referentiality (subsequently to be reincorporated in the sphere of high culture through the rhythms of capitalist conditioning of the cultural marketplace), returning us to the immediacy of relatively unprocessed sense data, dislocated statements about the meaning of collage lose any application. Richard Kostelanetz corroborates this when he says, "Collage has finally become a terribly hackneyed form, a familiar staple in every art today. Perhaps the surest test of this generalization is that I can think of no distinguished work, *in any art,* that is syntactically based on collage."[8] In spite of definite implications which collage engages (to be discussed below), the presence of collage in and of itself is a guarantee neither of the political status of a work of art nor of its degree of participation in something called "modernism."

The fact remains that artists almost obsessively continue to return to collage as a process for the genesis of their work. Leaving aside those visual artists who relied heavily upon collage—among them Schwitters, André Verlon, John Heartfield, Jiri Kolar, and Robert Motherwell[9]—virtually every artist in every art form has experimented with collage to one degree or another. To see this, one must accept an expanded definition of the term, as most critics have done, such as that offered by

Wescher: "It has been customary to apply the term 'collage' to all works in which components belonging to separate intellectual or perceptual categories are combined, even when, as in many instances, nothing has been pasted or glued."[10] Thus, for Stravinsky to "quote" Russian folk tunes in *The Rite of Spring* is as much collage as is Pound's unacknowledged use of (poorly) translated Chinese material in the *Cantos.* What counts is the rhythmic or arhythmic violation of strict, sequential development, the breaking of the narrative line, upsetting systematizing preconceptions about how a work *should* develop given its own aesthetic premises. The spectator must perceive this rupturing for collage to come into existence, to do its work. Thus, when Perloff says that "the word *collage* becomes an emblem of the 'systematic play of difference,' the 'mise en question' of representation that is inherent in its verbal-visual structure," although we can accept the highlighting of "difference," we must be careful about indiscriminate extensions to the party line on collage as a questioning of representation in art.[11] If some such questioning is taking place in the work of certain artists in Western societies, a full and careful analysis of its characteristics should be given, since one might easily argue that, just as with the examination of genre boundaries, one of art's most basic functions as it has been practiced in Western European societies is precisely to question representation, and there are many ways to do this, not only through distortion and elimination of the surface features of the "representational" mode, itself a highly suspect conceptualization.

Nevertheless, critics continue to resort to this formulation. Thus, the two main moments in modernist (visual) collage, the Cubist and the Futurist, have come to be seen as marking off the spectrum of possibilities explored by recent practitioners of this process. Representation as a concern of collage is touched upon by Poggi in her analysis of these two moments.

> For the Cubists, if it could be shown that no one representational schema was more 'true' than any other, then art became a specifically human creation, independent of nature. It would seem that the only legitimate way to re-present objects on the canvas was simply to place them there. In contrast, the Futurists attempted to counteract the arbitrariness of previous styles by basing their art on the inherently expressive properties of forms, colors, materials, and sounds in order to create a new, multi-sensory language.[12]

Additionally, although both groups were fascinated by increased simultaneity of vision, the Futurists were interested in addressing the issues of speed, dynamism, and technological violence in their work, whereas the Cubists seemed more intent on exploring the rational-intellective qualities of a pure visuality all but torn free from standard versions of representation. It is therefore not difficult to understand why the Russian avant-garde, after initial enthusiasm, reacted with such hostility to Marinetti's propositions during his visit to Moscow in 1914, since while the political implications of his project so closely paralleled their own, from the Russian point of view the uses to which collage was to be put had a specific, politically revolutionary content, whereas Italian practices seemed like a last stage of decadence. "The [Italian] Futurists strove to discover a new, naturally expressive artistic language. It was their subversion of rational means of communication and the appeal of their work to intuition that attracted the Dadaists, and, later, the Surrealists,"[13] These, of course, were not quite the intentions of the Russians, intent as they were on using the resources of art to build a new society on the ashes of a long bankrupt feudalism. Furthermore, the appeal to "naturally expressive artistic language" was closely bound up with a Fascist ideology.

As indicated above, by idealizing the "category" of collage among a variety of others, critics then can use it to advance their own arguments concerning modernism and postmodernism. This is the conceptual error which Rosalind Krauss makes when she outlines a series of claims about collage in relation to Cubism and modernism. "The extraordinary contribution of collage is that it is the first instance within the pictorial arts of anything like a systematic exploration of the conditions of representability entailed by the sign."[14] What about Cézanne's exploration of signs of living space in his Mt.-Sainte-Victoire series? What about the serial signs of Monet's cathedral facades or haystacks? Indeed, Cubism's uses of collage are not transparent. According to Barr, "Paradoxically, the Cubists, having destroyed in their paintings the image of the natural world, began to apply to their paintings actual fragments of the natural world," which could be taken as a regressive practice.[15] Krauss goes on to develop her notion of collage in the following manner: "It is the affixing of the collage piece, one plane set down on another, that is the center of collage as a signifying system . . . [it is] the literalization of depth . . ." and,

> The field is thus constituted inside itself as a figure of its own absence, an index of a material presence now rendered literally invisible. . . . It is this eradication of the original surface and the reconstitution of it through the figure of its own absence that is the master term of the entire condition of collage as a system of signifiers. . . . Collage thus effects the representation of representation . . . [It] is a metalanguage of the visual.[16]

This excessively formalist reading, although fashionably inflected by a loosely applied semiotics of the visual image, does not hold up; what, after all, does it mean to say that something is "literally invisible," or to speak of the "literalization of depth"? The common sense of the literal becomes the mystique behind Krauss's argument. As for the "metalanguage of the visual" and the "representation of representation," we have only to consider Jan Van Eyck's *The Arnolfini Wedding* (1434) or Velázquez's *Las Meninas*. As indicated above, the critical interrogation of representation by representation has been a central concern of perspectively structured visual art in European history since Alberti and is not an invention or even an effect of collage.

Later in her essay, we see Krauss's real goal, as she introduces a version of modernism which she would like to debunk. "For collage operates in direct opposition to modernism's search of perceptual plenitude and unimpeachable self-presence . . . . Collage problematizes that goal, by setting up discourse in place of presence."[17] Are discourse and presence, however, mutually exclusive? Krauss's comments sound very much like a covert response to Derrida; she seems to be simultaneously claiming that collage achieves presence through destroying it, which would indeed be something noteworthy. Furthermore, to assert that modernism was a search for "perceptual plenitude and unimpeachable self-presence" willfully ignores works by artists such as Giacometti, Schoenberg, Stein, Malevich, and Gabo, for whom absence was rather the favored but not exclusive term of the dialectic. As we can see, to work with bipolar diversions such as presence/absence without placing the work itself in a fully developed historical and social context leads to specious conclusions about the art and sets criticism free to elaborate its own categories of discourse.

In a final move, Krauss equates language and collage: "For it is collage that raises the investigation of the impersonal workings of pictorial form, begun in analytical Cubism, onto another level: the *impersonal* operations of language that are the subject of collage."[18] This opens the door for the critic to supplant the visual artist, but it leaves unexamined the question of whether and how in fact language can be said to be impersonal. Impersonality, very much a concern of many artists in the early twentieth century, must be viewed within the context of their understanding of its functions, their various embodiments of it in their work. The key formulation was Eliot's which grew out of a hieratic dimension in Symbolism. Says Steiner,

> The desire for a natural correlation between physical and mental states was also part of the ideology of many early modernists. Eliot's objective correlative, for example, calls for poets to depict emotions only through such objective situations as would give rise to them. He thereby assumes that such an absolute correlation between situation and emotion exists. . . . Eliot's approach is symptomatic of an academic conservatism intent on finding nature and universals where culture, in all its variability, reigns."[19]

In any event, when Flaubert, Yeats, Joyce, Eliot, Pound, and others sought to make art "impersonal" or more object-oriented, this came as a reaction to the sloppy effusions of Symbolism in which Yeats himself had participated in his early work. Impersonality in language, as these and others pursued it, was a strategy whereby poetry's net impact could be increased, not decreased, as Krauss seems to be suggesting.

For a more suggestive critical approach to the difficulties posed for theory by collage, we turn to Cavell's notion of acknowledgment as a part of the work of modernist art in achieving its sense of medium.

> What modernist painting proves is that we do not know *a priori* what painting has to do or be faithful to in order to remain painting. So there is no way, or ways, in which it does something differently from the way poetry does it. Its mode of existence is different. In insisting on its specific mode of existence, a modernist art seems to break down the concept of genre altogether: what a painter or poet or composer has to achieve in his painting or poetry or music is not a landscape or sonnet of fugue, but the idea of his art as such.[20]

This breaks the art medium free from an exclusive identification with its material support, while maintaining a meaningful relationship to it as an ontologically necessary substratum. To protect this understanding of the dialectical foundations of a medium, Jean Paris indicates the dangers of proceeding with a strictly linguistic model:

> [H]ow could criticism better stress the *secondary* character of visual arts than by submitting them to the methods of *linguistic* analysis? For example, by reducing pictures . . . to repertories of rhetorical figures and by decoding the painting surface as if it were a literary text? And how, then, could the structuralist critic not find in painting what he himself put into it, all those metaphors, antonomasias, hyperboles, synecdoches and the like, which completely negate the specificity of *visual* facts?[21]

Thus, as the above discussion has indicated, misunderstanding the different uses to which artists in varying social/cultural circumstances have put the process of collage can lead to conclusions about art which don't make much sense. To put this another way, the discourse on collage has passed through several stages of its own trajectory while leaving the implications of this practice unexamined.

Materials

For collage to be perceived as such, the phases in the composition process must be discernible; that is, one must *know* that collaging has occurred in the course of art-making. The artist must construct signs whereby the viewer is told that collaging has occurred. I want to emphasize the present perfect of this signalling, a way of conjoining past and present by blurring their artificial separation. ''Collage'' as substantive, referring to a process in art-making, has gotten appropriated by criticism which then makes statements about its own linguistic categorizations after the art has reached its final physical state, thus producing a kind of optical illusion. Beyond the level of sensory appreciation of the materials of art, collage in Western European modernism comes to equal *knowledge of the production of art.* The use of the practice constitutes a historically conditioned gesture which factors in this knowledge as a self-consciousness. This is coincidental with Saussure's bifurcation of the linguistic sign. The following account of Saussure's concept is offered as perhaps the closest theoretical analogue contemporaneous with early high modernism's exploitation of collage starting around 1914.

Saussure sets out a distinction between a noun and a thing. 'The linguistic sign unites not a thing and a noun, but a concept and an acoustical image . . . the psychic imprint of this sound, the representation that gives us the evidence of our senses.''[22] Saussure thus invokes the *metaphor* of the ''acoustical image,'' revealing a secondary splitting with the initial splitting upon which his theory will be erected. The evidence of the senses cannot be trusted but must be completed by a conceptual overlay; what we *know* must be brought to bear on what we *perceive.* This *splitting* is then developed through Saussure's move to replace ''acoustical image'' and ''concept'' with ''*signifiant*'' and ''*signifié.*'' ''We propose to retain the word *sign* to designate the whole, and to replace *concept* and *acoustical image* respectively with signified [*signifié*] and signifier [*signifiant*].''[23] In this way, in spite of the splittings which the linguist detects as inherent in the data he will examine, all is resolved at the level of the sign, by virtue of whose agency these contradictions are transcended. Collage as used by early modernist artists, instead of pursuing a similar transcendence through supposedly incorporating nature in art, acknowledges (in Cavell's sense of the term) contradiction. That is, it speaks against itself.

The Speedy Space Craft

Materiality is introduced into the discourse on art, then, by collage's negativizing or rejecting of craft or the physical acts involved in art making; inherent in taking objects and pasting them in or on, as indicated above, is a rejection of academy training and the ideology of power which it mediates. Time is not necessary for the collage artist to achieve mastery, itself an ideological token. Rather, he or she plugs directly into the instantaneous present of cultural artifacts. Craft becomes equivalent to labor, which is time itself in a material sense. The control of this time/experience is necessary in a structuring of society according to concentrations of wealth; in order for wealth to concentrate, a social hierarchy is established whereby the sedimented time which exists in the products of labor gets transferred differentially, selectively.

Fundamental to this buried process is the separation and subsequent reorientation to each other of the previously accepted categories of space and time, which are joined in the artists's life experience and conceptualized under the heading of "labor." Upon this two-part process as reflected in the post-Enlightenment project of the rationalization of power on secular grounds—the elaboration of political economy as an explanation of the meaning of the world, and the grandiose classifications according to the tree schemes of Linneaus, the language descent schemes of the German comparatists, and Darwin's branching model—is based the view of nature as a storehouse of potentiality, a source of life itself which must be tamed through reduction, division, hierarchical rationalization. Modernist practices with collage implicitly examine the subterranean nature of these relationships, whose access point is precisely the mystification of the labor necessary for the creation of art.

If the purpose of a spacecraft is to travel through space, the faster we move the shorter the amount of time elapsed. Pushing the model to its extreme, we see that instantaneous transport, the hypothetical ideal state of the system, in which speed is totalized, eliminates time as a category separable from any other, which logically eliminates space, its complement. Thus one can speak either of spatial or temporal simultaneity. "Ubiquity, instantaneity, the peopling of time supplants the peopling of space."[24] Collage, then, gestures towards this instantaneity, which perhaps suggests why the process has been so appealing to contemporary sensibility. This increasing popularity of collage art as a tool for materially conceptualizing what is unique about our historical experience argues for the extension of the term "modernism" beyond the arbitrary cut-off points assigned by various critics: World War II, Abstract Expressionism, Minimalism, and so on. The classical distinctions between sensory experience and knowledge thereof, between the worlds of nature and culture, image and text, the body and the mind have been superseded by a state of affairs which defies the institutional urge to incorporate them into its own drying structures. A separation of collage art practices from the critical discourse these practices have generated can help us to realize that the art has embodied these contradictions and indeed has become the key artistic process not in understanding the world, now an impossibility, but in interacting with it so as to change it.

Notes

Unless otherwise noted, translations in the text are by author.

1. Marjorie Perloff, "The Invention of Collage," in Jeanine Parisier Plottel, ed., *Collage* (New York: New York Literary Forum, 1983), p. 8.
2. Eddie Wolfram, *History of Collage: An Anthology of Collage, Assemblage and Event Structures* (New York: Macmillan, 1975).
3. Clement Greenberg, *Art and Culture: Critical Essays* (Boston: Beacon Press, 1961).
4. "El gesto alcanzaba la categoría de una *provocación* artistica contra el concepto y objeto de arte burgués. Y este gesto de provocación es considerado como arte." Simón Marchan Fiz, *Del arte objetual al arte de concepto: Epilogo sobre la sensibilidad "Posmoderna"* (Madrid: Akal, 1986), p. 161. On the modernist notion of "event" as an art form, see Stephen C. Foster, ed., *"Event" Arts & Art Events* (Ann Arbor: UMI Research Press, 1988).
5. "*Le montage n'est pas une catégorie subversive en soi* . . . la catégorie du montage est donc *anti-naturaliste* et anti-'réaliste' (ou si l'on préfère anti-matérialiste mécaniste)." Felicie Pastorello, "La Catégorie du montage chez Tretjakov, Arvatov, Brecht," in *Collage et montage au théâtre et dans les autres arts durant les années vingt* (Paris: La Cité, 1978), p. 119.
6. "Le débat sur le montage déborde massivement le problème du montage comme technique. Ce débat qui s'achève en U.R.S.S. en 1932 par un décret, qui se prolonge dans les années trente chez les exilés allemands, n'est pas un débat entre *formalistes* et *contenutistes*, mais une lutte entre deux lignes, entre deux conceptions de la révolution." Ibid., p. 127.
7. Werner Hofmann, in André Verlon, *Collage + Montage-Painting 1958–1983* (Vienna: Schriftenreihe des Museums moderner Kunst, 1983), p. 32.
8. Richard Kostelanetz, "Avant-Garde Past," in *The Old Fictions and the New* (Jefferson, N. C.: Macfarland, 1987), p. 11.
9. See E. A. Carmean, Jr., "The Collages of Robert Motherwell," in *The Collages of Robert Motherwell: A Retrospective Exhibition* (Houston: The Museum of Fine Arts, 1972).
10. Herta Wescher, *Collage* (New York: Harry N. Abrams, nd (after 1968), p. 163.
11. Perloff, p. 14.
12. Christine Poggi, "Marinetti's *Parole in Libertá* and the Futurist Collage Aesthetic," in *The Futurist Imagination: Word + Image in Futurist Painting, Drawing, Collage and Free-Word Poetry* (New Haven: Yale University Art Gallery, 1983), p. 9.
13. Ibid., p. 14.
14. Rosalind Krauss, "Modernist Myths," in *On the Originality of the Avant-Garde and Other Modernist Myths* (Cambridge, Mass.: MIT Press, 1985), p. 34.
15. Alfred H. Barr, Jr., *Cubism and Abstract Art* (Cambridge: The Belknap Press, 1986), p. 78.
16. Krauss, p. 37.
17. Ibid., p. 38.
18. Ibid., p. 39.

19. Wendy Steiner, *The Colors of Rhetoric* (Chicago: The University of Chicago Press, 1982), p. 25.

20. Stanley Cavell, *The World Viewed: Reflections on the Ontology of Film* (New York: The Viking Press, 1971), p. 106.

21. Jean Paris, *Painting and Linguistics* (Pittsburgh: The Carnegie-Mellon University, 1975), p. 7.

22. "Le signe linguistique unit non une chose et un nom, mais un concept et une image acoustique," and this latter is "l'empreinte psychique de ce son, la représentation que nous en donne le témoignage de nos sens." Ferdinand de Saussure, *Cours de linguistique générale,* Charles Bally and Albert Sechehaye, eds. (Paris: Payot, 1985), p. 98.

23. "Nous proposons de conserver le mot *signe* pour désigner le total, et de remplacer *concept* et *image acoustique* respectivement par *signifié* et *signifiant.*" Ibid., p. 99.

24. "Ubiquité, instantanéité, le peuplement du temps supplante le peuplement de l'espace." Paul Virilio, *L'Espace critique* (Paris: C. Bourgois, 1984), p. 155. See also Virilio's *Vitesse et Politique* (1977).

11

Rethinking Kurt Schwitters: An Interpretation of *Grünfleck*

Annegreth Nill

From 1918 to his death in 1948, Kurt Schwitters produced a vast number of collages, collecting from sidewalks, dustbins, trash barrels, and cast-off materials to create his own medium and idiom. Traditionally, Schwitters's work has been discussed in formal terms, concentrating on materials and forms. Annegreth Nill's work, however, focuses on Schwitters's masterful combination of visual and verbal elements, thereby creating multiple levels of meaning in the collages. Referring first to Schwitters's 1918 Hansi, *his first extant work to use material from the commercial world, and then concentrating on* Grünfleck *(1920) Nill points to the intricate fusion and relationship of art and commerce in Schwitters's world. Through collages such as* Grünfleck *one sees clearly, through Nill's argument, how art and the economy interacted at a variety of levels in Germany at that time. The collage elements in Schwitters's pieces are important in their concreteness and formal qualities, but beyond that, "their very concreteness, combined with Schwitters's formal and verbal manipulation of them, creates possibilities for meanings of a very real kind." As Nill points to the collages as "an autobiographical record, which bridged the gap between art and life," Schwitters's statement, "I myself am now called MERZ," becomes more meaningful to our contemporary world.*

In 1927 Kurt Schwitters exhibited eighty-two collages in the great MERZ exhibition at the Sturm gallery in Berlin. The prices listed in the accompanying catalogue ranged from 50 to 300 marks with the exception of the 1920 collage *Grünfleck,* listed at 600 marks.[1] An inflated price tag on a work

This article, the second of a two-part series on Schwitters, originally appeared in *Arts Magazine* 55, no. 5 (January 1981). Reprinted by permission of the journal.

of art may mean that the work is not for sale because it has a particular significance for the artist. In the case of *Merzzeichnung 94: Grünfleck* (fig. 11.1),[2] an iconographic analysis reveals that this collage embodies Schwitters's artistic, private, and public concerns during the inflationary period in Germany that followed World War I.

The destruction of the war and the ever-worsening monetary situation following the war brought the struggle for economic survival into the forefront of German existence. Small wonder that Schwitters thought of his first one-man exhibition at Herwarth Walden's Sturm gallery in 1920 as a marketing operation. Quite consciously he searched for a trade name with which to present his work to the public. He could not call it Dada, as he had been rejected by the Berlin Dadaists, and stylistically it did not fit under the label of any of the other contemporary art movements. Schwitters chose the word MERZ, the title of one of the works he was about to exhibit (fig. 11.2). In this assemblage of 1919, Schwitters had isolated the syllable "Merz" from the word "Kommerz," which derived from the name of a banking establishment, KOMMERZ UND PRIVATBANK, "commercial and private bank."[3] The fact that the very name Schwitters chose for his one-man art movement had commercial roots is highly revealing about the character of his work at the time, in which art and commerce are intricately fused. The exemplary integration of these two themes in *Grünfleck* constitutes the true significance of this collage.

Just as Schwitters's impressive statement of 1920, "I pasted up pictures and drawings so that sentences should be read in them,"[4] has been proved to be true for *Hansi*,[5] it is also true for *Grünfleck*. The artist's love for the creation of new compound words rich in compressed meaning, encountered in *Hansi*, is also present in *Grünfleck*. The very name of the work makes the link between the verbal and the visual content of the collage, just as the word "ade" had done in *Hansi*. If the title *Hansi* was found to be central to the interpretation of that work, in *Grünfleck* it is the word *Anlage*, its meaning extended by the artist through its function in the collage. *Grünfleck* possesses a richly expressive content. But with it, Schwitters has moved beyond the theme of apocalypse of the German Expressionists still found in *Hansi* to the pure manifestation of MERZ.

When compared to other known collages from 1919 and 1920, *Grünfleck* appears much less randomly composed. Its formal arrangement bespeaks an orderly creative process that is clearly concerned with the presentation of content. But while *Hansi*'s formal structure derived from the early collages of Hans Arp, that of *Grünfleck* is based on Cubo-Futurist sources. These influences first appeared in 1919 in what Schwitters calls his Merz pictures, to distinguish them from the collages, which he

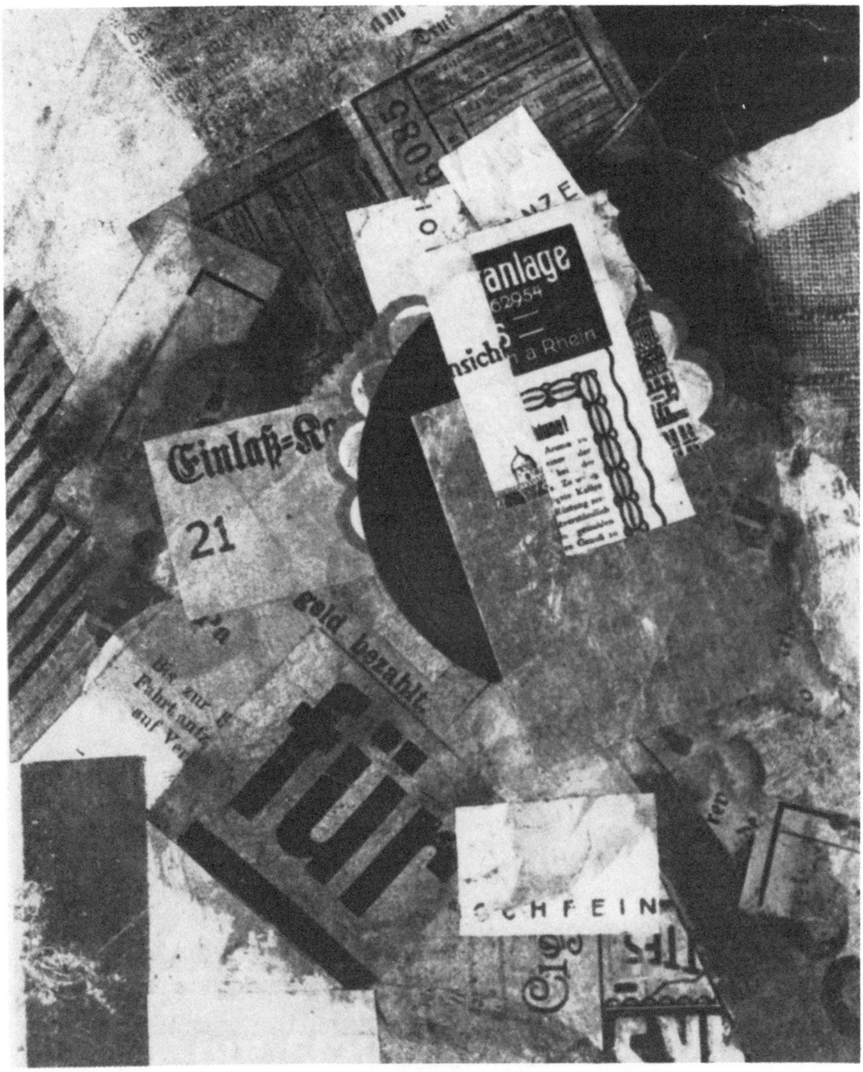

Figure 11.1 Kurt Schwitters, *Merzzeichnung 94: Grünfleck,* 1920
Collage, 6⅝″ × 5$\frac{5}{16}$″.
(Formerly in the collection of Pedro Vallenilla, Caracas. Present whereabouts unknown. Copyright © 1988, by COSMOPRESS, Geneva)

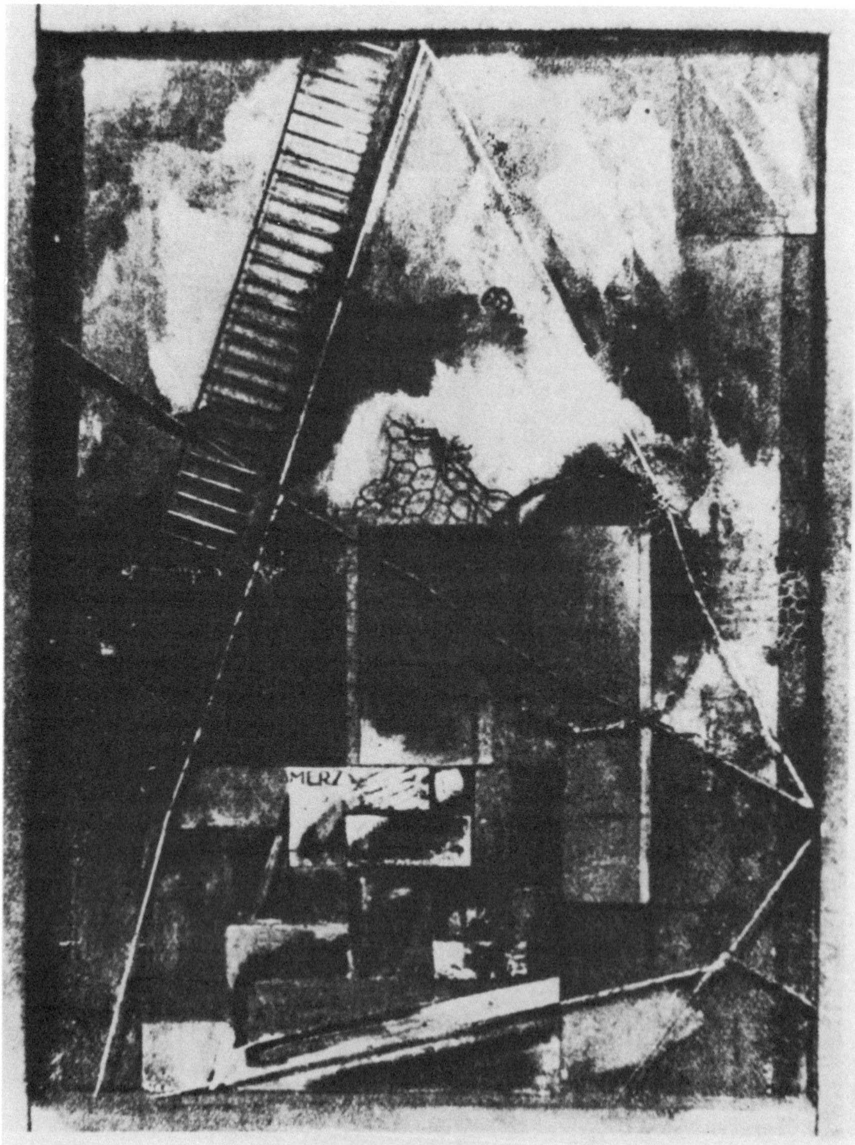

Figure 11.2 Kurt Schwitters, *Merzbild,* 1919
Assemblage.
(Lost)

sometimes calls drawings. Generally larger in size (i.e., *The Great Ich-Picture* measures 38-1/8 by 27-5/8 inches (fig. 11.3) vs. *Grünfleck*'s 6-5/8 by 5-5/16 inches), many of the Merz pictures are characterized by centralized circular motifs, partially pierced and obliterated by raylike wedges emanating from the edges.[6]

Grünfleck differs from the early Futurist-looking Merz pictures not only in size but also in paint handling. In the larger Merz pictures, the scraps of printed matter are too small to carry the structure by themselves; hence the composition relies heavily on painted elements. The smaller scale of *Grünfleck* is more commensurate with the size of the pieces used and allows the structure to grow out of the syntactical character of the pieces. Some painted passages have been retained, but in this case they are subservient to a different order—an order created by the syntax of the collage. The scraps have gained independence by retaining more of their individuality, while at the same time becoming more relational and therefore more interdependent.

The composition of *Grünfleck* is fanlike, centered around a circular core somewhat to the right of center. Diagonal lines of blue, beige, and red textiles move toward the core from the right edge, drawing attention to the center. A kind of smudge which is part of a larger stain obscures, and hence renders unimportant, the spatial relationships of the diagonals to the central core. Greater spatial clarity exists on the left side, where tickets and other rectangular printed matter relate to the primary circle in the manner of a hand of playing cards, but this time in a clearly spatially subordinated position. The tickets and other printed scraps come in "under" the black central core. Again, as in a hand of playing cards, the order in which these pieces relate to the core is important. The stain which Schwitters has applied over this area delineates it and anchors it in an upward sweep from the bottom right to the upper left-hand edge of the collage. This upward motion is introduced by the tapered red material at the bottom, and is then taken up by the three overlapping rectangles floating on top via a pair of streetcar tickets and a triangularly shaped piece of newspaper. This triangular shape is repeated on the left side of the collage by a pink- and black-striped piece of fabric. Its edges complement the diagonals on the right, and its apex, though obscured, points directly to the central core, helping to direct attention to it. Overall, there is a sense of a mounted jewel, the central core being held in position by its setting.

Turning to the verbal elements, one must first consider the title of the word, *Grünfleck,* written in Schwitters's own hand on the left, below the collage proper. Like *Witzgrund* in *Hansi,* this is a compound word which does not ordinarily exist in German and which was probably coined

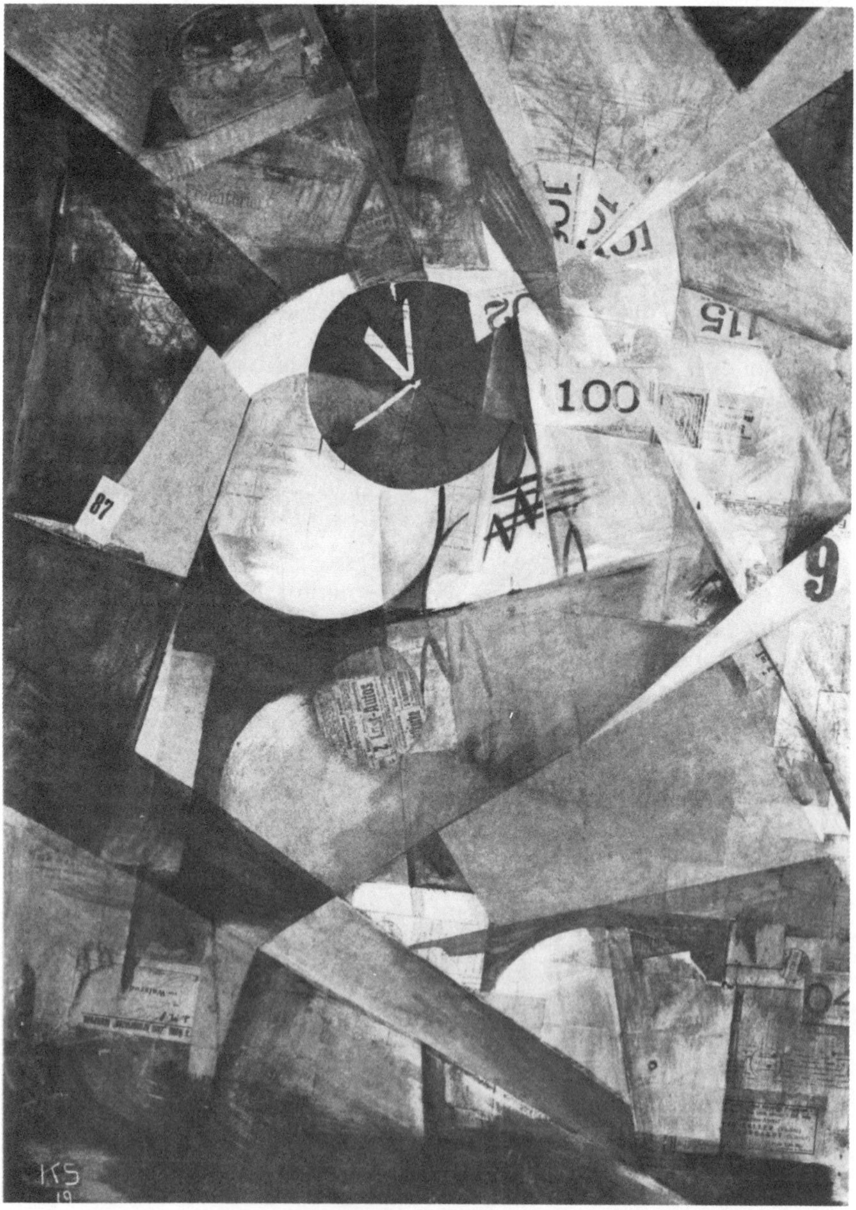

Figure 11.3. Kurt Schwitters, *Merzbild 9b: Das grosse Ichbild*, 1919
Collage, 38⅛″ × 27½″.
(Museum Ludwig, Cologne. Copyright © 1988, by COSMOPRESS, Geneva)

by Schwitters to describe the collage. Hence the meaning of *Grünfleck* must be derived from the meaning of its components *Grün* and *Fleck,* taking into consideration the context in which they appear.

To cite only relevant meanings, the noun *Grün,* according to a German-English dictionary of 1909, means "1. the colour green; 2. anything green, like verdure; and 3. spades, in a suit of playing cards." As an adjective it sometimes means "fresh" or "new."[7] The two relevant meanings of the noun *Fleck* are "1. spot, stain, blot, blur, blemish, taint and 2. patch, piece, botch."[8] The color green is conspicuously absent from the collage; hence the title seems to be problematic. Yet Schwitters is actually being quite concrete when one takes *Grün* to mean a suit of playing cards. The arrangement of the collage fragments around a central core has already been likened to a hand of cards. The outer range of the cards was described as being delineated by a "stain," which is one of the meanings of *Fleck. Grün* is the traditional color for spades in German cards. It is derived from a spadelike leaf pattern which decorated these cards.[9] Schwitters even incorporated some representations of leaves into the "card zone" of *Grünfleck.* The origin of these silvery-gray leaves is discussed below.

Combining *Grün,* meaning "fresh," with *Fleck,* meaning "patch," one gets the idea of a fresh patch. The correlation between "collage" and patching needs no elucidation. However, there is one more meaning to be derived from *Grünfleck* which will relate to the next word under discussion, *Anlage.* "Green" and "spot" may be put together to mean a "green spot" in nature, *Fleckchen Grün.*

Anlage (fig. 11.4) is the only major word printed in white letters on a black background. It appears on the narrow rectangular piece above the circular "center" of the collage. The word *Anlage* is rich in meanings, many of which determine the subthemes with which Schwitters deals in *Grünfleck. Anlage* is a noun meaning "1. beginning, foundation, construction, plan, design, outline, plot; 2. laying out; establishment, plantation, pl. -n. pleasure grounds, public walks; 3. investment, invested capital, stock; 4. natural aptitude, talent, predisposition; 5. annexed paper, enclosure; 6. tax, duty."[10]

How, then, does *Anlage* relate to *Grünfleck* and to the rest of the words in the collage? Or, to rephrase the question, what constitutes the meaning or message of the collage which Schwitters so carefully crafted? The answer to this question is twofold, although ultimately the meanings of the collage are joined. The division is mainly created for the sake of clarity, but it also reflects Schwitters's dual concern for art and commerce. First, *Grünfleck* is about the making and viewing of collages and other works of art, and the viewing of things in general. Secondly, it addresses

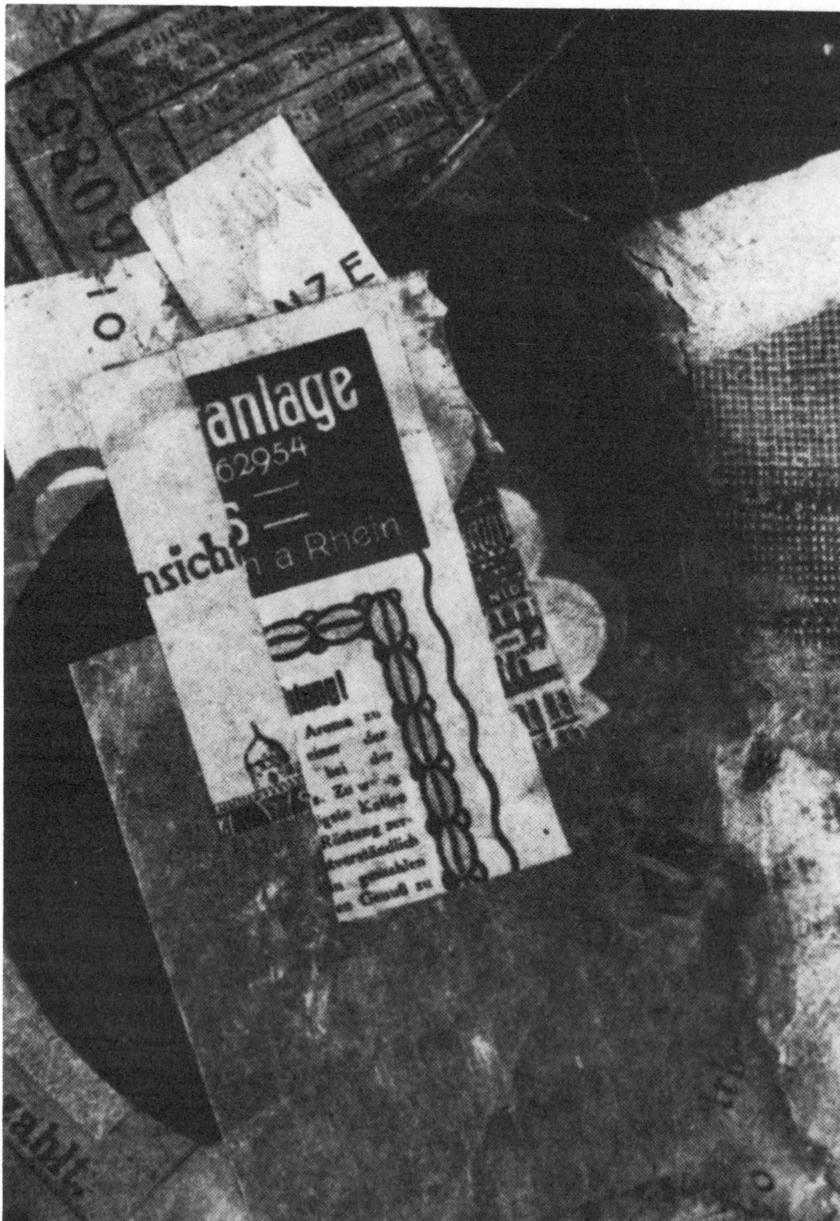

Figure 11.4. Kurt Schwitters, *Merzzeichnung 94: Grünfleck,* 1920
Detail.

itself to the economic situation of the inflationary period after World War I, a theme already touched on in *Hansi.*

The words *Grünfleck* and *Anlage* both relate foremost to the first of these issues, the issue of "collage" as an artistic medium. Schwitters uses a formal device to lead the viewer to make the association between the two words. *Grünfleck* is written below and a little to the right of the gold-colored rectangle at the lower left-hand corner of the collage.[11] First, by being strictly lined up with the edge of the collage, the rectangle seems to be identified with the entire collage. This serves to draw attention to the obvious fact that *Grünfleck,* as is the nature of titles, stands for the whole collage. Secondly, due to the similarity in shape, a visual syntactic link is created between the gold-colored rectangle and the topmost rectangle over the circular core, or the *Anlage* piece. Hence, one may reason, if the gold rectangular piece stands for the entire collage, so does the *Anlage* piece, or simply, so does the word *Anlage.* Schwitters has thus extended the meaning of the word *Anlage* (design) to include the meaning of "collage." *Anlage* also relates to *Grünfleck* in the sense of "playing cards." The process by which one lays one's cards on the table in a game of solitaire, for example, is called *anlegen* in German. Its connection with the creation of collages by assembling and gluing down pieces of paper is obvious. Schwitters may even hint at the scraps of paper which make up his collages via the popular German card game called Skat. "Skat" is a "tarot term, derived from the Italian 'scartare,' 'to discard,' or 'scatola,' a 'place of safekeeping.' "[12] Both meanings are directly applicable to Schwitters's collages, since they are a way of preserving some important (to Schwitters) fragments which have been discarded.

Returning to the *Anlage* piece, a further connection may be made between this word, in the sense of "pleasure grounds and public parks," and *Grünfleck* in the sense of *ein Fleckchen Grün* or a "green spot." Hanover, the city in which Schwitters grew up and lived during his most productive phase, was richly endowed with public parks, or *Anlagen.* One of these, Herrenhausen, the residence of the local ruling house, was a formal garden based on the gardens at Versailles.[13] Schwitters evidently has superimposed the idea of designing a garden and the idea of making a collage, both of which require *Anlage* or artistic talent.

Immediately below the *Anlage* fragment appears another carefully cropped piece on which are printed the letters "nsicht" above a domed architectural structure. The structure would have been recognized readily by everyone in 1920 as one of the earliest cigarette factories built in Dresden, in the shape of a mosque, as its image and the name of the firm were printed on every cigarette produced by that firm (fig. 11.5).[14] The factory was visible from the train and must have been a favorite landmark, as a quote by George Grosz seems to indicate: "Once on the train

Figure 11.5. Yenidze Cigarette Case, n.d.
Illustrated in *Tabago, a Picture Book of Tobacco and the Pleasures of Smoking* (Reemtsma Cigaretten-Fabriken GmbH., 1960), p. 89.

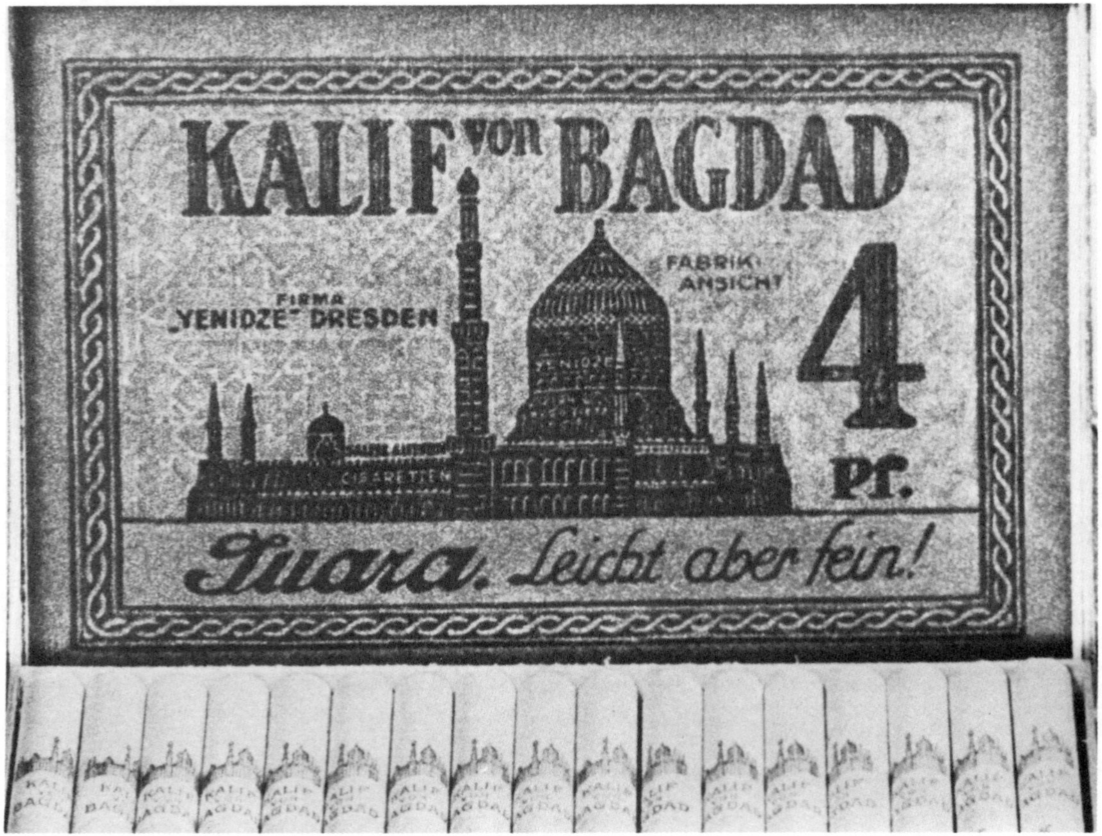

(for Radebeul), the rain beat relentlessly against the windows but it did not hide the view we had in passing of the Yenidze cigarette factory, which was built in pure Turkish style. Through the streams of rainfall it looked like a Moorish fairy castle''[15] (fig. 11.6).

The association of that factory with seeing a beautiful sight should have been made by anyone looking at *Grünfleck.* Schwitters purposely cropped *(Fabrik)Ansicht* in that ambiguous way for maximum effect, asking the viewer either to add the ''A'' to complete the word *Ansicht* or ''view,'' or remove the ''n'' to read *Sicht* or ''sight.'' So what was there to be seen besides a cigarette factory, which, being a plant, is also an *Anlage*? Immediately to the right of ''nsicht'' one finds the phrase *a. Rhein* printed, like *Anlage,* in white on black.

Now of course the Rhine River is Germany's most famous scenic area, almost to the point of being a cliché. One goes on holiday there, not to swim or climb mountains, but to take a boat ride in order to ''see'' the Rhine and the surrounding mountains covered with vineyards and dotted with castles. Schwitters has cut off the *Anlage* piece just below a word important in connection with the Rhine, namely *Genuss,* which means ''enjoyment,'' ''pleasure,'' or ''delight.'' In other words, Schwitters is equating the pleasure one experiences when looking at the beautiful scenery on the Rhine with that of looking at the cigarette factory in the shape of a mosque, and ultimately with that of looking at the collage.

Although in 1918 Schwitters officially became an ''abstract'' artist, he nevertheless continued to paint landscapes from nature for the rest of his life. As he later explained in a catalogue of his work in 1927:

> I have exhibited paintings 17 and 31 to show that alongside my abstract compositions I have always made studies from nature, devoting at least a little time to this every year. This is perhaps a purely private diversion; in any case, I should not like to lose the connection with earlier stages of my development . . . I have nothing to hide, not even that still, today, I cling to the sentimental pleasure of painting after nature, without any artistic intentions, merely for orientation.[16]

Thus, Schwitters not only delighted in seeing beautiful, picturesque scenery, but also took a great deal of pleasure in ''photographic painting.'' Schwitters may even have alluded to some kind of a recording process of the scenery in the *Grünfleck* collage. The ''nsicht'' piece is placed directly above a blank rectangular piece of paper ready to be transformed into a picture. This piece in turn is placed over the circular core. In 1920, at the time Schwitters made the collage, the black circular shape with the black number on the oval reddish-brown ground would have been recognized readily by everyone. Today, knowledge of its origin may be gathered by searching other collages for similar, more revealing aspects

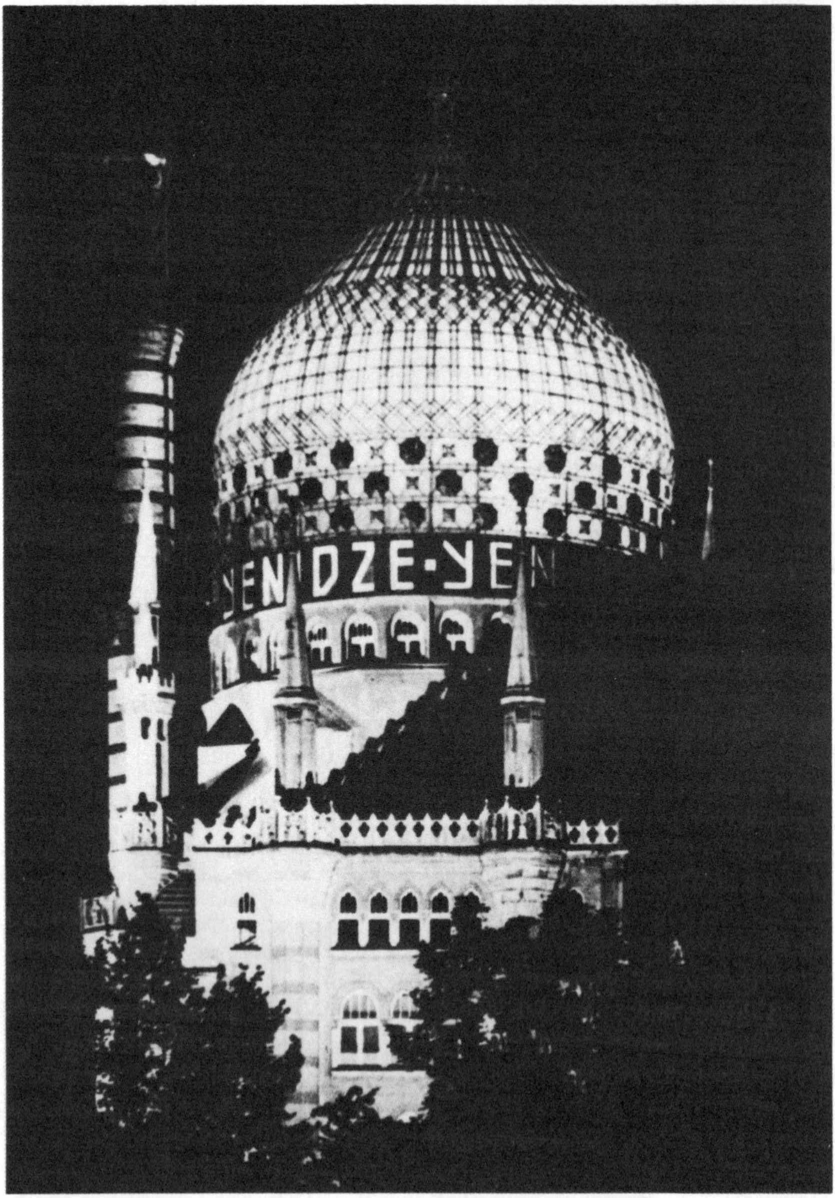

Figure 11.6. "Mosque" Yenidze Cigarette Factory, Dresden, n.d. Illustrated in *Tabago, a Picture Book of Tobacco and the Pleasures of Smoking* (Reemtsma Cigaretten-Fabriken GmbH., 1960), p. 88.

of the piece. Collages *Merzzeichnung 313: Otto* of 1921 (fig. 11.7) and *Merzzeichnung 26, 41: okola* of 1926 (fig. 11.8), among others, reveal the black circular paper to be "Agfa-Filmpack" paper. In *Otto* Schwitters even juxtaposes the film packaging with what appears to be a color magazine illustration of a landscape. Hence, in *Grünfleck* Schwitters seems to say that the beautiful scenery should be recorded either on canvas or on film.[17]

The kind of spectator phenomenon inherent in the idea of viewing beautiful scenery is reinforced by the stub of a ticket to an unspecified cultural event. The ticket is part of the larger circle of the collage and joins the center in a way that places the words printed on it in *Fraktur* in line with "nsicht" and *a. Rhein.* The ticket reads *Einlass-K* or "entrance-t(icket)." This adds to Schwitters's collage the commercial dimension which will prove ultimately to dominate the content of the work. Here, the viewing of the *Anlage* and the Rhein becomes something that one pays for by means of a ticket.

Since Schwitters has provided no clue as to what specific event the ticket was for, it must be regarded generically. The ticket allows for participation in some form of urban entertainment. That Schwitters is aware of entertainment as a category can be readily seen in another collage dating from 1921, *Merzzeichnung 222.*[18] That collage deals exclusively with urban entertainment, particularly with visual entertainment. The tickets include one for the Admirals-Palast, an ice arena where one goes to watch people perform on figure skates; another ticket allows one to enter the U.F.A. Palast, a popular movie theater,[19] a third provides admission to some event with the word *Vater* in its title at the Deutsches Kaffeehaus; and the fourth, interestingly enough, is an announcement to an event at Herwarth Walden's gallery Der Sturm on 16 February 1921. In covering up or tearing off the particular event for which the ticket had been bought, Schwitters was consciously alluding to the idea of entertainment generally rather than to a particular event.

In the light of this concern with urban entertainment it is, first of all, interesting that Schwitters would devote an entire collage to the subject of entertainment, and, secondly, that he should bring the Sturm gallery into association with the more commercial entertainment forms. The Sturm gallery was at this time a hotbed of controversy, not the least of which was created by Schwitters himself with his Merz works. Hence the activities of the Sturm ranked with the popular entertainment of the time. It was customary at the time to pay an entrance fee when visiting a gallery, which is probably what Schwitters is implying by requiring, so to speak, an entrance ticket to the viewing of the "Anlage-Collage."

The flourishing of the entertainment world was one of the most significant phenomena in postwar Germany. People supported many forms of entertainment in their attempt to flee from the problems of reality

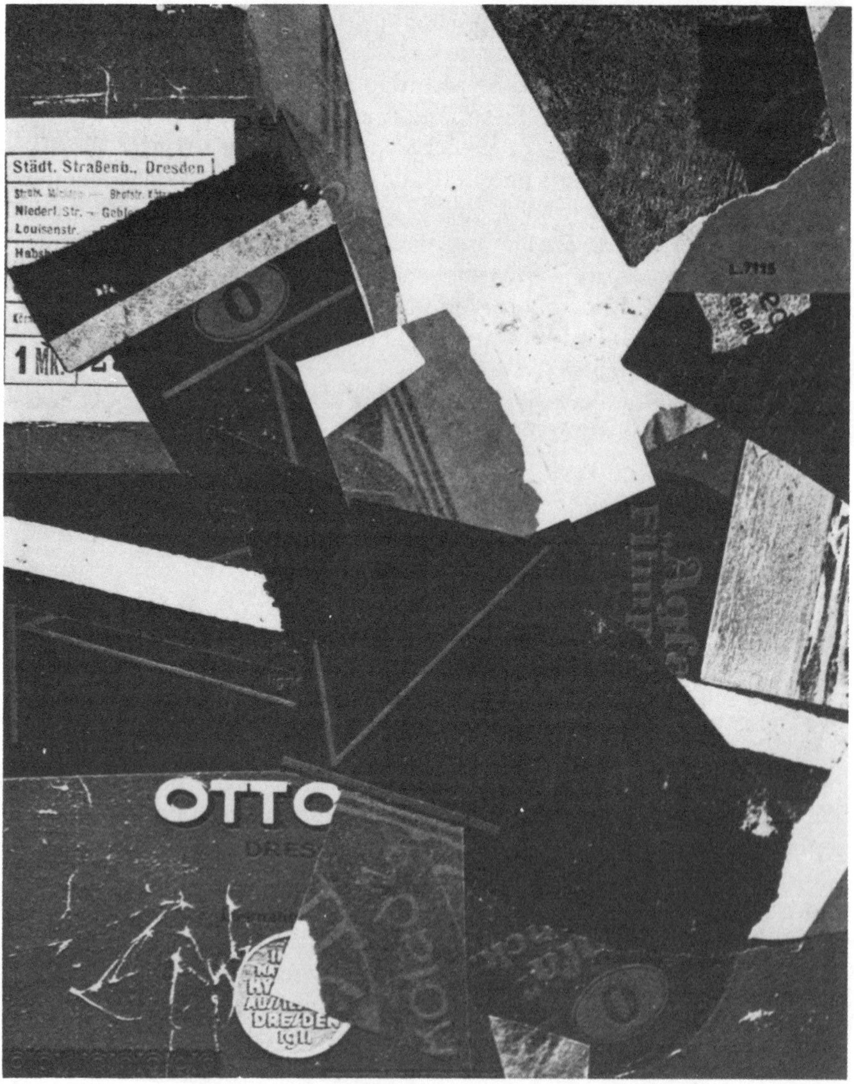

Figure 11.7. Kurt Schwitters, *Merzzeichnung 313: Otto,* 1921
Collage, 7″ × 5⅞″.
(Marlborough Fine Arts Ltd., London. Copyright © 1988, by COSMOPRESS, Geneva)

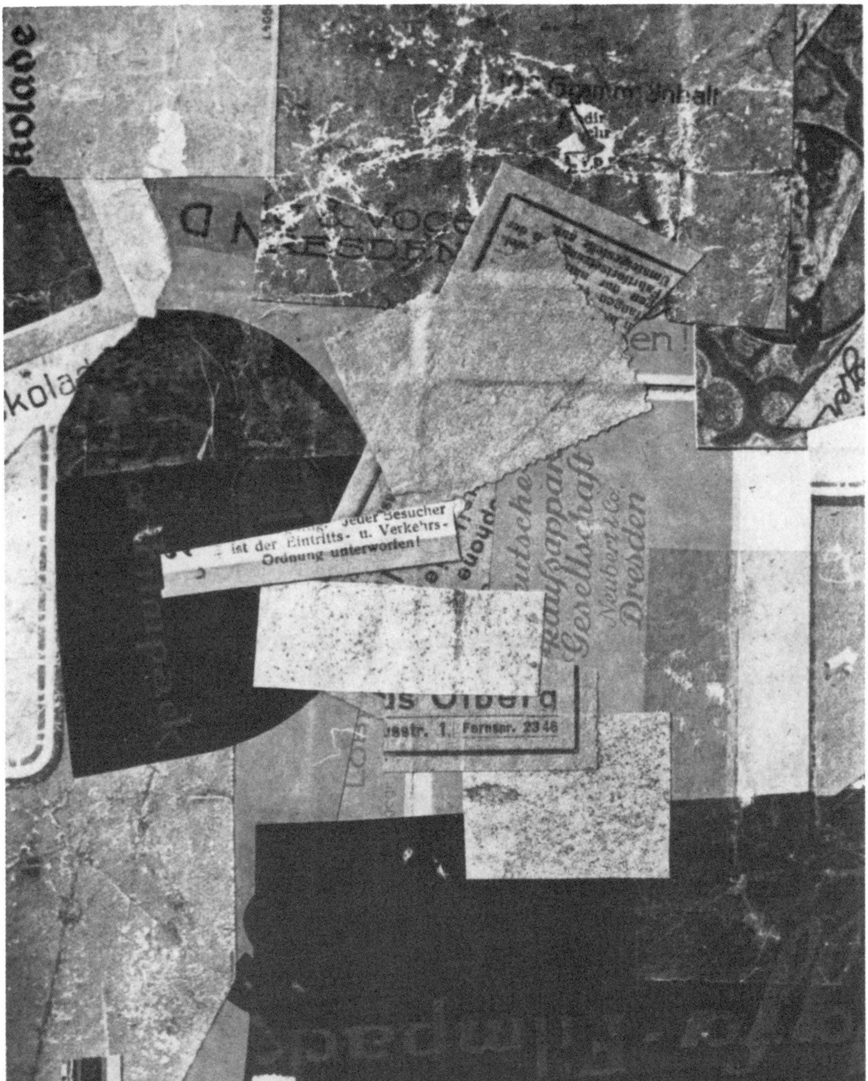

Figure 11.8. Kurt Schwitters, *Merzzeichnung 26, 41: okola,* 1926
Collage, $6\frac{7}{8}'' \times 5\frac{3}{8}''$.
(Private collection. Copyright © 1988, by COSMO-PRESS, Geneva)

into an imaginary world. Many times this involved an entire evening spent going from one place to another, as Lothar Schreyer describes in his *Erinnerungen an Sturm und Bauhaus* in the chapter entitled "Excursion into the Night." Herwarth Walden, George Blümner, and Lothar Schreyer stopped off at five places: The Admirals-Palast; Der blaue Vogel, a bar in the outskirts of Berlin to hear a Negro spiritualist, Claire Waldoff, a cabaret singer, who performed better after twelve. The tour ended in a private dancing "palace" which featured a Negro jazz band.[20]

Thus, one must "read" the "Entrance" ticket in the context of the artistic world and at the same time in a larger cultural context. By alluding to the theme of urban entertainment, Schwitters placed his work into a tradition which began with the Impressionists, who depicted boating scenes, horse races, concerts, and ballets.

Once the viewer's eye has left the central core, and its preoccupation with aesthetic matters, the problems and cares of the everyday world begin to impinge on the collage. These everyday concerns are emphatically announced through the phrase *Geld bezahlt,* meaning "money paid" and, in bold sans-serif type, the preposition *für* or "for." Schwitters used typography to expressive ends.[21] *Für* has an emphatic quality due to its large size and bold underlining. It precedes an entire list of things "for" which money must be paid besides the admission ticket, namely streetcar tickets, cigarettes, chocolate, and coffee, as an analysis of the other identifiable scraps will reveal. All of these items, which may be separated into "goods" and "services," had a special significance in postwar inflationary Germany.

The streetcar tickets which belong, like the entrance ticket, in the category of "services," join the central core from the top left-hand corner. There are obvious formal reasons for using streetcar tickets, which may account for the fact that they appear so frequently in Schwitters's collages. Their flat, rectangular shape fits readily into the rectangularly shaped format of the collage itself. The numbers, names, and lines printed on them add to their formal interest, without overloading the piece with content. In some collages it may be important to note the origin of the ticket (Hanover or Dresden appear most frequently) but on the whole they were probably not intended to be read. In all likelihood, Schwitters chose the streetcar tickets for their formal qualities and to mirror in a concrete way an important aspect of urban life at the time. Although Schwitters himself preferred riding his bicycle,[22] streetcars were the most common mode of transportation in Germany in the postwar years.[23] The tickets also reflect the restlessness of the age. People wanted to move about; however, transportation by train was limited owing to the poor state of the equipment. So people's *Wanderlust* was confined to their immediate surroundings. Schwitters was undoubtedly aware of these issues, as well as the fact that, all things considered, a streetcar ride was a good buy for the money. As he "advertised" as an aside in his inflation fairy tale "Er," of 1923, the trip to the neighboring town of Lüneburg by streetcar provided a relatively inexpensive Sunday excursion.[24]

Turning from Schwitters's concern with services, his references to "goods" (the cigar/cigarettes, the chocolate, and the coffee) must be analyzed. First, however, it is necessary to explain how these items may be recognized in the collage. The cigar/cigarette reference is easily discovered at the bottom of the collage. Schwitters uses one of his favorite devices in presenting that reference. He cuts up a word into several parts and leaves the process of reassembly to the viewer. One of the more provocative examples of this type occurs in *Merzzeichnung 280,* a 1921 collage entitled *Rotfeder (für Lisker)* (fig. 11.9). Here the name of the city of Hanover must be spliced together from three pieces of different typography: Ha-no-ver (the English or American spelling of the city, perhaps alluded to by the American stamps also in the collage). It appears that in *Grünfleck,* cigars can be assembled out of "Cig" and what appears to be a somewhat ambiguous upside-down "ars."[25] The word "cigarettes" is just composed of "cig . . . ttes," leaving out the middle "-are-".

The chocolate presents more of a problem to the modern viewer. It is incorporated into the collage by means of three rectangularly shaped pieces—two joining the circular center at the top, and the third, a large piece immediately above the cigarette piece (which it helps to create). All three scraps feature part of the very characteristic cocoa leaf already noted as alluding to the color green of early German playing-card spades. This cocoa leaf, still used today by certain chocolate manufacturers, would have been immediately recognized in Schwitters's day as coming from a chocolate wrapper. Today we must again call upon a collage created seven years after *Grünfleck* for the purpose of identification (fig. 11.10). There the leaf appears with the letters "scho" clearly readable and continued in another, bolder print with "kolad." Thus chocolate is the extrinsic content of those three pieces; their created content, or their function in the collage, is discussed below.

The reference to coffee is both visual and verbal. The most direct reference is the coffee bean pattern surrounding the finely printed text in the *Anlage* piece, which discusses the virtues of properly roasted coffee. From the text derives the verbal reference to coffee.[26] There is another nonverbal reference to coffee, immediately beyond the black circular core, in the form of the scalloped paper. The scalloped paper's extrinsic function, that is, its function in the real world, was to serve as a kind of blotter for spilled coffee between the cup and the saucer. This kind of paper

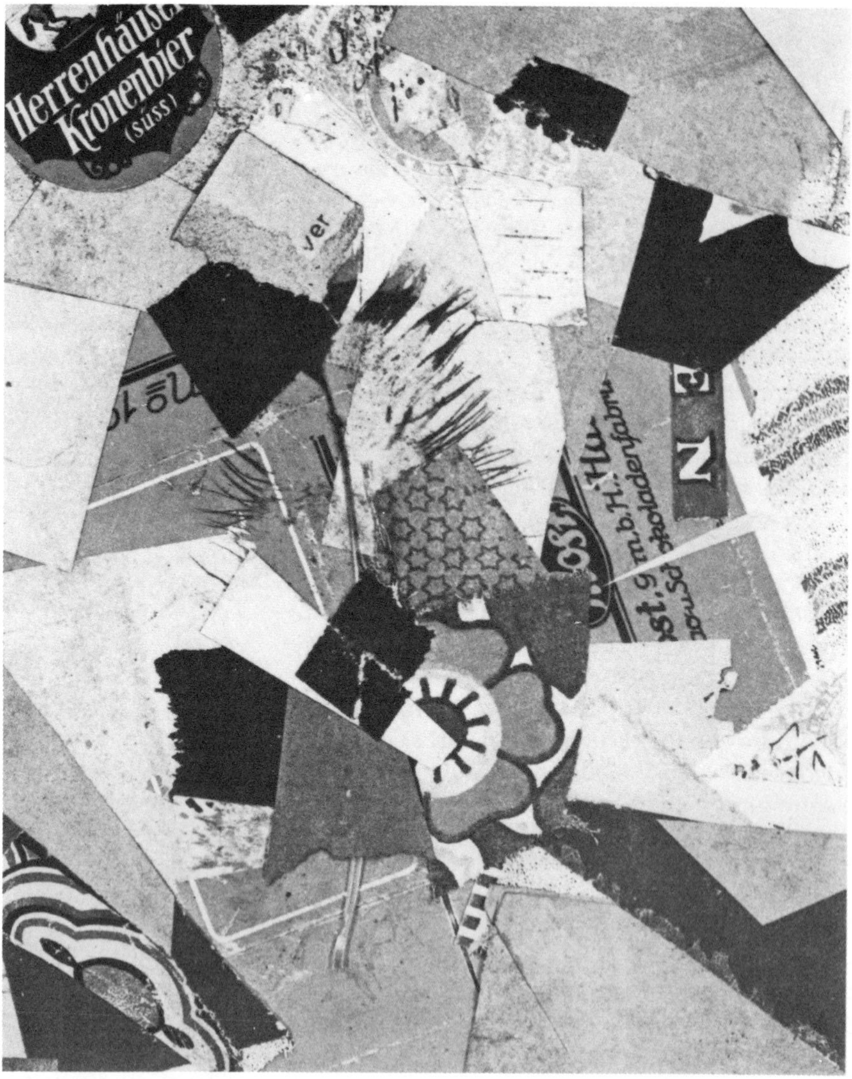

Figure 11.9. Kurt Schwitters, *Merzzeichnung 280: Rotfeder (für Lisker)*, 1921
Collage, 70⅞″ × 56¾″.
(Private collection. Copyright © 1988, by COSMO-PRESS, Geneva)

''doily'' is commonly used in German cafés and would have been recognized readily by people at the time.[27] Hence all references to the ''goods'' can be said to be organized primarily around the central core.

The question arises why Schwitters was motivated to select these three items (counting the cigar/cigarette product as one) for his collage from countless other possibilities. One reason may be that all three of them are processed from materials which must be imported, since tobacco, cocoa, and coffee are not grown in Germany. They are what one would call *Kolonialwaren* in the original sense of the word, meaning materials produced in the colonies, in short, imports. Before World War I the German merchant marine roamed the seas and consequently consumable luxury goods such as cigarettes, chocolate, and coffee were in plentiful supply. This was true to the extent that these items dominated the poster advertising of commodities.[28] The photograph from Breslau (*Hansi* article, fig. 3) from ca. 1911 may be cited again as an example of the kind of advertising favored during the Empire.[29] Entire walls of buildings were covered with advertisements of merchandise, especially with ads for the *Kolonialwaren* coffee, tea, and chocolate. This aggressive form of advertising bespeaks a society much concerned with material values. It was the environment in which Schwitters grew up and which may have been responsible for his reputed lifelong habit of studying newspaper advertisements with almost religious fervor.

Using poster advertising again as an index for the war and postwar economy, one finds its character totally changed after the war. Posters advertising goods, particularly those of the prewar period advertising luxury goods, became superfluous and nearly disappeared. They survived only in the form of small handbills advertising cigarettes, chocolate, or newspapers.[30] Since all of Germany's harbors were blockaded for the duration of the war, importation by sea was at a standstill.[31] Hence the *Kolonialwaren*, so plentiful before the war, truly became luxuries during and for years after the war, when the demand, especially for sweets and cigarettes, increased dramatically.[32] Significantly, Schwitters's paintings and collages containing references to the three ''goods'' under discussion cluster mainly around 1921–22, the years during which their rising cost made it more and more difficult to obtain them.

While Schwitters with his allusions to coffee and cigarettes places himself in the café tradition depicted by the Impressionists, and alluded to in Cubist still lifes,[33] his references are much more specific and concrete. Aware of the social function of coffee, Schwitters appears to have been much more concerned with its qualities as a beverage, its taste, and its availability. His concern with taste is directly stated in *Grünfleck* by the little word *Genuss* at the bottom of the *Anlage* piece. The coffee should be savored.

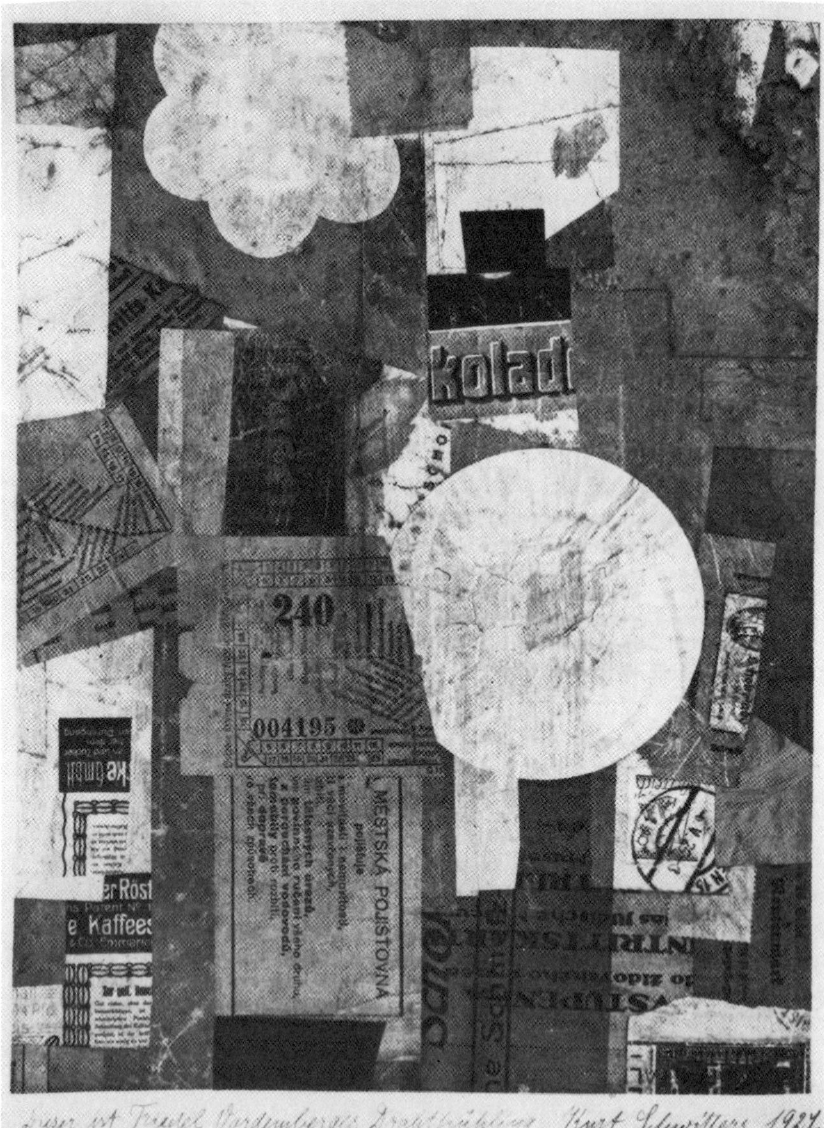

Figure 11.10. Kurt Schwitters, *Dieser ist Friedel Vordemberges Drahtfrühling*, 1927
Collage, 10⅝″ × 8″.
(Private collection. Photo courtesy Marlborough-Gerson Gallery, New York. Copyright © 1988, by COSMO-PRESS, Geneva)

In *Grünfleck,* however, Schwitters seems to have been most concerned with the economic aspects of the luxury products, as *Geld bezahlt für* implies. This commercial theme ties together the goods and the services. As mentioned above, this was the period of postwar inflation. In an interview with Pearl S. Buck, Erna von Pustau, who lived in Hamburg during the period 1920–30, paints the following picture of the times:

> Yet another very confusing picture of inflation was that part of life wasn't affected by it at all. There were ceiling prices, for instance. What was important for me, although I couldn't buy a cup of coffee with this money, a bit of candy or chocolate, the theatre prices had not gone up and the street car fares had a ceiling price and really, the things I had to pay for from my allowance did not go up.[34]

Schwitters must have been as aware as anyone else of this irrational economic situation. The things which ultimately had more value, or were more useful, were cheaper than the things which had been in such plentiful supply before the war. An anecdote from Sibyl Moholy-Nagy about Schwitters confirms that he was very much aware of the economic situation: "Schwitters dedicated a series of his bright 'Merz' collages to Moholy, and he gave him the first copy of his famous *Anna Blume,* bound in a multicolored paper cover made by himself, and inscribed: 'To Moholy on the last day of the reduced street car tariff.'"[35] Hence, it was no accident that Schwitters selected the scraps referring to chocolate, cigarettes, and coffee on the one hand and the streetcar and entrance ticket on the other.

This, however, does not exhaust the commercial connotations of *Grünfleck.* One final and very important link must be made. As has been shown, one had to pay to "see" the *Anlage* or collage. The phrase *Geld bezahlt für* may be extended through one additional association beyond the luxury goods and the tickets. The collage, *Anlage,* enters the commercial arena. It becomes one more commodity to be bought, but with an additional implication. It is transformed into another kind of *Anlage:* it becomes an investment.

There is good evidence that Schwitters thought about his art in commercial terms, especially during the "classic" Merz phase of his work. Schwitters came from a bourgeois, small business background. From 1886 on his parents owned a ladies' apparel store, from which his father retired at the age of forty and henceforth supported the family on the income from five houses he had purchased.[36] Perhaps through this intimate association with business matters, compounded by the economic situation of postwar Germany, Schwitters became fascinated by business. The commercial source for the word "Merz" has already been discussed. As Lach points out, Schwitters was in search of a trade-name, some word or expression that would collectively describe his products while distinguishing them from those of other artists.[37] Lach also cites a notation from one of Schwitters's notebooks which further illuminates his thinking about his art: "Commerce = com mercurio. Mercury is the messenger god and the god of commerce. Mercantile art."[38] Schwitters thus drew art and commerce together into an intimate whole.

However, the reference in *Grünfleck* to buying or selling the collage or *Anlage* is no hollow phrase. Schwitters was specifically concerned with "marketing" his collages in 1919–23, as he revealed in a letter addressed to Herwarth Walden concerning an upcoming one-man exhibition at the Sturm gallery in Berlin. In discussing the contents of the accompanying catalogue, he proposes a comprehensive list of his pictures, not just those to be exhibited. He would add the works already sold and would include the collectors' names to stimulate sales, especially since many of the collectors were well known. As Schwitters explained, "The artist is to be an artist solely in his art. I believe that whosoever is an artist may think after hours about how best to get his pictures into the hands of the collector. And the collector has confidence when he reads that numerous collectors already own work by that artist."[39]

In the light of these remarks there can be little doubt that commercial, or specifically marketing, concerns would find expression in Schwitters's collages. As Schmalenbach has asserted, Schwitters "was very clever with words, a definite asset in advertising, indeed a strong bent for advertising, for 'selling' his own products, was not just innate but was a stylistic element of his production, particularly his writing."[40] *Grünfleck* exemplifies this stylistic bent, which Schwitters himself called "Merz." The created meaning of *Grünfleck* expresses finally Schwitters's desire to market his collages.[41] The idea is communicated by the placement of *Anlage* (collage) into a context of extrinsic meanings, that of goods and services, which are obtainable only through money. Schwitters thus created an autobiographical record which bridged the gap between art and life.

In July 1919 Kurt Glaser published a critique in the *Berliner Börsenkurier* of Schwitters's first group exhibition at the Sturm gallery showing his early "Merz" work. Schwitters wrote a rebuttal in a letter to Christof Spengemann, with the hope of having it published, in which he contrasts his method of creation with that of the hypothetical student appearing in Glaser's article. It will be quoted at length here both to explain, in Schwitters's own words, his way of working, and to provide the explanation of why Schwitters's work has remained misunderstood for so long:

> Merz pictures are abstract works of art. (Read Valori Plastici.) The artist creates through choice, distribution, and dissociation of the materials. (Also slips.) If, for example, I would use Mr. Kurt Glaser, a pair of bloomers, and the *Berliner Börsenkurier* (Pardon curier) as materials (I would probably not make that arrangement), then I would perhaps use the B.B. Courier, in spite of its cute little articles, as paint support. I would fragment and dissociate the old gentleman and the bloomers and distribute them over the pictorial surface according to the laws of artistic logic. I would thus utilize Mr. Kurt Glaser as beautiful and expressive form, as rhythm and as chiaroscuro-modeled mass. My so-called student seems to prefer the wax museum over art. He would, for example, utilize Mr. Kurt Glaser as a real critic, with angry brow and inkpen in hand; in back of him he would 'tastefully' spread out the bloomers and he would respectfully place the *Börsencourier* on the table as a real paper, as the leading paper with respect to art criticism. (Add three supplements.) I, on the other hand, demand the abstract utilization of critics.[42]

The analyses of Hansi[43] and *Grünfleck* reveal two important ideas about Schwitters's working method: first, that he chose his raw materials, and second, that he transformed them according to the formal logic of each work. This is what he called ''working abstractly.'' He did not simply represent the subject as does the student in the quote above, because for Schwitters that would be too obvious. However, Schwitters's refusal to ''represent'' does not imply a dissociation from the world of real forms around him. Indeed, the collage elements themselves are too concrete for us to disconnect them from their original context, and thus their very concreteness, combined with Schwitters's formal and verbal manipulation of them, creates possibilities for meanings of a very real kind.

Notes

1. Kurt Schwitters, *Merz 20, Kurt Schwitters Katalog* (1927; repr. Bern and Frankfurt: Lang, 1975), p. 102.

2. *Merzzeichnung 94: Grünfleck* signed and dated at lower right: Kurt Schwitters, 1920. *Grünfleck*'s provenance is sketchy. The collage appears to have been in the possession of the artist at least until 1927, when it was exhibited as No. 124 in ''Die Grosse Merzausstellung'' (see n. 1). In Werner Schmalenbach's monograph, *Kurt Schwitters* (Cologne and New York, 1967), *Grünfleck* is listed in the collection of Eduard Neuenschwander, Zurich. Some time after that it went via Paul Haim et Cie, Paris, into the Vallenilla Collection, Caracas, which was housed temporarily at the University of Texas at Austin in 1977. Present whereabouts unknown. *Grünfleck* measures 16.8 by 13.5 cm (6-5/8 by 5-5/16 in.) by sight.

3. Schwitters, *Merz 20,* p. 99.

4. Translation mine. ''Ich habe . . . Bilder and Zeichnungen geklebt, auf denen Sätze gelesen werden sollen.'' Kurt Schwitters, ''Merz,'' *Der Ararat* (Munich, 1921), reprt. in *Kurt Schwitters* (Cologne: Galerie Gmurzynska, 1978), p. 47.

5. See ''Rethinking Kurt Schwitters, Part I: An Interpretation of *Hansi,*'' *Arts Magazine* 55, no. 5 (June 1981): 112–17.

6. Examples of these very dynamic compositions, which probably have their origin in the Italian Futurist Carrà's famous collage of 1914 *Manifestazione Interventista,* are Merz picture 9b *The Great Ich-Picture* of 1919, *Picture with Light Center* of 1919, and Merz picture *Thirty-One* of 1920. Whether Schwitters was directly familiar with Carrà's work is uncertain, but that such forms were common currency can be seen in the two similarly structured woodcuts by Johannes Molzahn published in *Der Sturm* (*Sternbewegung 1919, Der Sturm* 10:6 [1919/20], p. 85, and untitled woodcut, *Der Sturm,* 10:7 [1919/20] p. 101). Molzahn was a friend of Schwitters in those early years. They exhibited together with Paul Klee at the Sturm gallery in 1919. Not considered here are the constructed pictures which fell under the heading of Merz pictures and which are also large in size, but which contain three-dimensional elements, placing them into the category of relief sculpture.

7. Felix Flügel, Im. Schmidt, and G. Fanger, *Wörterbuch der Englischen und Deutschen Sprache für Hand- und Schulgebrauch,* vol. 2 (8th ed., 1909), p. 426.

8. Ibid., p. 338.

9. Detlef Hoffmann, *Die Welt der Spielkarte: Eine Kulturgeschichte* (Munich: Callwey Verlag, 1972), p. 22.

10. Flügel, *Wörterbuch,* pp. 64–65.

11. The gold rectangle is gold in color only. It does not have the proportions of the golden section, nor does the collage as a whole.

12. Geoffrey Mott-Smith, "Skat," *Encyclopaedia Brittanica,* vol. 20 (1968), p. 583. George Grosz painted three men playing cards in his *Café* painting of 1916. They may well represent skat players, since three is the usual number of participants in the game. Morton D. May Collection, St. Louis.

13. Marie Louise Gothein (Schroeter), *Geschichte der Gartenkunst II* (Jena: Eugen Diederichs, 1914), pp. 206–10.

14. *Tabago: A Picture Book of Tobacco and the Pleasures of Smoking* (Munich [?]: Reemtsma Cigaretten-Fabriken GmbH, 1960), p. 89.

15. George Grosz, *A Little Yes and a Big No,* illustr. by the author and trans. by Lola Sachs Dorin (New York: Dial, 1946), p. 99.

16. Schwitters, *Merz 20,* p. 100. Translation in Werner Schmalenbach, *Kurt Schwitters* (New York: Abrams, 1967), p. 76:

    > Die Bilder 17 und 31 habe ich mit ausgestellt, um zu zeigen, dass ich neben den abstrakten Kompositionen immer noch di Natur studiert habe, jährlich eine kleine Zeit lang. Es ist dieses vielleicht auch ein privates Vergnügen, jedenfalls möchte ich den Zusammenhang mit meinen früheren Entwicklungsstadien nicht verlierien. . . . Ich habe nichts zu verbergen, auch nicht, dass mir noch heute di Sentimentalität der Naturnachbildung so angenehm anhaftet, ohne irgendwelche künstlerischen Absichten, nur Orientierung.

17. Photography was very much in evidence in the work of the Dadaists, who manipulated photographs by cutting and pasting them into biting, satirical comments. Schwitters also made photomontages, but his utilization of the wrapper, which had outlived its usefulness, is unique.

18. Illustrated in John Elderfield, "The Early Work of Kurt Schwitters," *Artforum* 10 (November 1971): 65.

19. U.F.A. stood for Universum Film Aktiengesellschaft, a film company founded in 1917 at the instigation of the German government. The company opened the huge *U.F.A. Palast* am Zoo in Berlin in 1919 with the première of Lubitsch's *Madame Dubarry.* See Liz-Anne Bawden, ed. *The Oxford Companion to Film* (New York: Oxford, 1976), p. 707.

20. Lothar Schreyer, *Erinnerungen an Sturm und Bauhaus* (Munich, 1956), pp. 53–77.

21. Schwitters shared this sensitivity toward typography with the Cubists. However, Schwitters also worked with typography on a professional level, as did many artists in the twenties, especially Schwitters's Constructivist and Bauhaus friends.

22. Kate Trauman Steinitz. *Kurt Schwitters: A Portrait from Life* (Berkeley: University of California Press, 1968), p. 7.

23. "The Berlin streetcar company transported, for example, 873 million people in 1918 vs. 570 million in 1913" (tr. mine). Friedrich Hesse, *Die deutsche Wirtschaftslage von 1914 bis 1923* (Jena: Fischer, 1938), p. 145.

24. Kurt Schwitters, *Das Literarische Werk,* 5 vols., ed Friedhelm Lach (Cologne: Schauberg Verlag, 1973—), vol. 2: *Prosa 1918–1930,* p. 102.

25. "Ars," the Latin word for art, fits well into the context of the collage.

26. Small, black print, fifth line down.

27. There could be one more reference to another sort of commodity which will not be gone into here. At the bottom of *Grünfleck* is printed DIE SCH in white letters. In looking for something to match DIE SCH up with, the eye lights immediately on the lower chocolate "piece," in which the latter part of *hochfein* can be read. Schwitters could be making an allusion to pigs, since "die Schfeine" is a phonetic way of spelling *die Schweine* [pigs]. Pork was practically nonexistent in Germany after the war and hence would neatly fit into the category of luxury goods.

28. Münchener Stadtmuseum, *Plakate in München, 1840–1940* (Munich: Lipp Verlag, 1975), p. 97.

29. See "An Interpretation of *Hansi,*" fig. 3.

30. Münchener Stadtmuseum, *Plakate,* pp. 107, 113.

31. Gustav Stolper, *The German Economy, 1870 to the Present,* tr. Toni Stolper (New York: Harcourt, Brace, 1967; orig. ed. 1940), pp. 53–54. Speaking specifically of the cacao situation, Wolf Müller states in *Seltsame Frucht Kakao: Geschichte des Kakao und der Schokolade* (Hamburg: Gordian-M. Rieck, 1957), p. 198:

> During the First World War Germany's cacao trade nearly experienced a total collapse. Nevertheless, it was still possible at the beginning to supplement existing reserves through purchases from neutral neighbors: Holland, Sweden, Switzerland, Denmark, etc. Preventative measures undertaken by the countries concerned, however, either to secure their own needs or in response to pressure from Germany's enemies, made such large-scale importation impossible by 1915. In 1916 control of the cacao reserves was given to a War Cacao Agency, which regulated distribution of the stock (tr. mine).

32. Müller (*Seltsame Frucht,* p. 198) has the following to say about the cacao situation in postwar Germany:

> Although the political and economic situation in Germany after the First World War raised chocolate again to the status of a luxury item, pent-up demand for the sweet

> was so great that the chocolate industry had little trouble disposing of products manufactured from its record importation of 103,000 tones in 1921; however, this was not without quite a substantial loss due to the daily worsening monetary valuation (tr. mine).

In his autobiography, the writer Carl Zuckmayer states that "they" craved alcohol in the same way. It is interesting that, although liquor bottles have paper labels, there is only one example known to this writer of a reference to alcoholic beverages in Schwitters's collages. In *Mz 280: Rotfeder (für Lisker)* of 1921 (fig. 11.9) appears the label of a Hanover beer, "Herrenhäuser Kronenbier." In contrast, alcoholic beverages are frequently alluded to, both visually and verbally, in Cubist works.

33. Unlike coffee and cigarettes, chocolate has no longstanding tradition in art. Chocolate conquered Europe in the eighteenth century as a "nourishing" drink, especially good taken at breakfast. The drinking of a cup of chocolate was occasionally depicted during this period. Müller (*Seltsame Frucht,* plates I and XVI) illustrates two examples. A painting by the Italian artist Pietro Longhi (Museo Correr, Venice) depicts the morning ritual; the other painting by an unknown artist shows a mother and daughter (?) sharing a cup of chocolate (coll. Cadbury Brothers). More recently, but still predating Schwitters, is Marcel Duchamp's painting *Chocolate Grinder, No. 1* of 1913.

34. Fritz K. Ringer, *The German Inflation of 1923* (New York: Oxford, 1969), p. 125.

35. Sibyl Moholy-Nagy, *Moholy-Nagy: Experiment in Totality* (New York: Harper, 1950), p. 25.

36. Schmalenbach, *Schwitters,* p. 21.

37. Friedhelm Lach, *Der Merzkünstler Kurt Schwitters* (Cologne: Schauberg, 1971), p. 21.

38. Ibid., p. 22.

39. Translation mine. "Der Künstler soll nur Künstler sein in seiner Kunst. Ich glaube, wer das ist, darf im Civilberuf auch überlegen, wie er seine Bilder am besten an den Sammler bringt. Und der Sammler hat Zutrauen, wenn er liesst, dass von dem Künstler schon zahlreiche Sammler Arbeiten besitzen." Kurt Schwitters, *Wir spielen bis uns der Tod abholt,* ed. Ernst Nündel (Frankfort: Ullstein, 1975), p. 42.

40. Schmalenbach, *Schwitters,* p. 54.

41. The title of *Mz 405* of 1922, *kaufen Sie sehr preiswert* (Schmalenbach, *Schwitters,* black and white plate no. 54) and *Merzzeichnung 2010 man verkauft gern* (1924) (Schmalenbach, *Schwitters,* fig. 74) must allude to that phenomenon.

42. Translation mine, from Schwitters, *Wir spielen,* pp. 28–29:

> Die Bilder der Merzmalerei sind abstrakte Kunstwerke. (Lesen Sie Valorie Plastici.) Der Künstler schafft durch Wahl, Verteilen und Entformeln der Materialien. (Auch Unterröcke.) Wenn ich zum Beispiel Herrn Kurt Glaser, ein Damenbeinkleid und einen Berliner Börsenkurier (Verzeihung, curier) als Material verwendete (Ich würde diese Zusammenstellung übrigens wahrscheinlich nicht treffen.), dann würde ich etwa den BB Courier trotz seiner netten Artikelchen als Malgrund verwenden, den alten Herrn und das Damenbeinkleid würde ich zerteilen und entformeln und nach den Gesetzen der künstlerischen Logik auf die Bildfläche verteilen. Ich würde also Herrn Kurt Glaser als schöne und ausdrucksvolle Form, als Rhythmus und als helldunkel modellierte Masse verwenden. Mein sogenannter Schüler scheint das

Panoptikum mehr zu lieben, als die Kunst. Er würde beispielweise Herrn Kurt Glaser als richtigen Kritiker verwenden, mit einer Zornesstirn und einer Tintenfeder in der Hand, das Damenbeinkleid ''dezent'' dahinter ausbreiten und den Börsencourier als wirkliche Zeitung respektvoll auf den Tisch legen, als das führende Blatt in Bezug auf Kunstkritiken. (Hierzu 3 Beilagen.) Ich dagegen fordere die abstrakte Verwendung der Kritiker. . . .

43. See ''An Interpretation of *Hansi.*''

12

Collage as Jokework: Freud's Theories of Wit as the Foundation for the Collages of Max Ernst

Charlotte Stokes

In Beyond Painting *Max Ernst wrote, ''Max Ernst died the 1st of August 1914. He was resuscitated the 11th of November 1918 as a young man aspiring to become a magician and to find the myth of his time.'' Following his founding of the Cologne Dada group with Hans Arp and Johannes Baargeld, in 1919, Ernst plunged into exploring collage. Unlike Schwitters, Ernst did not frequently retrieve materials from the street. Instead, he was concerned with the ''collage idea,'' as rationalism was being shattered and the conscious and unconscious were being discovered. Ernst, like a number of artists of his time, particularly the Surrealists, was influenced by Freud. In her essay, Charlotte Stokes points not to the Freudian symbolism that is often seen as influencing visual artists, but to the verbal devices such as puns, double entendres, and allusions described in Freud's* Jokes and Their Relation to the Unconscious. *Stokes points to early concepts of play, wit, repetition, and self-analysis that have become so significant in the twentieth century. As her essay well documents, ''Ernst's ability to use Freud's ideas so successfully derives from a talent for manipulating language and images, seeing them as potentially interchangeable vehicles of communication. Thus, by using Freud's originally verbal devices to create visual ambiguities, Ernst was able to turn Freud's contention that the ambiguities of language made jokes possible into pictorial form.''*

It is hardly a new thought that a Surrealist artist was influenced by the psychological studies of Freud and others. Usually that influence has been described in terms of strange dreamlike images, which are seen as sym-

---

This article originally appeared in *Leonardo* 15, no. 3.

bolic representations of emotional states. Indeed, this is often psychology's main legacy to Surrealist art. But for artists such as Max Ernst (1891–1976), the debt to psychological study is on a more fundamental level, for psychology was able to provide not only a subject but a method of structuring it.

An awareness of the rich possibilities of psychological study is evidenced in Max Ernst's earliest post-World War I collages as well as in his later works. His knowledge and use of psychology are not haphazard. From 1910 to 1914 Ernst had been a college student at the University of Bonn, where he studied psychology among other subjects (Trier 63).* He even worked in a mental hospital. Because Bonn was an intellectually active city at the time, Ernst learned not only the more conventional psychological theories of the day, but also Freud's theories and writings through a friend, Karl Otten, who had been a student of Freud's in Vienna. When Ernst reentered the art world, on completion of his military service, he did not return to the Expressionist group, several of whose key members had been killed in the war. Instead, he developed with Hans Arp and Johannes Theodor Baargeld the Dada movement in Cologne, and began to explore the possibilities of collage as an expressive medium. He cut apart and combined fragments of engravings from popular nineteenth-century books, photographs, and even his own drawings. Ernst's Dada collages and paintings and then his Surrealist works were interpretations of the inner life in a modern and irreverent medium replacing the freely painted and more traditional emotional expressions of his college years.

In these later works Ernst concerned himself with their almost literary significance rather than their formal beauty. Penrose observed that the artist's comment, "ce tableau en trois couleurs élémentaires," written under the title on the face of the painting *Oedipus Rex,* was an indication of Ernst's lack of concern with the refinements of color demanded of conventional works of art (Penrose 11). Ernst's choices of visual symbols and the way in which they were combined were of central significance to his work. Ironically, this meant that form was of greater importance than subject. The form in question here is what Freud refers to in *Jokes and Their Relation to the Unconscious* when he writes that humor resides in the form of the joke rather than in the subject (Freud 17). For example, people have sexual feelings—true, but not funny nor very profound. But this idea couched in an apt set of words, or juxtaposed to another idea, or associated with a specific individual might be either funny or indeed profound. Form in this context is the configuration in which the parts of the

---

* All references are to bibliography at end of chapter.

idea have assembled. How efficiently a joke is communicated, how appropriately stated, and how cleverly worded are the gauges of its success.

Ernst's importance as a Surrealist artist lies in the fact that he used Freud's discussion of verbal mechanisms such as puns as the basis of organization in his collages, which like sentences, are made up of preexisting units that take on new meaning from their interrelationships with other units (Spies, *Return* 38, 40). Besides forming visual ideas, the devices described by Freud in *Jokes and Their Relation to the Unconscious* also frame or encapsulate them in order to present them to a public. This effective packaging of an idea is, as Freud points out, important because communication to a second person or a selected public is a necessary part of jokework (Freud, 140–58). Another important source of ideas and symbolism would have been *The Interpretation of Dreams,* but because dreams are both personal and vague in form, it would never have been as helpful as *Jokes and Their Relation to the Unconscious* in providing Ernst with structural models.

For Ernst, the mechanism of condensation is one of the most important concepts Freud discussed (Freud 16–29). In general, condensation is the pushing together of two or more elements into a new word or phrase so that each original element retains its own character while effectively interacting with the others. Freud gives as an example "alcoholidays," the term used for Christmas that combines the holy day and the season's secular association with drunkenness. Ernst translated this verbal device into a visual one in his personal symbol, the bird-headed man, who appears in many of his paintings and collages, as for example in figure 12.5. The body clearly establishes the figure's human nature, while the bird's head is associated with freedom from the inhibitions imposed by society (see Stokes). Even though the two elements retain their identities, their condensation into a new personality is consistent with Freud's description.

Among Ernst's works that demonstrate the artist's reliance on many of Freud's writings is the painting *Oedipus Rex* (1922) (fig. 12.1), made according to the collage method of combining images from apparently disparate sources. Each image preserves its own scale, shadow, and perspective. The title of the painting links it to Freud's theory of the relationship between parents and child. Further, as Freud pointed out, psychological wounds, though bloodless—the fingers in the painting are bloodlessly wounded—are traumatic nonetheless, but the basic organization of *Oedipus Rex* relies on other aspects of Freud's thought found in *Jokes and Their Relation to the Unconscious.*

Oedipus Rex is almost a catalogue of Freud's jokemaking devices that Ernst has translated into visual mechanisms. For example, Freud pointed out the importance to a joke of the unexpected recognition of the familiar.

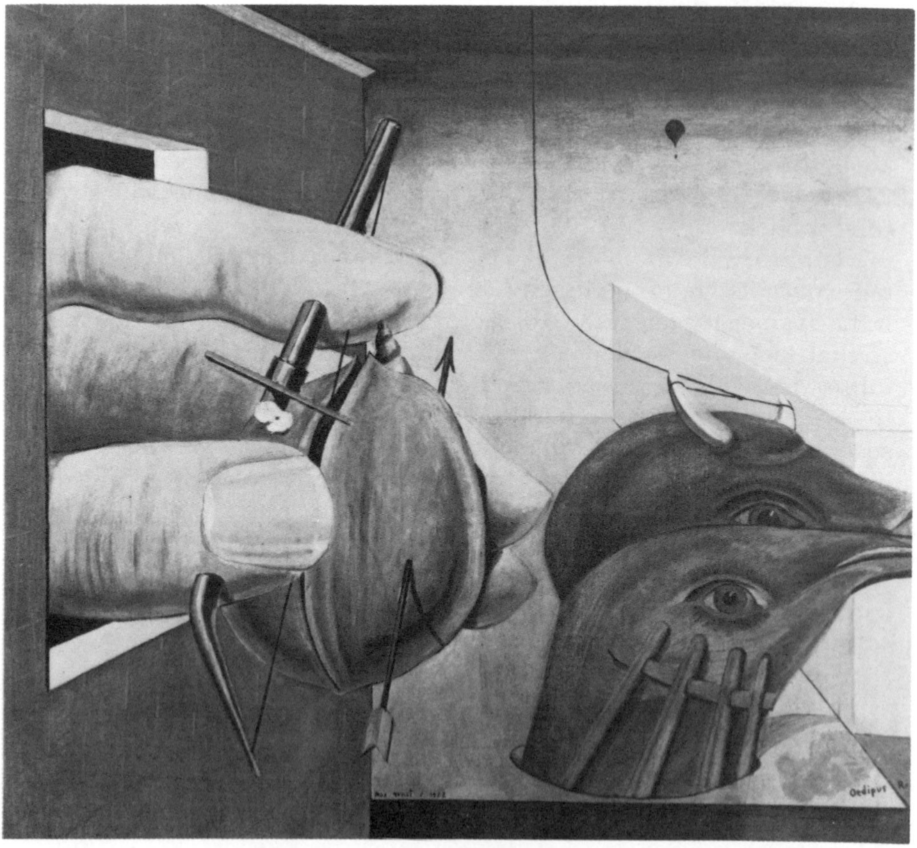

Figure 12.1. Max Ernst, *Oedipus Rex,* 1922
Oil on canvas, 93 cm × 102 cm.
(Private collection, Paris)

For this reason, allusions to myths and common stories are an important part of many jokes. Likewise the title *Oedipus Rex* is the familiar key to this painting's meaning: the fingers are pierced as the infant's feet were, and the nut like a half-closed or blinded eye recalls the ironies of seeing and blindness in Sophocles's play *Oedipus Rex. Oedipus Rex* is a Surrealist retelling of the old story with the modern methods of psychoanalytic practice and the juxtaposition inherent in the collage technique. Using these methods, Ernst gives an irreverent touch to the relationship between Oedipus and his father, King Laius, by putting horns on one of the birds and thereby evoking the plight of the cuckold. The hornlike end of the spike coming form the thumb also adds an equivocal note to the sadomasochistic thrust of the spike. The fingers are abused as they aggressively intrude into our view, squeezing the nut and dealing out punishment as they receive it.

The double entendre, which according to Freud is the meat of so many jokes, gives a sexual significance to the male hand that cracks the "female" nut. The repository of new life, the nut shown by Ernst as having a vulvalike opening, is an image rich in association with female sexuality. Ernst drew from an illustration that accompanied an article in *La Nature* (fig. 12.2), a popular French nineteenth-century science magazine. The article states that when the nut has been squeezed open, it may be allowed to close on the index finger above and thus to hang there almost magically. A nice metaphor for neurotic sexual attachment.

The fingertips on the other side of the nut exemplify another type of double meaning, the pun. A verbal pun is formed when a single sound can have more than one meaning; a visual pun is formed when a single shape can be seen as a literal representation of more than one thing. Ernst modified the fingertips just enough so that, even though they retain their original meaning, they can be taken for female breasts on the side of the nut.

The use of the image of the fingers and the nut in that way is what Freud would have called "misdirection." From *La Nature* Ernst took a not extraordinary image and, unexpectedly, brought out its dreamlike qualities. In the original illustration, the fingers showed that a walnut could be opened simply by the application of pressure along the seam. By putting this innocent image in another context and slightly modifying it, Ernst brought out its inherent sexual associations. Even though his changes modified the meaning, in the painting Ernst refers to the source of the original engraving; the isolated fingers as they come out of the window in the brick wall are a disturbed-perspective rendering of the illustration's isolated fingers in the flat black rectangle on the page surrounded by blocks of print.

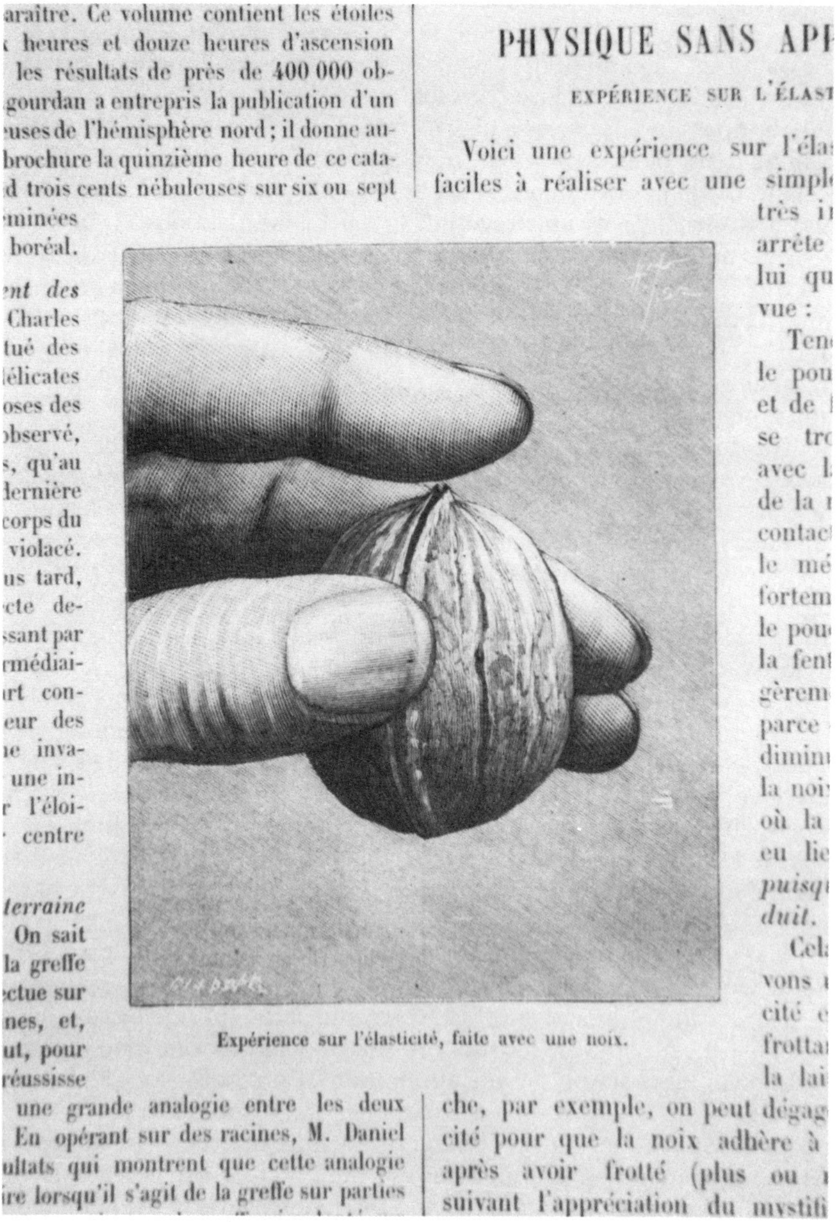

araître. Ce volume contient les étoiles
heures et douze heures d'ascension
les résultats de près de 400 000 ob-
gourdan a entrepris la publication d'un
uses de l'hémisphère nord ; il donne au-
brochure la quinzième heure de ce cata-
d trois cents nébuleuses sur six ou sept
minées
boréal.

nt des
Charles
tué des
délicates
oses des
observé,
s, qu'au
dernière
corps du
violacé.
us tard,
cte de-
ssant par
rmédiai-
rt con-
eur des
ne inva-
une in-
r l'éloi-
centre

terraine
On sait
la greffe
ctue sur
nes, et,
ut, pour
réussisse
une grande analogie entre les deux
En opérant sur des racines, M. Daniel
ultats qui montrent que cette analogie
ire lorsqu'il s'agit de la greffe sur parties

PHYSIQUE SANS APP

EXPÉRIENCE SUR L'ÉLAST

Voici une expérience sur l'éla
faciles à réaliser avec une simpl
très i
arrête
lui qu
vue :
Ten
le pou
et de
se tr
avec l
de la
contac
le mé
fortem
le pou
la fen
gèrem
parce
dimin
la noi
où la
eu lie
puisq
duit.
Cel
vons
cité
frotta
la lai
che, par exemple, on peut dégag
cité pour que la noix adhère à
après avoir frotté (plus ou
suivant l'appréciation du mystifi

Expérience sur l'élasticité, faite avec une noix.

Figure 12.2. Illustration from article, "Expérience sur l'élasticité, faite avec une noix," 1891
This article appeared in the popular French science magazine *La Nature* (pt. 2, 1891): 272.

The combination itself of disparate object—the birds with their upside-down eyes, the balloon, the wall, and over-sized fingers—illustrates yet another example of Freud's principles of organizing jokes: juxtaposition. According to Freud, simply putting a word in an unlikely context would be funny. Ernst and the other Surrealists would find this one of the most useful devices for eliciting a poetic response. (They found this concept not only in Freud but in the flamboyant and frantic *Les Chants de Maldoror* by Lautréamont.) The startling interrelationships in Surrealist art and literature are not created merely to surprise, but rather to bring out some new truth that the unlikely relationship provoked in the mind of the artist and eventually the mind of the spectator. For example, the "picket fence" and the tie around the horns of one of the earthbound birds have a special meaning when juxtaposed to the tiny but free balloon in the sky above them.

The painting, intended or not, is a fine pictorial allegory of the repression and release found in Freud's exercise of jokemaking. Freud stated that the two main purposes for making jokes are wishes to express hostility and sexual desires in situations in which direct expression of these emotions would be unacceptable (Freud 101). In *Oedipus Rex* the wall is an apt representation of social and personal suppression of natural and socially unacceptable feelings. The window is, like the joke, the hole punched in this wall of resistance. Unexpectedly, the feelings come out, like the oversized fingers, in the form of a joke that contains the repressed feelings in a cleverly, if not completely, disguised form. The jokemaker safely exposes himself. Obviously, the audience in *Oedipus Rex,* the birds who even turn away from indirectly exposed sexuality, is not amused.

For all the devices that Ernst took from *Jokes and Their Relation to the Unconscious,* the main point of the book is that jokes spring from the unconscious. This point was not lost on Ernst. From 1919 he cultivated methods of letting the unconscious guide his making of collages and paintings. *Oedipus Rex* was made by the method of taking images from the pages of books and magazines. According to his own accounts, Ernst leafed through publications such as *La Nature,* taking those images that struck a responsive chord in him. He described this process as a combination of "*acharnement et méthode*" (Ernst 235–69). After having discovered these images he treated them in several ways: he would cut out the things that appealed to him and paste them together directly; or he would make drawings from the images[1] or enlarge them to be included in paintings such as *Oedipus Rex.* Other motifs could be used in less obvious ways.

In *La Nature* certain subjects were discussed and pictured repeatedly. Ernst responded to this obsessive repetition in his primary source without copying any one image exactly. Three of the subjects that appear in *Oedipus Rex* had received considerable exposure in *La Nature:* balloon flight; animals, especially birds; and small clever mechanical gadgets, especially outrageous little handguns. Although Ernst probably did not copy any one of the many engravings illustrating balloon flight,[2] the cord, connecting the horns of a bird to perhaps some hovering device above (Russell 66), in juxtaposition with the balloon that is floating high in the distance, may be an ironic comment on freedom and captivity inspired by the magazine's engravings of the tethered balloons (fig. 12.3). The birds in the painting seem to refer to the stories that gave birds human characteristics, e.g., the illustrated article about two dissimilar birds who became friends and who are pictured side by side in their cage on page 192 in the article H. G. de Kerville, "Amité réciproque chez deux oiseaux" in *La Nature,* 1890, part 2. The strange little gadget that appears to pierce the fingers is like many of *La Nature*'s engravings of seemingly detached hands that demonstrate a wide variety of inventions and scientific principles, e.g., the illustration of the "pistols" on page 256 of 1891, part 1. Ernst saw in this limited vocabulary of images from *La Nature* a potential for expression not only by copying images but also by letting his mind work on the types of subjects offered. The naive and educational engravings like those in *La Nature* were found also in many German publications, e.g., *Die Gartenlaube,* popular during Ernst's childhood. For Ernst these engravings are part of the childhood experience that Freud considered so important. In this context it should be pointed out that the issue of *La Nature* in which the *Oedipus Rex* fingers-and-nut motif appears is 1891, the year of Ernst's birth.

Even the imagery of the pierced flesh may have been suggested by other engravings in the 1891 issues of *La Nature.* Two illustrations for an article on the magic tricks of Houdini that evoke *Oedipus Rex* most strongly are: one of an acupuncture technique and one of a man under hypnosis who feels no pain as a knife supposedly passes through his arm (fig. 12.4). The references to hypnosis would not have been missed by Ernst,[3] for hypnosis was one of Freud's early and well-documented tools in exposing the unconscious and controlling mental disease. *La Nature,* 1891, part 2, which provided the motif of the fingers and nut, suggested another pierced form in an engraving (p. 353) of an ancient Spanish relief of a bull pierced in the chest by a long, graceful spear. Although Ernst did not directly copy these images, their consistency with the themes in *Oedipus Rex* indicates that the unconscious play of the mind cultivated by the artist in himself found more than one expression in the painting.

Oedipus Rex also demonstrates the playful aspect of Ernst's work which is derived from Freud's belief that pleasure from jokes evokes the

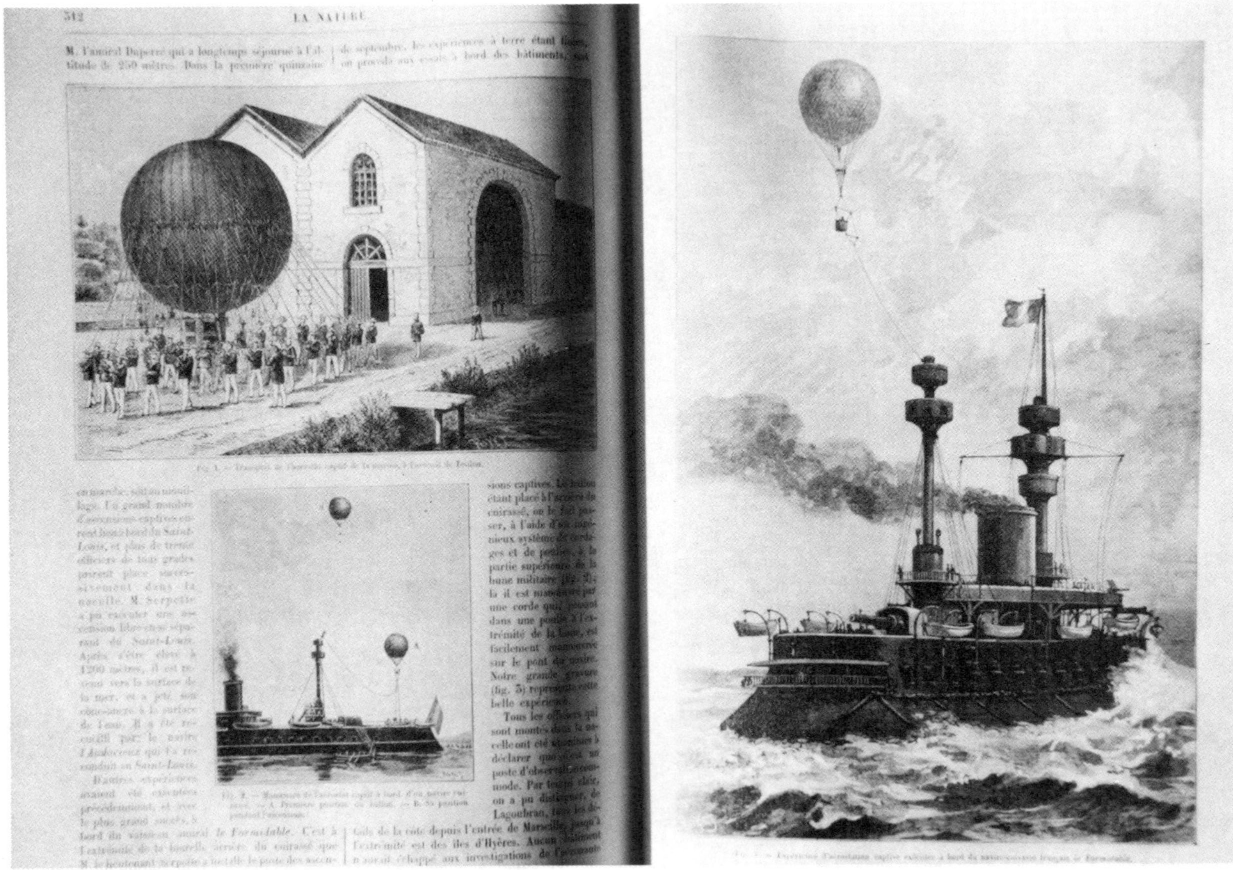

312 LA NATURE

sions captives. Le ballon étant placé à l'arrière du cuirassé, on le fait passer, à l'aide d'un ingénieux système de cordages et de poulies, à la partie supérieure de la hune militaire (fig. 2); là il est manœuvré par une corde qui, passant dans une poulie à l'extrémité de la hune, est facilement manœuvré sur le pont du navire. Notre grande gravure (fig. 3) représente cette belle expérience.

Tous les officiers qui sont montés dans la nacelle ont été unanimes à déclarer que c'est un poste d'observation commode. Par temps clair, on a pu distinguer, de Lagoubran, tous les détails de la côte depuis l'entrée de Marseille jusqu'à l'extrémité est des îles d'Hyères. Aucun bâtiment n'aurait échappé aux investigations de l'aéronaute

Figure 12.3. Pages from *La Nature,* 1890
Pt. 2: 312–33.

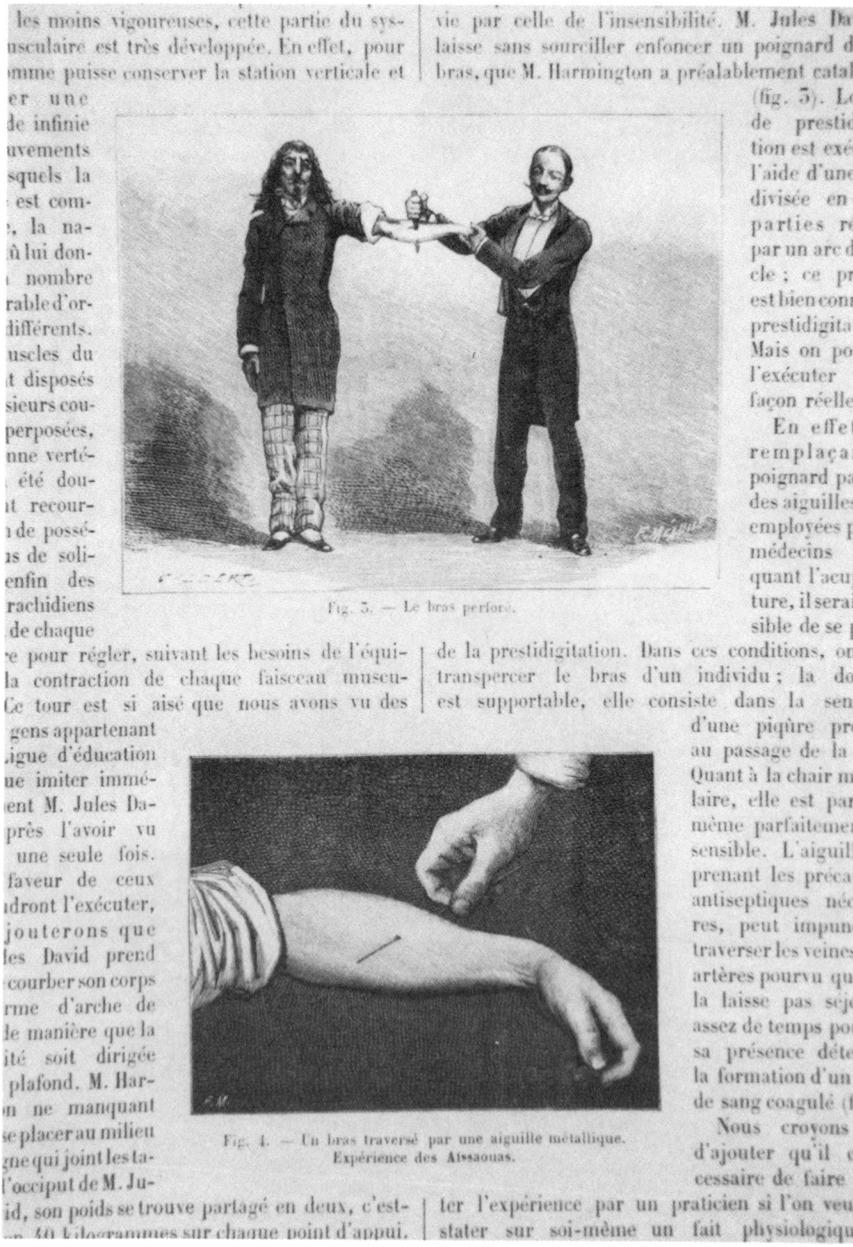

les moins vigoureuses, cette partie du sys-
usculaire est très développée. En effet, pour
mme puisse conserver la station verticale et
er une
de infinie
uvements
squels la
est com-
, la na-
û lui don-
nombre
rable d'or-
différents.
uscles du
t disposés
sieurs cou-
perposées,
nne verté-
été dou-
t recour-
de possé-
s de soli-
enfin des
rachidiens
de chaque
e pour régler, suivant les besoins de l'équi-
la contraction de chaque faisceau muscu-
Ce tour est si aisé que nous avons vu des
gens appartenant
igue d'éducation
ue imiter immé-
ent M. Jules Da-
près l'avoir vu
une seule fois.
faveur de ceux
dront l'exécuter,
jouterons que
les David prend
courber son corps
rme d'arche de
le manière que la
ité soit dirigée
plafond. M. Har-
n ne manquant
se placer au milieu
gne qui joint les ta-
l'occiput de M. Ju-
id, son poids se trouve partagé en deux, c'est-
40 kilogrammes sur chaque point d'appui.

vie par celle de l'insensibilité. M. Jules Dav
laisse sans sourciller enfoncer un poignard da
bras, que M. Harmington a préalablement catale
(fig. 3). Le
de prestidi
tion est exéc
l'aide d'une
divisée en
parties ré
par un arc de
cle ; ce pro
est bien conn
prestidigitat
Mais on pou
l'exécuter d
façon réelle.
En effet,
remplaçan
poignard par
des aiguilles
employées p
médecins p
quant l'acup
ture, il serait
sible de se p
de la prestidigitation. Dans ces conditions, on
transpercer le bras d'un individu ; la dou
est supportable, elle consiste dans la sens
d'une piqûre pro
au passage de la p
Quant à la chair mu
laire, elle est par
même parfaitemen
sensible. L'aiguill
prenant les précau
antiseptiques néc
res, peut impuné
traverser les veines
artères pourvu qu'
la laisse pas séjo
assez de temps pou
sa présence déte
la formation d'un
de sang coagulé (fi
Nous croyons
d'ajouter qu'il e
cessaire de faire
ter l'expérience par un praticien si l'on veut
stater sur soi-même un fait physiologiqu

Fig. 3. — Le bras perforé.

Fig. 4. — Un bras traversé par une aiguille métallique. Expérience des Aïssaouas.

Figure 12.4. Page from *La Nature,* 1891 Pt. 1: 29.

play of childhood and that "a joke is developed play" (Freud 179). That Ernst looked on collage in the same way is confirmed by his comment, "Les collages aussi sont des jeux d'enfant." In *Oedipus Rex* Ernst suggested the similarity to children's play by making it look like pictures by and for children in which letters are hidden in naturalistic forms. The area of the fingers, wires, and mechanisms at the left of the picture is a virtual alphabet of forms. But do these "letters" mean anything? Letters from Ernst's name seem to be present: the fingers as they come out of the window from the letter *E* in this mad monogram, but it is doubtful whether all the letters are present to spell out his name. Such teasing reference to the letters in his name by fingers can also be found in the self-portrait in the painting *Au rendez-vous des amis* (1922). Another visual/verbal game may also be found in the title. The words "Oedipus Rex" bear a suspicious resemblance to the words "Oiseaux Max" (bird Max) suggesting the artist's developing bird alter ego. If this is more than a chance similarity, it would be consistent with the word games that were the pleasure of both the Dadaists and Surrealists.

At about the same time Ernst was beginning work on the painting in 1921, he was also making a collage called *L'Invention* when it was reproduced in Paul Eluard's book of poetry *Répétitions* the following year. As in *Oedipus Rex* the collage shows fingers that are holding a mysterious device as they protrude from a window. The engraving of this strange bit of equipment, used to puncture the webbing between the toes of the birds in distinctive patterns in order to identify their age, was cut from a catalogue of poultry farming supplies (Spies, *Return* 44, 46). Although Ernst did not title the collage in reference to the Oedipus myth, the mutilation of the birds (Ernst's personal symbols), which indicates their maturity and thus their date of slaughter, is obviously similar to the mutilation of Oedipus when left as a child to die from exposure.

Ernst did not let the reference to the Oedipus myth go. In 1933 he composed *Une Semaine de bonté*. He named the chapters in the book for the days of the week. The Wednesday chapter is associated with Oedipus and with blood. One of the collages (fig. 12.5) in this violent chapter presents a replay of some of the themes in *Oedipus Rex,* as Werner Spies points out (*Collagen* 121). The now familiar hand protrudes from the window above two bird-headed men. Why does Ernst repeat and vary these themes? Such patterns of repetition are themselves allusions to the process of psychoanalysis, in which a single obsessive idea may show itself again and again in a person's life. Taking psychoanalytic theory as his base, Ernst formed a significant part of his aesthetics, in which the idea of repetition was enlarged to include variations and developments of the theme at each new presentation, adding depth and resonance to the theme as a whole. Whatever the personal psychological unity of these themes

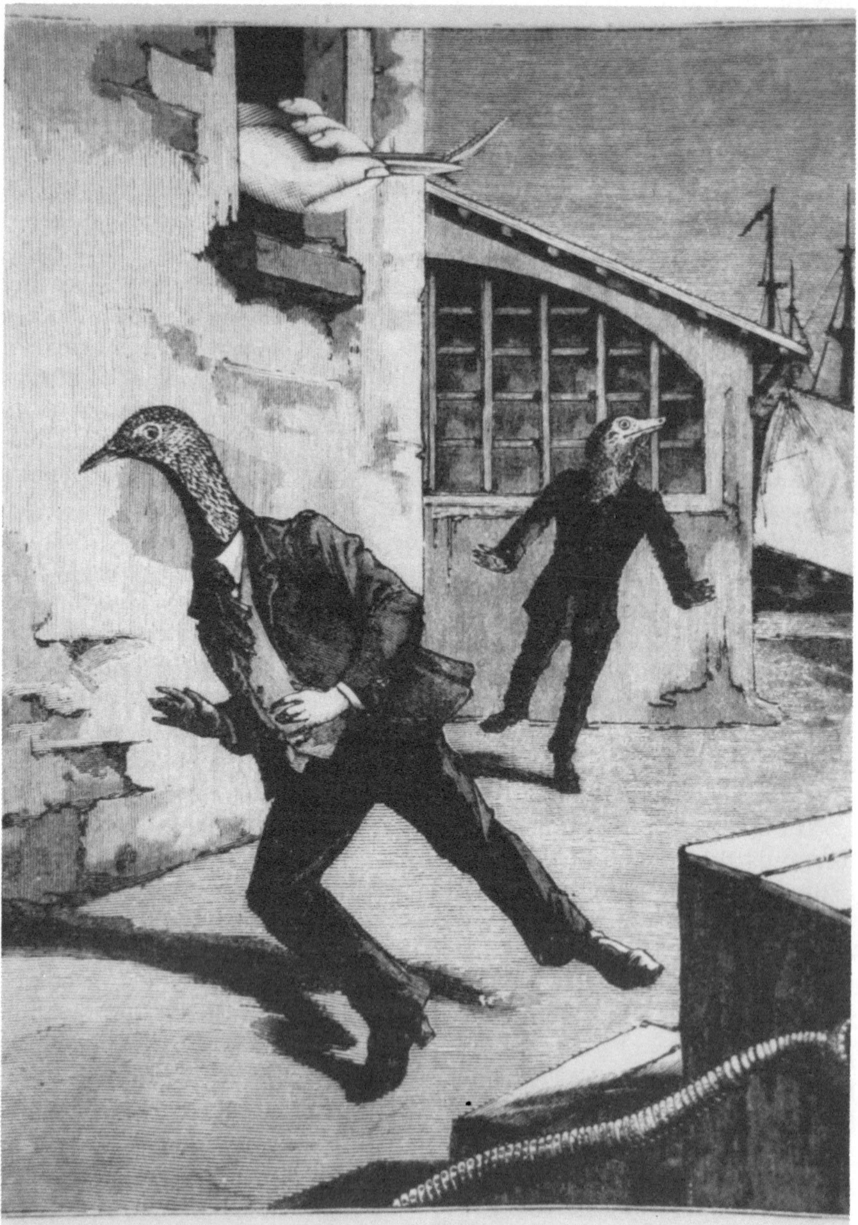

Figure 12.5. Max Ernst, Collage from "Wednesday" (the Oedipus Chapter) of *Une Semaine de bonté,* 1933

for Ernst, their mere repetition would have been meaningless to a viewer without modern art historical method, which entails looking at an artist's entire career, relating various aspects of the artist's work.[5] Thus when Ernst repeats themes it is not just an uncontrolled eruption of an obsession but rather a conscious quotation of his past work meant to elicit a knowing response in the viewer as well as in himself.

Even though Freud's *The Interpretation of Dreams* and the work of other psychologists play ever increasing roles in Ernst's works, he continued to refine the mechanisms found in *Jokes and Their Relation to the Unconscious.* For example, in 1949 when the artist was in the United States and working with new collage materials found there, he made the collage (fig. 12.6) and accompanying poem, "Oh Hercules oh Frau Cules oh Fraucles oh Herr Cules oh Herr Cules oh Frau oh Frau Cules oh Hercules oh Frau Cules oh Fraucules oh Hercules and Frau" in his book called *Paramyths* (published by the Copley Gallery, Beverly Hills). The poem combines the polite German titles *Herr* and *Frau* with the not-so-polite French word *cul* making a cross-language wordplay using the devices Freud described in *Jokes and Their Relation to the Unconscious.* But the poem teases the sex roles that Freud defined in other writings that influenced Ernst's later works.

The collage goes further than the poem in parodying traditional male-female or husband-wife relationships: the adoring little female at the big man's feet and the phallic club sprouting the elaborate parasol, a fitting object of female envy. For the basis of the collage Ernst took an illustration of Hercules from an edition of Bulfinch's famous *Age of Fable* (fig. 12.7). At the modified demigod's feet in the collage is a small figure, half female, half bird. She is one of the Harpies from another engraving in the same edition of Bulfinch (321).

In the section of *The Age of Fable* that provided Ernst with the engraving of Hercules, Bulfinch writes that Hercules was once condemned to be a slave of Queen Omphale, during which time he dressed as a woman and "lived effeminately" (185). Ironically, if we recall that Ernst's male alter ego is a bird-man, Bulfinch describes the Harpies as "disgusting birds with the heads of maidens" who attacked the great mythic heros (319–20). Ernst's additions to the engraving of Hercules and its juxtaposition to the Harpy are transcriptions of Freud's devices that amplify the twisted sex roles in the myths Bulfinch describes.

Through his writings Freud provided Ernst with many aspects of his aesthetic system. Later in Ernst's career the devices from *Jokes and Their Relation to the Unconscious* combined with concepts from others of Freud's books and became more smoothly integrated into his collages and paintings. But this book would always remain useful to him, for while it in-

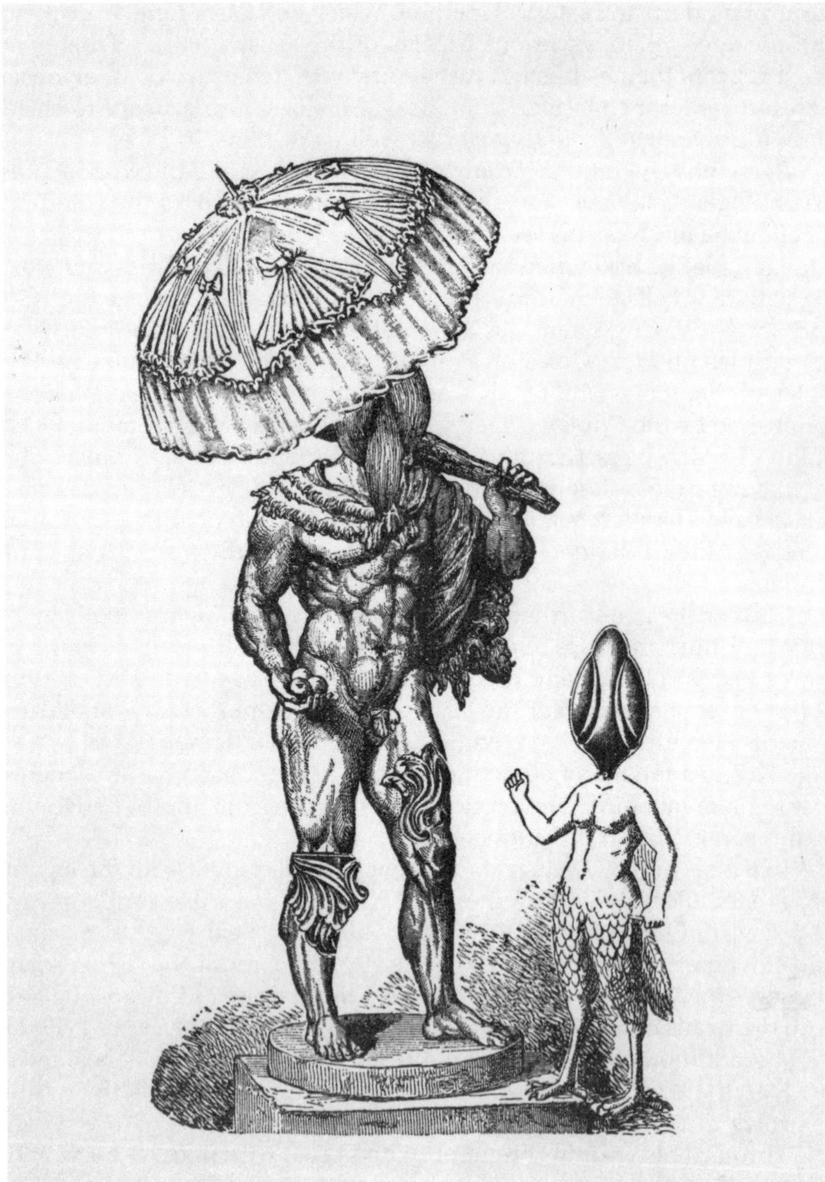

Figure 12.6. Max Ernst, *"Oh, Hercules . . . "*
Collage from *Paramyths* (Beverly Hills, Calif.: Copley Gallery, 1949), p. 35.

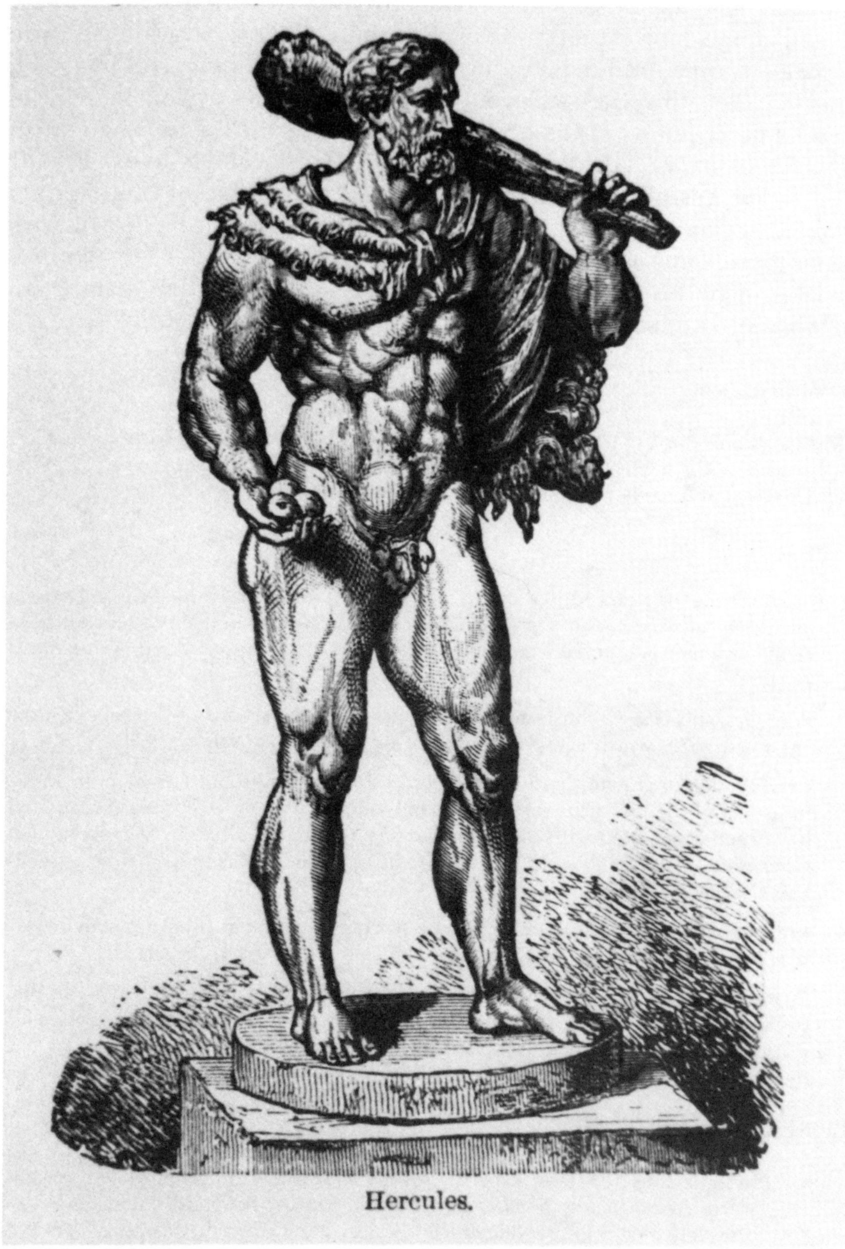

Figure 12.7. Drawing of Hercules
From Thomas Bulfinch's *The Age of Fable* (New York: Tudor Publishing, 1937), p. 179.

cluded some of the possibilities of dream symbolism, it provided the artist with important prototypes for combining preexisting images from disparate sources and making the resultant collages powerful images to others. In locating the subjects of his works, Ernst relied heavily on Freud's descriptions of his own self-analysis, as well as on the conclusions Freud drew on the nature of the mind. Ernst's ability to use Freud's ideas so successfully derives from a talent for manipulating language and images, seeing them as potentially interchangeable vehicles of communication. Thus, by using Freud's originally verbal devices to create visual ambiguities, Ernst was able to turn Freud's contention that the ambiguities of language made jokes possible (172) into pictorial form.

Acknowledgments

I wish to thank the Center for Advanced Study in the Visual Arts, National Gallery, Washington, D.C., at which I was a Visiting Senior Fellow, summer 1981. The photographs and the research for this article are part of the outcome of this fellowship.

Notes

1. See 1923 drawing reproduced as No. 183 in W. Spies, *Max Ernst—Collagen: Inventar und Widerspruch* (Cologne: DuMont, 1974). This drawing is in reality four sketches of elements which I observed were copied from pp. 260, 264, and 299 of *La Nature* (1890), pt. 1.
2. W. Spies, in *Collagen,* illustrates one possibility for the source of the balloon in the sky in No. 572, which is a photograph of page 197 of *La Nature* (1890), pt. 1.
3. Even though engravings and articles from *La Nature* arrived in Germany in various formats and the magazine itself varied in binding, it seems likely that Ernst would have been acquainted with the full range of this material while he was working on *Oedipus Rex* in 1921 and early 1922, before he came to Paris later in that year (see W. Spies, *Collagen,* p. 92).
4. Ernst quoted by A. Jouffroy. Max Ernst: "Ma peinture et mes procédés sont des jeux d'enfant," *Arts,* no. 765 (6–12 January 1960).
5. Ernst had studied art history as well as psychology while at the University of Bonn (E. Trier, "Was Max Ernst studiert hat," in Wulf Herzogenrath, ed., *Max Ernst in Köln* [Cologne: Rheinland-Verlag, 1980], p. 63), and had wanted to write a book on art made by the insane (P. Waldberg, *Max Ernst* [Paris: Jean-Jacques Pauvert, 1958], pp. 62–64).

Bibliography

Anon. "Physique sans appareils: expérience sur l'elasticité," *La Nature* (1891), pt. 2.

Bulfinch, T. *The Age of Fable or Beauties of Mythology.* New York: Tudor Publishing, 1937.

Ernst, M. "Au-delà de la peinture." Originally published in *Cahiers d'Art,* special Max Ernst issue, 1937:13–46. Repr. in M. Ernst, *Ecritures.* Paris: Editions Gallimard, 1970, pp. 235–69.

Freud, S. *Jokes and Their Relation to the Unconscious.* James Strachey, trans. New York: W. W. Norton, 1963.

Penrose, R. *Max Ernst's Celebes.* University of Newcastle upon Tyne, 1972.

Russell, J. *Max Ernst.* New York: Abrams, n.d.

Spies, W. *Max Ernst—Collagen: Inventar und Widerspruch.* Cologne: DuMont, 1974.

______. *Return of the Belle Jardinière: Max Ernst 1950–1970.* New York: Abrams, 1971.

Stokes, C. "Surrealist Persona: Max Ernst's Loplop Superior of Birds." *The Art Journal* (in press).

Trier, E. "Was Max Ernst studiert hat." In Wulf Herzogenrath, ed., *Max Ernst in Köln.* Cologne: Rheinland-Verlag, 1980.

13

Engendering Collage: Collaboration and Desire in Dada and Surrealism

Robin Lydenberg

Robin Lydenberg moves beyond a number of formalist and thematic interpretations of collage to a discussion of "engendering collage," particularly in Dada and Surrealist works. She writes, "Most critics acknowledge the collage artists' heightened attentiveness to the sensual *reality of their materials and to the complex relationships between the components of their works. Very few, however, pursue the implications of these characteristics—the notion that the process of collage experimentations, both verbal and visual, may be seen as an erotic encounter and its fertile outcome." Lydenberg carefully delineates how Dada and Surrealist collage may be connected with the body, eroticism, and natural cycles of birth and death. As she notes, "To perceive collage as an erotic and procreative encounter is to reemphasize its importance not just as an abstract experiment or a moment in art history, but as a continuous cosmic adventure."*

On the occasion of the "Art of Assemblage" exhibit at the Museum of Modern Art in 1961, Roger Shattuck addressed a symposium on the use of juxtaposition as an artistic technique. Of the two effects of juxtaposition that he identified, Shattuck characterized the first by its "negative esthetic"—the shocking convergence of elements which "cancel each other out and return us spiritually and esthetically to zero" (Shattuck 20).* He described the second type, in contrast, as creating a tension between its elements, offering the viewer "stability of design" and a "field of forces sustained by the association" (Shattuck 21). Shattuck worried that the intermingling of these two conflicting styles in the exhibit would work counterproductively, defusing the "historic interest" of one and the

*Page references are to sources found in the bibliography at the end of the chapter.

''esthetic values'' of the other. In his desire for ''rigorous distinctions'' between these opposing effects, Shattuck lost sight of the possibility of a cultural cross-fertilization between them. I would argue that as it functions in verbal and visual collage, juxtaposition can operate as a kind of erotic encounter, producing precisely this sort of hybrid offspring.

Shattuck's effort to isolate the two effects of juxtaposition is at odds with a collage aesthetic promoting the combination of heterogeneous elements. The Museum's gathering of collages, assemblages, and combines for the ''Art of Assemblage'' show thus mirrors the eclectic nature of collage itself. The discomfort of many critics with this collage aesthetic is also evident in Harold Rosenberg's dismissal [see ch. 3 of this volume] of the 1961 exhibit as producing ''chaos, intellectually and aesthetically'' (Rosenberg 60) and in Clement Greenberg's preference [see ch. 4 of this volume] for those collage experiments resulting in a ''seamless fusion'' over those in which juxtaposition and alternation leave the elements in unresolved ''confusion'' (Greenberg 75).

What is obscured by these assessments of collage as producing ''chaos'' and ''confusion'' is the way in which its juxtaposition of disparate elements leads to their productive and continuous interaction. Most critics acknowledge the collage artists' heightened attentiveness to the *sensual* reality of their materials and to the complex relationships between the components of their works. Very few, however, pursue the implications of these characteristics—the notion that the process of collage experimentation, both verbal and visual, may be seen as an erotic encounter and its fertile outcome.

This reluctance on the part of critics to acknowledge the sexual component of collage is particularly surprising because so many artists and writers working with collage techniques describe the interaction of elements in their work in terms of desire, copulation, and regeneration. I would propose, therefore, that Shattuck's typology be expanded to include a third effect that grows out of the combination of the other two. Neither purely self-destructive nor purely self-sustaining, collage works of this third type can be identified as erotic, procreative, and subject to continual metamorphosis.

Because the exploitation of collage's erotic potential is most explicitly developed in Dada and Surrealism, they are the primary focus of my analysis. By emphasizing the erotic rather than the abstract aspects of collage, I hope to draw attention to its sensual immediacy, to its creative power as continual process, and to its function, for many artists, as an emblem of the cycle of life and death.

Juxtaposition

In describing the early cubist collages of Picasso and Braque, most art critics focus on such technical aspects as the dislocation of planes and points of view. Even within this essentially abstract discourse, however, critics such as Greenberg note the effects of the''corporeal presence'' of pasted papers (Greenberg 71) and the ways in which different layers of the material or facets of the image ''touch'' each other. While critics may use a somewhat disquieting language to describe how the cubist canvas is ''invaded'' or ''infected'' by collage, how various planes are alternately ''thrust through the surface'' or ''drive[n] back into depth'' (Greenberg 68, 70, 72), their metaphors are rarely sexual.

In the work of early noncubist collage artists, however, the same techniques of flattening perspective and bringing all the elements of the composition into contact take on a more insistent sensual quality. For example, among the Italian Futurists there is a tendency to transform the spatial relations between objects into motion, a violent and reckless motion in which the human body penetrates and is penetrated by its environment. This Futurist goal is often declared in manifesto form:

> To paint the human figure . . . you must render the whole of its surrounding atmosphere.
>
> . . . How often have we not seen upon the cheek of the person with whom we were talking the horse which passes at the end of the street.
>
> Our bodies penetrate the sofas upon which we sit, and the sofas penetrate our bodies. The motor-bus rushes into houses it passes and in their turn the houses throw themselves upon the motor-bus and are blended with it. (Chipp 290)

The Futurists refuse to ''correct'' their perception with an acquired knowledge of reality. Instead, they employ optical effects in which a flattened field of perception produces a hallucination of vast inner spaces where objects sensuously engulf and invade each other. This confusion of surface and depth is described by Greenberg as essential to collage, but his recognition of a ''shuttling'' (70) and ''oscillation'' (72) between these two planes is a muted and abstract version of the abandoned sensual interpenetration which dominates many Futurist works.

The Surrealists extend this intense focus on spatial relations and points of contact and interpenetration to words as well as images. In more explicitly sexual terms, André Breton describes his discovery of the material and sensual properties of language: ''I had begun to pet and pamper words immoderately, attracted by the space that surrounded them, by their tangential relations with innumerable other words I left unpronounced'' (*Manifestes du Surréalisme* 33, my translation). Breton's thought process leads him naturally from an intellectual analysis of the "tangential relations" between words to images of erotic pleasure and limitless fertility. Imagining the way in which words are transformed by rubbing up against each other, he concludes elsewhere, "Words have finished playing. Words are making love" (*Les Pas perdus* 134, my translation).

Breton insists, however, that mere juxtaposition will remain sterile unless the individual *recognizes* the new relations created by this process. When the unexpected encounter of disconnected images, objects, or words is recognized, there is a momentary closing of the gap that separates them. For Breton, this is analogous to the moment when his desire at last recognizes and possesses its previously unknown object. Footbridges, crossroads, a thread stretched, or a spark shot across a gap dominate Dada and Surrealist descriptions of the convergence of unrelated elements in art or in life. The emphasis on connection, however, is rarely reassuring; the point of contact is always at the site of some abyss, at the intersection of invisible forces, at the meeting of paths to the unknown, or in a moment of total displacement from any frame of reference. As Breton says in a 1920 essay on Max Ernst: "[Collage] has the marvellous faculty of attaining two widely separate realities without departing from the realm of our experience; of bringing them together and drawing a spark from their contact . . . and of disorienting us in our own memory by depriving us of a frame of reference" (*What Is Surrealism?* 7).

What is striking in these new relations, then, is not so much the continuity of images or words as their discontinuity. Produced by chance encounter or magical accident, these juxtapositions are experienced as part of an aesthetic of adventure, risk, and desire, qualities often overlooked in critical analyses of collage. For example, using the electrical analogy that appears in many Surrealist descriptions of collage, Shattuck depicts juxtaposition as either a "brief bright spark that jumps the gap and thus destroys the whole rig" or as a process in which elements are brought "as close together as possible without ignition" so that the "field of forces [is] sustained" (21). The only possibilities envisioned here by Shattuck are careless self-destruction or cautious self-regulation. In the Surrealist version of this metaphor, the spark that jumps the gap in collage doesn't blow everything up, but rather sets in motion a machinery of desire. The risk of self-destruction is always there, but that is precisely what provides the excitement and energy that keep the machine running.

Chance Encounter/Erotic Encounter

The sense of danger associated with collage stems primarily from the role often played by the chance encounter as its source of inspiration and, for some, its method of composition. By chance the artist encounters the material elements of his work; by chance the elements within the work encounter each other and engender new elements. Not to be confused with a total abdication of artistic control, this willingness to collaborate with chance has the effect of blurring the distinction between artistic production and the direct experience of life. The early cubist collages of Picasso and Braque, in which a piece of reality intrudes into the artistic frame, challenge these categories on an abstract level. For Dada and Surrealist artists, the collage encounter takes place not just in the artwork but in the world itself. Breton and his companions, for example, roam aimlessly through the streets of Paris, leaving themselves open to any and all chance meetings. With his friend Vaché, Breton wanders in and out of movie theaters at random, creating his own film montage without any equipment.

Tristan Tzara also celebrates ''the pure delight of a random object encountered by a man out for a walk'' (''Max Ernst'' 187); in such daily adventures he finds the ordinary to be surprising, fruitful, and above all revolutionary. The anti-aesthetic of Dada insists on the arbitrariness of the chance encounter as part of a strategy to undermine all cultural hierarchies, all aesthetic and intellectual pretensions: ''[Dada] *is* the point where *yes* and *no* meet, not solemnly as in the castles of human philosophies, but quite simply on street corners like dogs and grasshoppers'' (*Seven Dada Manifestos* 112).

Critics often acknowledge the revolutionary nature of collage as a challenge to cultural hierarchies, to conventions of representation, to the binary opposition of art and life, but their context remains resolutely aesthetic and abstract. The revolutionary gestures of Dada collage, however, are insistently physical and sexual, and their transgressions against aesthetic norms are presented as a scandalous coupling of the high and the low. For example, Jean Arp's ''navel bottle'' is described by the artist as a monstrous invention in which ''a bicycle, a sea-serpent, a brassiere, and a Pernod spoon copulate'' (*Arp on Arp* 239). As one historical account points out, the term collage is related to the French slang expression for an illicit love affair, the scandal of ''nobly born oil paint'' coupling with ''the streetwalker newspaper'' (Janis 21). By emphasizing the scandalously sexual nature of the collage encounter, Dada and Surrealist artists assert their allegiance to a natural and creative life force which erupts joyously and dangerously in defiance of all social and political as well as aesthetic regulations.

In the elaborate mythology and psychology of Surrealism, the chance encounter often extends from social and political to mystical realms. Inspired by the radical poetic tradition of writers such as Lautréamont and Rimbaud, Ernst defines his artistic techniques in terms of the mysterious procedures of alchemy. He sees his collages of Victorian engravings as "something like the alchemy of the visual image" and his verbal experiments with word combinations as the "alchemy resulting from the unexpected meeting of two or more heterogeneous elements . . . directed toward systematical confusion and disorder of all the senses (Rimbaud)" (*Beyond Painting* 12). Unlike later critics of collage, Ernst sees "confusion" and "disorder" as the major goals of the technique. One example he gives of a verbal collage is the invention of the "phallustrade": "An alchemic product, composed of the following elements: the autostrade, the balustrade and a certain quantity of phallus" (*Beyond Painting* 16). With such composite wordplay Ernst wittily reminds us of the erotic component in the combinative procedures of collage.

In a reformulation of a phrase from Lautréamont's *Les Chants de Maldoror,* "beautiful . . . as the chance encounter of a sewing machine and an umbrella on a dissecting table" (322, my translation), Ernst develops a general formula for the juxtaposition of collage elements as an encounter that is erotic as well as mystical:

> I am tempted to see in collage the exploitation of the chance meeting of two distant realities on an unfamiliar plane. . . . A ready made reality, whose naive destination has the air of having been fixed, once and for all (a canoe), finding itself in the presence of another and hardly less absurd reality (a vacuum cleaner), in a place where both of them must feel displaced (a forest), will, by this very fact, escape to its naive destination and to its identity . . . [C]anoe and vacuum cleaner will make love. (*Beyond Painting* 13)

While Lautréamont's phrase is part of his rhetorical challenge to poetic analogy and conventions of beauty, Ernst's revision underlines instead the obsessive, erotic and alienating nature of the encounter. Noting the "obsession which held under [his] gaze the pages of an illustrated catalogue" containing an absurd collection of unrelated objects, Ernst feels his visionary powers intensified, "piling up [contradictory images] with the persistence and rapidity . . . peculiar to love memories" and "revealing dramas of [his] most secret desires" (*Beyond Painting* 14). While many commentaries on collage stress its humor and its playful mockery of conventions (Rosenberg 66), they overlook its disturbing intensity—an intensity that derives in part from its association with unconscious sexual desire. As Ernst points out here, releasing those subliminal associations gives the artist access to tremendous creative energies.

"A poem is no longer a formal act," Tzara argues, but an encounter of disparate elements which "love to be closely associated, truly hugging each other, like the cerebral hemispheres and the cabins of transatlantic liners" (*Seven Dada Manifestos* 76–77). Elaborating his own philosophy of collage, Tzara envisions a universe of multiple constellations and connection in which the single unifying element is the desire for interpenetration. The collage experiments of Dada and Surrealism bring everything into contact, producing not isolated erotic encounters but a pandemic sexuality, an all-inclusive polymorphous perversity.

Cocteau sees this quality already in Picasso's early Cubist collages where "furniture, animals, people, mingle like lovers' bodies in love" (Fry 164); and Breton comments similarly on the paintings and automatic drawings of André Masson: "In Masson's work eroticism must be considered the keystone: it supervises the compulsive activation of the limbs of men and women whose marvellous struggles eventually involve the participation of the furniture, which had hitherto been suspected only of retaining the imprint of their bodies." (*Surrealism and Painting* 154) Breton's own poetry offers a verbal equivalent of such erotic contagion, as in "Postman Cheval," where bodies, furniture, and architecture merge in a dreamlike sensuality:

> And may glowing gaps open up in his bed
> Gaps through which can be glimpsed stags with coral antlers in a clearing
> And naked women at the very bottom of a mine
> . . . While his house collapses and he wonders at the odd interconnections
> That his bed seeks with the hallway and the staircase
> But no it is content as we advance to open all its steps like drawers
> Bread drawers wine drawers soap drawers mirror drawers staircase drawers
> Flesh drawers with handles of hair
>
> (*Poems* 67)

The mysterious bed in Breton's epic fragment "Fata Morgana" similarly "hurtles along on its rails of blue honey," eroticizing everything in its path (*Poems* 137).

While many Dada and Surrealist collage works demonstrate the erotic nature of juxtaposition, it is in Breton's development of the philosophy of Surrealism that this effect becomes most explicit and essential. The chance encounter is the very crystallization of desire; the encountered Surrealist object, most often an object with a mysteriously dual nature, is its condensation in material reality. In collaboration with his friend Paul Eluard, Breton circulates a questionnaire in which they ask "What do you consider the essential encounter of your life?" (*Mad Love* 19). For Breton, the answer is the discovery of love, which he sees as the magical convergence of unconscious desire and objective chance. The legend of Cinderella haunts him as the essential narrative of the mysterious workings of desire and chance. In *Mad Love* Breton narrates in detail his own

Cinderella encounter: first, how he is enchanted by a composite phrase which came to him in half-sleep, "le cendrier de Cendrillon," the Cinderella ashtray; and then how he discovers this dream object at a flea market in Paris. In fact, the object he finds is not the slipper-shaped glass ashtray he imagined, but a wooden spoon whose handle is propped up by a little carved shoe at its tip.

Breton's narrative of the event is made up of a series of encounters: the composite object (the slipper-spoon) encounters the composite phrase (the Cinderella-ashtray) and in their convergence Breton recognizes the condensation of his desire. In the course of his narrative, he emphasizes certain aspects of the creative process that are essential to an understanding of collage: collaboration, metamorphosis, and engendering, and the association of creativity with desire and death. Because it can thus be read as a parable of what is at stake in the use of collage techniques, I will examine Breton's account of this episode in some detail.

Collaboration

Many factors contribute to the impact of this particular encounter on Breton. One is the presence of his friend Giacometti, a painter and sculptor with whose work Breton was intimately involved. At the time of the incident, Giacometti had been struggling to complete a sculpture of a female form, and his discovery—on that same day at the flea market—of a strange iron half-mask is recognized by both men as the solution to Giacometti's creative block. It is the companionship of the two friends, however, that establishes the necessary conditions for the found object to function as a catalyst: "I observe in passing that these two discoveries that Giacometti and I made *together* respond not just to some desire on the part of one of us, but rather to a desire of one of us with which the other . . . is associated. . . . [T]he two people walking near each other constitute a single influencing body, *primed*" (*Mad Love* 32–33). The peculiarly homoerotic quality of the episode is emphasized further by Breton's insistence that "any female interaction" in the sculptor's life at that time would have been "harmful," an interpretation which guarantees Breton's place at his friend's side. While critics locate the origins of collage in the collaborative work of Picasso and Braque and acknowledge the continued frequency of communal projects in its development, they give insufficient attention to the potentially erotic component in these collaborations.

Breton believes that certain personalities are connected by magnetic energies, energies that can be condensed and magnified in collaborative creative enterprises. He sees the Surrealist "group" as conducting this sort of electrical power, and particularly (as in this episode) when its members wander the streets of Paris, the city itself imagined as a vast magnetic field.* The Surrealists' collaborations on both verbal and visual collage are attempts to tap into the rich sources of collective creativity, collective desire, collective subconscious—to merge with a collective identity, cosmic and anonymous. Max Ernst sees this convergence of personalities, ideas, and desires as a kind of human collage in itself: "When the thoughts of two or more authors were systematically fused into a single work (otherwise called collaboration) this fusion could be considered as akin to collage" (*Beyond Painting* 17).

Both Dada and Surrealist artists understand that such an enterprise can only succeed if individual ego and self-expression are abandoned. Therefore, many collaborative collage works are either left unsigned or are signed by other artists; and from Braque and Picasso to Arp and Ernst, many declare their quest for an anonymous collective style. Some of them hope that the bonds of communal work will replace competition and enmity between artists, but Arp, for one, sees that the transition will not be an easy one: "These works . . . try to go beyond the human and attain the infinite and eternal. They reject our egotism. . . . The hands of our brothers, instead of being interchangeable with our own hands, have become enemy hands. Instead of anonymity, we have renown and masterpieces." (*Arp on Arp* 139)

The Surrealists approach a similar collective goal in the writing and drawing game known as "Cadavre exquis," a collaborative activity in which each player creates part of a story or drawing without seeing the contributions of the other players. In such a game, Eluard points out, "there were no losers. Each wanted his neighbor to win and go on winning" (Short 142). In this spirit of noncompetitive cooperation, Breton declares dialogue to be the most appropriate form of surrealist writing because it allows different thoughts to come together without the thinkers trying to dominate one another.

Freed from ego, fused in a collective and anonymous identity, Dada and Surrealist artists can then explore the unknown regions of desire and madness, as Breton and Eluard did in the collaborative poetic texts of *The Immaculate Conception*. After collaborating with Eluard on a poetic narrative in which they sought "new techniques in the practice of love" (*Beyond Painting* 17), Ernst declared: "Love cannot be reborn from isolated efforts of isolated men: reborn love will take its origins in a collective subconscious by the discoveries and efforts of all" (Maurer 70). So these artistic collaborations, like the collages themselves, are most often held

*See Anna Balakian's discussion of the influence of Eliphas Lévi's theories about magnetism on Breton, pp. 34–35.

together by the glue of desire—quite simply the desire for love that Breton discovers in the episode of the slipper-spoon (*Mad Love* 37).

Metamorphosis and Engendering

While Breton's initial discovery of the object of his desire occurs as part of an eroticized collaborative adventure, the subsequent unleashing of the object's fertile powers takes place in private. As he contemplates the spoon, Breton sees it mysteriously transformed before his eyes:

> From the side . . . the little wood spoon coming out of its handle, took on, with the help of the curvature of the handle, the aspect of a heel and the whole object presented the silhouette of a slipper on tiptoe. . . . [The] little slipper-heel presided over the spell cast, containing in itself the very *source* of the *stereotype* (the heel of this shoe heel could have been a shoe, whose heel itself . . . and so on). . . . From then on the slipper, with the shoe heel multiplying, started to look vaguely as if it were moving about alone. (33–34, Breton's italics)

At this impossible intersection of the fantastical and the banal, "the marvelous slipper potential in the modest spoon," the object is set free in a series of metamorphoses, as when the wood "took on the transparency of glass." In the replication of the heel of the slipper within the heel of the slipper, the reproductive power of the object approaches a vertiginous infinite regression.

This pattern of excessive multiplication or reproduction is characteristic of the indeterminacy and fluidity of collage creations. As we have seen, everything that is juxtaposed in collage—from furniture to ideas—can "make love"; the procreative possibilities, therefore, are staggering. As Tzara says of Ernst's collages, "so vastly do they multiply by series of perspectives that they seem to be cut up into segments within a single mass that loses itself in the infinite" (*Beyond Painting* 186).

As early as 1925, Aragon announced the beginning of the "age of metamorphosis" (Caws 46). Some subsequent discussions of collage have also recognized its metamorphic potential as a technique for "dissolving reality into endless visual absurdities" (Rosenberg 66). Donald Kuspit's essay, "Collage: The Organizing Principle of Art in the Age of the Relativity of Art" [see ch. 2 of this volume], has most explicitly recognized the indeterminacy of collage as the sign of a creative process of becoming: "The collage is a metaphor of universal becoming, . . . the restlessness of individuality in the process of becoming" (Kuspit 48). In emphasizing the "creative flux" of collage, Kuspit captures its dynamic potential. However, in ultimately describing the process of collage as a "dialectical response—a dialectical emergence" (54), he remains within the limits of an abstract discourse which is antithetical to the spirit of Dada and Surrealism. As Breton reminds his readers, for the Surrealists the "dialectical method in its Hegelian form was inapplicable . . . [and] it was imperative to have done with idealism proper" (*What Is Surrealism?* 130).

This rejection of idealism and abstraction is perhaps most evident in the tendency of Dada and Surrealist collage to focus on the body as the site of metamorphosis, and to describe the process of change not as a dialectical pattern but as an actual birth. Arp, for example, describes how relinquishing conscious artistic control can release the generative power of the artist's collage materials: "I allow myself to be guided by the work at the time of its birth, I have confidence in it. I don't reflect. The forms come, pleasing or strange, hostile, inexplicable, dumb or drowsy. They are born of themselves" (Read 117). A similar suppression of conscious artistic will allows Ernst to "assist as a spectator at the birth of all [his] works" (*Beyond Painting* 9).

In their effort to reach back to a time before social and aesthetic conventions, to a prenatal purity before individual consciousness and will, these artists produce works with such suggestive titles as Arp's chance-generated collage *Before My Birth* or Breton's experiments with simulated states of madness in the collection of prose-poems, *Intrauterine Life.* These artists thus attempt to gain access to a cosmic generative force which Tzara hails as "an Everlasting Sphere . . . without a begetter" (*Seven Dada Manifestos* 76).

Under the influence of this sign of inexhaustible fertility, Arp composes collage poems in which the "unending wealth of division, placing, arrangement" (Read 147) yields infinite permutations from a limited set of phrases and images. Using a process he calls "constellating," Arp composes the collage poem "Strasbourg Configuration" in which he plays variations on the titles of his previous volumes of poetry and at the same time narrates his own multiple births, playing variations on himself: "i was born in nature. i was born in strasbourg. i was born in a cloud. i was born in a pump. i was born in a robe" (*Arp on Arp* 47).* In verbal collages such as those by Arp and Tzara, nothing is allowed to remain fixed either in past or present time; everything—including one's origin and identity—is put back in circulation.

The association of the creative process with birth is, of course, a familiar aesthetic conceit. In the context of collage, however, the birth is never completed; its process is continuous and multiple. Through the

---

*In this and subsequent sections on Arp's poetry I am very much indebted to the five essays in *Arp 1886–1966,* particularly those by Bleikasten, Watts, and Hancock. For an excellent analysis of Arp's use of sexual and procreative images see Jane Hancock's essay "Jean Arp's *The Eggboard* Interpreted" in *The Art Bulletin* 65, no. 1 (March 1983): 122–37.

collage artist's abdication of his individual will to collaboration and to collective desire, not only the work but the very life and identity of the artist escape the finality of definition and totalizing systems. Liberated from a single origin and evolution, both artist and work are also liberated from the threat of a single death.

Desire and Death

One of the peculiar charms of collage is that its multiple births are most often resurrections of discarded and forgotten refuse—dead garbage brought back to life as art. In fact, collage offers a unique occasion for the reconciliation of life and death, of creation and destruction. Its multiple metamorphoses and births, after all, can only occur through the death of each displaced image. In a process Kuspit describes as continual "creative flux," everything in collage is endlessly recycled.

The Parisian flea market where Breton discovers the slipper-spoon embodies perfectly this merging of treasures and garbage, of desire and death. But it is only after long meditation on his experience there that Breton comes to fully understand how the desire that engenders his fertile imaginative vision of the spoon is intimately bound to death and loss. First Breton traces the series of associations that made the slipper-spoon function for him as an erotic symbol of "a woman unique and unknown": "So it became clear . . . that the whole movement of my thought before this had had as its starting point the objective equation: slipper = spoon = penis = the perfect mold of this penis" (*Mad Love* 36–37). Having perceived that the spoon functions in the encounter as the emblem of his desire, Breton then belatedly recognizes in the mysterious mask discovered at the same time by Giacometti an emblem of death, a reminder of "the loss of a beloved being" (38). It is the proximity of the death mask to the love object that gives the moment of discovery its power and significance. Sex and death are exalted, Breton says, in the "ultramaterial guise" of the two objects brought together in the episode and in the two photographs included in the text of *Mad Love.* Breton understands finally that the challenge posed by this convergence of death and desire requires of him a blind leap across an abyss and into an "endless unknown" (39). So the gap within collage, the discontinuity of its material components, is mirrored here in the metaphysical gap between life and death.

The connection between destruction and recreation in collage is perhaps most clearly and movingly evident in the evolution of the work of Jean Arp. In a crisis precipitated by his mother's death, Arp is first terrified by the evidence of the effects of time on his fragile paper collages. He then discovers, however, that the ephemeral nature of his material can be overcome and assimilated into the creative process: "I had accepted the transience, the dribbling away, the brevity, the impermanence, the fading, the withering, the spookishness of our existence. Not only had I accepted it, I had even welcomed transience into my work as it was coming into being" (Hancock 123). Obsessively, Arp begins to tear up his old collages and use the pieces to create new ones, making death and rebirth simultaneous.

In a poetic context, Arp and Tzara both use a similar recycling method of composition, accumulating scraps of paper in drawers and then one day assembling them into poems. Not only in their method of composition, but often in content as well, these poets dramatize the disintegration and reconstruction of language, even of individual letters. In his poem "Davos Configuration II" Arp describes such a cataclysmic moment in which "the air breaks up. the letters break up. / the capital A breaks up. the small a breaks up. the capital B breaks up. / the small b breaks up. / the letters of flesh climb up the trunk of flesh." The poem ends in what one critic has called "radical recombination, throwing the stocks of the collected letters against a host of flying eggs" (Watts 118). Thus Arp gives us a vision of the excessive fertility that grows out of total destruction.

The violent death and resurrection of words, images, and objects are seen by Dada and Surrealist artists as part of a natural and continuous process. Making no distinction between the garbage on city streets and the effects of time and the elements in nature, Arp elevates both alike to the level of art or dream:

> Who has shown the beauty of the sprigs and twigs, splinters, fragments, rubbish on the ground? Flooring, sidewalks, flagstones in plazas, the washed and dried out ground of a river bed, the sand on a beach ending in lace of underwater refuse . . . all are transformed into a sphere or a temple for dreamers alone. (*Arp on Arp* 211)

The overlooked beauty in the abandoned, the persistence of life in death, are captured in the works of collage masters such as Arp and Schwitters. This aesthetic of recycling continues to dominate more recent collage experiments such as the combines of Robert Rauschenberg.

In an essay which is itself a collage of fragments, John Cage describes a combine painting by Rauschenberg: "This is not a composition. It is a place where things are, as on a table or on a town seen from the air: any one of them could be removed and another come into its place through circumstances analogous to birth and death, travel, housecleaning, or cluttering" (99). For Cage and Rauschenberg, as for many Dada and Surrealist artists, collage juxtaposition is a natural process in which such opposites as life and death, cleaning and cluttering, are simultaneous and interchangeable.

Cage sees clearly that to make birth and death coincide in a collage of images, sounds, or words is to "transform our contemporary awareness of nature's manner of operation into art" (9). That manner of operation cannot be contained within Shattuck's dualistic typology or even within Kuspit's model of dialectical interaction. A fuller representation of the continuing tradition of collage, and of Dada and Surrealist collage in particular, would have to restore its connection with matter, with the body, with eroticism, and with the natural cycles of birth and death. Such an approach would reveal the source of collage in collaboration and collective desire, and its goal in an endless metamorphosis fueled simultaneously by creation *and* destruction. To perceive collage as an erotic and procreative encounter is to reemphasize its importance not just as an abstract experiment or a moment in art history, but as a continuous cosmic adventure.

Bibliography

Arp, Jean. *Arp on Arp: Poems, Essays, Memories.* Edited by Marcel Jean, translated by Joachim Neugroschel. New York: The Viking Press, 1972.

Balakian, Anna. *André Breton: Magus of Surrealism.* New York: Oxford University Press, 1971.

Bleikasten, Aimee. "Arp the Poet, or, The Voice of Origins," in *Arp 1886–1966.* Cambridge: Cambridge University Press, 1986, pp. 16–27.

Breton, André. *Mad Love.* Translated by Mary Ann Caws. Lincoln: University of Nebraska Press, 1987.

______. *Manifestes du Surréalisme.* Paris: J. J. Pauvert, 1962.

______. *Les Pas perdus.* Paris: Gallimard, 1969.

______. *Poems of André Breton: A Bilingual Anthology.* Translated and edited by Jean-Pierre Cauvin and Mary Ann Caws. Austin: University of Texas Press, 1982.

______. *Surrealism and Painting.* Translated by Simon Watson Taylor. New York: Harper & Row, 1965.

______. *What Is Surrealism?* Edited and introduced by Franklin Rosemont. New York: Monad Press, 1968.

Cage, John. *Silence.* Middletown, Conn.: Wesleyan University Press, 1961.

Caws, Mary Ann. *Poetry of Dada and Surrealism: Aragon, Breton, Tzara, Eluard & Desnos.* Princeton: Princeton University Press, 1970.

Chipp, Herschel B., ed. *Theories of Modern Art.* Berkeley: University of California Press, 1968.

Ducasse, Isidore (le comte de Lautréamont). *Oeuvres complètes.* Paris: Livre de Poche, 1963.

Ernst, Max. *Beyond Painting.* New York: Wittenborn, Schultz, Inc., 1948.

Fry, Edward F. *Cubism.* New York: Oxford University Press, 1966.

Greenberg, Clement. "Collage," in *Art and Culture* (Boston: Beacon Press, 1961); reprinted in present volume, pp. 67–77. Page references to this article are to pages in this volume's reprint.

Hancock, Jane. "Constellations and Cosmos," in *Arp 1886–1966.* Cambridge: Cambridge University Press, 1986, pp. 122–23.

Janis, Hariet and Blesh, Rudi. *Collage: Personalities, Concepts, Techniques.* Philadelphia: Chilton Book Company, 1967.

Kuspit, Donald B. "Collage: The Organizing Principle of Art in the Age of the Relativity of Art," in Betty Craig, ed. *Relativism in the Arts* (Athens: The University of Georgia Press, 1983), pp. 123–47; reprinted in present volume, pp. 39–57. Page references to this article are to pages in this volume's reprint.

Maurer, Evan M. "Images of Dream and Desire: The Prints and Collage Novels of Max Ernst," in *Beyond Surrealism.* New York: Oxford University Press, 1986, pp. 37–93.

Read, Herbert. *The Art of Jean Arp.* New York: Harry N. Abrams, Inc., 1968.

Rosenberg, Harold. "Collage: Philosophy of Put-Togethers," in *Art on the Edge* (New York: Macmillan Publishing Co., 1975), pp. 173–80; reprinted in present volume, pp. 59–66. Page references to this article are to pages in this volume's reprint.

Shattuck, Roger. "The Mode of Juxtaposition," in *About French Poetry from DADA to "Tel Quel": Text and Theory.* Detroit: Wayne State University Press, 1974, pp. 19–22.

Short, Robert. *Dada and Surrealism.* London: John Calmann and Cooper, Ltd., 1980.

Tzara, Tristan. "Max Ernst and his Reversible Images," in Max Ernst's *Beyond Painting.* New York: Wittenborn Schultz, Inc., 1948, pp. 186–90.

______. *Seven Dada Manifestos and Lampisteries.* Translated by Barbara Wright. London: John Calder, 1977.

Watts, Harriett. "Hans Arp and the Principle of Constellation," in *Arp 1886–1966.* Cambridge: Cambridge University Press, 1986, pp. 112–21.

14

Celebrating Intimacy

C. M. Judge

C. M. Judge explores the importance of tactility and its role in collage. In particular, she discusses various aspects of tactility and intimacy in Kurt Schwitters's "Merz" pieces, Carolee Schneeman's body collage performance works, and Atsushi Ogata's space-sound-video collages. For Judge, collage may be seen as "essentially an intimate artform. Materials are set in space and time to either repel or caress one another; regardless of which of these are represented, the issue still remains one of attachment, of close physical proximity."

> *Every physical form, every living form, every pattern of feeling or thought has its own unique identity, its boundaries, extension and its wider context; it contains or is contained by another pattern; it follows or is followed by another pattern. The unique identity, discrete shape, and nature of a space-occupying substance are shaped by the boundary that separates it from and connects it to the space outside. An organic form lives and grows only through its intricate transactions with its environment. An optical event becomes a visually perceived figure only when seen against its ground. The quality, feeling, and meaning of a sound is cast in the matrix of the physical processes that generated it; it is not independent of its surrounding silence or the other sounds that frame it. In the same way the physical, biological, or moral individuality of man is the function of his active relationship with the physical and social environment.*
>
> Gyorgy Kepes, *Arts of the Environment*

A Collection of Sensations

Tactility is not easy to write about—descriptions made of words seem initially only to confuse the obvious and direct partnering of self and world they seek to describe. Yet words seem to have become necessary in describing a human ''predisposition'' which many cultures, specifically those which are technologically advanced, seem intent upon stifling. Each and every moment of our lives we are involved in complex tactile interactions with our environment. We are tactile beings.

Cait, my six-year-old friend, picked a slightly premature, just barely opened dandelion from the lawn. With furrowed brows, she examined the huddled petals, carefully separating them with her thumbs. She raised the flower to her cheek, slowly stroking herself with it.

''Cathy!'' she exclaimed, ''look at this flower!''

Glancing over at her, I responded, ''It's quite beautiful.''

''No!'' she retorted, ''I said *look* at it!''

With great determination, she came over to me and tugged at my hand, pulling my shoulder and eventually my cheek down within her reach so that she could ever so gently brush the flower in a caressing motion along my face.

''See,'' she said softly.

Perhaps in a less visually oriented culture or, more precisely, a culture which is not touch deficient, as ''puritanical'' New England where Cait and I live is, she might have said, instead of ''look'' and ''see,'' words which more clearly described her experience—''feel'' and ''touch;'' words which, by their very nature, suggest and celebrate our physicality.

The flower was indeed beautiful, not only visually but tactually as well. And in a sense, without a direct physical involvement with the flower, I wasn't ''seeing'' what Caitlin felt was essential to her experience of this flower. Ernest Schachtel tells us that distance senses, sight and hearing, both phylogenetically and ontogenetically attain their full development later than the proximity senses, touch, taste, and smell. He notes that in Western society proximity senses are neglected and even tabooed. Further, he points to an issue with which Plato certainly would have found agreement: ''Both pleasure and disgust are more intimately linked with the proximity senses than with the distance senses. The pleasure which a perfume, a taste or a texture can give is a more bodily, physical one, hence more akin to sexual pleasure, than is the more sublime, aroused by sound and the least bodily of all pleasure, the beautiful.''[1] I dare say, if the intimate is beautiful, then let's free the beautiful from cerebral malnutrition and instead bathe it with our hands and adopt it with our hearts!

When I choose to brush the flower against my cheek, I am becoming involved in a direct experience—the sensation precedes the verbal interpretation. Often a tactual sensation precedes various visual perceptions, and inherently involves us in a direct participation of space if not ultimately a contemplation of space.

It seems that a collagist professes an intimacy with the world. S/he uses a method which juxtaposes different realities which combine to form an unexpected new reality. I find myself drawn to the details of creation, of life force when I experience Kurt Schwitters's *Merz,* Carolee Schneeman's body collage performance works, and Atsushi Ogata's space-sound-video collages. Through these artists' poetic articulations I am engaged and soothed (not always without pain as part of this process) simultaneously in various ways, but especially in a kinesthetic-tactile sense. In this essay, I will describe some impressions I've gathered from experiencing collage work by these artists from the particular vantage point of being an artist who admittedly believes she continues to experience the world in a profound way through the proximity sense—touch.

Perceptions of Reality through the Skin

Children seem more directly linked to their physical world and body than an adult counterpart, for a child who has not been tactually stimulated as an infant has little chance for survival.

Within the womb, we are enclosed and intimately bounded by the supporting, embracing walls of the uterus. It seems to be a comforting and reassuring experience. But with birth the experience of environment changes—we are now directly a part of a more or less open-ended space and we must learn to grow accustomed to these new and potentially radically diverse variations of our environment. Ashley Montagu describes the experience:

> The uterogestate fetus, embraced, supported, and rocked within the amniotic environment; as exterogestate requires the continued support of his mother, to be held and rocked in her arms, and in close contact with her body . . . he needs to be enclosed in his mother's arms, embraced in contact with her warm skin. The infant needs to learn, on the firm foundation of closeness, what closeness, proximity, distance and openness mean. In short, he needs to learn the greater meaning and manner of accommodating himself to a greater variety and complexity of spatial relationships—all of which is closely bound up with experiences of tactility, principally in relation to the mother's body.[2]

Our senses develop in a definite sequence: tactile, auditory, and visual. At the onset of adolescence, the order of precedence becomes reversed: visual, auditory and tactile. Montagu continues to tell us of eminent anthropologist Alfred Kroeber's observation:

> We all touch first, learn to see later, and in learning erect a nearby visual world on a tactile base, giving a double quality to all perceptions of objects, first within immediate reach, and later within ultimate or potential reach. All children and many adults, want to handle a new sight. The two senses of course are disparate: they operate through different receptors. But what is seen and touched is always made part of ourselves more intensely and more meaningfully than what is only seen. And so in art representation the representative picture we *only* see but cannot, in imagination, touch, does not carry the same attraction and concentration of interest as the one we can imaginatively, handle and touch as well as see clearly.[3]

Kurt Schwitters offers us part of this dynamic, for example, when he directs us to partake of his *Merz* collage work. Schwitters's process is a hands-on activity. He describes his artistic concerns as follows: "When I adjust materials of different kinds to one another, I have taken a step in advance of mere painting, for in addition to playing off color against color, line against line, form against form, etc., I play off material against material, for example wood against sackcloth."[4] It is the impulse to adjust materials in a particular kind of relationship to one another which seems to be at the heart of the experience of his intimately-scaled collage work (most works are no larger than a postcard). The implications of positioning specific kinds of matter in close physical proximity to one another suggests that collage is essentially an intimate artform. Materials are set in space and time to either repel or caress one another; regardless of which of these are represented, the issue still remains one of attachment, of close physical proximity.

The hand is involved most directly in every phase of production, from gathering material from the city sidewalks to carefully layering and gluing these varied materials together into a single panel, as did Schwitters. In the same way as Schwitters used his hands in his collage work, he used his voice in a variety of vocal performances given in Germany during his younger years. Moholy-Nagy referred to these as "verbal collages."[5] One such performance revolved around the pronunciation of the letter *W* with varying inflections and volume levels. This performance was a "throat-on" experience as opposed to a "hands-on" experience, lending to the experience the same kind of textured immediacy as the visual work.

Body Attachment—Textures of Experience

In various performances during the sixties, Schneeman's nude body and voice were collaged with paper, plastic, pigment, snakes, sausages, chicken carcasses, light projections, and other human bodies. Her body was used as an expressive vehicle in part because of her belief that "the life of the body is more variously expressive than a sex-negative society can admit." Although Schneeman's performance work was closely tied to the politics and culture of the sixties and it is difficult to sift out and sort political issues from strictly body experience issues, it seems that Schneeman has been an advocate of tactility in a unique way—as audience members at her performances became aware not only of the cultural taboos of the body she was trying to eradicate by way of establishing a new feminine mythology, but also of a clearly intimate view of our own physicality pushed to a limit of kinesthetic-tactual release. Her need to establish, as Lucy Lippard says, "a primitive unselfconsciousness about the body,"[6] allowed her to be direct enough in interpretation of her natural body empathies to shock an otherwise understimulated audience by introducing a collage of enticing material which challenged all of the human sensorium. For example, in her performance piece "Eye Body," Schneeman appeared nude with live snakes crawling on her torso. She was surrounded by plastic sheeting and various other found materials which emphasized her fleshiness. The snake-body juxtaposition in part was symbolic of her dedication to the myths of goddesses and serpents (symbols of rebirth and fertility, healing and water). Perhaps most important in this observation is the idea that Schneeman's work addressed all of the human senses at once, and geared toward expressing full body tactility certainly tabooed in the public forum, tactility we reserve for infants only. It has been noted that Schneeman's work was largely ignored by the "high art world," and scorned by many who disapproved of these works as unnecessarily "vulgar."[7]

In Schneeman's work of the sixties, I am both enticed and repulsed by her body collage images, I am equally enticed tactually, but more graciously reintroduced to nature by the cross-cultural sound-space-video collages of Atsushi Ogata. Ogata, currently a fellow at the Center for Advanced Visual Studies at M.I.T., creates meditative video collages which rely heavily on compositional tactility. By compositional tactility, I mean a composition which creates an intimate spatial relationship between viewer and subject matter, suggesting a reciprocal and nurturing harmony of organic and manmade matter. Atsushi describes his experience of fish, water, insect, and human in this account of his inspiration for the video collage, *semi no uta,* meaning "cicada songs":

> It was a hot summer day. All I heard were the cicadas singing. I noticed a carp resting still in the water. The water was still. I walked further and saw a few carps lying on their side attempting to breathe as they jerked their bodies out of the water. The drains had been clogged from rain the night before. As we unclogged the drains, we carried the carps in buckets to the other side of the pond where fresh water was coming out. Light reflected off the surface of the water creating shapes. The carps began to move. First slowly, then faster. As they swam, they created ripples. Concentric circles moving away from their body. Expanding and eventually disappearing. The ripples became light. Lines of light full of energy. The light danced on the shoji screens. The light danced on the tea-colored walls.[8]

The video collage becomes tactile in the sense that the viewer becomes empathetically locked into the natural rhythms, whether they be actual body rhythms, such as a fish swimming through water, or implied rhythms, such as an interlocking grouping of stones. Images of water in its various rippling manifestations are intercut as a large golden carp gently glides through the water, beneath patterns of light. The fish guides its body through the water, cutting a new direction of movement from the slightest motion of its tailfin. The audio, an intermittent high-pitched tone coupled with low, undulating, bubbling water sounds, creates an otherworldly spatial suggestion. It is the movement of the fish in complete harmony with its aquatic environment which strikes a familiar note with my own kinesthetic awareness. Water seems to caress water as images are intercut, fading in and out from a pure white ground of unoccupied space—"unoccupied" visually, yet I am there imaginatively waiting for the next caressing ripple of water to roll off my eyes—waiting, suspended in water (for me in time and motion) just like the carp.

Water imagery in this case, rather than carrying the additional weight of a symbolic meaning as in Schneeman's work, assumes a most directly tactual significance. The water imagery is used to unleash the viewer from the confines of his or her body denial into the freer realm of body affirmation through tactile suggestion. We are contained within this tactility, supported by multiple images, free to experience them all. One remembers womb space, the aquatic sack of complete nurturing space and motion.

The footage for the piece was shot in a Japanese garden, where zenlike experiences are fostered. Ogata, having spent half of his life in Tokyo and half in the States, bouncing back and fourth between the extremely diverse cultures, finds found images from nature, whether from the East or West, to be most satisfying in his work. For Ogata, beauty is an ephemeral concern, something experienced during international air travel, and is necessarily something he carries within himself, rhythms within his own sensibilities—inherently intimate.

Tactility helps us to contain ourselves. The collage process, through the suggestive force of its tactual, multitextured, multilayered, immediate experiential nature, nurtures and helps us to reintegrate ourselves with our worlds.

Gaston Bachelard, in his *Poetics of Space* tells us that "it would seem, then, through their 'immensity' that these two kinds of space—the space of intimacy and world space—blend. When human solitude deepens, the two immensities touch and become identical."[9]

As the tear distances from its port of origin,
a stone cooked in sunlight by day
frozen by starlight
at night
is cuddled by earth
while space is tickled by whispers of air around its belly
pressed against
a saline drop
which reflects a quick,
blue shiver of
sky

C. M. Judge

Notes

1. Ashley Montagu, *Touching: The Human Significance of Skin* (New York and London: Columbia University Press, 1971), pp. 221–22.
2. Ibid., pp. 236–37.
3. Ibid.
4. Harriet Janis, *Collage, Personalities, Concepts, Techniques* (Philadelphia: Chilton Book Company, 1967), p. 61.
5. Ibid., p. 64.
6. Lucy Lippard, *Overlay* (New York: Pantheon Books, 1983), pp. 66–67.
7. Art-talk meeting, Cambridge, Mass., January 1988.
8. Atsushi Ogata. Personal statement, 1988.
9. Gaston Bachelard, *Poetics of Space* (Boston: Beacon Press, 1958), p. 203.

15

Femmage

Miriam Schapiro

Miriam Schapiro calls out attention to the origins, development, and implications of Femmage, and its important contribution to twentieth-century art. Schapiro points to the significance of ''women's culture,'' and its integral part in Femmage, and notes the work of artists such as Betye Saar, Faith Ringgold, Marybeth Edelson, and Harmony Hammond. Schapiro also clearly elucidates the expanded role of Femmage as we enter the nineties—its ''coming to mean any deep concern with women's issues, values, and any ideas relating to gender, language, and media as they illuminate who women are and how they can redefine themselves in the light of deconstructing old mores, customs, style, and patriarchal meaning.''

In the winter of 1978, just ten years ago, Melissa Meyer and I belonged to a collective of women who produce a magazine called *Heresies* (a feminist publication on art and politics). As artists, we wished to contribute to the issue called *Women's Traditional Arts: The Politics of Aesthetics.* We wrote our article and called it ''WASTE NOT WANT NOT: An Inquiry into What Women Saved and Assembled—FEMMAGE.''

The article was a labor of love which affected the very way we worked. As time went on, Melissa, who had created some lovely collages in her youth, moved on to make her paintings, and I continued with the idea of attaching fabric to the surface of my paintings. I was propelled in this direction by my initial discovery of the word Femmage, which was lodged in my imagination and which I extracted for our article. Melissa was happy with it and we used it in our title.

Since that time, I have heard from countless women who appreciated the Femmage concept and described themselves as Femmagists. They hold exhibitions in various parts of the country and the word has come to fill a void in the language. What I learned about inventing it is that all one needs for change is a deep commitment to an idea for which no word exists.

Collage, another word invented in the twentieth century, is known to all interested in modern art. Following are some definitions:

COLLAGE: Pictures assembled from assorted materials. "Coller," a French verb meaning pasting, sticking, gluing as in application of wallpaper.

ASSEMBLAGE: A collection of things, often combined in the round. A specific technical procedure and form used in the literary and musical— as well as the plastic— arts, but also a complex of attitudes and ideas . . . . [C]ollage and related modes of construction manifest a predisposition that is characteristically modern.[1]

DECOUPAGE: (literally "cutting") A mode of decorating painted furniture with cutouts of flowers, fruit, etc. Also, the art of decorating surfaces with applied paper cutouts.

PHOTOMONTAGE: The method of making a composite picture by bringing photographs together in a single composition and arranging them, often by superimposing one part on another, so that they form a blended whole.

FEMMAGE: Takes its clues from all of the above with one difference. Femmage is many things. It is work by women of history who sewed, pieced, hooked, cut, appliquéd, quilted, tatted, wrote, painted, and combined materials using traditional women's techniques to achieve their art-activities (also engaged in by men but assigned in history to women). Femmage is also practiced by contemporary women who, like their ancestors, are clear about their womanly life and how it shapes their view of the world. Such artists, like Betye Saar, Mimi Smith, Harmony Hammond, Faith Ringgold, Marybeth Edelson, and I, were known to reshape artifacts from women's culture and give them new voice. As we move into the nineties, Femmage is also coming to mean any deep concern with women's issues, values, and any ideas relating to gender, language, and media as they illuminate who women are and how they can redefine themselves in the light of deconstructing old mores, customs, style, and patriarchal meaning. Jenny Holzer, Barbara Kruger, and Ida Applebroog are three artists whose work follows this direction.

Women's culture is the framework for Femmage. In the seventies a new reading was given to utilitarian works whose content had never been seriously considered. The domination of men in the recitation of history (the literature on which we raise our children) clearly elevates art over craft. This is a serious impediment to our cognitive and sensual appreciation of art produced by women. It also inspires the hieratic scale which finds women failing in the ways they think about making art and the ways they make it. Jehanne H. Teilhet in her article in the same issue of *Heresies* ("The Equivocal Role of Women Artists in Non-Literate Cultures") tells us that in the Marquesas a serving bowl not made by a male artist with a deep knowledge of magic and ritual would be just a bowl, because it had not been properly initiated into the universe. This is another way of saying that it is the male who makes the important art objects, since it is he who is privileged to do so. In many preliterate societies, men alone are permitted to make anthropomorphic and zoomorphic forms. Women are rarely allowed to make objects requiring the knowledge of ritual process or the skill of manipulating certain tools. For centuries it has been the male artist who is responsible for significant form and if the description of significant form as it makes its way into modern culture is described by the male archivists, it is not surprising to find out that women as artists are nowhere to be found, and if they *are* discovered, then it is easy to say of them that they do not measure up to patriarchal standards.

In preparation for our article, we read books by Herta Wescher, William Seitz, and Harriet Janis and Rudi Blesh and discovered the material we were looking for in their introductions and in the notes in the backs of their books. Janis and Blesh put it succinctly:

> Collage was once only the simple pleasant folk art or pastime of cutting and pasting bits of paper into pictures or ornamental designs. It was no concern of serious artists. . . . Its origins began so many centuries ago . . . . It is only with this century and the advent of modern art that this quondam delight of school girl and housewife came to the attention of serious artists grappling with revolutionary ideas.[2]

It is in fact the "school girl" and the "housewife" we must look at more carefully to understand the aesthetics of our ancestors and their processes. William Seitz includes this information in his work on assemblage: "Valentines, postcards and folk art of various kinds incorporating pasted elements as well as pictures and objects made of butterfly wings, feathers, shells, etc., were common much earlier. Indeed various stamped letters, passports and official documents can be looked at as a form of unintentional collage."[3]

As part of the revisionist view of history, women's culture is being redressed. Trivialization of women's art no longer serves a patronizing cause. The leftovers of history are under consideration. Art historians are finding aesthetic and technical contributions by women artist-makers and see the authenticity, energy and passion of the work. For example, when it becomes possible to appreciate a sewn object like a quilt because it employs thirty stitches to the inch and uses color which by all standards

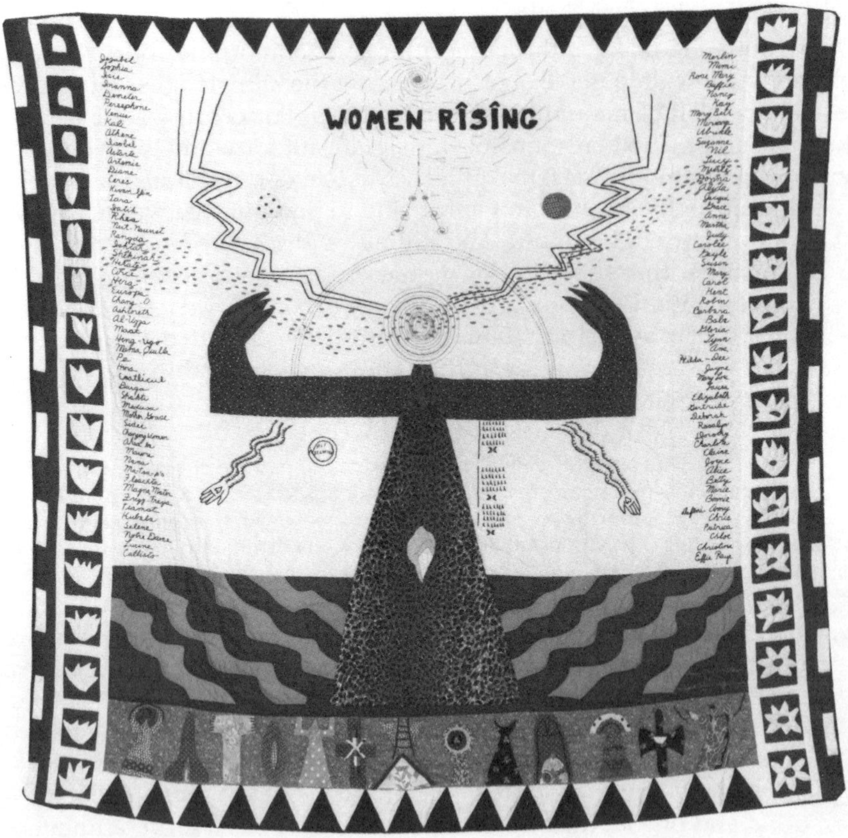

Figure 15.1. Mary Beth Edelson and Marie Ingalls, *Women Rising,* 1977
Cotton, 85″ × 85″.

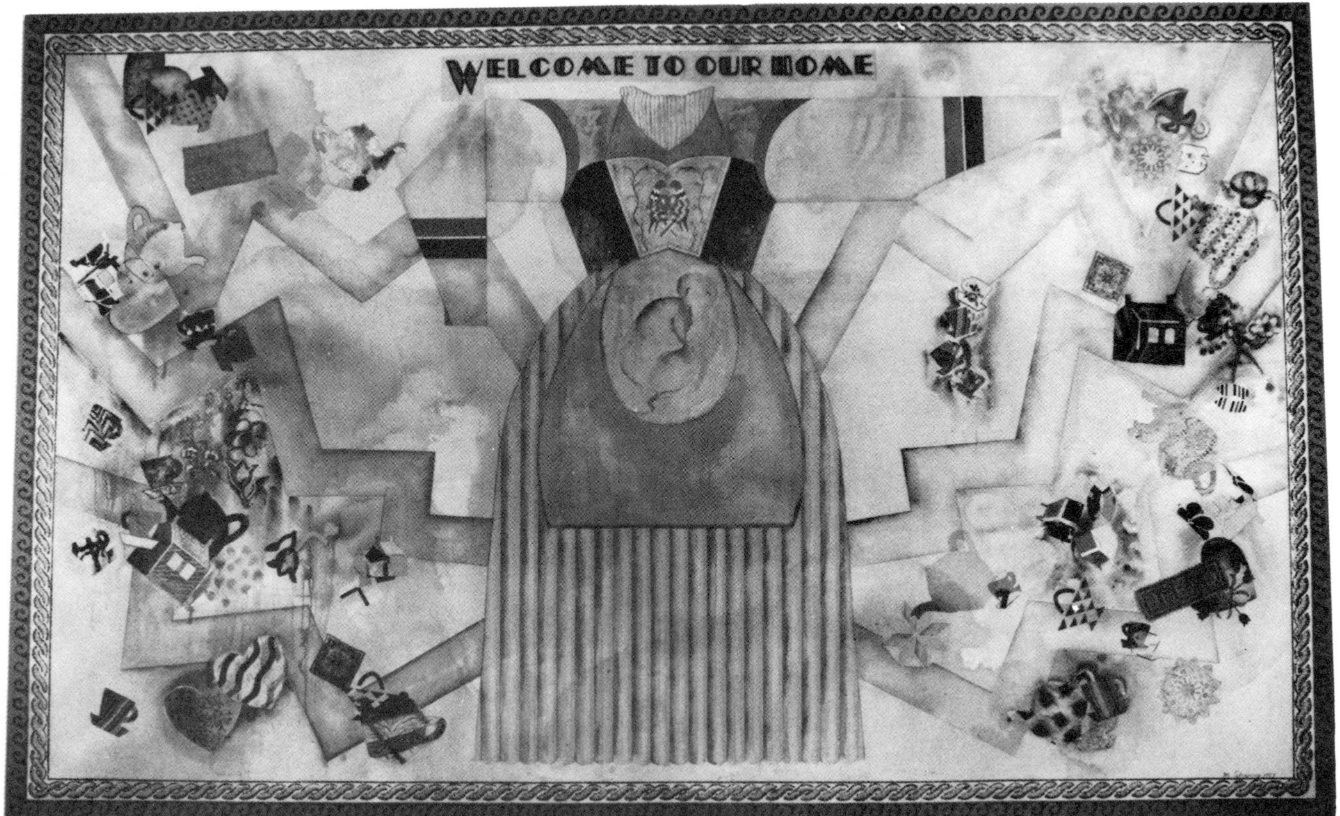

Figure 15.2. Miriam Schapiro, *Welcome to Our Home,* 1983
Fabric on canvas, 90″ × 144″.
(Courtesy Bernice Steinbaum Gallery)

Figure 15.3. Harmony Hammond, *Floor Piece VI,* 1973
Fabric, acrylic, 5′ diameter.
(Photo by eeva-inkeri)

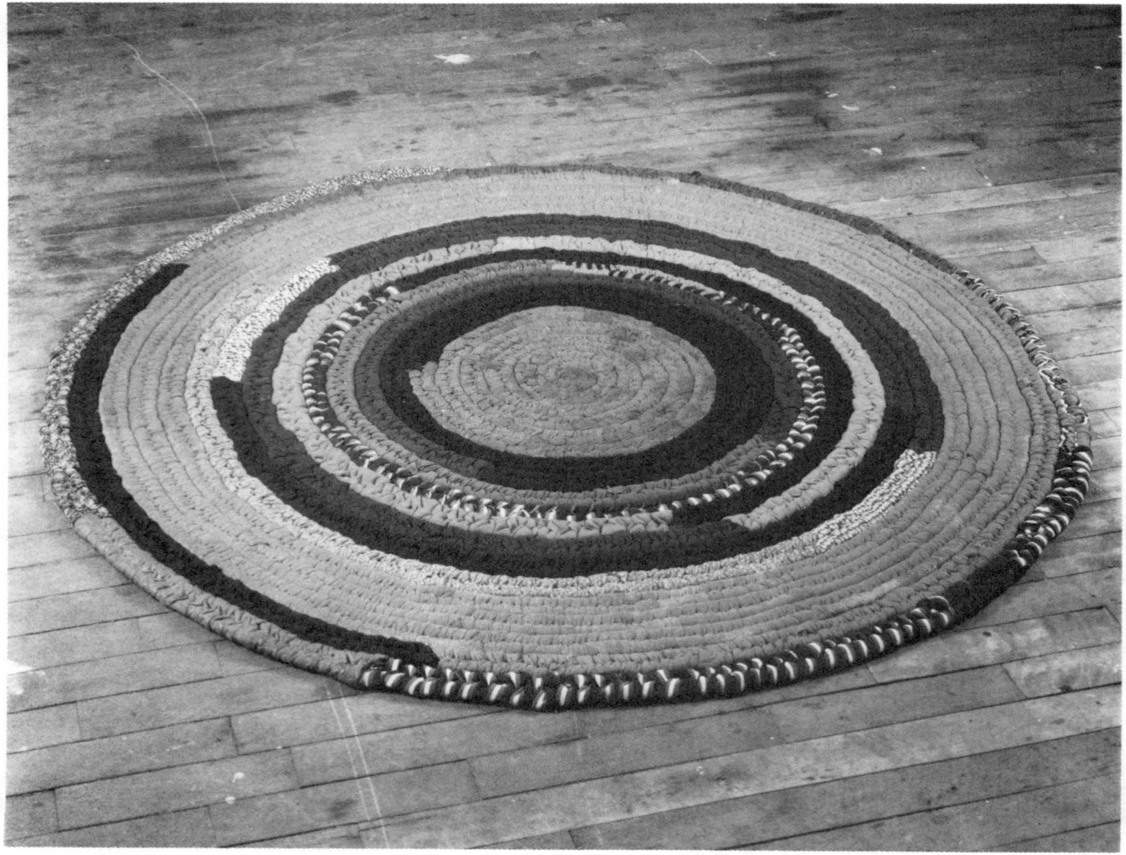

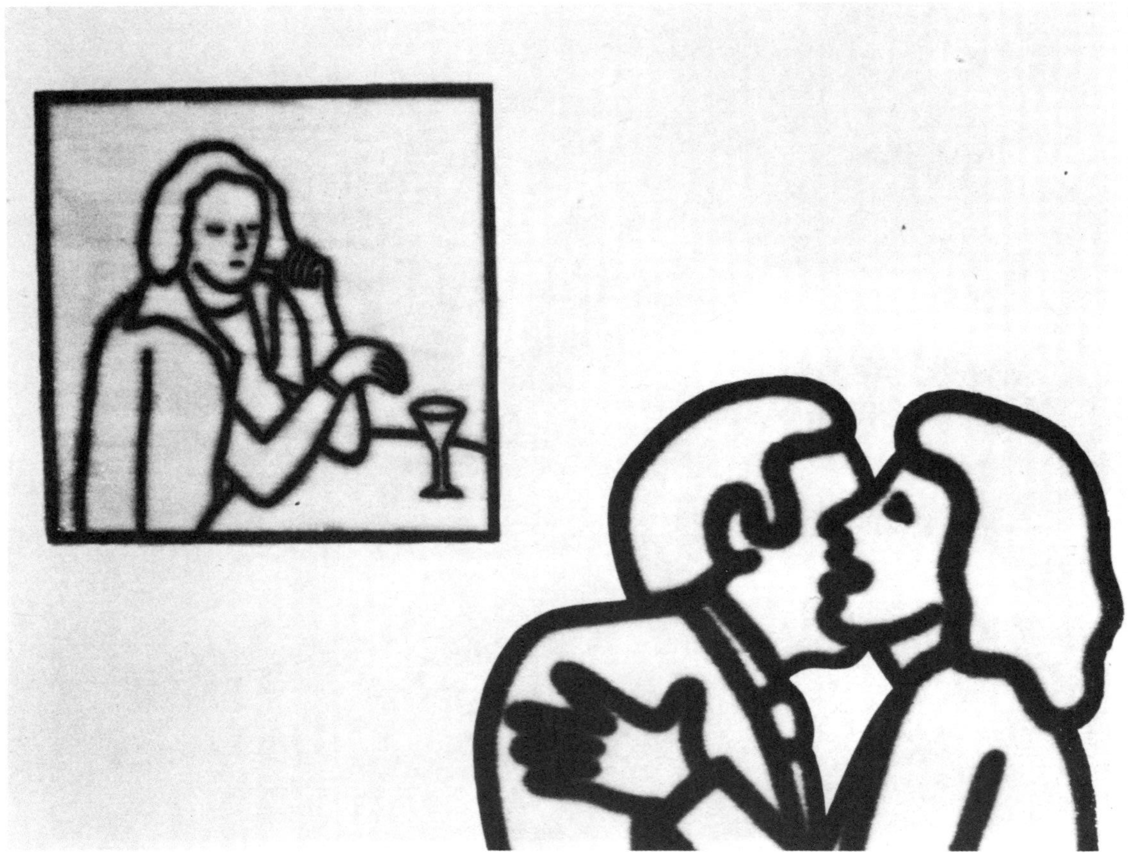

Figure 15.4. Ida Applebroog, *Happy Birthday to Me,* 1982
Rhoplex on canvas, 66″ × 84″.
(Photo by Jennifer Kottler; courtesy Ronald Feldman Gallery)

Figure 15.5. Anonymous, Pot Holders, ca. 1930
Crocheted cotton, dress (*left*), 9½″ × 7″; pitcher (*right*), 5½″ × 6″.
(Photo by Noel Rowe)

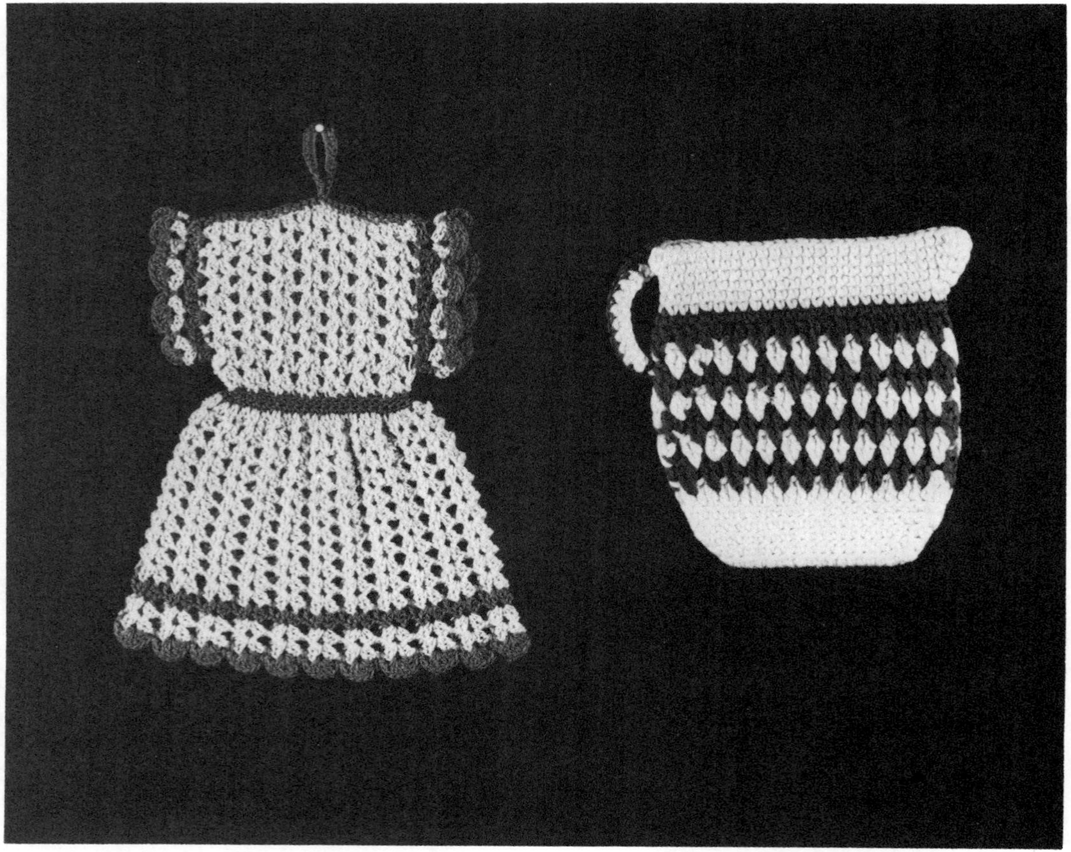

is rich and evocative, contains silhouetted forms which are skillfully drawn, and connects perfectly measured geometric units of fabric, then it will be clear that women's art invites a methodology of its own.

Cynthia Ozick tells us that a diary is a shoring-up of the ephemeral evidence that a writer (substitute artist-maker) takes up real space in the world.[4] One does not have to probe deeply to understand that she speaks of people who are fragile, who need to hold an elusive mirror to themselves to be certain they are there. Perhaps this holds true for all artists, Rembrandt and de Kooning included. In earlier America, as the people moved west, collected, saved, and combined materials represented acts of pride, desperation and necessity.

An Iroquois woman in 1775 sews five elliptical quillwork designs at the base of a black buckskin bag, quillwork borders at the top and additional moosehair embroidery at the bottom and sides.

Hannah Stockton, a New Jersey woman, dips into her scrap bag in 1830 in the tradition of waste not, want not and finds just the right pieces with which to appliqué her quilt.

In the 1860s Lady Filmer photographs the Prince of Wales and his shooting party. Later, she cuts up these photos and creates a composition of them in her album, producing the first photo-collage.[5]

In 1932 during the American Depression, a housewife selects variegated, colored mercerized cotton from her sewing box and tats a border at the edge of a plain white handkerchief purchased from the local five and dime store. With this simple embellishment, she provides us with a model of poetic behavior and a method of making more from less. Her impulse, the same as mine, is to work for beauty. She joins the nesters, the humanizers, the nurturers of civilization and is encoded with a gift for order and more—a desire for beauty—to see it—to make it. She must learn great discipline for the mastery of clear form to communicate subject and provide pictorial harmony within the functionalism of the work.

Patricia Mainardi in her essay tells us that in the decorative functional objects women made, they often spoke a secret language and bore a covert imagery. When we read these images in needlework, in paintings, in quilts, rugs, and scrapbooks, we sometimes find a cry for help, sometimes and allusion to a secret political alignment, sometimes a moving passage about the relationships between men and women. Mainardi says: "Women not only made beautiful and functional objects but expressed their own conviction on a wide variety of subjects in a language for the most part comprehensible only to other women . . . . There was more than one man of Tory persuasion who slept unknowingly under his wife's Whig Rose Quilt . . . . [W]omen named their quilts for their political belief . . . at a time when they were not allowed to vote."[6]

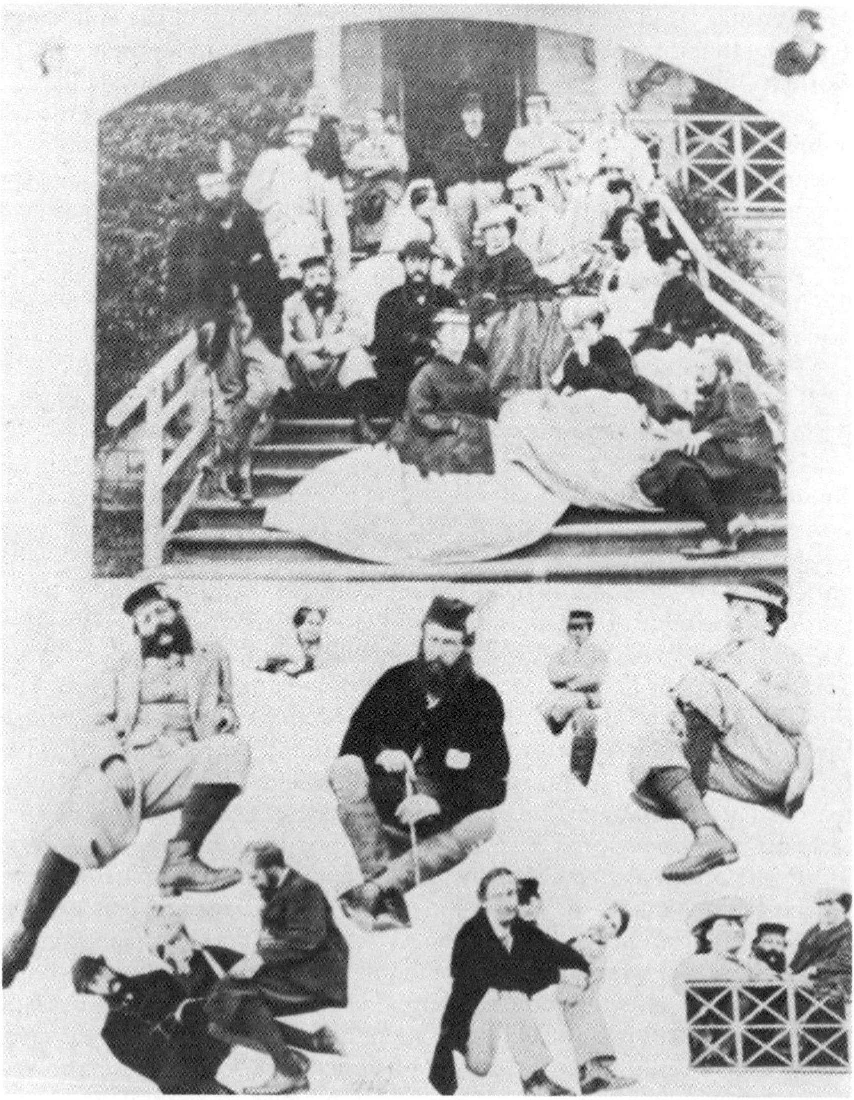

Figure 15.6. Lady Filmer, *Prince of Wales Shooting Party,* 1864
Photo-collage, $11\frac{3}{8}'' \times 9''$.

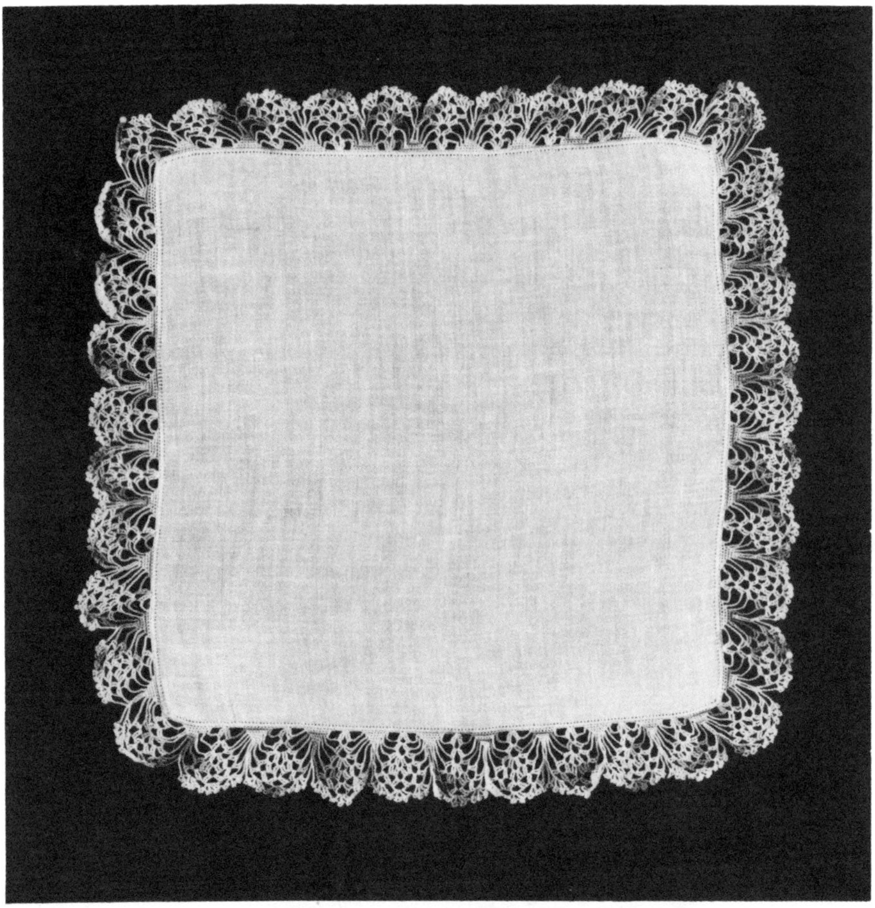

Figure 15.7. Anonymous, Handkerchief, ca. 1940
Linen with tatted embroidery thread (multicolored), 14″ × 14″.
(Photo by Noel Rowe)

Human relations received a familiar treatment in a small quilt appliquéd with chintz borders. The words ''Phoenix Factory'' appeared above the image of a man's top hat. Below the hat, the words ''Yonkers'' and ''1850'' were written above an image of a heart. Below the heart in small print was:

A HEART I SEND THEE SQUIRE BALDWINE
REJECT IT NOT, I DO IMPLORE THEE
A WARM RECEPTION MAY IT MEET
MY NAME A SECRET I MUST KEEP
OLD MAID

Femmagists interchange text and image frequently. I have made a simple etching by dipping a work already crocheted into a soft ground solution and printing the result on Arches paper. The work is called *Bread* because that is what the original work says. It is part of a series of ten such works called *Anonymous Was a Woman,* a phrase originated for us by Virginia Woolf who spoke of the loose, drifting material of life, describing how she would like to see it sorted and coalesced into a mold transparent enough to reflect the light of our life and yet aloof as a work of art.[7]

An honored and ancient way of working is called lap work. It is what it sounds like. In order to maintain an inconspicuous role in the family and for the sake of preserving the dictum which commended busy hands for keeping out of trouble and doing the Lord's work, women could sit in corners, take up the least amount of territory and let their minds run wild. A picture of Jane Austen comes to mind as she wrote her novels on the dining room table. Women, thus, did needlework, sewed on children's garments, maintained household possessions, and invented their art. A latter-day practice by contemporary women is seen in the immense subway installation of Joyce Kozloff in Wilmington, Delaware. Her entire work is built on the module of a tile which would fit in her lap. Jennifer Bartlett's *Rhapsody* (1975–76), containing 988 enameled plates, uses a 12-inch-by-12-inch 16-gauge steel unit with which to build her enormous work of art. Finally, Pat Steir has also made a large installation using a lap size module. Called *The Brueghel Series (A Vanitas of Style) 1982–1984,* it is polychromed, an eight-by-eight-foot grid, each panel 27″×22″.

The gridding is familiar in quiltmaking and appeared as newly energized after 1970 when liberated women artists like Michele Stuart, myself, Susie Shei, Yvonne Porcella, and Virginia Jacobs availed ourselves of old patterns and old techniques to be used as a basis for freshly vitalized statements about art and life.

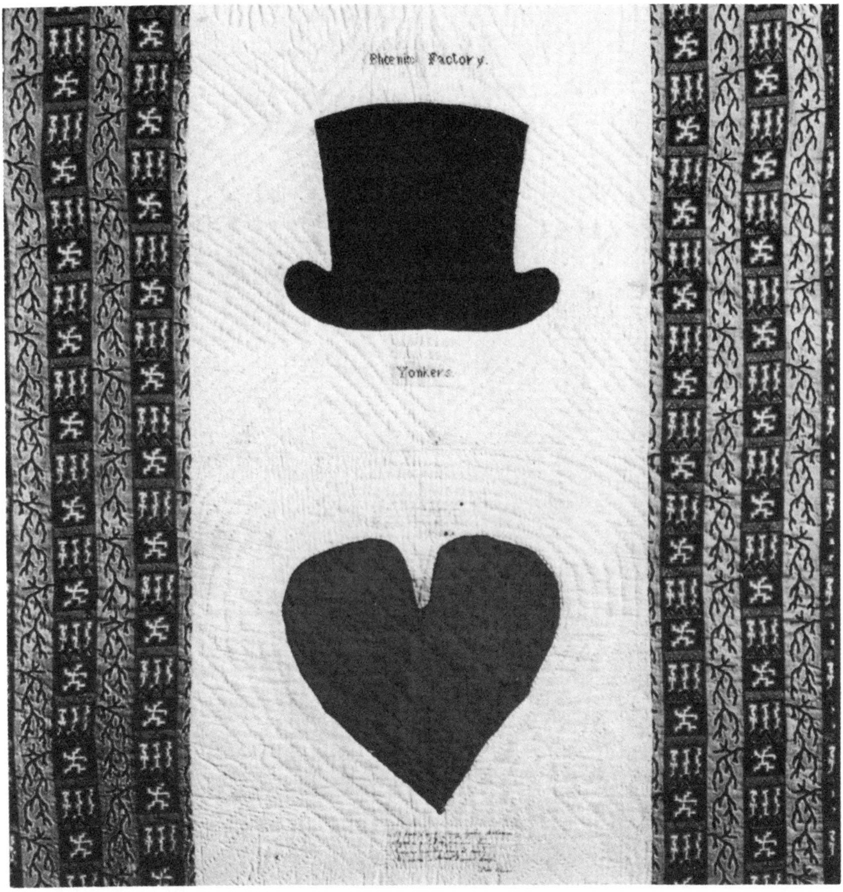

Figure 15.8. Anonymous, Appliqué Crib Quilt, 1850
Cotton, 34½″ × 32½″.

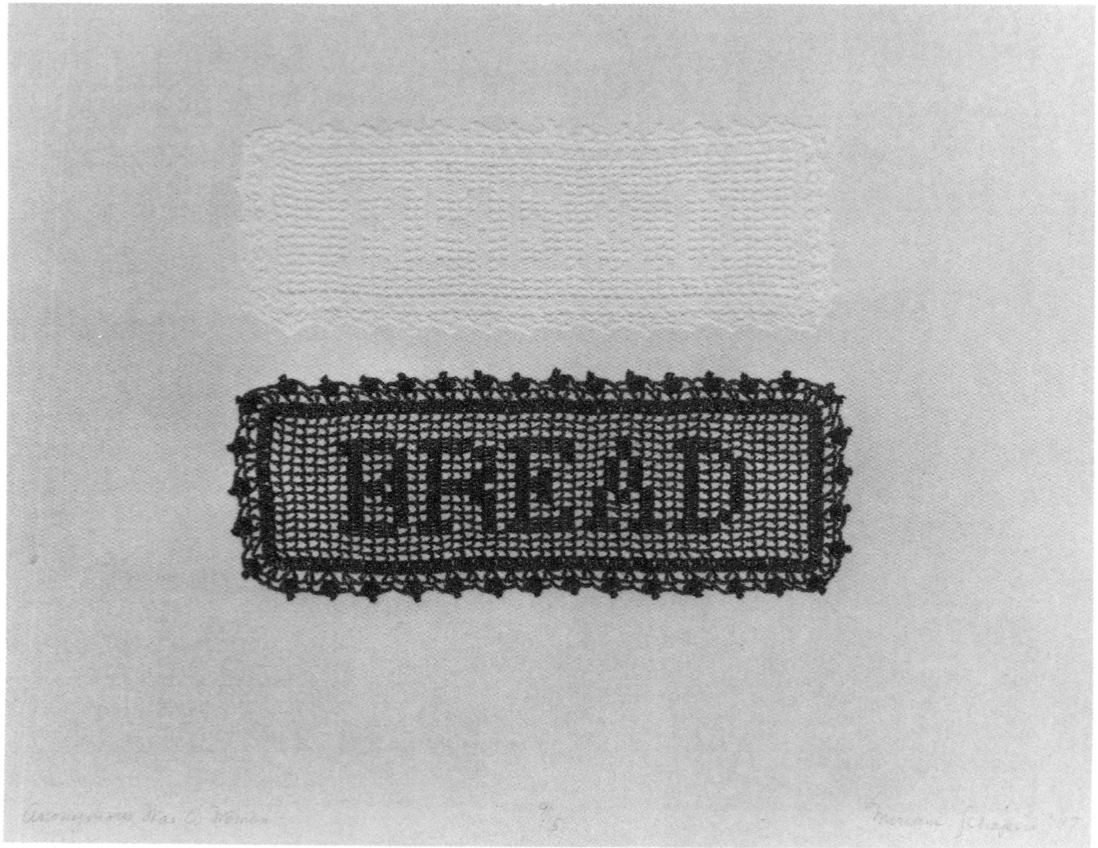

Figure 15.9. Miriam Schapiro, *Anonymous Was a Woman*, 1977
Etching, 18″ × 24″.
(Photo by James Dee; courtesy Bernice Steinbaum Gallery)

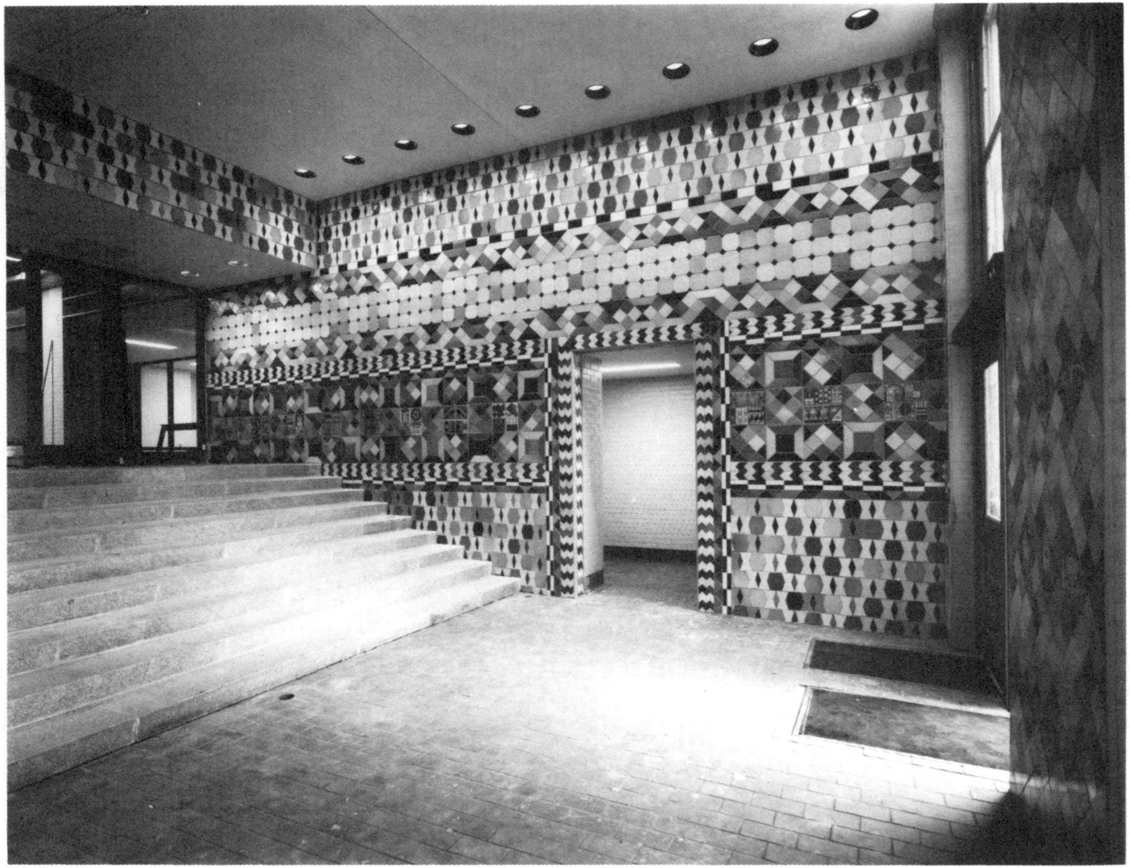

Figure 15.10. Joyce Kozloff, Vestibule, Wilmington, Delaware, Train Station, 1984
Hand painted, glazed ceramic tiles, 30′ × 20′ × 15′.
(Photo by eeva-inkeri; courtesy Barbara Gladstone Gallery)

Figure 15.11. Stephanie Brody Lederman, *He Got Her Started*, 1980
Acrylic, glitter, graphite, collage, 15″ × 33″.
(Photo by Anne Turyn)

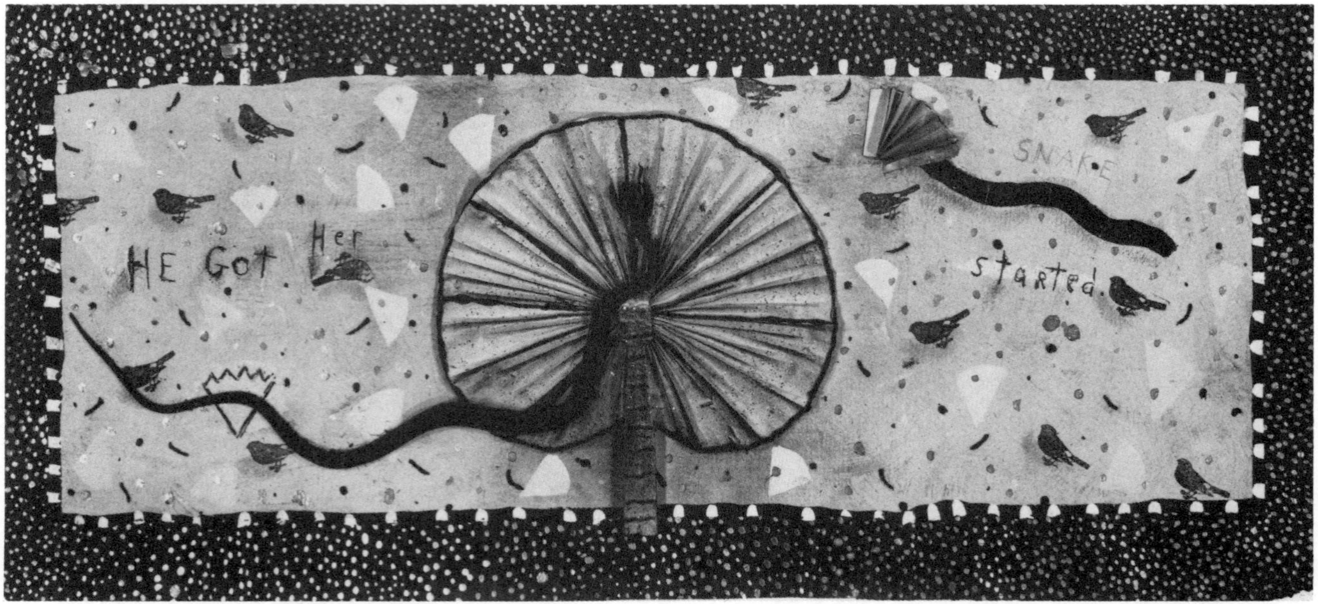

I have spoken of the exclusion of women artists from mainstream. What is mainstream? It is the codification of ideas for the illumination of history and the teaching of the young. Very little is known about how women artists think and how they function. For example, time is a conscious factor in the way women structure their art, particularly if they are at the same time responsible for the domestic engineering of a home and the nurturing of children. The family, as it is seen on the level of survival (life over death), can never take second place to aesthetic involvement. Recently, my friend told her father that she was contemplating marriage. Her training as an artist had already put her on an immutable course. He, a religious man, asked her, "Which will come first, your art or your husband?" She, for all her independence, living at the end of the twentieth century, was shocked to hear his archaic interpretation of the old theme.

If my friend's new husband calls to her for succor and love, if their children are in need, how precious will her special time be when she is alone with her thoughts and her creative impulse? Such momentary holidays cannot be seen except in contrast to the real space Cynthia Ozick mentions—the space of duty, the time of belonging to others. Guilt is the overriding demon of creative women who must steal time and space from others in order to work. No one as yet has recorded the extent to which women's artistic inhibitions arise out of the unbearable conflict between love, duty, and devotion on one hand and the glorious selfishness, the desire to reorder the world in the name of art, on the other.

The original femmagists:
saved, collected and recycled materials
made work with a woman-life context
often made subversive art
worked for an audience of intimates
celebrated private or public events in their work
combined image and text
used silhouetted forms
used narrative with recognizable images
created patterns with abstract geometric and floral forms
used photographs and printed matter
made functional and aesthetic combinations

Because of our respect for history from a woman's point of view, because of our desire to conserve such a past, women's work often shows

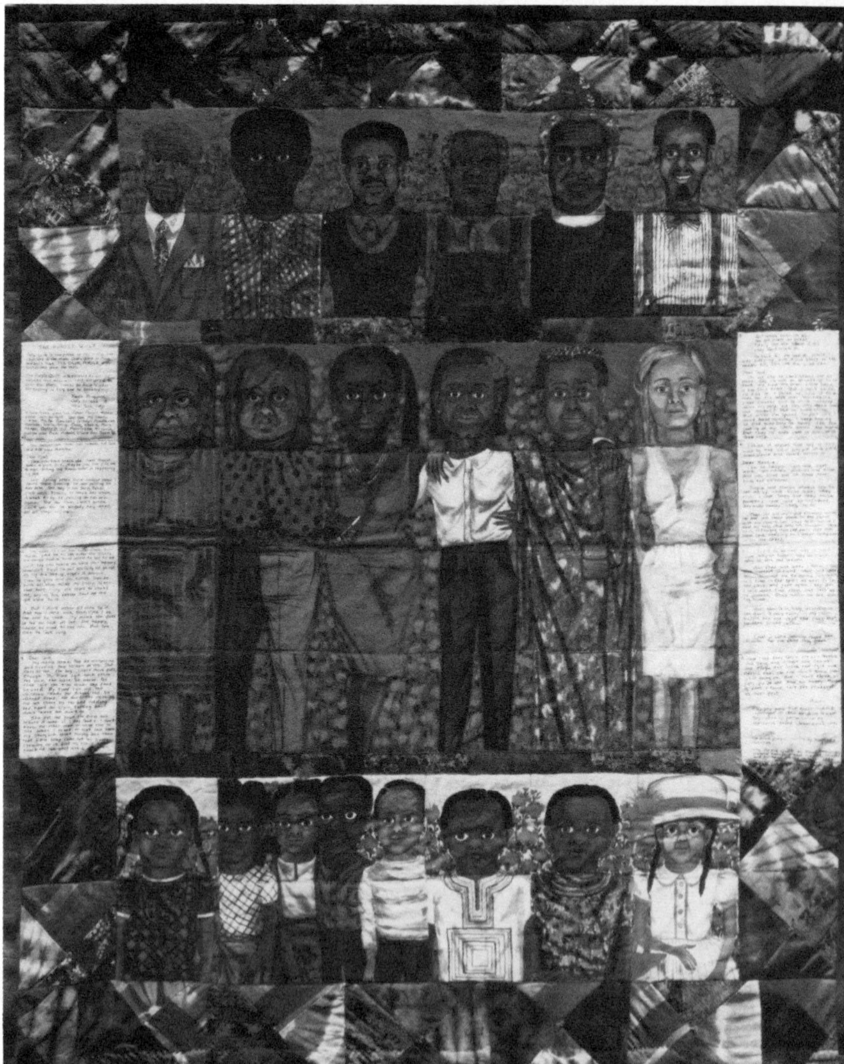

Figure 15.12. Faith Ringgold, *The Color Purple,* 1986
Acrylic on canvas, printed and pieced fabric,
91″ × 72″.
(Courtesy Bernice Steinbaum Gallery)

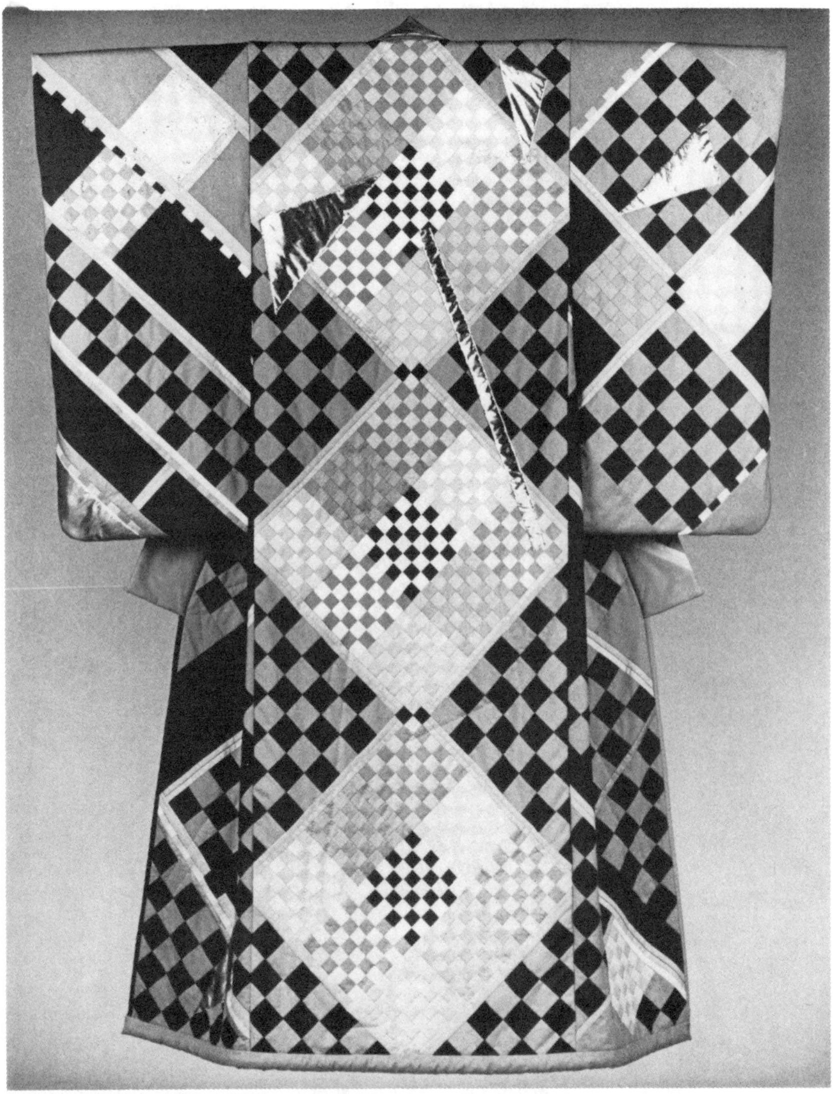

Figure 15.13. Yvonne Porcella, *When All Colors Come Dancing,* 1983
Pieced silk kimono, 72″ × 48″.
(Photo by Elaine F. Keenan)

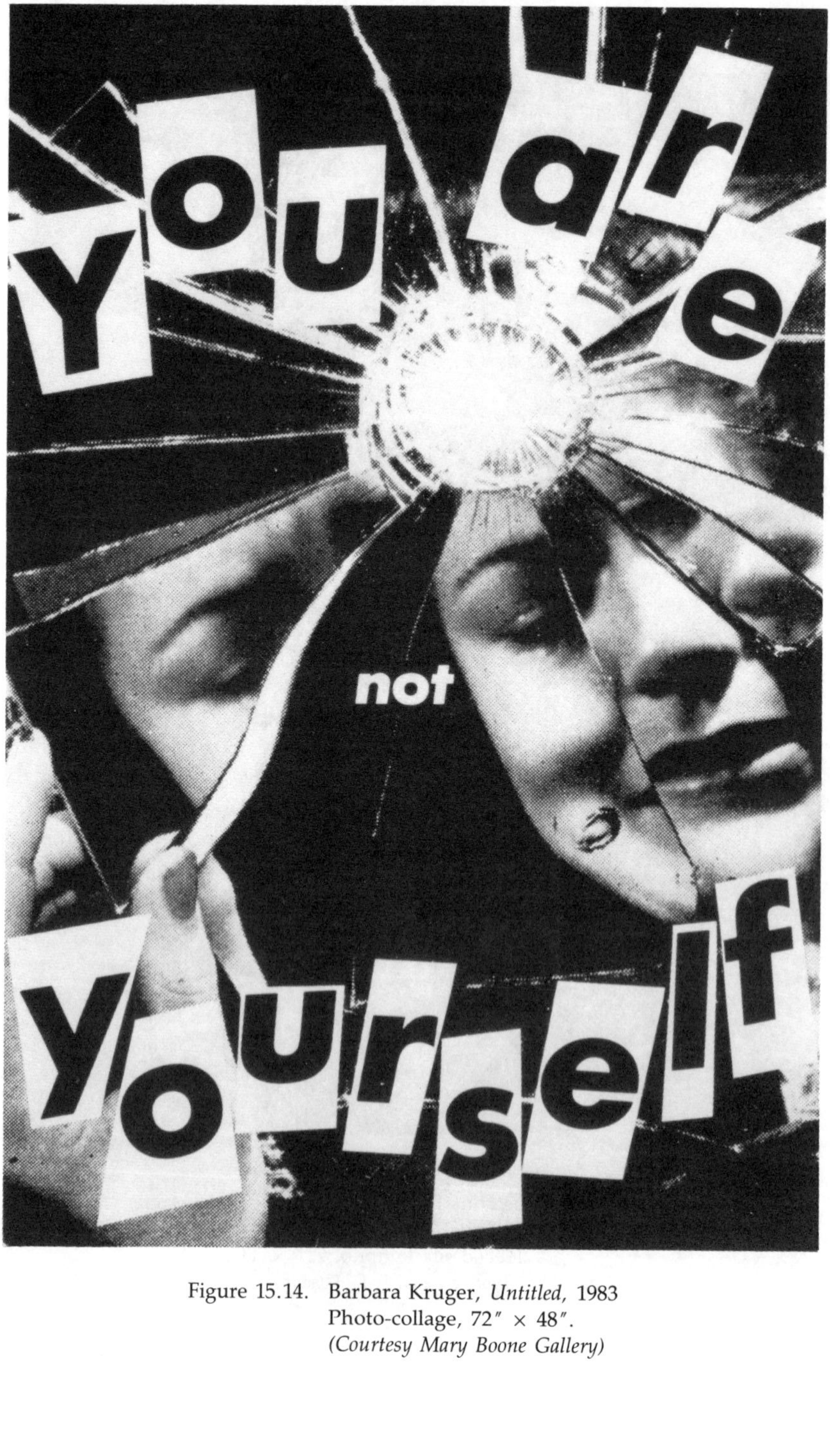

Figure 15.14. Barbara Kruger, *Untitled,* 1983
Photo-collage, 72″ × 48″.
(Courtesy Mary Boone Gallery)

us to be avowed ''sentimentalists.'' For some of us this word has lost its negative stigma. We incorporate our own form of ironic detachment, framing a view of the past (a feeling for the world of our grandmothers), recognizing its style. Our lack of fear comes from knowing the impossibility of such a style's substituting for our own. It also comes from confronting masculine power over the traditional arts of women and internalizing the politics of aesthetics. It comes from a desire to reconstruct the masculinist point of view in art (mainstream) and to produce an art of sentience which relies on female signifiers for aesthetic direction.

If we did not accept the profound dignity in the art of women, we would not have accepted Femmage as a word which opens up language to make room for specific entitlement.

Notes

1. William C. Seitz, *The Art of Assemblage,* catalogue (New York: The Museum of Modern Art, 1961), p. 10.
2. Harriet Janis and Rudi Blesh, *Collage Personalities, Concepts, Techniques* (Philadelphia/New York/London: Chilton Book Co., 1969), p. 3.
3. Seitz, p. 150, note 5.
4. Cynthia Ozick, ''The Loose Drifting Material of Life,'' *N. Y. Times Book Review* (2 October 1977).
5. *Women of Photography: An Historical Survey,* catalogue (San Francisco: San Francisco Museum of Art), 18 April–15 June, 1975.
6. Patricia Mainardi, ''Quilts: The Great American Art,'' *Feminist Art Journal* (Winter 1973): 19.
7. Virginia Woolf, quoted in *Self Explorations, Diarists in England and America,* exhibition catalogue (New York: 42nd Street Public Library), 2 May–15 September 1977.

16

Collages of the Spirit

Marjorie Agosin
Translated by Janice Molloy

The conception of collage as a collaboration between artistic creation and life itself is poignantly seen in Latin American culture. Moving far beyond the world of museums, galleries, dealers, etc., Marjorie Agosin sensitively portrays the roles of the animitas *and* arpilleras *as tools for survival of the spirit in Latin America. Agosin shows how the* animitas *and* arpilleras *are "vehicles of denunciation and resistance," as well as "therapeutic." And, as she writes, "the collage, formed from scraps of hope, is a work of art and a work of life, because it serves to bring back the missing and restore order to a fragmented reality."*

Throughout the history of popular Latin American culture, the collage has taken on different levels of significance, blurring the divisions between artistic creation and life. In Chile, the so-called cult of the *animitas* is a fascinating example of the use of collage. According to folk beliefs, *animitas* are the souls of people who died violently. Shrines are erected on the spot where the individual was killed. These shrines are scattered throughout Chile, and drivers frequently stop along the side of the road to pay tribute to the *animitas* and to ask for their protection in their travels.

The *animitas* possess the ability to perform miracles for people who pay them tribute in the form of collages. These collages are formed from various objects that are arranged around the small tomb marked by a cross. The elements of collage surrounding the *animitas* consist of personal objects, such as pieces of clothing, cigarettes, candles, coins, and family photographs. All of these items are attached to a surface of cardboard or metal, creating a mosaic of living objects.

The shrines of the *animitas* vary in form and size: some are tiny buildings that participants can enter, while others are smaller, but all have a cross and are continually surrounded by flowers. The place where an *animita* has died becomes a symbolic-mythical space occupied by the imagination and fantasy as well as by the physical artifacts that surround the tomb.[1]

The *animitas* and their cult are not associated with a formalized religion, but rather, with metaphors of life and death. In order to transcend the finality of death, the *animitas* take on magical qualities within the popular culture to establish an intimate relationship between the living and the dead.

In Chile, with the advent of the authoritarian government, the collage has taken on another type of significance, also associated with the metaphors of life and death. Since 1973, when the freely elected government of Marxist leader Salvador Allende was overthrown by a fascist junta, Chilean women have created their own collages, the *arpilleras,* where they defy death and reaffirm life.

Arpilleras are tapestries that function as texts written with scraps of material. A collage of three-dimensional figures relating to a single theme is sewn onto a burlap backing. The impact of these tapestries that speak has been so vast and powerful that women in other regions of Latin America have begun to use the same techniques to narrate the events of their daily lives.

The *arpilleras* were born as a way to communicate through an expressive, visual medium in the repressive Chile of Augusto Pinochet. The first *arpilleras* were created in 1974 by relatives of individuals who had either been detained by the government or had disappeared. This group of people decided to create tapestries as a way to express their feelings. Thus, these pieces of cloth present a vivid portrait of the country's political situation: the prisons of fear, the anguish caused by the disappearances and, more than anything, the realities of life under a military dictatorship.

The basic technique the women use to create the *arpilleras* is collage. In the context of Pinochet's Chile, this artistic element takes on a new level of ethical and moral significance. The *arpillera* combines both popular art and the culture of resistance in a single scrap of cloth.

A single *arpillera* represents the collective effort of numerous individuals and organizations. The scraps of cloth used to create the collages are obtained by chance. Different charitable organizations give rags to the Catholic church, and this material is later given to the *arpillera* workshops in the city of Santiago.

From these randomly collected scraps of material, the women create a mosaic of stories, a collage of life and death. In the workshops, although each woman begins her creation alone, she always knows she is part of a larger group. When a woman shares the theme of her *arpillera* with the other members of the workshop, the collage becomes the product of a collective consciousness, will, and experience.

Each individual fragment of an *arpillera* represents and reconstructs memories. The collage tells an intimate, individual story that later becomes the history of the entire country. One woman transcribes on the cloth the story of her son's detention through patches from the missing youth's clothing. Another woman, needing a scrap of blue cloth for the sky in her *arpillera,* cuts a piece from her own skirt.

I see the women inclined over their cloth, carefully cutting and sewing the mountains that surround Santiago and the generous Chilean sun that poeticizes the horror and desperation by creating the hope of a better future. A young woman uses pieces of her missing husband's pants in her work, as if, by incorporating her spouse's belongings in an *arpillera,* she could bring him back to life.

The *arpillera* uses physical elements and living material to destroy the artificial opposition between inanimate objects and life. The women who make *arpilleras* even use locks of their own hair in the creation of the collage. Thus, in this ritualized art, the separation between art and life dissipates, and the elaboration of the *arpillera*-collage becomes a testament to the transformational power of the human spirit.

The *arpillera* possesses an important, therapeutic quality. By presenting scenes of torture and individuals uprooted by violence in the form of carefully worked scraps of cloth, the women attempt to restore a broken and fragmented universe. The completion of an *arpillera* represents a process of rehabilitation. Despite the fact that the artists are immersed in the fragments of broken lives and the crevices of sadness, the collage permits them to reestablish a missing order through the scraps of material that recount the stories of their lives.

The workshops where the *arpilleras* are made are not alienating. We observe a group of women absorbed by the process of creating something that comes from within themselves and that expresses, through an artistic medium, a political testimonial. The *arpillera* tells the story of divided families and of a country imprisoned by the bonds of fascism.

Each *arpillera* reflects a different reality. Some of the tapestries articulate the historical and political experiences of the country, such as those that depict the discovery of mutilated corpses in a common grave, or the burning of protestors by the military forces. These events form part of Chile's collective history, and by memorializing them through cloth, the women who create *arpilleras* resist fascism and express both the horror and beauty of life in their country.

Vivid examples of the stories behind the *arpilleras* may also be seen in the verbal testimonies of the women.

Figure 16.1. Anonymous, *Soup Kitchen,* 1983
Arpillera.
(Photo by Emma Sepulveda)

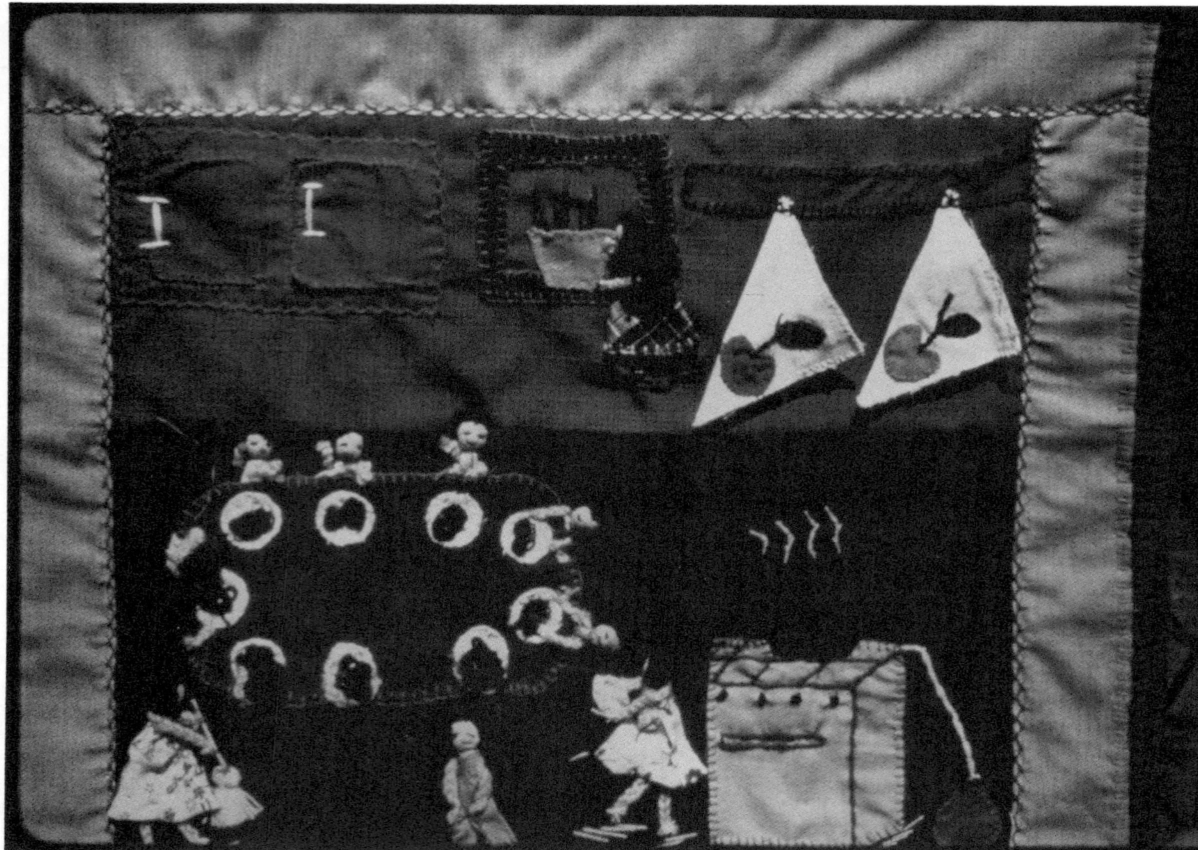

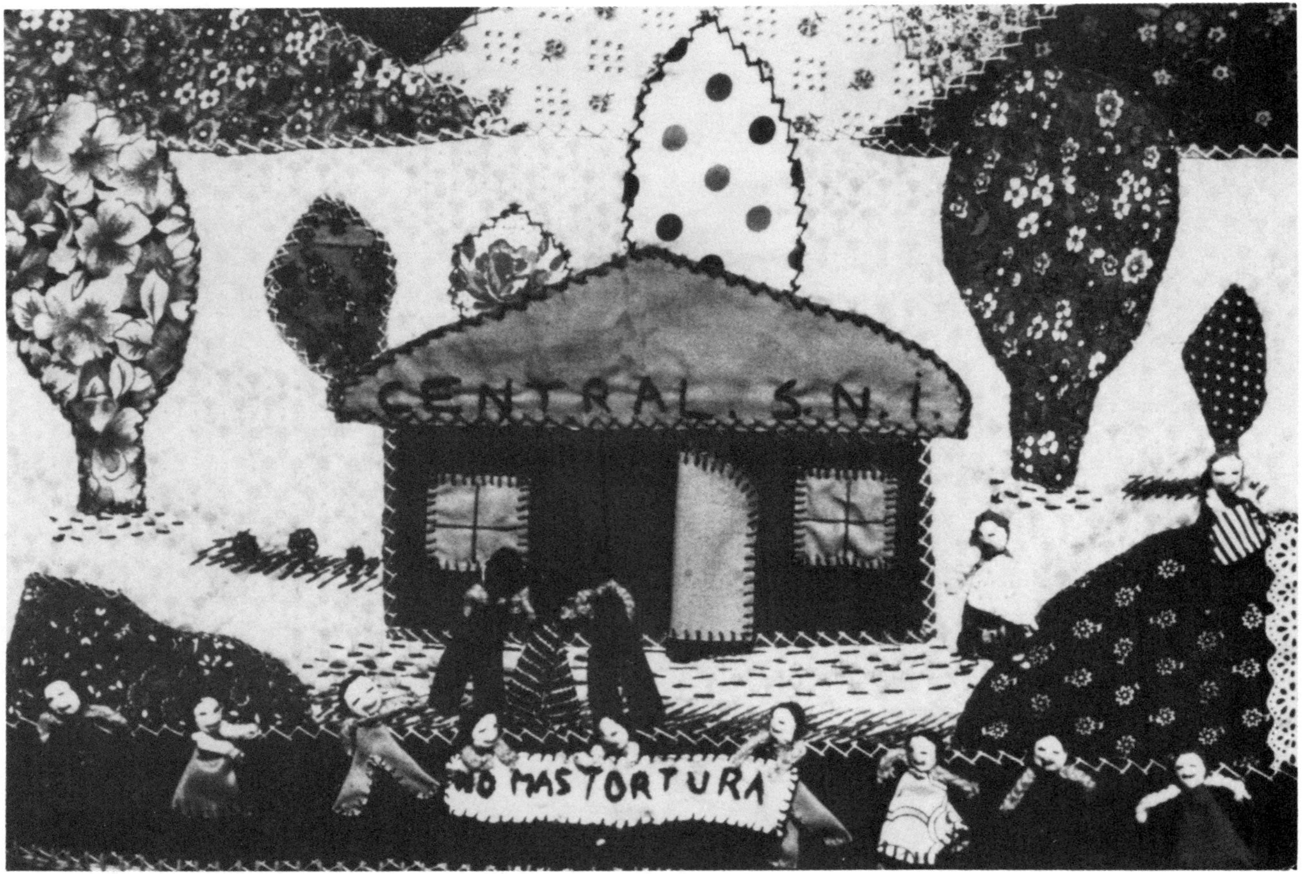

Figure 16.2. Anonymous, *No More Torture,* 1983
Arpillera.
(Photo by Emma Sepulveda)

Santiago, January 14, 1985

My story is very simple and more than that sad, I belong to the Association of Families of Detained-Disappeared and am arpillerista at the same time, when I make the arpilleras I am thinking not only of my own problem, but of all the families without distinction because of political beliefs. This work is done under the wing of the Vicarate, that also buys the work from us, that helps us to survive. The work began ten years ago, with the object of denouncing to the world what was happening in Chile, regarding the disappearance of thousands of Chileans beginning from the 11th of September, 1973. The suffering and anguish for my daughter, daughter-in-law and little grandchildren and myself is very great, but still I don't lose hopes of seeing my son alive again. In addition our association has a folklore group and from time to time we have a get-together in the Association where in spite of the sadness, we enjoy ourselves and have a good time.

Well, there's a lot to tell but I don't find the words to tell it, in addition, here I enclose a short biography of my son not very complete, because there is a tremendous lot to tell about my beloved son. I beg you to denounce what has happened and to ask in the name of our family especially that my son Agustin A. Mártinez Meza, be returned alive from the tyranny of the dictator.

Through you we send greetings to all people interested in our problem and especially to You.

Affectionately, a mother.[2]

Santiago de Chile 28 February, 1985

I received your letter dated the 14th of this month, and a few days later a card, I haven't answered you because I wasn't in Santiago, I went with my husband on a little vacation to the South, so that when I got back I had your letter, so I went to work immediately, it was a bit hard for me to get inspired because I came back too relaxed from the trip, to be with people there is as though they lived in another world, things don't happen to them such as we in the Capitol see and live every day.

At the same time I send this letter, I will send the order so hoping you will like it, as I told you earlier in every one of my works I put my life because I make my arpilleras thinking about all the immense painful problem here, in every pore of my being, and it hurts me every day the same way, it's not true that one forgets with time, perhaps when things happen in a natural way, but not the way it happened with my son Jorge. I could talk so much about this but I won't any more because I don't want to infect you with my sadness.

That's very good what you tell me about the article on the Association, I do hope you can send it, they would thank you many times over because we receive that type of material very rarely.

As for the orders in the future I believe it would be possible in general to send them from the workshop but we stumble against the problem that there are people in great need and they want to have their money immediately, it would be good if we could find a way to do it.

Thank you for considering me your friend, I hope you realize it is the same from my side.

With a big and affectionate embrace.[3]

TO MY SONS, IN EXILE

The echo of your voices come to me
they are calling me
painful knowing they are alone
not being able to accompany them
painful knowing them sad, without being able to console them
I only ask that they understand
the purpose of my intense battle
which is that hope will bring them back
so I can embrace them.

September, 1976[4]

FOR YOU

If you don't return I won't stay here waiting for you
I will wander the roads in search of you
to find you in every companion
that carries your banner through the world
If you don't return I won't stop looking for you
I will find you on the road.[5]

The women in the workshops often cannot complete certain *arpilleras* because they are overwhelmed by the pain surrounding the fate of their loved ones. Nevertheless, they continue to meet and turn scraps of material and pieces of thread into works of art. Each thread is a story, and each scrap of cloth brings the observer a step closer to a mutilated body. Each *arpillera* articulates the experience of a divided world: Pinochet's Chile and a free Chile; the rich, well-fed children and the poor, starving children; a world of violence and a world of hope.

The collages continue to spread throughout the country, and are now a type of living monument in which everyone can participate. On 2 July 1987, two adolescents were burned by the Chilean police. Gloria Quintana survived, while her companion, Rodrigo Rojas, died and became an *animita.* On the spot where the crime occurred, a living mural has been created. The walls are covered with photographs of political leaders such as Salvador Allende and Ché Guevara, and other objects, including embroidered *arpilleras.*

Like the *arpilleras* themselves, this shrine reflects the relationship that exists in Chile between popular culture and collage. For example, phrases appear on the Rojas-Quintana mural such as: "The police robbed you, Rodrigo." In this way, the *animitas,* as well as the *arpilleras,* become vehicles of denunciation and resistance.

The artifacts found in the shrines of the *animitas,* the Rojas-Quintana mural, and the *arpilleras* use many different materials, especially personal objects, to tell a story, overcome pain, and defy fear through an artistic creation. The use of collage thus takes on magical dimensions, where the creation of a work of art from fragments of material helps to overcome death, where popular culture is an arm of resistance and a challenge to fear. The collage, formed from scraps of hope, is a work of art and a work of life, because it serves to bring back the missing and restore order to a fragmented reality.[6]

Notes

1. For more information about the *animitas,* see José Donoso's article "Animitas," *Araucania de Chile,* no. 29 (1983): 19; and Oreste Plath's books on Chilean folklore.
2. Quoted in Marjorie Agosin, *Scraps of Life: The Chilean Arpillera* (Trenton, N.J.: Red Sea Press, 1988), pp. 115–16.
3. Ibid., p. 105.
4. Ibid., p. 133.
5. Ibid.
6. In this work, I have focused on the relationship between *arpilleras* and collage. For more information on *arpilleras,* see Agosin, *Scraps of Life: The Chilean Arpillera.*

17

Reflections on Collage/Assemblage: A Personal View

Richard Newman

Looking at the processes of artistic thought involved in collage and assemblage is the focus of Richard Newman's writing. Newman reflects on the role of collage and assemblage in his work as an artist, and on the creative process in which he has been involved. As he discusses aspects of his work such as the interplay "between the sacred and the profane," and "low- and highbrow culture," the role of myth, and the joining of yin and yang forces, one sees clearly the many levels of assemblage and collage that are possible and important to contemporary artists such as Newman. For Newman collage and assemblage provide a means by which he can "enter the realm of metaphorical thought" to find his "artistic voice."

I have always felt a strong inclination toward, as well as preference for, a mixed media approach to art. Collage, along with its counterpart, assemblage, continues to afford me the best access to my creative intelligence. Both of these forms provide a means by which I can enter the realm of metaphorical thought to find my artistic voice. Each medium responds well to my needs by presenting a process which is open-ended and which keeps alive the possibility of both an additive or subtractive action.

Compared to traditional drawing and painting, collage/assemblage offers me a less limited method of expression and provides a more varied means of image-making which can blur conceptual as well as media boundaries. This flexibility encourages me to tap more layers of my experience and to expose more levels of my psychic involvement during the creative encounter. It also offers me a better form of reentry into my work when I have to disengage from it for any length of time. This means that the opportunity to revise old works always remain open, so I have to be careful when I weigh any decision to return to a past encounter. Can this specific work benefit from a revision? Will I be able to call forth the dimensions of my original confrontation with these visual materials?

When I look back across the years to recover some memory of a formal introduction to these modes of expression the picture becomes quite dim. What I can recollect are traces of early creative urges, along with a view of how my childhood and education nurtured a sensibility which later welcomed the opportunity to engage the potential of mixed media avenues of expression. I can remember the excitement I felt as a young boy every time I was given the chance to help my parents strip wallpaper in the rooms of our house. That mysterious action which could reveal multilayers of juxtaposed colors and patterns stimulated my youthful imagination, encouraged my ability to fantasize, and satisfied my desire to be destructive within approved bounds. Armed with a putty knife I was allowed to create my own ways of removing the paper. Some of my decisions favored scraping down long vertical columns while others demonstrated the need to expand in diagonal directions. All these paths led to discovery and empowerment. By exercising choices about how to manipulate the wall's surface plane I could reveal designs and create images which nourished my vision and mind. While my attention was not directed toward producing art, it was engaging an act of expression as well as the impulse to order experience. Such a recollection takes on greater meaning now within the context of Leonardo's advice in his *Treatise on Painting,* which directs the young artist to gain inspiration from the act of examining the abstract stains or patches on a wall.

> If one but threw a sponge full of colors at the wall it would leave a patch in which one might see a beautiful landscape. It is probably true that one may see all sorts of things in such a patch—that is, if one wishes to look for them—such as human heads, different kinds of animals, battles, cliffs, the sea, clouds or forests, and other such things.*

I can equally recall that these early visual encounters with wallpaper could produce a dark side to life as well. I could frighten myself at night in bed while watching the magical play of shadows over the surface of the decorative figures on the walls of my room. This activity could prompt my imagination to find grotesque and disturbing shapes as easily as pleasant ones. That realization furnishes now still another connection to Leonardo's wise counsel that the study of deformity and ugliness must properly accompany the artist's search for absolute beauty or truth.

---

*Robert Wallace, *The World of Leonardo* (New York: Time Inc., 1966), p. 29.

I remember my first encounter with Leonardo's sketches of grotesque human faces as a first year student in art school. This brought about my increased awareness and validated the use of distortion in other works of art which I would confront later. Not only did this experience foster an understanding that artistic expression could expose contrasting emotions and conflicting ideas but it unlocked the door to modern art for me. It provided a reference point for my gradual acceptance of abstract and expressionistic art styles as well as fueled interest in the work of the contemporary English painter, Francis Bacon. I chose this artist as the subject of an art history term paper in my second year. In the process of conducting research I uncovered the following quote by the seventeenth-century English statesman and philosopher of the same name: "There is no beauty in nature which has not some strangeness in proportion." These words equipped me with a conceptual bridge and, therefore, enabled me to connect the process of art and nature. They still continue to resonate with meaning today.

The creative act is a manifestation of my attempt to integrate my experiences. It draws upon sensorial memories as well as my receptivity to nature's forms, textures, and rhythms. It presents me with a basis for understanding the relationship of beauty to ugliness, growth to decay, and stability to change. This recognition of dichotomies that reside in the human condition compels me to study the dark side along with the light side of existence. Yin and yang must join forces in my work if I am to create a full or complete statement.

My activity provides the manner by which I search for artistic unity and psychic equilibrium in life. It serves my need to find a magic vessel where I can dispose of fears and misgivings as well as store moments of joy and astonishment. It provides a format for examining and connecting the diverse material which floats into my field of perception.

I can visualize a particular summer from my youth when I had another formative experience. A number of neighborhood children, including myself, conducted a large paper drive to earn money and support the war effort in the forties. One result of this activity was an unexpected bonanza of visual stimuli in the form of comics and magazines which landed on my side porch for temporary storage, much to the envy of all my pals. It became obvious to me, a boy of seven, that I faced an important challenge. I had to consume every last *Captain Marvel, Batman,* and *Classics Illustrated* comic as well as search through every *Look, Life, Modern Romance,* and *National Geographic* magazine. There was no time to waste. I sensed the threat of a deadline. I knew that adult reality would prevail and soon would act to discharge these riches to their proper place. I could feel the pull of contradictory emotions. I was confronted with a storehouse of treasures which soon I would reluctantly turn loose to become bombs or parachutes to help our boys overseas.

My marathon attack must have lasted for no more than a week. I remember that the urgency of the matter necessitated that I gain permission to sleep out on the porch or battleground to maximize my effort. While I have no evidence that I ever completed this Herculean task, what strikes me today is the intensity of that memorable visual encounter. It must have left indelible imprints on my subconscious mind. When I couple this experience with other youthful ones, like the hours spent on scrapbooks, postage stamp, and matchcover collections, as well as the time logged at Saturday matinee movies, I can reconstruct the wide parameters of my early influential experience. I now also realize the many outlets I had for exposure to fantasy materials and the methods I used to impose some structure on my life.

Perhaps it is this personal history and storehouse of memories which leads me today to attend antique fairs or to search through antique shops. Am I reliving those days of singing cowboys and heroic crime fighters or do I only seek potential collage/assemblage items? I have only recently acknowledged what a strange mixture of forces now directs me to frequent these markets of the past. They can continue to supply relics of time and image composites in unpredictable patterns. Not only do these settings yield found objects but they provide me with sources for photographs. Antique fairs present me with visual shards of time and associative meaning. These can thrust their way into my perceptual frame of reference in unexpected ways. These random visual juxtapositions can produce mixed contexts, exciting relationships and seeds for studio works. I can find kitsch and kunst nestled together on the same tabletop or some other contrasting situation which begs to be preserved.

As an approach, collage/assemblage presents me with a framework for the integration of contrasting values, opposing ideas, and emotional tensions. At their core these methods of visualization promote contradistinction as well as the use of irony to enrich their articulated meaning. In fact, the history of their development since Cubism is marked by examples which act to either obscure the difference between illusion and reality, past and present, or art and life. Many employ a use of the pun, or provide colliding frames of reference to promote paradox or poetry. When one calls forth specific works one remembers either their confrontational nature or their ability to transcend precise categorization. These media possess the power to persuade or the ability to declare subtle blends of human concerns.

These visual art processes illustrate better than any other the adage that "art transforms life." They speak directly to the artist's need to physically or contextually alter his visual materials to create a new construct which embodies aesthetic value or universal meaning. Because potential items can exist anywhere in any guise, I must be alert to my environment. I must constantly screen my surroundings to uncover articles which hold the promise of application to my work.

These media furnish me with an appropriate means for letting the past inform the present. Relics from one time can be called upon to aid perception, clarify thought, and stimulate action in a new age. This realization colors the mind-set of the practitioner. Many of us become packrats and store up goods or treasures for future use. Without the practiced skill for mining our discoveries, along with the ability to relegate each to its proper place in some new world, our activities become insignificant. With each new work I seek to create a dynamic arrangement and new play of visual relationships. Every creative encounter attempts to produce a unified and resonant configuration. Selected items must be transformed, revitalized, or reborn. Individual elements must interact with one another to establish a family of relationships. Formal structure or expressive meaning can manifest itself through a use of analogy or contrast, and dissonance or consonance. Compositional form grows from many smaller acts of destruction or accidents of fate which liberate items or experiences from one context for use in another.

The danger which lies with a collage/assemblage approach is connected to its susceptibility for reflecting only autobiographical data or trips of nostalgia. I try to be sensitive to this in my work. I rely on my editing instincts and remain vigilant to the need to abandon materials which serve no essential function in the overall composition.

I was given a rather traditional education in both art school and college. I was trained as a painter and sculptor and given plenty of reinforcement for keeping these activities discretely apart from each other. My own decision to marry these forms in a mixed media approach came about in this manner: A few years after my formal training had been completed I decided to explore the field of photography. Up until that time I had experienced rather limited exposure to it as an artform. I set up a small darkroom and began to teach myself camera and printing skills. I soon discovered that I was producing many images which fell short of my idea of perfection. Some landed in the trash barrel but I recognized that others could be saved for another use. I began quite casually to experiment with cutting them apart for reassembly into a photocollage. At some point during this time of exploration I realized that my rejects or artistic seconds had become more valuable to me than most of my finished prints.

At this juncture I began also to become interested in the juxtaposition of these black and white images with drawing techniques. I produced

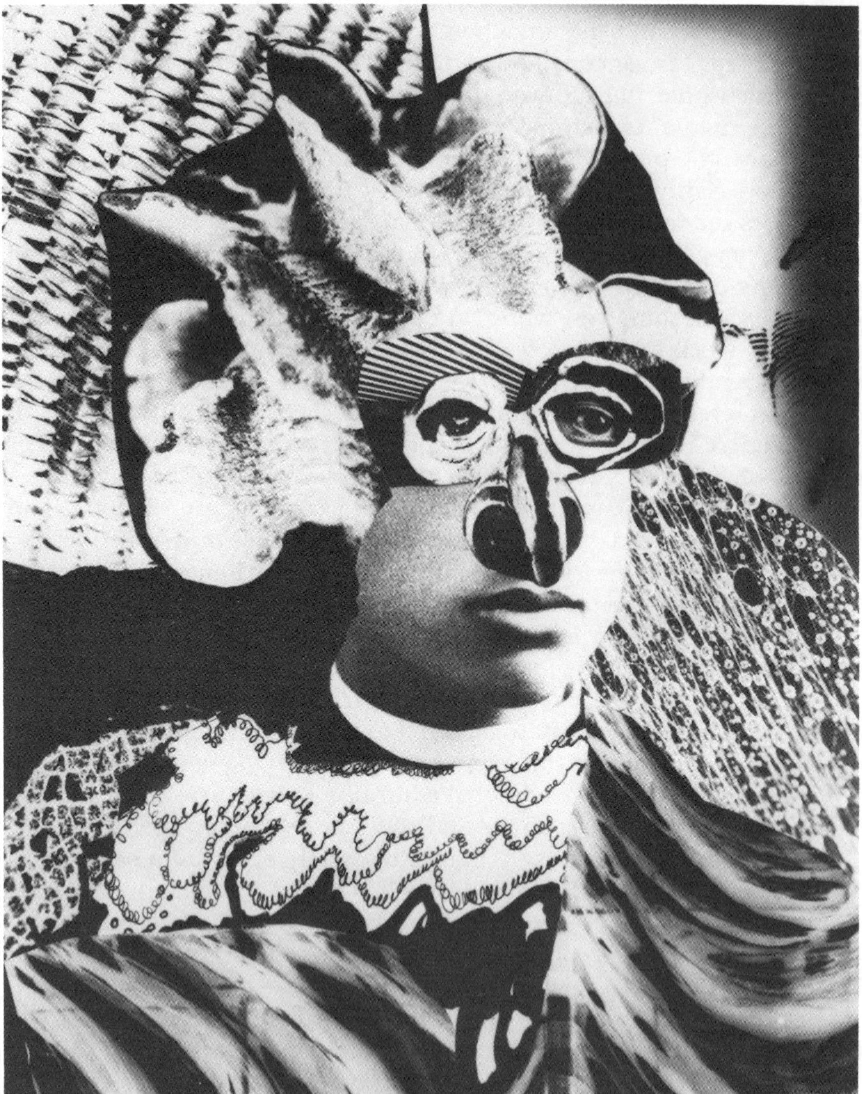

Figure 17.1. Richard Newman, *School Marm,* 1974
Photo-collage with hand-drawn passages in pen and ink, 14″ × 18″.
(Collection, Addison Gallery of American Art, Andover, Massachusetts)

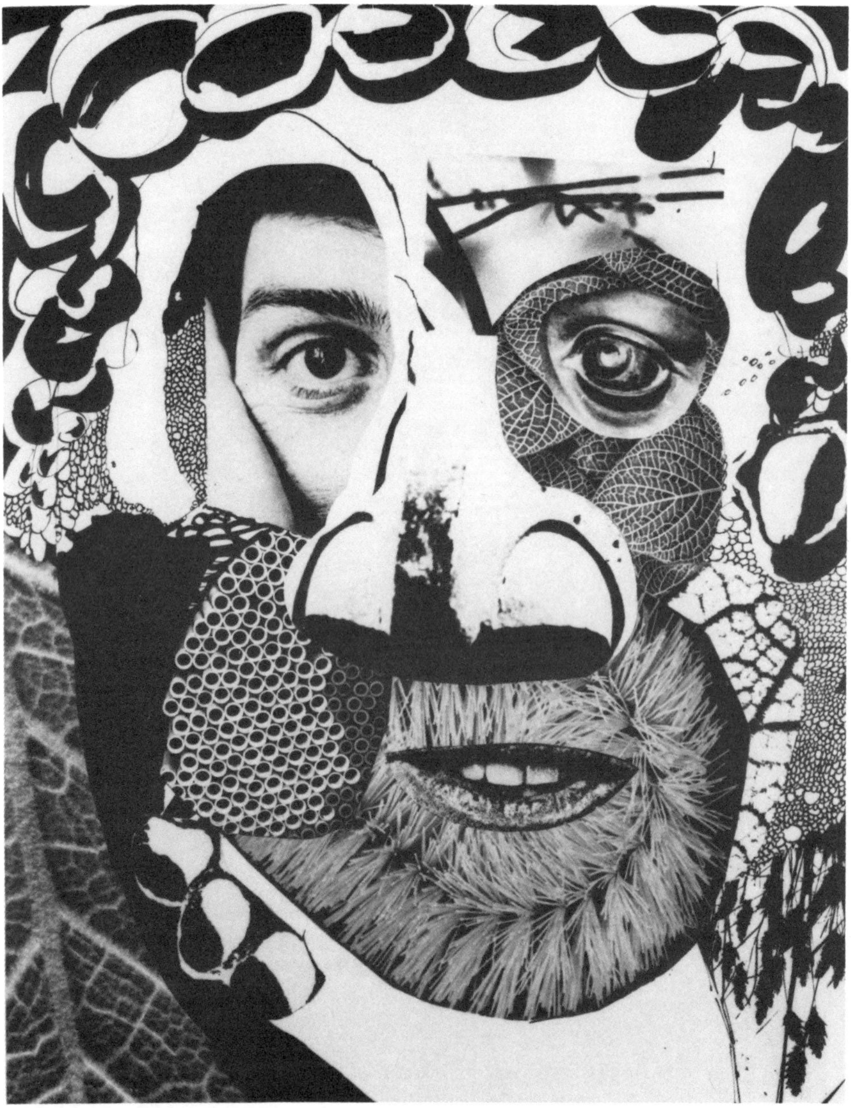

Figure 17.2. Richard Newman, *Bacchus,* 1974
Photo-collage with hand-drawn passages in pen and ink, 14″ × 18″.

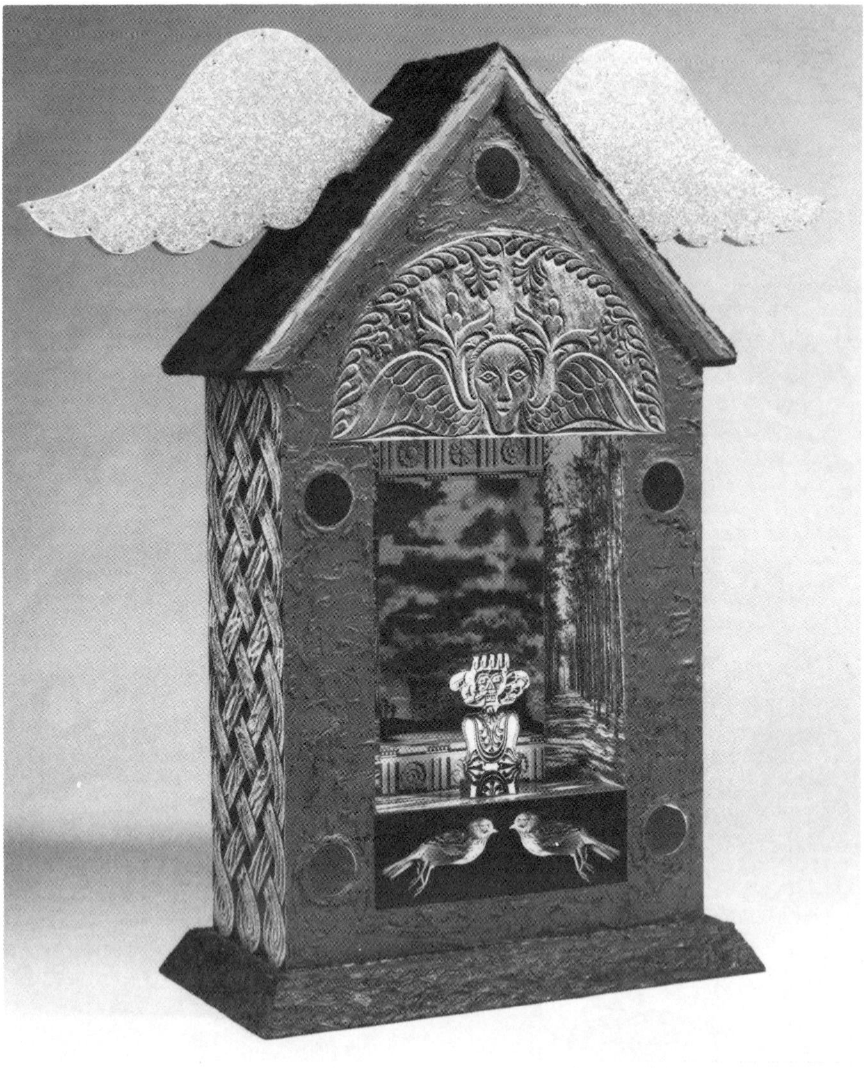

Figure 17.3. Richard Newman, *House of the Dead*, 1978
Mixed media sculpture, 36″ × 37″ × 8″. This work employs the use of New England gravestone imagery dealing with its theme of death. It features a stagelike setting along with assorted materials like photos, paint, fabric, and mirrors.

a series of collages called *Face Fabrications* which displayed a fascination for fusing photo techniques with hand-manipulated passages in pen and ink (figs. 17.1 and 17.2). These pieces attempted to blur the boundary between the two image-making fields of activity. I began eventually to call upon the need to marry photography to the color of painting and the form of sculpture in subsequent studio efforts (fig. 17.3).

Over the years those interests and exploratory actions have continued to evolve. My present work still moves back and forth between two-dimensional and three-dimensional encounters. It has widened its frame of reference to include the use of natural forms and manmade found objects but still attempts to blend formalistic and expressionistic concerns, organic and architectonic forms, gestural and mechanical marks, hard-edge and soft-edge shapes.

The collages tend to deal with faces, figures, and dreamscapes and they still join color and black/white elements along with referents to the areas of information and subjects I teach (figs. 17.4 and 17.5). The sculptural constructions take cues in their form and structure from religious and folk art objects. They frequently resemble icons or monuments but offer a play between the sacred and the profane as well as lowbrow and highbrow culture. For example they often contrast the use of intense color and symmetrical form, preferred by the folk artist, with references to the world of academia and studies of art and mythology (figs. 17.6 and 17.7). These references become visible through the use of photographs or found objects which act to complicate the work's meaning by providing another area of association. I have often built a complex work around a commonplace or kitsch object which gets elevated in status to that of a relic, given its new formal surroundings. In other pieces I have purposely taken religious articles and placed them in a rather fanciful environment.

My private research in preparation for teaching becomes intermingled with my studio work just as art feeds off of life and becomes part and parcel of one matrix. I can cite my appreciation for Egyptian art, African sculpture, medieval reliquaries, mannerist painting, German Expressionist prints, tramp art, and other folk objects. My comparative study of myth and ritual has contributed heavily to my works' content. It has led me to expand my knowledge of symbolism and to understand better why I gravitated early in my career to the use of such universal forms as the mandala or Jungian concepts like the anima/animus before I had names for them. It influences my need now to create an object whose presence of form produces an air of mystery for the viewer by charging its space with a sense of sanctity. A particular artist who has expanded my awareness and provided me with strong inspiration is Joseph Cornell.

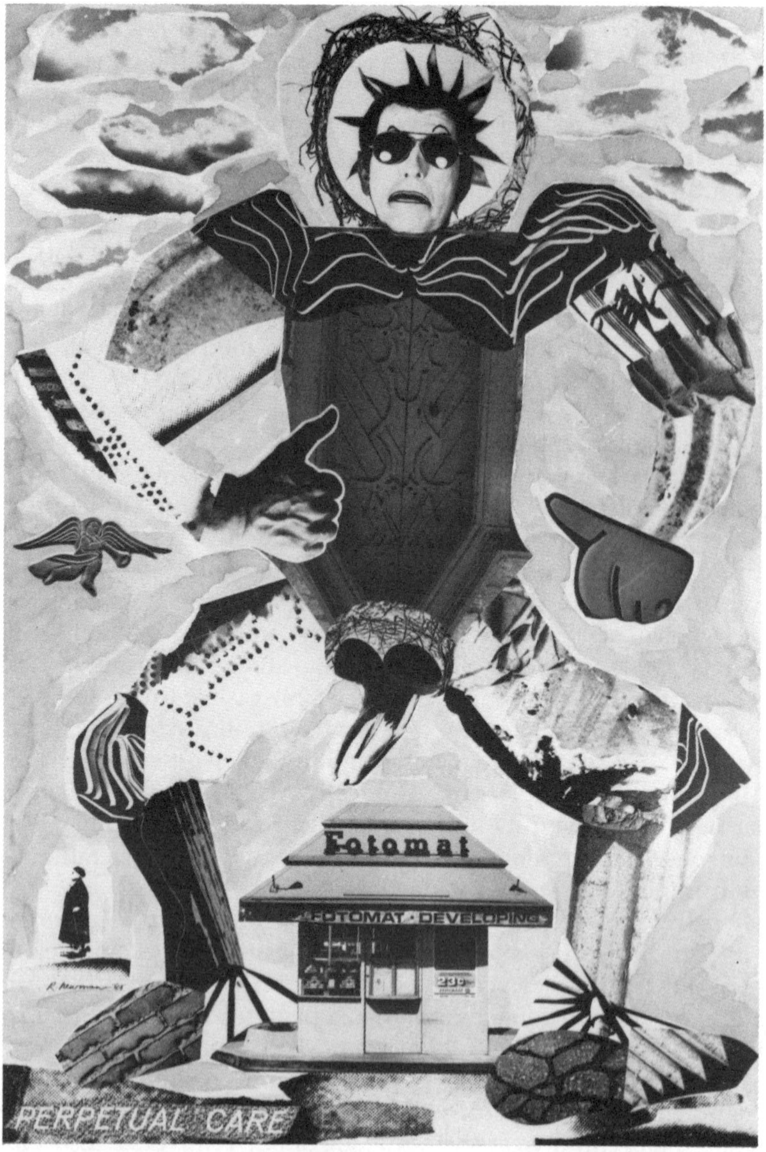

Figure 17.4. Richard Newman, *An Artist's Ego Needs Perpetual Care,* 1986
Photo-collage, 28″ × 38″. This work and figure 17.5 incorporate the use of color with black/white elements and draw upon a diverse set of references.

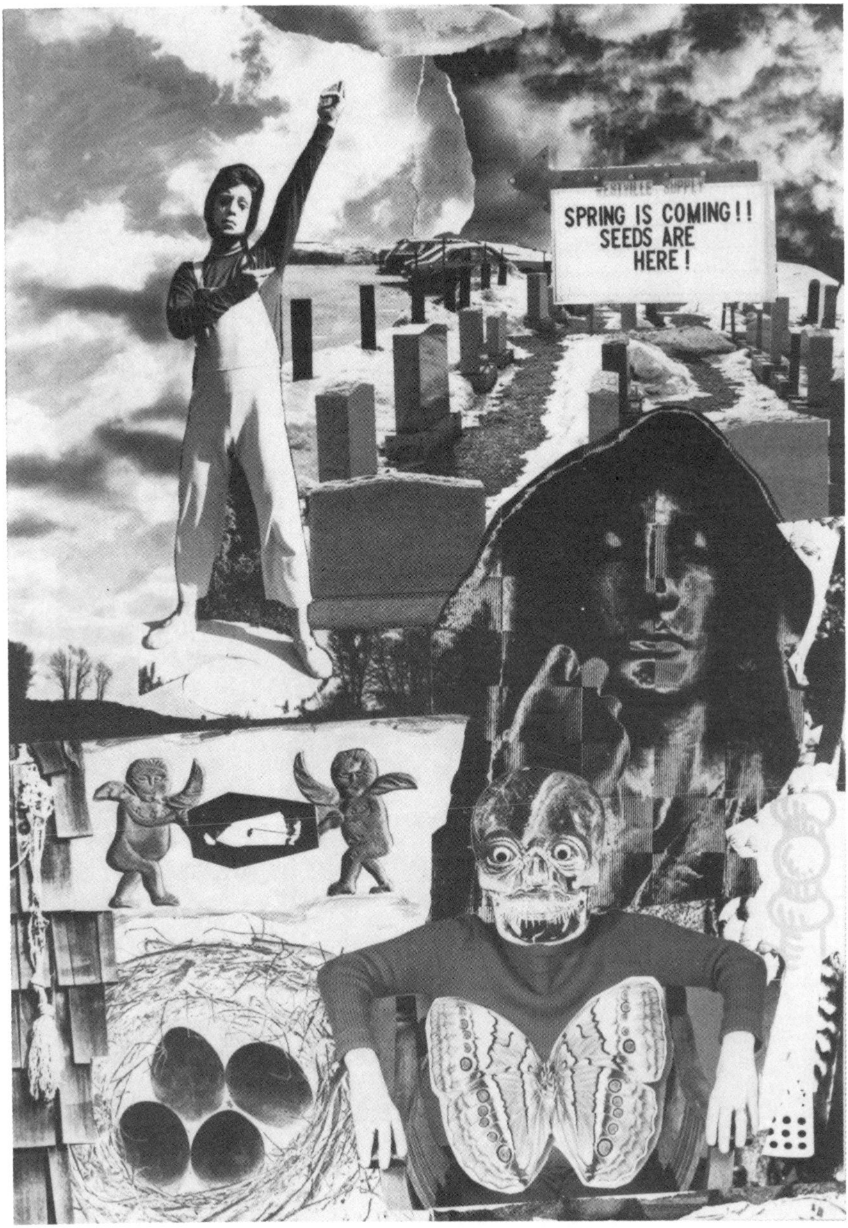

Figure 17.5. Richard Newman, *Spring Is Coming,* 1985
Photo-collage, 22″ × 28″.

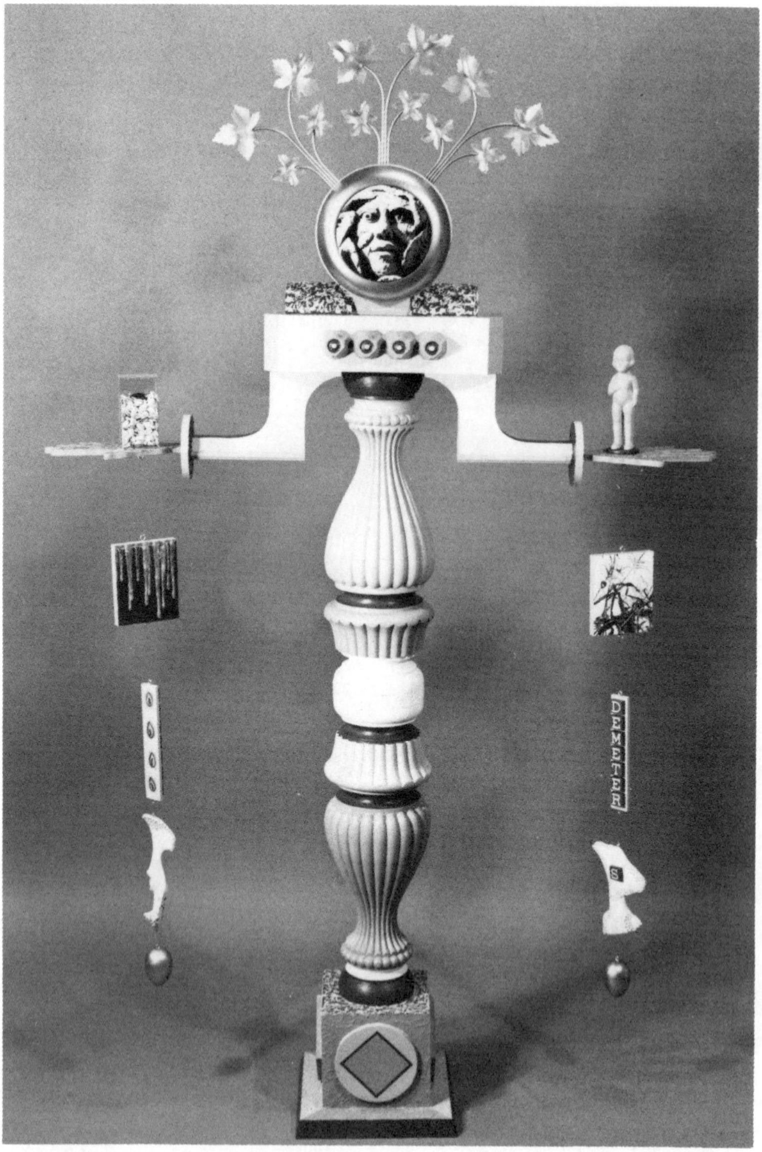

Figure 17.6. Richard Newman, *Demeter's Dilemma,* 1986
Mixed media sculpture, 68″ × 42″ × 10″. A recent work that assembles found objects and photographic elements. It marries painting to sculpture and revitalizes such materials as a clock, doll, piano legs, bones, and crafted wood parts.

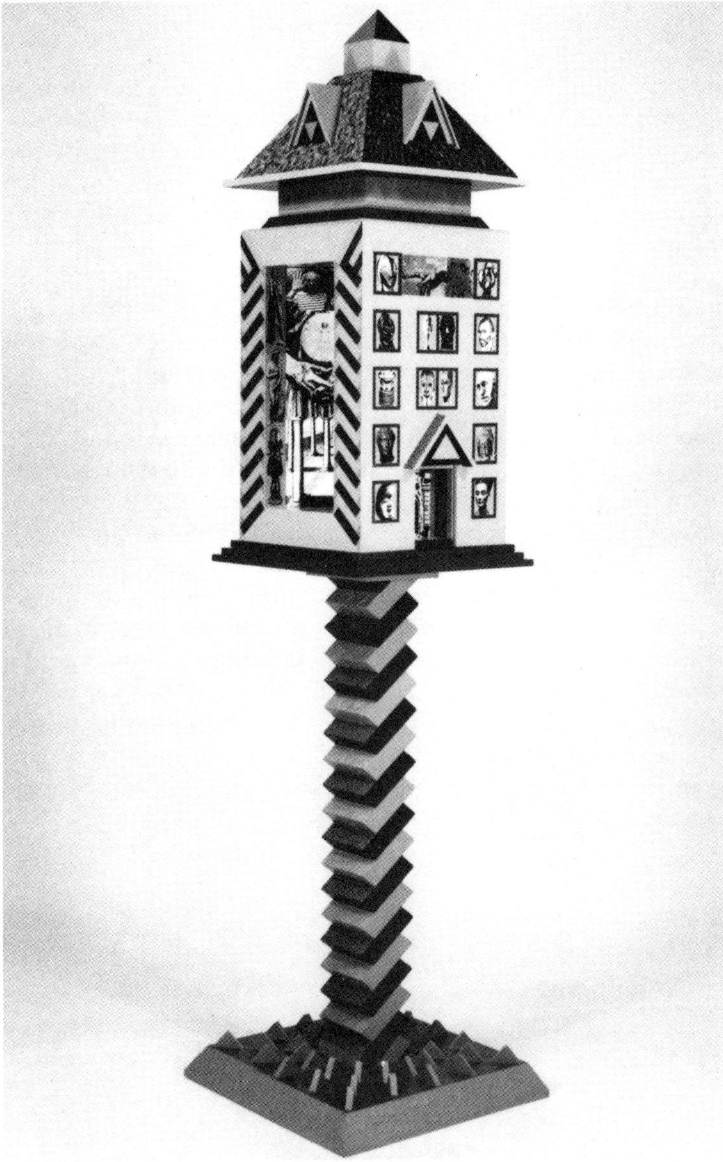

Figure 17.7. Richard Newman, *Kunsthaus,* 1985
Mixed media sculpture, 82″ × 20″ × 20″. This polychromed work incorporates the use of black/white photographic references to famous works of art along with found objects.

His boxes, which exhibit poetic reveries, persuaded me to employ enclosed sections in my own work to confront the viewer with added dimension and reference.

I also cannot fail to mention the naive artist James Hampton's *Throne of the Third Heaven.* I first viewed this work in Boston at the Museum of Fine Arts in the mid-seventies and have never forgotten its powerful presence and mystical meaning. Constructed from scraps of wooden furniture, lightbulbs, and jelly jars which are covered by tin and gold foil, this large environmental assemblage is now housed in the Smithsonian. While it was probably intended as a religious testament rather than an artistic statement, it offers a rich display of personal iconography as well as being a striking example of how symmetrical form can easily lend itself to the development of complex surface and shape detail.

In conclusion, I would say that all art speaks to our need to transform experience in order to discover our human relationship to the past as well as the present. Its pursuit by either the artist or the consumer stems from our craving for wholeness or self-affirmation. It casts its attention upon such polarities as self and other, life and death, or the known and unknown. As an activity it takes on the semblance of examining life through a looking-glass. Any prolonged gaze allows each of us to note private memories, reflected mysteries, or any manner of meaningful visions. But a looking-glass is dependent upon the disposition of its user and the perceptual skills or psychic proclivities that the user needs to call upon in putting such a device to use. It has the potential to intensify, clarify, exaggerate, distort, or even blur the images which fill the perimeters of its frame. Each of us makes use of it in our own way.

18

Passion and Politics: Eisenstein and Montage

Michael Selig

Sergei Eisenstein is the best known of the Soviet revolutionary filmmakers. His reputation developed initially through the international distribution of his films in the late twenties. However, his continuing significance to film scholarship derives as much from the body of writings he left behind as from the films. Although his films are not necessarily the best examples of his theories of montage in the cinema, his writings on montage are considered to be fundamental to the development of classical film theory.

Eisenstein's best-known writings are collected in Film Form *and* The Film Sense, *with new translations of his other writings appearing every few years. He was a leading figure in Soviet filmmaking in the twenties, with the production of* Strike *(1925),* The Battleship Potemkin *(1925), and* October *(1929). After his return from Europe, the United States, and Mexico in the late twenties his ''formalist'' work was out of favor with the new Stalinist regime, and Eisenstein spent several bitter years unable to get government support for his films. In the thirties, Eisenstein began to reorient his theories and filmmaking in a manner more in line with government policy.*

Michael Selig clearly analyzes the concept of montage as developed in Eisenstein's writings and demonstrates how the conception of montage changed ''over time as a function of both political necessity and discursive or theoretical unity.''

Both the philosophy of language and theories of film have been concerned primarily with the adequacy of forms of representation. Virtually all theories maintain that some link exists between the world of objects, our consciousness about the world, and the ''language,'' whether visual or verbal, which we use to represent that world of objects and ideas. Verbal language and visual representation are explored, judged, analyzed, and dissected based on their perceived adequacy (or in more recent times, inadequacy) in representing the external world of objects and the internal world of consciousness. Both language and the cinema are viewed as primarily functioning to represent, or literally re-present, absent objects or ideas. As Edward Said has noted,

> Representation [is] one of the key problems in all criticism and philosophy. Most accounts of representation, including Plato's, involve an original and copy or representation, the first coming first in time and higher in value, the second later in time and lower in value, the first determining the second; in principle a representative representation is meant to be a sometimes unavoidable, sometimes merely convenient substitute for the original, which for any number of reasons cannot be present to be itself, and act itself. The representative or substitute is thus qualitatively different from the original.[1]

The value associated with the ''original'' and with ''presence'' is no small matter. For many contemporary intellectual historians, these terms have generated virtually all of Western philosophical speculation. Jacques Derrida indicts this ''metaphysics of origins and presence'' as the ''ruling illusion'' of Western philosophy.[2] Some thing which preexists expression forms the foundation and ultimate sanction for language. In semiological parlance, the signified determines the signifier, the referent dominates and commands its expression—i.e., the world is there, before representation, in order to be represented. It is the ''metaphysics of origins and presence,'' then, which determines the search for an adequate ''language,'' a ''language'' that transcends its alienation from the world and from consciousness (its difference from the thing it represents; from Being), a ''language'' that liberates itself from the bonds of discourse.[3]

Sergei Eisenstein's theories of montage cinema, primarily developed during the twenties and thirties in the Soviet Union, reiterate a ''metaphysics of origins and presence'' in asserting the cinema's ability to overcome the alienation of representation, in asserting that the cinema, in its essence, adequately and ''truthfully'' re-presents the ordering process of consciousness. In doing so, Eisenstein's writings depend on a set of distinct philosophical or epistemological concepts which were characteristic of previous theories of language. For Eisenstein's writings, an epistemological foundation is provided by what Michel Foucault calls an ''episteme'' of ''representation,'' a discursive class which pervaded mechanistic philosophies, and specifically the development of general grammar in the work of philosophers like Condillac.[4] In an episteme of representation, words are thought to be arbitrarily related to their referent (in a fashion similar to early structuralist theory). But the specific rules of their *grammatical* combination form a system that fully, truthfully, and adequately re-presents both the process of logical reasoning, as well as a synthesis of logic and emotion, or in Eisenstein's words, ''sensual thinking.''

In a similar discursive fashion, Eisenstein's assertions of the representational adequacy and affectiveness of montage cinema depend on the assumption that montage cinema, that the ordering of images, can represent the ordering process of consciousness. Like the proponents of general grammar, who argued that "the art of speaking is the art of thinking and . . . reasoning, which develop in the same measure as languages approach perfection,"[5] Eisenstein argued that "a work of art must reproduce that process whereby . . . new images are built up in the human consciousness and feelings."[6] Also like the proponents of general grammar, who tended to suppress the signifying function of the word, Eisenstein's early writings and their emphasis on the montage relationship between images suppressed the representational value of the single image and its content, and by extension the representational significance of narrative form. Consequently, Eisenstein is faced with a set of discursive paradoxes similar to those in prior philosophies of language, paradoxes which continually reassert themselves in discourses which argue that expressive systems can adequately re-present that which is absent. Continually forced to recognize the meaning inherent in a single image (in the "montage cell"), and in particular forced to recognize that meaning by the demands of Socialist Realism, Eisenstein employed over time a variety of discursive strategies and tropes—the dialectic, "organicness," and finally his own concept of "inner speech." With each, he consistently asserted the primacy of meaning in montage juxtapositions over that in the content of the shot.

The Dialectic

For Eisenstein, the dialectic forms the foundation for virtually all his early writings on montage, making a system of conflicts his fundamental view not only on editing but on all aspects of cinema work. In "The Cinematographic Principle and the Ideogram" (1929), he wrote,

> The compression of all cinematographic factors and properties within a single dialectical formula of conflict is no empty rhetorical diversion. . . . [For example] the camera position, as a materialization of the conflict between the organizing logic of the director and the inert logic of the object, in collision, reflects the dialectic of the camera angle.[7]

Thus, for Eisenstein, dialectical conflict suffuses all aspects of cinematographic art. But the art of the cinema is not alone in this regard. As he writes in the essay "A Dialectical Approach to Film Form" (1929), all "dynamic" art embodies a system of conflict—"according to its social mission . . . according to its nature . . . according to its methodology."[8]

According to its social mission *because*: It is art's task to make manifest the contradictions of Being . . . According to its nature *because*: Its nature is a conflict between natural existence and creative tendency . . . Hypertrophy of the purposive initiative—the principles of rational logic—ossifies art into mathematical technicalism. . . . Hypertrophy of organic naturalness—an organic logic—dilutes art into formlessness. . . . The logic of organic form *vs.* the logic of rational form yields, in collision, the dialectic of the art-form.[9]

This principle of conflict is by no means limited to the realm of art, however, and Eisenstein is sure to make the connections between this process of artistic creation and the "process of thinking." "A Dialectical Approach to Film Form" opens,

Thus:
The projection of the dialectic system of things
into the brain
into creating abstractly
into the process of thinking
yields: dialectic methods of thinking;
dialectical materialism — PHILOSOPHY
And also:
The projection of the same system of things
while creating concretely
While giving form
yields: — ART

Later in the essay, he writes that dialectical conflict "is true in every field that can be understood as an art. For example, logical thought, considered as an art, shows the same dynamic mechanism."[10]

In making this connection between the "process of thinking" and cinematographic art, Eisenstein brings to bear that wide range of knowledge that always fascinates his commentators. Philosophy, the Japanese ideogram, architecture, music, physiology, language and speech, as well as art and the art of the cinema partake of a universal law of dialectical conflict. Eisenstein writes, for example,

From separate hieroglyphs has been fused—the ideogram. By the combination of two "depictables" is achieved the representation of something that is graphically undepictable. . . . It is exactly what we do in cinema, combining shots that are *depictive*, single in meaning, neutral in content—into *intellectual* contexts and series. . . . [H]uman expression is a conflict between conditioned and unconditioned reflexes.[11]

Most significantly, the discursive connection between cinematographic art, language, and thought forms an authoritative triad, making dialectical montage more than the mere *analogue* of a natural law, but is *identical* in process. With this triad, Eisenstein reifies the metaphysical ideal of a natural, nonalienated form for expression, based on the presumably universal condition of dialectical conflict, and more generally on an episteme of representation. The essay "A Dialectical Approach to Film Form" constructs this triad in the last three pages.

> Now why should the cinema follow the forms of theater and painting rather than the methodology of language, which allows wholly new concepts or ideas to arise from the combination of two concrete denotations of two concrete objects? Language is much closer to film than painting is. For example, in painting the form arises from *abstract* elements of line and color, while in cinema the material *concreteness* of the image within the frame presents—as an element—the greatest difficulty in manipulation. So why not rather lean towards the system of language, which is forced to use the same mechanics in inventing words and word-complexes?[12]

This "material *concreteness* of the image" leads Eisenstein to construct a theory of "film grammar . . . a *syntax* of film manifestations, in which visual counterpoint may determine a whole new system of forms of manifestation."[13]

But this is not all. For the combinatory rules of language are not merely functional and communicative; they are generative as well, capable of poetry and philosophy, pathos and intellection, emotion and deduction. As Eisenstein writes, while conflict and tension in the arts have been "calculated for purely physiological effect—from the purely optical to the emotional, we must mention here also the case of the same conflict-tension serving the ends of new concepts—of new attitudes, that is, of purely intellectual aims."[14] Here Eisenstein completes his authoritative triad of cinema, language, and thought in the "intellectual dynamization" of image juxtaposition. And in this triad, in the universality of dialectical conflict, not only does the opposition between emotion and intellection vanish, but so do the oppositions between mind and body, science and art. The conclusion of "A Dialectical Approach to Film Form" tells us,

> In these . . . experiments we have taken the first embryonic step towards a totally new form of film expression. Towards a purely intellectual film, freed from traditional limitations, achieving direct forms for ideas, systems, and concepts. . . . We may yet have a *synthesis of art and science.*[15]

In a lecture at the Sorbonne six months later in 1930, Eisenstein pursues this "synthesis" to a "primitive" source. He does so in a manner which reiterates a "metaphysics of origins and presence," valorizing the natural not only as the "presence" or nonalienation of consciousness and emotion to cinematic expression, but also as an original, pure state of human reasoning, opposed to modern, deteriorated forms of intellectual and emotional "dualism."

> In the earliest times, the time of magic and religion, knowledge was both an emotional element and an element of collective wisdom. Then, with dualism, things got separated and we find on the one hand speculative philosophy, pure abstraction, and on the other hand pure emotion.
>
> We must now go back, not to the primitive stage (the religious stage), but toward an analogous synthesis of he emotional and intellectual.
>
> I think film alone is capable of making this great synthesis, of returning the intellect to its vital, concrete, emotional sources.[16]

In sum, then, the dialectic serves as the source of authority in Eisenstein's earlier writings. Realized in montage editing, the dialectic serves to synthesize and unite not only conflicting cinematic images, but also the realms of emotion and intellect, art and science, a reunification that harks back to some ill-defined (pre)historic epoch prior to the degenerate "dualism" of advanced civilization. With the authority of the dialectic Eisenstein argues for a cinematic system of representation which, through its dialectical identity with the principles of montage, fully makes present the workings of consciousness. Further, Eisenstein reifies the Western philosophical tradition which associates the unity of perception, consciousness, and representation with some original, primitive social order, with the "vital, concrete, emotional sources" of the intellect.

"Organic-ness"

In Andrew Tudor's essay on Eisenstein, he asks,

> What are we to make of his declining concern with dialectics? . . . The fundamental assumption is that all things in the world are related in a dialectical manner, and so this "universal" dialectic must find its place in film as much as anywhere else. . . . There is, at least at first, a considerable pressure apparent in his work to use the mold of "dialectics" to hold his thoughts, accompanied by an equally obvious tendency for them to overflow the sides of the container.[17]

Tudor seems to suggest that Eisenstein's "declining concern with dialectics" was a function of his transcendent philosophical and intellectual range—the "tendency" for his thoughts to "overflow the sides of the [dialectical] container." But Tudor's interpretation of Eisenstein's diminishing regard for a dialectical theory of cinematic representation ignores the real pressure of Soviet political changes in the thirties, especially the changes in cultural production marked by Socialist Realism.

By the time Eisenstein returned to the Soviet Union, following aborted attempts at film production in the West, a new cultural order had been established, with the Soviet Film Office under the leadership of Boris Shumyatsky. Shumyatsky's lack of tolerance for Eisenstein's formalism is obvious in his 1937 statement halting work on his film *Behzin Meadow*:

> So there can be no doubt on this point: S. M. Eisenstein was interested in making *Behzin Meadow* only because it offered him an opportunity to indulge in formalistic exercises.
>
> Instead of creating a strong, clear, direct work, Eisenstein detached his work from reality, from the colors and heroism of reality. He consciously reduced the work's ideological content.[18]

Eisenstein's writings following his return to the Soviet Union should be treated as a reorientation of his earlier position, under political pressure which forced him to come to terms with his discursive disregard for the presence of meaning in a single shot—or put more baldly, with the content of the image. Near the beginning of *The Film Sense,* Eisenstein writes,

> *Representation* A and *representation* B must be so selected from all the possible features within the theme that is being developed, must be so sought for, that their *juxtaposition*—that is, the juxtaposition of *those very elements* and not of alternative ones—shall evoke in the perception and feelings of the spectator the most complete *image of the theme itself.*[19]

Eisenstein thus makes a discursive attempt to integrate the content of the image into his montage theories. This integration takes place under the authority of a metaphor of organicism, implying a natural, nonalienated representational form. This is not to say that Eisenstein rejected the principle of dialectics, but that as a formal guide to film expressiveness it was diffused (de-fused) into *general* laws of constructing emotionally and intellectually affective works of art, rather than as a precise form of image juxtaposition. In "Film Form: New Problems," Eisenstein writes,

> The dialectic of works of art is built upon a most curious "dual-unity." The affectiveness of a work of art is built upon the fact that there takes place in it a dual process: an impetuous and progressive rise along the lines of the highest explicit steps of consciousness and a simultaneous penetration by means of the structure of the form into the layers of the profoundest sensual thinking. The polar separation of these two lines of flow creates that remarkable tension of unity of form and content characteristic of true art-works.[20]

In "The Structure of the Film" (1939), Eisenstein repeats the same sentiments in a discussion of *Potemkin*.

> All these are elements of a dialectical movement of development, elements which enter into the comprehension of materialist dialectics. And from this—for the structure of the work we are analyzing as well as for the structure of any construction of pathos—we can say that a pathetic structure is one that compels us, echoing its movement, *to re-live the moments of culmination and substantiation* that are in the canon of all dialectical processes.[21]

But this "structure of the work" follows a theme of "organic-ness," a theme not entirely dissociated from the dialectic, but one which invests it with a series of metaphors from the natural world.

> However, in an organic work of art, elements that nourish the work as a whole pervade all the features composing this work. A unified canon pierces not only the whole and each of its parts, but also each area that is called to participate in the work of the composition. One and the same principle will feed any area. . . . And only in such a case may one speak of the organic-ness of a work, for an organism is here understood as defined by Engels in *Dialectics of Nature*: " . . . *the organism is certainly a higher unity.*"[22]

For Eisenstein, such an organically structured work overcomes not only the alienation of expressive form from nature but also its alienation from consciousness.

> We have before us a case where a work of art—an *art-ificial work*—is built on those same laws by which *non*—artistic phenomena—the "organic" phenomena of nature—are constructed.
>
> There is in this case, not only . . . a *truthful and full reflection of a canon peculiar to actuality.*
>
> Evidently, whatever may be the kind of organic-ness in it, the work has a completely individual affect on its perceivers, not only because it is *raised to the level of natural phenomena,* but also because the *laws of its construction are simultaneously the laws governing those who perceive the work,* inasmuch as the audience is also part of organic nature. Each *spectator feels himself organically related, fused, united with a work of such a type, just as he senses himself united and fused with organic nature around him.*[23] (emphasis added)

Thus, montage cinema obeys a set of unspecified natural laws in constructing representations that are deemed "organic" and which, as a function of "organic-ness," compel the spectator "to proceed along that selfsame creative road that the author travelled."[24] In these later writings of Eisenstein, in *The Film Sense,* the art of cinema consists less in the conflicting juxtaposition of images, which might potentially corrode the dualistic nature of modern civilization, than in the process of creating "partial representations which, in their combination and juxtaposition . . . evoke in the consciousness and feelings of the spectator . . . that same initial general image which originally hovered before the creative artist."[25] "Consequently, in the actual method of creating images, a work of art must reproduce that process whereby, *in life itself*, new images are built up in the human consciousness.''[26] Thus, the theory of dialectical montage juxtapositions, which was central to the earlier writings, is displaced into a theory of ''the construction of a chain of representations.''[27]

Eisenstein's search for a method and theory of creating organic representations is built on and authorized by a concept of ''inner speech,'' or ''internal monologue.'' Within this discursive context, Eisenstein employs the same primary set of oppositions between ''speech'' and ''writing'' that Derrida finds pervasive in the West's philosophical reification of an opposition between nature and culture—where ''writing'' is a degenerate form, alienated from and inadequate to the purity and fullness of ''speech.''[28] In Eisenstein's writings, ''inner speech'' conceptually reifies the historically and philosophically dominant opposition between ''speech'' and ''writing,'' associating ''speech'' with the original, with primitive, sensual forms of thought, with the promise of a return to a pure, affective, fully adequate ''language.'' In ''Film Form: New Problems'' (1935), Eisenstein writes,

> We know that at the basis of the creation of form lie sensual and imagist thought processes. Inner speech is precisely at the stage of image-sensual structure, not yet having attained that logical formulation with which speech clothes itself before stepping out into the open [in ''writing'']. It is noteworthy that, just as logic obeys a whole series of laws in its construction, so equally, this inner speech, this sensual thinking, is subject to no less clear-cut laws and structural peculiarities . . . If we turn to the immeasurable treasury of folklore, of outlived and still living norms and forms of behavior preserved by societies at the dawn of their development, we find that, what for them has been or still is a norm of behavior and custom-wisdom, turns out to be at the same time precisely what we employ as ''artistic methods'' and ''technique of embodiment'' in our art-works.[29]

Eisenstein's later writings are concerned increasingly with the discovery and development of these structures of ''inner speech.'' In these writings, ''inner speech'' and not the dialectic serves as the foundation and authority for a cinematic synthesis of the sensible and the intelligible, the affective and the logical, art and science.

In ''Dickens, Griffith, and the Film Today'' (1944), Eisenstein outlines the characteristic structures of ''inner speech,'' rediscovering their affinity with montage structures.

> Thus the secret of the structure of montage was gradually revealed as a secret of *the structure of emotional speech*. For the very principle of montage, as is the entire individuality of its formation, is the substance of *an exact copy of the language of excited emotional speech*.[30]

Eisenstein quotes linguist Joseph Vendryes to establish the priority of speech over writing as an affective embodiment of the speaker's emotions and feelings. In doing so, he further emphasizes the primacy of ordering in representation.

> The main difference between affective and logical language lies in the *construction of the sentence.* This difference stands out clearly when we *compare the written with the spoken tongue. . . .*
>
> The elements that the written tongue endeavors to combine into a coherent whole seem to be divided up and disjointed in the spoken tongue: even the order is entirely different. It is no longer the logical order of present-day grammar. It has its logic, but this logic is primarily affective, and the ideas are arranged in accordance with the subjective importance the speaker gives to them . . . rather than with the objective rules of an orthodox process of reasoning.[31] (emphasis added)

''The spoken tongue,'' then, manifests more directly than written language the contents of consciousness; it makes present what is absent, ''the subjective importance the speaker gives.'' Here ''speech'' is considered less alien to consciousness than ''writing'' because it follows primarily a logic of affect and emotion rather than ''orthodox . . . rules.'' For the later Eisenstein, then, montage juxtapositions should follow the structure of emotional speech rather than that of the dialectic. ''However, the chief thing remained—an understanding of montage as not merely a means of producing effects, but above all as a means of *speaking,* a means of *communicating* ideas, of communicating them by way of a special film language, by way of a special form of film *speech.*''[32] Again, Eisenstein reveals the teleology (''the chief thing'') of his artistic and theoretical endeavor, to communicate ideas with a new affective language, film language, without the necessary alienation from feeling and consciousness that characterizes the conventional (written) structures of reason and logic. Once again, the model form of affective language is primitive, original, an ''imagist'' language built from metaphor and trope.

> The primitive metaphor necessarily stands at the very dawn of language, closely linked with the period of the production of the first transfers, that is, the first words to convey meanings, and not merely *motor* and *objective* understanding. . . . At the threshold of the creation of language stands the simile, the trope and the image.[33]

Eisenstein's appeal to ''primitive'' forms of thought and expression validates his assertion of identity between montage constructions and some supposedly premodern, ''sensual'' thought. This identity was mirrored earlier in Eisenstein's writings when he first began to confront the political and discursive limits of his theory of dialectical montage. In ''Film Form: New Problems,'' the language of the Bushman, for example,

> turns out to be something familiar to every one of us—a shooting script, an instrument to transpose a fact, abstracted into a concept, back into a chain of concrete single actions, which also happens to be the process of translating stage directions into action. . . . Again we have an example to show how, the moment we have to pass from informative to realistic expressiveness, we inevitably pass over to structural laws corresponding to sensual thinking, which plays the dominant role in representations characteristic of early development.[34]

Thus, a strict identity between primitive forms of thought, sensual thinking, and film montage authorizes the potential for a nonalienated system of expression, within the same discursive modes of Western metaphysics. In fact, Eisenstein takes even further the historically dominant philosophical valorization of ''speech'' in his assertion of an ''inner speech,'' or ''inner monologue,'' which precedes not only the logic of ''writing'' but also the affective structures of ''speech.'' In ''Dickens, Griffith, and the Film Today,'' he asserts,

> Concerning ''affective logic'' . . . which lies at the base of spoken speech, montage very quickly realized that ''affective logic'' is the chief thing, but for finding all the fullness of its systems and laws, montage had to make further serious creative ''cruises'' through the ''inner monologue'' of Joyce, through the ''inner monologue'' as understood in film, and through the so-called ''intellectual cinema,'' before discovering that a fund of these laws can be found in a third variety of speech—not in *written,* nor in *spoken* speech, but in *inner speech,* where the affective structure functions in an even more full and pure form. But the formation of this *inner speech* is already inalienable from that which is enriched by *sensual thinking.*[35]

As such, even ''spoken speech,'' which according to Derrida is ''always already'' inhabited by ''writing,'' that is by the logical, articulate, nonpresent meaning of signs, grammar, syntax, etc., even ''spoken speech'' for Eisenstein exists as a form of expression alienated from sensual thinking. Instead of a speech ''always already'' inhabited by writing, Eisenstein asserts an ''inner speech . . . already inalienable from . . . sensual thinking.''

Conclusion

Montage centers Eisenstein's theories of cinematic art, but his conception of montage changes over time as a function of both political necessity and discursive or theoretical unity. Eisenstein asserts the unity of artistic form with the ordering process of consciousness, much as proponents of general grammar did with language. In the earlier writings, prior to Socialist Realism, this unity was premised on and authorized by the synthesizing power of dialectical materialism, a strictly formal system which

Eisenstein identifies with both the external processes of historical change and the internal processes of consciousness.

With the institutionalization of Socialist Realism in the early thirties, Eisenstein was forced to confront the theoretical limitations of his dialectical approach to film form, specifically its inattention to the "content" of the image. In a manner of political and theoretical recantation, the dialectic was increasingly absent from his writings, no longer functioning as the authorizing property of montage cinema. "Organic" form, a systematic explication of the relation of parts to whole, of image to image-juxtaposition, replaced the conflict and synthesis of colliding images. The assertion of an aesthetic unity of mind and body, intellect and emotion, art and science took the form of a natural, organic structuration. An "organic" work was seen to unify not only the formal structure of an artwork with each of its "parts," but also the artwork and its perceiver.

The organic metaphor, however, like the dialectic, has its discursive limitations, particularly in its lack of specificity regarding the actual, immediate structuring principles of an "affective" work of art. In search of these principles, Eisenstein employed a concept of "inner speech." Eisenstein's enthusiasm for Joyce was a function of his experiments with "'inner monologue' as a literary method of abolishing the distinction between subject and object."[36] For Eisenstein, the qualities of "inner speech," as a prearticulate, primitive, sensual mode of thought and expression, offered a model for the cinema to emulate in its realization of a nonalienated, montage form of cinematic representation. Just as Condillac found that arbitrary institutional signs ("les signes d'institution") were a developed form of natural, animalistic cries ("les cris naturels"),[37] Eisenstein asserts that montage principles are a developed form of the most basic, innate structures of consciousness.

For Eisenstein, however, the messianic age for art was part and parcel of, in fact dependent on, a messianic age for humankind. In contrast to Griffith, who was limited by the ideology of capitalist social structures and thus remained "on a level of *representation and objectivity,*" Eisenstein saw himself within a "new social structure, which . . . forever freed art from narrowly commercial tasks, [and which could] give full realization" to montage principles of artistic construction.[38] With this conception, the revolution was for Eisenstein the culmination of a great deal more than the conflict of opposing social and economic orders. The revolution made possible a unity of the conceptual and the political, the emotional and the intellectual, transcending both the natural unity of "primitive" cultures and the degenerate dualism of the modern age. From the dialectical synthesis of the "primitive" and the "modern," Eisenstein constructed an aesthetic in which the image/sign and the laws of montage juxtaposition are raised to the highest level of sensual unity—in the dialectical synthesis of art and science, emotion and intellect, passion and politics.

Notes

1. Edward W. Said, "The Problem of Textuality: Two Exemplary Positions," *Critical Inquiry* (Summer 1978): 689.
2. Christopher Norris, *Deconstruction, Theory and Practice* (London: Methuen and Co., 1982), p. 142.
3. Even as philosophers like Nietzsche and writers like Michel Foucault criticize language as bound by discourse, they nevertheless assert that certain language use is liberating. For Nietzsche, it's "Dionysian" Greek theater, in which "not only is man and man reaffirmed, but nature which has become alienated, hostile, or subjugated, celebrates once more her reconciliation with her lost son, man." *The Birth of Tragedy* and *The Case of Wagner,* Walter Kaufmann, trans. (New York: Vintage Books, 1967), p. 37. For Foucault, language is liberated from discourse in the literature of writers like de Sade, who practice "the simple naming of that which lies at the limit of what we can say." In Donald F. Bouchard, ed., *Language, Counter-Memory, Practice, Selected Essays and Interviews with Michel Foucault* (Ithaca: Cornell University Press, 1977), p. 62.
4. On p. 191 of *The Archaeology of Knowledge,* translated by A. M. Sheridan Smith (New York: Harper and Row, 1972), Michel Foucault defines an "episteme" as "something like a world-view, a slice of history common to all branches of knowledge, which imposes on each the same norms and postulates, a general stage of reason, a certain structure of thought that the men of a particular period cannot escape." Both Foucault and Timothy Reiss, in relatively similar fashion, carve out two "epistemes" or 'discursive classes" which characterize linguistic philosophy prior to our own modernist epoch. For Foucault, they are epistemes of "resemblance" and "representation"; for Reiss, they are "discursive classes" of "patterning" or "analytico-referentiality." Foucault, *The Order of Things: An Archaeology of the Human Sciences* (New York: Vintage Books, 1973): Timothy J. Reiss, *The Discourse of Modernism* (Ithaca: Cornell University Press, 1982). Eisenstein's discourse seems to reiterate the latter of these "epistemes."

   For the other major theorist of classical film theory, André Bazin, his theories of cinematic realism reiterate an "episteme" of "resemblance," based on the divine accord words maintain with their referent. This discursive context is well represented by Leibniz, who approached a discovery of natural language based on the belief that

   > words are not only of thoughts but also of things . . . not so arbitrary and accidental in origin as some suppose . . . for languages have a certain natural origin, from the agreement of sounds with the dispositions of the mind. . . . I truly believe that languages are the best mirror of the human mind, and that an exact analysis of the signification of words would give insight into the operations of understanding better than any other means. Quoted in Hans Aarsleff, *From Locke to Saussure: Essays on the Study of Language and Intellectual History* (Minneapolis: University of Minnesota Press, 1982), pp. 69, 88.

   Aarsleff provides, in these essays, a more traditionally historical approach to the discourse of philosophies of language.

5. Etienne Bonnot Condillac, *Oeuvres philosophiques de Condillac,* Georges le Roy, ed., vol. 1 (Paris: Presses Univ. de France, 1947–51), p. 403A, as quoted in Aarsleff, p. 166.
6. Sergei Eisenstein, *The Film Sense,* Jay Leyda, ed. and trans. (New York: Meridian Books, 1957), p. 18.
7. Sergei Eisenstein, "The Cinematographic Principle and the Ideogram," in *Film Form: Essays in Film Theory,* Jay Leyda, trans. (New York: Meridian Books, 1957), pp. 39, 40.
8. Eisenstein, "A Dialectic Approach to Film Form," in *Film Form,* p. 46.
9. Ibid., p. 46.
10. Ibid., pp. 45, 47.
11. Eisenstein, "The Cinematographic Principle and the Ideogram," in *Film Form,* p. 30.
12. Eisenstein, "A Dialectic Approach," p. 60.
13. Ibid., pp. 52–53.
14. Ibid., p. 61.
15. Ibid., p. 63. In "Methods of Montage," dated about three months later (in *Film Form,* p. 83), Eisenstein concludes by writing that "the intellectual cinema will be that which resolves the conflict-juxtaposition of the physiological and intellectual overtones. Building a completely new form of cinematography—the realization of revolution in the general history of culture; building a synthesis of science, art, and class militancy."
16. Eisenstein, quoted in Leon Moussinac, *Sergei Eisenstein: An Investigation into His Films and Philosophy,* D. Sandy Petrey, trans. (New York: Crown, 1970), p. 42.
17. Andrew Tudor, *Theories of Film* (New York: Viking, 1974), pp. 26, 30.
18. Boris Shumyatsky, *Pravda,* March 1937, n. pag., as quoted in Moussinac, p. 159.
19. Eisenstein, *The Film Sense,* p. 11. In a similar vein, Eisenstein writes of his earlier lack of concern with film narrative. In "Film Form: New Problems," dated 1935 (in *Film Form,* p. 125), he writes,

    > The theory of the "intellectual cinema" . . . set before it the task of "restoring emotional fullness to the intellectual process." This theory engrossed itself as follows, in transmuting to screen form the abstract concept . . . without intermediary. Without recourse to story, or invented plot, in fact directly—by means of the image-composed elements as filmed. This theory was a broad, perhaps even a too broad, generalization of a series of possibilities of expression placed at our disposal by the methods of montage. . . . The theory of the intellectual cinema represented, as it were, a limit, the *reductio ad paradox* of that hypertrophy of the montage concept with which film esthetics were permeated during the emergence of Soviet silent cinematography as a whole and my own work in particular.

    Even earlier, in 1934, in the essay "Film Language" (in *Film Form,* pp. 111, 121), he had written:

    > For many filmmakers montage and leftist excesses of formalism—are synonymous. Yet montage is not this at all.
    >
    > For those who are able, montage is the most powerful compositional means of telling a story. . . .
    >
    > At present Soviet cinematography is historically correct in entering the campaign for the story. Along this path are still many difficulties, many risks of falsely

understanding the principles of story-telling. Of these the most terrible is the neglect of those possibilities given us now and again to liberate from the old traditions of the story:

The possibility of principally and newly re-examining the foundations and problems of the film-story.

And to go ahead in a cinematographically progressive movement, not "back to the story," but "to the story ahead of us."

20. Eisenstein, "Film Form: New Problems," pp. 144–45.

21. Eisenstein, "The Structure of the Film," in *Film Form,* p. 173.

22. Ibid., p. 160.

23. Ibid., p. 161.

24. Eisenstein, *The Film Sense,* p. 32.

25. Ibid., pp. 30–31.

26. Ibid., p. 18.

27. Ibid., p. 19.

28. In *Positions,* translated by Alan Bass (University of Chicago Press, 1981), on pp. 22 and 24–25, Derrida recounts the historical privilege accorded "speech":

> When I speak not only am I conscious of being present for what I think, but I am conscious also of keeping as close as possible to my thought, or to the "concept," a signifier that does not fall into the world, a signifier that I hear as soon as I emit it, that seems to depend upon my pure and free spontaneity, requiring the use of no instrument, no accessory, no force taken from the world. Not only do the signifier and signified seem to unite, but also in this confusion, the signifier seems to erase itself or to become transparent, in order to allow the concept to present itself as what it is, referring to nothing other than its presence. . . . The reduction of writing—as the reduction of the exteriority of the signifier—was part and parcel of phonologism and logocentrism. We know how Saussure, according to the traditional operation that was also Plato's, Aristotle's, Rousseau's, Hegel's, Husserl's, etc., excludes writing from the field of linguistics—from language and speech—as a phenomenon of exterior representation, both useless and dangerous.

29. Eisenstein, "Film Form: New Problems," pp. 130, 131.

30. Eisenstein, "Dickens, Griffith, and the Film Today," in *Film Form,* p. 249.

31. Joseph Vendryes, *Language: A Linguistic Introduction to History,* Paul Radin, trans. (New York: Knopf, 1925), pp. 145–16, quoted in *Film Form,* p. 249.

32. Eisenstein, "Dickens, Griffith," p. 245.

33. Ibid., pp. 248, 247.

34. Eisenstein, "Film Form: New Problems," p. 138.

35. Eisenstein, "Dickens, Griffith," pp. 250–51.

36. Eisenstein, "A Course in Treatment," p. 104.

37. See the discussion of Condillac in Aarsleff, "The Tradition of Condillac," in Aarsleff, esp. pp. 163–65.

38. Eisenstein, "Dickens, Griffith," p. 240.

19

Video: Electronic Collage

Max Almy

Video artist Max Almy discusses the concept of video as collage, giving insights into the process and content of recent work in video by artists such as Ed Emshwiller, Woody and Steina Vasulka, John Sanborn, Larry Kaufman, and Teri Yarbrow. For the essay she interviewed a number of contemporary video artists. Almy clearly describes both the technical and aesthetic concerns of a number of video artists' "collaged" pieces, as she points to "the challenge of using the video collage to reflect the way man perceives the world." As she notes, in the words of Ed Emshwiller, "We live in a multi-layered world and in a world that is so aware of various perspectives, ideologies and of meaning of signs and images—it (collage) is something that enables one to reflect on the complexity of life and relish its mystery."

It has been just over two short decades since a few adventurous artists began exploring the potential of video as a creative medium. From its rudimentary "port-a-pak" beginnings amidst the avant-garde rebellions of the sixties to its current status of respectability in museums around the world, video art has had a dizzyingly fast-paced history.

Video art has had a first generation involved with Neodada, formalism, conceptualism, feminism, performance, installation, documentary, experimental, and abstract work plus a second generation pursuing the postmodern concerns of language, new narrative, media, culture, poetry, and perception. Surrounding this activity has emerged a supportive network of exhibition spaces, curators, festivals, funding, alternative broadcast, and a newly curious critical establishment anxious to discuss the growing body of work and to define a position for video somewhere between art, television, and cinema. It has been a whirlwind of aesthetic activity that has proven the creative potential of this very contemporary new art medium.

The concept of video as ''collage'' is surprisingly appropriate and useful in describing an entire genre of visual experimentation that a specific group of video artists have explored throughout its history. Video is a medium with inherent technical properties. The video image is an electronic signal that can be manipulated, distorted, shaped, colorized, cut out, and collaged in a variety of ways. Just as collage suggests a composition of images or image fragments, text and materials taken out of their original context and recomposed to create an abstracted new composition, video artists have innovatively utilized the specific technical properties of the medium to recompose or collage images and image fragments within the video composition or frame.

This fascination with the multilayering of images and the resultant multilayering of meaning in video works has been described by media theorist Gene Youngblood. He philosophically refers to ''the collision of codes within the frame'' and sees this type of video composition as inherently different than ''the classical language of film in which the codes are constructed from the collision of frames.''[1] Although the following video artists represent a variety of aesthetic and conceptual concerns, they share a fascination with the video collage and the properties of the medium that offer such infinite compositional possibilities.

One of the earliest and most audacious examples of video collage was the classic broadcast television project *Global Groove,* by Nam June Paik. Born in Korea, Paik studied classical and avant-garde music in Europe and became part of the Neodada group Fluxus in the 1960s. In New York, Paik pioneered the use of video in the avant-garde with TV sets that were crudely altered with magnets. These TVs with absurdly distorted video images were used in outrageous sculptures and in his notorious performance works.

Paik's increasing interest in the experimental use of video led to the development of one of the first video synthesizers. He collaborated with Shuya Abe to design a device that could manipulate the video signal to create strangely colored and altered images.

In 1971, Paik began work on *Global Groove* for the Television Laboratory at WNET in New York, It was a wild mix of multilayered, multicultural programming including performances by John Cage, Allen Ginsberg, Charlotte Moorman playing Paik's *TV Cello* sculpture, go-go dancers, and Japanese commercials. The performers and video images were electronically collaged using a conventional television switcher which combines multiple video sources plus the newly designed Paik-Abe synthesizer. *Global Groove* was a dynamic and highly innovative work that challenged the conventions of traditional broadcast television and demonstrated the potentials of the new video art form.

Another artist who combined conventional television studio processes with experimental techniques in the early seventies was Ed Emshwiller. His stunningly beautiful *Scape-mates,* produced at WNET in 1972, was an early example of his consistently innovative work with video.

Previously, Emshwiller had been involved with abstract expressionist painting and had worked professionally as an illustrator for science fiction publications. His interest in movement, time, and the tension between formal abstraction and representational imagery led to experimental film works that combined abstract animation with live performance. For Emshwiller, the video work *Scape-mates* was a further exploration of abstract synthesized video imagery combined with live dancers from the Alwin Nikolais dance group. It was a surreal, futuristic look at man and technology in an environment of imagery created on a Scanamate video processor.

The type of image processing that was used in *Scape-mates* and *Global Groove* is known as analogue processing. The image is translated electronically into a video signal or voltage flow within the video camera. That continuous flow of electronic information can be controlled and altered by devices like video switchers and video synthesizers. These devices can shape, distort, colorize, cut out (key), and recombine video images from one or more sources including live cameras and video tape playback. The result can be very subtly altered video images or complex collages combining many layers of images and processed video.

In 1974, computer technology was interfaced with video technology to help control and organize editing. Complex and sophisticated editing was possible for the first time with the help of specially programmed computer systems and software. Even video processing and collaging could be carefully programmed and controlled by computers and new digital special effects devices.

In this new type of digital processing, the video image itself was now being translated into digital information, thousands of discrete bits of image data or pixels that could be manipulated by a computer program. Artists like Ed Emshwiller and Woody and Steina Vasulka led the way, working with engineers to design the first programs and systems that could digitally process the video signal.

Ed Emshwiller's famous computer-video work *Sunstone,* produced at the New York Institute of Technology in 1979, was one of the first works to create, move, transform, and combine images digitally (figs. 19.1, 19.2). Using NYIT's highly advanced computer animation systems, Emshwiller and a group of talented computer scientists, including Alvy Ray Smith, worked for eight months to create programs and images for *Sunstone.* It was a remarkable demonstration of two-dimensional computer paint im-

Figure 19.1. Ed Emshwiller, Image from *Sunstone,* 1979
Computer-video work.

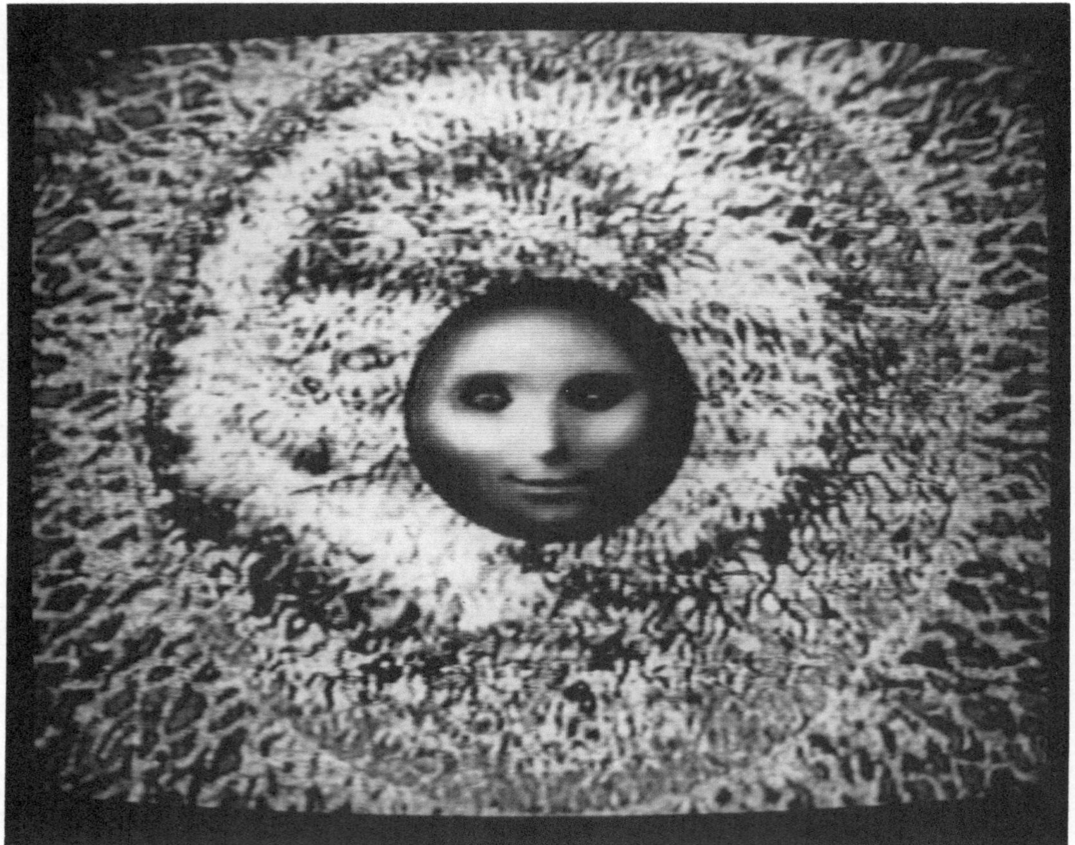

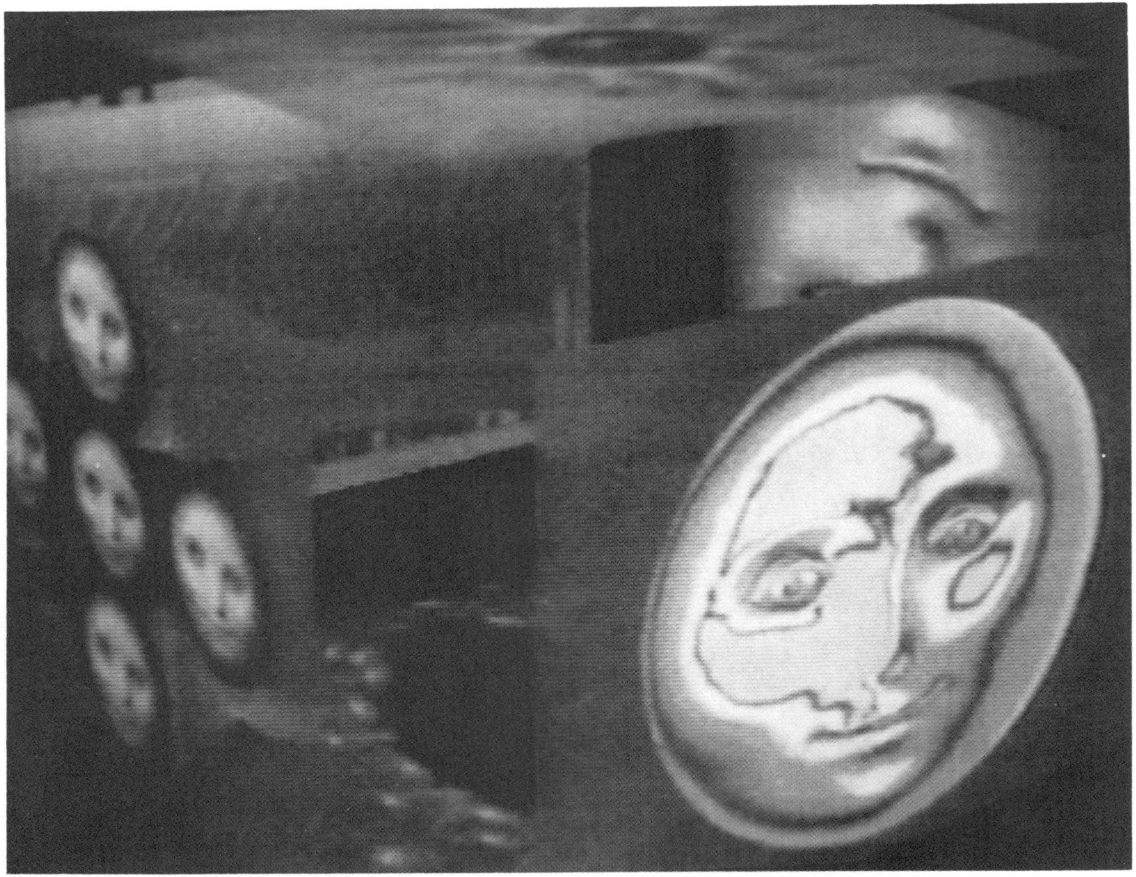

Figure 19.2. Ed Emshwiller, Image from *Sunstone,* 1979
Computer-video work.

agery and three-dimensional computer animation integrated to create a truly multidimensional computer-video work.

As an artist who is drawn to experiment with new techniques, Emshwiller states,

> I'm fascinated by the character of the mark that one is capable of using with different instruments. In my early training, I studied graphics and used engraving and etching tools, then water colors, crayons, movie cameras, video cameras—every one makes a different kind of mark and can combine things in different ways. That sort of thing has always fascinated me because the character of the mark has such an impact emotionally and stimulates thought relationships just as imaginative content does.[2]

In contrast to the highly sophisticated tools used for *Sunstone,* Emshwiller worked with an inexpensive home computer to create elaborate computer-generated traveling mattes for his video work *Skin Matrix.* A matte is a black and white high contrast shape or cut-out that is used in editing to combine two different video image sources. One video source is assigned to each color and then layered electronically.

Emshwiller programmed two hundred forty different moving black and white patterns that were then used to create complex moving collages of rock, sand, skin, ancient stone faces, and a variety of luxurious textures, images, and surfaces. It was a highly evocative and haunting portrayal of man, nature, age, and time.

His most recent work, *Hungers* (1988), is a large theater piece conceived and created with new music composer Morton Subotnick (fig. 19.3). *Hungers* involves layers of collaborative performance, dance, voice, acoustic and computer music, video and computer images. It is a precisely orchestrated collage of images and music expressing the basic human hungers, including food, sex, love, and power in poetic, nonnarrative movements. For this work, computers are not only used to help compose and generate the music and video imagery but are also relied on during the performance to help choose and combine images for specific musical passages.

As a video artist, Emshwiller creates work of great beauty and visual poetry. He reaches deep into the human experience toward the larger issues of man, environment, relationships, and technology to create powerful works. The ecstatic complexity of his video collages is a stunning reflection of his ideas about the way man perceives the world.

Woody Vasulka and his wife Steina have played an important role in the development of video art. In 1971, they founded The Kitchen, an important interdisciplinary art center in New York, which has continuously featured video screenings of new video work. Steina and Woody have been prolific artists, creating works that have systematically explored innovative techniques while addressing issues of visual aesthetic theory.

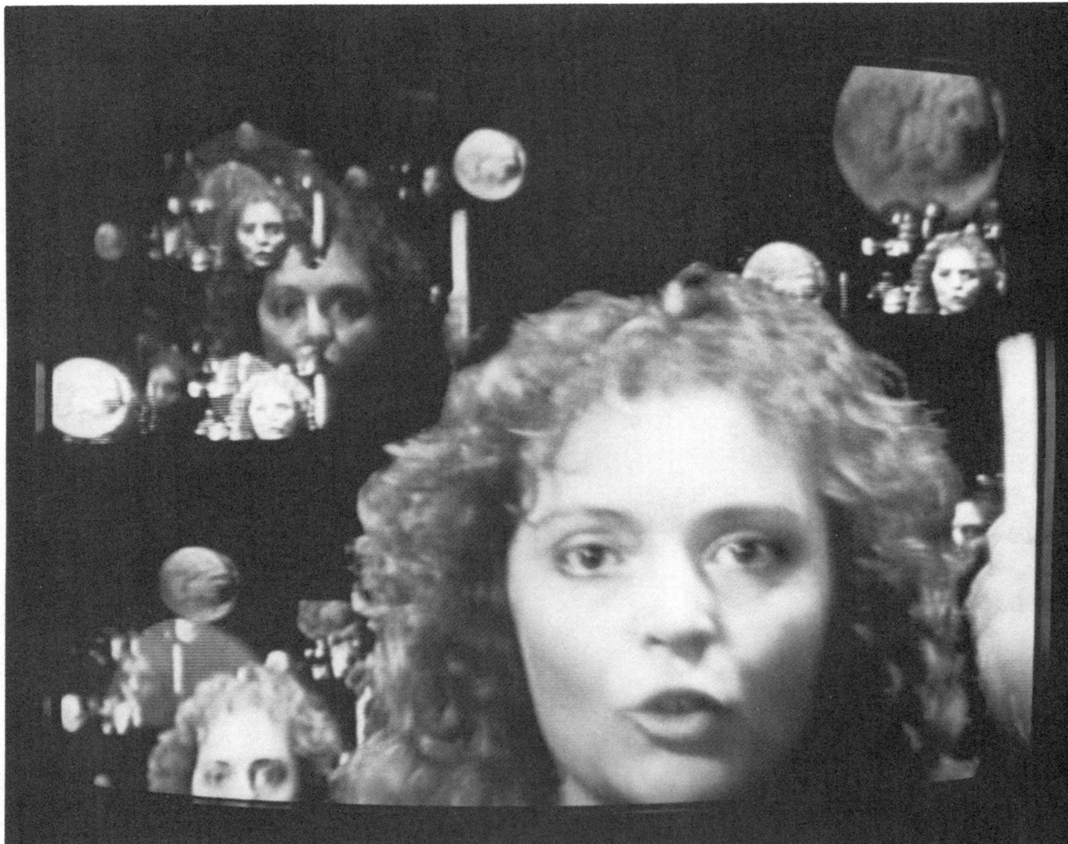

Figure 19.3. Ed Emshwiller, Image from *Hungers,* 1988
Computer-video work.

In 1978, Woody Vasulka and Jeffrey Schier developed the Digital Image Articulator, which stores processes, colors, and shapes, and layers multiple video image sources in real time. Vasulka has gradually added to this technology with the capacity to create totally computer-generated imagery in an attempt to further "identify the codes" of electronically generated imagery. "Vasulka has long argued for the possibility of producing an 'electronic reality' that would be more convincing than camera reality, reflecting a Modernist faith in science and the transformative powers of technology."[3]

Woody Vasulka's approach to video collage has some highly theoretical underpinnings. He respects the concepts of Austrian artist and theoretician Peter Weibel, who describes computer imagery as "polytropic" and "polychronic." Polytropic (an extension of concepts in modern paintings) is the ability of the frame to contain many planes of information, subject, image, and even concepts of time, such as present, past, future, and dream, within one space. Polychronic refers to the rate at which various images appear, their order and speed. The polytropic and polychronic concepts are useful to explain the layering of image and meaning, and the importance of time in video collage.

In his video work, Vasulka further demonstrates his own theories of figure-ground, image-object, texture-narrative and object-database. With his most recent work, *Art of Memory,* he has chosen powerful content and strong images to play out these formal inquiries (fig. 19.4). Historical images from World War II and the Spanish Civil War are collaged within images of the monumental Southwest landscape. He digitally shapes the historic images into three-dimensional image-objects. Vasulka describes this work as an attempt to move from the illusionistic view of the frame as cinematic "window on the world" with image as icon, to a view of the frame where the image becomes a new type of psychologically dimensional object. These polytropic and polychronic collages refer to war, media, memory, and loss with strikingly original and memorable imagery.

In the 1980s, the pioneering technical work that was done by artists and engineers has been further developed by the video and television industry. Digital processing has been perfected to the degree that each pixel can be manipulated with precise control. Sophisticated video effects and processing are now part of the everyday visual language of television sports, news, commercials, and music videos.

Meanwhile video artists have continued to pursue the medium with an intent to convey serious aesthetic and conceptual meaning. A new generation of artists have chosen video as an appropriate medium to

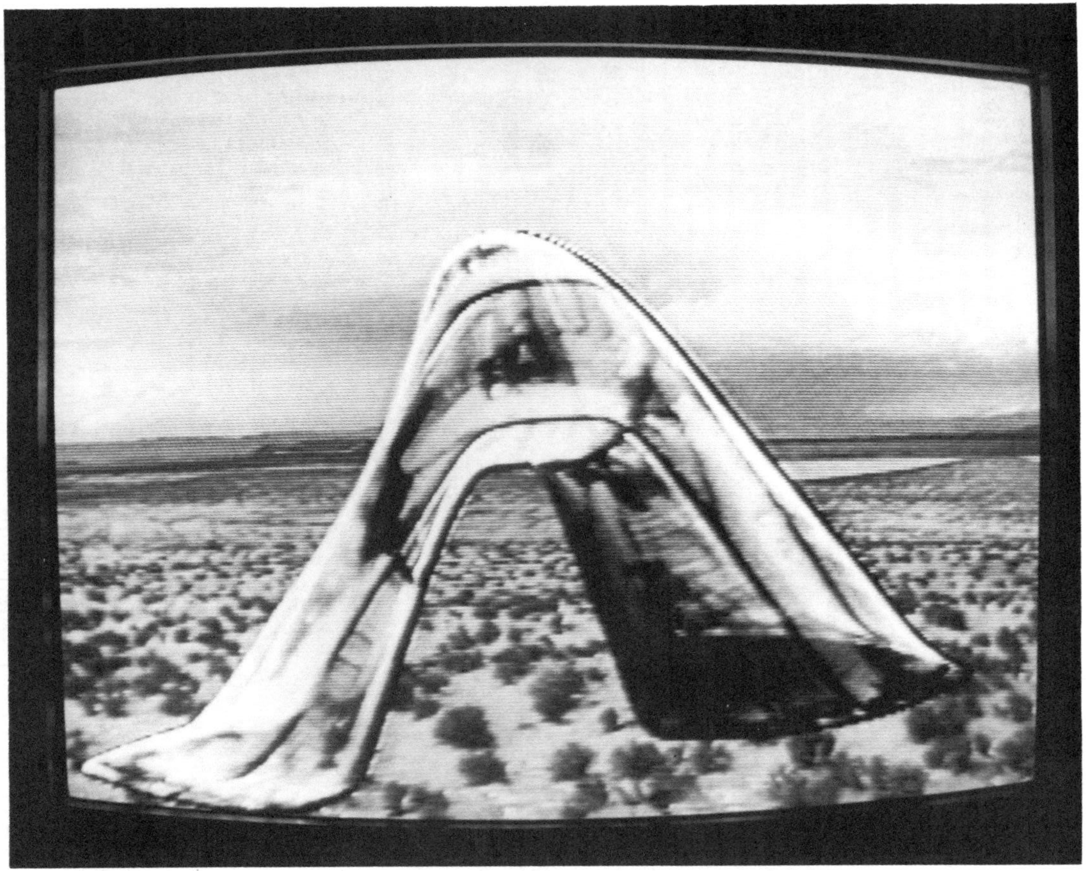

Figure 19.4. Woody Vasulka, Image from *Art of Memory,* 1987
Computer-video work.

reflect the dynamics of the postmodern world. In a milieu characterized by crossovers between art forms—painting, sculpture, video, film, media, music, theater, and design—where appropriation, collaboration, and eclecticism are the norm, video provides an expansive and articulate medium of expression.

John Sanborn has taken the video collage to a high level of development. Although he was initially interested in film, he wanted to move beyond the traditional linear construction and narrative techniques of film with works that would explore innovative visual and narrative structure. He recognized that with video he could "take the representational image out of its conventional context and place it seamlessly amongst other images to recontextualize and create a wholly new idiom with new readings and mental association."[4]

In 1981, Sanborn began work on a brilliant collaboration with avant-garde composer Robert Ashley. The work, *Perfect Lives,* was a new music opera described by the artists as a "Post-Modern version of the mythology of small town America." *Perfect Lives* was originally performed live as an elaborate multimedia performance with video by John Sanborn. But it had also been conceived as an opera for television, providing Sanborn with an opportunity to experiment with this innovatively structured work.

It was produced by The Kitchen and Channel 4 in London as a massive seven-part opera. The production was designed to use video framing, camera work, collaging, and effects as integral conceptual elements of the overall work. In each episode, visual themes and compositions were designed as metaphors carefully moved in and out of conceptual focus.

While working with leading contemporary dance choreographers like David Gordon and Charles Moulton, Sanborn has used a variety of approaches to recontextualize movement, activities, and events. He takes a specific dance metaphor created by the choreographer and by placing it in a different context, builds and elaborates on the metaphor.

In a recent work, *Luminaire* (1986), dancers move and interact within a transforming environment where space and camera movement are articulated by computer animations and digitally moved video elements (figs. 19.5, 19.6). In one memorable sequence, the viewer is moved through a completely computer-generated art museum with galleries that represent eras in the history of art. In the final, futuristic room, we float into one of the art works, a three-dimensional computer abstract that wryly suggests where the future of visual art may lie. It is a perfect metaphor for the merging of art and future technologies that Sanborn embraces in his work.

Larry Kaufman and Teri Yarbrow are two emerging artists who feel quite comfortable working with the highly sophisticated new tools of video and computer technology to create complex and compelling personal works.

After working with photography and film, Kaufman chose to work with video for its flexibility as a medium, particularly in editing. He finds a correlation between video and music as he builds rhythm and syncopation into the structure and layering of his work.

His newest work, *The Whole Truth* (1988), is a systematic analysis of the behavior involved in lying. Through hundreds of lies spoken by countless "talking heads," we hear a complexly constructed litany of lies (fig. 19.7). In one sequence, a visual collage of lies is taken apart as layer upon layer of performers telling lies are peeled away. Another sequence is carefully structured and designed to portray the contagion of lies. A long row of performers is moved across the screen; each one is digitally turned to tell his lie to the one following him before he leaves the frame.

Kaufman used a new digital recording device to construct these video collage sequences. With it, each performer was recorded separately as a moving cut-out until the entire sequence was complete. Digital recording allows each new image to be added to the frame as new data; there is never any generational loss of picture quality as in multiply recorded layers of analogue video. The video collage can now be digitally composed with an almost endless number of layers and elements.

Teri Yarbrow worked as a painter and had developed a series of intricate abstract collages based on Middle Eastern design when she started working with video as a way to move images spatially and in time. Her video work is elaborately designed and multilayered but with a primary concern of communicating highly focused personal and social statements.

Yarbrow's *Atomic Dreams* (1987) is an experimental narrative which portrays nuclear anxiety through a series of disturbing dreams. A woman has increasingly terrifying dreams that are a visual collage of old war footage, the dreamer, and computer-generated images and effects (fig. 19.8). At one point, a frightening tunnel of war is digitally constructed of twenty-seven separate moving video panels. Yarbrow skillfully orchestrates numerous elements to create a work that gradually transforms and suggests a hopeful resolution to fear and conflict.

As a video artist, I realize that I have always thought of video as collage. I have worked with video as an experimental medium since the early 1970s and through the years my work has become increasingly complex and visually layered. At the same time, the layers of text and meaning have moved from personal to social commentary and satire.

In the seventies, I used video very minimally and usually as one element within an elaborate installation or performance work. But as the

Figure 19.5. John Sanborn, Image from *Luminaire,* 1986
Computer-video work.

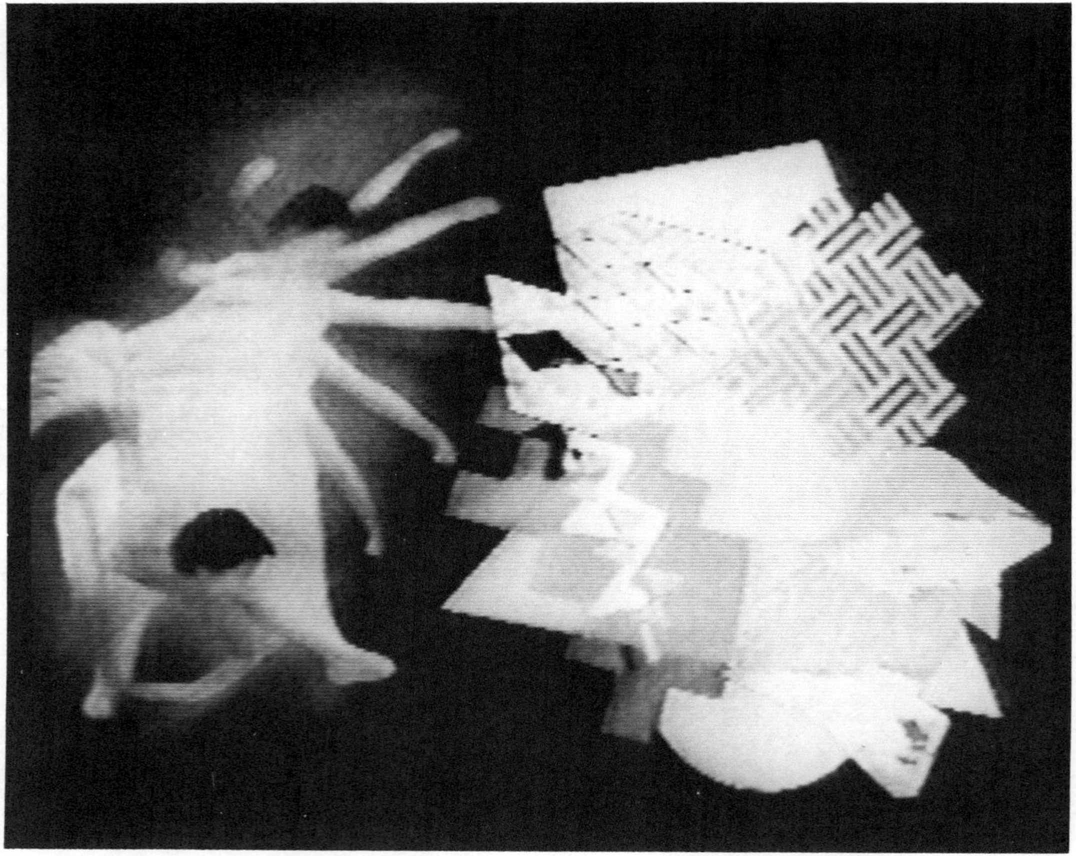

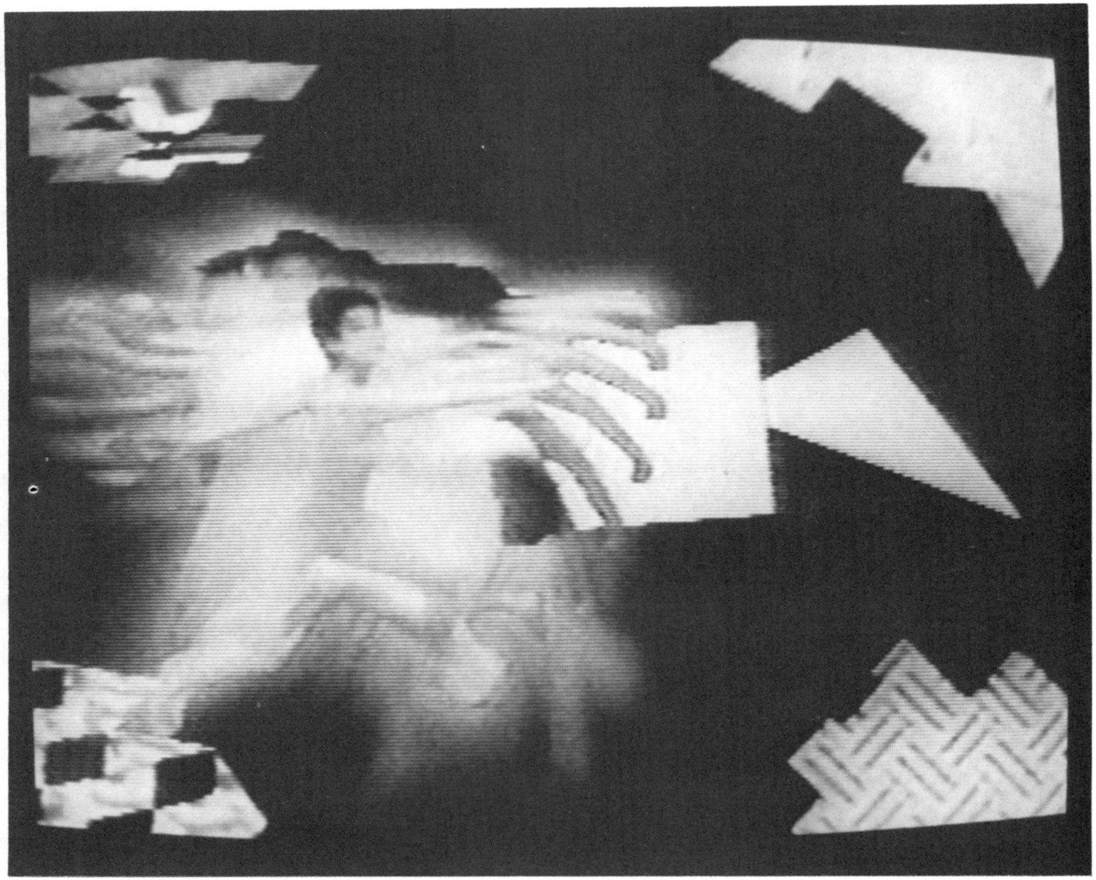

Figure 19.6. John Sanborn, Image from *Luminaire,* 1986
Computer-video work.

Figure 19.7. Larry Kaufman, Image from *The Whole Truth,* 1988
Computer-video work.

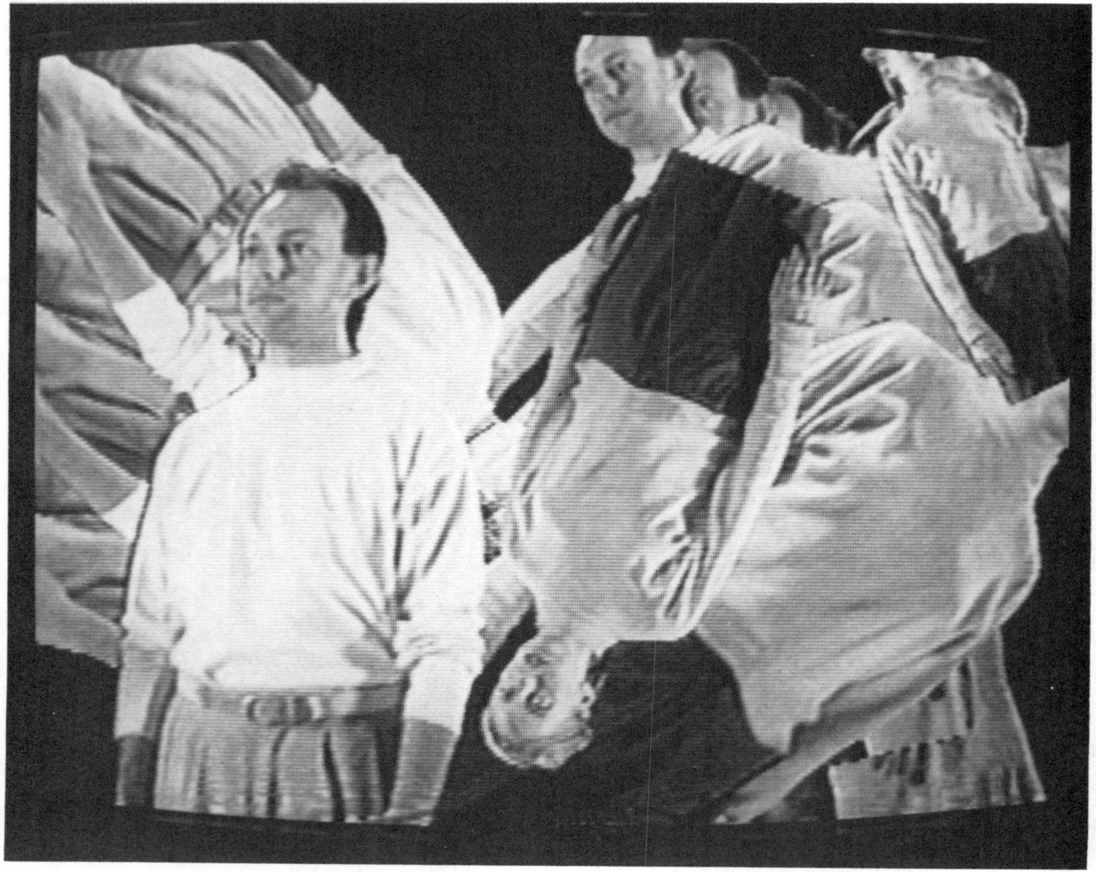

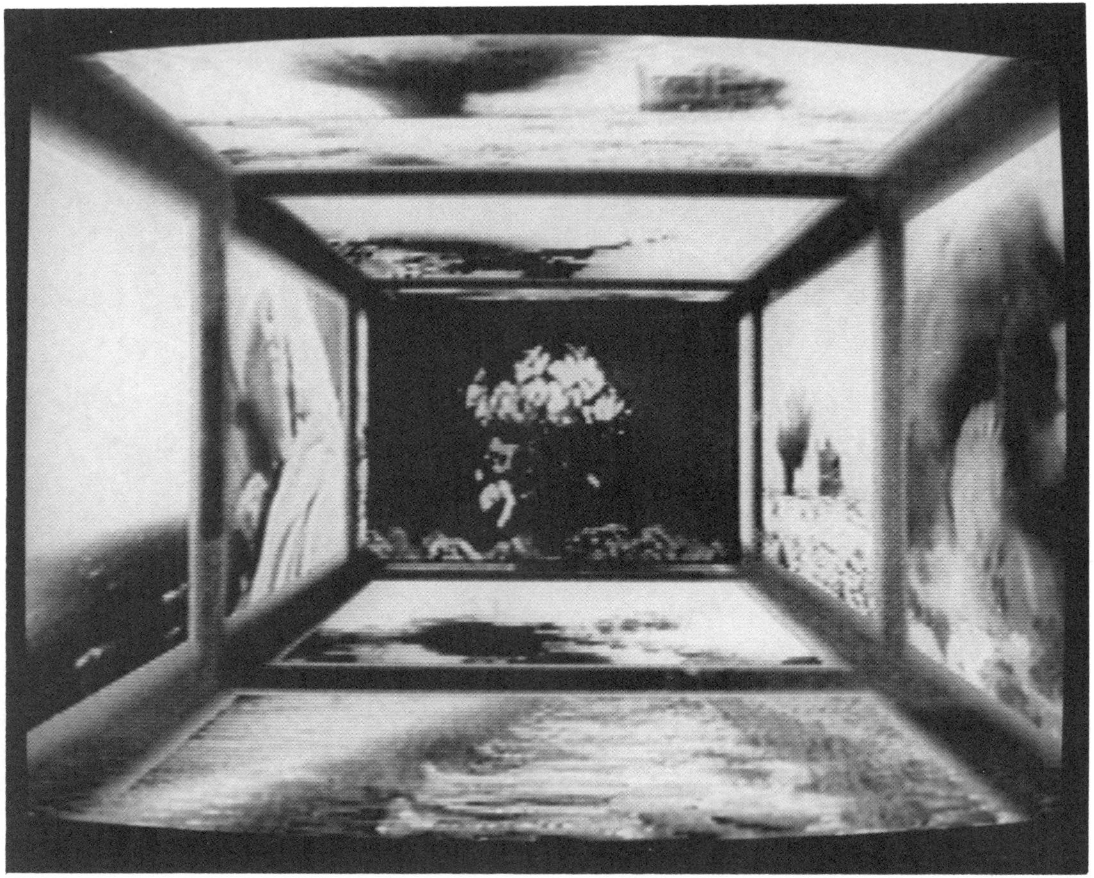

Figure 19.8. Teri Yarbrow, Image from *Atomic Dreams,* 1987 Computer-video work.

Figure 19.9. Max Almy, Image from *Perfect Leader,* 1983
Computer-video work.

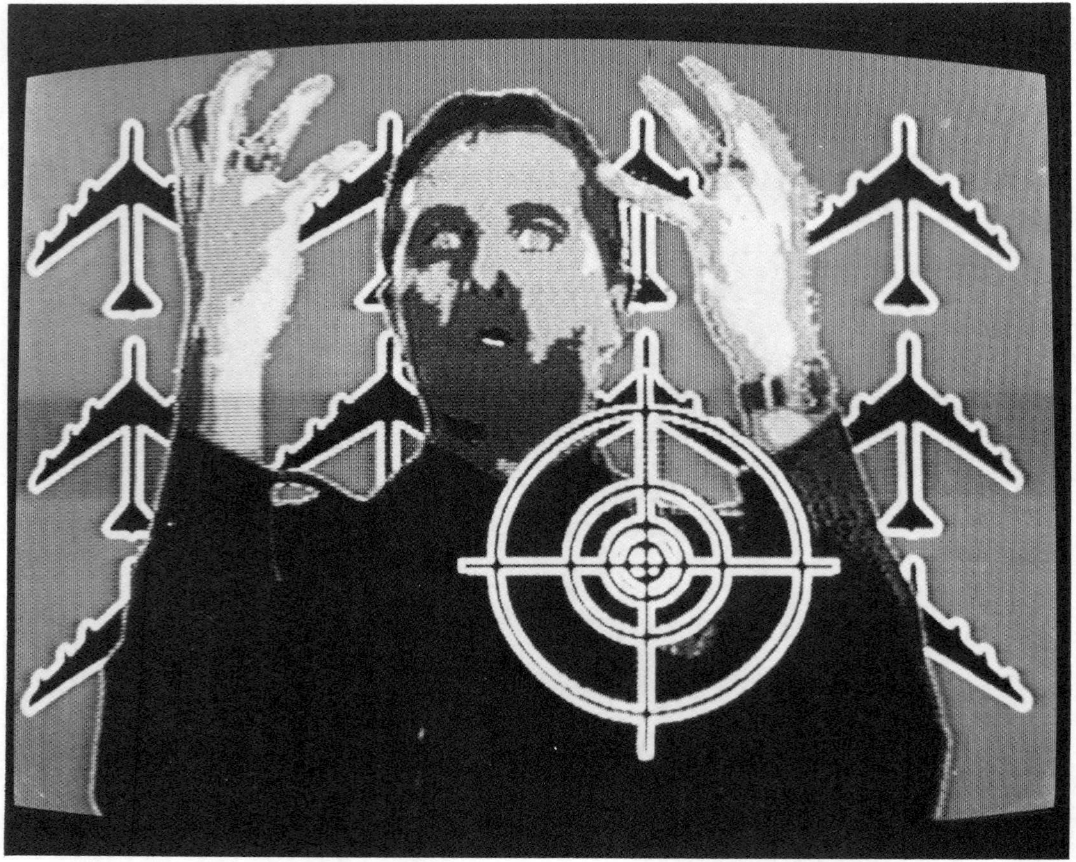

technology evolved, I became interested in using the emerging techniques to create complexity within the frame, moving images through and composing in unusual and interesting ways.

In *Leaving the 20th Century* (1981) I created a video-synthesized futuristic world for an experimental narrative work that examined life in the late twentieth century. A man and a woman portrayed in the work move through videoscapes created entirely on a video switcher. I was exploring unconventional narrative techniques and designing visual strategies to support them. Utilizing advanced editing and video collaging, I found that I had complete freedom to imaginatively control every element of the work. It is this ultimate imaginative and creative control that makes video such an expressive palette for the artist.

In 1983, I finished *Perfect Leader,* a short satire about the manufacturing and marketing of a political candidate in which an omnipotent computer creates the perfect leader. The entire work is structured to resemble interaction with a computer program. The visual design is calculated to portray the candidate's development in very graphic terms. The leader is constantly surrounded by a collage of visual information and icons that suggest the best ingredients for a successful candidate (fig. 19.9). The numerous collage elements carried an important amount of information additional to the performance and text. This type of collaging of visual information, image, and text has become a distinctive and important part of my continuing video work.

Whether using the concepts of polytropic space, polychronic time, ecstatic multiplicity, or a recontextualized video idiom, the video artists discussed have all responded to the challenge of using the video collage to reflect the way man perceives the world. As Ed Emshwiller has said, "We live in a multi-layered world and in a world that is so self aware of various perspectives, ideologies and of the meaning of signs and images—it [collage] is something that enables one to reflect on the complexity of life and relish its mystery."[5]

Notes

1. Gene Youngblood, "A Medium Matures: Video and The Cinematic Enterprise," *The Second Link* (Walter Phillips Gallery, 1983), p. 10.
2. Ed Emshwiller, interview with Max Almy, 1988.
3. Charles Hagen, "Breaking the Box: The Electronic Operas of Robert Ashley and Woody Vasulka," *Artforum* (March 1985): 57.
4. John Sanborn, interview with Max Almy, 1988.
5. Ed Emshwiller, interview with Max Almy, 1988.

20

Collage as Language: Further Thoughts on "Events"

Paul Vangelisti

Not only have the visual arts been liberated by the techniques of collage, but so, too, have literature and language. Indeed, it is interesting to note that much artistic innovation in this century has been rooted in literary work. Futurism and Dada began as literary and political movements. Surrealists were involved with automatic literary techniques. In the contemporary era, Paul Vangelisti, in his poetry, experiments with collage techniques and points to relationships between collage in the visual arts and collage in language. For him, "verbal collage," offered "a way to salvage the 'shipwreck,' to shift from the tragic to the comic, reclaiming the pluralities of language, the lyrical included. Comedy thus was assumed as the basis for collage, and ultimately, its synthetic force."

> *A week now that ragged black dog nuzzling the curb 400 miles north of here as if it were asleep. So we begin with an extensive appreciation of a woman called "Charlotte," a generous cocotte who simulates long nightingale-like cries of satisfied love because they give felicity and triumph to her dying young lover. As one drowsier with the wind whipping elm and cypress the odor of last night's fire a sky so blue the bottom looks fallen out. The elder of the two gentlewomen keeps a diary of continuous small joys, referring to her companion in terms such as "my Love" or "my Delight": "Read Mme. deSevigne. My Love drawing." Or: "At ten my Beloved and I drank a dish of tea. A day most delicious and exquisite in its refinement." Filled with information about people, companies, charitable organizations and churches, government bodies and absolutely amazing places that need quick wit and literacy to write on countless subjects. Or: "Sweet sunshine, blue sky, birds innumerable. My beloved and I went a delicious walk round Edward*

Evans' field.'' Since most of it is done evenings and weekends, sitting cross-legged in front of the typewriter, on a richly luxurious carpet in a penthouse with an incredible skyline view. Sir Walter Scott and other distinguished travellers finally begin calling on them, for the grace of their elegant manners and concentrated tenderness. Because brain-boggling as it might seem, there is a real shortage in this world of people who can write the English language without stubbing their toe on a comma. Think about this for a moment, then read the following. Rembrandt etched THE THREE TREES during a time when he was preoccupied with light and swirling action. While the principal motif is a group of trees, touched with highlights and shadows, their massed foliage interpenetrating, the etching is alive with sunshine and storm, and with wind that sends clouds flying. Now look at this etching again. Fire and flood sweep the world. Sinister hybrids break into every bedroom, electric paperweights play an unaccountable part in human affairs, torsos with severed heads make themselves comfortable in well-known Parisian archways, lion-headed men go undeterred to the guillotine, a commodious railway carriage makes its last stop half-way up the Sphinx. Now look at the etching again. A vision that is to say a device of snouts and raw fish clogged gutters and cabbages wet streets in an unfamiliar city mirrors that won't come clean twilight tiny spoons of coffee stirring all day long. Now look at the etching again. This classic makes its statement more strongly than ever, with a contemporary cut, attention to detail and the particular uniqueness of its fabric. Now look at the etching once more. Do you see more in it now? Feel greater involvement? If you do, you already see more, feel more, know more about Rembrandt—and about art.

''Event 19: Rembrandt''

This is one of a series of nineteen pieces from my book *Portfolio,* written in 1976, published in 1978, and now appearing in a bilingual Italian reedition. The verbal collages (or, if you will, poems-in-prose) of ''Events 7-25'' had as their starting point a sense of rupture with how I had defined my poetry up to that time. Even ''collage,'' borrowed from visual art as a model in assembling these pieces, did not seem then to emphasize enough the coincidences of meaning that had come to play in *Portfolio.* The term ''event'' (a collision of forces which forms, in physics, a basic observational unit) suggested more of a departure not only in compositional method but in the conception of these pieces as poems.

Subsequent work, with verbal and visual texts, has changed not so much the intrinsic value of the ''events'' as my evaluation of what influence these poems-in-prose have had on what I have done since.* In retrospect, what remains stable in *Portfolio* is the enterprise of collage. It grew from an urge (however fictively or artificially realized) to base art in physical reality, or in this case, in the language contemporary reality was speaking in me. As poet Jack Spicer put it in *After Lorca* (*Collected Books* 33):

> I would like to make poems out of real objects. The lemon to be a lemon that the reader could cut or squeeze or taste—a real lemon like a newspaper in a collage is a real newspaper. I would like the moon in my poems to be a real moon, one which could be suddenly covered with a cloud that has nothing to do with the poem—a moon utterly independent of images.

My poetic language then felt inadequate to perceive and organize the words that daily surrounded me. I would revise poems until they were lines awash on the pages of notebooks, seeming to lack context, frame, or purpose when translated onto the typed or printed page. Reduced to what I had considered its minimal, i.e., "poetic" essence, the verse seemed fragments of a misquoted and lost text, a text which betrayed itself and me—any unified sense it might have held in my consciousness—the more it was written or uttered.

In an afterword to the original 1978 edition, I tried to describe these misgivings and the rupture they ultimately led to (*Portfolio* 37):

> At this point the activity of writing poetry and, of course, the poem itself, are not self-defining. The verbal machine left by the modernists holds at best a tentative relationship to whatever it is we call language. The poems' linguistic situation—that area of human activity described by the poem's use of language—has become marginal, no longer including much of the self-justifying energy that we, like all dutiful post-modernists, have been more than willing to ascribe to it.

Besides the unfortunate, if then necessary, polemical tone, what now emerges is a challenge to the autonomy of lyric verse, that repetition of and belief in form without semantic and contextual differences. The indirection and coy formalism of the first and third sentences in "Event 19"

---

*In my next two collections, *Another You* (Red Hill, 1981) and *Abandoned Latitudes* (Red Hill, 1983), collage was a constructive method in visual poems, performance and exhibition texts, and in metrical experiments which combined Etruscan and Greek orthographies, as well as sound systems, with Anglo-Saxon and Anglo-American lyric models. From 1984 to 1986, I also used verbal collage to compose two texts, "River" (1985) and "Marx' Daughters" (1986), for the dance company Rime and another for the performance piece "Who Is God" (1986).

seemed to evade the life (the texture and chaos of verbal experience) out of which they were written):

> A week now that ragged black dog nuzzling the curb 400 miles north of here as if it were asleep. . . .
> As one drowsier with the wind whipping elm and cypress the odor of last night's fire a sky so blue the bottom looks fallen out.

These statements, from abandoned or unfinished poems here recomposed as sentences, acquire within the collaged "event" a way to be read which implies their linguistic origins as well as their peculiar emotional density. Such contexts had become so barely suggested in my poems that they appeared phantasmic, cynically formal and incomplete when the lines tried as verse to lie on the page. Why the images of dreaminess and absence? Was it an attempt at lyrical transcendance (a reaching for some farther shore) or a disquietude with what one had become or a combination of the two?

In any case, the other semiotic systems in the collaged "event" allow the poetical statements a background and/or foreground against which to cast their rather oblique shadows. It is as if the two sentences may float at times on the surface of semantic chaos and at other times be read through the surface like a screen.

The break with the lyric, however, was not only a formalistic dissatisfaction. I felt more and more trapped by a certain "tragic" ethos or stance for which the desire to write verse preordained me. Something curious was happening to my notion of the poet as artist-subject, not unlike a phenomenon persistent among the historical avant-gardes in the first third of the century. Once the subject was dislocated formally—spatially in painting, say, or rhythmically in verse—once, as Braque put it, "the subject is not the object" (*Cubism* 147), an interesting thing began to happen. Not only did the process of painting or writing become itself the subject but this process acquired certain historical and political values, thematic values, if you will.

After the first successes of rebellion, avant-garde practice often shifted from antagonism to agonism, i.e., became rarified and interiorized within a play of contradiction residing in the very notion of the artistic self. This play within modernism, and postmodernism as well, allows a drive toward contemporaneity (the historical peculiarity of a medium) to co-exist with the continually aggravated ethic (and perhaps economy) of individualism. The radical approach to a medium or set of signs—an approach grounded in a social reality seeming to demand a dismantling of individual art practice—finds its functional opposite in the psychology of self-risk, ultimate responsibility to the artistic self, etc. Avant-gardism may be viewed—historically and contemporaneously—as an activity by which this basic opposition gets worked out in art practice, though the contradiction in theory remains.

In my first ten years of writing poetry, I had worked on various means to analyze and dismantle the lyric. I had tried to dislocate it rhythmically and semantically, under the influence of literary translation and jazz, pushing the poem toward some minimal, philosophic rapture. Then I extended the sense of "silent music" into the long or book-length poem, fashioning a sort of lyrical and epistemological diary. Then came the break in *Portfolio* and its "events"; for over a year and a half I did not write verse.*

In experimenting with the lyric, I had found myself adopting an increasingly melancholic and, at least in schematic terms, "tragic" view of contemporary life. It became what George Oppen (a poet then most influential to me) named "the shipwreck/ Of the singular," a life of the mind in which "one may honorably keep/ His distance/ If he can" (*Of Being Numerous* 13, 18). This displaced view was not only thematic but essential, as if the activity of writing verse had become itself a "tragic" undertaking: the singular poetic utterance in a wasteland of semantic destruction.

Verbal collage offered a way to salvage the "shipwreck," to shift from the tragic to the comic, reclaiming the pluralities of language, the lyrical included. Comedy thus was assumed as the basis for collage and, ultimately, its synthetic force.

Before describing the composition of an "event," I would again like to quote my afterword:

> While in Burroughs' assemblages the most evident procedure is the disjunction of the material, the opposite is true of these "Events." The rupture of the sensibility chronicled by Burroughs in the 50s and 60s has by now become a given. One's instinctive response is not to balk at the fragmentation of cultural activity immersing us—e.g. reading an art or movie review while in front of the television while skimming a biography while attempting to sustain talk with the person next to you on the sofa—but instead to repair this disassociation, to make some connection among the fragments.

The salvage in *Portfolio* is precisely comic, an asssemblage of social and personal contexts within which poetic language may be renewed, albeit at times ironically or self-mockingly, at times wistfully, even on occasion ecstatically. Or, once more quoting my afterword: "In choosing to play

*After finishing *Portfolio* in 1976, and through all of the next year, I concentrated on two editions, published in xerox, of visual and verbal narrative: 2×2 (San Francisco: Invisible City Editions, 1977) and *Remembering the Movies* (Invisible City, 1977).

with this phenomenon, I find my poetry redefining itself in terms of language and, even more important, containing a criticism of itself and, in turn, a criticism of the language it is defined by."

A few words then about the specific construction of "Event 19: Rembrandt." The basic compositional unit, syntactically and rhythmically, is the sentence. The sentence allows the collage to become specific and public, a fundamental place for a society's linguistic behavior to convene. There is a certain democracy, if only formal and mechanical, in the encounter. The "performative" (persuasive) sentence, the PR aphorism, the manufacturer's instructions are somewhat neutralized outside of the informationally torrid climates within which these utterances customarily thrive. Also my salvaged lines no longer depend on the hierarchical context of verse; they are extended, stretched horizontal, if you will, into statement and sentence. Thus the collages are a forum in which linguistic codes attain a syntactic, multivocal equality, while in constant play with one another—prose and verse alike—as if they were rhythmical components in an oral epic.

Specifically, we have an encounter of sentences (occasionally syntax was adjusted to maintain the encounter's fluidity or sociability) which contain, in order, the following elements: fragments of verse from my notebooks; a citation from a biography of Colette; more verse fragments; an article on two nineteenth-century British lesbians, with quotations from one of the gentlewomen's diary; excerpts from an how-you-too-can-become-a-writer magazine ad; more of the gentlewoman's diary; more writer's ad; more about the nineteenth-century reputation of the lesbian couple; more of the writer's come-on; then the Rembrandt ad for some art-history-made-easy books; citations from Patrick Waldberg's *Surrealism;* more of the refrain, "Now look at the etching again," from the Rembrandt ad; more verse; the Rembrandt refrain again; captions from a fashion catalogue; once more the Rembrandt refrain; and finally the closing lines, the grand, clinching finale of the plea for Rembrandt and art appreciation.

Viewed rhetorically the sentences breakdown thus: poetic, in the broadest sense of the word, with a more often than not fugacious tone; narrative and vaguely sentimental; descriptive and diaristic; "performative" or persuasive from the ad copy, caption, slogan contexts; and false journalistic, from Waldberg's "history" of Surrealism.

More generally, in his introduction to the reedition of *Portfolio,* Peter Carravetta locates the book, and specifically "Event 19: Rembrandt," within the notions of "language, *topics* and form in the Modern-to-Postmodern curvature." He says of "Event 19":

> An apparently nonsensical section of sentences strewn upon the page. Now look again and notice how each of the sentences is stylistically complete, enclosed, and in most

> cases unrelated to what precedes and what follows it, yet calm and undistressed (the distress we may say is in the reader's mind as it searches feverishly for the proper master code to establish the referent of the sign strings). Clearly this collage or poem-in-prose displays, at the very least, an awareness of the multiplicity of semiotic systems which linguistic utterances can trigger and represent. But that's the first step. Then we consider the ''actual'' meaning of each of these sequential though unrelated sentences, and we tune in each code individually. Yet the material available is scant, so each word must charge itself symbolically, and each statement will tend to make a larger claim.

Whatever his critical agenda, I find Carravetta's analysis accurate and helpful. I hesitate, however, to analyse the thematics of this or any of the other texts in *Portfolio.* I prefer to distrust my intentions—retrospective or otherwise—and respect the ambiguous, plurivocal nature of the texts. As for any ''larger claim,'' this should be left to Carravetta:

> The ''Event'' is perhaps best understood as a poliphony of utterances, poetic and otherwise, within which the poet's voice is but one incidental sparkle constantly threatened by the magmatic and chaotic background, and whose speaking is furthermore straightlaced to the dominant tropes of short, lyrical, undifferentiating prosody. In this sense, the ''event'' is witness to the inner struggles and failures not only of the referential sentences that speak and represent the Babylonian essence of the American fiber, but also of a literary tradition (that of the ''lyrical'' poem) which insists on defining poetic being while forgetting poetic becoming in the meantime.

I would like to conclude with some further thoughts on the comic impulse of these collages. In his essay ''Laughter,'' Bergson points out several tendencies which seem to have bearing on the constructive urge behind collage, verbal or visual. Bergson makes three preliminary observations about the comic context (472–74): 1) the comic is strictly human, outside of nature; 2) it appeals to intelligence wherein an ''*absence of feeling* usually accompanies laughter'' or, put another way, ''Indifference is its natural environment, for laughter has no greater foe than emotion''; 3) laughter must maintain a certain life in common, a ''*social* signification,'' a societal purpose or, as Bergson sums it up, ''Laughter appears to stand in need of an echo.''

It is not hard to see how the comic context stands in opposition to the individualized poetic ego, the tragic and melancholic act of scribbling verse or ''shipwreck of the singular'' mentioned earlier. Laughter is above all societal—artificial (outside of nature), intellectually generated, socially meaningful. It is also not unreasonable to view these categories as valid indexes of the contextual nature of collage.

But Bergson goes on to develop a central and equivocal image of the comic: ''*something mechanical encrusted on something living*'' (475–77). Much, he argues, of what we find laughable is so because comedy draws our attention to the physical in a person, to the rigidity and fallibility of bodies, to ''*the impression of being a thing.*'' Surely in visual art the otherness of the collaged material is always present. The factuality, the physical autonomy of its mechanical introduction both frees and integrates space in a sort of foreground/background contextual play.

So too with the verbal collage of my ''events,'' where the mechanical, syntactic urgency of the sentences drives the various semiotic systems to line up on the stage, as it were, of our linguistic consciousness. The assembled proscenium, across which sentence after sentence dances in parody of basic verbal order, is as self-mocking as it is ironizing and satiric.

But this line-up (or collage) is, to say the least, ambiguous, problematic. Its comedy belongs, as Bergson notes, ''neither altogether to art nor altogether to life''; its pleasure is not ''exclusively esthetic or altogether disinterested'' (477). The amusement for me (and one hopes for the reader) in relentlessly moving from sentence to sentence through what Carravetta has called the ''magmatic and chaotic background'' is not so abstract or formal as it might appear. The thrust of the collage cannot help but be implicitly, if at times desperately, corrective.

The conjunction of radically disjunct verbal realities forms my attempt to salvage from the enterprise of poetry (whether labeled collage or poem-in-prose) some sort of public significance. It yields a pleasure which, once again Bergson notes, ''implies a secret or unconscious intent, if not of each one of us, at all events of society as a whole'' (477).

Put historically, Carravetta suggests that collage in *Portfolio* ''is exciting the multifaceted antagonisms of the avant-gardes as well as of Modernity in its broader configurations, and is beginning to clear the pathways for untried grafts between the aesthetic and the social, the poetic and the political.'' In essence the ''event'' is not a way out of any experimental contradiction found in the poetic self but a way forward. The collages marked a shift from a lyrical composition insisting on a tragic, or at least melancholic, isolation of poetic being to a more comic vision centered on the social nature of poetic becoming. As I concluded in my first musings on *Portfolio*:

> Then, like the Mayan serpents, poems begin to swallow their own tails. Sections or lines from poems discarded several years ago, even work-in-progress, become animated within the landscape of a particular ''Event.'' So new topographies and contexts are generated, which poetry may now situate or be situated by.

Bibliography

Bergson, Henri. ''Laughter.'' In Robert W. Corrigan, ed., *Comedy*. San Francisco: Chandler, 1965.

Braque, Georges. ''Thoughts on Painting.'' In Edward F. Fry, ed. *Cubism*. New York: Oxford, 1966.

Oppen, George. *Of Being Numerous*. New York: New Directions, 1969.

Spicer, Jack. *The Collected Books*. Los Angeles: Black Sparrow, 1975.

Vangelisti, Paul. *Portfolio*. San Francisco: Red Hill, 1978; bilingual reedition, Parma: Edizioni TamTam, 1988.

21

The Object of Post-Criticism

Gregory L. Ulmer

As concepts of what the nature of art is have changed in our times, so, too, has the nature and object of criticism. As Gregory Ulmer notes, a new "paraliterary" practice has evolved, as lines between creative and critical forms begin to be dissolved. Ulmer poses the question, "Will the collage/montage revolution in representation be admitted into the academic essay, into the discourse of knowledge, replacing the 'realist' criticism based on the notions of 'truth' as correspondence to or correct reproduction of a referent object of study?" Through a discussion of collage and montage, deconstruction, and allegory, Ulmer points to transformations in criticism, and to new cultural forms, such as the writing of Roland Barthes and the composing of John Cage. Ulmer's arguments illustrate the far-reaching effect that collage has had beyond the visual arts. As Ulmer states, "By most accounts, collage is the single most revolutionary formal innovation in artistic representation to occur in our century."

What is at stake in the controversy surrounding contemporary critical writing is easier to understand when placed in the context of modernism and postmodernism in the arts. The issue is "representation"—specifically, the representation of the object of study in a critical text. Criticism now is being transformed in the same way that literature and the arts were transformed by the avant-garde movements in the early decades of this century. The break with "mimesis," with the values and assumptions of "realism," which revolutionized the modernist arts, is now underway (belatedly) in criticism, the chief consequence of which,

This article originally appeared in *The Anti-Aesthetic: Essays on Postmodern Culture,* edited by Hal Foster (Port Townsend, Wash.: Bay Press, 1983).

of course, is a change in the relation of the critical text to its object—literature.

A rationale for this shift may be found in Hayden White's complaint that "when historians claim that history is a combination of science and art, they generally mean that it is a combination of late-nineteenth-century social science and mid-nineteenth-century art," modelled on the novels of Scott or Thackeray.[1] White suggests, instead, that historians of literature (or of any discipline, for that matter) should use *contemporary* scientific and artistic insights and methods as the basis for their work, pursuing "the possibility of using impressionistic, expressionistic, surrealistic, and (perhaps) even actionist modes of representation for dramatizing the significance of data which they have uncovered but which all too frequently they are prohibited from seriously contemplating as evidence" (*Tropics,* 47–48). I will argue, following White's lead, that "post-criticism" (-modernist, -structuralist) is constituted precisely by the application of the devices of modernist art to critical representations; furthermore, that the principal device taken over by the critics and theorists is the compositional pair collage/montage.

By most accounts, collage is the single most revolutionary formal innovation in artistic representation to occur in our century.[2] Although the technique itself is ancient, collage was introduced into the "high arts" (as is well known) by Braque and Picasso as a solution to the problems raised by analytic cubism, a solution which finally provided an alternative to the "illusionism" of perspective which had dominated Western painting since the early Renaissance.

> In a still-life scene at a café, with lemon, oyster, glass, pipe, and newspaper [*Still-Life with Chair Caning* (1912), the first Cubist collage], Picasso glued a piece of oilcloth on which is printed the pattern of woven caning, thus indicating the presence of a chair without the slightest use of traditional methods. For just as the painted letters JOU signify JOURNAL, a section of facsimile caning signifies the whole chair. Later Picasso would go one step further and incorporate into his collages actual objects or fragments of objects, signifying literally themselves. This strange idea was to transform Cubism and to become the source for much of twentieth-century art.[3]

The interest of collage as a device for criticism resides partly in the objectivist impulse of Cubism (as opposed to the nonobjective movements which it inspired). The Cubist collage, by incorporating directly into the work an actual fragment of the referent (open form), remains "representational" while breaking completely with the trompe-l'oeil illusionism of traditional realism. Moreover, "these tangible and non-illusionistic objects presented a new and original source of interplay between artistic expressions and the experience of the everyday world. An unpredicted and significant step in bringing art and life closer to being a simultaneous experience had been taken."[4]

It is not necessary to repeat here the historical account of how collage became the predominate, all-pervasive device of twentieth-century arts. Rather I will note the principles of collage/montage which have directed representations in a diversity of arts and media, including most recently literary criticism: "To lift a certain number of elements from works, objects, preexisting messages, and to integrate them in a new creation in order to produce an original totality manifesting ruptures of diverse sorts."[5] The operation which may be recognized as a kind of "bricolage" (Lévi-Strauss), includes four characteristics—découpage (or severing); preformed or extant messages or materials; assemblage (montage); discontinuity or heterogeneity. "Collage" is the transfer of materials from one context to another, and "montage" is the "dissemination" of these borrowings through the new setting (*Collages* 72). Two features of collage illustrated in *Still Life with Chair Caning* are worth noting here: 1) that the borrowed fragment is a signifier "that would summarize in one form many characteristics of a given object" (Fry 32–33); 2) the chair caning is in fact represented by a *simulacrum*—the printed oil cloth—which is nevertheless a readymade addition rather than an illusionistic reproduction.

Photography is an equally useful model for the mode of representation adopted by post-criticism—if it is understood not as the culmination of linear perspective, but as a means of *mechanical reproduction* (as described in Walter Benjamin's famous article). The analogy between postcriticism and the revolution in representation which transformed the arts, then, should include as well the principle of photographic representation in both its realist and semiotic versions. Considered at this level of generalization, photographic representation may be described according to the collage principle. Indeed, it is a collage machine (perfected in television), producing simulacra of the life-world: 1) Photography selects and transfers a fragment of the visual continuum into a new frame. The realist argument, most forcefully stated by André Bazin, is that because of mechanical reproduction, which forms the image of the world automatically without the intervention of human "creativity" (the reduction of this "creativity" to the act of selection, as in the readymade), "the photographic image is a kind of decal or transfer, . . . [it] is the object itself."[6] 2) Although semiotics prefers to designate this relation to the real in terms of iconic and indexical signifiers, the photographic image signifies itself and something else—it becomes a signifier remotivated within the system of a new frame. There are several versions of the argument that photography (or film) is a language, best summarized in Sergei Eisenstein's notion of "intellectual montage," in which the real is used as an element of a discourse.

The strongest version of the semiotic theory of photography is realized in the strategies of photomontage (in which are joined, in any case, the principles of photography and collage/montage). In photomontage the photographic images are themselves cut out and pasted into new, surprising, provoking juxtapositions, as in John Heartfield's *The Meaning of the Hitlerian Salute* (1933), which, besides the title, consists of:

> A caption which takes the form of one of Hitler's slogans: "I have millions behind me." An image: in right profile Hitler gives the Hitlerian salute, but reversed to the back [his unique version of the gesture, with palm flipped back, fingers extended beside his ear]. His silhouette reaches only to the middle of the image. Above his palm [is] a wad of banknotes being handed to him by a large-bellied figure, dressed in black, immense and anonymous (one barely sees his chin).[7]

Hitler's words as well as his image are turned against him in this recombination, revealing in a stroke the link between German capitalism and the Nazi party.

Photomontage illustrates the "productive" potential of collage promoted by Walter Benjamin and Bertolt Brecht (among others). "I am speaking of the procedure of montage: the superimposed element disrupts the context in which it is inserted," Benjamin says, describing Brecht's plays.

> The interruption of action, on account of which Brecht described his theatre as *epic,* constantly counteracts an illusion in the audience. For such illusion is a hindrance to a theatre that proposes to make use of elements of reality in experimental rearrangements. . . . [The spectator] recognizes it as the real situation, not with satisfaction, as in the theatre of naturalism, but with astonishment. Epic theater, therefore, does not reproduce situations, rather it discovers them.[8]

Brecht defended the mechanics of collage/montage against Georg Lukács's Socialist Realism (based on the aesthetics of nineteenth-century fiction) as an alternative to the organic model of growth and its classic assumptions of harmony, unity, linearity, closure. Montage does not reproduce the real, but constructs an object (its lexical field includes the terms "assemble, build, join, unite, add, combine, link, construct, organize"—*Montage* 121) or rather, mounts a process ("the relation of form to content is no longer a relation of exteriority, the form resembling clothes which can dress no matter what content, it is *process, genesis, result of a work*"—*Montage* 120) in order to intervene in the world, not to reflect but to change reality.

There is nothing innately subversive about the photomontage principle, or any other formal device. Rather, as we are often reminded, such effects must be continually reinvented. Part of the interest of this context for post-criticism is that the debates among Lukács, Brecht, Benjamin, Adorno, et al. with respect to the value of montage experiments in literature will no doubt be reiterated now with respect to criticism. Will the collage/montage revolution in representation be admitted into the academic essay, into the discourse of knowledge, replacing the "realist" criticism based on the notions of "truth" as correspondence to or correct reproduction of a referent object of study? The question of post-criticism was first posed in just this way by Roland Barthes in his reply to the attack made on his Racine book by Raymond Picard (who associated Barthes with Dadaism). Barthes explained that the modernist poets, beginning at least with Mallarmé, had demonstrated already the unification of poetry and criticism—that literature was itself a critique of language, and that criticism had no "meta"-language capable of describing or accounting for literature. Barthes concluded that the categories of literature and criticism could no longer be kept apart, that now there were only *writers*. The relation of the critical text to its object of study was to be conceived in terms no longer of subject-object but of subject-predicate (authors and critics both facing the same material—language), with critical "meaning" being a "simulacrum" of the literary text, a new "flowering" of the rhetoric at work in literature. The critic's text, he says, suggesting the systematic transformation relating the two writings, is an *anamorphosis* of its object—an analogy with distorted perspective which, in post-criticism, is joined by the analogy with collage/montage.[9]

The response to his "paraliterary"[10] initiative was violent and hostile, Barthes explained, because his project, following the lead of the artists themselves, touched language directly.[11] Jacques Derrida recently restated this criterion of critical vanguardism: "The deconstruction of a pedagogical institution and all that it implies. What this institution cannot bear, is for anyone to tamper with language. . . . It can bear more readily the most apparently revolutionary ideological sorts of 'content,' if only that content does not touch the borders of language and of all the juridico-political contracts that it guarantees."[12]

Grammatology

That Jacques Derrida should explore the lessons of the modernist revolution in representation is understandable, considering that he undertakes a deconstruction of the very concept and philosophy of mimesis.

''Mimesis,'' which Derrida labels ''mimetologism,'' refers to that capture of representation by the metaphysics of ''logocentrism,'' the era extending from Plato to Freud (and beyond) in which writing (all manner of inscription) is reduced to a secondary status as ''vehicle,'' in which the signified or referent is always *prior* to the material sign, the purely intelligible prior to the merely sensible.[13] ''It is not a question of 'rejecting' these notions,'' Derrida writes. ''They are necessary and, at least at present, nothing is conceivable for us without them. . . . Since these concepts are indispensable for unsettling the heritage to which they belong, we should be even less prone to renounce them'' (*Grammatology* 14–15). Derrida's alternative to ''mimetologism,'' then, does *not* abandon or deny reference, but rethinks reference in another way: ''It complicates the boundary line that ought to run between the text and what seems to lie beyond its fringes, what is classed as the *real.*''[14]

It is becoming apparent that in his reliance on collage/montage as the stylistic device with which to deconstruct mimesis, Derrida is doing for this new mode of representation what Aristotle, in the *Poetics,* did for ''mimetologism.'' In the same way that Aristotle provided at once a theory of tragedy (mimesis) and a method (formal analysis) for the study of all literary modes, Derrida in a text such as *Glas* (identified as the ''exemplary'' text of poststructuralism[15]) provides a ''theory'' of montage (grammatology) and a method (deconstruction) for working with any mode of writing whatsoever. Derrida is the ''Aristotle'' of montage.

In spite of its associated complexities and controversies, Derrida's basic formulation of the nature of language is relatively simple, a formulation which, placed in the context of the collage paradigm, takes on its fullest significance. Grammatology is ''poststructuralist'' in that it replaces the ''sign'' (composed of signifier and signified—the most basic unit of meaning according to structuralism) with a still more basic unit—the *gram.*

> It is a question of producing a new concept of writing. This concept can be called *gram* or *différance.* . . . Whether in the order of spoken or written discourse, no element can function as a sign without referring to another element which itself is not simply present. This interweaving results in each ''element''—phoneme or grapheme—being constituted on the basis of the trace within it of the other elements of the chain or system. This interweaving, this textile, is the *text* produced only in the transformation of another text. Nothing, neither among the elements nor within the system, is anywhere ever simply present or absent. There are only, everywhere, differences and traces of traces. The gram, then, is the most general concept of semiology—which thus becomes grammatology.[16]

Collage/montage, in other words, is the manifestation at the level of discourse of the ''gram'' principle, as will be made clear when its definition is compared with the following rhetorical definition of the collage effect:

> Its [collage's] heterogeneity, even if it is reduced by every operation of composition, imposes itself on the reading as stimulation to produce a signification which could be neither univocal nor stable. Each cited element breaks the continuity or the linearity of the discourse and leads necessarily to a double reading: that of the fragment perceived in relation to its text of origin; that of the same fragment as incorporated into a new whole, a different totality. The trick of collage consists also of never entirely suppressing the alterity of these elements reunited in a temporary composition. Thus the art of collage proves to be one of the most effective strategies in the putting into question of all the illusions of representation (*Collages* 34–35).

This undecidable reading effect, oscillating between presence and absence, is just what Derrida tries to achieve at every level of his "double science," from his paleonymic redefinition (remotivation) of concepts to his publishing of two books under one cover (*Glas*).

The notion of the gram is especially useful for theorizing the evident fact, much discussed in structuralist psychoanalysis (Lacan) and ideological criticism (Althusser), that signifieds and signifiers are continually breaking apart and reattaching in new combinations, thus revealing the inadequacy of Saussure's model of the sign, according to which the signifier and the signified relate as if they were two sides of the same sheet of paper. The tendency of Western philosophy throughout its history ("logocentrism") to try to pin down and fix a specific signified to a given signifier violates, according to grammatology, the nature of language, which functions not in terms of matched *pairs* (signifier/signifieds) but of *couplers* or *couplings*—"a person or thing that couples or links together." The following description of what Derrida calls "iterability" is also an excellent summary of the collage consequences of the gram:

> And this is the possibility on which I want to insist: the possibility of disengagement and citational graft which belongs to the structure of every mark, spoken or written, and which constitutes every mark in writing before and outside of every horizon of semio-linguistic communication; in writing, which is to say in the possibility of its functioning being cut off, at a certain point, from its "original" desire-to-say-what-one-means and from its participation in a saturable and constraining context. Every sign, linguistic or nonlinguistic, spoken or written (in the current sense of this opposition), in a small or large unit, can be *cited*, put between quotation marks; in so doing it can break with every given context, engendering an infinity of new contexts in a manner which is absolutely illimitable.[17]

In criticism, as in literature, collage takes the form of citation, but citation carried to an extreme (in post-criticism), collage being the "limit-case" of citation, and grammatology being the theory of writing as citation (cf. *Collages*, 301).

A useful point of departure for reviewing Derrida's own montage practice is the collection entitled *Dissemination* (a term which is listed as a synonym for collage/montage—*Collages* 23) of which he says that "the most general title of the problem treated in those texts would be: castration and mimesis" (*Positions* 84). In citing the object of study or in offering examples as illustrations, the critic is in the position of castrator: "Such a decision is a castration, at least acted out or feigned, or a circumcision. This is as it always is, and the knife that with obsessive frequency slashes the tree of *Numbers* [the text Derrida "studies" in the essay "Dissemination'] hones itself as a phallic threat. . . . The 'operation' of reading/writing goes by the way of *'the blade of a red knife'*" (*Dissemination,* 301). But rather than elaborating this connection between writing and psychoanalysis (exploited at length in Derrida's texts), I will confine myself to noting the two chief elements of Derrida's post-critical technique—grafting and mimicry:

1. *Graft.* Derrida's discussion of montage writing as "grafting" in *Dissemination* is itself couched in the collage style (it *does* what it *says*), in a text consisting of nearly equal portions of selections from *Numbers* (a French "new new novel" by Philippe Sollers) and Derrida's frame text. "To write," Derrida states, "means to graft. It's the same word" (*Dissemination* 355). Then, in a description of method which applies as much to his own as to Sollers's writing, he adds, distinguishing post-critical from conventional collage:

> Hence all those textual samples provided by *Numbers* do not, as you might have been tempted to believe, serve as "quotations," "collages," or even "illustrations." They are not being applied upon the surface or in the interstices of a text that would already exist without them. And they themselves can only be read within the operation of their reinscription, within the graft. It is the sustained, discrete violence of an incision that is not apparent in the thickness of the text, a calculated insemination of the proliferating allogene through which the two texts are transformed, deform each other, contaminate each other's content, tend at times to reject each other, or pass elliptically one into the other and become regenerated in the repetition, along the edges of an *overcast seam.* Each grafted text continues to radiate back toward the site of its removal, transforming that too, as it affects the new territory. (*Dissemination* 355)[18]

The new representation, the new status of the example mounted in the critical frame, has to do in part with the shift away from commentary and explanation, which rely on concepts, to work instead by means of examples—both in terms of the substitution of examples for arguments in one's own writing,[19] and of approaching the object of study (when it is another critical or theoretical text) at the level of the examples it uses.[20] "Clip out an example, since you cannot and should not undertake the infinite commentary that at every moment seems necessarily to engage and immediately to annul itself" (*Dissemination* 300). If the clipping is associated with "castration" ("So make some incision, some violent arbitrary cut"), the montage or dissemination of the fragments thus collected in the new frame is associated with "invagination" (collage/montage is a bisexual writing).

The logic of examples governed by the principle of invagination is itself illustrated by the "loop hole" of a figure borrowed from set theory (the modern heir of the notion of the "concept" as a "having" or "belonging to") in order to describe the paradoxical escape of the "example" from conceptualization (collage writing being a kind of theft which violates "property" in every sense—intellectual property protected by copyright, and the properties of a given concept). The illustration figures that which Derrida formulates as the "law of the law of genre":

> It is precisely a principle of contamination, a law of impurity, a parasitical economy. In the code of set theories, if I may use it at least figuratively, I would speak of a sort of participation without belonging—a taking part in without being part of, without having membership in a set. The trait that marks membership inevitably divides, the boundary of the set comes to form, by invagination, an internal pocket larger than the whole; and the outcome of this division and of this abounding remains as singular as it is limitless.[21]

Derrida's strategy with regard to "invagination" (matting or mounting the example) is to find a mode of critical "mimesis" which, like the law of the law of genre, would relate to its objects of study as an excess (and vice-versa)—the "law of participation without membership, of contamination," similar to the paradox of the hierarchy of classification in set theory: "The re-mark of belonging does not belong" ("Genre" 212).

The question Derrida poses, faced with the problem of comparing Blanchot's *L'arrêt de mort* with Shelley's *The Triumph of Life,* but seeking an alternative to "mimetological" commentary, is: "How can one text, assuming its unity, give or present another to be read, without touching it, without saying anything about it, practically without referring to it?" ("Borderlines" 80). His solution is to "endeavor to create an effect of *superimposing,* of superimprinting one text on the other," the text as "palimpsest" or "macula," a double band or "double bind" procedure which breaks with the conventional assumptions of criticism and pedagogy: "One procession is superimposed on the other, accompanying it without accompanying it." But, "You can't give a course on Shelley without ever mentioning him, pretending to deal with Blanchot, and more than a few others" ("Borderlines" 83–84). One version of the solution, utilized in *Dissemination* and *Glas,* is simply to interpolate rhythmically (the "art of interruption" as a kind of music) a series of citations from the "host" texts. But, as *Glas* proves, citation produces excessively long texts. The model for a writing which goes beyond juxtaposition to superimposition is not collage but photography. ''Borderlines'' itself is compared (with respect to the problem of translation) to a ''film for developing,'' for ''processing''—hence, the text as ''procession.'' ''This superimposing is readable,'' Derrida adds, referring to a double-exposed print in Blanchot's story, ''on a 'photograph''' (''Borderlines'' 77, 85). The task of post-criticism, in other words, is to think of the consequences for critical representation of the new mechanical means of reproduction (film and magnetic tape—technologies which require collage/montage composition) in the way that Brecht, as Benjamin noted in ''The Author as Producer,'' had done for theatrical representation. Derrida formulates his new mimesis of superimposition in terms of mime.

2. *Mime.* The most important innovation in Derrida's practice of montage is a ''new mimesis'' in which the text mimes its object of study.[22] *Dissemination* turns out to be a unified study in that the theory of a new mimesis worked out in the first two essays (''Plato's Pharmacy'' is a review of ''mimesis'' in Platonic philosophy; ''The Double Session'' is a review of Mallarmé's alternative to Platonic mimesis, discovered in mime) is applied in the concluding piece (''Dissemination''). The chief lesson of ''Plato's Pharmacy'' is that any composition which works according to the principle of mechanical reproduction falls under the category (despised in Platonic philosophy) of hypomnesis or artificial memory; hypomnesis can only mime knowledge. The sophist sells only ''the signs and insignia of science; not memory itself (*mneme*), only monuments (*hypomnemata*), inventories, archives, citations, copies, accounts, tales, lists, notes, duplicates, chronicles, genealogies, references. Not memory but memorials'' (*Dissemination* 106–07). Writing, in short, is a simulacrum of ''true science.'' But ''true science,'' from Plato to positivism, is what post-criticism puts in question.

> We are today on the eve of Platonism. Which can also, naturally, be thought of as the morning after Hegeliansim. At that specific point, the *philosophia,* the *episteme* are not ''overturned,'' ''rejected,'' ''reined in,'' etc., in the name of something like writing; quite the contrary. But they are, according to a relation that philosophy would call *simulacrum,* according to a more subtle excess of truth, assumed and at the same time displaced into a completely different field, where one can still, but that's all, ''mime absolute knowledge.'' (*Dissemination* 107–08).

Secondly, Derrida concludes from his extensive analysis of Mallarmé's *Mimique* (in ''The Double Session'') that mime models an alternative to Platonic mimesis.

> We are faced then with mimicry imitating nothing. . . . There is no simple reference. It is in this that the mime's operation does allude, but alludes to nothing. . . . Mallarmé thus preserves the differential structure of mimicry or *mimesis*, but without its Platonic or metaphysical interpretation, which implies that somewhere the being of something that *is*, is being imitated. Mallarmé even maintains (and maintains himself in) the structure of the *phantasma* as it is defined by Plato: the simulacrum as the copy of a copy. With the exception that there is no longer any model, and hence no copy. (*Dissemination* 206)

Once one realizes that the mime emblematizes (for Derrida) mechanical reproduction, it becomes apparent that representation without reference is a description of the way film or tape functions as a ''language,'' receiving exact copies of sights and sounds (in collage terms, mechanical reproduction removes or lifts sights and sounds from their contexts—*de*-motivates them, hence the *loss* of reference, the undecidability of allusion), only to *re*-motivate them as signifiers in a new system. Mallarmé earns the label of ''modernist'' by detaching mimicry from logocentric mimetology; Derrida becomes ''postmodernist'' by putting mimicry to work in the interest of a new reference (discussed as ''allegory'' in the next section).

Derrida's first experiments with mimed writing consisted largely of the collage procedure of direct, massive citation (''Here again I do nothing more, can do nothing more than cite, as you will come perhaps to see,'' [*Glas* 24]). The working assumption was that repetition is ''originary''—''Repeated, the same line is no longer exactly the same, the ring no longer has the same center, *the origin has played*.''[23] Derrida's desire to superimpose one text on the other (the program to which mimicry is addressed) is an attempt to devise a system of reference or representation which works in terms of *différance*, [24] with its reversible temporality, rather than in terms of the irreversible time of the sign. From the very beginning, then, the strategy of deconstruction has been repetition: ''There is probably no choice to be made between two lines of thought; our task is rather to reflect on the circularity which makes the one pass into the other indefinitely. And, by strictly repeating this *circle* in its own historical possibility, we allow the production of some *elliptical* change of site, within the difference involved in repetition.''[25] Here we have the earliest version of text as ''texture''—''touching'' language—in which the deconstructive writing *traces* the surface of the object of study (writing as ''tracing'') looking for ''flaws'' or ''faults''—the openings of joints, articulations, where the text might be dismembered. The deconstruction is accomplished in fact by borrowing the very terms utilized by the host work itself—''difference'' from Saussure, ''supplement'' from Rousseau, and so on—and remotivating them, detaching them (following the principle of the gram) from one conceptual set or semantic field and reattaching them to another (but always with the most systematic attention to the potentials or materials available in the word itself).

As the strategy of "literal" repetition developed, the borrowing of terms and the direct citations were supplemented with the construction of general simulacra of the object of study. The practice is clearly illustrated in an extreme case, such as "Cartouches" (in *La Vérité en peinture*), in which the task is to mime in discourse a *visual* work. The referent is a work by Gérard Titus-Carmel entitled *The Pocket-Size Tlingit Coffin* (1975–76), consisting of a "sculpture"—a mahogany box of "modest" dimensions—and one hundred twenty-seven drawings of this "model," each from a different angle. The relationship that exists within the *Tlingit Coffin* between the sculpture and the drawings emblematizes or remarks the relationship of Derrida's critical mimicry to its chosen referent ("model"). The sculpture (the box as model) "does not belong to the line of which it makes a part," but is heterogeneous to it (*Vérité* 217). Derrida's own discourse, as noted earlier, "touches nothing," leaves the reader or viewer alone with the work, "passes beside it in silence, as another theory, another series, saying nothing about what it represents for me, nor even for him" (*Vérité* 227).

Unlike Heidegger, who declared that art "speaks," Derrida insists on the muteness of the series, or on its capacity to work without concept, without conclusions: "Such would be the de-monstration. Let us not abuse the easy word-play. De-monstration proves without showing, without evidencing any conclusion, without entailing anything, without an available thesis. It proves according to a different mode, but proceeding with its step of demonstration [*pas de demonstration*] or non-demonstration. It transforms, it transforms itself, in its process rather than advancing a signifiable object of discourse."[26] The series of drawings, that is, demonstrates the problem of order and representation in the relation of examples to models, which is why Derrida selected it, mounted it. Indeed, his own text relates to this referent the way the drawings relate to the box, an example mounted because, like *Numbers,* it exposes exposition.

The strategy for miming the *Tlingit Coffin* is to ignore the plastic objects as such (in the way that the "content" of *Numbers* essentially was ignored) and to mime the structuring process of the work—to concentrate on the generation of a "contingent" of terms (cartouche, paradigm, article, duction, contingent, and the like) which are processed in a way parallel to the way Titus-Carmel runs through one hundred twenty-seven variations in his drawings of the model, "putting them in perspective, turning them about in every sense (direction) by a series of swerves [*écarts*], variations, modulations, anamorphoses,'' finally stopping after a predetermined number of pages, creating the same effect of contingent necessity or arbitrary motivation as the series of exactly one hundred twenty-seven drawings (*Vérité* 229). The anagram and the homonym operate on the lexicon the way anamorphoses operate on representational perspective. Derrida mimes the dated drawings further by composing as if in a journal, with dated entries, each entry constituting a variation on a theme. Such is the logic of the simulacrum as translation, as verbal mimicry of a visual scene—a mimicry which functions similarly in other texts, regardless of referent.

The implication of textual mime for post-criticism, informing paraliterature as a hybrid of literature and criticism, art and science, is that knowledge of an object of study may be obtained without conceptualization or explanation. Rather, as if following Wittgenstein's admonition that ''the meaning is the use,'' Derrida enacts or performs (mimes) the compositional structuration of the referent, resulting in another text of the same ''kind'' (genre—but ''different'' according to the ''law of the law of genre'' noted above.) Post-criticism, then, functions with an ''epistemology'' of performance—knowing as making, producing, doing, acting, as in Wittgenstein's account of the relation of knowing to the ''mastery of a technique.'' Thus post-criticism writes ''on'' its object in the way that Wittgenstein's knower exclaims, ''Now I know how to go on!''[27]—with this ''on'' carrying all the dimensions and ambiguities of the ''on'' in Derrida's ''Living On'' (beyond, about, upon, on—including the parasitical connotation). Writing may show more (and other) than it says—the ''surplus value'' of writing which interests Derrida. The name of this ''more'' is ''allegory.'' The importance of allegory for postmodernism has already been discussed by critics such as Craig Owens (among others) who in fact uses the writings of Derrida and Paul de Man to define the question. Owens identifies allegory with Derrida's notion of ''supplement'' (one of the many names Derrida assigns to the effect of the gram: ''If allegory is identified as a supplement ['an expression externally added to another expression,' hence 'extra,' yet supplying a lack], then it is also aligned with writing, insofar as writing is conceived as supplementary to speech.''[28] Owens also makes good use of Derrida's notion of ''deconstruction'' to suggest how postmodernism goes ''beyond formalism'':

> The deconstructive impulse is characteristic of postmodernist art in general and must be distinguished from the self-critical tendency of modernism. Modernist theory presupposes that mimesis, the adequation of an image to a referent, can be bracketed or suspended, and that the art object itself can be substituted (metaphorically) for its

> referent. . . . Postmodernism neither brackets nor suspends the referent but works instead to problematize the activity of reference.[29]

Objections have been raised concerning the possibility of sustaining this distinction between self-reference and a problematized reference—both to Owen's statement and to Derrida's project.[30] These doubts about the "post," about the possibility of working "beyond" modernism or structuralism, are based in thought which is still semiological rather than grammatological. Grammatology has emerged on the far side of the formalist crisis and developed a discourse which is fully referential, but referential in the manner of "narrative allegory" rather than of "allegoresis." "Allegoresis," the mode of commentary long practiced by traditional critics, "suspends" the surface of the text, applying a terminology of "verticalness, levels, hidden meaning, the hieratic difficulty of interpretation," whereas "narrative allegory" (practiced by post-critics) explores the literal—*letteral*—level of the language itself, in a horizontal investigation of the polysemous meanings simultaneously available in the words themselves—in etymologies and puns—and in the things the words name. The allegorical narrative unfolds as a dramatization or enactment (personification) of the "literal truth inherent in the words themselves."[31] In short, narrative allegory favors the material of the signifier over the meanings of the signifieds.

An idea of how this material reference functions may be derived from the examples Owens mentions, including his point (supporting my discussion of photography) that film is the "primary vehicle for modern allegory" because of its mode of representation: "Film composes narrative out of a succession of concrete images, which makes it particularly suited to allegory's essential pictogrammatism"; and, citing Barthes, "'an allegory is a rebus, writing composed of concrete images'" ("Allegorical Impulse, Part 2" 74). Owens also cites the example of Sherrie Levine, who literally "takes" (other people's) photographs, as an extreme version of the allegorical capacity of collage as "readymade." The point of a recent allegorical project by Levine, in which she "selected, mounted, and framed Andreas Feininger's photographs of natural subjects," Owens explains, is the deconstruction of the opposition between nature and culture. "When Levine wants an image of nature, she does not produce one herself but appropriates another image, and this she does in order to expose the degree to which 'nature' is always already implicated in a system of cultural values which assigns it a specific, culturally determined position."[32] Levine, that is, de-monstrates the grammatological writing appropriate to the age of mechanical reproduction in which "copyright" now means the right to copy anything, a mimicry or repetition which is originary, producing differences (just as in allegory anything may mean anything else.)

Post-critics write with the discourse of others (the already written) the way Levine "takes" photographs. In the words of the great montage-ist of electronic music, John Cage, "with magnetic tape, the possibility exists to use the literature of music as material (cutting it up, transforming it, etc.); this is the best thing that could have happened to it."[33] Roland Barthes typifies the relationship between science and art which exists in paraliterature. In this new "intellectual art," he explains, "we produce simultaneously theory, critical combat, and pleasure; we subject the objects of knowledge and discussion—as in any art—no longer to an instance of truth, but to a consideration of *effects*."[34] The point is that "one plays a science, one puts it in the picture—*like a piece in a collage*" (*Barthes* 100). In his own case, Barthes often played with linguistics: "You use a pseudo-linguistics, a metaphorical linguistics: not that grammatical concepts seek out images in order to express themselves, but just the contrary, *because these concepts come to constitute allegories,* a second language, whose abstraction is diverted to fictive ends" (*Barthes* 124). Barthes's statement is as precise a definition as it is possible to give of what postcriticism is, and of the way Derrida writes with, allegorizes, the gram.

Walter Benjamin, to whom Owens also alludes, is perhaps the principal precursor of the post-critical use of collage-allegory.

> Benjamin saw affinity between the allegoric imagination of the German baroque dramatists and the artistic needs of the twentieth century; first in the melancholy spirit of the former, with its emblematic but inscrutable insignia, which he rediscovered in Kafka; then in the cognate principle of montage which he found in the work of Eisenstein and Brecht. Montage became for him the modern, constructive, active, unmelancholy form of allegory, namely the ability to connect dissimilars in such a way as to "shock" people into new recognitions and understandings.[35]

Benjamin applied the collage/montage style in the early *One-Way Street* (the cover of which, when it was published in 1928, displayed a photomontage by Sascha Stone as an icon of the technique applied in the text[36]). Defining the conventional academic book as "an outdated mediation between two different filing systems,"[37] Benjamin wanted to write a book made up entirely of quotations in order to purge all subjectivity and allow the self to be a vehicle for the expression of "objective cultural tendencies"[38] (similar to Barthes's project in *A Lover's Discourse: Fragments*).

Benjamin's response to the problem of representation raised in philosophy by the modernist crisis was to abandon the conventional book form in favor of the essay—incomplete, digressive, without proof or conclusion, in which could be juxtaposed fragments, minute details ("close-ups") drawn from every level of the contemporary world. These details, of course, functioned allegorically. But there is an all-important difference between montage-allegory and the object as emblem in baroque and romantic allegory. In the latter, adhering to the model of the hieroglyph in which the particular object of nature or daily life is taken over as a conventional sign for an idea, the object is used "not to convey its natural characteristics, but those which we have ourselves lent it."[39] In collage, on the other hand, the allegorical significance is literal, derives from the natural characteristics themselves. "The 'truth' which Benjamin had discovered in this literary form [*Trauerspiel*], one which had been lost in the history of its interpretation, was that allegory was not an arbitrary representation of the idea which it portrayed. It was instead the concrete expression of that idea's material foundation."[40]

The style of the essay was to be an "art of interruption": "Interruption is one of the fundamental methods of all form-giving. It reaches far beyond the domain of art. It is, to mention just one of its aspects, the origin of the quotation" (*Brecht* 19). Benjamin's procedure was "to collect and reproduce in quotation the contradictions of the present without resolution"—"the dialectic at a standstill," juxtaposing the extremes of a given idea. This collage strategy was itself an image of the "break-up," the "disintegration" of civilization in the modern world, relevant to one of Benjamin's most famous formulas: "Allegories are, in the realm of thoughts, what ruins are in the realm of things" (*Tragic Drama* 178), the premise being that something becomes an object of knowledge only as it "decays," or is made to disintegrate (analysis as decay).

Theodor Adorno shares many of Benjamin's most basic assumptions about the value of the montage-allegory strategy. Adorno's method was derived in part from his studies with Arnold Schönberg. Adorno wanted to do to philosophical idealism what Schönberg, with his twelve-tone compositional procedure, had done to tonality in music. "Schönberg rejected the notion of artist-as-genius and replaced it with the artist as craftsman; he saw music not as the expression of subjectivity, but as a search for knowledge which lay outside the artist, as potential within the object, the material. For him, composing was discovery and invention through the practice of music-making" (Buck-Morss 123). The method is objective because the "object" leads, criticism being a translation into words of the *inner logic of the object*, thing, event, text itself. Once articulated, however, the material could be "rearranged" in order to render intelligible its "truth":

> The thinker reflected on a sensuous and non-identical reality not in order to dominate it, not to butcher it to fit the Procrustean beds of mental categories or to liquidate its particularity by making it disappear under abstract concepts. Instead the thinker, like the artist, proceeded mimetically, and in the process of imitating matter transformed it so that it could be read as a monadological expression of social truth. In such philosophy, as in artworks, form was not indifferent to content—hence the central

> significance of representation, the manner of philosophical expression. Aesthetic creation itself was not subjective invention so much as the objective discovery of the new within the given, immanently, through a regrouping of its elements. (Buck-Morss 132)

Benjamin perhaps put this attitude most concisely when he cited Goethe's notion of the symbol as suggestive of how photographs "mean": "there is a sensitive empiricism which makes itself most inwardly identical with the object and thereby becomes genuine theory."[41] But it is important to realize that this object-become-theory in montage-allegory functions in terms of a representation which is neither allegorical nor symbolic in the traditional senses (the meanings are neither purely unmotivated nor motivated—the opposition deconstructed by grammatology, according to which "meaning" is a continual process of demotivation and remotivation.) An important aspect of this "philosophy of the concrete particular," whose true interest is "with the nonconceptual, the singular and the particular; with that which since Plato has been dismissed as transitory and insignificant, and upon which Hegel hung the label of 'foul existence,'" (Buck-Morss 69), first intuited by Benjamin and then formalized by Adorno, is its ability to exploit the tension between science and art in a way that anticipates the strategy of post-criticism. Indeed, Adorno's description of the method as "exact fantasy" ("fantasy which abides strictly within the material which the sciences present to it, and reaches beyond them only in the smallest aspects of their arrangement: aspects, granted, which fantasy itself must originally generate" [Buck-Morss 86]), outlines the project of poststructuralist theory—to locate the "subject" of knowledge—and of "pragmatics"—to study the user's (knower's) attitude to the message.

What the baroque or romantic allegorist conceived of as an emblem, the post-critic treats as a model. A good example of Derrida's use of the quotidian object as a theoretical model is found in *Spurs, Nietzsche's Styles*. *Spurs* is a divagation on a fragment found in Nietzsche's Notebooks—"I have forgotten my umbrella"—apparently a meaningless citation, randomly noted. Derrida performs an "exact fantasy" apropos of this fragment, whose undecidable status, he argues, is replicated in Nietzsche's complete works (and in Derrida's own oeuvre as well). In the process of making this point, Derrida appropriates the umbrella as an icon marking or modeling the very structure of style as such:

> The style-spur, the spurring style, is a long object, an oblong object, a word, which perforates even as it parries. It is the oblongi-foliated point (a spur or a spar) which derives its apotropaic power from the taut, resistant tissues, webs, sails and veils which are erected, furled and unfurled around it. But, it must not be forgotten, it is also an umbrella.[42]

The "double" structure of style—relevant to the problem of allegorical representation which at once reveals and conceals—finds, in the "morphology" of the umbrella with its shaft and fabric, a concrete model. Derrida borrows the "umbrella" left behind in Nietzsche's Notebooks and remotivates it (its meaning was indeterminate in any case) as a demonstrative device. The umbrella counts for Derrida not as a "symbol," Freudian or otherwise, not as a meaning at all, but as a structural machine which, in its capacity to open and close, de-monstrates the unrepresentable gram.

A review of Derrida's texts turns up a small collection of such borrowed theoretical objects, including, besides the umbrella, a pair of shoes (from Van Gogh),[43] a fan (from Mallarmé), a matchbox (from Genet), a postcard (from Freud)—all displaying the double structure of the gram. Together they constitute a collage, to be entitled "Still Life" (as models of writing they necessarily manifest the death drive); or perhaps "Autoportrait," in the surrealist mode, since each of these objects occurs in a discussion of fetishism. Let it suffice to say that the "example" in post-criticism functions in the manner of a "fetish object," thus linking allegory with psychoanalysis in paraliterature.

Parasite/Saprophyte

A model for the relation of the post-critical text to its object of study, often mentioned in the debate between traditional and postcritics, is that of parasite to host. J. Hillis Miller, speaking for the deconstructionists in a conference session on "The Limits of Pluralism," offered a rebuttal of Wayne Booth's assertion (seconded by M. H. Abrams) that the "deconstructionist reading of a given work is plainly and simply parasitical on the obvious or univocal reading."[44] Given that Derrida describes grammatology as a "parasitical economy," this term may not be as "wounding" as Booth and Abrams intend. Miller's response is to problematize the meaning of "parasite":

> What happens when a critical essay extracts a "passage" and "cites" it? Is this different from a citation, echo, or allusion within a poem? Is a citation an alien parasite within the body of its host, the main text, or is it the other way around, the interpretative text the parasite which surrounds and strangles the citation which is its host?

The issue is compounded in the case of post-criticism, which carries citation to its limit—collage.

Miller's rebuttal is meant to undermine the very notion of "univocal" reading by showing the equivocal, paradoxical plurality of the meaning of "host" and "guest," which turn out to share the same etymological root and are interchangeable in their sense. The point of this etymological exercise, he says,

> is an argument for the value of recognizing the great complexity and equivocal richness of apparently obvious or univocal language, even the language of criticism, which is in this respect continuous with the language of literature. This complexity and equivocal richness resides in part in the fact that there is no conceptual expression without figure, and no intertwining of concept and figure without an implied story, narrative, or myth, in this case the story of the alien guest in the home. Deconstruction is an investigation of what is implied by this inherence of figure, concept, and narrative in one another. (Miller 443)

In short, Miller's definition of "deconstruction" is what Maureen Quilligan describes as the operation of narrative allegory.

It so happens that Michel Serres has provided a full elaboration—allegory—of the very story of deconstruction, of the alien guest in the home, in a paraliterary text entitled *Parasite.* Not only does Serres support Miller's point regarding the equivocality of the host-parasite terminology, he supplements it by noting that in French a third meaning is available which permits the story of the parasite to be explored literally as an allegory of communication theory (or rather, as with the gram, the theory itself produces the allegory):

> The parasite is a microbe, an insidious infection that takes without giving and weakens without killing. The parasite is also a guest, who exchanges his talk, praise, and flattery for food. The parasite is noise as well, the static in a system or the interference in a channel. These seemingly dissimilar activities are, according to Michel Serres, not merely coincidentally expressed by the same word (in French). Rather, they are intrinsically related and, in fact, they have the same basic function in a system. Whether it produces a fever or just hot air, the parasite is a thermal exciter. And as such, it is both the atom of a relation and the production of a change in this relation.[45]

Taking the luck of this homonym as a clue, Serres researches a selection of literary examples, stories about dinners, hosts, and guests, beginning with the fables of La Fontaine and including the return of Odysseus among the suitors, the *Symposium, Tartuffe,* etc., all examined in terms of *interruption,* interference, the noise which frightens away the mice, the call which took Simonides away from the table just before the roof collapsed (his recollection of which guest was sitting where, for purposes of identifying the bodies, is said to be the origin of "artificial memory"). Serres concludes that parasitism is "negentropic," the motor of change or invention—recalling Benjamin's art of interruption—consisting of a new logic with three elements: host, guest, and interrupter (noise is "the random element, transforming one system or one order into another"). The gram in the structure of language, and collage at the level of discourse, are operators of this inventive interruption.

This context provides an opportunity to demonstrate the usefulness of post-criticism not only as a compositional method but also as a method for reading paraliterature itself. I want to use the writings of John Cage as a test for allegorical reading, writings which in any case have exemplary value as some of the most important versions of paraliterature yet produced. Part of their value is that Cage is famous as a postmodernist musician. His "prepared piano" and early use of electronic equipment, along with his compositional innovations (graphic scores and aleatory procedures) and performance innovations (scores indeterminate as to performance), revolutionized—"postmodernized"—music. Students of post-criticism can benefit from the fact that Cage decided to apply his philosophy of composition to language ("I hope to let words exist, as I have tried to let sounds exist").[46]

It is worth noting in this context that Cage, like Adorno, studied music theory with Schönberg. Cage adopted a view, similar to Adorno's strategy of the "concrete particular," that music should be a kind of research, an exploration of the logic of materials, which in Cage's case became extended to include not just the materials of music but everything in the natural and cultural worlds: "Art changes because science changes—changes in science give artists different understandings of how nature works."[47] This attitude leads Cage to his own version—a musical one—of the "theoretical object":

> We know the air is filled with vibrations that we can't hear. In *Variations VII,* I tried to use sounds from that inaudible environment. But we can't consider that environment as an object. We know that it's a process. While in the case of the ashtray, we are indeed dealing with an object. It would be extremely interesting to place it in a little anechoic chamber and to listen to it through a suitable sound system. Object would become process; we would discover, thanks to a procedure borrowed from science, the meaning of nature through the music of objects. (*Birds* 221)

Moreover, this procedure is explicitly identified with the collage/montage principle, identified here as "silence" (or what Barthes calls the "death of the author"): "*The Gutenberg Galaxy* is made up of borrowings and collages: McLuhan applies what I call silence to all areas of knowledge, that is, he lets them speak. The death of the book is not the end of language: it continues. Just as in my case, silence has invaded everything, and there is still music" (*Birds* 117). Cage acknowledges McLuhan, who has been credited with inventing a kind of *essai concret,* and Norman O. Brown—both major representatives of postcritical writing—as important influences on his work.

Cage postmodernizes the critical essay by bringing to bear on its *inventio* and *dispositio* the same collage and aleatory procedures used in working with tape recorders and other electronic equipment in his musical compositions. The selection of the texts—Thoreau's journals and Joyce's *Finnegans Wake*—is not itself random but, as in Derrida's selection of *Numbers,* a major part of the critical statement. (The Journals and the *Wake* are appropriated, literally or in a mimed version, and signed by Cage, remotivated as signifiers in a new frame.) Cage does not write about Thoreau, but uses the Journals for the generation of others texts which are in fact musicalized simulacra. These simulacra are collage constructions in that all the words, letters, phrases in them are derived directly from the Journals, selected according to chance operations. "Mureau" ("music"+"Thoreau"), for example, is

> a mix of letters, syllables, words, phrases, and sentences. I wrote it by subjecting all the remarks of Henry David Thoreau about music, silence, and sounds he heard that are indexed in the Dover publications of the Journals to a series of *I Ching* chance operations. The personal pronoun was varied according to such operations and the typing was likewise determined."[48]

A more elaborate version of this operation, entitled *Empty Words,* reveals that such works are intended for performance, which is how Cage uses them to produce "lecture-events" (thus fulfilling the original logic of collage/montage which "represents" not in terms of *truth* but of *change*—indeed, the *I Ching* is the "book of changes").

> Subjecting Thoreau's writings to *I Ching* chance operations to obtain collage texts, I prepared parts for twelve speaker-vocalists (or -instrumentalists). . . . Along with these parts go recordings by Maryanne Amacher of breeze, rain and finally thunder and in the last (thunder) section a film by Luis Frangella representing lightning by means of briefly projected negatives of Thoreau's drawings.[49]

When confronting such a text in print, the full import of Barthes's advice about writerly reading becomes apparent, for something like "Mureau" may not be read "conceptually." Rather, by skimming the eye over the page, letting it be arrested momentarily by different typefaces so that the sense of those randomly noted words is allowed to register, a powerful effect emerges—the simulacrum of walking through the woods of Concord with the senses open and the attention floating. Cage explains that Thoreau listened "just as composers using technology nowadays listen; . . . and he explored the neighborhood of Concord with the same appetite with which they explore the possibilities provided by electronics."

Another example of Cage's procedure is *Writing for the Second Time through "Finnegans Wake."* This text was generated out of the *Wake* using Cage's mesostic form: "not acrostics: row down the middle, not down the edge. What makes a mesostic as far as I'm concerned is that the first letter of a word or name is on the first line and following it on the first line the second letter of the word or name is *not* to be found. (The second letter is on the second line)" (*Words* 134). In this manner Cage produced, in his first version of the piece, one hundred fifteen pages of mesostics such as this one:

Just
A
May i
bE
for She'll be sweet for you as i was sweet when
i came down out of me mother.
Jhem
Or shen/brewed by arclight/
and rorY end
through all Christian
ministrElsy.

By restricting further which syllables would be allowed, the second version was reduced to forty pages, of which Cage says:

> From time to time in the course of this work I've had my doubts about the validity of finding in *Finnegans Wake* these mesostics on his name which James Joyce didn't put there. However I just went straight on, A after J, E after M, J after S, Y after O, E after C. I read each passage at least three times and once or twice upside down. (*Words* 136)

If texts such as *Empty Words* exemplify the post-critical penchant for mimicry and collage, Cage's other writings display equally well the montage-allegory principle in a way that illuminates the allegorical power of the host-parasite theme. "Where Are We Eating? And What Are We Eating?" is a good example (an account of Cage's travels with Merce Cunningham's dance troupe entirely in terms of what they ordered when they stopped to eat) with which to mark the parallel between Cage's narrative allegory and Serres's *Parasite,* with the latter alerting us to the "extra" import of the many anecdotes concerned with guests, hosts, and dining to be found throughout Cage's writings. The extraordinary insight made available through Serres's elaboration of the French meaning of "parasite" (which means "noise" as well as "guest" and "parasite") is that Cage—

who is famous as the composer who opened music to noise ("Since the theory of conventional music is a set of laws exclusively concerned with 'musical' sounds, having nothing to say about noises, it had been clear from the beginning that what was needed was a music based on noise, on noise's lawlessness. . . . The next steps were social" [*M* v])—when he is writing about dining, is *still* talking about noise. His anecdotes about eating are the essayistic, discursive equivalents of utilizing noise in his musical compositions. They are also a commentary on the "parasitical" invention process of citation, upon which his music and essays depend.

At the center of this allegory about noise and dining is Cage's passion for mushrooms. Cage, founder of the New York Mycological Society, owned one of the world's largest private collections of books about mushrooms. Again, although anecdotes having to do with mushrooms are disseminated throughout Cage's writings, they are the exclusive topic in *Mushroom Book,* whose collage construction may be seen in this prospectus:

> To finish for Lois programmed handwritten mushroom book including mushroom stories, excerpts from (mushroom) books, remarks about (mushroom) hunting, excerpts from Thoreau's *Journal* (fungi), excerpts from Thoreau's *Journal* (entire), remarks about: Life/Art, Art/Life, Life/Life, Art/Art, Zen, Current reading, Cooking (shopping, recipes), Games, Music mss., Maps, Friends, Invention, Projects, $ Writing without syntax, Mesostics (on mushroom names). (*M* 133–34)

Why mushrooms? Cage remarks that it is because "mushroom" is next to "music" in most dictionaries. But read as paraliterature, the mushroom may be understood as a model mounted in a discourse for allegorical purposes. Indeed, the mushroom turns out to be the best emblem yet for what Derrida calls the "pharmakon," a potion or medicine which is at once elixir and poison (borrowed from Plato), modelling what Derrida calls (by analogy) "undecidables" (directed against all conceptual, classifying systems). The undecidables are:

> unities of simulacrum, "false" verbal properties (nominal or semantic) that can no longer be included within philosophical (binary) opposition, but which, however, inhabit philosophical opposition, resisting and disorganizing it, *without ever* constituting a third term, without ever leaving room for a solution in the form of speculative dialectics (the *pharmakon* is neither remedy nor poison, neither good nor evil, neither the inside nor the outside, neither speech nor writing. (*Positions* 43)

What the pharmakon is in the pharmaceutical (and the conceptual) realm, the mushroom is in the plant world, for, as Cage remarks, "The more you know them, the less sure you feel about identifying them. Each one is itself. Each mushroom is what it is—its own center. It's useless to pretend to know mushrooms. They escape your erudition'' (*Birds* 188). Cage's fascination with mycology is due in part to this undecidability of classification, as indicated in his anecdotes about experts who have misidentified poison species as edible, or of people who have become ill, even died, from eating a variety which had no effect on other people (different individuals react differently to the same species sometimes). When he suggests, in the context of anecdotes about his own experiences of poisoning by mushrooms, that it is too bad that books are not edible, Cage seems to be making a point similar to the one Barthes made in *S/Z* with respect to the *risk* in reading. Sarrasine, having mistaken the castrato Zambinella for a woman, dies ''because of an inaccurate and inconclusive reasoning'':

> All the cultural codes, taken up from citation to citation, together form an oddly joined miniature version of encyclopedic knowledge, a farrago: this farrago forms the everyday 'reality' in relation to which the subject adapts himself, lives. One defect in this encyclopedia, one hole in this cultural fabric, and death can result. Ignorant of the code of Papal customs, Sarrasine dies from a gap in knowledge.[50]

The mushroom, in other words, de-monstrates a lesson about survival.

According to the montage-allegory principle, Cage's mushroom anecdotes constitute collaged fragments alluding to the entire science of mycology. To determine the larger significance of the mushroom as allegory, then, one must review the ''logic of the material'' thus paradigmatically evoked (just as the absent terms of a semantic field are implied negatively by the specific term used in a sentence). The connotation relevant to our specific context has to do with the parasite-host relationship as a model for the status of the citation in post-criticism. The lesson taught by the kind of fungi hunted (emblematizing the research activity in general) and eaten by John Cage in particular—the fleshy, fruity, ''higher'' fungi, Boletus, Morels, and the like—is *symbiosis.* These fungi are not parasites, but *saprophytes* (any organism that lives on dead organic matter), and exist in a symbiotic, mutually beneficial relationship with their hosts (the green plants and trees which supply the organic ''food''). The genus ''Cortinarius,'' for example, as described by C. H. Kauffman (whose study, *The Agaricaceae of Michigan,* Cage lists among the ten books which most influenced him), may be found ''in the region of pine and spruce, or in old beech forests, where the shade is dense and the ground is saturated with moisture,'' growing, of course, on a substratum of decaying matter. The trees benefit from the fungi growing among their roots by absorbing the nutrients made soluble as a result of the decomposing process to which the mushrooms contribute.[51]

This symbiotic ecology (related to the usefulness of the lower fungi, whose fermentations are essential to the production of wine, cheese, and bread) is Cage's version of what Benjamin was talking about when he compared allegory to ruins, for it could be said that the saprophyte, living off the decay of dead organisms in a way that makes life possible for living plants, is to nature what the ruin is to culture, or the allegory to thought. For Adorno and Benjamin, the ruins were signs of the *decay* of the bourgeois era, requiring in philosophy a "logic of disintegration." For Derrida, too, deconstruction is a process of decomposition at work within the very *root* metaphors—the philosophemes—of Western thought. But we may see that this work is symbiotic, similar to the "mycorrhizal formation" in which tree roots and fungi supplement one another, enabling each to "live *on,*" *sur*vive. The point is that if normal critics adhere to the model of the poem as living plant—the critic M. H. Abrams, for example, one of those accusing the deconstructors of being "parasites," whose *Mirror and the Lamp* provides the definitive study of the organic model in poetry—it might be useful to emblematize post-criticism as the saprophyte, growing among the roots of literature, feeding off the decay of tradition.

Cage suggests that his mushrooms could be read allegorically, even if he himself (being, as he says, the "grasshopper" of the fable) is too lazy to undertake the labor required for the comparison (*Silence* 176). The social philosophy which he derives from his theory of music, however, manifests the symbiotic theme of ecology, of cooperation and an end to competition. For, as he warns, referring to the current world situation, to the same global implications of the parasite theme which inform Serres's study, "The party's nearly over. But the guests are going to stay: they have no place else to go. People who weren't invited are beginning to arrive. The house is a mess. We must all get together and without saying a word clean it up" (*M* vii).

The immediate lesson for post-criticism, however, is found in this statement in the diary: "Mushrooms. Teaching-machines" (*M* 196). In other words, what those who attack postcriticism as "parasitical" have not yet realized is that montage-allegory (the mushroom as teaching-machine) provides the very technique for popularization, for communicating the knowledge of the cultural disciplines to a general public, which the normal, so-called humanist critics claim to desire. Wayne Booth, in his recent presidential address to the Modern Language Association, decried the drift of critical writing into solipsism, unaware that in *La Carte postale,* to take just one example, Derrida makes available a working model capable of de-monstrating with utter simplicity the teleological essence of the logocentric tradition:

> Everything in our bildopedic culture, in our encyclopedic politics, in our telecommunications of all kinds, in our telematicometaphysic archive, in our library, for example the

> marvelous Bodleian, everything is constructed on the protocolary charter of an axiom, which one could demonstrate, display on a card, a post card of course, it is so simple, elementary, brief, stereotyped. (*Carte postale* 25)

—that axiom being that Socrates comes *before* Plato, that the signified comes before the signifier; in short, the rigid order of an irreversible sequence. And when one mails a postcard, confident that it will be delivered to the addressee, one displays the ideology of identity. Cage remarks that "something needs to be done about the postal services. Either that or we should stop assuming just because we mailed something it will get where we sent it."[52] In *La Carte postale* Derrida suggests the possibility of a communications network without "destiny" or "destination," in which all mail (messages) would be addressed only "to whom it may concern"—a system which values "noise" or invention over transparent meanings. Moreover, he shows us the writing which is appropriate for such an era: "It suffices to manipulate," he says, referring to the model postcard, "to cut out, glue, and set going or parcel out, with hidden displacements and great tropic agility" (*Carte postale* 121). The image one the card (the one he found in the Bodleian library, depicting Socrates taking dictation from Plato) by means of *collage* becomes "articulate," "is capable of saying everything."

Such texts represent or mime not by means of signs but by signing—the signature. What remains of "identity" in a post-critical text is constituted by the new mimesis—the contamination between language and its user, the effects of which may be seen in the fact that the man who composed "Music of Changes," who composes all his productions by means of the "Book of Changes" (*I Ching*) in order, he hopes, to change society, is named *Jo Change* (John Cage).

Notes

1. Hayden White, *Tropics of Discourse* (Baltimore: Johns Hopkins, 1978), pp. 42–43, 45–47.
2. See Richard Kostelanetz, ed. *Esthetics Contemporary* (Buffalo: Prometheus, 1978).
3. Edward Fry, *Cubism* (New York: McGraw-Hill, n.d.), p. 27.
4. Eddie Wolfram, *History of Collage* (New York: MacMillan, 1975), pp. 17–18.
5. Group *Mu*, eds., *Collages* (Paris: Union Générale, 1978), pp. 13–14.
6. André Bazin, "The Ontology of the Photographic Image," in James B. Hall and Barry Ulanov, eds., *Modern Culture and the Arts* (New York: McGraw-Hill, 1972), p. 427.
7. John Heartfield, *Collage et Montage au Théâtre et dans les autres Arts durant les Années Vingt* (Lausanne: La Cite, 1978), p. 98.
8. Walter Benjamin, "The Author as Producer," in A. Arato and E. Gebhardt, eds., *The Essential Frankfurt School Reader* (New York: Urizen, 1978), p. 266.

9. Roland Barthes, *Critique et Vérité* (Paris: Seuil, 1966), pp. 68–69. Also see Barthes, "The Structuralist Activity," in R. and F. DeGeorge, eds., *The Structuralists from Marx to Lévi-Strauss* (Garden City, N.J.: Doubleday, 1972), pp. 148–54.

10. The most recent statement of this generic conflation of literature and criticism is Rosalind Krauss's notion of "paraliterature."

> If one of the tenets of modernist literature had been the creation of a work that would force reflection on the conditions of its own construction, that would insist on reading as a much more consciously *critical* act, then it is not surprising that the medium of a *post*modernist literature should be the critical text wrought into a paraliterary form. And what is clear is that Barthes and Derrida are the *writers*, not the critics, that students now read.

See Rosalind Krauss, "Poststructuralism and the 'Paraliterary,'" *October* 13 (1980): 40.

The insight of paraliterature is that although by the 1960s the collage revolution seemed to have run its course, it was in fact being renewed in critical discourse, which was itself finally being affected by experiments with representation. Indeed, as Elizabeth Bruss proposes in *Beautiful Theories* (concerned with the criticism of Susan Sontag, William Gass, Harold Bloom, and Roland Barthes), theory is not only the most interesting of contemporary literary forms, it is the mode best suited for moving out of the impasse reached by the modernist movements in the arts.

11. See S. Doubrovsky, *Pourquoi la Nouvelle Critique?* (Paris: Mercure de France, 1966).

12. Derrida, "Living On: Borderlines," in *Deconstruction and Criticism* (New York: Seabury, 1979), pp. 94–95.

13. This is the topic of Jacques Derrida, *Of Grammatology*, Gayatari Spivak, trans. (Baltimore: Johns Hopkins, 1976).

14. Derrida, *Dissemination*, Barbara Johnson, trans. (Chicago: University of Chicago, 1981), pp. 41–42.

15. Philip Lewis, "The Post-Structuralist Condition," *Diacritics* 12 (1982): 16.

16. Derrida, *Positions*, Alan Bass, trans. (Chicago: University of Chicago, 1981), p. 26.

17. Derrida, "Signature Event Context," in *Glyph* 1 (1977): 185.

18. Elsewhere Derrida writes: "What is in question here, this time at last, finds itself not displayed but given play, not staged but engaged, not demonstrated but *mounted*, mounted with a confectioner's skill in some implacable machinery" (*Dissemination*, p. 291). The verb is *monter*, from which "montage" derives. In a later text Derrida, playing on the meanings of *monter*, introduces the image of *passe-partout* or matting (used to frame pictures) as an analogy for the way a critical text "mounts" its examples. See Derrida, *La Vérité en peinture* (Paris: Flammarion, 1978), pp. 5–18.

19. See Derrida, "Title (to be specified)," *Sub-Stance* 31 (1981).

20. This is the strategy used to deconstruct Kant in *La Vérité en peinture* and Saussure in *Glas* (Paris: Galilée, 1974).

21. Derrida, "The Law of Genre," *Glyph* 7 (1980): 206.

22. "Dissemination" is written using the same montage technique practiced in *Numbers*—indeed, *Numbers* is selected as a tutor-text for just this reason—so that what is "re-marked" here (the term Derrida prefers to "represented," "illustrated," "displayed," etc.) in the critical version is the structuration of the object of study:

> We will hence be inscribing—simultaneously—in the angles and corners of these *Numbers,* within them and outside them, upon the stone that awaits *you,* certain questions that touch upon "this" text "here," the status of its relation to *Numbers,* what it pretends to add to "that" text in order to *mime* its presentations and representations, in order to seem to be offering some sort of review or account of it. For if *Numbers* offers an account of *itself* then "this" text—and all that touches it—is already or still "that" text. Just as *Numbers* calculates and feigns self-presentation and inscribes presence in a certain play, so too does what cold still with a certain irony be called "this" text mime the presentation, commentary, interpretation, review, account, or inventory of *Numbers.* As a *generalized simulacrum,* this writing circulates "here" in the intertext of two fictions, between a so-called primary text and its so-called commentary. (*Dissemination,* p. 294)

23. Derrida, *Writing and Difference,* Alan Bass, trans. (Chicago: University of Chicago, 1978), p. 296.
24. The very repetition that permits a sign to be a sign—to be recognized as the same as what it signifies—also produces a difference, as Saussure emphasized (the sign is not the referent itself). The temporal oscillation generated in this play between presence and absence is what Derrida terms *différance,* naming that which is opposed to the rigid first-second ordering between signifier and signified dictated by logocentric semiotics from Plato to Saussure.
25. Derrida, *Speech and Phenomena,* David Allison, trans. (Evanston, Ill.: Northwestern University, 1973), p. 128.
26. Derrida, *La Carte postale* (Paris: Flammarion, 1980), p. 317.
27. Ludwig Wittgenstein, *Philosophical Investigations,* G. Anscombe, trans. (Oxford: Blackwell, 1968), p. 105.
28. Craig Owens, "The Allegorical Impulse: Toward a Theory of Postmodernism," *October* 12 (1980): 84.
29. Owens, "The Allegorical Impulse (Part 2)," *October* 13 (1980): 79–80.
30. See Stephen Melville, "Notes on the Reemergence of Allegory," *October* 19 (1981); and Jonathan Culler, *On Deconstruction* (Ithaca: Cornell University, 1983).
31. Maureen Quilligan, *The Language of Allegory* (Ithaca: Cornell University, 1979), pp. 30–33.
32. Owens, "(Part 2)," 64, 66. Cf. Douglas Crimp, "The Photographic Activity of Postmodernism," *October* 15 (1980), for a discussion of Sherrie Levine, Benjamin.
33. Richard Kostelanetz, ed., *John Cage* (New York: Praeger, 1970), p. 115.
34. Barthes, *Roland Barthes,* Richard Howard, trans. (New York: Hill & Wang, 1977), p. 90.
35. Stanley Mitchell, "Introduction," in Walter Benjamin, *Understanding Brecht,* Anna Bostock, trans. (London: New Left Books, 1977), p. xiii.
36. Rainer Hoffmann, *Montage im Hohlraum zu Ernst Blochs "Spuren"* (Bonn: Grundmann, 1977), p. 92.
37. Benjamin, *"One-Way Street" and Other Writings,* E. Jephcott, K. Shorter, trans. (London: New Left Books, 1979), p. 62.

38. Martin Jay, *The Dialectical Imagination* (Boston: Little Brown, 1973), pp. 176, 200. Jay mentions Norman O. Brown's *Love's Body* as perhaps a realization of Benjamin's plan.

39. Benjamin, *The Origin of German Tragic Drama,* J. Osborne, trans. (London: New Left Books, 1977), p. 184.

40. Susan Buck-Morss, *The Origin of Negative Dialectics* (London: MacMillan, 1977), p. 56.

41. In Benjamin, "Short History of Photography," Phil Patton, trans., in *Artforum* 15 (1977): 50.

42. Derrida, *Spurs, Nietzsche's Styles,* Barbara Harlow, trans. (Chicago: University of Chicago, 1979), p. 41.

43. In this case, Derrida appropriates the materials of a debate between Heidegger and Meyer Schapiro regarding the ownership of the shoes figured in Van Gogh's paintings—a theme which emblematizes the whole question of property and the signature involved in collage writing. Like the umbrella borrowed from Nietzsche, Van Gogh's shoes are detached from the critical argument and remotivated as a model for the frame—an act which by itself refutes the attempts of the critics to fix the shoe-signifier to a specific signified, to determine whether the pictured shoes were owned by a peasant woman (Heidegger) or by Van Gogh himself (Schapiro). Indeed the fact that the shoes are depicted as partially (un)laced is the clue to the process by which the gram-coupling works.

> Like a lace, each "thing," each mode of being of the thing, passes inside then outside the other. We will often avail ourselves of this figure of the lace passing and repassing through the eyelet of the thing, from outside in, from inside out, *over* the outer surface and *under* the inner one—and vice versa when this surface is turned inside out like the top of the left shoe, the lace remains the "same" on both sides, shows itself and disappears (fort/da) in the regular crossing of the eyelet, insures the thing of its resemblance, bottoms tied to tops, inside fastened to outside, by a law of stricture.

Derrida goes on to mock those who insist on viewing language in terms of the sign, seeing pairs (signifier-signified) everywhere, in the way that Heidegger and Schapiro assume they are looking at a pair of shoes. On close inspection of the paintings, Derrida argues wryly, it is not at all clear that the shoes are matched; rather, they appear to be two left shoes—left behind, in any case, like Nietzsche's umbrella, for the next user, or writer. See Derrida, "Restitutions of Truth to Size," John P. Leavy, Jr., trans., in *Research in Phenomenology* 8 (1978): 32 (a partial translation of "Restitutions, de la vérité en peinture," in *Vérité en peinture*).

44. J. Hillis Miller, "The Critic as Host," *Critical Inquiry* 3 (1977): 439.

45. Michel Serres, *The Parasite,* Lawrence Schehr, trans. (Baltimore: Johns Hopkins, 1982)—Schehr's introduction, p. x.

46. John Cage (in conversation with Daniel Charles), *For the Birds* (Boston: Boyars, 1981), p. 151.

47. John Cage, *Silence* (Cambridge, Mass.: M. I. T., 1961, 1970), p. 194.

48. John Cage, *M: Writings 67–72* (Middletown: Wesleyan University, 1974), p. i.

49. John Cage, *Empty Words* (Middletown: Wesleyan University, 1981), p. 3.
50. Roland Barthes, *S/Z*, Richard Miller, trans. (New York: Hill & Wang, 1974), pp. 184–85.
51. For a discussion of mycology, see G. C. Ainsworth, *Introduction to the History of Mycology* (Cambridge: Cambridge University, 1976).
52. John Cage, *A Year from Monday* (Middletown: Wesleyan University, 1969), p. 150.

Afterword

Where does the road go from here? Where will collage and its extensions lead as the twenty-first century approaches? As seen in the diversity of the preceding essays, collage is a medium and process that can be approached and used in a variety of ways. It appears that its multiple facets may help us better deal with our contemporary and future world, as we cope with continuing changes and the possibilities of countless new realities. As we have seen, the medium of collage in this century has inspired revolutionary experiments in the making of art and in approaches to art criticism and theory. As artists and writers continue to explore new forms and content while seeking the unknown, collage will continue to be an important tool. It may well accomplish what Marcel Proust wrote concerning the role of art:

> Only through art can we get outside of ourselves and know another's view of the universe which is not the same as ours and see landscapes which would otherwise have remained unknown to us like the landscapes on the moon. . . . [I]nstead of seeing a single world, our own, we see it multiply until we have before us as many worlds as there are original artists—more different from each other than those which revolve in space.*

---

*Marcel Proust, *Le Temps retrouvé* (Paris: Gallimard, Editions de la Nouvelle Revue Francaise, 1923–27), p. 491; translated by Justin O'Brien in *The Maxims of Proust* (New York: Columbia University Press, 1948), p. 176.

Contributors

Marjorie Agosin is a Chilean poet and associate professor of Spanish at Wellesley College. She has written several books on literary criticism, including *Pablo Neruda* and *Silencio e imaginacion: metaforas de la escritura femenina,* and is the author of several collections of poetry. Her most recent work is *Women of Smoke.* She has been very involved with the political life and culture in her native land, and her recent work, *Scraps of Life: The Chilean Arpilleras,* deals with the way in which women from the Santiago shantytowns have resisted and fought against the Chilean dictatorship.

Max Almy is currently teaching at the University of California, Los Angeles. Since the early 1970s she has worked with video as an experimental medium. Utilizing complex video and audio effects, she creates compelling images which portray critical issues affecting life in the contemporary urban environment. She has been the recipient of a number of awards, including an NEA fellowship and Independent Filmmakers Production grant.

Clement Greenberg is a dominant figure in twentieth century art and cultural criticism. His first article, on Brecht, was published in 1939, in *Partisan Review.* Among his positions, he has been editor for *The Partisan Review,* art critic for *The Nation,* and book reviewer for *The New York Times.* He is the winner of the 1988 Morton Dauwen Zabel Award of the American Academy and Institute of Arts and Letters.

Katherine Hoffman is an associate professor of Art History at Bradford College, Bradford, Mass. She has published a variety of articles on 19th and 20th century art, and has exhibited her paintings and photographs in group and solo exhibitions. She is the author of *An Enduring Spirit: The Art of Georgia O'Keeffe* and is currently working on a book on contemporary art.

Wendy Holmes is an associate professor of Art at the University of Rhode Island, where she teaches art appreciation, art theory, and occasionally, studio art. She has published in *Semiotica* and contributed "Semiotics of Visual Art" to the recent *An Encyclopedia Dictionary of Semiotics.*

C. M. Judge is a painter, environmental sculptor, and videographer. Her most recent work, sponsored by Sealed Air Corporation, is a series of large-scale, interactive sculptures made of polyurethane foam, which initiate and celebrate "receptive space" and the mysteries of life force. Ms. Judge holds a Master of Science degree in Visual Studies from M.I.T.

Donald B. Kuspit is a professor of Philosophy and Art at S.U.N.Y. at Stony Brook, as well as contributing editor at *Art in America,* staff member at *Artforum,* and editor of *Art Criticism.* In 1983 he was the winner of the Frank Jewett Mather Prize for Distinction in Art Criticism given by the College Art Association. Among his numerous publications are two books by UMI Research Press: *The Critic is Artist: The Intentionality of Art* (1984) and *The New Subjectivism: Art in the 1980s* (1988).

Patricia Leighten received her Ph.D. from Rutgers in 1983. Her book, *Re-Ordering the Universe: Picasso and Anarchism, 1897–1914,* on which this article is based, will be published by Princeton University in fall 1989, and was given Special Mention as U.S. nominee for the 1988 C.I.N.O.A. (Confédération Internationale des Négociants en Oeuvres d'Art) Art History Prize for best book manuscript. She was Guest Editor of a special issue of *Art Journal* "Revising Cubism," which appeared in Winter 1988, and is currently working on her second book, *Art and Social Radicalism in France, 1900–1914,* for which she received a J. Paul Getty Postdoctoral Fellowship in the History of Art and the Humanities in 1985–86.

Robin Lydenberg is associate professor of English at Boston College. She has published articles on Lautréamont, Barthes, Dinesen, Borges, and Gothic fiction and architecture, and has recently published a book on William Burroughs' experimental fiction, *Word Cultures: Radical Theory and Practice in William S. Burroughs' Fiction.*

Richard Newman is chairperson of the Creative Arts Department at Bradford College. A graduate of Cranbrook and Cornell University, he has worked in collage and assemblage for a number of years. He has shown his work throughout the country and is currently president of the Society of Layerists in Multi-Media.

Annegreth T. Nill is Assistant Curator of Contemporary Art at the Carnegie Museum of Art, Pittsburgh. There she has curated a variety of exhibitions, including "Abstract Prints from the Collection," "The Art of Propaganda: Twentieth Century Prints from the Collection," and "Pittsburgh Photography: A New Generation." From 1980–82 she was a Fulbright Scholar in Germany. She is the author of several articles on Kurt Schwitters and is currently finishing her Ph.D. at the University of Texas at Austin, where her dissertation is titled, *Romantic Dada: The Iconography of Kurt Schwitters' Early Work.*

Christine Poggi received her Ph.D. from Yale University in 1988, where her dissertation was entitled "In Defiance of Painting: The Invention and Early Practice of Collage, 1912–1919." She has been the recipient of a number of awards, including a Georges Lurcy Fellowship at the Whitney Humanities Center at Yale, a Kress Travel Grant, and a Fulbright-Hays Full Grant. She is currently an assistant professor at the University of Pennsylvania.

Harry Polkinhorn is an associate professor of English and Art at San Diego State University. Having graduate degrees in both literature and art, he has been involved in a number of projects as writer, editor, and visual artist. His publications include *War* (1982), *Anesthesia* (1985), and *Bridges of Skin Money* (1986). He is currently working on a book, *Seeing Power: The Politics of Verbal/Visual Art.*

Harold Rosenberg (1906–1978) contributed much to the field of art criticism through his writing and teaching. From 1966–78 he was professor at the University of Chicago, and from 1967–78 he was art critic for *New Yorker* magazine. His books include *The De-Definition of Art, Discovering the Present,* and *Art on the Edge.*

Robert Rosenblum is a professor of Fine Arts at New York University, and the author of many articles on Picasso. He is also the author of *Cubism and Abstract Art* (1960), *Transformations in Late Eighteenth Century Art* (1967), *Ingres* (1967), *Frank Stella* (1970), *Modern Painting and the Northern Romantic Tradition* (1975), *19th Century Art* (with H. W. Janson) (1984), and *The Dog in Art from Rococo to Post-Modernism* (1988).

Miriam Schapiro has an international reputation as a painter and femmagist. She exhibits regularly at the Bernice Steinbaum Gallery in New York City, and is the recent winner of a Guggenheim award.

Michael Selig is an assistant professor in Mass Communication at Emerson College in Boston. He has published in a number of academic journals, including *Wide Angle, Journal of Popular Film and Television, Jump Cut,* and *Velvet Light Trap.* He is the editor of the *Journal of Film and Video.*

William C. Seitz (1914–1974) was a curator at the Museum of Modern Art, New York City from 1956–65. He was professor of Fine Art and director of the Rose Art Museum, Brandeis University from 1965–70. He was also a practicing artist, and author of a number of books, including *The Art of Assemblage, The Responsive Eye,* and *George Segal.*

Charlotte Stokes is chairperson of the Department of Art and Art History at Oakland University in Rochester, Michigan. She has written a number of articles on Max Ernst and Surrealism, and is currently working on a book on the collages of Max Ernst. She has won a number of awards, including two Center for Advanced Study of the Arts Visiting Senior Fellowships at the National Gallery.

Gregory L. Ulmer, professor of English at the University of Florida, is the author of the forthcoming book, *Teletheory: The Making of "Derrida at the Little Bighorn."*

Paul Vangelisti is a poet, editor, and instructor at the Otis Art Institute of Parsons School of Design. His most recent works include *Portfolio* (Edizioni Tam Tam, Parma, 1988, bilingual), *Domain: Works-in-Progress,* and exhibitions of his visual poetry. He was the recipient of a National Endowment for the Humanities Poetry Fellowship in 1988.

Selected Bibliography

Acatos, Sylvio. "Rudolf Haas et ses reliefs-assemblages: jetés vont ailleurs." *L'Oeil,* no. 375 (October 1986): 60–65.

Ades, Dawn. *Photomontage.* London: Thames and Hudson, 1976.

Aliteri, C. "Picasso's Collages and the Force of Cubism." *Kenyon Review* 6 (Spring 1984): 8–33.

Arnason, H. H. *History of Modern Art.* New York and Englewood Cliffs, N.J.: Harry N. Abrams, Inc. and Prentice Hall, 1986.

Bauer, G. "Max Ernst's Collageroman *Une Semaine de bonté.*" *Wallraf-Richartz Jahrbuch* 39 (1977): 237–57.

Becker, J. and Vostell, W. *Happenings.* Hamburg: Rowalt, 1965.

Bergius, H. "Ambiguous Aesthetic of Dada: Towards a Definition of Its Categories." Translated by B. H. Mann and R. W. Sheppard. *Journal of European Studies* 9 (March/June 1979): 26–38.

Berman, Avis. "Romare Bearden." *ARTnews* (December 1980): 60–67.

Bohn, W. "Circular Poem Paintings by Apollinaire and Carrà." *Comparative Literature* 31 (Summer 1979): 246–71.

Bois, Yve-Alain. "Kahnweiler's Lesson." *Representations,* no. 18 (Spring 1987): 33–68.

______. "Jean Arp: Chance and Necessity." *Art in America* 71 (September 1983): 41–43.

Botar, Oliver A. I. "Constructed Reliefs in the Art of the Hungarian Avant-Garde: Kassak, Bortnyik, Uitz and Moholy-Nagy, 1921–1926." *The Structuralist* Nos. 25/26 (1985–1986): 87–98.

Bouisset, M. "John Heartfield et 'la beauté' révolutionnaire." *XXe Siècle,* no. 44 (June 1975): 164–65.

Buchloh, B. H. D. "Allegorical Procedures: Appropriation and Montage in Contemporary Art." *Artforum* 21 (September 1982): 43–56.

Buchloh, Benjamin, Guibaut, Serge, and Solkin, David, eds. *Modernism and Modernity.* Halifax: Press of Nova Scotia College of Art and Design, 1981.

Calin, W. "The Poets' Poet: Intertextuality in Louis Aragon." *Symposium* 40 (Spring 1986): 3–15.

Chipp, Herschel B., ed. *Theories of Modern Art: Source Book by Artists and Critics.* Berkeley: University of California Press, 1968.

Cinquante ans de collages. Sainte-Etienne: Musée des Arts Décoratifs, 1964.

Cohen, R. H. "Collages and Reliefs 1910–45, La Boetie Gallery," *Artforum* 21 (February 1983): 74–75.

Cooper, Douglas. *The Cubist Epoch.* London: Phaidon, in association with the Los Angeles County Museum of Art and the Metropolitan Museum of Art, 1971.

Cowart, J. "Matisse's Artistic Probe: The Collage." *Arts Magazine* 49 (May 1975): 53–55.

Daix, Pierre. *Cubists and Cubism.* New York: Rizzoli/Skira, 1982.

______. "Des bouleversements chronologiques dans la révolution des papiers collés (1912–1914)." *Gazette des Beaux-Arts* 82 (October 1973): 217–27.

______. *Picasso: The Cubist Years, 1907–16.* Boston: New York Graphic Society, 1979.

Davis, Douglas. *Art and the Future: A History/Prophecy of the Collaboration between Science, Technology and Art.* New York: Praeger, 1973.

Digby, John and Joan. *The Collage Handbook.* New York: Thames and Hudson, 1987.

Dills, Keith. "A Powerful New Tradition." *Artweek* 17 (October 18, 1986): 3–4.

Dunnett, James. "On the Sadness of Juan Gris." *Architectural Review* (May 1987): 89–92.

Eisenstein, Sergei. *Film Form and the Film Sense.* Ed. and trans. by Jay Leyda. Cleveland and New York: Meridian Books, 1957.

Elderfield, J. "Early Work of Kurt Schwitters." *Artforum* 10 (November 1971): 54–67.

______. "Merz in the Machine Age." *Art and the Artists* 5 (July 1970): 56–59.

Ellenzweig, A. "Private Objects: The Sculpture of Kurt Schwitters." *Artforum* 12 (September 1973): 45–54.

______. "Still Life with Art History: The Collage Paintings of Josef Levi." *Arts Magazine* 51 (December 1976): 92–94.

Environments, Situations, Spaces. New York: Martha Jackson Gallery, 1961.

An Exhibit of the Work of Robert Motherwell. Northampton: Smith College Museum of Art, 1963.

Flam, Jack. *Robert Motherwell: The Collaged Image.* Minneapolis: Walker Art Center, 1985.

Foster, Hal. "The Problem of Pluralism." *Art in America* 70 (January 1982): 9–15.

______. "Subversive Signs." *Art in America* 70 (November 1982): 88–92.

______, ed. *The Anti-Aesthetic: Essays on Post-Modern Culture.* Port Townsend, Wash.: Bay Press, 1983.

Fox, Howard. *Avant-Garde in the Eighties.* Los Angeles: Los Angeles County Museum of Art, 1987.

Friar, K. "Imagery and Collages of Odysseum Elytis." *Books Abroad* 49 (Autumn 1975): 703–11.

Friedman, B. H. "Homage to La Belle Epoque: Conrad Marca-Relli's New Work." *Arts Magazine* 58 (October 1983): 76–77.

Fry, Edward. *Cubism.* New York: McGraw-Hill, 1966.

Gerke, H. "Gestaltung mit Fotografie: Collage, Montage, Übermalung." *Kunstwerk* 28 (January 1975): 44.

Glenn, C. W. "Art—Contemporary Collage—The Mixture of Form and Medium." *Architectural Digest* 39 (May 1982): 104–9.

Glimcher, Arnold. *Louise Nevelson.* New York: Dutton, 1976.

Golding, John. *Cubism: A History and Analysis, 1907–1916.* London: Faber and Faber, 1959.

Greenberg, Clement. *Art and Culture.* Boston: Beacon Press, 1961.

______. "The Pasted Paper Revolution." *ARTnews* 57 (September 1958): 46–49, 60–61.

Hancock, Jane, and Poley, Stefanie, curators. *Arp 1886–1966.* Minneapolis: Minneapolis Institute of Arts, 1987.

Harkavy, D. "Alexander Liberman's Recent Collages and Gate Constructions." *Arts Magazine* 57 (June 1983): 74–77.

Haroutunian, H. H. "Joseph Cornell's *The Crystal Cage,*" *Arts Magazine* 55 (March 1981): 102–8.

Heller, Steven. "Passionate Collagists." *Print* 37 (September/October 1983): 47–67.

Henning, E. B. "Jean Hatchet and Charles the Bold: Surrealist Collage by Max Ernst." *Cleveland Museum Bulletin* 69 (October 1982): 273–78.

Henry, G. "Ray Johnson: Collage Jester." *Art in America* 72 (December 1984): 139–41.

Hornbacher, Sara, ed. *Video: The Reflexive Medium. Art Journal* 45 (Fall 1986).

Hubert, R. R. "Apollinaire and Dine: A Re-enactment of the Poet's Assassination." *Symposium* 34 (Winter 1980/81): 333–51.

______. "Max Ernst: The Displacement of the Visual and Verbal." *New Literary History* 15 (Spring 1984): 575–606.

Ivory, James. "'In the American Grain': Robert Helm." *Artforum* 23 (November 1984): 74–76.

Janis, Harriet and Blesh, Rudi. *Collage—Personalities, Concepts, Techniques.* Philadelphia and New York: Chilton Book Co., 1962.

Johnson, Dorothy Rylander. *Arthur Dove: The Years of Collage.* College Park, Md.: University of Maryland Art Gallery, 1967.

Johnson, R. "Picasso's Musical and Mallarmean Constructions." *Arts Magazine* 51 (March 1977): 122–27.

Jouffroy, A. "L'Influence des ready-mades Marcel Duchamp." *XXe Siècle,* no. 41 (December 1973): 63–69.

Kalil, S. "American Collage since 1950." *Artweek* 13 (September 18, 1982): 1ff.

Kaplan, P. "On Jasper Johns' 'According to What.'" *Art Journal,* no. 3 (Spring 1976): 247–50.

Kaprow, Allan. *Assemblages, Environments and Happenings.* New York: Abrams, 1966.

Krauss, Rosalind E. *The Originality of the Avant-Garde and Other Modernist Myths* (see especially the essay, "In the Name of Picasso," pp. 23–41). Cambridge, Mass.: MIT Press, 1985.

______. "Rauschenberg and the Materialized Image." *Artforum* 13 (December 1974): 36–43.

______. "Re-presenting Picasso." *Art in America* 68 (December 1980): 90–96.

Kuspit, Donald. "Oyvind Fahlstrom's Political Puzzles." *Art in America* 70 (April 1982): 106–11.

Lajer-Burcharth, Ewa. "Urban Disturbances." *Art in America* 75 (November 1987): 147–53.

Lavin, M. "Heartfield in Context." *Art in America* 73 (1985): 85–92.

Leighten, Patricia. "The Dream and Lies of Picasso." *Arts Magazine* 62 (October 1987): 50–55.

Lichtenstein, T. "Collage Expanded." *Arts Magazine* 59 (December 1984): 34–35.

Linker, K. "Jiri Kolar and the Alexandrian Imagination." *Arts Magazine* 50 (September 1975): 58–60.

Lorenz, Melinda. *Contemporary Collage: Extensions (Work from Southern California).* Claremont, Calif.: Galleries of the Claremont Colleges, 1983.

Loss, A. D. "Joyce's Use of Collage in 'Aeolus.'" *Journal of Modern Literature* 9 (May 1982): 175–82.

Loughery, John. "Contemporary Assemblage." *Arts Magazine* 62 (November 1987): 106–7.

McCullagh, J. "Image to Collage." *Arts Magazine* 60 (December 1985): 80–85; 61 (January 1986): 74–76.

Meilach, Dona Z., and Ten Hoor, Elvie. *Collage and Assemblage—Trends and Techniques.* New York: Crown Publishers, 1973.

Michaelsen, K. J. "Early Mixed Media Constructions." *Arts Magazine* 50 (November 1976): 58–65.

Monod-Fontaine, Isabelle, with Carmean, E. A. eds. *Braque: The Papiers Collés.* Washington, D.C.: The National Gallery, 1982.

Myers, John. "Naming Pictures: Conversation between Lee Krasner and John Bernard Myers." *Artforum* 23 (November 1984): 69–73.

Nadelman, Cynthia. "Gabo's Progeny." *ARTnews* 86 (December 1987): 123–27.

Nechvatal, Joseph. "Post-Simulation Decadence." *Arts Magazine* 62 (Summer 1987): 28–29.

Néret, G. "Max Ernst: Alphabet pour une autre vie." *L'Oeil,* no. 238 (May 1975): 36–41+.

Nill, Annegreth. "Rethinking Kurt Schwitters, Part One: An Interpretation of *Hansi.*" *Arts Magazine* 55 (June 1981): 112–17.

Nochlin, L. "Miriam Schapiro: Recent Work." *Arts Magazine* 48 (November 1973): 38–41.

O'Doherty, B. "Inside the White Cube: The Eye and the Spectator." *Artforum* 15 (April 1976): 26–34.

Otlet-Moutoy, S. "Les étapes de l'activité créatrice chez E. L. T. Mesens et l'esprit du collage comme aboutissement d'une pensée." *Musées Royaux des Beaux-Arts de Belgique* Bulletin (Brussels) 22, nos. 1–4 (1973): 171–90.

Owens, Craig. "Representation, Appropriation and Power." *Art in America* 70 (May 1982): 9–21.

Parada, E. "Women's Vision Extends to the Map of Memory." *Michigan Quarterly Review* 6 (Winter 1987): 196–217.

Paulhan, Jean. *La peinture cubiste.* Paris: Denoel, 1970.

Perrone, Jeff. "Robert Rauschenberg." *Artforum* 15 (February 1977): 24–31.

Picon, Gaetan. *Surrealists and Surrealism, 1919–1939.* New York: Rizzoli, 1977.

Plottel, Jeanine Parisier, ed. *Collage.* New York: New York Literary Forum, 1983.

Richardson, Nan, ed. *The Return of the Hero.* Aperture Foundations, no. 110 (Spring 1988).

Robins, Corinne. *The Pluralist Era—American Art, 1968–1974.* New York: Harper and Row, 1984.

Ronca, F. C. "Influence of Rimbaud on Max Ernst's Theory of Collage." *Comparative Literature Studies* 16 (March 1979): 41–47.

Rose, B. "Lee Krasner and the Origins of Abstract Expressionism." *Arts Magazine* 51 (February 1977): 96–100.

Rosenberg, Harold. *Art on the Edge: Creators and Situations.* New York: Macmillan, 1975.

Rosenblum, Robert. *Cubism and Twentieth-Century Art.* New York: Abrams, 1961.

______. "Picasso and the Coronation of Alexander III: A Note on the Dating of Some Papiers Collés." *Burlington Magazine* (October 1971): 604–6.

Rowe, Colin, and Koetter, Fred. *Collage City.* Cambridge, Mass.: MIT Press, 1978.

Schear, C. K. "Photomontage in the Early Work of R. B. Kitaj." *Arts Magazine* 59 (September 1984): 74–77.

Schwartzman, M. "Romare Bearden Sees in a Memory." *Artforum* 22 (May 1984): 64–70.

Schwarz, Dieter. "Look! Books in Plaster: On the First Phase of the Work of Marcel Broodthaers." *October,* no. 42 (Fall 1987): 57–66.

Seitz, William. *The Art of Assemblage.* New York: The Museum of Modern Art, 1961.

Sergeant, P. "Erro et le Silence Collectif." *XXe Siècle,* no. 50 (June 1978): 40–45.

Slatkin, Wendy. *Women Artists in History: From Antiquity to the Twentieth Century.* Englewood Cliffs, N.J.: Prentice Hall, 1985.

Solomon, Andrew. "Something Borrowed, Something Bloom." *Artforum* 26 (May 1988): 122–26.

Stapanian, J. R. "Universal War 'Ъ' and the Development of 'Zaum': Toward a New Pictorial and Literary Realism." *Slavic and Eastern European Journal* 29 (Spring 1985): 18–38.

Steinberg, Leo. *Other Criteria—Confrontations with Twentieth-Century Art.* New York: Oxford University Press, 1972.

Steinitz, K. T. "Kurt Schwitters: A Portrait from Life." *Comparative Literature Studies* 12 (September 1975): 199–217.

Stokes, Charlotte. "Dadamax: Max Ernst in the Context of Cologne Dada." In *Dada/Dimensions,* ed. by Stephen Foster, pp. 113–28. Ann Arbor, Mich.: UMI Research Press, 1985.

______. "From the Edges of Floating Worlds: Meaning in Max Ernst's Collages." *Arts Magazine* 61 (April 1987): 37–41.

______. "The Thirteenth Chair: Max Ernst's 'Capricorn.'" *Arts Magazine* 62 (October 1987): 88–93.

Tashjian, Dickran. *Skyscraper Primitives—Dada and the American Avant-Garde, 1910–1925.* Middletown, Conn.: Wesleyan University Press, 1975.

Temin, Christine, "Tim Rollins and K.O.S." *The Boston Sunday Globe* (April 17, 1988), B1, 12.

Thomsen, Christian W. "Architektonische Traumflüge." *Du*, no. 1 (1987): 58–65.

Toman, Jindrich. "Wort, Bild und Objekt: Zum Werk des tschechischen Surrealisten Jindrich Heisler." *Pantheon* 43 (1985): 165–70.

Tomkins, Calvin. "Profiles—Putting Something over Something Else—Romare Bearden." *New Yorker* (November xx, 1977): 53+.

Troy, N. J. "Abstraction, Decoration and Collage." *Arts Magazine* 54 (June 1980): 154–57.

Tsai, E. "The Unknown Smithson." *Arts Magazine* 60 (March 1986): 33–35.

Van der Marck, J. "The Modernist Schwitters." *Art in America* 73 (October 1985): 32+.

Van Hook, L. B. "Robert Motherwell's *Mallarmé's Swan*." *Arts Magazine* 57 (January 1983): 102–6.

Varian, Elayne. *Art in Process: The Visual Development of a Collage*. New York: Finch College Museum of Art, 1967.

Violand, Heidi E. "Jean Tinguely's *Cenodoxus Isenheim Altarpiece*." *Arts Magazine* 62 (October 1987): 80–85.

Wallis, Brian, ed. *Art after Modernism: Rethinking Representation*. New York: New Museum of Contemporary Art, 1984.

Warde, W. B., Jr. "A Collage Approach" Donald Barthelme's Literary Fragments." *Journal of American Culture* 8 (Spring 1985): 51–56.

Warlick, M. E. "Max Ernst's Alchemical Novel: *Une Semaine de bonté*." *Art Journal* 46 (Spring 1987): 61–73.

Welish, M. "Texas, Japan, etc.: Robert Rauschenberg's Sense of Place." *Arts Magazine* 60 (March 1986): 52–54.

Wescher, Herta. *Collage*. New York: Abrams, 1968.

Weschler, L. "David Hockney's Camerawork." *Du*, no. 10 (1984): 24–31.

Withers, J. "Artistic Collaboration of Pablo Picasso and Julio Gonzalez." *Art Journal* 35, no. 2 (Winter 1975/76): 107–14.

Wolfram, Eddie. *History of Collage*. New York: Macmillan, 1978.

Wyrick, D. "Dadaist Collage Structure and Nathanael West's *Dream Life of Balso Snell*." *Studies in the Novel* 11 (Fall 1979): 349–59.

Index